Advanced Research on Asian Economy and Economies of Other Continents – Vol. 7

EU-Asia and the Re-Polarization of the Global Economic Arena

Advanced Research on Asian Economy and Economies of Other Continents

(ISSN: 1793-0944)

Series Editor: Manoranjan DUTTA
(Rutgers, The State University of New Jersey, USA)

Published

Vol. 1 Asian Economic Cooperation in the New Millennium: China's Economic Presence
Edited by Calla Wiemer (East Asian Institute, National University of Singapore) & Heping Cao (Peking University, China)

2 China's Industrial Revolution and Economic Presence
by Manoranjan Dutta (Rutgers, The State University of New Jersey, USA)

3 International Economic Integration and Asia
Edited by Michael G Plummer & Erik Jones (Johns Hopkins University SAIS-Bologna, Italy)

4 Economic Dynamism of Asia in the New Millenium: From the Asian Crisis to a New Stage of Growth
Edited by Yoshinori Shimizu (Hitotsubashi University, Japan)

5 Future Perspectives on the Economic Development of Asia
by John Malcolm Dowling (Singapore Management University, Singapore)

6 Asean Economic Integration: Trade, Foreign Direct Investment, and Finance
by Michael G Plummer (Johns Hopkins University, SAIS-Bologna, and East-West Center, Italy)

7 EU-Asia and the Re-Polarization of the Global Economic Arena
Edited by Lars Oxelheim (Lund University, Sweden & Research Institute of Industrial Economics, Sweden)

Advanced Research on Asian Economy and Economies of Other Continents – Vol. 7

EU-Asia and the Re-Polarization of the Global Economic Arena

edited by

Lars Oxelheim

Lund University, Sweden &
Research Institute of
Industrial Economics, Sweden

World Scientific

NEW JERSEY • LONDON • SINGAPORE • BEIJING • SHANGHAI • HONG KONG • TAIPEI • CHENNAI

Published by

World Scientific Publishing Co. Pte. Ltd.
5 Toh Tuck Link, Singapore 596224
USA office: 27 Warren Street, Suite 401-402, Hackensack, NJ 07601
UK office: 57 Shelton Street, Covent Garden, London WC2H 9HE

British Library Cataloguing-in-Publication Data
A catalogue record for this book is available from the British Library.

Advanced Research on Asian Economy and Economies of Other Continents — Vol. 7
EU-ASIA AND THE RE-POLARIZATION OF THE GLOBAL ECONOMIC ARENA

ISBN-13 978-981-4366-52-6
ISBN-10 981-4366-52-8

In-house Editor: Yvonne Tan

Typeset by Stallion Press
Email: enquiries@stallionpress.com

Printed in Singapore.

Preface

The end of World War II left a bi-polar world built up of two superpowers: the US and the Soviet Union. After *glasnost* and the eventual breakdown of the Soviet Union at the beginning of the 1990s, a tri-polar world emerged consisting of the US, the European Union and Japan. However, the economic turbulence of the first decade of the 2000s changed the prerequisites of this tri-polar world. The burst of the IT bubble at the beginning of the decade and the severity of the economic and financial crisis at the end of it makes it appropriate to ask in what direction the balance of the global economic arena will be heading. What will the economic configuration look like in the decades to come? Will the old poles fade away and be replaced by new ones like China and India? As of the early 2010s, China is facing a momentum making it rank number one on a global scale as an exporting country and number two according to the size of its economy. However, China is also climbing to top position in terms of the magnitude of investments in research and development (R&D), making promises for a sustained economic position of tomorrow. The 12th strategic five-year plan released in March 2011 further emphasizes the ambition of Chinese politicians in that respect.

In this book we discuss the probability of different tentative global economic power balances to emerge. In the decades to come, will we see one superpower, a bi-polar world, or a tri-polar world of the kind we are having at the early 2010s? Will the US keep its position as a superpower despite all the economic troubles it is currently facing? We assume here that the control of the world's reserve currency will grant the US a continued role as a superpower, if not necessarily the only one, in the decades to come. The book then focuses on the other contestants — the EU, China and Japan. At the beginning of the 2010s, the EU is having its own economic problems with the EMU being under severe pressure, a sovereign debt crisis looming and the cohesion of the entire EU at stake. Japan, meanwhile, has for long periods faced very weak economic growth and suffered from problems related to deflation. The debt-ridden country was in early 2011 further stressed by a serious earthquake, a tsunami and a radioactive contagion in large areas. With such troubled contestants, the momentum of China may render it an advanced position in the global economic arena. Will China replace Japan in the tri-polar world of the early 2010s, or will it advance even further and become a superpower matching the US in a G2? Other powerful economic constellations of the next decades — though not discussed in detail in this book — may be the BRICS, the G7 or the G20, with the latter constellation having shown impressive decision-making power and a willingness among its members to cooperate during the financial crisis.

Different drivers of the re-polarization process are discussed in the 16 chapters of this book. What role will the global climate and energy policies play for the outcome of the re-polarization process? If all firms are to be responsible for taking care of their own pollution, then a country like China may find itself of less interest as a production or assembly site for European firms with end-users in Europe. What role will Africa play as a strategic platform for the contestants in the re-polarization process? As of the early 2010s, China, India and the EU are all very active on the African economic front. What will their different modes of entry mean for the outcome of the re-polarization process? What lessons can be learnt from the long-term innovation waves for the outcome of the process? How important for the process is the outcome of the social reforms in China? What role will a high degree of corruption play for the probability of a country like China becoming one of the poles in a bi- or tri-polar world? Are the Sovereign Wealth Funds (SWF) to be seen as strategic weapons in the re-polarization process? These and many other relevant questions for the re-polarization process and the future economic order of the global economic arena will be explored in this book.

The book is organized along three sections. The first six chapters address general and trend-wise developments relevant to the outcome of the re-polarization process. Chapters 7–9 examine the major Asian contestants — China, Japan and India — for a polar position. The final seven chapters address special issues such as the role of climate policies, corporate governance, social reforms and cross-border economic alliances for the outcome of the re-polarization process.

It is a delicate task and a challenge for me to try to summarize the findings of this book, since the many drivers discussed lead to different combinations of power centers as a result of the re-polarization process. However, as a common denominator, most findings of the book point in the direction towards the US and the EU continuing to be the most powerful economic centers of the world in the decades to come, whereas it is likely that China will need more time for reforms before it can overtake the role of Japan in the tri-polar world at the beginning of the 2010s.

The interdisciplinary approach required for a proper analysis of the many dimensions of the re-polarization process makes most traditional scientific journals less well-suited as an outlet for the result of such an analysis; hence, my motivation to present the results in the form of a book. The process behind the book was similar to that behind refereed journals. Following the main ideas of the re-polarization as outlined by me at the outset of this project, a number of research teams were invited to contribute and to address different parts of the research question as presented above. The first drafts were discussed at a three-day workshop held at the Trolleholm Castle in the south of Sweden in February 2010. Each contribution was refereed by two of the participating contributors to the book, in addition to the editor, and then discussed at a seminar during the workshop where the appointed referees acted as discussants. A second draft of each chapter was presented and discussed at the 12th annual conference of the Swedish Network for European Studies in Economics and Business (SNEE) in Mölle, in May 2010. Also on this occasion, each contribution had two appointed discussants. The final manuscript was then delivered to me in March 2011.

My greatest gratitude now goes to all those who have contributed different chapters and who participated in the Trolleholm workshop and the Mölle conference. I am grateful for their efforts and constructive attitudes in working with their own chapters, but also in reading and commenting on the other contributions. I would also like to thank Marcus Thorsheim for his work on coordinating the different versions of the chapters. Finally, I would like to thank my colleagues at the Lund School of Economics and Management and at the Research Institute of Industrial Economics (IFN) for their support and contribution in individual discussions.

One target audience of this book consists of researchers and students interested in the multidimensional development of the global economic power balance. However, the book should, on the academic side, attract interest from not only economists but also political scientists and researchers and students in the area of international relations. Moreover, as a second target audience, politicians and business leaders will benefit from reading this book in their search for a view on what is going to happen to the global economic map in the next couple of decades.

I am most grateful to the SNEE for providing necessary support, particularly for the three-day workshop at Trolleholm. SNEE's support made it possible to bring together scholars from many countries and to develop this network of colleagues conducting research on the different dimensions of the new global economic map.

Lars Oxelheim
January 2012

Contents

Notes on Contributors

Raj Aggarwal is the Sullivan Professor of International Business and Finance and former Dean of the College of Business Administration at the University of Akron. Before that, he was the Firestone Chair in Finance at Kent State University and the Mellen Chair in Finance at John Carroll University. He has received several teaching and research honors including university-wide distinguished scholar and distinguished faculty awards, and has also taught at Harvard, Michigan, and South Carolina. He has worked at Dana Corporation and Owens-Illinois, and is a member of the board at Manco (Duck, Loctite, and Lepage brands) and Ancora Mutual Funds. He has been a consultant to the US SEC, Comptroller of the Currency, the UN, the World Bank, and Fortune 100 and foreign companies. Dr. Aggarwal is a Fellow of the Academy of International Business, has been a Senior Fulbright Research Scholar in Asia, and received a Larosiere award for an essay on global finance presented at the 2000 Prague World Bank/IMF annual meeting. He attended the Indian Institute of Technology, Kent State University, and the University of Chicago, and is a Chartered Financial Analyst.

Anders Ahnlid is Director-General for Trade in the Swedish Ministry for Foreign Affairs and Sweden's representative in the EU Trade Policy Committee, in which the European Commission consults EU Member States on trade matters. Previously, he was Minister and head of the Department of Trade and Economic Affairs at the Embassy of Sweden to the USA, head of the Department for International Trade Policy at the Ministry for Foreign Affairs in Stockholm, and Deputy Permanent Representative of Sweden to the

Organization for Economic Cooperation and Development in Paris. Mr. Ahnlid formed part of Sweden's negotiating team in the Uruguay Round of multilateral trade negotiations in 1996–2004. He started his professional career as a trade policy analyst at Sweden's National Board of Trade. He has a background as a researcher and has co-operated with several universities and research institutions, and is the author of numerous articles on trade policy and trade negotiations.

Claes G. Alvstam is a professor in international economic geography at the School of Business, Economics and Law at the University of Gothenburg, and chairman of the Centre of European Research at the University of Gothenburg. His research deals with spatial patterns of foreign trade, foreign direct investment, global production networks and international business, as well as with economic integration and trade policy issues, in Europe and Asia. Recently published papers include studies on supplier upgrading in the value chains of transnational corporations, and the long-term economic integration process between Western and Eastern European countries.

Rym Ayadi is Senior Research Fellow and Head of Research of the Financial Institutions, Prudential Policy and Tax Unit at the Centre for European Policy Studies. She is Director of MedPro (Mediterranean Prospects), a 3 million-EU funded consortium to Think Ahead for the Mediterranean and the Euro-Mediterranean Partnership. Dr. Ayadi is an expert in economic, financial and political developments in Europe, Africa, and the Middle East. She has managed projects on financial services, trade, enterprise, consumer and foreign policies, funded by the European Union institutions; she is a member of several high-level expert groups at the European Commission and at the newly established European Supervisory Authorities, and external advisor to the European Parliament. She is also Rapporteur for several high-level CEPS working parties, which are chaired by senior officials and executives and attended by business representatives and officials; and Vice President of the European Financial Inclusion Network (EFIN), a European network that promotes mutual learning on financial inclusion. She is author of several books on financial markets and regulation, SME financing, banking mergers & acquisitions, banking diversity, and financial market integration in Europe and the Mediterranean.

Andrew Chiu is a Ph.D. candidate in Finance at the Hong Kong University of Science and Technology. His research interests include asset pricing, behavioral finance, and trading strategies. He has a Bachelor's degree in Computer Engineering from the University of Waterloo, and an M.B.A. from the Hong Kong University of Science and Technology. In between his studies, he has worked for 10 years at major software companies in the US and manufacturing firms in China.

Chun Ding, professor of economics, is the director of Center for European Studies, Dutch Study Center, Fudan University, as well as the secretary-general of the Chinese Society for EU Studies. He is acting editor of the Chinese journal, *World Economy Outlook*, and the chief editor of *Annual Report on European Economic Development*. Dr. Chun Ding specializes in the fields of world economy, European economic and social integration, European welfare state, and European and Chinese social security systems. He has taken charge of over 20 significant national and international research projects, and has published over 100 articles, theses and treatises. His monograph, *Comparative Studies on Performances of Four Major Health Care Systems in the World*, was awarded the Second-Class Prize for Eminent Monographs on Philosophy and Social Sciences in Shanghai in 2008.

Andrew Delios is Professor, Department of Strategy & Policy, at the National University of Singapore. He is a General Editor of the *Journal of Management Studies*, and is author or co-author of more than 70 published journal articles, case studies and book chapters. His articles have appeared in journals such as the *Academy of Management Journal*, *Administrative Science Quarterly*, *Strategic Management Journal*, and *Journal of International Business Studies*. Dr. Delios has authored six books including *International Business: An Asia-Pacific Perspective* (2nd Edition, Pearson), and *Strategy for Success in Asia* (Wiley). He has written case studies and conducted research on companies based in Canada, China, India, Italy, Hong Kong, Japan, Singapore and Vietnam. His research looks at foreign direct investment and strategy issues in emerging economies in Asia.

Roberto N. Galang is Assistant Professor, Department of Leadership and Strategy, at the John Gokongwei School of Management of Ateneo de Manila University. He is concurrently a doctoral student at the IESE Business School in Barcelona, where he is completing his dissertation on the impact of government regulation on the international diffusion of technology. Before joining the academe, he served as an economic consultant for Navigant Consulting-LECG in New York, Manila and Washington, working on engagements concerning the analysis of regulatory issues for private corporations. He has been involved in various research projects for companies in the Philippines, Vietnam, Canada, Jamaica, Dubai and the US. He has co-written a book on the impact of elitist politics on Philippine economic development for the French research agency, IRASEC.

Shubhashis Gangopadhyay is Managing Trustee and Research Director of India Development Foundation, and Director of the School of Humanities and Social Sciences, Shiv Nadar University. In 2008, the year of the global financial crisis, he was appointed Advisor to the Finance Minister, Government of India. He was awarded an honorary doctorate by the University of Gothenburg, Sweden in October 2006, where he is currently a Visiting Professor. He received his Ph.D. in Economics from Cornell University, USA in 1983; his Bachelor's degree from Presidency College, Kolkata in 1978; and did his schooling at Calcutta Boys' School. He joined the Indian Statistical Institute as a lecturer in 1983 and was promoted to full professor in 1991. He took over as founder-director of IDF, an independent research organization, in 2002. Dr. Gangopadhyay is the Chief Editor of the *Journal of Emerging Market Finance* (Sage Publications), and has been a member of the South Asia Chief Economist's Advisory Council of the World Bank. Currently, he is also an advisor to the Competition Commission of India and is on the Board of the Centre for Analytical Finance, ISB. He is also the founder-president of the Society for the Promotion of Game Theory and Its Applications. He has published widely in international journals, and has a number of books on economics and finance.

Janti Gunawan is a lecturer at Sepuluh Nopember Institute of Technology, Indonesia. She holds a B.Sc. (Industrial Engineering) from Sepuluh Nopember Institute of Technology, a Master of Engineering Science in Industrial Management from the University of New South Wales Australia, a Master of Commerce in International Business from the University of Auckland, and a Ph.D. in International Business from Victoria University of Wellington. She worked for the International Labor Organization during 2008–2010, served as a local programme coordinator for the Job Opportunities for Youth (JOY) project, and was involved in the feasibility investigations pertaining to the Vulcania Indonesia project. Her core research interests are in the fields of entrepreneurship, internationalization and international fair trade.

Michael Hutchison is a professor of economics at the University of California, Santa Cruz. He is also co-director of the Santa Cruz Institute for International Economics, Visiting Scholar at Federal Reserve Bank of San Francisco, Research Associate of the National Institute of Public Finance and Policy (New Delhi), and Senior Research Fellow at the Economic Policy Research Unit (University of Copenhagen). Dr. Hutchison joined the faculty of economics at the University of California at Santa Cruz in 1985. He has served as Chair of the Economics Department (2001–2003) and Dean of Social Sciences (2003–2006). Previous full-time appointments include research economist at the Federal Reserve Bank of San Francisco (1983–1985) and economist/head of section at the Bank for International Settlements (1999–2001) in Basle, Switzerland. He has also held visiting and consulting appointments with the International Monetary Fund, the Bank of Japan, the Reserve Bank of New Zealand, the Hong Kong Monetary Authority, the Bank of Sweden, and other institutions. He has taught at the University of Gothenburg, the Copenhagen Business School, the Haas School of Business at UC Berkeley, and the Marshall School of Business at the University of Southern California. Dr. Hutchison specializes in international finance, monetary economics and emerging market economies, and frequently consults with central banks and international institutions around the world. His recent research focuses on the causes and costs of financial crises, the role of the IMF in the international financial system, financial instability, and the effectiveness of central bank foreign exchange market intervention. He has published over 100 articles and 8 books and monographs on these topics.

Michael Keller is a research assistant and Ph.D. candidate at the Department of Economics and Social Policy, Faculty of Economics and Social Sciences, at the University of Fribourg, Switzerland. His Master's degree in Economics and Social Sciences from the University of Fribourg, Switzerland was obtained in 2009. He has been working as a researcher and consultant at the Center for Competitiveness, University of Fribourg, Switzerland since 2008.

Ari Kokko is a professor of international business at Copenhagen Business School, and an associate professor at the Nordic Institute of Asian Studies in Copenhagen. He runs the Center for International Business and Emerging Markets at CBS and focuses in particular on the role of trade and foreign direct investment in the development process. In recent years, his work has had a clear bias towards China, Vietnam, and other parts of East Asia. Before joining CBS, he was director of the China Economic Research Center at the Stockholm School of Economics, and he has also held positions as professor of international business at Abo Akademi University in Finland, and as research director at the European Institute of Japanese Studies in Stockholm. Dr. Kokko was a member of the board of directors of Sida for nine years, chairman for a Swedish government inquiry into the development of Swedish export competitiveness, and has been a consultant to several governments, international organizations, and private firms. In 2008, he received an honorary doctorate in Economic Sciences from Tartu University, Estonia.

Lena Lindberg holds a Ph.D. in international economic geography, and is a research fellow at the Centre for European Research at the University of Gothenburg (CERGU) and the School of Business, Economics and Law, University of Gothenburg. Currently, she acts as special adviser to the Ministry for Foreign Affairs, Sweden. Her specialization is in the external relations of the EU, in particular the trade relations and free trade negotiations between the EU and countries in South and North East Asia. Her dissertation dealt with regionalization and economic integration in the ASEAN region.

Peter MacKay is a professor at Hong Kong University of Science and Technology. He publishes in top journals such as *The Journal of Finance*, *The Review of Financial Studies*, *The Journal of Financial and Quantitative Analysis*, and the *Journal of Banking and Finance*. His research spans several areas of corporate finance, namely, capital structure, corporate risk management, corporate investment, working capital management, and corporate governance. His work on capital structure examines how firms' production technology and product-market environment affect their financial policy. His work on corporate risk management shows how much value a firm can create (or destroy) through its risk-management policy. He is currently extending this work to examine how far ahead firms hedge their risks. In related work, he is tackling the controversial question of whether corporate diversification creates or destroys firm value. His work on corporate investment shows how industry competition affects corporate capital expenditures. His work on working capital management compares the working-capital policies and practices of firms in Canada, the United States, and Australia. His work on corporate governance examines how shareholders' ability to redeem the money they entrust to mutual-fund managers bears on fund performance. Dr. MacKay has experience of teaching in universities in Canada, the United States, Europe and Asia, in undergraduate, postgraduate (M.B.A., M.Sc., Ph.D.) and executive education programs. He has industry experience from Reed Paper (Quebec, Canada); Legal Department, Postipankki (Helsinki, Finland); and Alberta Treasury (Calgary, Canada). Dr. MacKay has also launched and managed several small business ventures.

Cal B. Muckley is a lecturer at the University College in Dublin, Ireland. Previously he was a lecturer at Durham Business School. Dr. Muckley specializes in international finance. His many scholarly publications include papers in the *Journal of Common Market Studies*, *Journal of International Markets, Institutions & Money*, and *International Journal of Finance and Economics*.

Yumiko Okamoto is a professor of economics at Doshisha University in Japan. She holds a Ph.D. in economics from the University of Hawaii at Manoa in the US. Previously, she was an associate professor at both Kobe University and Nagoya University in Japan. Dr. Okamoto has been visiting professor at Brandeis University in the US, Universidad Nacional de La Plata in Argentina, Universidad de Chile and the Instituto de Estudios Internacionales in Chile, and Nanjing Audit University in China. Between April 2009 and March 2010, she served as a visiting research fellow at both Gothenburg University in Sweden and the Science and Technology Policy Research Unit (SPRU) at the University of Sussex. Her major research fields are international economics and economics of innovation.

Lars Oxelheim holds a Chair in International Business and Finance at the Lund Institute of Economic Research, Lund University, and is affiliated with the Research Institute of Industrial Economics (Institutet för Näringslivsforskning), Stockholm, and with the Fudan University, Shanghai. He is chairman of the Swedish Network for European Studies in Economics and Business (SNEE). He has authored or edited some 35 research monographs, and authored or co-authored a number of research articles published in international business, finance, and economic journals. His recent research monographs include *How Unified is the European Union?* (Springer Verlag), *Corporate Decision-Making with Macroeconomic Uncertainty* (Oxford University Press), *Markets and Compensation for Executives in Europe* (Emerald Group Publishing), *National Tax Policy in Europe — To Be or Not to Be* (Springer Verlag), *Corporate and Institutional Transparency for Economic Growth in Europe* (Elsevier), *European Union and the Race for Inward FDI in Europe* (Elsevier), and *Money Markets and Politics — A Study of European Financial Integration and Monetary Policy Options* (Edward Elgar). Dr. Oxelheim is a member of several editorial boards.

Rebecca Piekkari is Professor of International Business at Aalto University, School of Economics (formerly Helsinki School of Economics), Finland. She holds a Ph.D. from the Helsinki School of Economics and Business Administration. Her research interests focus on the management of multinational corporations, particularly on control, coordination and communication challenges in these organizations. She has also developed considerable expertise in the use of qualitative case studies in international business research, and is a member of several editorial review boards.

Dr. Piekkari has published many journal articles and has edited a *Handbook of Qualitative Research Methods for International Business*. She is actively involved in providing methodological training to Ph.D. students in Europe.

Apanard Penny Prabhavivadhana is a Senior Research Analyst in the Financial Research group at the Milken Institute. Her research focuses on financial institutions, open economy macroeconomics, emerging market economies and financial crises. Her work has been published in the *Journal of International Money and Finance*, *International Review of Finance*, *Open Economies Review*, *Journal of International Financial Markets, Institutions & Money*, and *International Journal of Economics and Finance*. Prior to joining the Milken Institute, Dr. Prabhavivadhana was an assistant professor of economics at the University of Illinois at Springfield. While completing her Ph.D., she also held visiting scholar positions at the Claremont Institute for Economic Policy Studies and the Freeman Program in Asian Political Economy at the Claremont Colleges, and was a lecturer of economics at Pitzer College and the University of Redlands. She received a Ph.D. in economics from Claremont Graduate University in 2005.

Elizabeth L. Rose is Professor of International Business at Aalto University, School of Economics (formerly Helsinki School of Economics), Finland. She holds a B.S.E. (Civil Engineering) from Princeton University, and an M.S.E. (Civil Engineering), an A.M. (Statistics) and a Ph.D. (Business Administration) from the University of Michigan. Her core research interests pertain to various aspects of internationalization and global strategy, especially foreign direct investment and multimarket competition, and she has a long-standing interest in the business contexts of Asia. She is a member of several editorial review boards, and has served on the committees charged with selecting the best doctoral research for both the Academy of International Business and the International Management Division of the Academy of Management. Currently, she is serving her second term as President of the Australia and New Zealand International Business Academy (ANZIBA). Dr. Rose is also the President of the Association of Japanese Business Studies, and the foundation Chair of the Australia and New Zealand Chapter of the Academy of International Business (AIB).

Lennart Schön is Professor (chair) in economic history at Lund University. His research is mainly devoted to industrialization and modern economic growth, with technological, structural and cyclical changes in long-term perspective. He has, *inter alia*, presented models of long waves and structural crises, and he led the construction of Swedish Historical National Accounts 1800–2000 and its regional composition. Dr. Schön is also co-founder of the Centre of Innovation Research in the Learning Economy (CIRCLE) at Lund University, as well as being a trustee and former president of the European Historical Economics Society. Recent publications include "Electrification and energy productivity", *Ecological Economics*, vol. 68 (2009); and *Sweden's Road to Modernity* (2010).

S. K. Shanthi is an economist currently serving as the Chair-Professor of the Union Bank Center for Banking Excellence at the Great Lakes Institute of Management, Chennai, India. Throughout her career as teacher and researcher, she has worked at a few other institutions like the Indian Statistical Institute, New Delhi and the University of Southern California, Los Angeles. She was with the Institute for Financial Management and Research, Chennai during 1990–2006. There, she started out as a research scholar and went on to become an Associate Professor. She also has a widespread interest in research and has made contributions to the areas of local body public finance, applied finance, and financial markets and banking. Dr. Shanthi has consulted with the first State Finance Commission of Tamil Nadu, and with other governmental departments like the Finance Ministry and the Planning Commission, Tamil Nadu. She has also consulted with the Confederation of Indian Industry, Southern Region, India.

Weiqi Tang is currently a Ph.D. candidate in Economics at Fudan University, Shanghai, China, majoring in energy, resource and environmental economics. He is also an assistant director of the Center for Energy Economics and Strategy Studies, Fudan University. He started his research on international and Chinese energy markets in 2007, and has a few publications including one paper in *Energy Economics* (Vol. 32, Supplement 1, September 2010, pp. S3–S14). His research interest also includes international climate policy analysis, and he is currently working on energy-environment-economy modeling of Chinese and international energy systems.

Clas Wihlborg is the Fletcher Jones Chair of International Business at the Argyros School of Business and Economics, Chapman University. He received his Ph.D. in Economics from Princeton University in 1977, and has held faculty positions at New York University, University of Southern California, Gothenburg University in Sweden and Copenhagen Business School in Denmark. His teaching and research focus on international finance, corporate finance and financial institutions. Publications include numerous articles in scientific journals and books in the areas of international finance, corporate finance and financial regulation. His most recent book is *Corporate Decision-Making with Macroeconomic Uncertainty*, Oxford University Press, 2008, co-authored with Lars Oxelheim. Dr. Wihlborg is a member of the European Shadow Financial Regulatory Committee, and a board member of Global Medical Excellence, LLC.

Libo Wu is a senior scholar in environmental and natural resource economics at Fudan University. She received her Ph.D. in environmental and natural resource economics from Hiroshima University in Japan in 2004. Dr. Wu has been executive director of the Center for Energy Economics and Strategies Studies at Fudan University since its establishment in 2007, and deputy director of the Center for Environmental Economics at Fudan University since 2005. She has been the principal of dozens of projects funded by the National Ministry of Science and Technology, National Ministry of Education, National Funding of Philosophy and Social Science, Shanghai Municipal Development and Reform Commission, and Shanghai Municipal Science and Technology Commission, to name a few. As an outstanding overseas returnee, she was honored with the title of "Pujiang Excellent Overseas Returnees" in 2007 and "Aurora Scholar" in 2010 by the Shanghai government. She has published more than 30 academic papers on SSCI, SCI and other journals.

Wenshi Yu is a junior researcher in the School of Economics at Fudan University. Her major research interest is in finance and she received her basic training from Zhejiang University, majoring in finance.

Chapter 1

Long-Term Innovation Waves and the Potential Dissonance between Europe and Asia

Lennart Schön

1.1 Introduction

During the last few decades, dramatic events have transformed the global economy. The breakthrough of microelectronics and the diffusion of digital information and communication technology, often referred to as the Third Industrial Revolution, interacted with a new flood in globalization. While the industrial leaders placed their imprint upon the breakthrough period of ICT, globalization and economic growth was increasingly dominated by developments in China and India from the 1990s onwards. These two giant economies attained a new significance in international matters from the turn of the millennium — particularly demonstrated after the Asian financial crisis at the end of the 1990s that saw a retardation in growth in large parts of Eastern and Southeastern Asia but a further acceleration in the Chinese and Indian economies. Contrasts and contradictions in the new global situation were even more acutely expressed in the global crisis that emerged in 2008, which signifies the need for thorough adaptations to new structural conditions and may also indicate a historical turning point into a new trend period.

The main idea of this chapter is to put the present economic situation into a long-term historical perspective and discuss the prospects of new innovation waves over the next decades and their implications for Europe and Asia, with a particular emphasis on the role of China. These prospects are also put into a more general perspective on structural change as an ingredient in economic growth and as a pertinent question in the present global crisis. In particular, the question is raised whether we are witnessing the awakening of a Chinese giant as a new leading polar in the global economy, overtaking Europe and the USA, or if old leaders will come out of the crisis in a refreshed manner.

In Section 1.2 of this chapter, a historical generalization is presented from the observation of different structural epochs in modern economic history, forming long waves. In Section 1.3 some general implications are discussed regarding economic growth and innovations for the next decades of upswing in a new long wave that may come out of the present crisis. In Section 1.4 two different innovation systems — based on formal science and market-led interaction, respectively — are contrasted in relation to assumed trends in innovation. Comparing economic growth internationally is, however, a rather complicated issue, since changes in both production structures and prices are involved. In Section 1.5 measurements of economic growth over the last two decades are critically assessed, which provides a basis for further analysis of structural change and comparative speed in income development in Europe, Asia and USA. Thereafter, in Section 1.6, prospects over the next decades for innovation and growth in these three major regions are discussed, followed by conclusions in Section 1.7 on global leadership in innovative behavior in a tri-polar world.

1.2 A Framework of Big Waves and Long Waves

In the economic history of the modern world, there is a conception of a long-term pattern of centennial *big waves* that have been initiated by industrial revolutions (cf. Gordon, 1999). Such revolutions do not occur overnight and do not immediately lead to any marked acceleration in economic growth. Rather, they create, within a couple of decades, a new basis for further growth in the unfolding of the ensuing big wave. Under such a perspective, the Third Industrial Revolution may have marked the beginning of a third big wave that will characterize much of the 21st century. From temporal, technological and geographical perspectives, the industrial revolutions have had the following features[1]:

- The First Industrial Revolution took off in the late 18th century with steam engines and the factory system as the major innovations. The revolution was geographically centered in Britain, with strongholds in the regions surrounding the Channel.
- The Second Industrial Revolution accelerated from the late 19th century with the electrical motor and the combustion engine as central innovations in a sophisticated machinery industry and with scientifically-based industries. This revolution had a geographically widened center with Germany and parts of Continental Europe as well as Northeastern USA as leading parties within the evolving North Atlantic Economy.
- The Third Industrial Revolution was a late 20th century phenomenon with the breakthrough of microelectronics and with increased knowledge-intensive interaction between industry and services. Once again, the geographical strongholds widened considerably with Western USA and Japan, around the buoyant Pacific Economy, joining the regions of the old North Atlantic Economy.

Furthermore, there is a pattern within each big wave with two structural epochs of about 40–50 years forming *long waves.* The first long wave comprises the periods of the industrial revolutions and the wave is focused on the technological breakthrough of radical innovations in the production sectors. The second long wave is focused on the wider infrastructural, social and institutional developments that have turned the radical innovations into General Purpose Technologies (Bresnahan and Trajtenberg, 1995), becoming an integral part of the backbone of the social organization. Historically, the second waves have entailed the following enlargement of the radical innovations:

- From the 1850s and 1860s, upswings were directed to the wider construction of railway networks, telegraphs and steam ships combined

[1] The model of waves in this chapter builds upon Schön (1998, 2000 and 2009).

with institutional adaptations to enlarged global interaction on all markets. While states became more involved in the infrastructural development at the national level, interaction over markets for goods, capital and labor intensified globally.

- From the 1930s and 1940s (and gaining wider and stronger momentum in the 1950s), upswings saw the wider social diffusion of combustion engines and electrical motors into national systems of infrastructures, concomitant with institutional adaptations to urbanization and to the industrial mass consumption society that had evolved from the beginning of the 20th century.
- If we follow the same pattern in time and context, we can envisage an upswing from the 2010s with the wider diffusion of networks and infrastructure based upon microelectronics (with the Internet as one early expression) integrated with other means of communication, and with institutional and juridical adaptations to these new conditions.

One can further add that these second upswings have created greater scope for diffusion of modernization and economic growth globally based upon reduced transaction costs institutionally and technologically. However, that has also meant the appearance of bottlenecks or new obstacles to growth that have had to be addressed by innovations, both in technology and in institutions. The contemporary menace of global climate change is a dramatic illustration of this point, challenging technology and institutions at a higher level than at earlier junctions in history.

These sequences fit largely to the observation, which Nikolai Kondratieff made in the 1920s, of long waves back to the First Industrial Revolution. Since the time of Kondratieff (1926), much new empirical evidence has amassed and long waves of roughly 40 years have reappeared. Each long wave has been demarcated by international or global crises that have been both financial and structural in character. These crises have been the lower turning points in the long waves. Such crises occurred in the late 1840s, early 1890s, early 1930s and mid-1970s. They were all preceded by decades of increased competition and fierce rationalization, and they were succeeded by decades of decisive thrusts of long-term investments, enlarging capacity in new trajectories of growth that either brought forward radical innovations or diffused applications of the innovations in transformed structures at a broader plane socially.

So far, the events after the beginning of the 2010s combine the characteristics of prior financial and structural crises and, furthermore, appear according to the time pattern of the long waves. Thus, it is the assumption in this chapter that historical experiences provide relevant perspectives for the future, at a rather general level which is summarized in Figure 1.1.

The waves have, furthermore, had a number of common characteristics. Three such characteristics are important for the launching of new innovation trajectories and should be emphasized in the present discussion; namely, shifts in relative prices, diffusion of industrialization to new regions, and new patterns in consumption. These three characteristics are important since they contribute to the creation of platforms for further innovations and structural change and, thus, for long-term economic growth.

The timing of Kondratieff's observation of long waves in the international price level was largely corroborated by Walt Rostow's (1978) analysis of relative prices. Rostow indicated trend periods in the relative price of primary to secondary goods with a rising ratio corresponding to the upswing phase of the long wave that fits to shifts in demand for primary goods in periods of long-term investments into new capacity, and to shifts in supply from that capacity when it was fully installed in the later stage of the wave. Thus, the swings in relative prices were provoked by the time lag from investment to production in the primary

1790s — 1st Industrial Revolution (Steam engines)
1850s — Railways, steam ships
1890s — 2nd Industrial Revolution (Motors)
1930s — Automobiles, electrification
1970s — 3rd Industrial Revolution (Micro-electronics)
2010s — Internet, social media

Figure 1.1: Long-term pattern of innovation waves.

goods sector. Historically, these waves saw an increased demand for raw materials in investment booms and a subsequent but belated widened production capacity, at a time when reduced investments into plants and infrastructure decreased demand for these resources. Such trend periods due to difference in the timing of demand and supply shift are still very important aspects of the waves, even if the relative prices of primary and secondary goods have developed slightly differently in the previous decades than in the Rostowian pattern, largely because of the Chinese expansion (see further below).

Furthermore, in each wave, the global economy was enlarged. Increased investments and expanding new trajectories of growth have stimulated demand in the global economy with the diffusion of modernization and industrialization. New industrializing economies and emerging markets have appeared. For a time, the diffusion of industrialization has stimulated overall demand since the emerging economies have had high investment ratios and deficits in their trade balances; but over a couple of decades, the output from these economies has expanded, leading to increased competition and to downward pressure on prices on large segments of the world market. Imbalances in trade appear more widely and are aggravated by a combination of structural crises and debt crises at the end, resulting in increased pressure towards structural transformation in many economies, both in the center and in the periphery of the world market. The past two decades bear ample witness to this mechanism.

Lastly, at the final stage of the wave, consumption has increased in the center and social patterns have changed more rapidly. The initial technological breakthroughs, with a basis in the production sphere or in infrastructure, have over a couple of decades led to a rich flow of new consumption goods that increasingly have been supplied at falling prices from emerging markets. The combination of technological change and new low-cost producers contributes to a deflationary tendency overall on the markets, which was the original observation by Kondratieff. Entrepreneurial profits are depressed in the center, but real wages are rising — nominal wages are stickier than prices. Thus, such decades as the 1880s, 1920s, 1960s and 2000s have been happy decades in the centers from a consumer point of view. These consumer booms have been important, moreover, from a long-term perspective since the change in consumer behavior is a necessary experience for furthering the innovative trajectory. Such change in behavior is to a large extent the unforeseeable effect of prior innovations, which basically fits to an evolutionary comprehension of economic growth.

In this evolutionary perspective, structural crises are critical, since during these events a broader spectrum of choice of future trajectories is open within a rather narrow timeframe of opportunities, until the mechanism of path dependency increases over the next wave. In this perspective the present crisis is structural, and raises a number of long-term issues that need to be handled, with indications of a possible shift of future trends.

The historical pattern of waves and structural crises also indicates that the modern society evolves over epochs with a certain stability or inertia, and furthermore, that institutions and structures stay stable over periods of roughly the same length despite the fact that the pace of change in a number of areas is increasing over time. The fact that structures and institutions have seemed to evolve at the same pace over the modern history of the past two centuries indicates that some elements of social and human behavior, fundamental to long-term development, are rather constant. Our time is not different in that respect.

The historical pattern of a widening global economy purveys another experience relevant for the present situation and for present apprehensions in industrialized countries of becoming increasingly marginalized due to Chinese or Asian expansion. The global economy has developed from uni-polar to bi-polar and to multi-polar. Old centers have not disappeared with the emergence of new ones; the precondition to stay in a polar position has been, though, that old centers have been capable of thorough structural transformation in relation to new circumstances.

Two questions, then, are central to the following discussion. Firstly, which economies will be likely to take the lead in the innovative trajectories that will characterize the next long wave? Secondly, within what timeframe will Asia overall — or perhaps we should confine the question to China as a new giant economy — converge with today's leading countries in overall social and economic capacity, measured as GDP per capita?

1.3 Drivers for Further Growth

Global economic growth in each wave has been characterized by two mechanisms, namely ***innovations*** that shift the technology frontier in production and consumption and ***catch-up*** processes with the leaders in the different sectors. Thus, global growth rates have been determined by the magnitude of innovative shifts and by the ability of economies to diffuse innovations widely and to catch-up with leaders.[2]

Innovations and catching-up have, quite naturally, different importance in different economies. The closer the economy is to the frontier of production and consumption possibilities, the more dependent the economy is upon innovation for further growth, i.e., upon the ability to turn knowledge and learning into new combinations of resources, while the mechanisms of catch-up (which involve a number of elements such as structural change from agriculture to industry and services, investments in modern social and material infrastructures, increase in capital intensity, transfer of technology, etc.) approach depletion or decreasing marginal returns.

In each wave, a number of new countries have caught up with the leaders. In that sense, the pool of potential catch-up economies is diminishing. This does not mean, however, that catch-up will disappear or even diminish as a mechanism for global growth over the next decades or the next century. Firstly, new countries are likely to enter the global scene, increasing competition from below upon all economies, particularly upon recent latecomers such as China and India. Secondly, there is still much scope for further catch-up in India and China and other emerging markets, with a wide gap to leading economies still existing from technical, economic and social aspects. Thirdly, new scope

---

[2] On catch-up and forging ahead, see Abramovitz (1989).

for catch-up appears over and over again in modern history since, in the upswing of the waves, some economies are able to open up innovative trajectories and forge ahead by shifting the frontier outwards — in some cases, even catching-up economies of the preceding waves have had the drive to forge ahead, thanks to very strong connections between knowledge creation institutions and production sectors. Such examples were the US and German economies in the late 19th century and the Japanese economy in the late 20th century, at least in some sectors of industry and services.

Thus, the two questions raised in the preceding section of this chapter concern the major mechanisms for global growth. The first question asks what innovations will be central to enable further growth globally and what economies will take the lead in that respect. From the perspective of long-term innovation waves, a leading economy does not have to be the richest economy or the largest economy, but it has to have the capacity to take the lead in crucial innovations over the next decades. Thus, conditions for innovation in Europe and Asia as well as in the USA are certainly central aspects for long-term innovation and for further growth. The second question may be phrased as to whether the very strong catch-up drive behind growth in parts of Asia over the last decades will continue or if it will taper off. The answer is dependent upon what conditions will characterize growth globally and the ability in these economies to change the structures behind growth, in order to meet new conditions.

Trends in Prices and in Demand for Innovations during the Next Decades

In the recent wave during the past two decades, the widening of the global economy has been unprecedented in scope due to Chinese and Indian growth. Their growth rates are perhaps not spectacular from a historical point of view, but the numbers are. More than 2 billion people have become actively integrated into the global economy at a path of high annual growth rates. This has meant a fundamental change in the relationship between factors of production. The increase in the supply of labor has been enormous, while at the same time the pressure on natural resources is augmenting rapidly. Shifts in relative prices between resource-intensive and labor-intensive goods have already appeared during the past decade (in contrast to the earlier Rostowian pattern), but these shifts will most probably be reinforced over the next decade, even if growth rates in India and China will be some percentage points lower. Thus, two major trends may be forecasted, originating in the Asian expansion.

First, the Asian expansion will continue to put a downward pressure on the relative price of labor in large segments of both industry and services — particularly in areas where the labor process is fairly standardized and is suitable for large-scale operations and for catch-up processes. On the other hand, demand pressure will continue to increase, even accelerate, on goods that are intensive in natural resources such as construction materials, energy and food. With further growth in China and India likely, the contribution to total demand for such resources will increase for every year over the next decade or two. This is particularly so, since output increases in this area need long-term investments, which during the construction phase tend to further increase demand for material and energy (cf. the mechanisms of the Rostowian relative price cycle between primary and secondary sectors). Price increases of energy and of natural resource-intensive materials may be further sustained by institutional measures taken to restrict climate change.

Another reasonable trend is that demand will shift towards new services with little material content. This will be particularly pronounced among medium- and high-income earners and thus, on an aggregate social level, in high-income nations. So far, both USA and Europe have been dominant in advancing new consumption patterns. This has been due to factors such as high income levels, a prominent role of consumption in economic growth, and a high degree of openness in societies regarding new trends and variation in habits. With a shift in demand towards more complex or more consumer-oriented services — and with a less elastic supply of human capital — the relative price of less standardized or more complex services will increase over the next decade.

Prices are important for the formation of value-added and for the distribution of income between economies. Shifts in relative prices are the combined effect of shifts in supply and demand. They may, hypothetically, be inversely related to changes in productivity, in which case the effect of the price change on income is minimal since it would be directly offset by an equivalent volume change per production factor. However, relationships are not that direct in all economies. Rather, one could say that the pressure to increase productivity is particularly strong in areas of falling relative prices (due to increased competition), while the anticipated remuneration to innovation is highest in areas of rising prices (due to increased demand).

This has a bearing on economic growth and income in different regions. Price movements are essential in relation to innovations and to the appearance of *development blocks* (Dahmén, 1988) or new configurations of complementary activities around important innovations. Major development blocks have some technological innovation at the center which usually provides goods or services at falling prices (through a decisive supply shift), which at the same time leads to an increase in demand for complementary goods or services that are less elastically supplied and thus meet rising prices. It is not certain that a concentration of resources in the innovation area, usually defined as high-tech, leads to a more favorable development in terms of income than allocation to complementary activities (such as a number of services).

The best situation is, of course, if demand shifts and innovative supply shifts are combined. Knowledge and innovations that combat bottlenecks and enhance the supply or reduce the demand of e.g., energy, material or food may be richly remunerated over a period of some decades (until competition in such innovative areas increases again at the ending decades of the anticipated new wave). Knowledge of energy-intensive processes, both in traditional industries and in new areas such as biotech, will be important to meet the challenges. Thus, mergers between the more mature information technology and the research-intensive biotechnology, which is still awaiting major commercialization breakthroughs, are highly ranked candidates for new development blocks in the next wave. A logical next step in the microelectronic revolution into nanotechnology and its fusion with biotechnology would also replicate the historical development during earlier "second winds" in the big waves. On one hand, the ability to construct smaller and more powerful units of the original radical innovation has been instrumental for the wider application into General Purpose Technologies, which could be applied effectively both in small units and in large social systems. On the other hand, complementary innovations in the area of materials that have dissolved or reduced bottlenecks in the supply of natural resources have been of utmost importance for further global growth. New steel processes as well as new plastics and metal alloys served such functions in the 19th and 20th centuries, respectively.

New trends in consumer behavior may be another important component behind growth, particularly since a coming second wave of the Third Industrial Revolution will very likely have a strong focus on the wider social diffusion and consequences of the microelectronic revolution. Such a trend involves two major preconditions. The first and perhaps most important precondition is that the contemporary rich economies are able to change their structures in relation to new global markets (i.e., taking advantage of relative shifts in prices) and keep increasing their GDP and income at a rate of 1–2 percentages per capita annually. That would sustain the consumer demand into new directions in conjunction with the demand from a rising and numerous middle-class in emerging markets. The second precondition is that consumer demand changes in the direction of more knowledge-intensive and less material-intensive goods and services. Innovative and knowledge-intensive services in a broad spectrum would in that case become a more substantial part of global growth. These perspectives raise a number of questions concerning future innovative trajectories as well as the direction of structural change in different economies.

1.4 Innovation in the Learning Economy

In studies of innovation and innovation systems, two distinctly different mechanisms have been distinguished. On one hand, there is the science- and technology-based innovation process, labeled STI; and on the other hand, there is the experience-based learning process, labeled DUI (Doing-Using-Interacting).

The STI process has been much targeted by research and innovation policy. It is characterized by investments in universities, in research institutes and in R&D, mainly by large firms. It is also characterized by increased interaction between these organizations in National Innovation Systems, and leads to a greater number of trained academics in all organizations.

The STI system is advantageous when it comes to following a certain technological trajectory and exploiting possibilities at the frontier of knowledge through basic research. It is also of great importance for the ability of an economy to import and adopt technology and innovations at an early stage.

The DUI process emphasizes interaction in different respects, between groups of employees within the firm, between employees in different firms and, perhaps most of all, between firms and customers. Innovations come out of learning from experience and from tests of a multitude of ideas. It goes without saying that DUI is more important in innovative areas related to new consumer behavior and to social change.

The structure of DUI processes means that such innovations tend to come out of less hierarchical organizations, built up from rather autonomous groups that are open to communication. Such organizations are more prevalent in open societies. The DUI process is of course still dependent upon a high level of knowledge among employees, particularly upon problem-solving abilities on all levels related to the doing-using-interacting functions.

In reality, the STI and DUI systems are not totally separated from each other or mutually exclusive, since all processes rely upon formal knowledge and science to some extent as well as upon experience and communication. It is, however, held by innovation economists that the two systems dominate different spheres of the economy and characterize different economies.

These systems played different roles historically, in different stages of economic growth. Thus, it was largely the Second Industrial Revolution that gave rise to formalized STI innovation processes. With the breakthrough of more sophisticated technology at the end of the 19th century, cooperation between universities and industry really took off. During that period, large firms established laboratories for R&D, superseding experience-based trial and error in the sphere of doing-using that had dominated in the First Industrial Revolution. The Third Industrial Revolution, however, created scope for much broader interactive innovation processes within firms, between firms and with consumers, thanks to *inter alia* dramatically reduced transaction costs. Thus, DUI reappeared in a novel form and with a new significance for innovations.

The major trends in growth and in relative prices have different implications for the innovation procedure. On one hand, the increased pressure on natural resources will in turn increase the pressure to advance knowledge in science-based technologies. Thus, innovations in areas such as energy, materials, medicine and food will be highly valued. STI processes will be fundamental in opening up new spheres of knowledge and innovative trajectories, particularly regarding the use of natural resources. On the other hand, shifts in demand to services and to virtual economies will induce innovations related to new consumer behavior, and thus build upon interaction and trial-and-error in a more open, evolutionary manner. Therefore, the broader array of services and consumer goods in future growth will most probably increase the importance of DUI processes.

In both areas, innovation will require that many disciplines cooperate in knowledge creation. Hence, the ability to communicate and coordinate is of utmost importance. While science-based innovations may be met by concentrated efforts that to some, but only to some, extent have a better fit in more hierarchical organizations and societies, the area of DUI innovations is definitely dependent upon an open society with flat organizations and with close connections to experimenting consumers.

1.5 Economic Growth, Structural Change and Purchasing Power

What is the growth rate of GDP in China? How does it compare to European growth rates? These questions are straightforward, but straight answers are more difficult to get, notwithstanding the very prominent role figures of economic growth rates have in every discussion or analysis of performances.

Every measure of economic growth is based upon a set of fixed prices for all goods and services produced, in order to eliminate the effect of inflation or deflation upon the sum of value-added produced in the economy. This may seem a trivial procedure but in fact it is not trivial, especially not when comparisons of growth rates should be made between countries.

In international comparisons of economic growth and levels, two principles are usually combined. Firstly, growth rates are calculated within each country with a set of fixed prices from each country. Thus, the different branches and sectors are weighted according to price relations within the country. Secondly, the level of the time series of GDP is adjusted for each country at one benchmark according to a measure of purchasing power parity (PPP) — i.e., a large set of "world market prices" for all goods and services in GDP is constructed for the benchmark year, and each country's GDP is recalculated for that particular year. Thus, the level of all series is adjusted at this PPP benchmark, but not the slopes of the series (i.e., the growth rates), which are determined by the domestic calculation.

Since different economies have different structures both in production and in prices, and since there are structural changes both in production and in prices, the use of fixed prices from different points in time will give different growth rates. Such variation is an abomination to the statistician, but varying results may also be an analytical tool to indicate the magnitude and direction of structural change in different economies.

In this section, the rate of economic growth in Asia, Europe and the USA will be adjusted for changes in purchasing power between two points in time, 1990 and 2005. The adjustment will serve a double purpose. Firstly, adjusted growth rates provide internationally more comparable growth rates in income per capita. Secondly, the size and the direction of the adjustment — upwards or downwards — will indicate the direction of structural change in relation to international price movements.

Nationally calculated growth rates may deviate from the growth rate at purchasing power parities, mainly for two reasons. Firstly, the national price structure is different from the constructed world price structure. This is particularly the case if large sectors of an economy are closed from world trade. In many economies at an early stage of industrialization, there are "traditional" sectors, particularly in agriculture and services, that usually produce at much lower prices than at the world market prices. The opposite may be the case in some industrialized countries that have protected sectors producing at relatively high prices. If growth rates differ much between closed and open sectors — as a general rule, the production volume of a closed sector grows more slowly — these differences in relative prices affect aggregate growth rates. Secondly, prices change over time. With fixed prices, only the volume of goods and services is accounted for, but the purchasing power of an economy is affected if relative prices change in any direction.[3]

In economic history, a so-called Gerschenkron effect has been identified in industrialization processes, characterized by a rather general phenomenon of falling relative prices and rising quantities of advancing, innovative commodities. During industrialization, such a development indicates increased productivity in modernizing branches. However, it may also indicate increasing pressure from external competition, while the opposite development of prices rising together with rising quantities may indicate a more favorable orientation to demand.

Constructing PPPs covering all economies in the world is labor-intensive and is performed only with rather long intervals. More

[3] A third reason for deviations is, of course, measurement errors that may be larger in countries at low income levels than in rich countries. The error is supposed to be unbiased and may affect adjustment in both directions.

recently, PPPs were constructed in 1990 and 2005. One approach to adjust growth rates between these benchmarks is to recalculate the national growth rates according to the annual percentage change in per capita purchasing power from a global supply of goods and services at fixed world prices.[4] The adjustment will be the combined effect of differences between internal and world price structures and of national orientation to segments of relatively rising or falling prices at the world market.

In Table 1.1, the traditional, domestically determined growth rates for a number of countries in Western Europe and Asia and for USA are presented together with growth rates adjusted for changes in purchasing power between the PPP benchmarks of 1990 and 2005.

The result is very striking. In traditional measures, using domestic price relations to quantities in the calculation, the difference between Asian and European growth rates is indeed large — excluding Japan, the Asian average rate is more than three times the European rate, and including Japan it is twice the European rate. When growth rates are adjusted for purchasing power parities in 1990 and 2005, however, a rather different picture emerges. All European countries increase their growth rates, some quite substantially. On the whole, one may hypothesize a positive demand effect, i.e., a European orientation to areas with increasing relative price. In the Norwegian case it is presumably to a large extent a contribution from oil, while the substantial German and Dutch effects are reached without such natural resources. There may also be a "reverse" effect from slow-growing and highly priced domestic service sectors, which may reduce growth rates in traditional calculations.

One may also notice that Europe compares very favorably with the USA in the PPP-adjusted growth rates. A slight American lead over Europe is turned into a decisive American lag. This is noteworthy for

---

[4] The procedure is to recalculate the 1990 GDP for every country in 2005 price level but with 1990 global PPP structure according to this formula: (Country share of world GDP 1990 in 1990 PPP) × (World GDP 1990 in 2005 PPP) and then calculate the difference in growth rates between series with the adjusted and non-adjusted base year of 1990.

Table 1.1: Annual growth rates in GDP per capita 1990/1994–2005/2010 in a number of Asian and European countries and in the USA. Traditional growth rates and PPP-adjusted growth rates.

Region/ country	Traditional	PPP-adjust.	Region/ country	Traditional	PPP-adjust.
China	8.2	7.0	Germany	1.3	2.4
India	4.9	2.2	UK	2.1	2.5
S. Korea	4.5	4.3	Ireland	4.4	5.3
Taiwan	4.0	4.2	Netherlands	1.9	2.8
Thailand	3.0	0.3	Norway	2.3	4.4
Indonesia	2.7	−0.6	Sweden	2.3	2.8
Asia (excl. Japan)	5.7	4.1	France	1.3	1.6
Japan	0.9	1.1	Italy	1.1	1.5
Asia (incl. Japan)	4.1	3.1	Spain	2.2	3.4
USA	1.8	1.6	Europe	1.6	2.3

Source: Calculations from the Conference Board.
Note: Europe = Austria, Belgium, Denmark, Finland, France, Germany, Greece, Iceland, Ireland, Italy, Netherlands, Norway, Portugal, Spain, Sweden, Switzerland, UK. Asia = Bangladesh, Cambodia, China, Hong Kong, India, Indonesia, Japan, Malaysia, Pakistan, Philippines, Singapore, South Korea, Sri Lanka, Taiwan, Thailand, Vietnam.

a number of reasons. The American lag had already appeared by 2005 (i.e., before the financial crisis), over a period encompassing the much praised "roaring nineties" in the USA. Rhode and Tonniolo (2006) argue that American growth in the 1990s gave rise to European fears of a new technological and economic gap opening up to the USA, which *inter alia* was a motivation for the Lisbon strategy in the European Union. Furthermore, the USA is the only rich country that has a negative effect from the purchasing power adjustment of the growth rate. Hypothetically, this reduction may be due either to a relatively large share of domestically low-paid and slow-growing services that have been "up-weighted" by international prices or, more positively, to a large IT sector with falling prices. Actually, American growth figures of the 1990s were boosted by the use of so-called hedonic prices of IT equipment to a much larger extent than in Europe — i.e., calculation methods increased production volumes in relation to the technical capacity of the equipment, which deviated from the value-added produced in a sector with rapidly falling prices. Overall, the adjustment of the American growth rates rather depicts an economy with increasing structural weaknesses, which contributed to accelerating deficits in the period preceding the financial crisis.

The Asian cases are generally the opposite of the European cases and follow a logical pattern. Thus, the effect of the PPP adjustment is clearly correlated to the income level or to the stage of industrialization. Only two small and commercially developed city-states — Singapore and Hong Kong — have substantial positive adjustment effects comparable to the European level. Of the major Asian economies, only Japan and Taiwan have positive effects at all from PPP adjustment, but in both cases the effect is very small. In Korea, the effect is only slightly negative, while the effect is strongly negative in all other Asian countries, in some cases catastrophically so. This pattern may be interpreted as an effect of the two reasons for deviations discussed earlier — firstly, that poor countries have large traditional sectors with slow or even negative growth at per capita basis that are given much greater weight in the PPP calculations than in the internal calculations, and secondly, that much of the volume growth in new industrializing countries is in sectors with falling prices, such as the provision of goods and services that are standardized and open to low-price competition.

Among the rising giants, the adjustment effect is particularly strong for India. This indicates that the modern sector is still very narrow in this overwhelmingly rural country, with much slower growth in the agricultural sector where the positive effects of the "green revolution" may be waning. The negative adjustment effect is substantial also in China, but much weaker than in India. Even the PPP-adjusted Chinese growth rate is very respectable, if not outstanding. One reason why the adjustment effect is so much weaker in China than in India may be that growth in China is broader-based with more upgrading undertaken, but it may also be due to a large and increasing share of domestic production of raw materials, notably of coal, at rising prices that counteracts negative influences from falling prices of manufactured goods and slow growth in extensive traditional sectors.

These calculations give further emphasis to the importance of consecutive structural changes and of social and regional broadening of modernization as part of economic growth and development.

1.6 Growth and Innovations in Three Continents

In this section, the three major economic regions — USA, Europe and Asia — will be revisited with prospects for further economic growth and, in particular, for leadership in the next wave of innovations.

USA a Leader in the Next Wave?

The leading US economy seems, to some extent, very fit to meet many of the challenges of our time. The USA was the leading economy in both the Second and the Third Industrial Revolutions. Thus, it has shown great potential in both STI and DUI processes of innovation. The present challenges facing the USA, however, are to a large extent of a different character than advancing new radical innovations. Basically the challenges are more social in character, with the adaptation of institutions to a number of new imbalances. In that sense, the situation has greater similarities with the crisis of the 1930s, which placed a heavy transformation pressure on US politics. At the beginning of the 2010s, the challenge is to come to grips with the imbalances that have emerged in relation to foreign markets and to natural resources due to a too-lavish consumption. While on one hand, the political and economic US hegemony has weakened in the face of growing competition, on the other hand, the US demand for resources has stayed at a high level both from consumers and from the global political apparatus. In particular, the American lifestyle — developed over two centuries with an extremely rich supply of natural resources — is at stake. An innovative change in the direction of economizing with natural resources, above all with energy, would represent a new American leadership, involving as well rearmament of the social and material infrastructures. It is still an open question whether such an American response to global questions will materialize within the next decade.

Rather low rates of PPP-adjusted economic growth over the past few decades may indicate structural conditions that raise more problems. That the USA forged ahead to global leadership in the 20th century was to a large extent based upon the combination of rich domestic resources and a wide integrated market that opened the way for standardization and mass production technologies at an early stage. Globalization and IT certainly enhanced some comparative advantages for US companies in the 1990s, but at the same time competition increased in the field of standardization. Furthermore, with the technologies of the Third Industrial Revolution, quality and flexible customized production have come to the fore — traditions that have been stronger developed in Europe.

European Innovative Leadership?

The European economy clearly faces new possibilities but also challenges of adaptation to a new competitive world and of catching up in new areas. The Lisbon strategy addressed some of these challenges, mainly arising from the new growth trends that appeared in the USA in the 1990s, by advocating enhanced knowledge intensity in Europe with a more rapid shift to an economy driven by innovation and services. It also entailed a number of European cooperative efforts in typical STI systems of knowledge creation and innovation, such as the enormous venture into the ESS center in Lund, Sweden.

A new European handicap to the integrated United States of America emerged out of the Third Industrial Revolution with the potential of large-scale service integration that became very visible with the expansion of the Internet and globalization in the 1990s. Hence, one of the major political challenges confronting Europe is within services, where markets to a large extent are fragmented nationally, despite decades of increased integration. Transformation pressure is augmented upon national social systems that were strengthened following the crisis of the 1930s — particularly in small open economies such as in Scandinavia and the Netherlands that once took the lead in the 1930s recovery.

Conditions for innovation and growth are, however, very different in different parts of Europe. This is due both to macroeconomic circumstances and economic structures at large, but also to differences in systems of innovation and learning organizations. Conditions for economic growth have shifted radically over the last few decades, as shown by the annual growth figures in Table 1.2, and new trends may be perceived from the 1990s.[5]

The overall picture of European growth is clear. In the post-war period of high growth rates, there was a strong convergence with

Table 1.2: Annual percentage growth in GDP per capita and GDP per capita in international dollars of 1990 price level in European regions, 1951/1955–2006/2010.

	Northwestern Europe	Continental Europe	Southern Europe	Central and Eastern Europe
Annual percentage growth in GDP per capita				
1951/1955–1971/1975	2.8	4.0	4.9	3.8
1971/1975–1991/1995	1.8	1.8	2.3	–0.2
1991/1995–2006/2010	2.3	1.4	1.8	3.6
GDP per capita in international dollars of 1990 price level				
1951/1955	6828	5406	3377	2315
1971/1975	11851	12095	8942	5057
1991/1995	16995	17460	14250	4823
2006/2010	24028	21495	18673	8317

Sources: Maddison and the Conference Board.
Note: Northwestern Europe: Ireland, Great Britain, the Netherlands, Denmark, Norway, Sweden, Finland and Iceland; Continental Europe: Austria, Belgium, France, Germany and Switzerland; Southern Europe: Portugal, Spain, Italy and Greece; Central and Eastern Europe: Poland, Czech Republic, Slovakia, Hungary, Yugoslavia, Bulgaria and Romania.

[5] These growth rates are not PPP-adjusted, mainly because no benchmarks prior to 1990 are available. One may also add that the effect of PPP-adjustment for the last period is rather similar over the European regions; it is positive in the range of 0.6–0.9 percentage points annually.

rapid growth in the economically more backward regions of Southern, Central and Eastern Europe. The whole of Europe was catching up with the USA, while European integration got rid of the fragmentation that had hampered modernization of industry. There was also a strong internal catch-up with the more affluent Northwestern Europe region. During the crisis-stricken decades of the 1970s and the 1980s, growth rates slowed down and the catch-up process withered, both externally to the USA and internally in Europe. Since around 1990, however, a new pattern has emerged. Growth rates have increased in Northwestern Europe and in Central and Eastern Europe, while there was a further deceleration of growth in Continental and Southern Europe. Thus, growth accelerated in the richest and the poorest regions of Europe — divergence and convergence co-existed.

These differences in growth performance over the last decades may be discussed in relation to changing structural conditions to meet the innovative waves of IT and globalization that took off in the 1990s. In particular, work organization and systems of innovation changed, but with different characteristics in different parts of Europe. In Lorenz and Valeyre (2006), a matrix of different systems of work organization with regard to learning processes and innovations is applied to characterize the EU-15 countries.

The analysis is made from a scheme of four types of work organization: (a) *discretionary learning* characterized by high level of problem solving in work with high complexity in problems and high level of discretion or latitude for the initiative of the individual employees; (b) *lean production* with high level of problem solving in work but with lower complexity in problems and with low level of discretion or latitude for the initiative of the individual employees (thus, the initiative is more with central administration); (c) *taylorism* characterized by low level of problem solving and very low level of discretion for the individual employees; and (d) *traditional handicraft organization* with low levels of learning and complexity.

Adaptation to new conditions of growth in the 1990s was most significant in Northwestern Europe, according to Lorenz and Valeyre (2006). Structural change in private enterprise was combined with new economic policies. Thus, macroeconomic measures, such as tax reforms, were undertaken in order to increase flexibility and labor supply. Even new political constructions were launched to meet the needs of both flexibility and social security, such as the Danish flexicurity in the 1990s. As regards work organization, the Scandinavian countries and the Netherlands took the lead in Europe as well as worldwide in developing discretionary learning processes within companies. The hierarchic Taylorist or Fordist model gave way for an organization where more responsibility was allocated to employees who were expected to solve problems on their own and where knowledge creation and learning developed in a more interactive form both within the company and with customers. With this structural change, the innovation process of the DUI type was strengthened. These countries also performed very well with two critical and complementary investments — in IT equipment and English. They were able to adapt to the new conditions of globalization at an early stage. Apart from being comparatively successful in the ICT sector, economies such as the Netherlands, Denmark and Sweden were also well-advanced in more complex knowledge-based innovation areas such as biotechnology. In Norway, economic growth was not only related to oil resources but also to non-R&D-based innovation underlying the exceptional productivity performance of the private services sector (OECD, 2008). Once again — as in the 1930s — small open economies in the northwest of Europe showed apt reactions to the structural challenges of the early 21st century.

The two other countries in Northwestern Europe — Great Britain and Ireland — were certainly well-prepared in respect of the complementarity between IT and English as well. Ireland could furthermore profit from educational reforms undertaken in the 1960s, enhancing supply of well-educated labor from the 1980s, while Great Britain took advantage of global expansion in services. Work organization in these two Anglo-Saxon countries differed, however, from Scandinavia and the Netherlands. It was characterized more by lean production in the Japanese sense with a work organization that was more structured or bureaucratic and with more narrowly defined tasks of problem solving, i.e., with less complexity for the employee. In general, learning processes in the Anglo-Saxon countries were weaker and more concentrated to the upper layers of the hierarchy.

In continental countries such as Germany and Austria, work organization was close to the Scandinavian or Dutch type with more discretionary learning processes undertaken by the employees. In France, on the other hand, work organization was closer to the British or Irish type with a more standardized labor process. The weak economic performance of this group of countries may partly be seen in relation to greater difficulties in adapting to new conditions of growth — not least with the strong complementarity between global services, IT and English. It was also the result of the economic strain that arose in the 1990s from the German unification. The very pronounced positive effect of PPP-adjustment of German growth rates indicates, however, a strong structural transformation to new conditions in the world market that partly may have come out of the unification and the further integration with liberalized Central European countries.

Deceleration in growth was similarly very marked in Southern Europe. In this region, structural difficulties were furthermore augmented over the period into the 2000s. Favorable catch-up conditions were to a great extent exhausted, while competition from expanding economies in Eastern Europe and from China became more intense. Above all, however, work organization in all these Southern countries was still either Taylorist in character or traditional with low knowledge intensity. This probably made them more vulnerable to the new low-price competition in manufacturing. One may envisage a rather high structural threshold into a new phase of more innovative and integrated learning processes, in combination with severely restrictive economic policies over a period of time to come to grips with large deficits.

The expansion in Central and Eastern Europe was very much of a catch-up character, driven largely by strong growth in manufacturing industries in countries with traditions in this area such as Poland, Czech Republic, Hungary and Slovakia, now open to the market economies. Very high PPP-adjustments of growth rates indicate positive structural changes in all these countries. These former planned economies certainly have scope for further catch-up — showing growth figures over the last decade in manufacturing exports of machinery, vehicles and other equipment that are close to the Chinese performance — but they will probably be rather weak players in terms of innovations over the next decades.

Overall, the indications of structural change in Europe in relation to new market conditions with traditions of customizing rather than standardization as well as political willingness, at least, to tackle some of the major problems confronting further global growth may give Europe, or some European countries, an important role for leadership in technological and institutional innovations of the 2010s.

Asian Dynamics and Structural Change

The spectrum of Asian economies is very wide in terms of income and economic development. There is much scope for further dynamics with catching-up countries at different levels. There are also strong pressures for structural change in this process. At the top, there are economies such as Japan, South Korea and Taiwan at income levels comparable to or close to the OECD average with similar situations as many European countries, confronted with new competition and in need of structural transformation. In the midst, there are the catch-up giants of China and India that will have a strong impact on both the Asian and the global economy in the near future. And below, there are countries and regions in Southeast and South Asia that are candidates to become new low-cost and high-growth industrializing economies, among them the next-to-giant economy of Indonesia.

High-growth countries such as South Korea and Taiwan have, in many respects, been very successful in terms of technology and productivity. Substantial efforts have been put into education, organization and technological upgrading of the economy. The rise of competition from new low-cost countries, not least China, increases the need for further upgrading and the creation of greater variety in more complex systems. Work organization and systems of innovation suffer, however, from some weaknesses that are rather common to the newly industrializing countries in Asia. Concentration to the ICT sector is very high and furthermore, it is concentrated to process rather than product innovation, often in close cooperation with advanced industrial customers (Edqvist and Hommen, 2008). Structural transformation in relation to new market conditions increases the need for greater variety and greater discretion and cooperation beyond the lean production concept. Thus, there is a need to shift from catch-up to creative innovation systems. In the case of Korea, however, the continued reliance upon large *chaebols* creates lock-ins that may place obstacles on such a restructuring (OECD, 2009).

The ensuing discussion of Asian innovation systems will concentrate on the Chinese perspectives, since China's future path will be very significant for global development. In an absolute sense and at the macro level, China has clearly advanced to a position close to the global frontier in terms of total gross domestic expenditure on R&D (GERD), second only to the USA and Japan. In relative terms, the Chinese level is certainly much lower than in most OECD countries, but its R&D intensity has increased rapidly, with R&D expenditures rising from 0.6 to 1.4 percent of GDP between 1995 and 2006.

China's innovation system still has a number of weaknesses, though. The OECD review (2008) of the Chinese innovation system concluded that some "framework conditions for innovation are insufficiently conducive to market-led innovation, especially those relating to corporate governance, financing of R&D and technology-based entrepreneurship, and enforcement of intellectual property rights". It also concluded that there was a too-great separation between knowledge producers and potential users and regions of science parks, which appear as "a very large number of 'innovative islands' with synergies insufficiently developed between them, limiting spillovers beyond them". Overall, conditions are very much characterized by massive resources channeled into catch-up, and are far from those of discretionary learning and DUI processes that characterize northwestern Europe.

Given the strong orientation in the catch-up process to manufacturing for foreign markets, such weaknesses of institutions for market-led innovation are understandable. It is also quite natural that Chinese R&D is mostly dedicated to experimental product development while expenditure in basic research has been low. Furthermore, patenting has been dominated by foreign firms in China, while exports of high-technology goods have been strongly, and increasingly so, dominated by foreign-owned companies or by joint ventures with foreign companies.

In a wider perspective, Chinese economic growth will be highly dependent upon reactions to the present crisis. In the upswing from the crisis, China will face the need for profound structural transformation. On one hand, international price development will probably turn negatively for the Chinese specializations hitherto, with price increases in the primary and tertiary sectors and with a further relative price decrease in the secondary sector of manufacturing. This will be particularly the case if industrialization maintains its global momentum and spreads to new regions of low-cost labor. Furthermore, consumer demand for Chinese exports from the American and European markets may weaken due to policies to get rid of current imbalances, not least in the USA but also in parts of Europe. On the other hand, internal pressure for transformation will probably increase; particularly if the present global crisis is prolonged and if the two main driving forces over the last 15–20 years — investments and exports — are faltering. Demand for social reforms and regional balance within China will increase, which is a situation similar to the one that confronted industrial countries in the crisis of the 1930s.

These issues are targeted by the Chinese leadership in the 12th five-year plan, taken in March 2011. The intention is for China to give up its position as a global factory with export-driven growth, by performing a structural shift to service sector growth, based to a large extent upon domestic demand. These reforms will raise consumption and wages. Higher wages and social expenditures will strengthen internal growth forces and increase pressure towards structural change, since profits will decrease within those companies that have been a mainstay in growth so far. Productivity will have to be raised further, particularly when confronted with competition from new low-cost countries or regions. The profit squeeze from falling prices and rising costs is already felt in "hot" regions in southern China, where firms have moved to adjacent low-cost countries in Southeast Asia — such mobility has been part of the Asian dynamics since the 1950s. This is a transformation pressure for structural upgrading that all industrial countries have to confront and react to. A number of much smaller Asian countries have done so in a rather orderly fashion and very successfully since the 1960s, while industrialization has been diffused to new countries. The new five-year plan is clearly intended to meet the needs of profound structural reforms.

Such reforms are necessary in order to achieve the overarching goal of keeping the nation intact. Structural change is, however, a problematic issue in many ways. For one thing, such shifts generally lead to periods of slow growth and unemployment, since old engines are choked before new ones really get to full steam. A slow-down may increase social and political pressure on the regime. For another thing, reforms to strengthen consumption and regions in Western China will at the same time work against strong groups in Eastern China that have become prosperous and established interests over the last decades. Social contradictions of this kind pose particular challenges to the political leadership in an economy that is both market-driven and planned. In particular, it raises the question of the political power to implement the reforms. What instruments does the leadership have to carry through reforms in a very wide and multi-layered economy such as China, where much of the initiative over the past decades has been handed over to those who had much to gain from the previous policy but little to win from the new one? It may take more than five years to realize the basic structural shift in Chinese growth.

The prospects for the effect on R&D and innovative capacity are mixed. Reforms may, on one hand, reduce the surplus for R&D investments in the short run but, on the other hand, they may improve the degree of market-orientation in R&D and innovation in the longer run. Above all, a successful realization of the five-year plan may create scope for somewhat lower but sustained growth rates in China over the next wave. This would at the same time undoubtedly have benign effects upon the stability of the global economy, reducing the pressure from present imbalances between China and USA.

A very last question with regard to China: How long will it take for China to reach the level of Western Europe in terms of per capita income? If one assumes that China and Western Europe continue on the PPP-adjusted paths that characterized the last 15 years, the answer is comparatively simple. With a differential in annual growth rates of roughly 4 percentage points, it will take 40 years — that is over the span of the next long wave!

1.7 Innovations and Institutional Change in a Tri-polar World

If global growth is to continue at an average rate of 1–2 percent per capita over the next decades with a further diffusion of industrialization, there is a need for innovations in areas of natural resource bottlenecks and for a concomitant shift in consumption into less resource-intensive goods and services. Innovations and shifts will take some time to mature and, in the meantime, trends in relative prices and competition will have a strong effect on the world economy and on needs to restructure. Such pressure will be hard not only for established industrial countries but also for new giants such as China and India. In this perspective, innovation, diffusion and structural transformation will be integral parts of a new long wave from the 2010s, and the national trajectories for the next decades are very much dependent upon abilities to meet the present structural crises. The impact from the rising Asian giants will most certainly continue to grow over the next wave, but they will hardly oust the present polar structure; rather, they will add new dimensions to the global economy.

Pressure towards structural change is particularly augmenting in the leading centers of USA and Europe, confronted with fundamental trend shifts, structural imbalances and acute debt crises in the early 2010s. In USA, the traditional lavish consumption lifestyle is put under heavy transformation pressure in conjunction with rather poor economic performance over the last decades. While political tensions increase within USA, the global American hegemony since the mid-20th century is weakend in a world that turns tri-polar. Thus, adaptation to new conditions is a profound challenge to the USA.

The European situation is very mixed. Long-term trend shifts towards complex services and customization favor some traditional European qualities; while at the same time widespread debt crises put the institutional structure of monetary and financial integration into jeopardy. Catching-up countries — such as Greece, Spain and Ireland — are caught in a financially fragile position with grave public deficits and with an economic structure open to low-cost competition in many fields, despite reasonably high growth rates over the last decades. The outcome of the crisis may be a deeper financial and political integration in Europe, or the reverse — a break-up of the monetary integration.

Northern Europe stands out as a strong region both in terms of economic structures and financial position. Just as important as innovative technological change are institutional changes that combine social security with structural flexibility in an increasingly urbanized and integrated global economy. In this area, a number of small and open economies in northwestern Europe have been comparatively successful over the last couple of years, strengthening their position both within Europe and internationally.

Institutional and technological leadership into the next long wave is not a question of being the richest economy or the largest economy, but rather, being able to meet and grapple with the major challenges. In an evolutionary perspective of long-term economic development, successful innovations come out of variety, and strong variants of institutional adaptation may appear in surprisingly small economies, as was the case in northwestern Europe from the 1930s. History may repeat itself in some fashion, but in the longer term it is necessary that large economies also follow suit.

References

Abramovitz, M. (1989). *Thinking about Growth and Other Essays on Economic Growth and Welfare*. Cambridge: Cambridge University Press.

Bresnahan, T. F. and Trajtenberg, M. (1995). General purpose technologies: engines of growth? *Journal of Econometrics*, 65(1), 83–108.

Dahmén, E. (1988). Development blocks in industrial economics. *Scandinavian Economic History Review*, 36, 3–14.

Edqvist, C. and Hommen, L. (Eds.) (2008). *Small Country Innovation Systems: Globalization, Change and Policy in Asia and Europe*. Cheltenham: Edward Elgar.

Gordon, R. J. (1999). US economic growth since 1870: one big wave. *American Economic Review*, 89(2), 123–128.

Kondratieff, N. D. (1926). Die lange wellen der konjunktur. *Archiv für Sozialwissenschaft und Sozialpolitik*, Band 56:3.

Lorenz, E. and Valeyre, A. (2006). Organizational forms and innovative performance: a comparison of the EU-15. In: E. Lorenz and B. Å. Lundvall (Eds.), *How Europe's Economies Learn: Coordinating Competing Models*. New York: Oxford University Press.

Maddison, A., *Statistics on World Population, GDP and Per Capita GDP, 1–2006 AD*; http://www.ggdc.net/Maddison.

OECD (2008). *Reviews of Innovation Policy: China*.

OECD (2008). *Reviews of Innovation Policy: Norway*.

OECD (2009). *Reviews of Innovation Policy: Korea*.

Rhode, P. and Tonniolo, G. (Eds.) (2006). *The Global Economy in the 1990s: A Long-Run Perspective*. New York: Cambridge University Press.

Rostow, W. W. (1978). *The World Economy: History and Prospects*. London: Macmillan.

Schön, L. (1998). Industrial crises in a model of long cycles: Sweden in an international perspective. In: T. Myllyntaus (Ed.), *Economic Crises and Restructuring in History*. Stuttgart: Scripta Mercaturae Verlag.

Schön, L. (2000). Electricity, technological change and productivity in Swedish industry, 1890–1990. *European Review of Economic History*, 4(2), 175–194.

Schön, L. (2009). Technological waves and economic growth — Sweden in an international perspective, 1850–2005. CIRCLE Working Paper 2009/06.

The Conference Board (2010). *Total Economy Database: Output, Labor and Labor Productivity, country details, 1950–2009*. September.

Chapter 2

Obstacles to Global Financial Adjustment: Economic Re-polarization and the Euro Area

Michael Hutchison

2.1 Introduction

The rate of economic and export growth in China has been phenomenally high for more than two decades, thrusting China into the position as the second largest economy in the world. This may be termed the re-polarization of economic power towards China, and more broadly emerging Asia, and away from the traditional advanced industrial economies, mainly the US and Western Europe. The emergence of China relative to the traditional economic powers may be a medium-term phenomenon or, as discussed in the previous chapter, may be the beginning of a "long wave" of economic development that continues for many decades. During most of this time, China did not run large external surpluses. These began with its ascension to WTO status in 2001, at which time current account surpluses jumped and, combined with sustained FDI inflows, created a large structural imbalance in China's balance of payments. Pressure on its quasi-fixed exchange rate regime was offset by the Chinese government's demand for reserve money and other relatively liquid assets (Glick and Hutchison, 2009). The result has been more than a decade of large sustained external imbalances between the US and China with a quite rigid USD-RMB parity. External competitiveness of the US has deteriorated, while that of China has grown. These developments are well-documented in the literature on global imbalances.

Alongside asymmetries in economic development between China (and Asia more broadly) and the West, the Euro Area experienced similar asymmetries between its "core" and "periphery" groups of countries. While implicitly maintaining fixed nominal exchange rates across countries in the Euro Area, large external surpluses and growing international competitiveness have emerged in the core group, led by Germany, and external deficits and a loss of international competitiveness have emerged in the periphery, Portugal, Ireland, Italy, Greece and Spain. These external pressures exacerbated tensions within the Euro Area and, arguably, played part of a causal role in the European fiscal crisis that emerged in 2010.

This chapter investigates the connections between global imbalances and rising economic imbalances within the Euro Area. We address whether global re-polarization associated with the rise of China and large external imbalances has contributed to tensions between Euro-zone core and periphery countries by changing patterns of competitiveness, economic performance and, ultimately, fiscal sustainability. The focus in this chapter is on a medium-term perspective, complementing the discussion of long-term waves of economic development in the previous chapter of this volume.

It is evident that global imbalances have been, at least in part, attributable to rigidity in the USD-RMB rate, a parity only maintained by massive Chinese international reserve accumulation and extensive capital controls. This policy has hindered adjustment between the US and China. An indirect effect of China's exchange rate policy, however, has been RMB depreciation against the Euro — when exactly the opposite would be suggested by fundamentals — thereby increasing Chinese competitiveness against the Euro Area. Moreover, rigid nominal exchange rates across countries in the Euro Area — the central tenet of monetary union — combined with *widely divergent unit labor costs* have led to wide swings in real exchange rates between the core and periphery. Divergent patterns of international competitiveness across the Euro Area, in turn, have contributed to growing discrepancies between surplus and deficit countries. This is a major reason for deteriorating economic performance and deteriorating fiscal conditions in the Euro Area periphery. Overvaluation against China, with associated large bilateral trade deficits, is a secondary cause of the deterioration in economic performance of the periphery. By contrast, German competitiveness against China is strong and roughly stable over the past decade, with fairly balanced bilateral trade or small surpluses with China.

The next section documents the rise of global imbalances and the rise of China as an economic power. Section 2.3 considers the implications for the Euro Area from global imbalances. Section 2.4 concludes.

2.2 Global Imbalances

Figure 2.1 shows current account positions as a percent of *world* GDP for the United States, Germany, and three groups of countries: oil producers in the Middle East, large exporter economies of Asia (i.e., China,

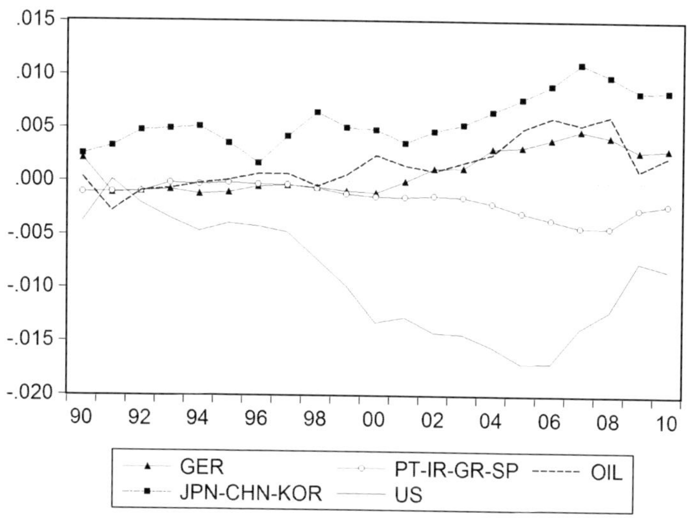

Figure 2.1: Global imbalances: Current account balances (percent of world GDP).

Sources: World Economic Outlook Database (WEO) and IMF.
Notes: PT-IR-GR-SP refers to Euro-zone periphery: Portugal (PT), Ireland (IR), Greece (GR) and Spain (SP). Oil Producers (Oil) consists of Middle Eastern oil producers. US and GER refer to United States and Germany, respectively, while JPN-CHN-KOR refers to the group consisting of Japan, China and South Korea. Global imbalances reflect annual CA balance of each region (in US dollars) as percent of annual world GDP (in US dollars based on 183 countries total in WEO).

Japan and South Korea), and the periphery countries in the Euro zone (i.e., Portugal, Ireland, Greece and Spain). The period covered is 1990 through 2010. Five years prior to the Asian financial crisis of 1997–1998 saw a roughly stable US current account deficit at –0.5% of world GDP, a corresponding 0.5% surplus for the large Asian exporters, and roughly balanced positions for the other countries and regions. However, a major shift in the pattern of global imbalances occurred after the Asian financial crisis. The US current account deteriorated dramatically, falling from –0.5% of world GDP in 1997 to almost –2% of world GDP in 2005–2006. The US deficit shrank during the financial crisis and was about –1% of world GDP by the end of the decade. The region seeing the largest rise in current account position was the exporters of Asia at about 1% of world GDP, largely due to the emergence of China as a major exporting and surplus country. China's current account surplus has surged since the Asian financial crisis and especially since its ascension to the WTO in 2001. Large surpluses were also observed in the Middle Eastern oil-exporting nations and in Germany.

Global imbalances have been very persistent and have been mainly attributable to three factors: (1) the worldwide demand by emerging economies for a larger stock of the reserve currency (US dollars)[1]; (2) China's exchange rate policy, unprecedentedly large international reserves and trade surpluses[2]; and (3) fiscal deficits and low private saving in the United States.[3]

Emerging Economies and the Demand for International Reserves

The first major contributing factor toward global imbalances has its roots in what occurred in Emerging Asia after the 1997–1998

[1] This argument is consistent with the publications of Aizenman and Lee (2007), Aizenman and Sun (2010), and others.

[2] This argument is consistent with the publications of Dooley *et al.* (2004, 2009). They argue that China purposefully follows a mercantilist policy with an undervalued exchange rate and trade surpluses to ensure rapid industrialization and absorption of surplus labor from the countryside.

[3] This argument is consistent with Obstfeld and Rogoff (2010), amongst others.

regional financial crisis and the demonstration effect it had on other emerging markets. The Asian Crisis that struck the region during 1997–1998 caused large downturns in economic activity in many countries (Hutchison and Noy, 2006). Many countries relied heavily on IMF programs to secure foreign currency to shore up their currencies and financial systems, but these came with stringent conditionality on monetary, fiscal and financial policies. This was a very difficult period for the countries that simultaneously faced currency crises, banking crises and sudden stops in capital flows. Sudden and unexpected financial and economic turmoil, and the tough conditions imposed on loans from the IMF (especially fiscal contraction and high-interest rate policies), created a great deal of resentment (Stiglitz, 2002).

Based on this experience and the desire to avoid the necessity of borrowing US dollars from the IMF if a crisis were to erupt in future, many emerging nations — in Asia and elsewhere — pushed strongly to "self-insure" against future currency attacks by accumulating large stocks of international reserves (US dollars), while at the same time continuing soft-pegs to the US dollar with limited home currency appreciation despite growing current account surpluses starting around 2000. The result was rapidly rising international reserves — referred to in the literature as both "precautionary" and "hoarding," primarily held in US dollars. Global reserve holdings rose from US$1.6 trillion in early 1999 to about US$9 trillion by the end of 2010. This is shown in Figure 2.2. The buildup in reserves was concentrated in Emerging Asia, but also was characteristic in many emerging nations around the world (Aizenman and Lee, 2007; Aizenman and Sun, 2010).

China's Exchange Rate Policy

The second major impetus to Emerging Asia's growing current account surpluses shown in Figure 2.1 was growing current account surpluses in China, and pressure on its exchange rate regime, after its ascension to the WTO in 2001. These surpluses, together with large long-standing inflows of foreign direct investment, have presented

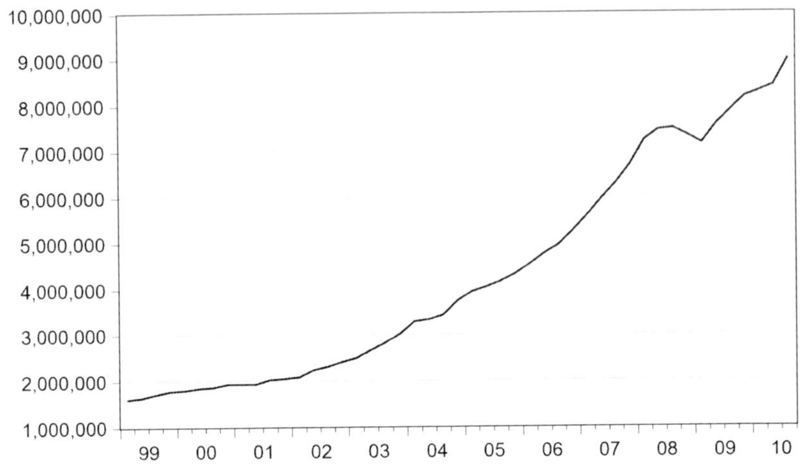

Figure 2.2: Global holdings of international reserves (thousands USD).

Source: International Monetary Fund.

China's authorities with a structural imbalance in the country's balance of payments. This imbalance, combined with bouts of "hot money" capital inflows spurred by speculation on RMB appreciation against a backdrop of greater capital account openness, has led the Chinese government to engage in ever-increasing foreign exchange market purchases and foreign asset accumulation to dampen appreciation of the currency.

China's foreign exchange holdings, shown in Table 2.1, have risen from US$166 billion in December 2000 to US$2.5 trillion in June 2010. China surpassed Japan as the largest reserve-holding nation. The increase in foreign reserves has been mainly associated with growing current account surpluses and FDI inflows. China's annual current account balance rose from $17 billion in 2001 (1.3% of GDP) to $326 billion in 2007 (almost 10% of GDP) and continued to rise in 2008 before falling during the 2009 global recession. Direct investment inflows have grown steadily over this period, though less rapidly. Despite the global downturn in 2009, and sharp decrease in international trade and reduction in China's current account surplus, international reserves continued to climb to even higher levels. Since

Table 2.1: China's foreign exchange reserves.

Date	Billion USD
2000	166
2001	212
2002	286
2003	403
2004	610
2005	819
2006	1066
2007	1528
2008	1946
2009	2399
2010*	2454

Source: Government of the People's Republic of China, SAFE database.
Note: 2010 amount is June 2010 officially reported figure.

2005, the Chinese government has allowed some very modest appreciation of the RMB against the US dollar, but this did not significantly reduce pressure on the exchange rate.

Figure 2.3 shows China's bilateral trade balances against the United States, Germany, the EU, and the Euro-zone periphery countries (Portugal, Ireland, Greece and Spain). The figures show the bilateral balance as a percentage of the focus country/region GDP. Only Germany maintained balanced trade balance with China. The United States had the largest bilateral trade deficit with China, but in terms of percentage of GDP, the EU in aggregate and the Euro-zone periphery countries also had very large deficit positions. Clearly, Chinese competitiveness was substantial, grew rapidly, and there was no indication of slowing.

RMB Undervaluation?

Two major trends were contributing to China's international reserve accumulation: large current account surpluses and sustained FDI

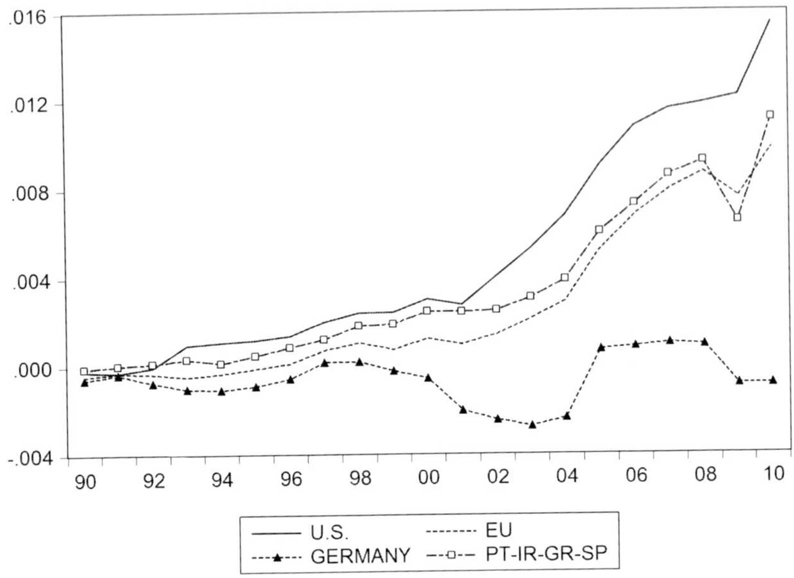

Figure 2.3: China's trade surpluses with the US, Germany, European Union and Euro-zone periphery (PT-IR-GR-SP) (percentage of focus region GDP).

Sources: Direction of Trade Statistics (DOT) and IMF.
Notes: Euro-Zone Periphery consists of Portugal (PT), Ireland (IR), Greece (GR) and Spain (SP). China's bilateral surplus as percent of gross domestic product (GDP) of the trading partner; calculated as China's annual trade surplus (in US dollars) divided by that year's GDP of the trading partner country/region (in US dollars).

inflows. These two forces put enormous pressure for RMB appreciation, but this was offset by a combination of controls on capital inflows and, mainly, purchases of USD by the Chinese authorities.

How large was the undervaluation of the RMB? There are two basic methods for estimating an "equilibrium" exchange rate — a modified purchasing power parity (PPP) method and the Fundamental Equilibrium Exchange Rate (FEER) method.[4] Cline and Williamson

[4] There is no consensus in the literature as to which methodological approach is preferable to measuring disequilibrium or even whether it is possible to empirically estimate a unique equilibrium value for the currency. As discussed in the text, some

(2009), using a FEER estimation approach, found substantial undervaluation of the Chinese Renminbi and several other Asian currencies. Their estimate of the equilibrium value of the RMB suggested a 40% undervaluation of the RMB against the USD as of February 2010. They concluded that global imbalances were mainly attributable to China's exchange-rate policy.

China's structural current account surplus and FDI inflows grew markedly after the Asian financial crisis. At times this was complemented by surging short-term capital inflows. China allowed very little currency appreciation against the dollar and — to maintain its exchange rate regime — purchased unprecedented amounts of USD foreign exchange reserves, i.e., foreign exchange market intervention. Other countries in Emerging Asia, especially South Korea, also saw a buildup of foreign exchange reserves through intervention, both to limit exchange rate appreciation and to build up a stockpile of reserves for defensive purposes to weather a financial crisis such as occurred in 2008–2009. But the magnitude of reserve accumulation in these Asian countries was much smaller than in China, and the flexibility of their exchange rates was greater.

Going beyond FEER and PPP-based measures of disequilibrium in exchange markets, the most compelling evidence of undervaluation was the purchase of billions of dollars of foreign exchange by the Chinese authorities each month. Market pressure on the RMB to appreciate, even with extensive and tightly enforced capital controls, was enormous. These actions were clearly designed to stop exchange rate adjustment to an appreciated equilibrium value. This was strong market-based evidence of RMB undervaluation, consistent with evidence put forth by Dooley *et al.* (2004, 2009), Cline and Williamson (2009), Krugman (2010) and others.

---

authors have argued that the RMB is substantially undervalued (e.g., Cline and Williamson, 2009), while others suggest that there is little or no statistical evidence that the RMB is undervalued (Chinn *et al.*, 2007 and 2009). Others, such as McKinnon and Schnabl (2009), suggest that China should follow an even tighter peg with the USD and not allow any appreciation of the currency (and that appreciation in recent years has been a policy mistake).

Saving in the United States

The mirror image of large and growing imbalances in Emerging Asia has been sustained current account deficits in the US (Figures 2.1 and 2.3). There has been considerable debate about the causes of US imbalances, but two arguments are generally put forward (e.g., Obstfeld and Rogoff, 2010). The first argument focuses on the rise of US government budget deficits since 2001, the collapse in private saving and a boom in residential and commercial real estate investment. These elements — increased national investment and reduced national saving — translated into current account deficits.

The second argument concerns the ease of financing. The US current account deficit was largely financed by inflows of capital, in large part from oil-exporters and emerging markets as they built up foreign exchange reserves. China was the largest importer of capital into the US among the emerging markets. Foreign financing contributed to maintaining low interest rates in the US and the boom in the asset markets, especially in residential and commercial real estate, from 2001–2007. The ease of finance via capital inflows to the US contributed to the investment boom and asset price inflation, or at a minimum did not put a "brake" on the surge in credit creation. Asset price inflation in turn reduced the US private saving rate since capital appreciation in housing and elsewhere substituted for personal saving.

2.3 Implications for Europe

European Imbalances and Deteriorating Competitiveness of the Periphery

Europe has been significantly affected by the shift in global imbalances associated in large part with policies emanating from Asia, especially China, and the United States. The Euro has appreciated significantly against the USD and also against other emerging currencies and the RMB in particular (Figure 2.4). This longer-term trend was interrupted by the 2007–2008 financial crisis and the Euro was again under pressure in the first half of 2010 due to the European sovereign debt crisis. Nonetheless, RMB depreciation against the

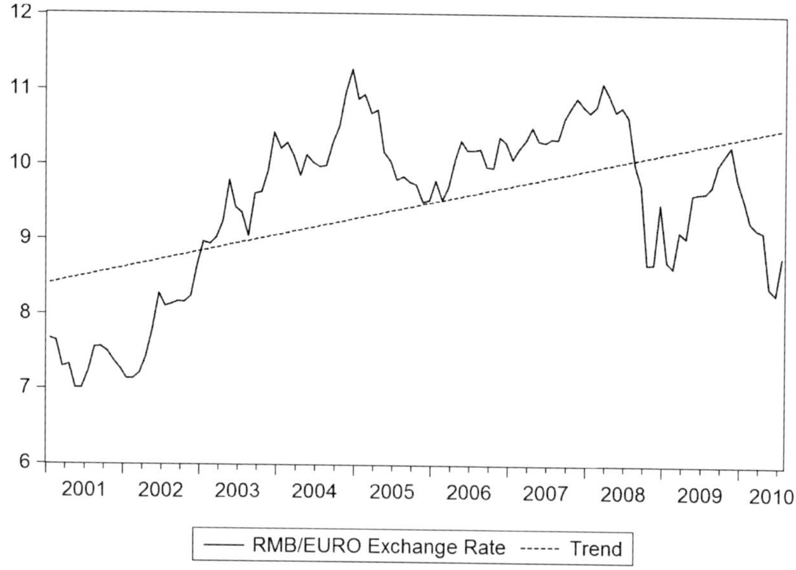

Figure 2.4: RMB exchange rate against the Euro.

Sources: International Financial Statistics (IFS) and IMF.

Notes: Yuan (RMB) per Euro; calculated as China, P.R.: Mainland national currency per US dollar divided by Euro Area national currency per US dollar, MARKET RATE, END OF PERIOD.

Euro continued in late 2010 and early 2011. In a longer perspective, the nominal value of the RMB against the Euro depreciated more than 10% from January 2000 to April 2011. Moreover, the real trade-weighted exchange value of the RMB rate in early 2011 was at its 2002 level, despite moves to revalue the currency in 2005.

As discussed above, large-scale purchases by China to keep the RMB parity with the USD kept the USD much stronger than it otherwise would have been and continued to keep the currency overvalued against the backdrop of a very large and persistent current account deficit. What is the counterfactual without Chinese purchases of US assets on such a massive scale? The USD would presumably have depreciated markedly against the RMB and further depreciated against the Euro, i.e., Chinese USD purchases are keeping the general valuation of the USD above its no-intervention equilibrium value by increasing the demand for the US currency in world markets.

The loss of international competitiveness against the RMB affected all EMU members. However, Euro appreciation had asymmetric effects as well. In particular, Germany maintained a relatively strong competitive position, whereas countries in the Euro-zone "periphery" — which we define here as Portugal, Ireland, Greece and Spain — fared much worse.[5] One way to illustrate this asymmetry is to compare the international competitiveness positions of the periphery group of countries compared to Germany.

Figures 2.5 and 2.6 illustrate real exchange rate appreciations of Portugal, Ireland Greece and Spain relative to Germany. Figure 2.5

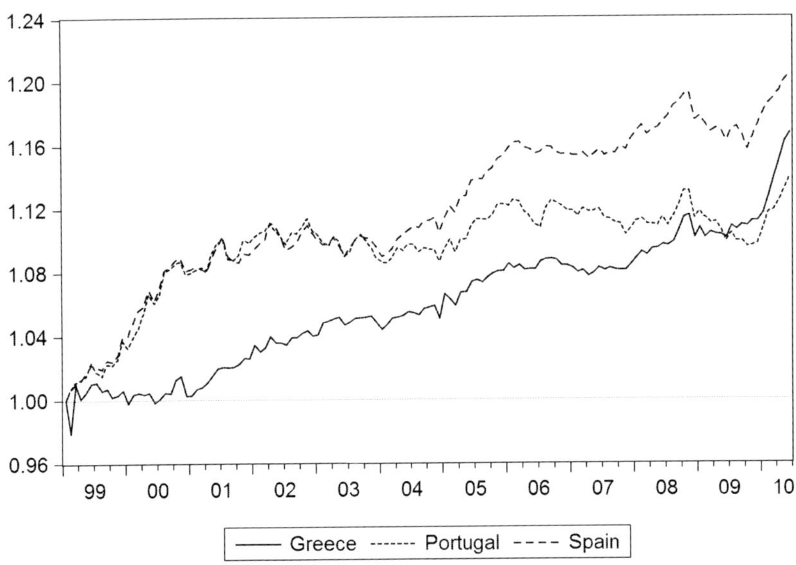

Figure 2.5: Real exchange rate relative to Germany (based on CPI levels).

Source: IMF: International Financial Statistics.

Notes: Calculated as real exchange rate (based on CPI) of focus country relative to German real exchange rate (based on CPI). Normalized at unity in January 1999. Ireland excluded due to missing data.

[5] Other "periphery" groups could be considered, but the group of Portugal-Ireland-Greece-Spain has been the subject of much scrutiny and debate and we therefore focus our attention on this group.

Figure 2.6: Real exchange rates relative to Germany (based on relative unit labor costs).

Source: IMF: International Financial Statistics.

Notes: Calculated as real exchange rate (based on ULC) of focus country divided by German real exchange rate (based on ULC). Values normalized to unity at date 1999Q1.

reports a measure based on CPI levels (base year normalized to unity in January 1999) and Figure 2.6 reports a measure based on Unit Labor Costs (ULC; base year normalized to unity in 1999Q1). The CPI measure shows an appreciation of the Euro-zone periphery countries against Germany of between 12%–20%, while the Unit Labor Cost measure shows an appreciation of between 10%–65%. Since 2000, the CPI in Spain has risen 20% relative to Germany and its ULC has risen 65% relative to Germany. This is a stunning loss of international competitiveness and, together with long-term appreciation of the Euro against the USD and RMB, had severe consequences for the Spanish economy in terms of weak production of tradable goods and high unemployment.

The loss of international competitiveness was manifested by the development of large bilateral trade imbalances in the Euro-zone periphery against China, shown in Figure 2.3. While Germany had a roughly balanced position with China, the Euro-zone periphery countries had very large bilateral deficits (over 10% of GDP in 2010). In addition, the periphery countries were running substantial current account deficits for a sustained period. Figure 2.7 reports the current account balances of the Euro-zone periphery. At their high point in 2008, deficit positions ranged from 5% (Ireland) to 14% (Greece) of GDP.

European imbalances versus China and Emerging Asia, and the regional imbalances within Europe, have been exacerbated by membership in the European Monetary Union. The Euro area has many

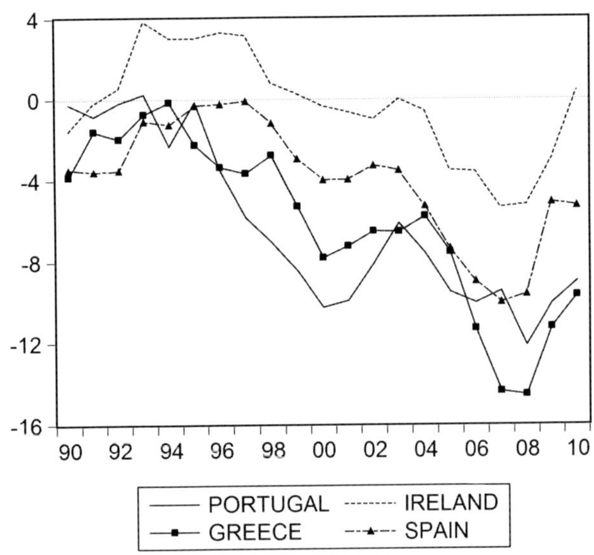

Figure 2.7: Current accounts in Portugal, Ireland, Greece and Spain (percent of GDP).

Sources: World Economic Outlook Database (WEO) and IMF.

Notes: Current account (CA) balances as percentage of GDP; calculated by dividing annual CA balance (in US dollars) of each country/region by its GDP (in US dollars).

positive features, but one problem is that nominal exchange rate adjustment is not possible for individual member states. This problem became acute since wage/productivity developments in the periphery did not grow in line with Germany. Countries in the Euro area that had sustained current deficits and weak economies, i.e., Greece, Spain and Portugal, did not have the option of currency devaluation to enhance international competitiveness, boost exports and lower current account deficits. Moreover, the problems of imbalances were not immediately self-correcting. Policy actions and institutional changes in labor markets to enhance productivity and limit wage growth could complement market forces to restore competitiveness in the periphery countries.

Another economic factor influencing currency values was the trend shift away from the USD as a reserve currency and towards other currencies, especially the Euro, as shown in Figure 2.8. If this trend were to continue, or intensify, pressure on the Euro to appreciate against the USD would increase. This shift in reserve holdings

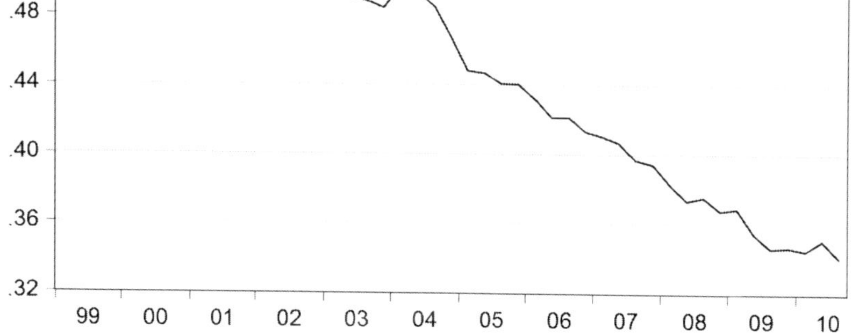

Figure 2.8: USD currency share of total international reserves.

Source: IMF, Currency Composition of Official Foreign Exchange Reserves (COFER) database.

Note: Author's calculations.

partly reflects a move by China to diversify its international reserve holding and partly reflects a "valuation" effect due to USD depreciation. This tendency to shift away from the USD increases pressure for Euro appreciation and further worsens the international competitive positions of the Euro-zone "periphery" countries.

Competitiveness, Growth and Fiscal Sustainability: The 2010 European Sovereign Debt Crisis

The gradual loss of international competitiveness associated with EMU membership also adversely impacted the sustainability of public finances and contributed to the 2010 sovereign debt crisis.

Figure 2.9 shows the development of budget deficits in Germany and the Euro-zone periphery (aggregate, weighted average), as a

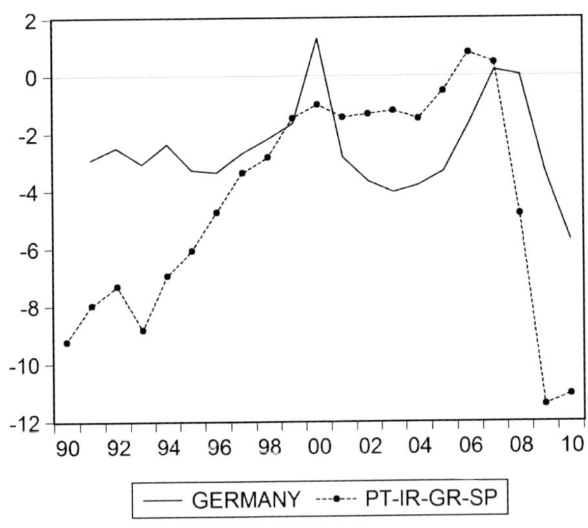

Figure 2.9: Government budget deficit (percent of GDP) in Germany and Euro-zone periphery (Portugal-Ireland-Greece-Spain).

Sources: IMF: World Economic Outlook Database (WEO).

Note: General government net lending/borrowing, percent of GDP. The regional series is a weighted average, with weights based on GDP contribution of each country to the total GDP of the region. Weights adjusted each period to account for changes in relative contributions and data omissions.

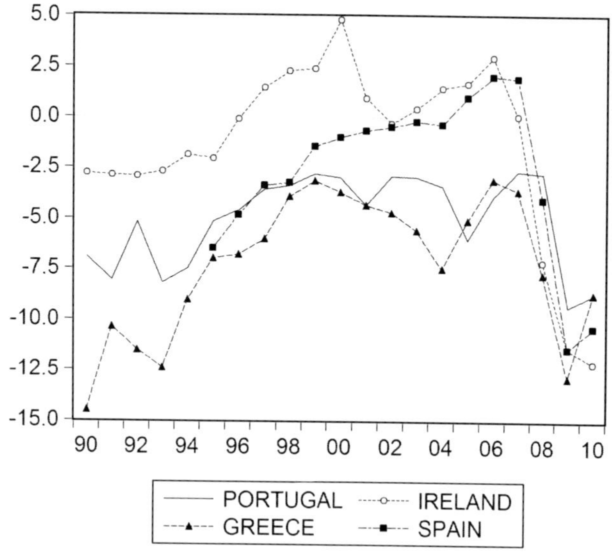

Figure 2.10: Budget deficits in Euro-zone periphery countries (percent of GDP).

Source: OECD.

percentage of GDP, over the 1990–2010 period. Budget positions did not appear to be a pressing issue until the financial collapse and recession in 2008–2009. At that point, budget positions deteriorated in both Germany and the periphery. However, the periphery saw budgets drop to almost −12% of GDP by 2009, twice the deficit position of Germany. Budgetary developments in individual periphery countries, shown in Figure 2.10, saw a distinct pattern. In particular, Portugal and Greece ran substantial budget deficits during the two-decade period, with a very sharp deterioration in 2008–2009. Spain started the period with deficits on par with Portugal and Greece, but gradually improved fiscal finances during the last decade until the 2008–2009 recession. Ireland generally had a much more solid fiscal footing during this entire period, but also experienced a massive deterioration in public finances during the 2008–2009 downturn, made even more acute by the public bailout of the banking system.

The budget deficit is one indicator of fiscal sustainability, as are the level and evolution of government debt as a percent of GDP.

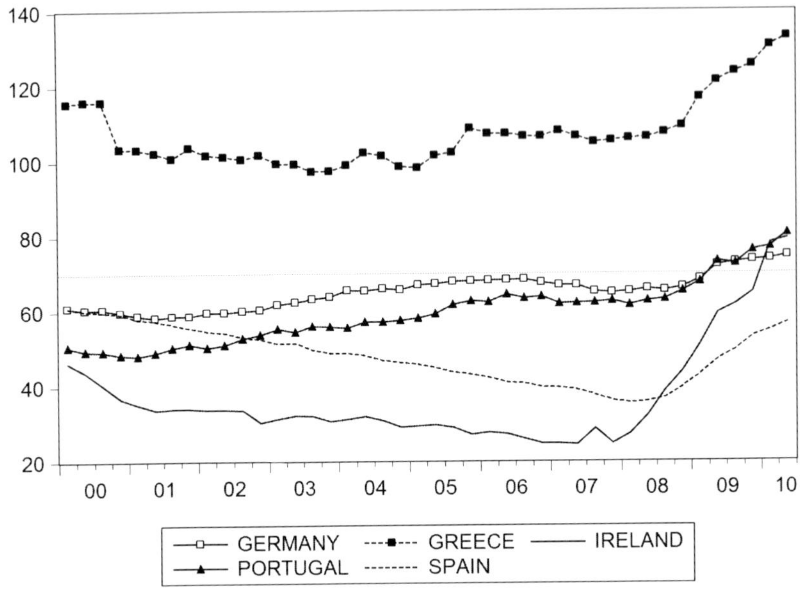

Figure 2.11: National debt level of Germany, Portugal, Ireland, Greece and Spain (percent of GDP).

Source: Eurostat, DSI Data Service & Information GmbH.

Figure 2.11 shows the level of government debt for Germany and the periphery countries for 2000–2010. The figure shows that Greece was an outlier among the periphery countries for its high level of government debt — over 130% of GDP in 2010. German and Portuguese debt levels grew slowly during this period, reaching over 70% of GDP in 2010. Spain and Ireland had substantially lower debt levels during the period, but grew quickly at the end of the decade, reaching about 55% and 75%, respectively, in 2010.

Given the general loss of competitiveness, current account deficits, deterioration in public finances and growing levels of government debt, it was not surprising that a sovereign debt crisis emerged in Euro-zone periphery countries. The 2010 European sovereign debt crisis was the biggest challenge faced by the EMU since its inception. Given its particularly high debt level, Greece was at the center of the crisis. Moreover, investor confidence in Greek debt was undermined by the "revision" of the national accounts which tripled the reported size of government budget deficits. When the key EMU member states, France and Germany, could not agree on a program of financial support for Greece, the premium paid on its debt jumped (interest rate relative to Germany) to very high levels. The high cost of refinancing, in turn, made the cost of servicing existing levels of Greek debt unsustainable. Confidence in the EMU suffered another major setback when Greece was forced to turn to the International Monetary Fund (IMF) for support, even though participation was (belatedly) forthcoming by its EMU partner countries. Ireland followed a similar path by turning to the IMF for financial assistance.

2.4 Exchange Rate Rigidities Forcing Global and Regional Imbalances: How Can Economies Adjust?

This paper argues that two fundamental obstacles are hindering adjustment of global and European financial imbalances — the rigid nominal USD/RMB exchange rate maintained by massive Chinese purchases of the USD, and the rigid (implicit) nominal exchanges across core and periphery countries within the Euro Area maintained by participation in the EMU. We demonstrate that the global financial imbalance is linked to the Euro Area financial imbalance. By financing current account deficits of the US (recycling current account surpluses of China) by buying dollars in the foreign exchange market, China has kept the dollar value higher and the RMB value lower in foreign exchange markets than it would otherwise have been. This policy has also had the effect of slowing USD depreciation against the Euro and stopping RMB appreciation against the Euro. Indeed, the RMB has depreciated about 30% against the Euro over the past decade, although exactly the opposite course would be justified by strong Chinese fundamentals — Chinese competitiveness and sustained trade surpluses against the Euro Area. The appreciation of the Euro against the RMB has deteriorated international competitiveness of all countries in the Euro Area, but the most severe consequences have fallen mainly on a set of "periphery" Euro-zone countries.

The second obstacle to financial adjustment is the fixed rate parity implicit across the core and periphery countries in the Euro Area, combined with the inability of the periphery countries to maintain international competitiveness. Firstly, the periphery countries have lost competiveness due to the general appreciation of the Euro. Secondly, Portugal, Ireland, Greece and Spain have seen further appreciations of their *real* exchange rates — exacerbating deterioration of current account balances — due to spiraling unit labor costs. Prices and unit labor costs in the periphery countries have climbed much more than in Germany over the past decade, in some cases as much as 55% more (Spain in terms of unit labor costs), making their economies increasingly uncompetitive but without recourse to currency devaluation. These factors have contributed to slower economic growth, higher unemployment, worsening public finances and, most recently, a sovereign debt crisis. There are clearly benefits to belonging to the Euro club, but mainly the costs are being felt by the Eurozone periphery countries.

This chapter has shown that the costs to EMU for the periphery members have been exacerbated by the emergence of large and persistent global imbalances associated with re-polarization of economic power and the rise of China and its international economic policies. Economic conditions in the periphery of the Euro Area would be improved if China were to allow greater appreciation of the RMB's parity with the USD. Alternatively, China could reduce imbalances and pressure on the RMB by adopting policies more focused on domestic demand (e.g., personal consumption). Indeed, the rise in private consumption is a key element of economic restructuring contained in China's 12th five-year plan announced in early 2011. Some analysts consider this a major turning point in Chinese economic policy.[6] If this policy were to effectively increase domestic demand, it would reduce China's external imbalances and help reduce global imbalances.

Another factor that would improve economic performance in the European periphery would be greater flexibility in labor markets and

[6] See Roach (2011).

other institutions that would improve productivity and limit wage growth to restore international competiveness. To some extent, this is a process that was accelerated by the fiscal crisis of 2010–2011 in the European periphery. Ultimately, participation in a monetary union necessitates substantial internal adjustment to adapt to both external shocks and productivity differentials across participating countries. Global imbalances have made the need for internal adjustment within EMU much more acute.

Acknowledgements

I am grateful to Vlad Sushko for excellent research assistance.

References

Aizenman, J. and Lee, J. (2007). International reserves: precautionary versus mercantilist views, theory and evidence. *Open Economies Review*, 18(2), 191–214.

Aizenman, J. and Sun, Y. (2010). Globalization and the sustainability of large current account imbalances: size matters. *Journal of Macroeconomics*, 32(1), 35–44.

Baldwin, R. and Tagalini, D. (2009). The illusion of improving global imbalances. 14 November 2009 posting on www.voxeu.com.

Chinn, M., Cheung, Y. W. and Fujii, E. (2007). The overvaluation of Renminbi undervaluation. *Journal of International Money and Finance*, 26(5), September, 762–785.

Chinn, M., Cheung, Y. W. and Fujii, E. (2009). Pitfalls in measuring exchange rate misalignment: the Yuan and other currencies. *Open Economies Review*, 20(2), 183–206.

Cline, W. R. and Williamson, J. (2009). Equilibrium exchange rates. 18 June 2009 posting on www.voxeu.com.

Dooley, M., Folkerts-Landau, D. and Garber, P. (2004). The revived Bretton Woods System: the effects of periphery intervention and reserve management on interest rates and exchange rates in center countries. NBER Working Paper No. 10332.

Dooley, M., Folkerts-Landau, D. and Garber, P. (2009). Bretton Woods II still defines the international monetary system. *Pacific Economic Review*, 14(3), August, 297–311.

Glick, R. and Hutchison, M. (2009). Navigating the trilemma: capital flows and monetary policy in China. *Journal of Asian Economies*, 20(3), 205–224.

Hutchison, M. and Noy, I. (2006). Sudden stops and the Mexican wave: currency crises, capital flow reversals and output loss in emerging markets. *Journal of Development Economics*, 79(1), 225–248.

Krugman, P. (2010). Chinese New Year. *The New York Times.* January 1, 2010.
McKinnon, R. and Schnabl, G. (2009). China's financial conundrum and global imbalances. BIS Working Papers No. 277 (March).
Obstfeld, M. and Rogoff, K. (2010). Global imbalances and the financial crisis: products of common causes. In: R. Glick and M. Spiegel (Eds.), *Asia and the Global Financial Crisis.* San Francisco: Federal Reserve Bank San Francisco.
Roach, S. (2011). China's Turning Point. Published online in Project Syndicate, The Asia Portfolio, February 22, 2011 (http://www.project-syndicate.org/commentary/roach2/English).
Stiglitz, J. (2002). *Globalization and Its Discontents.* New York: W.W. Norton.

Chapter 3

Interregional Trade Facing Re-polarization: The EU Trade Negotiations with ASEAN Countries

Lena Lindberg and Claes G. Alvstam

3.1 Introduction

The objective in this chapter is to describe and analyze the ambition to strengthen the interregional trade relation between the EU and the Association of Southeast Asian Nations (ASEAN) in times of an ongoing re-polarization of the global economic arena. This endeavor should be seen in the light of the EU's attempts to maintain its position in international trade. Its previously strong role has been challenged by the rapid growth of East Asia in the global economy, particularly at a time when the multilateral negotiations within the World Trade Organization (WTO) and its Doha Development Agenda (DDA) have shown very poor progress, and the world has faced the deepest economic downturn since the early 1930s, caused by the economic and financial crisis in 2008–2009.

This limited progress at the multilateral level has contributed to the FTA trend that took off in the 1990s. The number of bilateral and regional FTAs (BTAs and RTAs) has increased rapidly during the last two decades. As of mid-2011, around 300 trade agreements were in force.[1] The issue whether such agreements should be seen as purely negative to the attempts to further liberalize international trade, or

[1] See WTO (2011).

whether they can play a role as stepping-stones to future trade liberalization in a time when the multilateral route seems to be closed, has been vividly debated among trade economists (cf. Baldwin, 2006; Bergsten, 1997; Bhagwati, 1991, 2004, 2008; Bhagwati *et al.*, 1998; Desker, 2004; Hufbauer and Schott, 2007; Kawai and Wignaraja, 2007, 2009; Lamy, 2002; Lindberg and Alvstam, 2007; Low, 2003; Michalak and Gibb, 1997; Sally, 2007a, 2007b, 2010).

The starting-point is that BTAs and RTAs have come to stay for the foreseeable future. We do not aim to assess the potential economic impacts of these agreements, nor their advantages or disadvantages in relation to a strategy to avoid any kind of agreement that is not truly multilateral. Rather, our ambition is to put the EU's efforts to conclude FTAs with separate countries and groups of countries in the larger context of a geopolitical and geoeconomic strategy to play a major role in the world economy. There is a growing insight among its members that the external relations of the EU should not be overshadowed by the previously prioritized attempts at bringing about ever-deeper economic and political integration within its own realm. This is reflected in the so-called "Global Europe" strategy from late 2006, under which the EU has set its trade policy agenda since then. Here, broad FTAs are seen as essential complements to the WTO negotiations.[2] The Global Europe strategy has been followed up in 2010 by the new EU strategy for growth and competitiveness, "Europe 2020", and in a new communication from the Commission to the Council and Parliament, named *Trade, Growth and World Affairs.*[3] The need by the EU to formulate a more active external trade policy towards Asia is discussed in this volume as well in Chapter 4.

Among the different alternatives in all cardinal points, the EU's need to strengthen its economic ties with Asia stands out as the top

---

[2] Cf. European Commission/External Trade (2007): "Global Europe: A Stronger Partnership to Deliver Market Access for European Exporters." Available via http://trade.ec.europa.eu/doclib/docs/2007/april/tradoc_134591.pdf, accessed on March 19, 2011.

[3] European Commission (2010a, 2010b); see also Ahnlid–Alvstam–Lindberg (2011, p. 420f).

priority. Asia is today the fastest-growing region in international trade, accounting for 31% of global trade in 2010 (compared to 26% in 2000 and 15% in 1980),[4] at the same time that Asian dependence on the EU as a trading partner is stagnating or even falling. Negotiations have been completed with South Korea,[5] and are ongoing with India. Negotiations for a region-to-region FTA between the EU and ASEAN started in 2007, and numerous meetings were held during the following two years. However, they were characterized by diverging views of the two sides regarding the level of ambition, the general scope of such an agreement, as well as the participation. Consequently, a major success in the interregional negotiations was conspicuous by its absence. As the economic and financial crisis broke out in late 2008, hitting both regions, the talks also faced the risk of not being given precedence to, due to the subsequent sharp decline of world trade, which, in turn, was a direct result of the global recession. With limited substance reached in the interregional negotiations, the two sides started to explore an alternative route — going bilateral — that will be addressed in this paper.

This issue is also related to the theoretical discussion regarding the "decoupling" hypothesis, which was extensively debated in East Asia during the years before the economic downturn. The idea of decoupling is based on the empirical observation of the rapid growth of East Asian intra-regional trade and the parallel decline in relative shares of North America and the EU, i.e., the proposition that East Asia has emerged as "a self-contained economic entity with potential to maintain its own growth dynamism independent of the economic outlook for the traditional developed market economies" (Athukorala

[4] Based on January–October. IMF DOTS Database, accessed in March 2011; IMF DOTS Yearbook; and the 'Bureau of Foreign Trade' for Taiwan statistics.

[5] The agreement was initialled on October 15, 2009; approved by the Council on September 16, 2010; and officially signed on October 6, 2010 (http://ec.europa.eu/trade/creating-opportunities/bilateral-relations/countries/korea/, accessed on March 19, 2011). The European Parliament gave its assent in February 2011. The agreement has been provisionally in force since July 2011.

and Kohpaiboon, 2009). The decoupling hypothesis should also be seen in the context of the theoretical debate regarding horizontal specialization versus the emergence of growing production fragmentation in global and regional production networks (*ibid.*).

One of the most striking changes in EU-Asia trade in general during the past decades has been the accelerated pace of the upgrading of the commodity composition in Asian exports to Europe. This process has occurred simultaneously with an equally rapid upgrading of intra-Asian trade, and can be measured through the share of medium- and high-technology products compared to total exports of manufactured products (Yueh, 2010; Yusuf and Nabeshima, 2010). The process of upgrading can also be demonstrated in terms of a higher trade-to-value-added ratio, where China is underway to catch up with old as well as new "tiger" economies in Asia (Low, 2010). It is also increasingly becoming integrated with other countries in the region when it comes to the formation of regional production chains. EU-ASEAN trade should, subsequently, not be seen as isolated from the larger East Asian context. The production chains that one or two decades ago often had their assembly hub in one of the "tiger" economies, e.g., Singapore, before exporting to Europe, have today to an increasing extent been redirected towards China. In a detailed and comprehensive study of China's role as an endpoint of a giant Asian assembly line, it is shown that China is still acting as a "conduit", importing parts and components from other countries in the region, and assembling them into final goods (Haltmaier *et al.*, 2010). This development is confirmed by a similar study by Athukorala (2010), who shows that China's imports of intermediate products from countries in Southeast Asia have increased rapidly, at the same time as the exports from China of manufactured final goods to extra-regional markets, mainly to North America and the EU, have soared.

Accordingly, due to the application of the rules of origin in products subject to regional accumulation under recently implemented FTAs, China is increasingly recorded as the country of origin in imports to the EU, even though many Asian countries, not least within ASEAN, have to a great extent contributed to the compound export value. Even though the EU's huge negative trade balance with Asia is foremost concentrated to a deficit with China, it is likely that it should be more evenly distributed within the East and Southeast Asian region as a whole if a more appropriate composition of country origin was adopted (cf. Erixon *et al.*, 2010). An account of the EU-ASEAN trade relations that better mirrors the true location of value-added manufacturing should probably reveal an even more negative bilateral trade balance with ASEAN countries than is currently reported.

The EU's strategic challenge is thus to cope with the fact that the Asian dependence on trade and investment with the EU has stagnated and even declined, not only as a result of the rapid growth of intra-regional trade in Asia, but also due to shifting power relations within Asia. China has replaced Japan as the main trading partner to most Asian countries, and the third largest economic power in the region, India, has gravitated more and more away from Europe towards Asia. This re-polarization can be visualized in a simplified manner as in Figure 3.1.

The specific questions addressed in this chapter are:

(1) How has the interregional trade between the EU and ASEAN developed in a time characterized by a re-polarization of the global economic arena, where intra-regional trade in Asia is growing and China is taking on an ever more dominant role?
(2) How have the FTA negotiations between the EU and ASEAN developed since the launch in 2007? What were the main motives behind a region-to-region FTA, and what are the prospects that bilateral negotiations with separate ASEAN countries will bring about an interregional FTA at a later stage?
(3) Which countries in the respective trade bloc are likely to have a particular interest in promoting FTAs and who have other priorities?

The chapter is outlined in the following way. Section 3.2 gives the broader and more long-term picture of the EU-Asia trade, aiming at demonstrating the shift from Japan to China as the main trading partner of the European countries. Then follows in Section 3.3 a description of the decline in relative terms of Europe in ASEAN's external trade. The EU trade with the Southeast Asian countries is furthermore unevenly distributed among member states, which is discussed

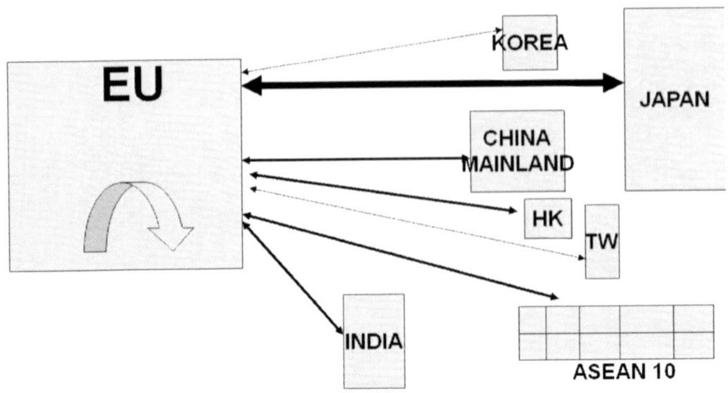

EU-Asia in 1980

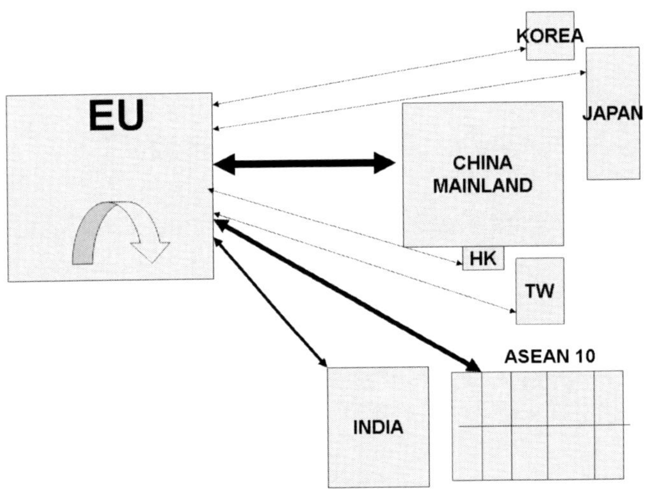

EU-Asia in 2010

Figure 3.1: EU-Asia in 1980 and 2010.

Source: IMF DOTS Database.
Note: Data for 2010 refer to January–October.

in Section 3.4. The major explanation, though, of the declining role of the EU, despite a rapid growth in absolute trade volumes, has to do with the even more rapid growth of intra-regional trade in Asia (Section 3.5). Then follow descriptions of the FTA negotiations between the EU and ASEAN, concluded by an analysis of potential scenarios (Sections 3.6–3.8). The development of the EU trade with Singapore during the last ten years is described, with a special focus on the dramatic downturn between the second half of 2008 and the first half of 2009, followed by a strong resilience. The development of the trade between the EU and Singapore is then put in a broader ASEAN context by a comparison with other current or potential FTA partners. It is finally concluded in Section 3.9 that the present situation of the EU-ASEAN region-to-region negotiations should be seen in the larger context of the re-polarization of the global economic arena, and particularly the rise of China.[6]

3.2 EU-Asia Trade: The Big and Long-Term Picture

The extraordinary growth of foreign trade in Asia over the past decades has also resulted in an increase of the EU-Asia trade relations, measured in both absolute and relative terms. Whereas EU intra-trade has contributed roughly between 55% and 65% to EU total trade over the period 1980–2010, remaining trading partners by the end of the period accounted for some 35%. Figure 3.2 shows the distribution of these among selected key regions, where Asia's share doubled from 5% to 11% over the period. This rise took place during the first half of the period, between 1980 and 1993, whereupon the share has stagnated around the 10% level, and has its origin in Northeast Asia. This growth can be compared to the decline of North America, whose share fell to about 5%.

The fact that EU trade with Asia has soared at such a remarkable pace becomes even more evident when visualized in absolute terms (Figure 3.3). The strong emergence of China is particularly striking. As is revealed in the graph, the decline in 2009 ended a long period of exceptional growth. The downturn generally brought the volumes back to the situation in 2007.

During the entire 1980s, and up to the time of the Asian financial crisis in 1997/1998, there was a strong growth in Asia's shares of the

[6] The latest data are from October 2010 (IMF DOTS Database, accessed in March 2011).

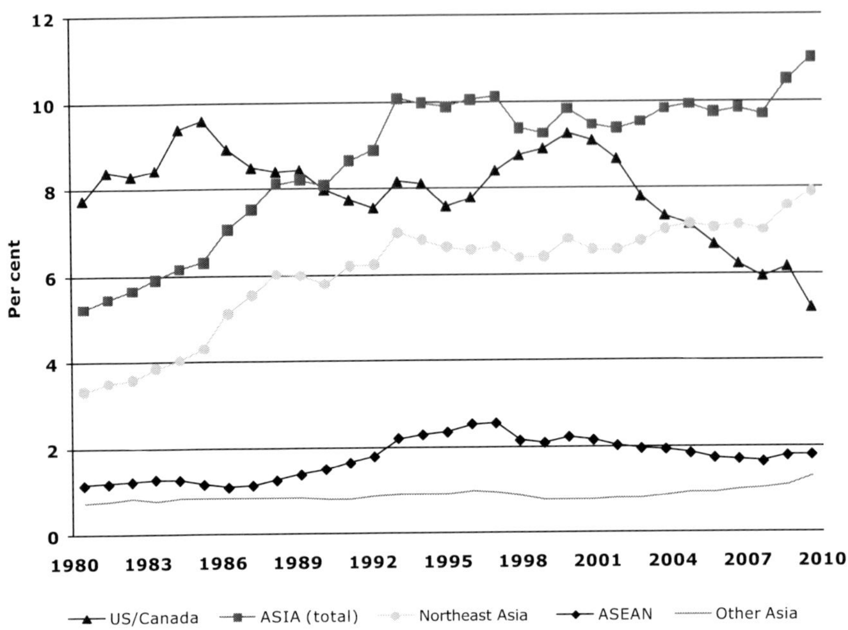

Figure 3.2: EU-27 total trade per selected partners (per cent), 1980–2010.

Source: IMF DOTS Database.

Note: Data for 2010 refer to January–October.

EU's extra-regional trade (i.e., excluding EU intra-trade). Asia's share of exports grew from 11% in 1980 to 26% in 1997, and its share of imports climbed from 14% to 34% (see Figure 3.4).

However, in recent years, this overall spectacular development has not resulted in a further increase of the EU-Asia trade relations, measured in relative terms and seen from the EU perspective. On the contrary, during the 2000s, the share of Asia in the extra-regional exports of the EU principally stagnated and remained stable just over the 20% level, although the most recent figures indicate a remarkable increase, possibly as a result of Asia's stronger resilience after the global downturn. The growth of Asia in the EU's extra-regional imports also slowed down after the Asian crisis, with the share settling down around the 35% level in the late 2000s. The relative decline of the EU-Asia trade relations should, though, also be viewed in the larger

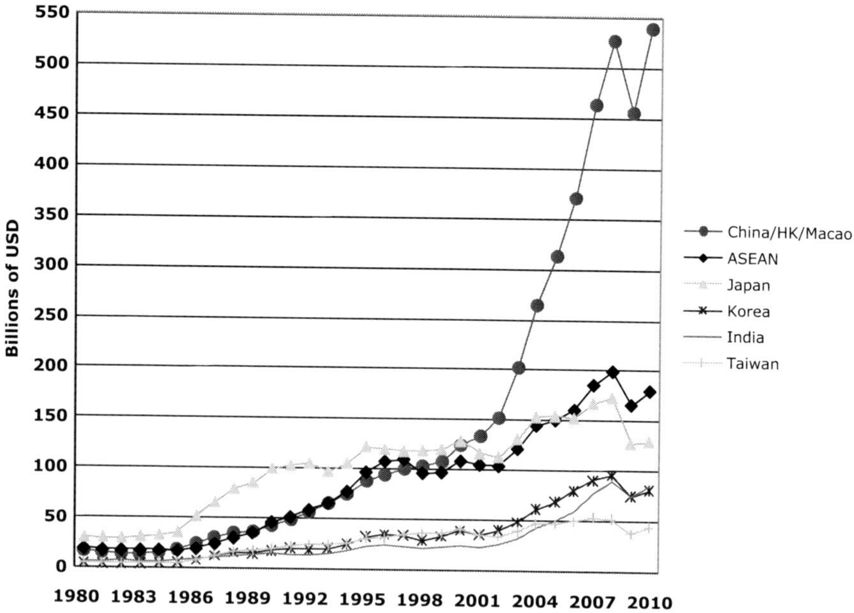

Figure 3.3: EU-27 trade with Asia, 1980–2010 (absolute values).

Source: IMF DOTS Database.

Note: Data for 2010 estimated from January–October.

context of whether European foreign direct investments (FDI) in Asia up until now have, to a certain extent, substituted trade. During the first phase of growing outward FDI to Asia in general and China in particular, i.e., roughly until 2005, the main part of manufactured production emanating from inward FDI to Asian countries went to exports; but there has in recent years been a gradual shift to European- and American-owned production serving domestic and regional markets to a larger extent. This trend is expected to continue, and will probably be even more reinforced when China's 12th five-year plan is implemented in 2011–2015. The plan signals an accelerated emphasis on growth of domestic consumption.[7] It is therefore assumed that the stagnation of EU-Asia trade in relative

[7] China's 12th five-year plan, March 5, 2011.

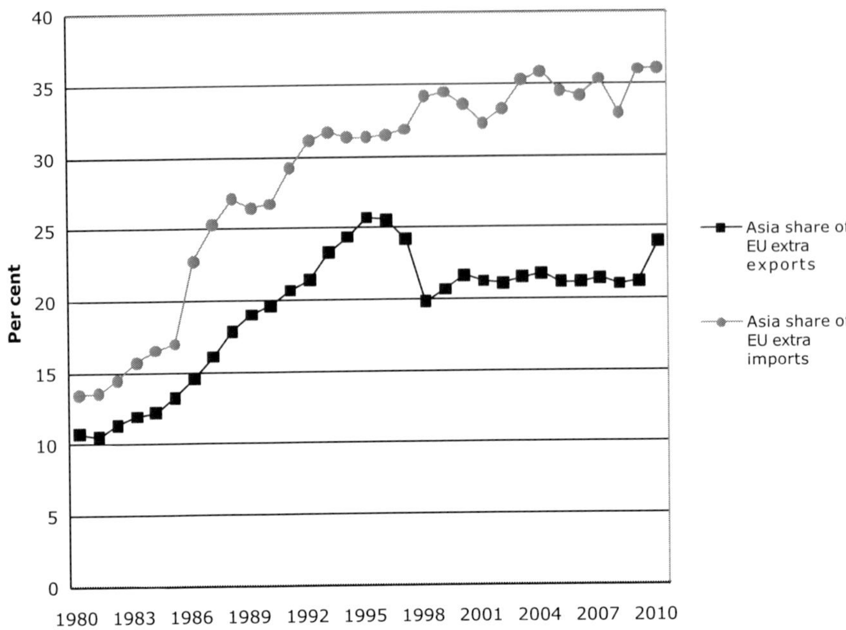

Figure 3.4: Asia's shares of EU-27 extra-regional trade, 1980–2010.

Source: IMF DOTS Database.

Note: Data for 2010 refer to January–October.

terms cannot so far be explained by replacement of trade by investment, but that such a substitution effect may become more prominent in the future development of the pattern of compound economic interaction between Europe and Asia.

This stagnation, measured in relative terms, can in the longer time perspective be related to the remarkable shift from Japan to China in the EU's trade with Asia. As illustrated in Figure 3.5, Japan accounted for between 35% and 40% of the EU's trade with Asia during the 1980s, while the same share had declined to 12% in 2010. This contrasts with trade with China (Mainland/Hong Kong/Macao), which grew from 15%–20% of the EU's trade with Asia during the 1980s, to almost 50% in 2010.

The share of ASEAN, on the other hand, has varied between 15% and 25% of the EU's total trade with Asia during the whole period

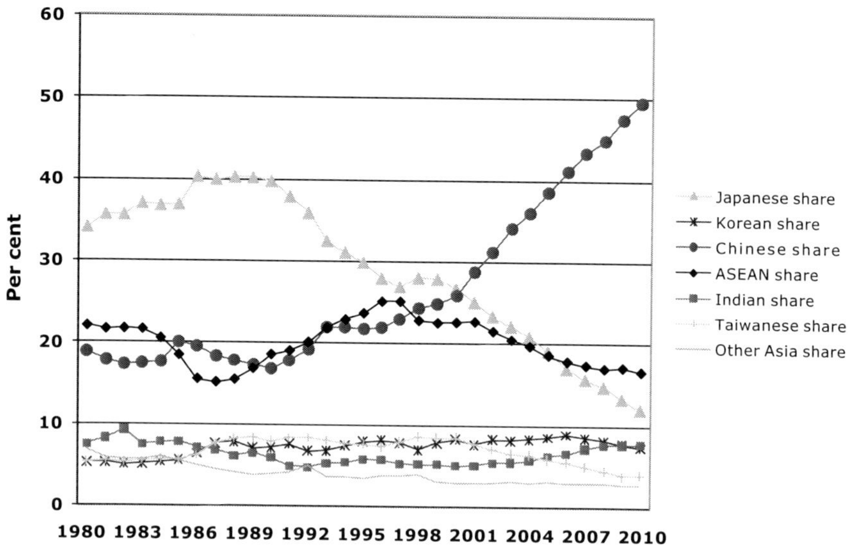

Figure 3.5: Selected Asian economies' shares of EU-27 trade with Asia, 1980–2010 (per cent).

Source: IMF DOTS Database.
Note: Data for 2010 refer to January–October.

1980–2010. It declined in the 1980s, and grew during the 1990s up to a peak of 25% when the Asian economic and financial crisis started in 1997, and has thereafter declined again to a level that is close to the period's all-time low in the mid-1980s. It should be noted, however, that ASEAN has recently surpassed Japan and has become the second largest trading partner to the EU after China.

When it comes to Asian dependence on the EU in the long-term perspective, the shares have either remained stable or declined slightly, as illustrated in Figure 3.6. A notable exception is India, where the EU's share has decreased dramatically since the 1980s. This development reflects the fact that India's foreign trade profile has undergone a dramatic shift from Europe to Asia during the last two decades. India has traditionally been an example of low trade intensity. When the country started to open up, the lion's share of trade growth was directed to newly emerging markets in Asia rather than to the UK and other European countries.

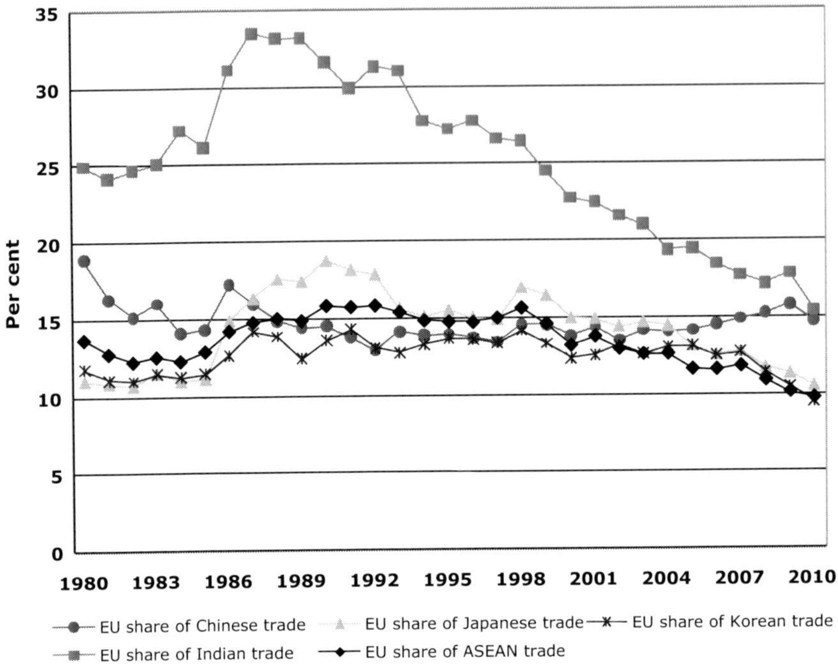

Figure 3.6: Asian dependence on EU-27, 1980–2010 (per cent).

Source: IMF DOTS Database.

Note: Data for 2010 refer to January–October.

3.3 The Decline of Europe in the Foreign Trade of ASEAN

Figure 3.6 also shows the relative decline of Europe in Southeast Asian foreign trade over the last few decades. This downward trend actually already started in the 1960s, when American and Japanese influences increased through large-scale foreign direct investment in manufacturing — initially in labor-intensive production, but gradually in more advanced sectors along the value chain. European investment in Southeast Asian manufacturing industries, particularly electronics, grew considerably in the 1980s, which resulted in a break in the downward trend in the shares of trade during the following years, but the Asian crisis in 1997/1998 signalled a return to the decrease. As shown in Figure 3.6, the EU share of ASEAN's total trade grew in the 1980s, stagnated in the 1990s around the 15% level, and has thereafter declined continuously since the crisis. This decline of Europe in relative terms has continued also during the last ten years, although the rapid growth of EU-ASEAN trade in absolute terms has concealed this deterioration. In 2010 it reached the lowest level ever: less than 10% of ASEAN's total trade took place with the EU (see Table 3.1).

The most rapid growth in Southeast Asian foreign trade since the beginning of this millennium has, though, not taken place with the United States and Japan, but with Mainland China. Furthermore, the intra-bloc trade within ASEAN has climbed slowly but steadily during

Table 3.1: EU-ASEAN trade, 1980–2010 (percentages).

	1980	1985	1990	1995	2000	2005	2008	2009	2010
Share of EU in ASEAN exp.	13.1	11.4	16.0	14.6	15.0	12.7	11.8	11.1	10.9
Share of EU in ASEAN imp.	14.3	14.5	15.7	14.9	11.1	10.3	9.9	9.9	8.5
Share of EU in ASEAN trade	13.7	12.9	15.9	14.8	13.0	11.6	10.9	10.5	9.7
Share of ASEAN in EU total exp.	1.2	1.2	1.5	2.3	1.6	1.4	1.4	1.5	1.5
Share of ASEAN in EU total imp.	1.1	1.2	1.5	2.4	2.9	2.3	1.9	2.1	2.1
Share of ASEAN in EU total trade	1.2	1.2	1.5	2.3	2.2	1.8	1.6	1.8	1.8
Share of ASEAN in EU extra exp.	3.0	2.9	4.5	6.9	4.9	4.3	4.2	4.6	4.5
Share of ASEAN in EU extra imp.	2.5	2.7	4.2	6.7	7.6	6.1	5.0	5.7	5.8
Share of ASEAN in EU extra trade	2.7	2.8	4.3	6.8	6.2	5.3	4.7	5.1	5.2

Source: IMF DOTS Database, March 2011.

Notes: (a) In order to facilitate comparison over time, the figures are based on EU-27 during the entire period. All ten countries that comprise today's ASEAN have been incorporated during the entire period. (b) Data for 2010 refer to January–October.

recent years, resulting in an intra-trade ratio of close to 27% in 2010 (IMF DOTS Database, March 2011 (based on January–October)).

The bilateral trade between the EU and ASEAN was for a long time well-balanced, but it turned into a large EU deficit after the Asian financial crisis in 1997/1998. A number of Southeast Asian countries then introduced import restrictions, at the same time that their currencies depreciated heavily towards Western Europe. The bilateral imbalance has thereafter remained within the interval of US$30–35 billion during the last few years, i.e., an export/import ratio of 0.65–0.70, seen from the EU perspective. It should also be noted that the EU deficit, recorded by Eurostat, is larger than the ASEAN surplus reported by its member states (Lindberg and Alvstam, 2008).

3.4 EU Trade with Asia by Member States

The EU's trade with Asia at large is highly unevenly distributed between the member states. Twelve out of the 27 countries account for 96% of the exports and 92% of the imports (2009 figures; IMF DOTS). Germany is the dominant country representing a third of the EU's exports to Asia and a fifth of its imports. It should be noted that whereas Germany's position as an exporter has been strengthened during the past ten years, it has weakened when it comes to imports. The other main countries are France, the UK, Italy and the Netherlands. The British and the French shares have declined over the past ten years, while the Netherlands in particular has grown in importance. The huge bilateral deficit of US$320 billion (2010) in the EU trade with Asia is concentrated to a few countries, where the Netherlands and the UK alone account for 50% (IMF DOTS). The implementation of the single internal market, with a geographical shift of customs clearance to the main gateways of imports, has resulted in an overrepresentation of these countries. Yet, the fact remains that certain EU members have stronger commercial reasons to give FTAs with Asian countries top priority.

Looking more specifically at the EU-ASEAN trade, the same pattern persists. Twelve countries out of 27 represent 93% of the EU exports and 94% of its imports (2009). Germany, the Netherlands, the UK and France together account for two-thirds of the total trade turnover. The large deficit of the EU is equally unevenly distributed, since almost US$27 billion of the total deficit of US$35 billion in 2008 and 19 out of 23 billion in 2009 were recorded in the UK and the Netherlands alone — once again partly an effect of the statistical reporting of these countries as first destinations of imports from Asia/ASEAN (IMF DOTS). It should also be noted that the UK and the Netherlands play a more dominant role in the EU's trade with ASEAN than in the trade with Asia as a whole. This is presumably due to the fact that actors in Germany, France and Italy more frequently tend to trade directly with their larger Northeast Asian partners, particularly with China, than what is the case with ASEAN partners.

3.5 The Rapid Growth of Intra-regional Trade in Asia

At the same time, there has been a remarkable growth of Asian intra-regional trade during the last decade. This spectacular development has been spearheaded by China, whose presence in the region has changed from being a minor partner in the early 1980s to become the totally dominant actor in the 2000s. The intra-regional share of East Asian non-oil trade grew from 33% in the mid-1980s to 52% in 2007 (Athukorala and Kohpaiboon, 2009). Behind these aggregated figures regarding total trade, however, an asymmetrical structure is concealed, in the sense that the intra-regional imports are considerably higher than the intra-regional exports. The intra-regional import share grew from 40% to 62% during the same period, while the corresponding figures for intra-regional exports were only 29% and 45%, respectively (*ibid.*). The explanation for such an asymmetric relation has to do with the development of fragmented production and export specialization in the region, and the resulting pattern of regional and global production networks. While imports in many Asian countries are sourced along the commodity chain from other Asian countries, the final export destination of the assembled consumer product is to a larger extent found outside Asia, e.g., in Europe or North America.

As was mentioned above, the development of intra-bloc trade within ASEAN, relative to its total foreign trade, has been fairly modest, despite nearly two decades of attempts to promote regional integration through the creation of the ASEAN free trade area, AFTA, and the objectives to strengthen its supranational decision-making within the framework of a common "Charter", with the long-term aim to realize a common market (Lindberg, 2007b). On the other hand, the general expansion of foreign trade in Southeast Asia and the participation by the ASEAN member states in the accelerating process of economic globalization have been extremely successful. Several states can boast of a foreign trade intensity, measured by trade as a share of GDP, that is among the highest in the world (cf. Singapore and Malaysia), and also much higher than in many countries in Western Europe.

ASEAN's trade with neighbouring Northeast Asia has generally been stable in relative terms throughout the entire period after the Asian financial crisis in 1997/1998, accounting for roughly 30%–34% of ASEAN's total exports and 35%–37% of its imports. However, behind these seemingly stable shares, a dramatic shift has occurred between the previous dominant partner, Japan, and the emerging Greater China (Mainland China, Hong Kong and Macao). Greater China's share of ASEAN's total exports to Northeast Asia has increased from 31% to 55% between 1997 and 2010, while Japan's has declined from 44% to 27%. At the same time, the share of Taiwan has decreased from 13% to 7%, and that of Korea has been stable around 11%–12%. The same shift has taken place in ASEAN's imports from Northeast Asia. Greater China's share has increased from 18% to 44%, while Japan's has declined from 57% to 32%. ASEAN reports a large bilateral surplus to Greater China with an export/import ratio amounting to 1.15 in 2008 and 1.25 in 2010, while the previously great deficit towards Japan has evened out somewhat. The export/import ratio amounted to 0.84 in 2010. ASEAN also runs large deficits with both Taiwan and Korea. There are notable variations in the country composition of trade with Northeast Asia between the ASEAN members, among which the Philippines reports the highest level of dependence, followed by Vietnam, while

Singapore and Malaysia show levels below the ASEAN average. On the other hand, the Philippines and Vietnam are much less dependent on intra-ASEAN trade than their larger bloc members. The exports of advanced manufacturing inputs from Singapore, Malaysia and Thailand for final assembly in China result in large trade surpluses with China. In contrast, Indonesia and Vietnam, which to a less extent are integrated in the regional production networks ending up in China, report deficits. ASEAN's total deficits with Japan, Korea and Taiwan can largely be attributed to Singapore and Thailand.

3.6 The Prelude to and Launch of EU-ASEAN Negotiations

At the time of an Asia trying to recover from the economic and financial crisis in 1997/1998, the EU trade policy was characterized by a strict focus on the multilateral negotiations within the WTO. As noted by Woolcock (2007), the EU exercised a *de facto* moratorium on new FTA negotiations after 1999, and in effect was a "one-track trade operator".[8] However, as the outlook for the DDA deteriorated, and as non-EU countries such as the US became increasingly active in signing FTAs, economic partnership agreements or the like with the trading partners of the EU, such as ASEAN, the EU position changed. This is most clearly reflected in the "Global Europe" strategy, where the complementary role of FTAs is highlighted. This changed position reflects the EU's recognition of the importance to look after its interests by means of a stronger presence in certain key markets, as well as the need to integrate its trade policy with its wider approach to competitiveness in a globalized world, where new economic powers are emerging.

As a consequence, in 2007, 30 years after the EU and ASEAN formalized their political dialogue,[9] the EU and ASEAN were prepared to take the next step towards interregional economic integration.

---

[8] Interview with official at DG Trade, November 2008.

[9] For a brief yet informative account of the evolution of EU-ASEAN relations since the 1970s, see, e.g., Severino (2006).

Negotiations for an FTA were launched on May 4, 2007, at the ASEAN Economic Ministerial Meeting in Brunei, with the aim to conclude these within two years.

From the EU point of view, an interregional FTA would facilitate balancing its external trade relations and regaining lost positions *vis-à-vis* other major economic actors, not least China. Moreover, over the past decade, the EU has watched ASEAN sign a number of trade agreements with China, Japan, Korea, India, Australia/New Zealand, and the US. By refraining from following suit, the EU would risk losing competitiveness in relation to ASEAN's other trading partners, and possibly find its relative position in the region further diminishing. In addition, strengthening trade relations with the Southeast Asian region would also provide a better balance in the EU's overall relationship with Asia, which today is highly skewed towards China.

From ASEAN's point of view, an FTA with the EU would secure improved market access as well as potentially breaking the downward trend in ASEAN's share of EU foreign trade since the Asian crisis. It could also facilitate the attainment of an overall better balance in ASEAN's foreign trade patterns, which have largely been dominated by the US and Japan in the past, and are now characterized by the ardent Chinese expansion in the region. Furthermore, achieving a region-to-region agreement with the EU could also further accelerate the internal market process, and may well be regarded as a way to reinforce the ASEAN integration as such.

3.7 Recent Events and State of Play

When the negotiations for an interregional FTA were launched in 2007, the original aim was to conclude these within two years. However, in March 2009, the EU and ASEAN agreed to "pause" the negotiations, for reflection on how to best move the process forward. Later that year, the development took a new direction when the parties opened up to the possibility of bilateral, rather than interregional, talks. What led up to this state of affairs?

In the run-up to the launch of the negotiations, the outlook was actually not that gloomy. A so-called Vision Group, consisting of EU and ASEAN representatives of national administrations and academia, had previously been set up to explore the possibilities of an interregional FTA. They produced a joint report[10] in May 2006 that summarized ideas for how to take the economic partnership to a higher level.

In the EU version of the subsequent course of events, the report was a common understanding on the level of ambitions. The EU negotiation mandate was therefore drafted on the basis of this report.[11] However, once the negotiations started within a trade negotiating committee known as the Joint Committee, it became clear that the perceptions of what the two sides wanted to achieve were different. In the views of one of the EU representatives, ASEAN started to "backpedal" on the level of ambition in the Vision Group report, the justification being that the report was a vision, an academic exercise, and not endorsed by the ASEAN ministers. This development took the Commission by surprise.[12] In the ASEAN version of the same story, the EU presented some unconditional requirements that not all ASEAN countries could accept, and some of them therefore accused the EU of lack of flexibility.[13] The two sides struggled to reach a consensus on how to move the process forward in subsequent Joint Committee meetings and working groups focusing on specific issues.

As the different positions became increasingly evident, a new idea emerged. It involved having a fast track with frontrunners in parallel with the regional approach. This idea was not foreseen at the beginning of the process, but gradually evolved towards the end of the first year of negotiations. It would mean having a subgroup of countries to be the first to sign an agreement with the EU, whereas full openness for others to join as soon as they would feel ready to do so would gradually result in having the subgroup widened towards the region.

---

[10] The Vision Group report is available via http://trade.ec.europa.eu/doclib/docs/2006/may/tradoc_128860.pdf, accessed on March 19, 2011.

[11] Interview with official at DG Trade, November 2008.

[12] Interview with official at DG Trade, November 2008.

[13] Interviews with officials at the Ministry of Foreign Affairs and the Ministry of Commerce in an ASEAN country, March 2010.

Singapore, Brunei and Thailand seemed to be the most willing and able countries to go ahead with this proposal, as indicated in meetings in June 2008.[14] However, political turmoil in Thailand severely affected the possibilities for any trade negotiations, and the idea of forming a core group of the three countries fell flat. At the Joint Committee meeting in Kuala Lumpur on March 4–5, 2009, both sides thus agreed to make a "pause" in the negotiations; not to suspend them. Whereas several EU officials have stressed that the idea was only to make a pause in the region-to-region negotiations, an ASEAN official noted that on the ASEAN side this was rather interpreted as a "freeze", pushed for by the EU.[15]

This development reflects the fact that the process was characterized by numerous aggravating circumstances even from the beginning. There were different perceptions of what the agreement should entail. While ASEAN's other FTAs and economic partnerships mainly focus on trade in goods, the EU vision was more ambitious, going beyond old generation trade in goods agreements to a "comprehensive and ambitious third millennium FTA."[16] This means that the EU envisioned an FTA that includes liberalization of trade in goods as well as in services, investment liberalization, simplification of rules and regulations, protection of intellectual property rights, transparency in legislation procedures, reduction of non-tariff barriers, as well as the inclusion of environmental and social dimensions (Lindberg, 2007a). The fact that the EU had its own visions and models, and ASEAN had its own, is one of the reasons why the process did not move forward. One aspect that has also been highlighted in the previous description of trade flows in this chapter is the fact that the EU-ASEAN trade cannot be viewed in isolation from the EU's commercial relations with China. A fair share of the value-added in goods that are finally assembled in China and exported to the EU, is actually created in ASEAN.

[14] Interviews with officials at DG Trade and EU delegations in Bangkok, Jakarta, Manila and Singapore, as well as with an official at the ASEAN Secretariat, Jakarta, November 2008 and March 2010.

[15] Interview with official at the ASEAN Secretariat, Jakarta, March 2010.

[16] Interview with official at DG Trade, November 2008.

Moreover, a crucial factor is that ASEAN does not have one single common trade policy, like the EU, but ten different ones, ranging from ultra-liberal Singapore to a number of more protectionist members. Closely related to this point is the fact that there is a "development gap" between the six older and richer member states and the so-called CLMV countries (Cambodia, Laos, Myanmar/Burma and Vietnam), which obstructed the ambitions to agree on a common negotiation platform in the free trade negotiations with the EU. Furthermore, as least developed countries (LDCs), Cambodia and Laos already enjoy free access to the EU market for Everything But Arms (EBA) and thus do not need an FTA in order to gain market access.[17] Hence, they would have little incentive to join in an interregional agreement at present. In fact, the negotiation mandate of the European Commission did not include Cambodia, Laos or Myanmar, the latter due to its political situation. Whereas Cambodia and Laos would presumably be welcome to join at any time, after a necessary adjustment of the negotiation mandate, the EU early on declared itself not to be ready to engage in negotiations with Myanmar, as long as the country lacks democratic governance.

This position clashed with the demand of ASEAN for all its ten members to be allowed into the process. The result was an impasse. Former Secretary-General of ASEAN, Ambassador Ong Keng Yong, once suggested that it all comes down to wordings, and to whether some reference could be made in the agreement to future possibilities for Cambodia, Laos and Myanmar to join.[18] The EU compromise was to allow all ten to be present at the negotiation table, where the three were basically only observers. The EU position was clear throughout the entire period, as was that of ASEAN to have all members on board. This infectious issue certainly contributed to the break in the negotiations in 2009, indicating that unless the political situation in Myanmar changes, a full interregional agreement will simply not be concluded.

[17] Myanmar's EBA status is temporarily suspended due to its political and human rights situation.

[18] Interview with Mr. Ong Keng Yong, February 2007.

Shortly after the parties agreed to take a pause, the original two-year deadline for the negotiations was reached. It was time for reflections on and an evaluation of the achievements made so far, not only for the EU-ASEAN process, but for all the FTA negotiations that were launched in 2007. It was then concluded that alternative routes were necessary, since the region-to-region process had not delivered. Hence, it was agreed that the EU would now be ready to engage in *bilateral* negotiations with individual ASEAN members, as long as their level of ambition matched that of the EU. While the region-to-region approach was allegedly still the one preferred by the ASEAN Secretariat, with the shift to the bilateral track, it was now up to each member country to make its own decision as to whether to engage in these talks or not.[19]

3.8 Potential FTA Scenarios: ASEAN-X or EU+Y

The central question now concerned which countries were interested in bilateral talks. There were a number of feasible alternatives or models at hand, which could gradually evolve into more comprehensive ones, with the optimal outcome of a full region-to-region agreement. Borrowing the within ASEAN sometimes used language of geometry, bilateral discussions between the EU and individual ASEAN countries would call for an ASEAN minus X (ASEAN-X; 10-X) constellation, implying that not all ten ASEAN members would be on board. A bilateral deal (BTA) with only one ASEAN country would thus mean an ASEAN-9 solution. From the EU point of view, this endeavor could also be seen as an EU+Y, where separate ASEAN members are gradually added.

The country that first signalled a strong interest in closer economic ties with the EU was Singapore, the EU's main trading partner in Southeast Asia. In December 2009, the EU member states gave the Commission green light to pursue negotiations towards BTAs with individual countries, starting with the island state. The first round of negotiations took place in March 2010, with the original ambition to

[19] Interview with official at the ASEAN Secretariat, Jakarta, March 2010.

conclude them by mid-2011. This BTA could serve as a good first example of how the two regions could be more closely related. During 2010, it became clear that other countries were also prepared to look into the bilateral option. In March, Vietnam signalled a readiness to launch negotiations, yet did not seize the opportunity to become the second BTA partner. Instead, in October, Malaysia and the EU went ahead. In mid-2011, Indonesia also expressed a strong interest.

The First Mover: Singapore

Singapore is the dominant partner among the ASEAN states in the EU-ASEAN trade relation, being the destination for over 40% of EU exports, as well as the origin of more than 20% of EU imports from ASEAN. As is shown in Figure 3.7, there is thus a clear asymmetry between exports and imports. On the other hand, the shares of Thailand, Malaysia, Indonesia and Vietnam are higher in EU imports than its exports. This gap reflects, firstly, Singapore's role as a hub for loading/unloading in the region, which means that the final destination may be another ASEAN country. Secondly, the difference between imports and exports is a result of the fragmented and specialized production within ASEAN, where goods are assembled in countries with lower production costs for sales on the European market.

The bilateral trade between the EU and Singapore was for a long time characterized by an EU deficit. As is shown in Figure 3.8, there was a sharp decline in 2001 of imports from Singapore. This fall was a result of a downturn in the telecommunication industry, which diminished the gap between imports and exports. Thereafter, a period of steady growth followed, both in exports and imports. The growth of EU imports from Singapore started to stagnate in late 2004, while exports continued to soar steadily up to a peak during the second quarter of 2008. The time lag between the decline of exports compared to imports resulted in a growing EU bilateral surplus, which remained during the subsequent downturn.

The development of Singapore's total foreign trade (Figure 3.9) similarly shows a rapid growth during 2002–2008, normally running a surplus in the overall trade balance. The sharp decline of foreign

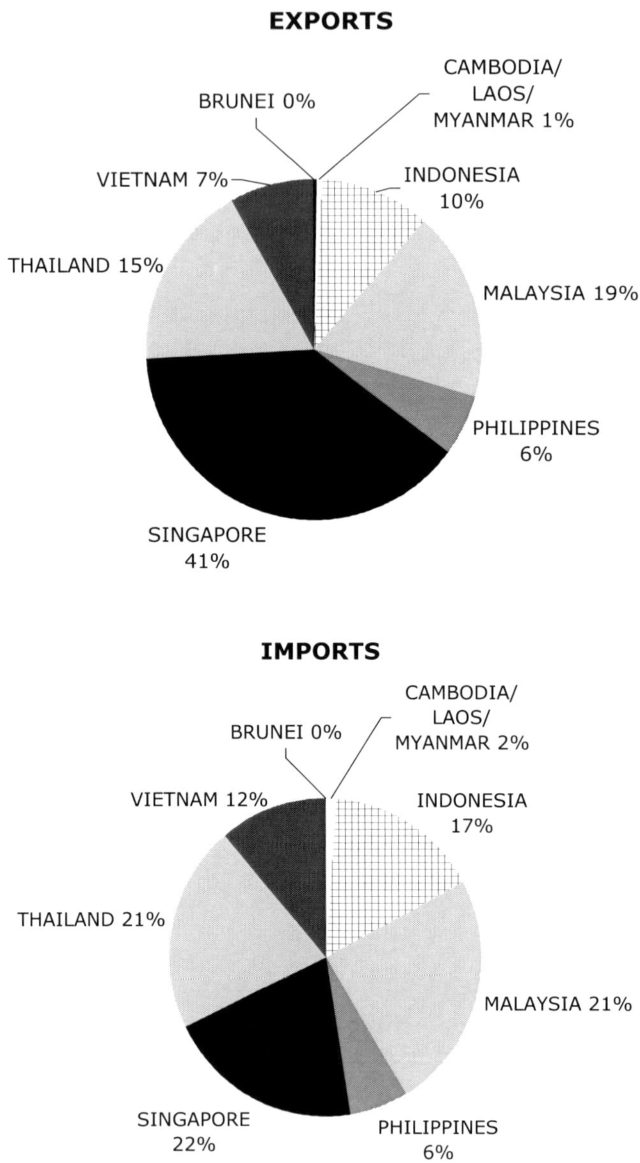

Figure 3.7: EU-27 imports and exports from ASEAN per partner, 2010.

Source: IMF DOTS Database.

Note: Data for 2010 refer to January–October.

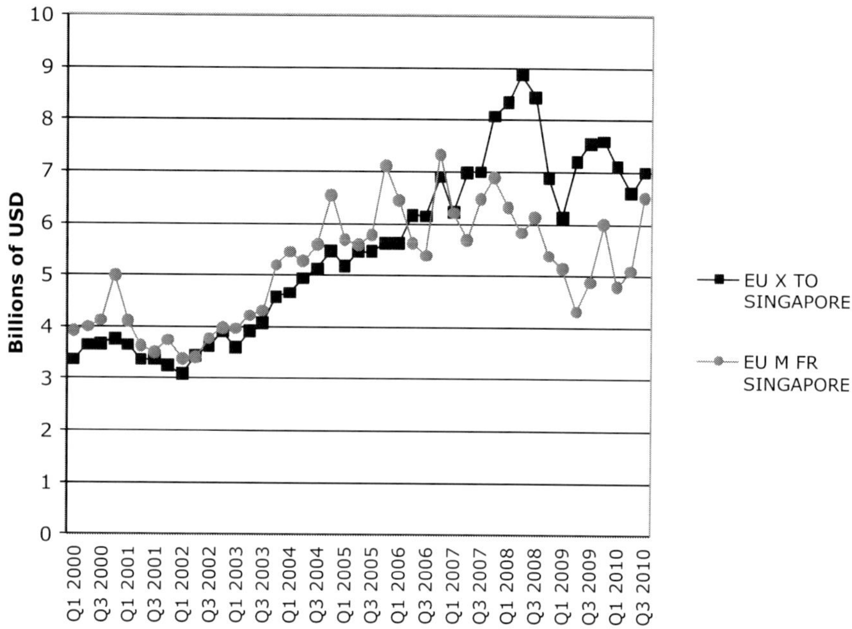

Figure 3.8: EU-27 trade with Singapore, 2000–2010 (absolute values, current prices).

Source: IMF DOTS Database.
Note: 2010: Q1–Q3.

trade that commenced in the third quarter of 2008 brought the turnover back to the level of early 2006. However, the volumes started to grow again in the early months of 2009, bringing the figures back to the level of the second half of 2007.

An important difference in the statistical reporting between the EU and Singapore is revealed when comparing the quarterly EU figures, shown previously in Figure 3.8, with the Singaporean statistics, featured in Figure 3.10. The Singaporean figures are normally much higher, presumably a result of the inclusion of transit trade. Furthermore, Singapore's exports to the EU were time-lagged in relation to its imports in the downturn in 2008, that is, the imports dropped earlier than the exports, and also started to recover earlier in 2009. One interpretation might be that Singapore was affected earlier than the EU by the global financial crisis, and commenced the recovery earlier.

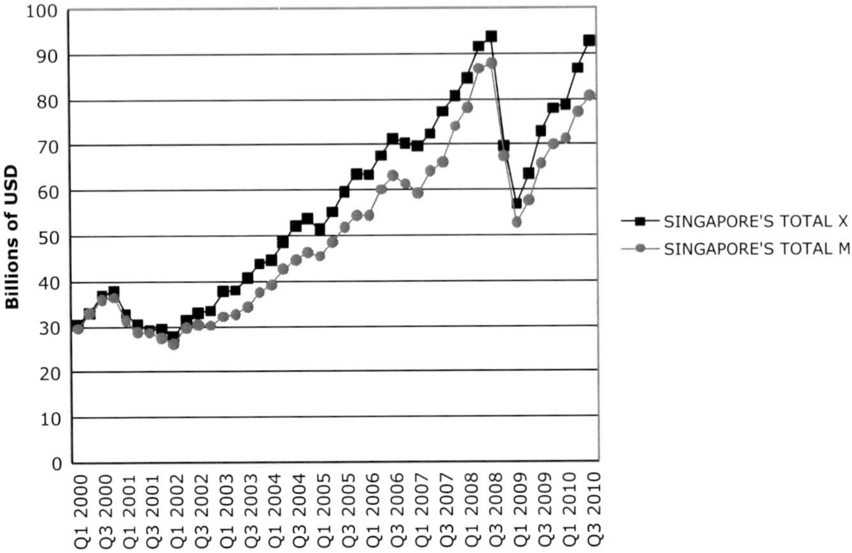

Figure 3.9: Singapore's total foreign trade, 2000–2010 (absolute values, current prices).

Source: IMF DOTS Database.
Note: 2010: Q1–Q3.

Despite the rapid growth in absolute values in the bilateral trade between the EU and Singapore, Singapore's long-term relative dependence on the EU as a final destination for its exports has declined during the 2000s (cf. Figure 3.11). The EU share of Singapore's total imports has been relatively stable throughout the period, but, interestingly enough, has increased since the economic crisis set in.

Real and Potential Followers: Malaysia, Vietnam, Thailand and Others

The decision by the EU and Singapore to launch negotiations also paved the way for similar processes with other ASEAN members, which was the idea behind the EU's desire to proceed along this route. Since Singapore has the role of an important transit point

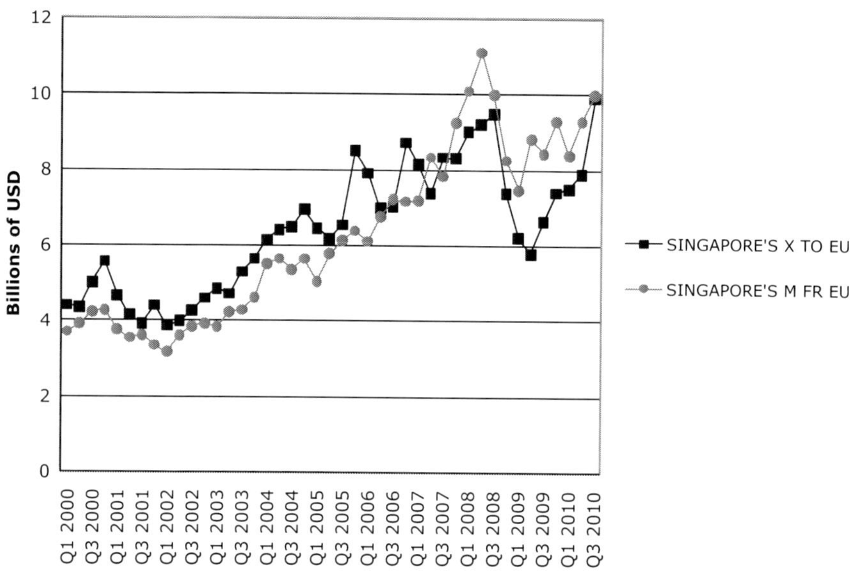

Figure 3.10: Singapore's trade with EU-27, 2000–2010 (absolute values, current prices).

Source: IMF DOTS Database.
Note: 2010: Q1–Q3.

between the EU and other ASEAN members, there are obvious reasons from the EU perspective to conclude agreements with other countries in the region as well. This would pave the way for a return to region-to-region talks at a later stage.

In October 2010, a key step in this direction was taken, as Malaysia followed Singapore's example and launched negotiations with the EU. This decision followed upon a so-called "scoping exercise", which served to examine the potential benefits of an agreement. Like in the case of Singapore, this BTA is envisaged to be an ambitious and comprehensive one. Malaysia is a logical FTA partner given its position as the EU's second largest trading partner in Southeast Asia, and also given the closely interconnected production networks. The key issue now is which ASEAN countries will follow in Singapore's and Malaysia's footsteps, and in which order. Several countries have formally or informally

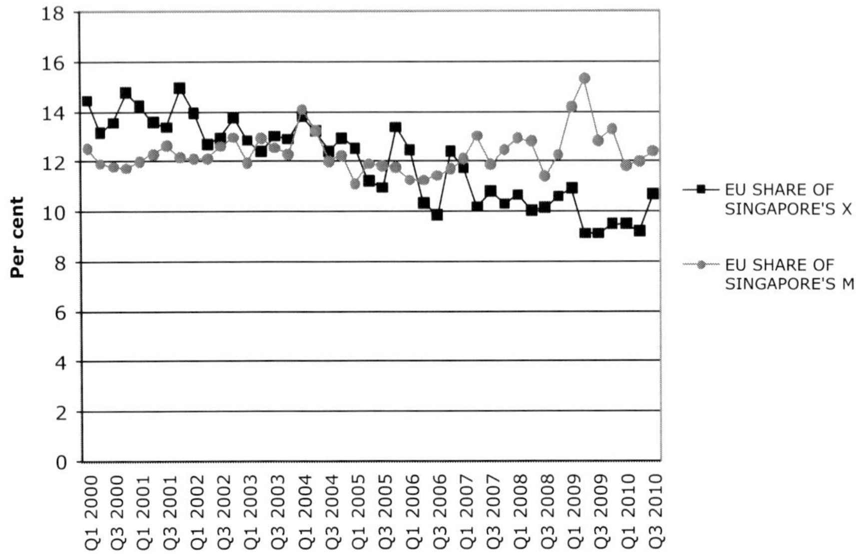

Figure 3.11: EU-27 share of Singapore's total trade, 2000–2010 (per cent).
Source: IMF DOTS Database.
Note: 2010: Q1–Q3.

signalled an interest in doing so. It should be noted, however, that the EU Commission has a limited capacity for FTA negotiations, and it is unlikely that more than three agreements can be negotiated in parallel.[20] Hence, whichever ASEAN country that would like to join should make a swift move.

One candidate is Vietnam, which in fact in March 2010 agreed to launch negotiations,[21] after which a scoping exercise was launched. Seen from a pure economic perspective, Thailand should also be a natural candidate due to its volume of trade with the EU as well as interlinked production networks. The domestic political situation has constituted a restraint on engaging in new FTA

[20] Interviews with EU delegation officials in Bangkok, Jakarta and Manila, March 2010.

[21] http://trade.ec.europa.eu/doclib/press/index.cfm?id=504, accessed on March 19, 2011.

negotiations, however. Moreover, since 2007, the Thai constitution requires the approval of the Parliament, which has further complicated the decision process. The Thai government needs to be convinced of the benefits of a BTA in order to be willing to take it into consideration.[22] Having said that, Malaysia's decision to join the bandwagon is likely to put the Thais under pressure to do the same. As regards the other ASEAN members, an EU-Indonesian Vision Group in May 2011 recommended the parties to move towards negotiations for a Common Economic Partnership Agreement (CEPA). Brunei and the Philippines have also in different ways expressed a certain interest in BTAs with the EU, but have not yet been very active.

Returning to trade statistics, as shown in Figure 3.12, the EU exports to Thailand, Malaysia and Vietnam show similar patterns as in the Singaporean case although at lower levels, i.e., presenting a steady growth over the period until the global economy ran into the major downturn in late 2008. While Singapore is the dominant destination for EU exports to ASEAN, it does not play the same role as a source of EU imports, where it is challenged by Thailand and Malaysia. All three countries suffered from the economic crisis, as evident in Figure 3.13. The imports from Vietnam show the most rapid growth among the examined countries over the period, reflecting the high pace of industrial transformation and its gradual inclusion in the regional and global production networks.

Irrespective of the growth of EU trade with ASEAN countries in absolute values since 2000, the underlying factor behind the EU interest in FTAs with the region is the fact that the EU is losing ground as a trading partner in this part of the world. This is not a new phenomenon caused by the recent economic crisis, but a long-term trend, as demonstrated in Figures 3.14 and 3.15, which reveal the EU shares of these countries' exports and imports, respectively, since 2000. There is a certain difference between exports and imports, in

[22] Interviews with Thai government officials and representatives of EU delegations in Bangkok, Jakarta, Singapore and Manila, March 2010.

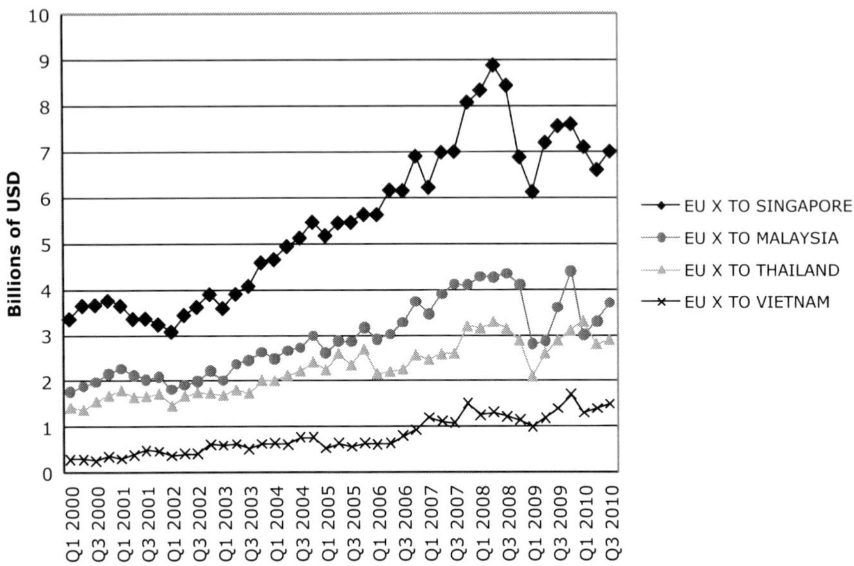

Figure 3.12: EU exports to selected ASEAN countries, 2000–2010 (absolute values, current prices).

Source: IMF DOTS Database.
Note: 2010: Q1–Q3.

the sense that the EU export shares declined in all four countries, whereas its import shares reflect a more stable pattern when it comes to Singapore and Malaysia than for Thailand and Vietnam. The Vietnamese interest in negotiating a BTA with the EU can be explained by the fact that the EU plays a larger role in Vietnamese exports than in the majority of other ASEAN countries.

Other Singaporean and ASEAN Options

In an assessment of various options of ASEAN in general and Singapore in particular, when it comes to initiating FTAs within and outside the Asian region, Low (2010) argues that ASEAN and Singapore "fit the emerging trade paradigm in Asia, in the presence of China's size, dominance and role". Both Singapore and China

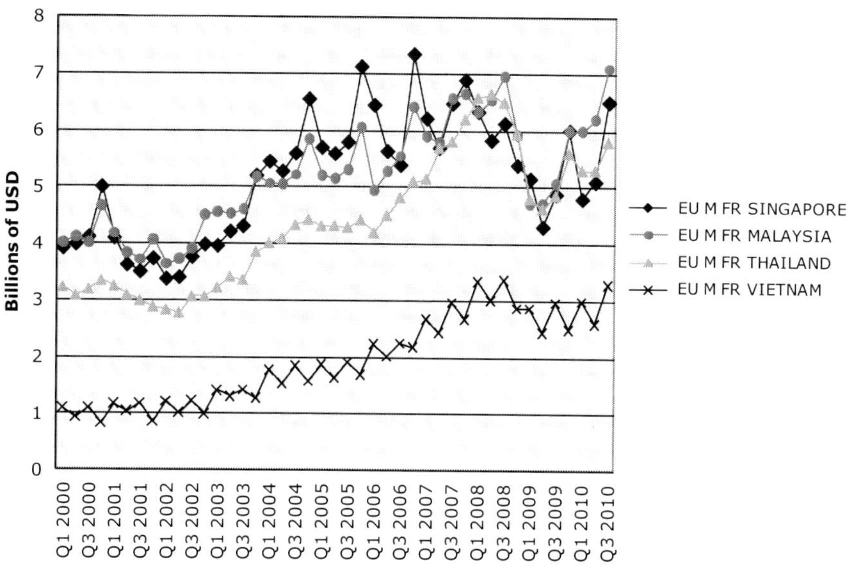

Figure 3.13: EU imports from selected ASEAN countries, 2000–2010 (absolute values, current prices).

Source: IMF DOTS Database.
Note: 2010: Q1–Q3.

have systematically implemented a strategy to engage in various constellations of FTAs, cross-regionally, as well as intra-regional agreements (*ibid.*). Singapore has 31 FTAs at various stages plus another 4 proposed, while China is engaged in 25, with another 8 proposed.[23] In this respect, Singapore's FTA policy has been a role model, not only for China, but also for other Asian countries in their FTA negotiations. This has particularly been the case when it comes to defining market access, national treatment and rules of origin (*ibid.*). Blomqvist (2010) shows that the Singaporean economy is highly complementary to that of China, but he also demonstrates that Singapore's trade intensity with China was more or less unchanged between 1981 and 2005 (*ibid.*). He urges that the

[23] Data from the ADB's ARIC database (www.aric.adb.org, accessed on October 23, 2010).

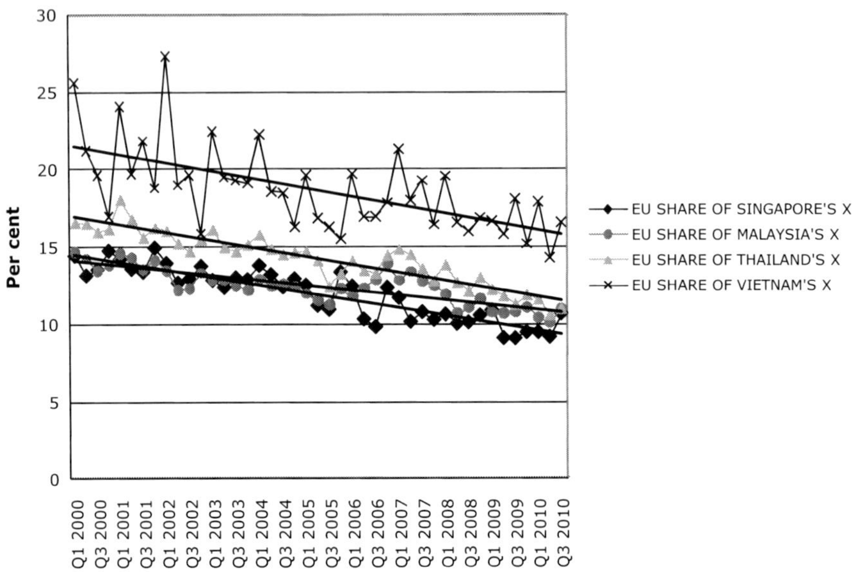

Figure 3.14: EU-27 shares of selected ASEAN countries' exports, 2000–2010 (per cent).

Source: IMF DOTS Database.
Note: 2010: Q1–Q3.

largest potential for improvement of Singaporean manufacturing exports to China would be within highly sophisticated components and niche products, given the role of China as an assembler of final products, but even more promising prospects would be found within the business service sector (*ibid.*).

Low points out that cross-regional FTAs (CRTAs) can be looked upon either from an "outside-in" or, reversely, from an "inside-out" perspective. In the former case, ASEAN and Singapore are secondary partners in CRTAs driven from outside of ASEAN (e.g., APEC, the APT or the EAS[24]), while, on the other hand, an inside-out perspective implies that ASEAN and Singapore steer from inside, and that the CRTA becomes a buffer in the APT/EAS and within APEC. Low

[24] APEC: the Asia-Pacific Economic Cooperation; APT: ASEAN Plus Three (ASEAN plus China, Japan and Korea); EAS: the East Asia Summit.

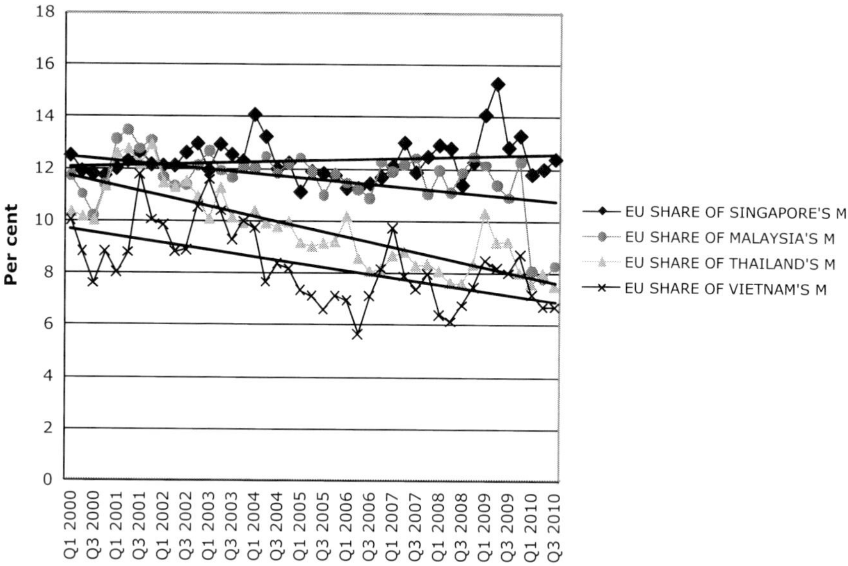

Figure 3.15: EU-27 shares of selected ASEAN countries' imports, 2000–2010 (per cent).

Source: IMF DOTS Database.
Note: 2010: Q1–Q3.

urges that Singapore's best scenario is incremental bilateral FTAs to CRTAs (Low, 2010), and she concludes that Singapore and China can "lend some leadership to the evolving all-inclusive EAFTA[25] as the mother-of-all FTAs, with India, Australia and New Zealand co-opted for political expediency, rather than geography in the Asian trade paradigm" (*ibid.*). In this context, the EU is left out as a preferred FTA partner to Singapore in an environment with more promising policy options. Brooks *et al.* (2010) show that in the long-term economic growth perspective, the ASEAN economies have the most to gain from further deepening of Asian economic integration, not least because they have the potential to emerge as a growth bridge between China and India. If such a scenario holds true, this would even further diminish the ambitions by ASEAN as a whole, as well as by Singapore or

[25] EAFTA: the East Asian Free Trade Area.

other separate member states, to push for the conclusion of comprehensive FTAs with the EU, unless significantly improved market access is given in sectors where ASEAN countries face restrictions.

3.9 Quo Vadis EU-ASEAN? Concluding Remarks

The interregional trade between the EU and the ten members of ASEAN has, despite a rapid growth in absolute values during the past decade, not developed at the same pace as the intra-regional trade in Asia. ASEAN's role as an important trading partner to the EU, measured in relative terms, has continued to weaken ever since the peak before the Asian economic and financial crisis in 1997/1998. The share of the EU in ASEAN trade has also decreased. The two regional blocs are thus slowly, but steadily, drifting apart. The economic turmoil between the second half of 2008 and the third quarter of 2009, causing the largest fall in world trade in recent history at an annual basis, does not seem to have affected the trend of relative decline of interregional trade flows between the EU and ASEAN significantly. There is no indication of a sharper drop in either interregional or intra-regional trade flows. The more detailed investigation whether there are diverging patterns between certain selected ASEAN countries reveals no major deviation from the aggregate picture.

These observations give tentative support to the assumption that the interconnectivity in global production networks has reached a level where trade policies are "blind", i.e., preferences to the own trade bloc are overshadowed by the logic of intra-firm trade in transnational corporations. Even though the EU and ASEAN can be said to be drifting apart in relative terms, the interdependence between the two blocs is high when it comes to the division of labor and product specialization and geographical fragmentation. A breaking down of global production networks into separate regional networks would be a costly and time-consuming procedure. Furthermore, there are no signs of a new trend of increased national or regional protectionism that has affected the process towards deeper globalization in the trace of the economic downturn (cf. WTO, 2009, 2010; WTO/OECD/UNCTAD, 2010). The "decoupling" hypothesis can be seen in view of a shift away from the previously skewed Asian dependence on Europe and North America towards more "equal" trade relations and an increased intra-regional dependence within Asia. This shift has occurred from an initially low level of intra-regional economic integration, and need not be seen as a contradiction to maintained and strengthened interregional trade relations.

It is in this larger context of a re-polarization of the global economic arena that the present situation of the EU-ASEAN region-to-region negotiations should be seen. Even though it is demonstrated in this chapter that the larger process of re-polarization has resulted in a shift in the general pattern of foreign trade, it could likewise be argued that the recent FTA arrangements can give rise to new patterns of re-polarization, and thus, that trade and general economic growth patterns will mutually reinforce each other. There is a mutual interest from the EU as well as from the ASEAN side, not only to maintain, but also to speed up the process of further liberalization of trade, at the multilateral as well as the interregional level. In a situation when the multilateral process has slowed down, FTA initiatives have become more frequent. Simultaneously, when the complexities of creating a consensual framework for an interregional FTA have become too difficult to overcome, the pragmatic response has been to investigate the opportunities to launch bilateral agreements between the EU and separate ASEAN member states, in order to "pave the way" for a more comprehensive deal in the future.

The readiness among ASEAN countries to engage in FTA negotiations varies. The idea is that Singapore and Malaysia will gradually be followed by their regional partners. While negotiating jointly on the EU side, individual EU members may nonetheless also have different priorities when it comes to the ambition to conclude BTAs, due to large differences in trade volumes with ASEAN countries and differing geopolitical considerations. Germany, the Netherlands, the UK and France are the largest trading partners and are thus the ones to gain the most from further trade liberalization with ASEAN.

In sum, an overwhelming part of the interregional trade takes place between a few dominant countries in each respective bloc. The interregional relations should therefore be seen in the context of the intra-bloc regimes of trade. While the European economic integration has reached an advanced stage with a common supranational policy under the supervision of the Trade Policy Committee (formerly the 133 Committee), ASEAN's free trade area, AFTA, is still not complete and there is a large degree of national sovereignty in trade policy matters, which led to difficulties in reaching a consensus on the common denominator in the region-to-region negotiations in 2007–2009.

It is now imperative for the EU to ensure that the current negotiations with Singapore and Malaysia will result in ambitious and far-reaching bilateral agreements, which may serve as role models for future agreements in the region. Negotiating incrementally separately for ambitious BTAs with the different "spokes" could finally lead to a successful deal with the "hub", ASEAN. The fact remains that in spite of all the difficulties involved in concluding a region-to-region FTA, such a deal would be mutually beneficial.

References

Articles, Monographs, Documents, Statistical Sources

ADB: Asia Regional Integration Center (ARIC) Database. www.aric.adb.org, accessed on October 23, 2010.

Ahnlid, A., Alvstam, C. G. and Lindberg, L. (2011). A world without Verona walls: new challenges for the external trade policy of the EU in a resilient global economy — with a special focus on Asia. In: C. G. Alvstam, B. Jännebring and D. Naurin (Eds.), *I Europamissionens Tjänst*, Forskning om Europafrågor, nr 25. Göteborg: Centrum för Europaforskning vid Göteborgs universitet, 413–429.

Athukorala, P. (2010). China and Southeast Asia in the new regional division of labour. In: L. Yueh (Ed.), *The Future of Asian Trade and Growth: Economic Development with the Emergence of China*. London and New York: Routledge.

Athukorala, P. and Kohpaiboon, A. (2009). Intra-regional trade in East Asia: the decoupling fallacy, crisis and policy challenges. ADBI Working Paper 177. Tokyo: Asian Development Bank Institute. http://www.adbi.org/working-paper/2009/12/11/3416.intra.regional.trade.east.asia/

Baldwin, R. (2006). Multilateralising regionalism: spaghetti bowls as building blocs on the path to global free trade. *The World Economy*, 29, 1451–1518.

Bergsten, C. F. (1997). Open regionalism. In: C. F. Bergsten (Ed.), *Whither APEC? The Progress to Date and Agenda for the Future*. Washington, D.C.: Institute for International Economics.

Bhagwati, J. N. (1991). *The World Trading System at Risk*. Princeton, New Jersey: Princeton University Press.
Bhagwati, J. N. (2004). *In Defence of Globalization*. New York: Oxford University Press.
Bhagwati, J. N. (2008). *Termites in the Trading System: How Preferential Agreements Undermine Free Trade*. Oxford: Oxford University Press.
Bhagwati, J., Greenaway, D. and Panagariya, A. (1998). Trading preferentially: theory and policy. *The Economic Journal*, 108, 1128–1148.
Blomqvist, H. C. (2010). The rise of China: new openings for Singapore? In: L. Yueh (Ed.), *The Future of Asian Trade and Growth: Economic Development with the Emergence of China*. London and New York: Routledge, 253–270.
Brooks, D. H., Roland-Holst, D., Verbiest, J.-P. and Zhai, F. (2010). Asian integration and the region's long-term economic prospects. In: L. Yueh (Ed.), *The Future of Asian Trade and Growth: Economic Development with the Emergence of China*. London and New York: Routledge, 321–350.
The Bureau of Foreign Trade, Directorate General of Customs, Ministry of Finance, Republic of China (Taiwan). http://cus93.trade.gov.tw/english/FSCE, accessed in April–October 2010 and March 2011.
China's 12th five-year plan. Submitted to the National People's Congress on March 5, 2011. http://www.gov.cn/english/2011–03/05/content_1816822.htm.
Desker, B. (2004). In defence of FTAs: from purity to pragmatism in East Asia. *Pacific Review*, 17(1), 3–26.
Erixon, F., Messerlin, P., Sally, R. and Wang, J. H. (2010). China's trade policy post-WTO accession: focus on China-EU relations. In: L. Yueh (Ed.), *The Future of Asian Trade and Growth: Economic Development with the Emergence of China*. London and New York: Routledge, 33–74.
European Commission/External Trade (2007). Global Europe: a stronger partnership to deliver market access for European exporters. Available via http://trade.ec.europa.eu/doclib/docs/2007/april/tradoc_134591.pdf, accessed on March 19, 2011.
European Commission/DG Trade. Press release: EU to launch FTA negotiations with individual ASEAN countries, beginning with Singapore. December 22, 2009. Available via http://trade.ec.europa.eu/doclib/press/index.cfm?id=504, accessed on March 19, 2011.
European Commission/DG Trade: South Korea. Available via http://ec.europa.eu/trade/creating-opportunities/bilateral-relations/countries/korea/, accessed on March 19, 2011.
European Commission (2010a). Europe 2020: a strategy for smart, sustainable and inclusive growth. Available via http://ec.europa.eu/eu2020/index_en.htm, accessed in January 2011.
European Commission (2010b). Trade, growth and world affairs. Available via http://trade.ec.europa.eu/doclib/docs/2010/november/tradoc_146955.pdf, accessed in January 2011.

Haltmaier, J. T., Ahmed, S., Coulibaly, B., Knippenberg, R., Leduc, S., Marazzi, M. and Wilson, B. A. (2010). The role of China in Asia: engine, conduit or steam-roller? In: L. Yueh (Ed.), *The Future of Asian Trade and Growth: Economic Development with the Emergence of China*. London and New York: Routledge, 131–198.

Hufbauer, G. C. and Schott, J. J. (2007). Multilateralizing regionalism: Fitting Asia-Pacific agreements into the WTO System. Paper presented at the Conference on Multilateralising Regionalism, organised by WTO-HEI, co-organised by the Centre for Economic Policy Research (CEPR). September 10–12, 2007, Geneva. Available via www.wto.org/english/tratop_e/region_e/con_sep07_e/hufbauer_scott_e.pdf, accessed on October 22, 2010.

IMF: Direction of Trade Statistics Database, visited on numerous occasions from May 2009 to March 2011.

IMF: *Direction of Trade Statistics Quarterly*, various issues. Washington, D.C.: International Monetary Fund.

IMF: *Direction of Trade Statistics Yearbook*, various issues. Washington, D.C.: International Monetary Fund.

Kawai, M. and Wignaraja, G. (2007). ASEAN+3 or ASEAN+6: which way forward? Paper presented at the Conference on Multilateralising Regionalism, organised by WTO-HEI, co-organised by the Centre for Economic Policy Research (CEPR). September 10–12, 2007, Geneva. Available via www.wto.org/english/tratop_e/region_e/con_sep07_e/ kawai_wignaraja_e.pdf, accessed on October 22, 2010.

Kawai, M. and Wignaraja, G. (2009). Multilateralising regional trade agreements in East Asia. In: R. Baldwin and P. Low (Eds.), *Multilateralizing Regionalism: Challenges for the Global Trading System*. Cambridge, UK: Cambridge University Press.

Lamy, P. (2002). Stepping stones or stumbling blocks? The EU's approach towards the problem of multilateralism vs. regionalism in trade policy. *The World Economy*, 25, 1399–1413.

Lindberg, L. (2007a). A status report on the ASEAN & EU-ASEAN economic integration in 2007 — including a pilot study on the interests of the Swedish business sector in Singapore. April, 2007. Singapore: ISEAS/Embassy of Sweden.

Lindberg, L. (2007b). The regionalization process in Southeast Asia and the economic integration of Cambodia and Laos into ASEAN. Series B, No. 113. Ph.D. dissertation, Göteborg University.

Lindberg, L. and Alvstam, C. G. (2007). The national element in regional trade agreements: The role of Southeast Asian countries in ASEAN-EU trade. *ASEAN Economic Bulletin*, 24(2), 267–275.

Lindberg, L. and Alvstam, C. G. (2008). EU-ASEAN trade facing free trade negotiations. In: R. Lindahl and P. Cramér (Eds.), *Forskning om Europafrågor*. Centrum för Europaforskning vid Göteborgs Universitet, 21, 1–19.

Lindberg, L. and Alvstam, C. G. (2009). Interregional trade facing economic downturn: the EU trade negotiations with ASEAN. Paper presented at the Annual Conference of the Swedish Network for European Studies in Economics and Business, Mölle, May 2009.

Low, L. (2003). Multilateralism, regionalism, bilateral and crossregional free trade agreements: all paved with good intentions for ASEAN? *Asian Economic Journal*, 17(1), 65–86.

Low, L. (2010). How ASEAN fits the Asian and China emerging trade paradigm. In: L. Yueh (Ed.), *The Future of Asian Trade and Growth: Economic Development with the Emergence of China*. London and New York: Routledge, 222–250.

Michalak, W. and Gibb, R. (1997). Trading blocs and multilateralism in the world economy. *Annals of the Association of American Geographers*, 87(2), 264–279.

Report of the ASEAN-EU Vision Group: Transregional partnership for shared and sustainable prosperity. May 10, 2006, Hanoi. http://trade.ec.europa.eu/doclib/docs/2006/may/tradoc_128860.pdf, accessed on October 22, 2010.

Sally, R. (2007a). Trade policy in Asia — where next with a crippled WTO and weak FTAs? *ECIPE Policy Briefs*, No. 1. Brussels: ECIPE.

Sally, R. (2007b). Looking East: the European Union's new FTA negotiations in Asia. *Jan Tumlir Policy Essays*, No. 3. Brussels: ECIPE.

Sally, R. (2010). Regional economic integration in Asia: the track record and prospects. *ECIPE Occasional Paper*, No. 2/2010.

Severino, R. C. (2006). *Southeast Asia in Search of an ASEAN Community: Insights from the Former ASEAN Secretary-General*. Singapore: Institute of Southeast Asian Studies.

Woolcock, S. (2007). European Union policy towards free trade agreements. ECIPE Working Paper, No. 03/2007. Brussels: ECIPE.

WTO (2009). Overview of developments in the international trading environment: Annual report by the director-general. Document WT/TPR/OV/12, November 18, 2009. www.wto.org/english/news_e/archive_e/trdev_arc_e.htm, accessed on October 24, 2010.

WTO (2010). Report to the TPRB from the director-general on trade-related developments. Document WT/TPR/OV/W/3, June 14, 2010. http://www.wto.org/english/news_e/news10_e/report_tprb_june10_e.pdf, accessed on October 24, 2010.

WTO (2011). *World Trade Report 2011 — The WTO and Preferential Trade Agreements: From Co-existence to Coherence*. Geneva: World Trade Organization.

WTO/OECD/UNCTAD (2010). *Report on G20 Trade and Investment Measures (September 2009 to February 2010)*. March 8, 2010. www.wto.org/english/news_e/archive_e/trdev_arc_e.htm, accessed on October 24, 2010.

Yueh, L. (Ed.) (2010). *The Future of Asian Trade and Growth: Economic Development with the Emergence of China*. London and New York: Routledge.

Yueh, L. (2010). The China effect: how the emergence of China affects the global economy, export-led growth models and relations to the United States. In: L. Yueh (Ed.), *The Future of Asian Trade and Growth: Economic Development with the Emergence of China*. London and New York: Routledge.
Yusuf, S. and Nabeshima, K. (2010). *Changing the Industrial Geography in Asia: The Impact of India and China*. Washington, D.C.: The World Bank.

Interviews

Mr. Ong Keng Yong, then Secretary-General of ASEAN, the ASEAN Secretariat, Jakarta, February 21, 2007; Director of the Institute of Policy Studies, Lee Kuan Yew School of Public Policy at the National University of Singapore (NUS), Singapore, January 14, 2009.
Officials at the Ministry of Foreign Affairs, Bandar Seri Begawan, Brunei Darussalam, April 8, 2008.
Official at DG Trade, European Commission, Brussels, November 18, 2008.
Officials at the Ministry of Foreign Affairs, Bangkok, March 22, 2010.
Officials at the EU delegation in Bangkok, March 22, 2010.
Official at the EU delegation in Jakarta, March 24, 2010.
Official at the ASEAN Secretariat, Jakarta, March 24, 2010.
Mr. Rodolfo Severino, former Secretary-General of ASEAN, Head of the ASEAN Studies Centre at the Institute of Southeast Asian Studies (ISEAS), Singapore, March 25, 2010.
Official at the EU delegation in Singapore, March 26, 2010.
Mr. Ganeshan Wignaraja, Principal Economist, Office of Regional Economic Integration, ADB, Manila, March 29–30, 2010.
Official at the EU delegation in Manila, March 30, 2010.
Officials at the Ministry of Commerce, Bangkok, March 31, 2010.

Chapter 4

The EU Meeting the Asian Trade Challenge — From Follower to Forerunner?

*Anders Ahnlid**

4.1 Introduction

The ongoing re-polarization of the global economy, in which China and Asia are playing an increasingly important role, has led to fundamental challenges for EU policymakers. Among them is a need to seriously reassess economic and trade links with Asian partners.

This chapter discusses the evolution in broad terms of contemporary Euro-Asian trade policy relations. Trade-liberalizing initiatives are examined against the backdrop of the shift in economic power from Europe and the United States to China and Asia, and the relative decline of the EU as a trading partner to key Asian countries, as shown in the previous chapter. While the preceding chapter departed from an analysis of EU-Asian trade flows and concentrated on EU-ASEAN relations, this chapter deals with EU-Asian trade policy developments in a broader context. A comparison between Euro-Asian trade relations and Trans-Pacific ditto, which provide an appropriate yardstick, forms the basis for a discussion of the prospects for future EU-Asian trade relations and liberalization initiatives on the global, regional and bilateral level.

The trade policy challenge for the EU — the world's largest trading entity — is to accommodate emerging Asian countries in the current and rapidly evolving architecture of trade and investment

* The views expressed in this chapter are the views of the author, and do not necessarily reflect the official policy or position of the Swedish Government.

arrangements, and to do so in a way that upholds and improves EU trade performance and, thereby, economic growth and living standards for EU citizens. This, in turn, will require the EU to reassess its trade policy approach towards Asia, taking into account the fact that the evolution of trade policy arrangements is characterized by "competitive liberalization."

The chapter contributes to the discussion on whether the EU should and could move from a largely reactive stance in its Asian trade relations, in which it has for the most part followed the US, to embarking upon a more proactive path, setting its own agenda and maybe even taking the lead in developing trade relations with Asia, including with its emerging economies.

After a brief account of the re-emergence of Asia on the international economic scene in Section 4.2, this chapter discusses and compares EU and US trade policy relations and strategies with Asian partners on the multilateral (Section 4.3), regional (Section 4.4) and bilateral (Sections 4.5 and 4.6) level. It elaborates on similarities and differences in the EU and US trade approach to Asian countries, and discusses which of the three levels of co-operation might be politically most conducive to expansion of trade in the future. In Section 4.7, the chapter concludes by assessing the prospects for the EU to further develop its trade relations with Asia. Thereby, some specific challenges that have to be overcome are identified.

4.2 The Economic Re-emergence of Asia

The recent financial and economic crisis — the "great recession" — has further accentuated the shift in relative economic power from Europe and the US to Asia. The re-emergence of China as a giant in the global economy not only fuels strong growth in Asia, it also serves as an engine for the rest of the world. This development creates numerous new opportunities for further economic gains in the EU and the US. At the same time, it is increasingly evident that it also poses numerous challenges for the former leading duo in the trading system (Figure 4.1). China recently overtook Germany as the world's largest exporter, and it is surpassing Japan as the second largest national economy. It is expected

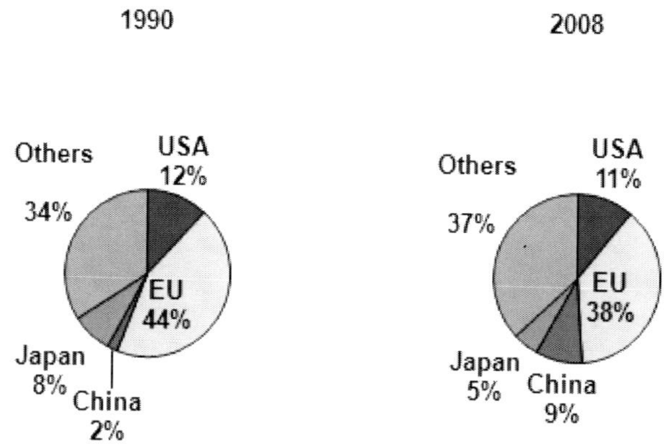

Figure 4.1: Share of world trade, 1990 and 2008.

Source: WTO.

to become the world's largest economy some time in the 2020s. Meanwhile, many other Asian countries are also experiencing stronger economic growth than "old" economies in Europe and North America.

The geo-economic shift in favor of Asia changes the conditions for international relations in general and for economic and trade relations in particular, and it does so with regard to both substance and process. Today, China and other Asian countries play a more prominent role in foreign and security policy than before. The challenges experienced at the Copenhagen climate summit in 2009 is a recent illustration. The economic crisis put China and Asia in a new light. The region is at the core of economic recovery, with China as the main economic engine. In addition, China controls a significant share of US debt.

The crisis has seen the establishment of the G-20, with China and India as key participants, which rapidly has taken over from G-8 as the main body for global economic co-ordination. For the EU the possibility of an emerging G-2, consisting of the US and China, forms an additional challenge at a point in time when the EU is seeking to improve its capacity as an international actor through the Lisbon Treaty.

The international governmental framework conditions for trade — as embodied in the trade regime — have been considerably affected by Asia's economic re-emergence and the new balance of power in the trading system. The future prospects for global, regional and bilateral trade relations, including through formal agreements, have changed substantially following in particular China's re-emergence as a leading trade nation, but also due to new accomplishments by economies such as India, South Korea and the ASEAN region.

The EU and the US still face the shifting balance of economic power from strong positions. Together, they hold about 50 percent of world GDP. The EU is the world's largest economic bloc in terms of GDP, and the US is still the largest national economy. The EU-US Trans-Atlantic link continues to be the most important bilateral economic relationship. Yet, Euro-Asian and Trans-Pacific economic relations are at the forefront of policy-making in Brussels as well as in Washington, D.C., and rightly so.

Over the past few decades, Brussels and Washington have approached the Asian challenge differently in terms of priority, timing, strategies used and measures deployed. For quite some time the Euro-Asia economic link played a less pronounced role in Brussels than the Trans-Pacific ditto in Washington, and so far, EU trade policy *vis-à-vis* Asia has to a large extent been formed in reaction to steps taken by the US. Thus, US trade relations with Asia constitute an appropriate yardstick for evaluating EU-Asian trade policy links.

On the global level, the shift in economic power has contributed to a stalemate in the Doha-round of trade negotiations in the World Trade Organization (WTO), which started in 2001. The fact that liberalizing results have not come about for a long time — not least due to disagreement between the US and Asian partners — has turned the attention of policymakers away from multilateral solutions towards regional and bilateral initiatives. Hence, the number of Asian initiatives of the latter kind has increased dramatically in recent years, which, in turn, has affected Euro-Asian as well as Trans-Pacific trade relations and policies significantly.

The priority attached to Trans-Pacific economic relations in the US since the 1980s led to the inception of the Asia-Pacific Economic Cooperation (APEC) in 1989. In response, the EU formed the Asia-Europe Meeting (ASEM) with Asian partners in 1996. However, neither APEC nor ASEM have so far delivered much, if anything, in terms of real trade liberalization. While APEC is the more specific and action-oriented of the two processes, ASEM has largely remained a forum for discussion.

Given the lack of liberalizing results in the WTO and APEC, the US started to negotiate bilateral free trade agreements (FTAs) with Asian partners well before the EU decided to pursue such negotiations and try to catch up. In addition, the US also initiated a high-level Strategic Economic Dialogue with China before the EU, who followed suit with its High-Level Economic and Trade Dialogue in 2006.

The EU decision to launch negotiations on FTAs with economically important Asian countries and to improve its trade strategy *vis-à-vis* China was taken on the initiative of the Commission on the basis of internal debate in 2006. It formed part of the so-called Global Europe strategy (European Commission, 2006) for international trade and trade policy, which aimed to improve EU trade policy by making it more coherent and result-oriented in terms of its contribution to EU competitiveness and economic growth.

Is the EU ready — willing and able — to play a more proactive, leading and offensive role in Euro-Asian trade relations, as indicated by the Global Europe strategy? The question remains unanswered and the remainder of this chapter seeks to develop a factual basis from which a response can be given. It does so by examining relevant multilateral, regional and bilateral trade policy developments.

4.3 EU and Asian Co-operation on the Multilateral Level

Since the conclusion of the previous multilateral trade negotiation, the Uruguay-round, in 1994 and the inauguration of the WTO in 1995, the multilateral trading system has been affected by two related, major changes in the structure of global economic power. First, the definitive abdication of the US from the role as sole leader in the trading system and the still unsuccessful attempt by the EU to fill the void. Second, the increasing power and role of emerging economies, with China, India and Brazil together at the forefront. In this context, China's accession to the WTO in 2001 changed the balance of power in the organization in a way that significantly affected the prospects for further liberalization.

On the multilateral level, the EU, through the European Commission as its trade negotiating body, has sought to take on a role as global leader, which would correspond to its position as the world's largest trading entity. Since the Uruguay-round, the EU has sought to substitute for previous US leadership. In 2001 this effort met with success in terms of process. The EU was instrumental in launching the Doha Development Agenda (DDA), or the Doha-round. For the first time the US was not the main instigator of a new round. On the contrary, the US had for quite some time, from 1996 when the EU first proposed to launch a new round, resisted the idea. In addition, major emerging countries sought to limit the agenda for the negotiations.

When it comes to substance — in the form of trade-liberalizing results — EU multilateral leadership has so far, however, not been successful. An overall EU position that has been restrained by defensive interests held by several EU member states, has not been sufficient to break up other blockages in the overall negotiating game. The US has remained unwilling to contribute as a leader, and is holding back due to perceived "free riding" by emerging economies. In parallel, Asian and other emerging economies, including China, have not translated their new structural position as great trade powers into free trade leadership. Instead, they have largely retained relatively defensive positions, and thereby performed as spoilers rather than leaders. Thus, following the DDA inception, the EU and other WTO member states have — so far — not been able to provide collective leadership of the kind that is necessary absent a hegemonic leader. Without collective leadership which includes the EU, the US and the most important emerging economies, the long overdue successful conclusion of the DDA will not come about.

China's entry into the WTO in 2001, and thereby participation in the Doha-round, has significantly affected the negotiation process in two ways. First, China has held the view that its terms of accession to the WTO were so far-reaching, compared to the WTO obligations of other emerging economies, that China should not be required to make additional "concessions" and lower its tariffs and other trade measures even further in the DDA. Second, other participants, including emerging economies such as India, have no doubt taken a more defensive stance in the round due to China's partaking, for fear of even fiercer competition from Chinese products, should these emerging economies be forced to lower their border protection further.

In this negotiating landscape the EU, on the one hand, and Japan and emerging Asian economies, on the other hand, have nevertheless been able to co-operate quite closely and have found ground for mutually acceptable solutions. This has become possible due to the fact that the EU has been willing to forego ambitions concerning liberalization for industrial goods due to its own relatively fragile position relating to trade in agricultural goods. In agriculture, the Commission has stretched the EU position, regarding access to the EU market, limitation of internal subsidies and abolition of export subsidies, to the limit in terms of what defensive EU member states are willing to accept.

While Japan and South Korea, too, have politically important defensive interests in agriculture, emerging Asian economies have appreciated relative EU restraint with regard to requests relating to the lowering of tariffs for industrial goods. Thus, Japan as well as emerging economies have all been more or less content with the overall offer of the EU in the negotiation, as has the US, which, however, has requested more from emerging economies with regard to industrial goods in particular. Against this background, an informal alliance between the EU, Japan, South Korea, China and India as well as other emerging economies in the Doha-round has come about at the expense of reduced scope for closer EU-US co-operation, with the EU taking on the role as a mediator between the US and emerging economies.

The consequences of this state of affairs were made evident in the summer of 2008 when the more than 150 WTO member states were close to a breakthrough in the round, which would have led to quite substantial results relating to trade in agricultural and industrial goods, as well as a substantial push forward in the negotiations on trade in services. The nearly-agreed package was brokered by WTO Director-General Pascal Lamy and pushed forward by an informal steering group of seven key trading partners, G-7, the composition of which reflected the new structure of power in the organization. In addition to the EU and the US, the group encompassed Australia, Brazil, China, India and Japan.

However, the attempt failed due to the fact that the US, after consultations with stakeholders and relevant congressmen and senators, deemed the package insufficient in terms of its liberalizing ambitions in key emerging economies. The proposal did not solve the free-rider problem, as defined by the US. Officially, the negotiating process stumbled due to US-Indian disagreement on the conditions for safeguarding small farmers from rapid increases in trade in agricultural products. In this game China was never forced to show its final negotiating cards, and neither was Japan. EU mediation did not suffice to break the deadlock, even as EU negotiators creatively sought to develop technical compromises for the agricultural problem at hand.

Since this failed attempt to reach a breakthrough, additional efforts to push the negotiations forward have largely stumbled due to a continued mismatch between US ambitions concerning liberalization for industrial and agricultural goods as well as services, on the one hand, and China's, India's and other emerging economies' unwillingness to agree to liberalize entry conditions for these products in order to meet the US requests, on the other hand.

China has so far not been willing to expand liberalization in specific sectors of industrial goods, or for specific products, to the extent requested by the US. Neither has India, who is also careful when it comes to binding its domestic trade regime through international law. At the same time, it is worth noting that the tariff solution on the table would result in real cuts of Chinese industrial tariffs while it would largely only lead to a lowering of bound Indian tariff rates, without significantly affecting applied tariffs. China is the only emerging economy in which bound tariffs largely equal applied rates.

In agriculture, it has been commonly held that the US and India can work out their differences, and India is presently seen as less of a spoiler in the negotiations than China. In this context, it is worth noting that Japan, until presently the world's second largest national economy, and South Korea have largely been passive in terms of playing additional substantive negotiating cards on the DDA table. This is largely explained by the defensive position in agriculture that these countries hold. Consequently, Japan and South Korea have been less active in the DDA than they were in the Uruguay-round (Sally, 2006: 18).

Under these circumstances the EU has sought to continue in its mediator or broker role, including between the US and Asian countries, *inter alia* by taking the lead on trade in G-20 discussions and by hosting a large number of informal high-level meetings between negotiators. At the same time, however, the EU has been hampered in its attempt to arbitrate due to the fact that it cannot itself offer more in agriculture to obtain more from emerging economies in industrial goods.

While the US is requesting larger concessions from China and India, as well as from other emerging economies, the EU continues to be more prone to settle for an agreement on the basis of what is already on the negotiating table. From a US point of view, this is seen as EU defection from a line involving sufficient liberalization in the trading system. The EU, on the other hand, holds that its position is more realistic, given the positions of other WTO members, including emerging economies, and thereby also more responsible from the point of view of a system leader. The EU has accepted that the offer on industrial goods by emerging economies is what the EU offers on agriculture "buys" in the DDA. This has led to less confrontational Euro-Asian relations in the WTO, while the US link to Asian emerging economies continues to be more strained.

The unequivocal statement from the G-20 summit in Pittsburgh in the autumn of 2009 to finalize the DDA before the end of 2010 did not do much to change the gloomy outlook; neither did the declaration from Toronto in the spring of 2010. At its autumn 2010 meeting in Seoul, G-20 leaders again sought to inject momentum into the Doha-round. The negotiating activity in Geneva has been speeded up, but at the time of writing, the indications from Washington continue to be such that the prospects for a successful DDA outcome still seem dim. It is unclear whether the new Republican majority in the House of Representatives will make it possible to use the "window of opportunity" that 2011 might open up for the round. The emerging economies still largely hold the key to progress. By offering larger tariff cuts, they could break the deadlock. However, there are no indications that such steps will be taken absent additional US precisions and offers. Under these conditions, the EU has largely exhausted its options in terms of substantive negotiating initiatives, but continues to seek to mediate in order to break the logjam.

On the global level, the EU effort to show leadership encompassing improved co-operation with Asian partners in both quantitative and qualitative terms, has not led to desired liberalizing results. In fact, no previous trade round has dragged on for as long as the Doha-round, and never before during the GATT/WTO era has so much time elapsed between the conclusion of two multilateral trade rounds, as is presently the case. This, in turn, has inevitably drawn the attention of policymakers to other, complementary means of trade liberalization, including regional and bilateral agreements.

4.4 Region-to-Region — Dead End for Trade Liberalization?

Since the debate on the consequences of the re-polarization of global economic activity towards Asia started in the 1980s, policymakers in Europe and the US have come up with different policy responses outside the realm of the GATT and later the WTO, aimed at adapting to the new balance of power and improving trade and economic relations. Region-to-region approaches have been tried, and found problematic, by both the US and the EU (Aggarwal and Fogarty, 2004). The US started out by developing and adopting an interregional response, including on the level of heads of state or government, through APEC. The EU followed suit some time thereafter and initiated ASEM. These steps were at least partly taken based on the hypothesis that it would be easier to make progress in smaller groups. It is evident that the large number of WTO members — 153 at the beginning of 2011 — has rendered negotiations more difficult. Prospects ought to be better in APEC, which presently has 21 members, and ASEM with 45. However, so far this hypothesis has not been confirmed. Neither APEC nor ASEM has delivered much, if anything, in terms of real trade liberalization.

In parallel with the Uruguay-round in 1986–1994, the US was instrumental, together with Australia, in forming APEC in 1989, not without some initial resistance from in particular ASEAN countries. APEC institutionalized yearly leaders' summits, which oversaw a growing number of meetings on lower political and expert level.

Initially, APEC mainly pushed for the conclusion of the Uruguay-round. Once this was successfully achieved, APEC set specific targets for Trans-Pacific free trade. The summit in Bogor, Indonesia, in 1994 declared that free trade should be established between developed APEC members by 2010, and between all APEC countries, including the developing ones, by 2020. The following summit in Osaka, Japan, in 1995 agreed in quite some detail on how these objectives should be achieved. The approach was described as one of "open regionalism." On US initiative it was supplemented with an agreement on seeking full liberalization within selected sectors, and the Vancouver, Canada, summit in 1997 launched a plan for *Early Voluntary Sectoral Liberalization* in nine designated goods sectors. However, despite all these efforts, APEC members could not agree to move forward on the sectoral approach, and therefore soon referred the initiative to the WTO. According to Aggarwal (2005), what appeared in the mid-1990s to be "… a promising avenue to pursue trade liberalization (at least from the American perspective) in the world's most dynamic region began to look more like a dead end, or, at the very least, a very bumpy road."

The developments during the following years supported the claim that APEC would not become the driver for trade liberalization that was initially envisaged. The 9/11 atrocities in the US in 2001 contributed to moving the focus of APEC from trade to security issues and anti-terrorism. Concerning trade, APEC has recently developed more into a body that presses for progress in the Doha-round, than into an organization that seeks to establish trade liberalization between its members in its own right. However, at its summit in Yokohama in the autumn of 2010, APEC renewed its pledge to free trade and agreed to speed up negotiations on the matter, including through the Trans-Pacific Partnership (TPP). It remains to be seen if these words are more prone to be translated into action than previous free trade rhetoric. So far, APEC's contribution to real trade liberalization is limited, if at all existing.

Compared to Trans-Pacific trade relations, historical and cultural differences have so far kept Euro-Asian ditto on a lower and less intensive level. In the 1990s the EU feared that the US, through APEC, would marginalize the EU in trade with East Asia. An EU-East Asia strategy was adopted in 1994, and in 1996, after additional consideration, the EU followed in US footsteps and set up ASEM, the first summit of which was held in Bangkok (Aggarwal, 2005).

Some saw successful EU economic integration, with the formation of an internal European market, as a suitable role model for closer economic ties between East Asian countries. Yet, ASEM never produced trade talks on the same level of specificity as APEC. Efforts did not go further than declarations relating to the desirability of open trade between the EU and Asia. Concerning trade, ASEM was from the outset mainly conceived of as a forum in support of the multilateral system and, later, the Doha-round.

The second ASEM summit in London in 1998 launched an Asia-Europe Vision Group, again following the pattern of an APEC Eminent Persons Group. The Vision Group proposed adoption of a goal of free trade between participants by 2025, but refrained from recommending how or through which institution this should be achieved. Since then, ASEM — including in numerous meetings at lower levels — has not reached much further on trade. The Seoul summit in 2000 was dominated by divisions over North Korea and human rights issues. Copenhagen 2002 and Hanoi 2004 mainly dealt with other issues than trade, such as security and co-operation against terrorism. Diverging views on how to handle Myanmar led to cancellation of lower level meetings and reduced enthusiasm for deeper co-operation. Thus, the recent meetings in Helsinki in 2006 and Beijing in 2008 have been characterized by a broad scope of issues debated by a growing number of participants, including India and Pakistan from 2008. The summit in Brussels in 2010 discussed global economic governance after the financial crisis, but did not focus particularly on trade. The conclusion by Aggarwal (2005) that ASEM, on the whole, has "… clearly done little to foster any degree of economic integration between the EU and East Asia" still holds.

In addition, the example of the EU internal market has not led Asian countries to follow suit. The ASEAN experience in economic integration is, for example, still far behind EU standards. Asian trade strategies differ substantially from both EU and US strategies, and there are no signs of China or any other major Asian country taking the lead in fostering real interregional economic integration through APEC or ASEM.

Thus, so far, region-to-region approaches to trade liberalization have not met with much success. Neither APEC nor ASEM has produced results in terms of real trade liberalization. Due to this fact, and absent progress in the Doha-round, it comes as no surprise that first the US and thereafter the EU have gradually turned to bilateral agreements in order to achieve free trade with Asia (Aggarwal, 2005), and they have done so against the backdrop of a recent rapid evolution of bilateral trade agreements between Asian countries. Again, this shift rests on the assumption that a further reduction of the number of participants, in this case to only two (counting the EU as one), would further increase the likelihood of successful trade liberalization.

4.5 Noodle Bowl or Bird's Nest?

For quite some time, Asian countries did not engage substantially in the negotiation of bilateral preferential or free trade agreements. The multilateral system, as embodied in the GATT and thereafter in the WTO, was given priority; unilateral and multilateral trade liberalization was preferred to preferential ditto. At the same time, the opposite held true in Europe, Africa, North and South America. This has changed, however. According to Sally (2006), since 2000 "… Asia is playing catch-up, with RTA [regional trade agreement] initiatives spreading like wildfire …". In 2009 54 Asian FTAs had been concluded, up from only three in 2000, while 40 of the 54 agreements were implemented and in effect. An additional 78 were under negotiations or proposed, with the largest Asian economies acting as hubs for FTAs, with other large partners as well as with smaller economies (Kawai and Wignaraja, 2009).

This evolution should largely be seen as a consequence of the slow progress in the Doha-round and, hence, as "... insurance policies against continuing WTO weakness ..." (Sally, 2006). Kawai and Wignaraja (2009) have pointed out two additional explanations for the deepening of market integration in Asia, namely European and North American economic integration and the 1997–1998 Asian financial crisis.

Most Asian FTAs are relatively shallow, weak and partial. Their sectoral coverage is often limited as is their coverage in terms of trade-related measures. For instance, only half of the Asian agreements have comprehensive coverage of agricultural products (Kawai and Wignaraja, 2009). In addition, the rules of origin found in the agreements, that determine if a product is eligible to FTA treatment, are often complex and burdensome for business. In fact, many of the Asian FTAs would probably not meet the WTO requirements for FTAs, even if they would pass the less stringent test for preferential trade arrangements between developing countries.

The extent to which formal FTAs are driving Asian economic integration, or if it is rather pushed by unilateral trade measures and companies' supply chains, is subject to debate (Sally, 2010). China apparently seeks to establish FTAs with other Asian countries as a means of asserting leadership in the region. In 2009 China had 10 FTAs in place and considered negotiating up to 30 more (Kawai and Wignaraja, 2009; Sally, 2006). New Zealand recently clinched a free trade agreement deal with China as the first OECD country to do so, and China is negotiating with Australia in the region, as well as with Norway.

Japan for a long time refrained from entering into bilateral FTAs, but is now part of the game with presently 11 FTAs at hand. In addition, Japan has expressed an interest in an EU-Japan FTA.

By Asian standards, ASEAN is a success story in terms of regional integration (Lindberg, 2007). As shown in the previous chapter, members of the ASEAN Free Trade Area (AFTA) are still struggling to form a really integrated regional market. ASEAN has emerged as the major regional Asian hub for FTAs. The agreement in force with China, Japan and South Korea forms ASEAN Plus Three. The recent additions of India, Australia and New Zealand create ASEAN Plus Six (Kawai and Wignaraja, 2009; Sally, 2010). On top of this, individual ASEAN members have entered into numerous bilateral FTAs with non-ASEAN countries. Singapore has taken the lead in this respect. In addition to its ASEAN membership, Singapore has all in all 18 FTAs, several of which are relatively far-reaching.

On the one hand, the web of Asian FTAs has been seen as a sticky and complex "noodle bowl" that diverts, not creates, trade and that complicates life for companies through the use of different and arbitrary rules of origin. On the other hand, the network of agreements has been said to resemble a "bird's nest" (with reference to the Beijing Olympic Stadium), holding the promise of bringing new life to more comprehensive liberalization, including on the multilateral level, by providing stepping stones towards wider and deeper free trade arrangements. The jury is still out concerning which view will prevail. Given the rapid increase in the number and coverage of Asian FTAs, the discussion on whether and how to create an East Asia-wide free trade zone is becoming more intense, as is the debate on whether and how to include the United States and/or the EU in the project (Kawai and Wignaraja, 2009).

The Asian web of FTAs poses an evident challenge to both the US and the EU, who have approached it differently. After 2000 the EU started the new decennium by refraining from launching new free trade agreement negotiations. Instead, clear and uninterrupted priority was given to multilateral negotiations. This approach was upheld and reinforced by the start of the Doha-round. The US, on the other hand, deviated from its original hesitation to FTAs by entering into NAFTA in 1994. When APEC did not deliver concrete free trade results, the US started FTA negotiations with selected Asian partners, pursuing a policy of "competitive liberalization" as formulated by then USTR Robert Zoellick (Evenett and Meier, 2007).

The US first looked at ASEAN members. Negotiations with Singapore were launched in 2000 and concluded in 2003. The agreement entered into force after Congressional approval in 2004 as the first US free trade agreement with an Asian country. The US-Singapore FTA has been considered a success since bilateral trade between the two countries has increased by more than 70 percent between 2004 and 2008. As a next step among ASEAN members, the US launched negotiations with Thailand in 2004, but the process was suspended in 2006 due to the Thai political turmoil and subsequent military-led coup. In addition, the US co-operates with several other ASEAN countries under so-called Trade and Investment Framework Agreements (TIFAs).

After successful negotiations and implementation of a free trade agreement with Australia in 2005, the US started negotiations with South Korea in 2006 and signed the Korea-US Free Trade Agreement (KORUS) in 2007. It would become the economically most important US FTA since NAFTA. However, the agreement was stalled in the US Congress for quite some time. In the autumn of 2010 the USTR, under the Obama administration, managed to renegotiate issues in the agreement that had been subject to domestic US criticism, mainly in the area of automobiles. With the changes, it is hoped that Congress will approve the deal in 2011. The prospects of an EU-South Korea agreement have to a large extent spurred the renewed US efforts to finalize KORUS, and the intended decision by Congress coincides with the planned entry into force of EU's agreement.

In 2008 the US sought to revive the interregional approach, albeit on a smaller scale, and announced its willingness to start negotiations to join the Trans-Pacific Partnership agreement between Singapore, Chile, New Zealand and Brunei as a means to forge Trans-Pacific economic integration, which was deemed important not only economically but also for strategic reasons. Additional countries have since declared a willingness to join the initiative, under which negotiations are under way. The US interest was reiterated in late 2009 as one of the first offensive steps taken by the Obama administration on trade, with the aim of "… shaping a high-standard, broad-based regional pact …." which through expansion to more Pacific countries should become "… the largest, most dynamic trade collaboration of our time" (USTR, 2009). The TPP might be a more realistic initiative than other attempts to form

Trans-Pacific formal trade ties, but it remains to be seen if the US Congress is willing to accept such a deal, should it be negotiated and sent to Congress for approval.

The EU took a pause in bilateral free trade negotiations after having concluded agreements with South Africa in 1999 and with Mexico and Chile in 2000. It thus initially largely observed the increase in Asian free trade arrangements without taking part. The stance was motivated with reference to the importance of safeguarding the multilateral trading system and giving priority to the Doha-round. This line was supported by both more defensive Mediterranean EU member states, on the one hand, and more ideologically prone liberal countries, such as United Kingdom and the Netherlands, on the other hand. The former saw increased Asian competition as a threat, while the latter objected to bilateral agreements due to the fact that they might lead to trade diversion rather than trade creation. However, absent progress in the Doha-round and facing an increasing number of Asian free trade arrangements being negotiated, including by the US, the embargo on new EU FTA negotiations became increasingly difficult to maintain. After internal debate the European Commission proposed a new, more active and result-oriented trade approach in 2006, the *Global Europe* strategy.

Global Europe re-affirmed that the multilateral trading system and a successful conclusion of the Doha-round remained the number one priority for the EU. However, it also opened the door for new negotiations on regional or bilateral FTAs as a complement to the WTO. Particular importance was given to Asia. The strategy noted that while EU's existing FTAs "... support our neighborhood and developing objectives well, our main trade interests, including in Asia, are less well served" (European Commission, 2006). Thus, the strategy stressed that new FTAs must drive European growth and employment and that economic factors therefore should play a primary role in the choice of negotiating partners. Three criteria were provided for the selection of partners. First, negotiating counterparts should have market potential in terms of economic size and growth. Second, the level of protection against EU exporters should be taken into account, with less emphasis given to partners with low trade barriers. Third, potential partners' negotiations with EU competitors should also be considered, adding a strategic element to the process. Furthermore, free trade agreements under the strategy should be broad and comprehensive, encompassing not only traditional trade in goods and services, but also areas such as investment, intellectual property rights, public procurement and sustainable development-oriented provisions.

Based on the *Global Europe* trade policy strategy and its criteria, EU member states, through a decision in the Council, mandated the European Commission to launch FTA negotiations with South Korea, the ASEAN countries and India in 2007. The fact that the US had already finalized or were involved in negotiations with South Korea and ASEAN countries at this time was an important consideration behind the start of EU negotiations with these partners, while the EU placed itself in a privileged position by starting negotiations with India before the US.

The EU negotiations with South Korea were concluded after eight negotiating sessions in the fall of 2009. Compared to the Korea-US agreement, the EU reached an outcome that was both wider in scope and deeper in terms of measures covered. For example, the EU agreement contained more discipline on non-tariff barriers, including in the automotive sector. Despite this achievement, the deal was questioned by EU member states in the Council and members of the European Parliament, as well as by many European car manufacturers. The EU automotive sector held that the agreement is skewed to the advantage of Korean car companies, and to the detriment of European ditto. The economic crisis was used as an additional argument for why the deal should not be accepted. Italy led the resistance within the Council. This pressure resulted in the inclusion of various safeguard provisions in the agreement towards the end of the negotiations. On top of this, the Commission incorporated additional safeguard measures in the EU implementation package, without departing from the agreement reached with Korea, in order to satisfy the interests of the European car industry.

While the EU member states formally backed the deal in the Council in September 2010, the European Parliament, which has to give its assent to the agreement under the Lisbon Treaty that entered into force in December 2009, was initially more hesitant towards the agreement. However, in early 2011 the Parliament voted to approve the agreement with a large majority, thereby proving its willingness to contribute to an open EU trade policy. The substance of the EU-Korea deal entered into force later in 2011. The EU deal with Korea has led to concern in the US, where it has been used by the Obama administration as an argument for pushing the Korea-US agreement through Congress in order to avoid that US companies be given worse access to the Korean market than EU competitors, once the EU-Korea deal enters into force.

The EU FTA negotiations with ASEAN — the EU's third largest trading partner outside Europe — were also launched in 2007 (Lindberg and Alvstam, 2008). The negotiations originated from dialogue and regulatory co-operation that had been started in 2003 under the so-called Trans-Regional EU-ASEAN Trade Initiative, which in turn was based on advice from a "Vision Group". However, and as discussed in more depth in the previous chapter, the region-to-region set-up for the process proved cumbersome. Progress was slow and the negotiations stalled quite rapidly. The fact that the EU was not in a position to include Myanmar in real negotiations for political reasons contributed to the complexity. In early 2009 both sides agreed to take a pause. The impasse was broken by the EU when the Commission, towards the end of the year and after protracted internal debate between member states, was given green light to begin FTA negotiations with individual ASEAN countries, starting with Singapore, which is the EU's most important trading partner amongst the ASEAN countries. This phase of the negotiation started in 2010, while the parties are upholding the ultimate objective of reaching a full region-to-region final arrangement. In September 2010 the Commission was also granted authority to start FTA negotiations with Malaysia. Simultaneously, preparatory talks were under way with Vietnam.

In addition to Korea and ASEAN, the EU also started FTA negotiations with India in 2007, based on recommendations from a "High-Level Trade Group". This negotiation differs from the other two due to the size of the parties involved. The negotiation seeks to integrate the EU's internal market, which encompasses about half a billion consumers, with India's market, with more than one billion inhabitants. In addition, the EU is a more dominant actor in India than in other markets in East and South-East Asia. For India, trade with the EU is larger than trade with the US, and it was just recently that China overtook the EU as India's largest trading partner. Several negotiating rounds have been held. An attempt to finalize the accord by the 2010 EU-India summit did not hold. A new deadline has been set to the 2011 summit. Hard bargaining no doubt remains in relation to traditional trade policy topics as well as "trade-related" or "non-trade issues".

Concerning market access, the EU and India still differ on the possible level of asymmetry in tariff cuts. The EU seeks 95 percent coverage for full tariff elimination for both parties, while India seems to be willing to grant 90 percent coverage in return for 95 percent from the EU side. Fierce negotiations will also take place on the possible exclusions from full liberalization and on the possible complete coverage of the textiles and chemical sectors. Concerning trade in services, India has offensive interests relating to both cross-border provision of services, for instance in the form of call-centers, and movement of individual service suppliers, computer consultants being one important example. The EU, on the other hand, wants to have better access to the Indian financial and telecommunication services markets. The inclusion of public procurement under the agreement is yet a disputed issue. Such procurement is of considerable size. The EU seeks rules that open up the sector, while the Indian negotiators have, so far, not been mandated to enter into the area.

In addition, different views persist between the EU and India regarding sustainable development. The EU attaches considerable importance to "trade-related" topics such as "trade and environment/climate" and "trade and labor rights", while India dismisses such "non-trade" issues, and seeks to get them off the negotiating agenda. The EU also insists on a link between the FTA and Indian commitments concerning human rights and non-proliferation of weapons of mass destruction, which, according to the EU, could be included in a general Partnership and Co-operation Agreement. In this respect, the EU maintains that there should be a possibility to abandon the FTA if the partner is in breach of these "political clauses". "Non-trade issues" of this sort are firmly rejected by India, but constitute a political must for the EU.

While EU and Indian business representatives generally support the negotiations, defensive sectors in both parties will no doubt have objections to liberalization. Civil society groups in both parties, but probably more so in India than in the EU, will also raise opposition, as will no doubt also parliamentarians in New Delhi and Brussels. The still unanswered question is whether these interests will be strong enough to block a deal.

In addition, it is worth noting that as the EU-India process has advanced, Pakistan has turned to the EU with a request for the initiation of FTA negotiations. The request has, however, so far not rallied sufficient support, neither by EU member states, nor in the Commission.

The web of Asian FTAs still poses a significant challenge to both the EU and the US. The EU is seeking to catch up with the US in terms of its Asian FTAs, and might be in the process of overtaking the US with regard to both the Korea agreement and, possibly, the Indian agreement in the making. However, neither in Brussels nor in Washington is the way ahead straightforward. Political opposition to FTAs is at hand in both capitals, and it remains to be seen to what extent it can be overcome. The South Korean FTAs act as important test cases. The EU also has to come to grips with how to handle the link between FTAs and so-called political clauses concerning human rights and non-proliferation of weapons of mass destruction, in particular in its negotiations with India.

4.6 Trade Relations without FTAs with China and Japan?

In addition to the intensification of FTA negotiations, the bilateral relations with Asia's two largest economies — China and Japan — are evidently also of utmost importance for the EU as well as for the US. In neither case is a FTA foreseen in the near future, while other ways and means dominate these relations.

China poses the biggest trade challenge for the EU and the US for several reasons. While factors in all three economies have contributed to current global economic imbalances, including in currency markets, the rapid export-led growth of the Chinese economy has resulted in the need for far-reaching structural adjustment in the EU as well as in the US. The questions of when and how China will embark upon a more balanced growth model than the present one remain to be answered. Trade policy making *vis-à-vis* China is also affected by the non-democratic political system of the country, which limits the scope and depth of potential economic integration with both the EU and the US.

Still, the EU *Global Europe* trade strategy concluded that "China is the single greatest test of Europe's capacity to make globalization an opportunity for jobs and growth ... Europe must get China right, as an opportunity, a challenge and prospective partner" (European Commission, 2006). From this point of departure the EU has developed a bilateral trade strategy *vis-à-vis* China, for which the EU is the largest trading partner. The strategy builds on economic engagement and focuses on enforcement of intellectual property rights, market access challenges and investment opportunities. Institutionally, however, the EU has yet again followed the US in terms of how to handle trade relations with China.

The US instituted a high-level "Strategic Economic Dialogue" with China in 2006, which was later amended into an expanded "Strategic and Economic Dialogue" by the Obama administration. This Dialogue deals with all overarching economic and trade challenges between the two countries. In 2008, the EU followed suit and launched its High-Level Economic and Trade Dialogue with China, with the aim of providing a tool to address issues of mutual concern. In addition to yearly summits, the dialogue has emerged as the key forum for EU-Chinese trade and investment policy relations. Since 2007 the EU and China have also been negotiating a comprehensive Partnership and Co-operation Agreement (PCA). These negotiations are conducted on the basis of the 2006 EU strategy on Partnership and Competition with China, according to which the EU, on the basis of engagement and partnership, pledges to accept strong

Chinese competition, on the one hand, while pushing China to trade fairly, on the other hand.

The bilateral trade relation with China has come under additional strain during the economic crisis in both Washington and Brussels. The alleged Chinese currency manipulation has dominated much of the debate. Concerning trade, US-China relations have deteriorated following the US imposition of tariffs on imports of car tyres, which made China retaliate by imposing anti-dumping measures on goods from the US. Recently, the currency dispute has dominated US-China economic relations. Legislative proposals in the US Congress, according to which a "manipulated" Chinese currency could result in US import restrictions on Chinese goods in order to "level the playing field", have fueled the debate. While recent G-20 co-operation has somewhat reduced the level of tension, it remains to be seen to what extent the Chinese leadership is willing to accept a higher degree of market determination of the value of the yuan, and thereby to what extent this issue will continue to dominate international economic diplomacy and trade policy debate.

While the EU has backed the US view that the yuan ought to appreciate faster, it has not let this issue dominate the bilateral relationship. Concerning traditional trade measures, the EU has prolonged anti-dumping measures on imports of Chinese shoes, despite severe Chinese criticism, and imposed new anti-dumping duties on imports of other manufactured goods. Both the US and the EU have reacted to an increasing use of "buy national" provisions in China. The past years have also witnessed an increase in the resort to WTO dispute settlement between these major trading partners. This trend is likely to become even more pronounced in the future, as trade flows continue to grow.

More demanding conditions for foreign direct investment in China have also been on the agenda. This has led the European Commission to consider a proposal to launch negotiations on an EU-China investment treaty in accordance with the Commission's newly acquired competence over investment relations with third countries under the Lisbon Treaty. At the same time, the increase in Chinese foreign direct investment into EU member states, such as Geely's recent acquisition of Volvo Cars, has opened up a new debate on the EU openness for such investments. The Italian EU Commissioner, with support from others, at the beginning of the 2010s put forward the idea that the terms and conditions for inward direct investment into the EU should be reassessed, and that the EU ought to consider the establishment of a review mechanism, the purpose of which should be to safeguard EU control over "strategic" EU companies. The suggestion was made with reference to similar devices in other countries, including the US, but it immediately triggered criticism from countries such as Germany, the Netherlands and Sweden.

While "G-2 strains" as the ones mentioned above risk hampering trade relations between the US and China, the EU has an opportunity to continue to develop its trade and investment links with China provided that it manages to uphold the balance between accepting competition and enforcing trade rules in a responsible manner. A proposal such as the one on screening of foreign direct investment would not seem appropriate in this context. However, the main question in this is, rather, to what extent China itself is willing to play by the international rulebook, including by the obligations that WTO membership brings.

While US-Japan trade relations in the 1970s and 1980s resembled the US-China relations of today, trade relations between the EU and Japan have been less confrontational over the years. Nevertheless, the EU, just like the US, has criticized Japan for maintaining a very large amount of non-tariff measures that hinder exports from entering the Japanese market. Since 2000 Japan, like other Asian economies, has moved from having no bilateral FTA to entering into several. As would be assumed under conditions of "competitive liberalization", the increasing resort to FTA by the US and the EU in the region has led Japan to follow suit.

Thus, in 2009 Japan started to lobby for the initiation of a free trade agreement with the EU. The quest led to a lukewarm response from several EU member states. Mediterranean member states shunned Japanese competition. Members like Germany and the Netherlands held that Japan had not shown sufficient willingness to do away with non-tariff barriers. The European Commission held the same view, while the United Kingdom, Sweden and Denmark belonged to those member states that were willing to seriously consider the possibility of an EU-Japan FTA. The diverging positions among EU member states led to a compromise at the EU-Japan summit in 2010, under which the EU and Japan will conduct a joint study concerning how to organize their future bilateral economic and trade relations. After intense Japanese lobbying, the support among EU members for launching FTA negotiations has increased and additional steps towards that end are likely at upcoming summits.

4.7 Future EU Trade Relations with Asia — from Follower to Forerunner?

While the EU since the turn of the century has sought to provide leadership in the multilateral trading system — with some procedural but still not much substantive success — it has so far been more of a follower than a forerunner in Asian trade relations. The 2006 *Global Europe* and China strategies call for a more proactive approach. It remains to be fulfilled, however. It is evident that the EU faces several challenges if it is to move from being a reactive to becoming a proactive player in trade relations with Asia.

The establishment of economically sustainable free trade relations between the EU and Asia is possible, but it requires that responsible trade policies are implemented in the EU, as well as in Asia. In order to attract necessary political support in democracies, such policies, in turn, require national social safety-nets for those individuals that stand to lose from the structural adjustment that trade liberalization fosters in the short run, and bridge the period between unemployment and re-employment with regard to income and re-training, if necessary.

Despite the gains from international trade, unilateral EU dismantling of trade barriers on a larger scale remains unlikely for political economy reasons. Proposals in this direction would not render sufficient support, neither among EU member states in the Council nor in the European Parliament, and the Commission will therefore not submit them. Even if substantial unilateral liberalization has taken place in Asia in past decades, additional steps of this kind are unlikely to drive further and wider liberalization, should such steps be taken. Therefore, negotiated liberalizing agreements continue to hold the best prospects for progress.

Developments and negotiations on the multilateral level will continue to influence Euro-Asian, as well as Trans-Pacific, trade relations, and global liberalization remains the preferred outcome of most, if not all, actors involved. However, the inability of the EU to break the Doha-round deadlock despite more intensive cooperation with Asian partners, the unrealistically high US expectations and the unwillingness of emerging economies, including the Asian ones, to improve their offers, continue to negatively affect the prospects for a successful conclusion of the Doha-round in the near future. In addition, while ASEM provides an even more improbable platform for trade liberalization than APEC, neither APEC nor ASEM is likely to deliver results in terms of real liberalization. Therefore, the FTA route is the most viable one for the EU as well as for the US.

The "great recession" and the 2008–2009 collapse in world trade have damped the appetite for trade liberalization. Economic recovery could motivate new attempts in this direction. However, so far, stalemate regarding trade initiatives seems to persist in Washington, D.C. It remains to be seen if the new Republican majority in the House of Representatives will change this state of affairs. If not, the EU could be given an opportunity to move from follower to forerunner on the FTA track in Asian trade relations.

One of the criteria for embarking upon FTA negotiations under the *Global Europe* strategy is the extent to which potential partner countries have already entered into agreements or negotiations with competing countries, foremost the US. This criterion has no doubt been important to the EU, and it is evident that many developments in terms of initiation of FTA negotiations follow the principle of "competitive liberalization".

The EU negotiation with Korea is a case in point. It followed upon successful US negotiations with the same country. By deciding to accept and implement the agreement, the Commission, the EU member states and the European Parliament have overtaken the US and passed the first test with regard to the ability of the EU to seize the opportunity to take the lead. In addition an EU-India FTA would put the EU in a privileged position in Asia, compared to the US, and the EU could overtake the US in terms of FTAs with ASEAN countries provided that it manages to conclude agreements with Singapore and Malaysia, and move into negotiations with additional ASEAN countries such as Vietnam and the Philippines, in order to pave the way towards an accord with most ASEAN countries. As shown in the previous chapter, such an outcome would be beneficial to all parties concerned, even if it still seems to be quite difficult to achieve. An eventual opening up for negotiations with Japan would further enhance the role of the EU as a forerunner.

In a positive scenario, a web of FTAs between G-20 members and other relevant economies could serve as a stepping stone towards progress on the multilateral level. In a negative scenario, FTAs may lead to a further weakening of domestic coalitions in support of global liberalization. EU leadership could help pave the way towards the preferable option.

However, it is still far from certain that the EU will be able to lead the way. It is questionable if the EU has reached a level of trade policy maturity that permits it to grab the opportunity at hand. The "great recession" has strengthened defensive, not to say protectionist, sentiments — in business circles as well as among labor unions and workers — in many EU member states. This has led several EU governments to take defensive stances in trade policy matters. In addition, some member states continue to pursue individual initiatives that are not always in line with overall EU interest.

Presently, Brussels and Washington have faced similar tests in terms of addressing the EU-Korea and US-Korea FTA, respectively. While the KORUS has been stalled in the US Congress for quite some time, the decision-making process on the EU-Korea agreement has advanced and been finalized in Brussels. While the European automotive industry lobbied heavily against the agreement, European business has — overall — been supportive. Italy has led attempts to stop, delay or diminish the agreement in the internal EU process; nevertheless, the necessary decisions have been taken by the Council and the European Parliament.

The Lisbon Treaty involves both challenges and opportunities for EU trade policy strategy. The treaty leads to EU gains in negotiating strength due to the fact that the Commission is given more comprehensive competence over trade and trade-related issues, including with regard to services and investment. At the same time, the increasing power granted to the European Parliament might give protectionist interests additional room for maneuver.

The new division of power between the EU institutions remains to be tested in several ways. In the negotiations on the EU-Korea agreement, the link between the FTA and the "political clauses" in the simultaneously negotiated Partnership and Co-operation Agreement did not pose any major difficulties. However, in other negotiations, this link might inflict more troublesome hurdles. The foremost example in this regard so far is the EU-EFTA negotiation with India. India has adamantly rejected any EU attempt to tie a possible FTA to provisions relating to nuclear non-proliferation or human rights.

The handling of the "political clauses" poses a major challenge to the EU negotiating strategy. How should the relation between the objective to negotiate economically meaningful free trade agreements, on the one hand, and the need to link such agreements to legally binding "political clauses" covering human rights and non-proliferation, on the other hand, be handled? Clarification on behalf of the EU will be needed. How far should it push the use of its so-called "soft power"? What is most conducive to the observance of human rights — increasing trade under FTAs or the threat of sanctions in terms of withdrawal of trade opportunities? So far, the EU and the US have differed in their respective approaches in this regard. While it is not yet clear whether the Obama administration will bring the US closer to the EU position, the EU will, no doubt, have to consider its options if it wants to conclude a FTA with India.

A result-oriented EU trade strategy *vis-à-vis* Asia would have to build on acceptance of additional competition from emerging Asian economies. This requires a willingness to adjust to new comparative advantages. To a considerable extent, domestic EU support of a strategy of this kind hinges on how Asian partners implement and on how the EU manages to enforce trade agreements. This, in turn, stresses the importance of detecting and monitoring protectionist measures, particularly in the aftermath of the "great recession". The EU "market access strategy" plays an important role in this regard, as does resort to WTO dispute settlement, including *vis-à-vis* China, as well as using dispute settlement procedures in FTAs, if and when trade commitments are breached.

The rapid economic development in several, if not all, Asian countries makes it necessary for any trading partner to optimize its regulatory conditions for trade with Asian partners if it wants to stay competitive. Despite still being the largest trading entity, the EU is no exception in this regard. This chapter has argued that the EU has an opportunity to become a forerunner in trade relations with Asia. However, it remains to be seen if the EU — with its newly established division of power between the Commission, Council and Parliament — is willing and able to seize this opportunity.

References

Aggarwal, V. K. (2005). The evolution of APEC and ASEM: implications of the new East Asian bilateralism. Paper prepared for the 46th Annual International Studies Association Convention, Honolulu, 2005.

Aggarwal, V. K. and Fogarty, E. (2004). *European Union Trade Strategies: Between Globalism and Regionalism*. London: Palgrave.

European Commission (2006). Global Europe: competing in the world. Strategy proposed by the EU Trade Commissioner.

Evenett, S. and Meier, M. (2007). An interim assessment of the US trade policy of competitive liberalization. University of St. Gallen, Discussion Paper No. 2007–18.

Kawai, M. and Wignaraja, G. (2009). Asian FTAs: Trends and challenges. ADBI Working Paper 144. Tokyo: Asian Development Bank Institute.

Lindberg, L. (2007). The regionalization process in Southeast Asia and the economic integration of Cambodia and Laos into ASEAN. Series B, No. 113. Ph.D. dissertation, Göteborg University.

Lindberg, L. and Alvstam, C. G. (2008). EU-ASEAN trade facing free trade negotiations. In: R. Lindahl and P. Cramér (Eds.), *Forskning om Europafrågor*. Centrum för Europaforskning vid Göteborgs Universitet (CERGU), 21, 1–19.

Sally, R. (2006). FTAs and the prospects for regional integration in Asia. ECIPE Working Paper, No. 01/2006.

Sally, R. (2010). Regional economic integration in Asia: the track record and prospects. ECIPE Occasional Paper, No. 2/2010.

United States Trade Representative (2009). USTR Ron Kirk remarks on Trans-Pacific Partnership negotiations. Press Release, 15 December 2009.

Chapter 5

The Growing Financial Interdependence between Europe and Asia

Andrew Chiu and Peter MacKay

5.1 Introduction

Are European and Asian economies becoming more closely related, more interdependent? This seems like a natural question to ask in a book premised on the idea of global re-polarization. This chapter therefore sets out to provide some answers. Following a brief discussion of contagion (Section 5.2), we propose three levels of analysis.

First, in Section 5.3, we estimate simple correlations between the stock markets of Europe, Asia, and the USA. Consistent with a general trend toward globalization, we find that the correlations among all three regions have roughly doubled since 1992. Consistent with a re-polarization of the global arena, we find that Europe and Asia experienced the greatest increase in correlation (from 0.30 in 1992 to 0.70 in 2009), testifying to the growing economic interdependence of these two regions.

Second, in Section 5.4, we apply the methods of financial contagion analysis to examine how much of this interdependence remains once we control for existing economic relations between the regions. The resulting partial correlations tell a similar story as the above-mentioned simple correlations: greater globalization and a re-polarization along the European-Asian axis. However, Forbes and Rigobon (2002) caution that evidence of financial contagion may reflect correlation in risk more than correlation in returns. Applying the Forbes–Rigobon correction, we find that any evidence of financial contagion vanishes once we control for concurrent changes in volatility, i.e., we find no evidence of financial contagion in the narrowest sense. This does not negate our evidence of greater interdependence and re-polarization, which indeed emerge as indisputable trends.

Third, in Section 5.5, we relate Bae, Karolyi and Stulz (2003) co-exceedances (the number of markets that experience extreme negative or positive returns on a given trading day) to intra-regional factors (regional volatility, exchange rates, and interest rates) and inter-region factors (volatility, exchange rates, and co-exceedances in other regions). We find that the number of European markets that experience extreme returns is affected by volatility and co-exceedances in Asia. Conversely, the number of Asian markets that experience extreme returns is affected by volatility and co-exceedances in Europe. By this standard, Europe and Asia are interdependent. However, we find no statistically significant evidence that their interdependence is time-varying.

5.2 Contagion, Transmission, or Interdependence?

Although the term "contagion" might seem straightforward in common parlance or in the vernacular of epidemiologists, to financial economists it has become quite controversial. This is why any discussion of financial contagion must first spell out what one has in mind.

The term "financial contagion" is often used to describe the spread of negative shocks across financial markets (e.g., Claessens and Forbes, 2001; Oxelheim *et al.*, 2011). Below are some examples cited from media reports of the recent financial crisis:

> "The financial contagion that has swept Europe has now infected every stock market in the world. Is this catastrophe heading 1929-wards?", journalist Jon Snow (Channel4.com, October 6, 2008).

> "Financial contagion has already reached the LAC (Latin America & Carribean) Economies", Augusto De la Torre, the chief economist for the Bank's Latin American and Caribbean region (October 8, 2008).

> British Prime Minister Gordon Brown says a number of countries must join forces to stop the spread of the "financial contagion" (October 29, 2008).

The major problem with the analysis of financial contagion is that there is no consensus on definitions. The World Bank proposes three definitions. Broadly speaking, contagion is the general cross-country transmission of shocks (i.e., innovations), either negative or positive. This is the definition often employed in the media. In a more restrictive definition, contagion is the transmission of shocks beyond fundamental linkages and beyond common shocks, also known as "excess co-movement". Finally, the narrowest definition limits contagion to when excess co-movements increase in times of crisis. Although more definitions exist, we focus on the three just outlined.

Under the broadest definition, all co-movements are termed "contagion". Consequently, we start by charting the time variation in correlations between Europe, Asia and the USA. This paints a broad picture of the co-movement patterns that ignores the underlying transmission channels. This basic analysis shows a clear increase in the co-movements of the three markets, particularly between Europe and Asia, where the correlation has more than doubled.

But these simple correlations do not distinguish between increased fundamental linkages and narrower notions of financial contagion. Filtering out co-movements transmitted through fundamental linkages and common shocks produces partial correlations known as excess co-movements or "pure contagion". Fundamental linkages include financial links, real economic links, political links, liquidity effects, and capital flows.[1] In measuring excess co-movements, we follow Forbes and Rigobon (2002) who find that, for all crises since 1987, any evidence of contagion vanishes after controlling for concurrent changes in volatility. The limitation of the Forbes–Rigobon test is that we must identify a crisis and the source of transmission. In this study, we test for the evidence of pure contagion during the 2008 Financial Tsunami.

Finally, following Bae, Karolyi and Stulz (2003), we also examine contagion as the joint occurrence of extreme returns. The advantage of this method is that we can study contagion over a long time period, with the crisis being endogenously determined rather than a single

[1] For a detailed discussion, see Dungey and Tambakis (2005).

event. Using multinomial logit regression, we can study the determinants of joint extreme returns within regions and between regions. This methodology has been used extensively in epidemiology research on contagious diseases. Furthermore, this method allows the study of both negative and positive returns. With the other correlation-based methods, it is often difficult to identify a specific date for positive shocks — a difficulty which this method avoids.

5.3 Analysis of General Co-movements of Stock Returns

For each region (Europe, Asia, and the USA), we retain countries whose stock-market capitalizations fall in the global top 30.[2] In addition, we include some smaller Asian markets used in past studies on contagion. For each market, we choose a representative stock market index to proxy for the broad market.[3] We use Morgan Stanley Capital International (MSCI) indices for Europe and Asia to analyze co-movements at the regional level. For each country and region, we download daily prices and exchange rates from Thomson Reuters' Datastream and calculate daily US-dollar-based returns from January 1, 1992 through October 30, 2009.

To study the time path of co-movements over the sample period, we calculate a moving window of parametric Pearson correlations using one year of daily returns (updated annually). We refer to these as *simple correlations.* We plot these time-varying correlations between the three regions and between each region and individual countries in another region. These graphs give a sense of the general co-movement trends under the broadest definition of contagion.

For a narrower measure of contagion, we filter out co-movements caused by fundamental linkages and common shocks. We use a five-period vector-autoregression (VAR(5)) procedure to calculate these excess co-movements. However, Forbes and Rigobon (2002) caution that excess co-movements are conditional on volatility and that failure

---

[2] Stock market capitalizations are taken from Bloomberg on October 12, 2009.

[3] Appendix 5.A lists all indices used for each country.

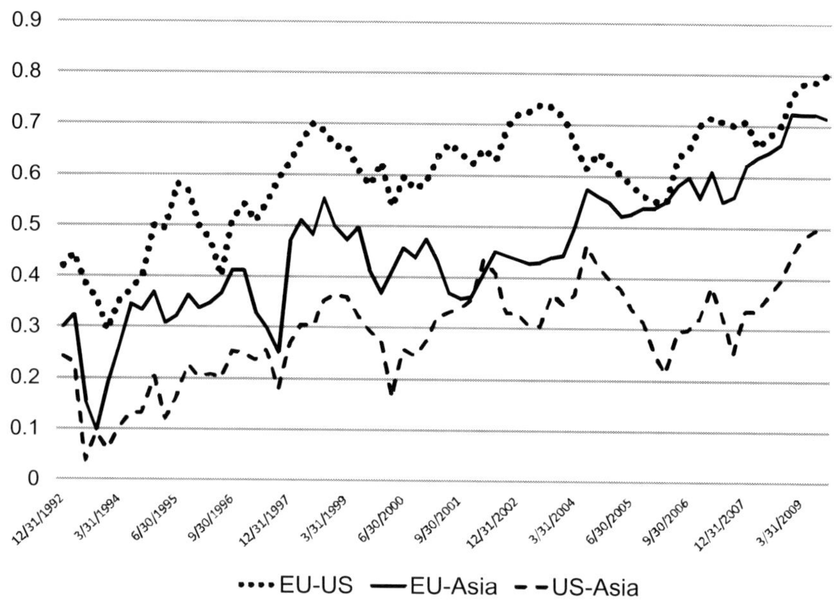

Figure 5.1: Simple correlations between Europe, Asia, and the USA.

Notes: Annually-moving correlations between the MSCI Europe Index, the MSCI Asia Index, and the S&P 500 Index for January 1, 1992–October 30, 2009.

to correct for this yields misleading contagion estimates because of correlated omitted-variable bias and residuals heteroskedasticity. The Forbes–Rigobon correction only applies with reference to a crisis country (and time), which is not possible over the long time-series analysis we consider. Although the resulting plots are thus incomplete, they are still informative. We return later to the issue of conditional volatility.

Figure 5.1 plots annually-moving simple correlations between the three regions from January 1, 1992 through October 30, 2009. All three lines exhibit a positive trend, with the correlation between Europe and Asia growing the most, and the correlation between Asia and the USA growing the least. Furthermore, the Europe-Asia line is consistently above the USA-Asia line, with the gap widening since 2004. This is one piece of evidence that Asia is becoming more interdependent with Europe than with the USA and is suggestive of a re-polarization of the global arena along the European-Asian axis.

Appendix 5.B plots time-varying simple correlations between Europe and 13 Asian countries. We find that Japan, Hong Kong, Singapore, South Korea, Taiwan, India, Malaysia, Indonesia, Philippines, and Thailand are the main drivers for the increased co-movement between Asia and Europe. Sri Lanka and China have recently risen in their co-movement with Europe, although the magnitude of the correlations remains relatively low.

Appendix 5.C plots the flip-side, namely, time-varying simple correlations between Asia and ten European countries. We observe an increasing trend in every case, and all ten correlations reached all-time highs of between 0.6 and 0.7 in 2009. Moreover, correlations for all ten countries jumped following the 1997 Asian Financial Crisis and the Russian Default of 1998. This sudden increase in co-movement, ostensibly because a crisis in one corner of the globe spreads elsewhere, is perhaps what the media and industry pundits mean by "financial contagion".

Figure 5.2 tracks partial correlations (excess co-movements) between the three regions over time. Figure 5.2 looks surprisingly similar to Figure 5.1 in that all lines trend upward. To the extent that Forbes–Rigobon's argument holds, these trends might not reflect increasing contagion (in the purest sense) but rather increasing volatility of one or both of the regions within each pair. In other words, the increased excess co-movement might reflect a correlation in risk more than a correlation in returns.[4] But it is well-known that volatility reverts to the mean, and the period 1992–2009 is no exception. For instance, even after volatility peaked following the Lehman Brothers bankruptcy, it eventually fell back to normal levels in 2009. Therefore, rising volatility is not likely to be the primary driver of the upward trend that we observe in excess co-movements. However, it is possible that we have omitted common factors from the VAR analysis and that rising volatility in such omitted factors is driving up the residual correlations. In following the procedure set out by Forbes and Rigobon, we have only used national interest rates as a proxy for

[4] This dichotomy points to the contentious nature of the debate surrounding the definition of financial contagion. An agnostic might argue that the form of contagion (risk or return) is, in a sense, immaterial.

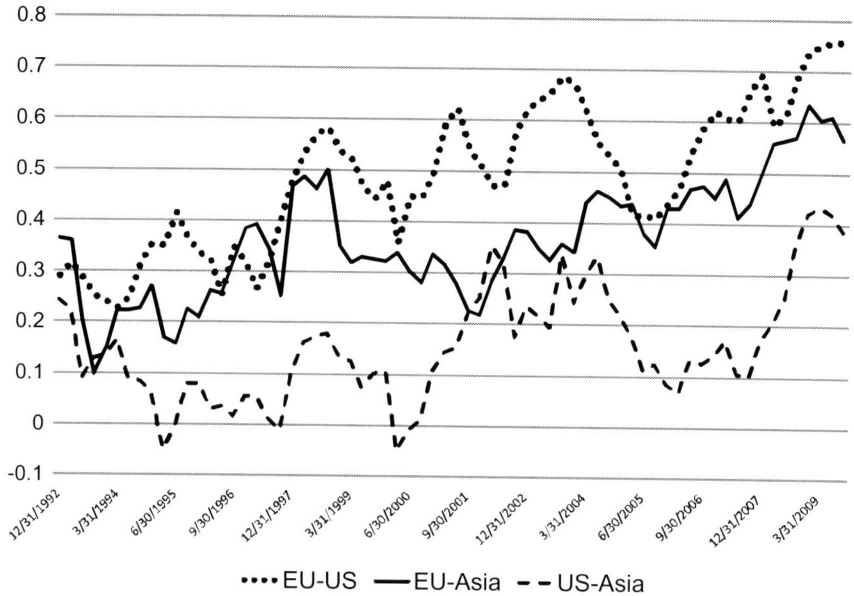

Figure 5.2: Excess correlations between Europe, Asia and the USA.

Notes: Annually-moving excess correlations between the MSCI Europe Index, the MSCI Asia Index, and the S&P 500 Index for January 1, 1992–October 30, 2009.

aggregate shocks. With these issues in mind, it will always be difficult to extract pure excess co-movements that do not stem from fundamental linkages and common shocks.

Appendix 5.D plots excess co-movements between Europe and 13 Asian countries. The strongest upward trends are seen for Hong Kong, Singapore, South Korea, Taiwan and India. Malaysia, Indonesia, Philippines and Thailand show a rapid increase, but only between 2002 and 2009. China, Sri Lanka and Pakistan exhibit low excess co-movement with Europe, while Europe-Japan excess co-movements appear very volatile and mean-reverting. Appendix 5.E shows excess co-movement plots for Asia *versus* ten European countries. All the correlation time series exhibit upward trends that reach all-time highs of between 0.5 and 0.7.

Overall, European markets are becoming increasingly correlated with both the USA and Asia, with the former relation just slightly stronger. On the other hand, Asia is noticeably more correlated with Europe than with the USA. European markets underwent a permanent jump in co-movements following the Asian Financial Crisis, tying them ever-more closely to Asia.

5.4 Financial Contagion and the 2008 Financial Tsunami

The subprime mortgage crisis evolved into a global financial tsunami following the collapse of Lehman Brothers on September 15, 2008. This shock eroded investor confidence across the world. A combination of de-leveraging and flight to quality helped push stock prices to the floor. Analysts, economists, and politicians all employed the term "financial contagion" to refer to the rippling effect of this shock to world stock markets during that difficult period. In this section, we test whether financial contagion, defined in its narrowest sense as an increase in excess co-movements during times of crisis, actually occurred in connection with this shock.

Figure 5.3 shows the time series of returns for the stock markets of four geographic regions. We use MSCI indices to proxy for Asia, Europe, and Latin America. The indices are normalized to start from the same value as the S&P 500 as of January 2, 2006. Roughly speaking, it appears that Asia and Europe are positively correlated with the US, both before and after the shock. Latin American equity prices are much more volatile than those of other regions, but generally trace the peregrinations of US equity prices, albeit with a wider amplitude.

We adopt the test method proposed by Forbes and Rigobon (2002).[5] This is a conservative test for financial contagion which shows that contagion, in the strictest sense, was not present in any of the crises studied by Forbes and Rigobon (beginning with the 1987 Crash). Their method recognizes that increases in volatility experienced in the crisis country can mechanically inflate correlations, even when interdependence between

[5] As of November 2, 2010, Forbes and Rigobon (2002) are cited 1,113 times on Google Scholar.

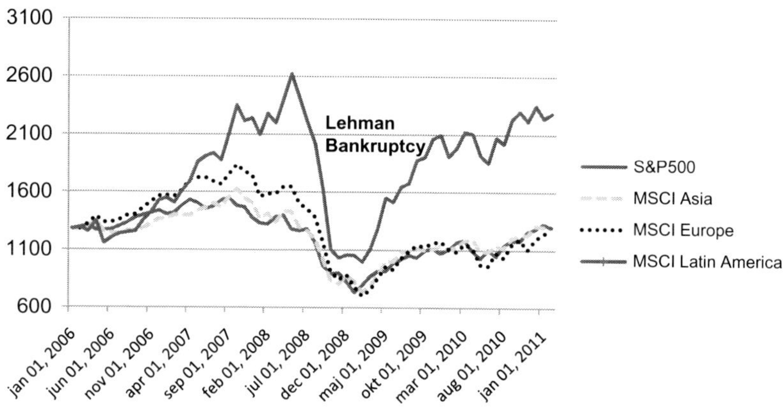

Figure 5.3: Global stock prices.

Notes: Historical stock price levels for the S&P 500 Index, the MSCI Asia Index, the MSCI Europe Index, and the MSCI Latin-America Index for January 3, 2006 to March 3, 2011. The indices are normalized to start at the same level as the S&P500 as of January 2, 2006.

countries is unchanged. After adjusting for this effect, we cannot reject the hypothesis that excess co-movements are unchanged across normal and crisis periods. Applying their method, we reach the same conclusion for the 2008 financial tsunami.

We now turn to the details of the Forbes–Rigobon (FR) test and its implementation here. First, the FR test uses a VAR framework to estimate the excess correlations between the crisis country, namely the USA in the case of the 2008 financial tsunami, and other countries. We run the estimation for the stable period (pre-shock), the crisis period (post-shock), and the full period. Second, we calculate the unconditional correlations by adjusting the excess correlation estimates for the change in volatility in US equity returns associated with the crisis. Finally, we compute a statistic to test the null hypothesis that the unconditional excess correlation surrounding the crisis period is not statistically different from the unconditional excess correlation for the full period. Although the formal definition of financial contagion compares the correlations between the crisis period and the stable period, the original FR test uses the full period instead. We begin by following their method strictly, and then examine variants of the

FR test in our robustness checks, such as testing for differences between the crisis period and the stable period.

We are interested in whether the shock propagated by the Lehman Brothers bankruptcy had a contagious effect on other countries. We choose this event because it is broadly viewed as the catalyst for the financial tsunami. Before this event, the US subprime mortgage crisis appeared to be contained locally. Problematic financial institutions, such as Countrywide Financial, Bear Stearns, Fannie Mae and Freddie Mac, were bailed out either by other institutions or by the US government. The failure of Lehman Brothers signaled that the problem was bigger than believed. Stock prices around the world fell by 33.8% within two months (source: MSCI World Index).

We define the crisis period as the two months from September 15 to November 17, 2008. We arbitrarily choose the period from January 1, 2007 to September 15, 2008 as the stable period. Following the FR test, we also estimate the correlation for the full period, from January 1, 2007 to November 17, 2008. In robustness checks, we find that extending the length of the full period does not materially affect the results.

We collect daily returns for the S&P 500 and thirty-six (36) other stock market indices that are representative of the countries we study. All data are from Thomson Reuters' Datastream. Appendix 5.F shows the list of countries and descriptive statistics for each stock-market index. The 36 countries comprise 30 countries with the largest market capitalization in the world as of October 12, 2009, and six other countries found in past studies on financial contagion. Appendix 5.F shows that the correlation with the USA increased during the crisis period for all countries except for Taiwan and Mexico. However, this does not constitute contagion in the strict sense until we account for fundamental linkages, common shocks, and the increase in volatility. In general, countries in North America, Europe, and Latin America exhibit the largest correlation with the USA, while countries in Asia and other regions are less correlated with the USA.

A few adjustments must be made to the data before it can be used. We replace missing values, usually due to country-specific holidays, by the previous trading day's closing price. In previous studies, researchers have either used this approach or simply deleted the dates with missing values. Another issue is that the indices are calculated in different currencies: we need to control for exchange rate fluctuations. We convert all index prices to US dollars using historical exchange rates, also from Datastream. The third issue is the wide range of time zones involved. We adopt the adjustment in the original FR test by calculating rolling-average, two-day returns. In subsequent analysis, we use this two-day average return rather than the daily return. And in robustness checks, we find that even using daily returns does not change the final results.

Following the FR test, we use a VAR(5) model to estimate excess correlations. Let us use an example to illustrate this method. Suppose we are testing for contagion between the USA and Hong Kong. We regress the returns for the USA with lagged returns for the USA itself and lagged returns for Hong Kong (Equation (5.1), below). We use five (5) lags of returns to control for serial correlation and any within-week variations. We also include short-term interest rates for the USA and Hong Kong to control for exogenous aggregate shocks. For interest rates, contemporaneous values are included along with lagged values. Similarly, the regression for Hong Kong (Equation (5.2), below) uses the same right-hand side variables. Using ordinary least squares, we estimate the variance-covariance matrix of the residuals (e.g., e^{US} and e^{HK}), and from this matrix, the conditional correlation between the two markets. We run the analysis for both the full period and the crisis period, and obtain the two corresponding conditional correlations:

$$\begin{aligned} US_t = &\sum_{i=1}^{5} \beta_{US,i} US_{t-1} + \sum_{i=1}^{5} \beta_{HK,i} HK_{t-i} + \sum_{i=0}^{5} \beta_{r1,i} R_{t-i}^{US} \\ &+ \sum_{i=0}^{5} \beta_{r2,i} R_{t-i}^{HK} + e_{t}^{US}, \end{aligned} \tag{5.1}$$

$$\begin{aligned} HK_t = &\sum_{i=1}^{5} \beta_{US,i} US_{t-1} + \sum_{i=1}^{5} \beta_{HK,i} HK_{t-i} + \sum_{i=0}^{5} \beta_{r1,i} R_{t-i}^{US} \\ &+ \sum_{i=0}^{5} \beta_{r2,i} R_{t-i}^{HK} + e_{t}^{HK}, \end{aligned} \tag{5.2}$$

where

US_t = US 2-day average returns (S&P 500),
HK_t = HK 2-day average returns (Hang Seng Index in USD),
R_t^{US} = US short-term interest rate (Fed Funds Rate),
R_t^{HK} = HK short-term interest rate (Hong Kong Interbank Call Rate).

Next, we need to adjust for the bias due to heteroskedasticity. Forbes and Rigobon (2002) show that correlations increase with larger volatility even when interdependence between two countries is constant. Using the volatility of the crisis period and full period, we can calculate the unconditional (heteroskedasticity-corrected) excess correlations using Equation (5.3) below:

$$\rho \overset{*}{C} = \frac{\rho C}{\sqrt{1 + \left(\frac{\sigma_C^{US}}{\sigma_F^{US}} - 1 \right) (1 - \rho C^2)}}, \tag{5.3}$$

where

ρC^* = unconditional correlation for crisis period,
ρC = conditional correlation for crisis period,
ρF = unconditional correlation for full period (same for conditional),
σ_C^{US} = variance of US market during crisis period,
σ_F^{US} = variance of US market during full period.

Finally, we test the null hypothesis that the unconditional excess correlation is less than or equal to the excess correlation in the full period. The test statistic (5.4) is calculated to test the following one-sided hypothesis:

$$FR = \frac{\frac{1}{2} \ln \left(\frac{1 + \rho \overset{*}{C}}{1 - \rho \overset{*}{C}} \right) - \frac{1}{2} \ln \left(\frac{1 + \rho F}{1 - \rho F} \right)}{\sqrt{\frac{1}{N_C - 3} - \frac{1}{N_F - 3}}}, \tag{5.4}$$

where

N_C = sample size for crisis period,
N_F = sample size for full period.

$$H_0\text{: } \rho_C^* - \rho_F \leq 0 \text{ (No contagion)}$$
$$H_a\text{: } \rho_C^* - \rho_F > 0 \text{ (Contagion)}$$

For robustness, we repeat the tests using a variety of different parameters. The results are reported in Appendix 5.G. We also run the following robustness checks:

(1) Different lengths of crisis period (2 months, 4 months, 6 months);
(2) Different lag lengths (1 to 5);
(3) Using local currency returns (uncorrected for exchange rate movements);
(4) Using a longer full period (January 1, 2006 to November 17, 2008);
(5) Excluding without interest rate controls;
(6) Using daily returns (rather than 2-day moving average returns);
(7) Stable period against crisis period (rather than full period against crisis period).

The results in Table 5.1 show very little evidence of contagion during the financial tsunami. First, comparing conditional (*uncorrected* for heteroskedasticity) excess correlations between the full period and the crisis period, we find that nine countries appear to experience contagion (left panel of Table 5.1). Robustness checks further show that this number fluctuates between 0 to 31 countries depending on the choice of test parameters, period lengths, and lag lengths (see Appendix 5.G for the full set of robustness check results). It is difficult to draw conclusions from these disparate numbers. Moreover, we learn from Forbes and Rigobon (2002) that this test is biased because correlation depends on the level of volatility in the contagious (crisis) country. After adjusting for heteroskedasticity, the unconditional excess correlations between the full period and the crisis period are not statistically different for all 36 countries (right panel of Table 5.1). This indicates that the increase in conditional excess correlation for the above-mentioned nine countries probably stems from a jump in volatility in the US market after the Lehman Brothers

Table 5.1: Financial contagion test results.

		Stable ρ	Full ρ	Crisis ρ	Test Stat.	Contagion?	Stable ρ	Full ρ	Crisis ρ	Test Stat.	Contagion?
	Country	Conditional Correlation					Unconditional Correlation				
Asia	China	−0.037	0.078	0.436	2.36	Yes	−0.014	0.078	0.183	0.65	No
	Hong Kong	0.153	0.419	0.776	3.58	Yes	0.059	0.419	0.427	0.06	No
	India	0.211	0.427	0.614	1.57	No	0.083	0.427	0.286	−0.98	No
	Indonesia	0.199	0.257	0.176	−0.51	No	0.078	0.257	0.069	−1.18	No
	Japan	0.012	0.106	0.022	−0.51	No	0.005	0.106	0.009	−0.60	No
	Malaysia	0.198	0.245	0.424	1.23	No	0.078	0.245	0.177	−0.43	No
	Pakistan	0.006	0.031	−0.263	−1.82	No	0.002	0.031	−0.104	−0.82	No
	Philippines	0.153	0.247	0.620	2.87	Yes	0.059	0.247	0.291	0.28	No
	Singapore	0.259	0.456	0.698	2.26	Yes	0.102	0.456	0.351	−0.76	No
	South Korea	0.227	0.328	0.480	1.11	No	0.089	0.328	0.206	−0.80	No
	Sri Lanka	0.052	0.027	−0.255	−1.75	No	0.020	0.027	−0.101	−0.78	No
	Taiwan	0.157	0.194	0.366	1.14	No	0.061	0.194	0.149	−0.28	No
	Thailand	0.202	0.392	0.643	2.13	Yes	0.079	0.392	0.307	−0.59	No
Europe	Belgium	0.505	0.672	0.785	1.48	No	0.220	0.672	0.437	−2.10	No
	France	0.527	0.646	0.684	0.42	No	0.232	0.646	0.339	−2.52	No
	Germany	0.472	0.675	0.746	0.88	No	0.202	0.675	0.396	−2.44	No
	Italy	0.468	0.568	0.415	−1.23	No	0.200	0.568	0.173	−2.86	No
	Netherlands	0.502	0.650	0.725	0.87	No	0.218	0.650	0.375	−2.31	No
	Norway	0.243	0.502	0.632	1.17	No	0.096	0.502	0.299	−1.48	No
	Russia	0.238	0.336	0.014	−2.04	No	0.094	0.336	0.005	−2.09	No
	Spain	0.442	0.567	0.652	0.82	No	0.186	0.567	0.313	−1.94	No

(Continued)

Table 5.1: (*Continued*)

		Stable ρ	Full ρ	Crisis ρ	Test Stat.	Contagion?	Stable ρ	Full ρ	Crisis ρ	Test Stat.	Contagion?
	Country	Conditional Correlation					Unconditional Correlation				
	Sweden	0.455	0.612	0.740	1.44	No	0.193	0.612	0.389	−1.83	No
	Switzerland	0.436	0.628	0.709	0.89	No	0.183	0.628	0.360	−2.19	No
	Turkey	0.379	0.461	0.583	1.02	No	0.155	0.461	0.266	−1.38	No
	U.K.	0.523	0.671	0.579	−0.92	No	0.229	0.671	0.264	−3.30	No
Latin America	Argentina	0.520	0.594	0.677	0.85	No	0.228	0.594	0.333	−2.05	No
	Brazil	0.625	0.772	0.839	1.17	No	0.294	0.772	0.510	−2.82	No
	Chile	0.397	0.576	0.789	2.51	Yes	0.164	0.576	0.442	−1.10	No
	Colombia	0.224	0.346	0.603	2.05	Yes	0.088	0.346	0.279	−0.45	No
	Mexico	0.722	0.768	0.823	0.91	No	0.372	0.768	0.486	−2.95	No
	Peru	0.235	0.502	0.679	1.67	Yes	0.093	0.502	0.335	−1.24	No
	Venezuela	−0.022	−0.004	−0.112	−0.66	No	−0.008	−0.004	−0.043	−0.24	No
Others	Canada	0.579	0.695	0.601	−1.00	No	0.263	0.695	0.277	−3.48	No
	Australia	0.202	0.423	0.741	3.04	Yes	0.079	0.423	0.390	−0.24	No
	Saudi Arabia	0.405	0.551	0.465	−0.70	No	0.168	0.551	0.198	−2.55	No
	South Africa	0.405	0.551	0.703	1.54	No	0.168	0.551	0.355	−1.51	No

Note: Conditional and unconditional excess correlations between the USA and 36 country stock-market indices during the stable, full, and crisis periods. The stable period runs from January 1, 2007 to September 15, 2008. The crisis period is from September 15, 2008 to November 17, 2008. The full period runs from January 1, 2007 to November 17, 2008. The test statistic tests the null hypothesis that the correlation in the crisis period is smaller than or equal to the correlation in the full period. A country experiences financial contagion if the test statistic is larger than 1.65.

bankruptcy. There is no transmission of additional co-movements, and therefore no contagion.

One interesting observation is that for European countries, neither the conditional nor the unconditional tests suggest contagion during the financial tsunami. That is, the excess correlations between European countries and the USA do not increase significantly after the Lehman shock. Under this interpretation, the fall of European stock markets is merely a reflection of the strong interdependence between the US and European economies, which pre-dates the Lehman shock. It is not the result of a new fundamental linkage or a new channel of shock transmission.

The robustness checks reported in Appendix 5.G show consistently that there is no evidence of contagion once we account for heteroskedasticity. In every comparison of full period with the crisis period, there are no cases where countries exhibit contagion. Tests that contrast the stable period and the crisis period indicate between zero to six countries with contagion. This number is still relatively small considering the sample size of 36 countries. Clearly, there is no strong evidence to reject the null hypothesis of no financial contagion during the financial tsunami.

To conclude, after adjusting for heteroskedasticiy, there is no evidence of global financial contagion during the 2008 Financial Tsunami, at least not in the narrowest sense of contagion. The strong co-movements seen after the Lehman Brothers bankruptcy no doubt reflect existing strong interdependence and a jump in volatility in the US stock market. Media and industry pundits must have had general co-movements in mind, not *excess* co-movements, in which case they are right that the crisis was contagious, but not in the clinical sense used in the literature.

5.5 Measuring Financial Contagion by Co-exceedance Counts

An alternative method to study contagion is to examine the coincidental occurrence of extreme returns across countries. We adopt the method devised by Bae, Karolyi and Stulz (2003) (BKS) to study joint occurrences of extreme positive and negative returns within countries in Europe. Then we use a multinomial logit regression to find out whether extreme events in other regions, namely Asia, can affect the probability of observing extreme events in Europe. We then repeat the reciprocal exercise for Asian markets and their relation to extreme returns in Europe.

The countries chosen for Europe and Asia are the same as in earlier sections. Index prices, exchange rates, and interest rates are all collected from Datastream. The sample period is January 1, 1992 to October 30, 2009: 4,652 trading days. For missing data, such as holidays, we fill in with the previous available trading day. We convert all returns to US-dollar returns.

Bae, Karolyi and Stulz (2003) introduce the term exceedance to define an extreme return, either negative or positive, that lies below (above) the 5th (95th) quantile of the daily-return empirical distribution. This 5% threshold is arbitrary; however, we follow the same convention. Our method differs from theirs in one important way: we compare each day's return against the historical return distribution using all available daily prices from January 1, 1980 up to that particular day. In contrast, the original BKS method compares each day's return against a distribution that is built from the same sample period. This in-sample approach uses information before and after the relevant trading date to determine whether an exceedance occurs. We alter the method slightly to use only information up to a particular day to determine exceedances. Because of this updating, the fraction of exceedance days will not be exactly 5% as in BKS.

BKS define "coexceedance" as the joint occurrence of many exceedances on a particular day. To avoid confusion, we use the expression n-coexceedance to denote the joint occurrence of n exceedances from n countries. Thus, a 1-coexceedance is the same as an exceedance.

We wish to study negative and positive n-coexceedances with a large n: these are the days when several markets experience large, same-signed returns together. The literature focuses on large *negative* n-coexceedances, which typically mark a crisis. The question is whether these n-coexceedances exist naturally through fundamental linkages and common shocks, or whether they are a result of contagion in the narrower sense.

The analysis proceeds as follows. First, we identify the days when each market experiences a negative or positive exceedance. We do this for all stock markets in Europe, Asia, and the USA. Second, for each geographic region, we identify the days with coexceedances and count the number of countries involved. BKS perform Monte Carlo simulations to calibrate the observed sample of coexceedances. Using different models for the joint return distribution as benchmarks, they find that the large number of observed n-coexceedances — those with a large n — cannot be reproduced by the simulations, confirming that such events indeed "exceed" the norm. We do not conduct such simulations in this study, but our results show that the coexceedance counts for Europe are even harder to reconcile than the regions studied in BKS. In particular, the negative 9-coexceedance count is significantly larger than the negative 8-coexceedance count, which is highly unlikely if we assume any return distribution with diminishing tails.

The main purpose here is to test whether the probability of an n-coexceedance in one region can be explained by an n-coexceedance from another region. Following BKS, we estimate multinomial logit regressions for each region, controlling for exchange rate changes[6], interest rates[7], and conditional volatility estimated by once-lagged Exponential General Autoregressive Conditional Heteroskedastic, EGARCH(1,1)[8]. Consistent with BKS's results, these local factors are

[6] Exchange rate changes are calculated as the equally-weighted average exchange rate changes of all countries studied in the region. For countries that adopted the Euro, we use the relevant exchange rates for each country before adoption of the Euro. The unit for the exchange rate is per USD.

[7] Interest rates are calculated as the equally-weighted average interest rates of all markets in the region. For countries that adopted the Euro, we use the relevant interest rate for each country before adoption of the Euro.

[8] The conditional volatility for the region is estimated using MSCI indices. For Europe, we use MSCI Europe and for Asia, we use MSCI Asia. For the US, we use the S&P 500 Index.

significant in explaining regional coexceedances. We also include the conditional volatility and coexceedance count from other regions to detect inter-regional effects. Results are mixed.

Table 5.2 shows coexceedance counts for Europe and the ten European countries we study. The table shows negative coexceedances on the left and positive coexceedances on the right. Along the top of the table, numbers from 0 to 10 represent the number of countries contributing to the coexceedance. 0-coexceedance means no countries have an exceedance. A 1-coexceedance is an exceedance of just one particular country. A 10-coexceedance indicates that all 10 countries are experiencing an extreme negative or positive return together. The coexceedance counts for each country indicate the number of times the particular country experienced an *n*-coexceedance event over the sample period. The Mean Return is the average return for the country during the 10-coexceedance events. Along the bottom of the table, the Total row refers to the overall coexceedance counts and mean returns for the European region as defined by the ten countries.

Out of the 4,652 trading days from January 1, 1992 to October 30, 2009, Europe recorded 1,186 days (25.5%) with a negative coexceedance and 1,194 days (25.6%) with a positive coexceedance. The mean returns for the 10-coexceedance trading days are -5.28% and 5.33%. This shows that both the probability of an extreme event and the magnitude of the extreme return are symmetric across highly-negative and highly-positive returns. However, the number of coexceedances with nine or more countries is 79 for negative returns and 51 for positive returns. For these extreme cases, there is a larger likelihood of a negative coexceedance. Also, there is an odd result that the number of negative 9-coexceedances (58) is over 40% greater than the number of negative 8-coexceedances (41). This implies that it is more likely to have an extreme negative return with 9 countries than with 8 countries.

Turkey seems to be the outlier that rarely participates in coexceedances in either direction, altough it tends to have a large number of individual exceedances. But when it does participate in the 10-coexceedance events, it exhibits a significantly larger absolute

Table 5.2: Coexceedance counts for European countries.

	Mean Return	Number of Negative (Co-)exceedances											Number of Positive (Co-)exceedances											Mean Return
	10	10	9	8	7	6	5	4	3	2	1	0	0	1	2	3	4	5	6	7	8	9	10	10
U.K.	–4.73%	21	56	37	28	32	33	20	26	37	53	3466	3458	50	43	26	19	28	23	30	34	37	13	4.91%
France	–5.28%	21	58	38	39	46	25	22	22	18	18	3466	3458	29	26	28	25	32	33	40	38	38	13	5.62%
Germany	–5.29%	21	58	36	39	51	28	34	33	42	56	3466	3458	60	49	44	25	39	39	39	33	38	13	5.33%
Switzerland	–3.72%	21	56	25	21	21	16	20	25	30	37	3466	3458	37	37	30	19	21	14	23	26	37	13	3.78%
Spain	–5.17%	21	57	40	32	46	32	40	35	51	59	3466	3458	49	39	47	25	31	32	39	39	37	13	5.09%
Italy	–5.36%	21	55	35	32	36	26	17	26	28	48	3466	3458	56	26	23	18	19	18	35	33	37	13	5.13%
Sweden	–4.91%	21	58	37	32	40	29	35	39	65	128	3466	3458	115	68	53	34	37	24	31	33	38	13	5.45%
Netherlands	–5.38%	21	57	40	39	47	32	43	26	28	14	3466	3458	15	34	33	36	43	37	41	37	38	13	5.79%
Belgium	–4.41%	21	57	36	28	39	28	28	44	37	50	3466	3458	79	45	43	38	33	28	33	34	38	13	4.50%
Turkey	–8.55%	21	10	4	4	8	6	5	12	24	107	3466	3458	100	25	9	5	7	4	4	5	4	13	7.68%
Total	–5.28%	21	58	41	42	61	51	66	96	180	570	3466	3458	590	196	112	61	58	42	45	39	38	13	5.33%

Note: Number of times a country is involved in a coexceedance with n countries. The numbers in the first row correspond to n. A negative (positive) coexceedance is a joint occurrence of an extreme negative (positive) return, defined as a return that lies below (above) the 5th (95th) quantile of the historical daily return distribution. The last row is the coexceedance counts for the region. The period counted is from January 1, 1992 to October 30, 2009. The historical return distribution is formed from all existing prices between January 1, 1980 to the trading day of interest.

mean return (over 44% higher than average in the region). Sweden is the only country with more individual exceedances than Turkey, although unlike Turkey, it typically does participate in coexceedances. France and Netherlands rarely show individual exceedances. These countries are more likely to experience joint exceedances with other countries in the region.

Switzerland has an overall low participation in coexceedances, except for the extreme cases with nine or more countries. It also has the lowest mean return during 10-coexceedance events. In these regards, Switzerland has the lowest risk out of the ten European countries.

In Figures 5.4 and 5.5, we plot the negative and positive coexceedance events over time. A bar below (above) zero indicates a negative (positive) coexceedance event. The length of the bar indicates the number of participating countries. Bouts of high coexceedance seem to coincide with crises. Most of the extreme events are concentrated around the 1997 Asian Financial Crisis, the 1998 Russian Default, the 2000 Internet Bubble Burst, the 2002 European Downturn, and the 2008 Financial Tsunami. As our earlier analysis suggests, the centering of coexceedances around crises is probably caused by increasing volatility during crisis periods, which produces extreme returns and — perhaps mechanically — higher international correlations.

Next, we use multinomial logit regressions to model the probability of a coexceedance event in Europe and Asia (see Tables 5.3 and 5.4). The number of coexceedances is modeled as an ordered polychotomous variable with five categories: 0, 1, 2, 3, and 4, with 4 representing coexceedances of four or more countries. Turning to Table 5.3 (model (1) for lower tails), we find that the three independent variables we consider first are statistically significant in explaining coexceedance, namely, EGARCH(1,1) conditional volatility (h_{it}), exchange rate changes (e_{it}), and interest rates (i_{it}). Because logit-regression coefficients are hard to interpret directly, we also report the average partial derivative of the probability with respect to each independent variable. From these marginal probabilities, we learn that exchange rate changes have the largest effect. For example, if the average exchange rate (against the USD) goes up by 1%, the probability

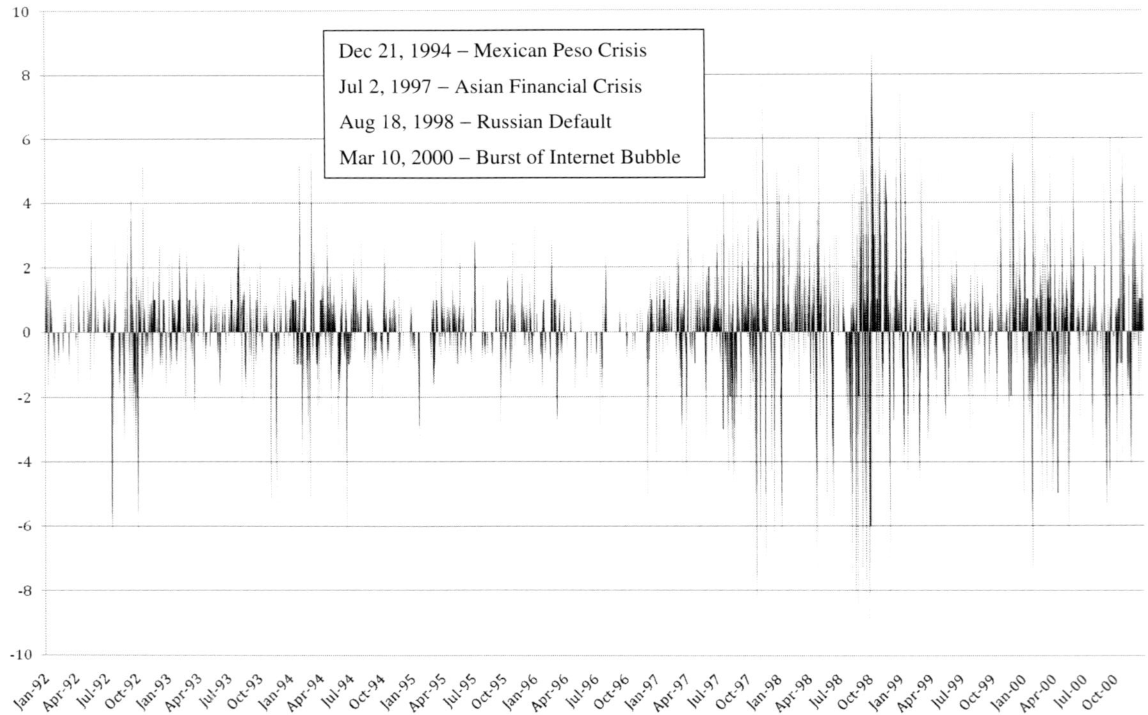

Figure 5.4: Europe coexceedance timeline (January 1992–December 2000).

Note: This figure plots the number of countries involved in a coexceedance on a particular day. Negative (positive) coexceedances are plotted below (above) the zero line.

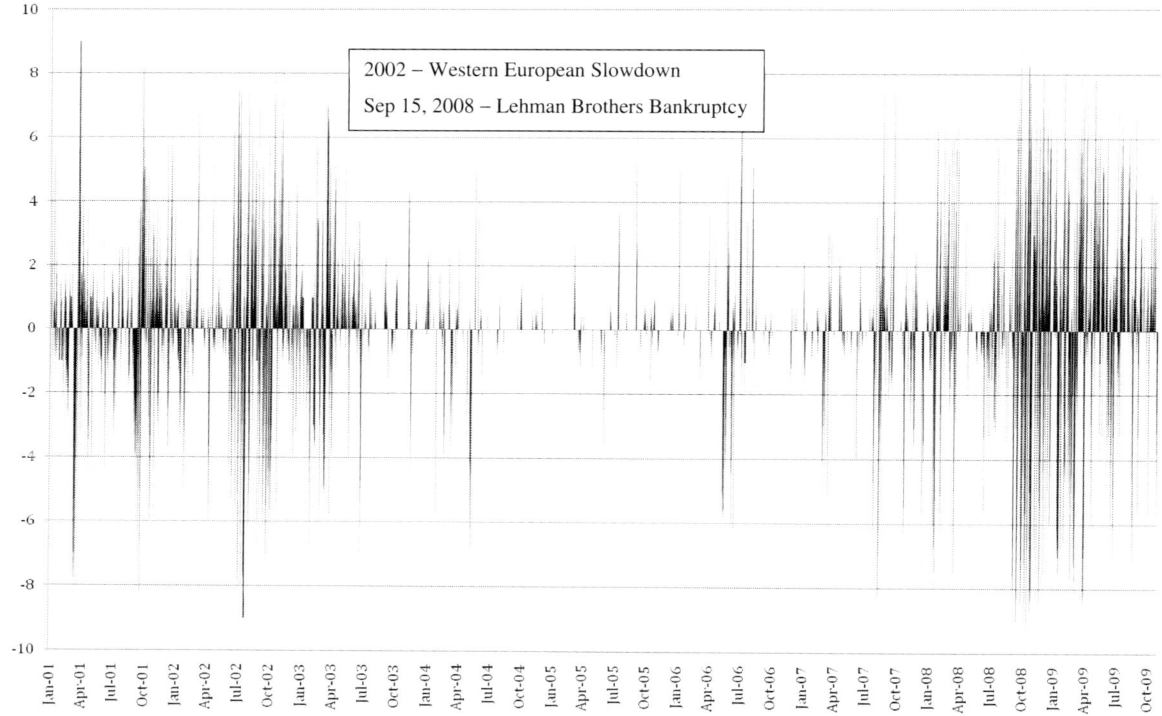

Figure 5.5: Europe coexceedance timeline (January 2001–October 2009).

Note: This figure plots the number of countries involved in a coexceedance on a particular day. Negative (positive) coexceedances are plotted below (above) the zero line.

that Europe will experience a negative coexceedance involving four or more countries increases by 20%. Out of the 4,652 trading days, this event happens about 7.3% of the time. Likewise, the probability of a single-country exceedance increases by 25.5%. On the upper-tail side, when the European exchange rates rise against the US dollar, the probability of a positive European coexceedance falls.

Conditional volatility in Europe has the second largest effect, while interest rates are of minor importance. In particular, conditional volatility has the largest effect on both the negative and positive 4-coexceedances, with marginal probabilities of 12% and 11.7%, respectively. Interest rates have negligible effects for both negative and positive coexceedances.

In order to test for financial contagion within the BKS framework, we extend these regressions to include two international variables, namely, conditional volatilities and coexceedance counts for Asia and the USA (see Table 5.3, model (2) for lower and upper tails). Asia's conditional volatility is only significant for negative coexceedances, i.e., lower tails. On the other hand, coexceedance counts from both regions are significant for both tails. The US coexceedance count has a greater marginal probability than Asia's. The Pseudo-R^2 rises in all cases, suggesting a better specification.

Marginal probabilities are consistently higher for single exceedances and 4-coexceedance cases. This is because the coexceedance brackets are aggregated: the number of coexceedances involving four or more countries is much larger than the number of 2-coexceedances and 3-coexceedances. But if we had used 11 brackets rather than five, we would observe a uniform decline in the marginal probabilities as the number of countries involved per coexceedance increased.

Overall, we can conclude that coexceedance in Europe is determined mainly by indigenous factors such as own-market conditional volatility, and by international factors such as exchange rate changes and coexceedances from Asia and the USA, with a greater effect from the latter region. Also, the magnitude of these effects is roughly symmetric for negative and positive coexceedances.

Table 5.4 shows the multinomial logit regression results for coexceedances in Asia. In this case, the most important explanatory

Table 5.3: Multinomial logit regression (dependent variable: Europe co-exceedances).

	Lower Tails						Upper Tails					
	(1)		(2)		(3)		(1)		(2)		(3)	
	Coeff.	Δ prob.	Coeff.	Δ prob.	Coeff.	Δ prob.	Coeff.	Δ prob.	Coeff.	Δ prob.	Coeff.	Δ prob.
Europe												
β_{01}	−3.229[a]	−0.387[a]	−2.979[a]	−0.359[a]	−3.145[a]	−0.378[a]	−3.058[a]	−0.378[a]	−2.982[a]	−0.369[a]	−3.015[a]	−0.376[a]
β_{02}	−5.209[a]	−0.265[a]	−4.703[a]	−0.244[a]	−5.181[a]	−0.271[a]	−4.811[a]	−0.260[a]	−4.844[a]	−0.267[a]	−4.805[a]	−0.270[a]
β_{03}	−5.738[a]	−0.174[a]	−5.336[a]	−0.170[a]	−5.712[a]	−0.183[a]	−5.276[a]	−0.179[a]	−5.453[a]	−0.188[a]	−5.241[a]	−0.188[a]
β_{04}	−4.296[a]	−0.306[a]	−4.107[a]	−0.274[a]	−4.607[a]	−0.294[a]	−4.886[a]	−0.301[a]	−4.857[a]	−0.289[a]	−4.898[a]	−0.269[a]
β_{11} (h_{it})	0.584[a]	0.070[a]	0.894[a]	0.108[a]	0.684[a]	0.082[a]	0.408[a]	0.050[a]	0.512[a]	0.063[a]	0.361	0.045
β_{12}	1.166[a]	0.059[a]	1.830[a]	0.095[a]	1.093[a]	0.057[a]	0.931[a]	0.050[a]	0.876[a]	0.048[a]	0.739[b]	0.041[b]
β_{13}	1.300[a]	0.039[a]	1.825[a]	0.058[a]	1.194[a]	0.038[a]	1.122[a]	0.038[a]	0.735[a]	0.025[a]	1.041[a]	0.037[a]
β_{14}	1.682[a]	0.120[a]	1.969[a]	0.131[a]	0.857[a]	0.055[a]	1.898[a]	0.117[a]	2.121[a]	0.126[a]	2.299[a]	0.126[a]
β_{21} (e_{it})	2.129[a]	0.255[a]	2.069[a]	0.249[a]	2.250[a]	0.270[a]	−1.549[a]	−0.192[a]	−1.487[a]	−0.184[a]	−1.631[a]	−0.203[a]
β_{22}	2.120[a]	0.108[a]	2.056[a]	0.107[a]	2.312[a]	0.121[a]	−1.339[a]	−0.073[a]	−1.259[a]	−0.069[a]	−1.492[a]	−0.084[a]
β_{23}	2.336[a]	0.071[a]	2.210[a]	0.070[a]	2.483[a]	0.080[a]	−2.275[a]	−0.077[a]	−2.111[a]	−0.073[a]	−2.472[a]	−0.089[a]
β_{24}	2.808[a]	0.200[a]	2.512[a]	0.168[a]	2.925[a]	0.187[a]	−2.673[a]	−0.164[a]	−2.418[a]	−0.144[a]	−3.049[a]	−0.167[a]
β_{31} (i_{it})	0.094[a]	0.011[a]	0.092[a]	0.011[a]	0.092[a]	0.011[a]	0.106[a]	0.013[a]	0.100[a]	0.012[a]	0.107[a]	0.013[a]
β_{32}	0.119[a]	0.006[a]	0.115[a]	0.006[a]	0.120[a]	0.006[a]	0.121[a]	0.007[a]	0.111[a]	0.006[a]	0.125[a]	0.007[a]
β_{33}	0.089[a]	0.003[a]	0.077[a]	0.002[a]	0.089[a]	0.003[a]	0.082[a]	0.003[a]	0.067[a]	0.002[a]	0.087[a]	0.003[a]
β_{34}	−0.002	0.000	−0.025	−0.002	0.021	0.001	0.024	0.001	0.009	0.001	0.025	0.001

(*Continued*)

Table 5.3: (*Continued*)

	Lower Tails						Upper Tails					
	(1)		(2)		(3)		(1)		(2)		(3)	
	Coeff.	Δ prob.	Coeff.	Δ prob.	Coeff.	Δ prob.	Coeff.	Δ prob.	Coeff.	Δ prob.	Coeff.	Δ prob.
			Effects from Asia		*Effects from U.S.*				*Effects from Asia*		*Effects from U.S.*	
β_{41} (h^*_{it})			−0.601[a]	−0.072[a]	−0.237	−0.028			−0.286	−0.035	−0.062	−0.008
β_{42}			−1.299[a]	−0.067[a]	−0.117	−0.006			−0.048	−0.003	0.043	0.002
β_{43}			−1.101[a]	−0.035[a]	−0.024	−0.001			0.351	0.012	−0.146	−0.005
β_{44}			−0.817[a]	−0.054[a]	0.589[a]	0.038[a]			−0.524[a]	−0.031[a]	−0.735[a]	−0.040[a]
β_{51} (Υ^*_{it})			0.177[a]	0.021[a]	1.144[a]	0.138[a]			0.255[a]	0.032[a]	1.200[a]	0.150[a]
β_{52}			0.356[a]	0.018[a]	1.717[a]	0.090[a]			0.288[a]	0.016[a]	1.594[a]	0.089[a]
β_{53}			0.438[a]	0.014[a]	1.378[a]	0.044[a]			0.339[a]	0.012[a]	1.994[a]	0.072[a]
β_{54}			0.601[a]	0.040[a]	2.486[a]	0.159[a]			0.494[a]	0.029[a]	2.784[a]	0.153[a]
Log-likelihood	−3738.14		−3629.93		−3615.2		−3794.35		−3729.55		−3672.85	
Pseudo-R^2	8.0%		10.7%		11.0%		7.4%		9.0%		10.4%	

Note: [a, b] denotes significance levels at the 1% and 5%, respectively.

Table 5.4: Multinomial logit regression (dependent variable: Asia co-exceedances).

	Lower Tails						Upper Tails					
	(1)		(2)		(3)		(1)		(2)		(3)	
	Coeff.	Δ prob.	Coeff.	Δ prob.	Coeff.	Δ prob.	Coeff.	Δ prob.	Coeff.	Δ prob.	Coeff.	Δ prob.
Asia												
β_{01}	−2.299[a]	−0.477[a]	−2.328[a]	−0.482[a]	−2.429[a]	−0.502[a]	−1.889[a]	−0.396[a]	−1.778[a]	−0.372[a]	−1.866[a]	−0.391[a]
β_{02}	−4.630[a]	−0.548[a]	−4.818[a]	−0.563[a]	−4.893[a]	−0.574[a]	−4.159[a]	−0.482[a]	−4.014[a]	−0.463[a]	−4.167[a]	−0.483[a]
β_{03}	−6.310[a]	−0.387[a]	−6.595[a]	−0.407[a]	−6.555[a]	−0.401[a]	−5.372[a]	−0.333[a]	−5.341[a]	−0.333[a]	−5.417[a]	−0.335[a]
β_{04}	−6.866[a]	−0.487[a]	−7.770[a]	−0.465[a]	−7.385[a]	−0.494[a]	−6.629[a]	−0.370[a]	−6.768[a]	−0.362[a]	−6.731[a]	−0.369[a]
β_{11} (h_{it})	0.610[a]	0.127[a]	0.480[a]	0.099[a]	0.364[a]	0.075[a]	0.293[a]	0.061[a]	0.528[a]	0.110[a]	0.324[a]	0.068[a]
β_{12}	1.142[a]	0.135[a]	0.705[a]	0.082[a]	0.647[a]	0.076[a]	0.880[a]	0.102[a]	1.145[a]	0.132[a]	0.855[a]	0.099[a]
β_{13}	1.424[a]	0.087[a]	0.686[a]	0.042[a]	0.951[a]	0.058[a]	1.445[a]	0.090[a]	1.351[a]	0.084[a]	1.270[a]	0.079[a]
β_{14}	1.976[a]	0.140[a]	0.817[a]	0.049[a]	0.678[a]	0.045[a]	1.982[a]	0.110[a]	1.707[a]	0.091[a]	1.580[a]	0.086[a]
β_{21} (e_{it})	1.775[a]	0.369[a]	1.765[a]	0.365[a]	1.819[a]	0.376[a]	−1.644[a]	−0.345[a]	−1.571[a]	−0.328[a]	−1.646[a]	−0.345[a]
β_{22}	3.550[a]	0.420[a]	3.393[a]	0.396[a]	3.500[a]	0.411[a]	−2.788[a]	−0.323[a]	−2.661[a]	−0.307[a]	−2.799[a]	−0.324[a]
β_{23}	3.479[a]	0.214[a]	3.320[a]	0.205[a]	3.441[a]	0.211[a]	−4.023[a]	−0.249[a]	−3.757[a]	−0.234[a]	−3.988[a]	−0.247[a]
β_{24}	3.573[a]	0.253[a]	3.426[a]	0.205[a]	3.524[a]	0.236[a]	−4.351[a]	−0.243[a]	−4.069[a]	−0.218[a]	−4.288[a]	−0.235[a]
β_{31} (i_{it})	0.141[a]	0.029[a]	0.145[a]	0.030[a]	0.155[a]	0.032[a]	0.131[a]	0.028[a]	0.117[a]	0.025[a]	0.130[a]	0.027[a]
β_{32}	0.235[a]	0.028[a]	0.257[a]	0.030[a]	0.265[a]	0.031[a]	0.204[a]	0.024[a]	0.187[a]	0.022[a]	0.206[a]	0.024[a]
β_{33}	0.277[a]	0.017[a]	0.309[a]	0.019[a]	0.306[a]	0.019[a]	0.146[a]	0.009[a]	0.144[a]	0.009[a]	0.156[a]	0.010[a]
β_{34}	0.299[a]	0.021[a]	0.365[a]	0.022[a]	0.367[a]	0.025[a]	0.216[a]	0.012[a]	0.222[a]	0.012[a]	0.237[a]	0.013[a]

(Continued)

Table 5.4: (*Continued*)

	Lower Tails						Upper Tails					
	(1)		(2)		(3)		(1)		(2)		(3)	
	Coeff.	Δ prob.	Coeff.	Δ prob.	Coeff.	Δ prob.	Coeff.	Δ prob.	Coeff.	Δ prob.	Coeff.	Δ prob.
			Effects from Europe		*Effects from U.S.*				*Effects from Europe*		*Effects from U.S.*	
β_{41} (h^*_{it})			0.095	0.020	0.294[a]	0.061[a]			–0.372[a]	–0.078[a]	–0.052	–0.011
β_{42}			0.366[b]	0.043[b]	0.580[a]	0.068[a]			–0.519[a]	–0.060[a]	0.022	0.003
β_{43}			0.704[a]	0.043[a]	0.509[b]	0.031[b]			–0.115	–0.007	0.164	0.010
β_{44}			1.076[a]	0.064[a]	1.379[a]	0.092[a]			0.005	0.000	0.344	0.019
β_{51} (Υ^*_{it})			0.128[a]	0.027[a]	0.335[b]	0.069[b]			0.143[a]	0.030[a]	0.073	0.015
β_{52}			0.322[a]	0.038[a]	0.554[a]	0.065[a]			0.290[a]	0.034[a]	0.073	0.008
β_{53}			0.347[a]	0.021[a]	0.847[a]	0.052[a]			0.337[a]	0.021[a]	0.284	0.018
β_{54}			0.679[a]	0.041[a]	0.691[a]	0.046[a]			0.504[a]	0.027[a]	0.776[a]	0.042[a]
Log-likelihood	–5075.317		–4933.759		–5029.655		–5004.012		–4942.975		–4995.425	
Pseudo-R^2	8.1%		10.6%		8.9%		7.0%		8.2%		7.2%	

Note: [a, b] denotes significance levels at the 1% and 5%, respectively.

variable is average regional exchange rate changes, with conditional volatility ranking second. Unlike Europe, in Asia, interest rates play a more significant role judging by their greater marginal probabilities.

We noted earlier that Asia's coexceedance count has a small but significant effect on Europe's coexceedance count. Europe affects Asia's coexceedance count reciprocally, with similar magnitude. The effect is symmetric in both tails. In contrast, coexceedances in the US play a significant and substantial role in explaining the lower tail of Asia's coexceedance count, but not in the upper tail. In this regard, Asia is more interdependent with Europe than with the USA.

We also examine whether the inter-regional effects noted above are time-varying. To study this question, we run additional (unreported) regressions that include an interaction term between foreign coexceedance counts and a time index. In all of these tests, the interaction term is both statistically and economically insignificant. From this, we conclude that the magnitude of the inter-regional effects did not change over time over the sample period we consider.

Overall, we conclude that Europe is affected by extreme returns from Asia and the USA, with a larger effect from the latter. According to Bae, Karolyi and Stulz (2003), this is evidence for contagion between regions. For Asia, there is a similar effect from Europe. A weakness with the BKS method is that it does not tell us the direction of causality. Between Asia and the USA, the only channel of contagion is negative extreme returns transmitted from the USA to Asia. European coexceedances have significant but small effects on the USA.

5.6 Conclusion: Growing Interdependence and Gradual Re-polarization

The prevailing winds are blowing east: the ascent of the BRICS, the PRC in particular, changes everything. Demography is replacing ideology and economics is replacing history in steering the distribution of power. The world's political and economic geography is being redrawn through the anti-meridian — not Greenwich. These changes, imperceptible a decade ago, have profound implications for the world economy and politics. As our findings show, these trends are taking hold firmly. It is indeed the growing awareness of these trends that lies at the foundation of this book.

So, what can we conclude on the thesis that the world is re-polarizing along a European-Asian axis? The least we can say is that there is growing interdependence between the economies we study (America, Europe, and Asia), or at least between the stock markets of the countries involved. We can also say that this decades-long trend accelerated in recent history: we find that simple (and partial) correlations between these markets have roughly doubled since 1992. However, based on a narrower definition of interdependence ("financial contagion") that accounts for changes in volatility, we find no evidence that partial correlations increased during the 2008 Financial Tsunami.

We also document that the number of European markets with extreme returns (coexceedances) is affected by volatility and coexceedances in Asia, and *vice versa*. By this standard, Europe and Asia are interdependent; however, this interdependence does not appear to be time-varying. Our evidence therefore corroborates the notion that world economies are not only becoming more interdependent but also that they are gradually re-polarizing along a European-Asian axis.

Acknowledgements

We thank Jonathan Batten, Lynn Pi, and Mark Seasholes for useful discussions and comments.

References

Bae, K. H., Karolyi, A. G. and Stulz, R. M. (2003). A new approach to measuring financial contagion. *Review of Financial Studies*, 16(3), 717–763.

Claessens, S. and Forbes, K. J. (Eds.) (2001). *International Financial Contagion*. Norwell, MA: Kluwer Academic Publishers.

Dungey, M. and Tambakis, D. N. (2005). *Identifying International Financial Contagion*. New York: Oxford University Press.

Forbes, K. J. and Rigobon, R. (2002). No contagion, only interdependence: measuring stock market co-movements. *Journal of Finance*, 57(5), 2223–2261.

Oxelheim, L., Wihlborg, C. and Østrup, F. (2011). The origins and resolution of financial crises: a policy dilemma. In: R. W. Kolb (Ed.), *Financial Contagion: The Viral Threat to the Wealth of Nations*. New York: John Wiley & Sons.

Appendix 5.A: Stock market indices.

Market Cap. Ranking	Country/ Region	Index	Market Cap. Ranking	Asian Countries	Index	Market Cap. Ranking	European Countries	Index
1	U.S.	S&P 500	2	Japan	Topix	4	U.K.	FTSE 100
	Europe	MSCI Europe	3	China	Shanghai SE Comp	6	France	CAC 40
	Asia	MSCI Asia	5	Hong Kong	Hang Seng Index	8	Germany	DAX 30
			9	India	BSE(100) National	12	Switzerland	Swiss Performance
			14	South Korea	Kospi	13	Spain	Madrid SE General
			16	Taiwan	Taiwan SE Weighted	15	Italy	FTSE MIB Index
			20	Singapore	Straits Times Index	19	Sweden	OMX Stockholm

(Continued)

Appendix 5.A: (*Continued*)

Market Cap. Ranking	Country/ Region	Index	Market Cap. Ranking	Asian Countries	Index	Market Cap. Ranking	European Countries	Index
			25	Malaysia	FTSE Bursa Malaysia	24	Netherlands	AEX Index
			30	Indonesia	Jakarta SE Composite	26	Belgium	BEL 20
			33	Thailand	Bangkok S.E.T.	28	Turkey	ISE National 100
			45	Philippines	Philippines SE I			
			53	Pakistan	Karachi SE 100			
			67	Sri Lanka	Colombo SE All Share			

Note: Stock market indices and their market capitalization ranking for each country. Rankings are taken from Bloomberg on October 12, 2009.

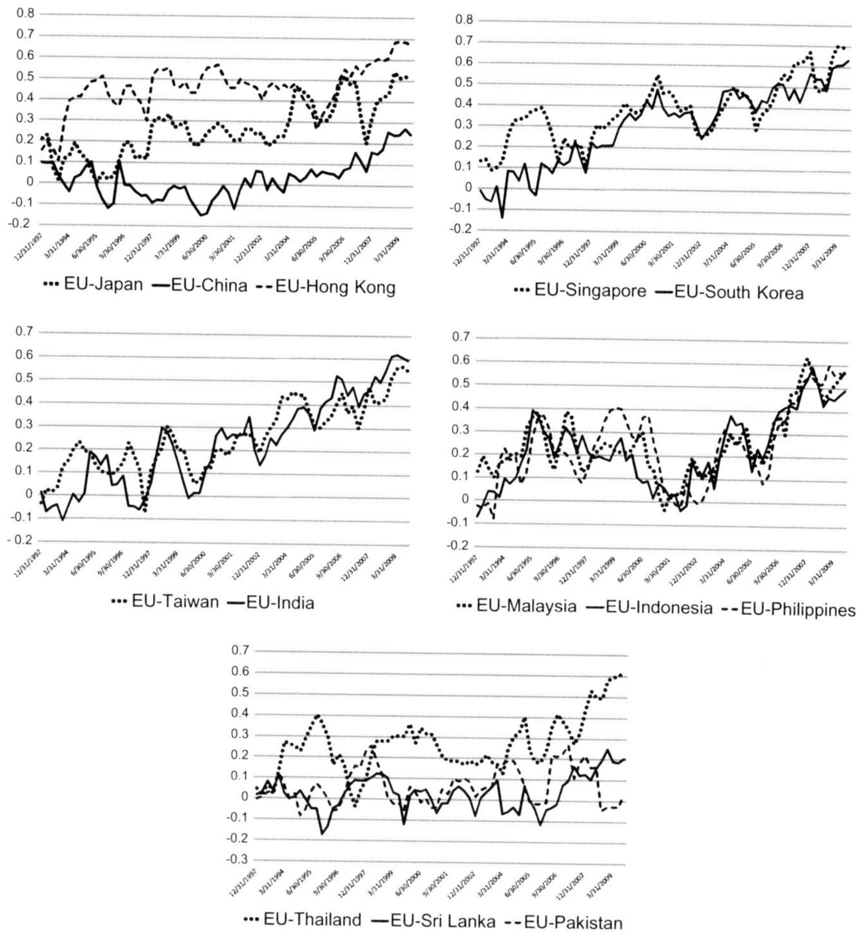

Appendix 5.B: Simple correlations between Europe and Asian countries.

Note: January 1, 1992–October 30, 2009.

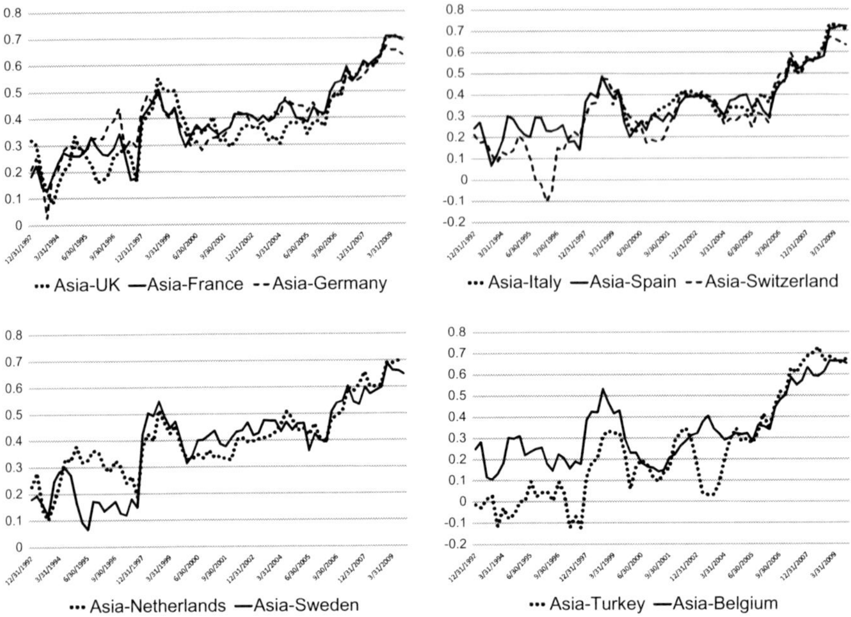

Appendix 5.C: Simple correlations between Asia and European countries.

Note: January 1, 1992–October 30, 2009.

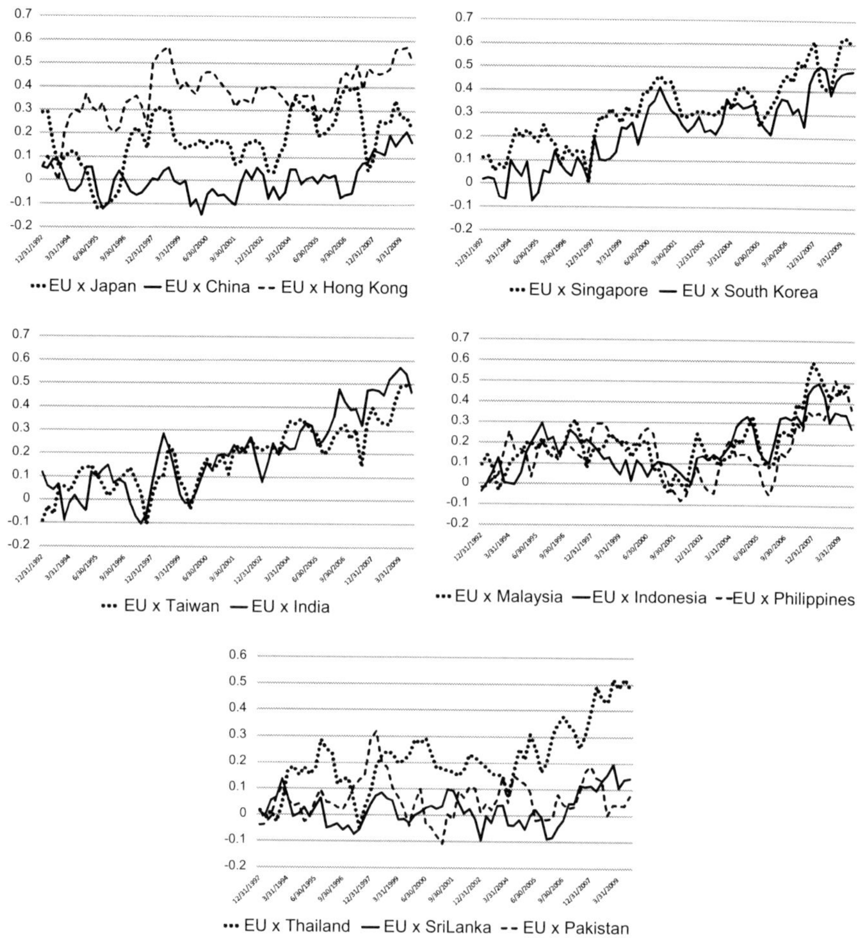

Appendix 5.D: Excess correlations between Europe and Asian countries.

Note: January 1, 1992–October 30, 2009.

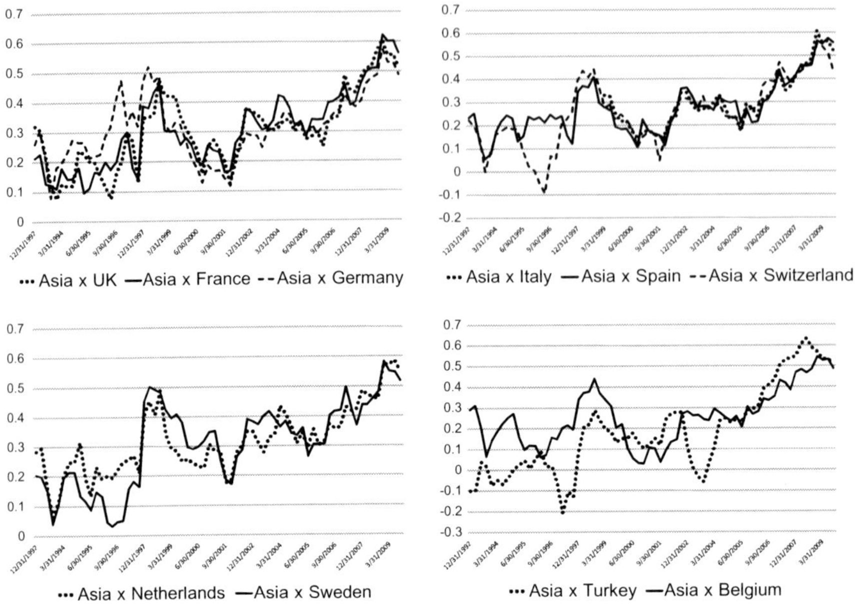

Appendix 5.E: Excess correlations between Asia and European countries.

Note: January 1, 1992–October 30, 2009.

Appendix 5.F: Stock market indices and descriptive statistics.

			Stable Period (Jan 1, 2007–Sep 15, 2008)				Crisis Period (Sep 15, 2008–Nov 17, 2008)			
Region	Country	Stock Market Index	Mean Return	Std. Dev.	N	Corr with U.S.	Mean Return	Std. Dev.	N	Corr with U.S.
North America	Canada	TSX COMP	0.0002	0.013	446	0.57	–0.0094	0.053	45	0.65
	U.S.	S&P 500	–0.0003	0.012	446	1.00	–0.0069	0.046	45	1.00
Asia	China	SHANGHAI SE COMP	0.0000	0.024	446	–0.05	–0.0006	0.033	45	0.28
	Hong Kong	HANG SENG	0.0001	0.019	446	0.05	–0.0063	0.055	45	0.47
	India	BSE 100	0.0002	0.021	446	0.12	–0.0098	0.046	45	0.56
	Indonesia	JAKARTA SE COMP	–0.0001	0.018	446	0.13	–0.0116	0.043	45	0.17
	Japan	TOPIX	–0.0004	0.014	446	–0.09	–0.0041	0.041	45	–0.01
	Malaysia	BURSA	0.0000	0.013	446	0.09	–0.0045	0.020	45	0.16
	Pakistan	KARACHI SE 100	0.0156	0.385	446	0.03	–0.0012	0.007	45	–0.08
	Philippines	PSEi	–0.0001	0.018	446	0.03	–0.0069	0.039	45	0.08
	Singapore	STRAITS TIMES	–0.0001	0.015	446	0.14	–0.0090	0.039	45	0.38

(*Continued*)

Appendix 5.F: (*Continued*)

			Stable Period (Jan 1, 2007–Sep 15, 2008)				Crisis Period (Sep 15, 2008–Nov 17, 2008)			
Region	Country	Stock Market Index	Mean Return	Std. Dev.	N	Corr with U.S.	Mean Return	Std. Dev.	N	Corr with U.S.
	South Korea	KOSPI	–0.0002	0.017	446	0.13	–0.0094	0.074	45	0.19
	Sri Lanka	COLOMBO SE ALL	–0.0003	0.007	446	0.04	–0.0064	0.019	45	–0.09
	Taiwan	TAIWAN SE	–0.0004	0.016	446	0.10	–0.0080	0.031	45	0.05
	Thailand	S.E.T.	0.0001	0.015	446	0.11	–0.0087	0.038	45	0.44
Europe	Belgium	BEL 20	–0.0006	0.014	446	0.40	–0.0103	0.046	45	0.60
	France	CAC 40	–0.0004	0.014	446	0.42	–0.0072	0.051	45	0.53
	Germany	DAX 30	0.0001	0.013	446	0.38	–0.0075	0.047	45	0.65
	Italy	FTSE MIB	–0.0007	0.013	446	0.39	–0.0080	0.051	45	0.44
	Netherlands	AEX	–0.0003	0.014	446	0.39	–0.0111	0.053	45	0.55
	Norway	OSLO OBX	0.0000	0.019	446	0.19	–0.0133	0.067	45	0.53
	Russia	RUSSIA RTS INDEX	–0.0008	0.017	446	0.19	–0.0130	0.081	45	0.24
	Spain	MADRID SE GENERAL	–0.0004	0.014	446	0.38	–0.0070	0.050	45	0.50
	Sweden	OMXS	–0.0006	0.016	446	0.35	–0.0092	0.049	45	0.57

(*Continued*)

Appendix 5.F: (*Continued*)

Region	Country	Stock Market Index	Stable Period (Jan 1, 2007–Sep 15, 2008)				Crisis Period (Sep 15, 2008–Nov 17, 2008)			
			Mean Return	Std. Dev.	N	Corr with U.S.	Mean Return	Std. Dev.	N	Corr with U.S.
	Switzerland	SWISS PERFORM.	–0.0001	0.011	446	0.31	–0.0054	0.037	45	0.55
	Turkey	ISE 100	0.0003	0.026	446	0.28	–0.0124	0.062	45	0.32
	U.K.	FTSE 100	–0.0005	0.014	446	0.45	–0.0086	0.050	45	0.61
Latin America	Argentina	MERVAL	–0.0006	0.015	446	0.51	–0.0107	0.053	45	0.57
	Brazil	BOVESPA	0.0008	0.023	446	0.60	–0.0104	0.083	45	0.79
	Chile	CHILE GENERAL	0.0002	0.012	446	0.42	0.0024	0.032	45	0.65
	Colombia	COLOMBIA IGBC	0.0000	0.015	446	0.19	–0.0086	0.036	45	0.20
	Mexico	BOLSA	0.0000	0.015	446	0.71	–0.0090	0.055	45	0.71
	Peru	LIMA SE GENERAL	0.0002	0.019	446	0.21	–0.0100	0.058	45	0.60
	Venezuela	VENEZUELA SE GEN.	–0.0005	0.019	446	–0.03	–0.0023	0.008	45	–0.03
Other	Australia	ASX ALL	–0.0001	0.017	446	0.08	–0.0095	0.056	45	0.21
	Saudi Arabia	TASI	0.0001	0.016	371	0.14	–0.0082	0.042	45	0.38
	South Africa	JSE ALL	–0.0001	0.019	446	0.31	–0.0099	0.056	45	0.37

Note: This table lists the market indices for each country and their mean return, standard deviation, and Pearson correlation with the US. The figures are calculated for the stable period and the crisis period. The number of trading days are indicated in the column "N".

Appendix 5.G: Robustness tests.

					Number of Countries with Contagion from U.S. Shock					
					Crisis Period Length					
					2 months		4 months		6 months	
Tranquil Period	Return Frequency	Interest Rate Control	Currency	Lags Included	Conditional ρ	Unconditional ρ	Conditional ρ	Unconditional ρ	Conditional ρ	Unconditional ρ
Full	2-day avg.	Yes	USD	1	19	0	10	0	5	0
Full	2-day avg.	Yes	USD	2	19	0	8	0	6	0
Full	2-day avg.	Yes	USD	3	11	0	0	0	0	0
Full	2-day avg.	Yes	USD	4	16	0	4	0	1	0
Full	2-day avg.	Yes	USD	5	9	0	6	0	5	0
Full	2-day avg.	Yes	Local	1	20	0	10	0	7	0
Full	2-day avg.	Yes	Local	2	20	0	11	0	8	0
Full	2-day avg.	Yes	Local	3	15	0	3	0	2	0
Full	2-day avg.	Yes	Local	4	18	0	5	0	4	0
Full	2-day avg.	Yes	Local	5	10	0	6	0	5	0
Long Full	2-day avg.	Yes	USD	1	22	0	13	0	14	0
Long Full	2-day avg.	Yes	USD	2	22	0	13	0	13	0
Long Full	2-day avg.	Yes	USD	3	13	0	7	0	3	0
Long Full	2-day avg.	Yes	USD	4	22	0	9	0	9	0

(*Continued*)

Appendix 5.G: (*Continued*)

					Number of Countries with Contagion from U.S. Shock					
					Crisis Period Length					
					2 months		4 months		6 months	
Tranquil Period	Return Frequency	Interest Rate Control	Currency	Lags Included	Condit-ional ρ	Uncondit-ional ρ	Condit-ional ρ	Uncondit-ional ρ	Condit-ional ρ	Uncondit-ional ρ
Long Full	2-day avg.	Yes	USD	5	14	0	13	0	14	0
Long Full	2-day avg.	Yes	Local	1	22	0	15	0	13	0
Long Full	2-day avg.	Yes	Local	2	23	0	15	0	14	0
Long Full	2-day avg.	Yes	Local	3	16	0	7	0	6	0
Long Full	2-day avg.	Yes	Local	4	20	0	8	0	8	0
Long Full	2-day avg.	Yes	Local	5	13	0	13	0	9	0
Full	2-day avg.	No	USD	1	19	0	11	0	11	0
Full	2-day avg.	No	USD	2	20	0	10	0	8	0
Full	2-day avg.	No	USD	3	15	0	8	0	6	0
Full	2-day avg.	No	USD	4	15	0	10	0	9	0
Full	2-day avg.	No	USD	5	16	0	9	0	8	0
Full	2-day avg.	No	Local	1	17	0	10	0	10	0
Full	2-day avg.	No	Local	2	14	0	11	0	10	0
Full	2-day avg.	No	Local	3	15	0	9	0	6	0
Full	2-day avg.	No	Local	4	16	0	9	0	9	0

(*Continued*)

Appendix 5.G: (*Continued*)

					Number of Countries with Contagion from U.S. Shock					
					Crisis Period Length					
					2 months		4 months		6 months	
Tranquil Period	Return Frequency	Interest Rate Control	Currency	Lags Included	Condit-ional ρ	Uncondit-ional ρ	Condit-ional ρ	Uncondit-ional ρ	Condit-ional ρ	Uncondit-ional ρ
Full	2-day avg.	No	Local	5	15	0	9	0	8	0
Full	Daily	Yes	USD	1	7	0	1	0	1	0
Full	Daily	Yes	USD	2	14	0	4	0	3	0
Full	Daily	Yes	USD	3	15	0	7	0	3	0
Full	Daily	Yes	USD	4	13	0	1	0	0	0
Full	Daily	Yes	USD	5	9	0	4	0	2	0
Full	Daily	Yes	Local	1	9	0	3	0	3	0
Full	Daily	Yes	Local	2	15	0	5	0	5	0
Full	Daily	Yes	Local	3	16	0	7	0	4	0
Full	Daily	Yes	Local	4	13	0	4	0	3	0
Full	Daily	Yes	Local	5	11	0	4	0	3	0
Stable	2-day avg.	Yes	USD	1	26	3	25	2	27	4
Stable	2-day avg.	Yes	USD	2	26	2	28	3	29	6
Stable	2-day avg.	Yes	USD	3	23	0	22	0	24	3
Stable	2-day avg.	Yes	USD	4	26	0	25	1	26	2

(*Continued*)

Appendix 5.G: (*Continued*)

					Number of Countries with Contagion from U.S. Shock					
					Crisis Period Length					
					2 months		4 months		6 months	
Tranquil Period	Return Frequency	Interest Rate Control	Currency	Lags Included	Condit-ional ρ	Uncondit-ional ρ	Condit-ional ρ	Uncondit-ional ρ	Condit-ional ρ	Uncondit-ional ρ
Stable	2-day avg.	Yes	USD	5	20	0	25	2	25	3
Stable	2-day avg.	Yes	Local	1	27	3	28	1	27	4
Stable	2-day avg.	Yes	Local	2	31	3	29	3	29	5
Stable	2-day avg.	Yes	Local	3	23	1	20	1	23	2
Stable	2-day avg.	Yes	Local	4	28	1	24	1	25	2
Stable	2-day avg.	Yes	Local	5	21	1	25	2	24	2

Note: This table reports contagion test results for tests with different parameters. The numbers under conditional and unconditional correlation indicate the number of countries that are found to have contagion effects using the respective correlation measures. Full period is between January 1, 2007 to November 17, 2008. Long Full period is between January 1, 2006 to November 17, 2008. Stable period is between January 1, 2007 to September 15, 2008.

Chapter 6

Asian Currency Basket Peg: Feasibility and a Move Towards a Multi-polar World

Raj Aggarwal and Cal B. Muckley

6.1 Introduction

There are many reasons for continuing interest in Asian exchange rate regimes. First, are the trade and financial imbalances that originate in Asia. Indeed, one of the reasons given for the global financial crises that started in 2008 is the persistent imbalance in international financial flows. It has been noted that some Asian countries have savings rates that are considered too high, resulting in rising current account surpluses and foreign exchange reserves considered to be excessive (e.g., China). In addition, the US is encouraged to run large international deficits to supply financing needed for world trade, including especially exports from these Asian countries. It is further contended that much of this problem of imbalances in global financial flows originates in Asian exchange rates that are held at unrealistic levels.

Second, it is often contended that free markets in exchange rates cannot be relied on to reflect fundamentals, and so there is a case for policy stabilization of exchange rates (Engel, 2009; Obstfeld and Rogoff, 2005). Third, the experience of European countries in forming a sometimes strained currency union, possibly due to a lack of fiscal cohesion across the union, may have lessons for the Asian region — lessons that may facilitate the formation of a similar or better currency union or at least the formation of a more coordinated currency region in Asia. Fourth, given the stresses currently being experienced by the European currency union (Forssbaeck and Oxelheim, 2007), the Asian experience in forming an Asian currency bloc may be more useful for other groups of developing countries such as those in South Asia, the Middle East, the Mediterranean, Central and/or Latin America, or sub-Saharan Africa.

Lastly, another reason for the continuing interest in the possibility of an integrated Asian currency regime is its implications for the re-polarization of the global economy. If the governments in the region act to form an Asian currency bloc, it is likely to facilitate greater intra-regional trade and economic integration. The formation of such an Asian currency bloc and trading group is a move away from global economic integration and a move closer to a multi-polar world.

Thus, there are many reasons to study the feasibility and possible nature of a more coordinated currency area in Asia. This chapter assesses the feasibility of pegging prospective Asian exchange rate regimes to a basket of the US dollar, the Euro, and the Yen, with the dynamics in a set of four European currencies prior to the introduction of the Euro providing a benchmark.

Our empirical findings can be summarized as follows. *First*, we find that a select set of Asian currencies — the Indonesian rupiah, the Korean won, the Philippine peso, the Taiwan dollar and the Thailand baht — exhibit more pronounced interdependencies, whether transient or long-run in nature, when expressed in terms of an equally-weighted basket of global currencies (the Euro, the Japanese yen and the United States dollar) as opposed to when they are expressed in terms of just the United States dollar. *Second*, we find that the dynamics of the aforementioned Asian currencies in the context of the common basket peg, are similar to the dynamics documented in Europe in the run-up to the European Economic and Monetary Union[1] (EMU). *Third*, our study accounts for generalized autoregressive conditional

[1] Consistent with our findings, Volz (2010) recommends gradual increase in monetary cooperation in East Asia. In contrast to our findings, Chow and Kim (2003) find that Asian countries react to external shocks more differently than did European countries prior to the formation of the EU. In addition, as was the case in Europe prior to the inception of the common currency, there may be significant regional political impediments to the solidarity required to support a co-ordinated regional exchange rate regime in Asia. Nevertheless, there is a developing institutional framework in Asia which is gradually extending its collective remit to further co-ordinate regional financial and monetary arrangements (e.g., Dutta, 2000; Moshirian, 2009).

heteroscedasticity (henceforth, GARCH) effects when estimating long-run time series properties in the exchange rate levels. This phenomenon may have compromised the power of tests utilized in earlier articles (e.g., Aggarwal and Mougoue, 1998; Tse and Ng, 1997).

Our findings have important policy implications for the Asian countries. While we have shown here that an Asian currency bloc is feasible, it is now up to the governments in the region to possibly act on this opportunity. The formation of an Asian currency bloc would be a move away from the global integration of national economies and would likely lead to the increased re-polarization of the global economy, moving us closer to a multi-polar world. These issues are fertile grounds for additional research.

The remainder of this chapter is organized as follows. Sections 6.2 and 6.3 discuss the inception of the Euro zone from financial, institutional and macroeconomic perspectives. Comparisons are drawn with features of the Asian environment from these fundamental vantage points with a view to assessing the prospect of a more coordinated exchange rate regime in Asia. Section 6.4 describes the data and the econometric methodology adopted. Section 6.5 presents the estimation of empirical results. Section 6.6 concludes.

6.2 Feasibility of a Basket Peg in Asia

While flexible exchange rates allow greater macroeconomic policy freedom, fixed exchange rates facilitate the economic integration between co-operating countries. This "two-corner solution" debate, however, has become less compelling in light of the revealed vagaries of foreign exchange markets (see Frankel and Rose, 1996; Froot and Ramadorai, 2005). Furthermore, Esaka (2009) finds no evidence that, as the "two-corner solution" argues, intermediate exchange rate regimes have a significantly higher probability of currency crises than both hard pegs and free floats.

In this vein, an important strand of the extant literature examines relevant macroeconomic criteria, e.g., the level of correlation of economic shocks and the level of intra-regional trade (see Mundell, 1961; McKinnon, 1963; Johnson and Swoboda, 1973), and advocates the inception of a more coordinated Asian exchange rate regime as an interim step towards an optimal currency area (see Eichengreen and Bayoumi, 1996; Ling, 2001; Huang and Guo, 2006). A recent example is Shirono (2008), who estimates trade-creating and welfare effects of various common currency arrangements in East Asia using a gravity model with bilateral trade data for 1980 and 1990. The study finds that a single currency in East Asia will stimulate regional trade substantially and regional currency arrangements can generate economically significant welfare gains for the region (see also Dutta, 2000).

While these studies show the potential benefits of a currency union, they and other prior literature say little about the feasibility or costs of forming such a currency union. In this regard, prior research is not very positive about the possibility of a coordinated Asian exchange rate regime. For example, while Aggarwal and Simmons (2006) find some PPP-based evidence of economic integration in the Caribbean area, Wilson and Choy (2007) who applied the theory of Generalized Purchasing Power Parity (GPPP) could not find persuasive evidence that East Asia as a whole constitutes a potential currency area with either the US or Japan. Similarly, Chow and Kim (2003), using a structural vector autoregression (SVAR) approach, note that East Asian countries are likely to be subject to asymmetric shocks, and thus, are not suitable for a single currency bloc.

Virtually all of the Asian authorities appear to have traditionally followed a United States dollar standard at some point in the past (see Frankel and Wei, 1994; McKinnon and Schnabl, 2004; Kearney and Muckley, 2007). However, growing intra-Asian trade and investment linkages have largely eroded the significant merit of that system with respect to price stability, financial market and trade integration, and current account imbalances, culminating (in part) in the Asian financial crisis of 1997–1998 (see Ito *et al.*, 1998; Kwan, 2001; McKinnon and Schnabl, 2003). Chow *et al.* (2007) find that the role of the US dollar declined in East Asia after the 1997 crisis, while that of the yen and other currencies remains mostly the same. In addition, the volatility of the US dollar-Japanese yen exchange rate has weakened the desirability of a US dollar-based exchange rate system for

Asia (see McKinnon, 2000). As a result, a reversion to the dollar standard in Asia implies undesirable fluctuations in effective trade-weighted exchange rates, unless the exchange rates of important trading partners are stabilized relative to one another. However, this seems unlikely (see Engelmann *et al.*, 2008).

Alternative hypotheses concerning the likelihood of a reversion to a United States dollar peg exchange rate regime are also present in the literature. Specifically, it is reported that the East Asian economies have pursued a strategy of development based on currency undervaluation with a view to stimulating exports and hence trade surpluses (see Dooley *et al.*, 2004). Alternatively, McKinnon and Schnabl (2004) and McKinnon (2007) indicate that the East Asian economies may be ineluctably trapped into experiencing trade surpluses on the current accounts of their international balance of payments as a result of their high savings rates and a reluctance to allow their currencies to appreciate relative to the United States dollar, with a resulting accumulation of dollar-denominated assets by these economies. However, as noted earlier, this imbalance in global financial flows is unsustainable in the long run (Bergsten, 2009).

There are a number of reasons to re-examine the feasibility of a currency union in Asia. First, in the last couple of decades, the economic situation of various countries in Asia has changed significantly. While the Japanese economy has long stagnated ("lost decades") and even its real income has declined, East Asian economies have continued to grow impressively despite the 1997 currency crisis. While it is undeniable that Japan is still a dominant economy in East Asia, the economic footing of Japan relative to its neighboring countries has declined, and this trajectory may be exacerbated in light of the March 2011 earthquake, tsunami, and nuclear accident in Japan and the corresponding economic costs, so as to raise questions as to whether there is any room for Japan to play a significant role in the exchange rate policy or a currency union in East Asia. Second, as noted above, reverting to a US dollar-based Asian exchange rate regime is also not a desirable alternative. Third, while the development of the prior literature on currency unions in Asia is engaging, they neglect to address the important issue of the relative feasibility of alternative exchange rate regimes. Finally, a new Asian coordinated exchange rate regime might draw some lessons from the earlier introduction of such a system in Europe.

In spite of continuing stresses, the integrated European Economic and Monetary System (EMS) introduced about two decades ago is considered mostly a success, albeit with the exception of the incoherence of fiscal stances across members of the union.[2] Nevertheless, there is ongoing debate regarding not just the merits and disadvantages of fixed versus flexible exchange rates with respect to realizing the objectives of Asian financial stability, economic development, and sustained economic growth, but also about the optimal transition path to a new regime (e.g., Frankel, 1999; Dutta, 2000; Fischer, 2001; Guillermo and Mishkin, 2003; Aggarwal *et al.*, 2006; Huang and Guo, 2006; Forssbaeck and Oxelheim, 2007; Jeon and Zhang, 2007).

By way of a benchmark, in the spirit of Eichengreen and Bayoumi (1996), the statistical time series properties of the select sets of Asian currencies are compared and contrasted with those of a group of European exchange rates prior to the inception of the European Economic and Monetary Union, January 1, 1999 (comprising the Belgian franc, the Dutch guilder, the French franc, and the German mark, expressed in terms of the European Currency Unit, henceforth the ECU).[3]

Thus, this chapter assesses prospective, more coordinated Asian exchange rate regimes with particular attention to the feasibility of their inception. *First*, this chapter examines the feasibility of a currency basket system in Asia (see Ogawa and Ito, 2002; Kawai, 2002; Williamson, 2005). The Euro area, Japan, and the United States are the largest trading partners of the Asian countries (see Williamson, 2005). Consequently, we calibrate the feasibility of introducing a

---

[2] The European system was subject to severe stress in 2010 due to the possibility of default by Greece, a member state. In addition, a number of other member states also had fiscal imbalances that were being judged by financial markets as being possibly unsustainable.

[3] In addition, Chow and Kim (2003) and Dutta (2000) also note the implications of the European single currency area for a similar single currency in Asia.

common basket peg exchange rate regime in Asia oriented around the corresponding currencies: the Euro, the Japanese yen, and the United States dollar. *Second*, more as a benchmark and less as a viable alternative, this chapter also examines the feasibility of a reversion to the United States dollar standard in Asia (see McKinnon and Schnabl, 2004; Dooley *et al.*, 2004).

By "feasibility" we refer to the costliness of the introduction of these regimes in terms of the expenditure of foreign reserves likely required to sustain them in light of the expected currency and economic divergence among the cooperating countries. Large inter-country macroeconomic variations among the countries in a peg would require large foreign exchange positions to defend the currency peg, while smaller variations would require smaller foreign exchange reserves to defend the peg. While it appears that the East Asian economies are in a credible position, in terms of foreign reserves, to defend a more co-ordinated foreign exchange rate system, the relative costs of the introduction of alternative exchange rate regimes and of defending such a system are still very relevant.

Specifically, how feasible is the adoption of a common basket peg exchange rate regime in Asia? Or would it be relatively more feasible to revert to an exchange rate regime focused exclusively on keying to the United States dollar? With a view to addressing this question, the statistical time series properties — internal transient and long-run dynamics — of select sets of Asian currencies, expressed in terms of the United States dollar and expressed in terms of the aforementioned common basket of currencies, are considered.

The greater the magnitude of the estimated interdependencies, the more inter-connected are the set of Asian currencies, and the more feasible a target currency or the adopted numeraire, the more readily these currencies may be managed coherently relative to the target currency or currency basket.[4] Significant interdependence is

[4] While the introduction of a more coordinated exchange rate regime will alter the dynamics of the currencies concerned, the case is nonetheless cogent that the cost of altering these dynamics declines *pro rata* with an increase in the estimated interdependence among the candidate currencies.

indicative of commonalities across the exchange rate determination procedure, whether introduced by intervention or by the machinations of the market system. It is more feasible to introduce a relatively coordinated exchange rate regime if regional exchange rates are *prima facie* compatible with that proposed exchange rate system.

6.3 Issues in Managing Coordinated Currency Pegs

Coordinated currency pegs offer a number of advantages and some disadvantages. Among the advantages is the elimination or a great reduction of any costs or risks of exchanging currencies among agents in the member countries — leading to significant increases in regional trade and economic welfare. Among the costs are likely to be the costs of transition in switching to a possible new common currency and the costs of defending an arrangement against possible speculative attacks. But the major costs are likely to be indirect, i.e., the loss of national monetary independence implicit in the need to coordinate monetary and fiscal policies among parties to a currency peg.

These costs and benefits have been accrued over the last dozen years in the countries that are members of the common European currency, the Euro. Thus, in assessing the feasibility of a currency peg in Asia, it seems that it would be useful to study the aspects of the European Community Treaty which relate to the required criteria for membership of the Euro zone, which succeeded the EMS in 1999.[5] As these criteria are not precisely coherent with optimal currency area (OCA) criteria, these latter criteria are also discussed. Perhaps as a result of the significant extent to which these criteria were satisfied by the European Community, monetary unification was achieved despite considerable regional political segmentation. Of interest is the extent to which Asian countries may perform on the outlined criteria, as well as the significance of the political impediments to eventual monetary

[5] The two situations are not entirely comparable as the European single currency is a basket of internal currencies, while the Asian currencies in this study are being assessed against a basket of external currencies. Nevertheless, the European experience may hold some lessons for the prospective Asian basket peg.

unification in Asia. Particular attention is paid to the Indonesian, the Korean, the Philippine, the Taiwanese and the Thailand economies.[6]

European Economic and Monetary System

With a view to attaining price stability, Article 121(1) of the European Community Treaty specifies four so-called "euro convergence criteria" to which each member country should subscribe. These criteria relate to various aspects of the macro-economy including: government finances, the inflation rate, the exchange rate, and the long-term interest rate. In particular, each member state should exhibit an inflation rate not in excess of 1.5 percentage points above the average of the three lowest inflation member states of the European Union. In addition, at the end of the preceding fiscal year, the ratio of the government deficit to gross domestic product (GDP) should not exceed 3%, and gross government debt to GDP should not exceed 60%. Moreover, candidate countries for membership of the Euro area should have joined the exchange rate mechanism under the European Economic and Monetary System for two consecutive years without devaluing their currency during this period. Finally, nominal long-term interest rates should not be more than two percentage points higher than in the three lowest inflation member states.

In contrast, the optimal currency area (OCA) criteria differ somewhat from the "euro convergence criteria". This may imply certain costs in terms of ultimate aggregate welfare benefits for the European Community. The OCA criteria may be listed as follows (e.g., Mundell, 1961): the degree of labor mobility, intra-regional trade intensity, the degree of regional risk sharing, *e.g.*, a monetary fund, and the extent of symmetry of shocks to real gross domestic product (GDP). Wyplosz (2001) adopts various specifications of the gravity model to explicate cross-sectional bilateral trade dynamics and finds that the results indicate considerable trade integration in Europe. However, Wyplosz

---

[6] These currencies have shown *de facto* evidence of unilateral basket peg exchange rate policies since the Asian financial crisis in 1997–1998 (the Chinese Yuan is excluded as its dollar value was fixed for most of this period).

(2001) also reports that despite 40 years having lapsed since the creation of the Common Market in Europe, Asia already appears more integrated with respect to trade than does Europe. In contrast, with regard to the symmetry or otherwise of shocks, Wyplosz (2001) specifies an AR(2) model on real GDP and reports that shocks are significantly more highly correlated in Europe than they are in Asia. Hence, despite the outlined difference in trade integration across Asia and Europe, Asia appears to exhibit greater segmentation, during the 1990–1998 period, with regard to economic shocks than does Europe.

Perhaps in light of the extent to which these OCA criteria were satisfied in the European context prior to 1999, a path of increasing political integration was pursued by a steadily growing set of European economies.[7] Thus, in the end, despite two world wars and a period of so-called "Cold War", political segmentation did not deter the European economies from forming a monetary union, conceding monetary authority and irrevocably defining their exchange rates *vis-a-vis* one another whilst floating against the currencies of the rest of the world.

Given that a common exchange rate policy will necessitate both compromises and costs, there is a mandatory political precondition in the form of "collective support" to the success of the process. In particular, relatively strong currencies may be reticent to support relatively weak currency counterparts, without the confidence that the latter's economic policies can be influenced. In Europe, there has been a unique socio-political history that has culminated in the Maastricht Treaty and, since 1999, the inception of a single currency alongside the establishment of the European Central Bank. While this process was not without its difficulties, for example, the refusal of the recommendations of the Werner Report in the early 1970s to largely concede national government fiscal powers, it does have its conceptual foundations in the liberal and democratic principles of the Enlightenment

[7] Also, considerable financial market integration has been achieved in the region, both in respect to stock markets (Aggarwal *et al.*, 2010) and more broadly across financial markets (Baele *et al.*, 2004). This heightened integration in part will also have followed from the development of the Euro zone and the consequent minimization of currency risk (Forssbaeck and Oxelheim, 2003).

(Eichengreen and Bayoumi, 1999), including such noteworthy intellectuals as Jeremy Bentham (who advocated a European Assembly), Jean-Jacques Rousseau (who advocated a European federation) and Henri Saint-Simon (who advocated a European monarch and parliament), as well as Victor Hugo (who spoke of a United States of Europe). During the 20th century, the most significant catalyst to establish collective governance across Europe was instigated by the Marshall Plan. This post-war United States aid established the principle of multilateralism in Europe, thus recognizing the legitimacy of international law and institutions in Europe. It is clear that Europe has undergone a process of political integration that spans several centuries.

Comparisons of Europe with Asia

In regard to the macroeconomic and financial criteria required to form a monetary union, Asian economies have generally performed well relative to their European counterparts. For example, Bayoumi and Mauro (2001) report that the ASEAN (Association of Southeast Asian Nations) economies exhibit increasing intra-regional trade *per se* and intra-regional trade as a percentage of GDP that is similar to that of the Euro area and higher than that of regions such as Mercosur or NAFTA during the 1980–1998 periods. Eichengreen (2004), Eichengreen *et al.* (2004) and Huang and Guo (2006) provide corroborative evidence. Indeed, Rana (2006) finds that many of the Asian economies including Indonesia, the Philippines and Thailand exhibit intra-regional trade integration in excess of 40%. In addition, Kawai (2008) indicates that for East Asia as a whole, the proportion of intra-regional trade in its total trade has expanded from 37% in 1985 to 52% in 1995, and to 55% in 2005.

With regard to labor mobility, a high level of mobility of labor allows migration to facilitate adjustments to asymmetric shocks, thus precluding the requirement of flexible exchange rates. In Asia, according to Huang and Guo (2006), while there remains strict immigration regulations, within ASEAN there has been a significant rise in migratory dynamics since the 1980s. While there were approximately 1 million migrants at the beginning of the 1980s, there were some 6.5 million in 2002. Park and Bae (2002) and McCauley *et al.* (2002) find that, from a financial viewpoint, these economies are becoming increasingly integrated both with globally important economies such as the United States and the Euro zone, as well as with neighboring Asian economies.[8] Asian regional efforts to enhance financial risk sharing are outlined against the background of Asian political history and primarily in terms of the Chiang Mai Initiative.

As with European political history, the countries of East Asia have also experienced a fragmented and often harsh political history, although over recent decades there have been significant overtures towards heightened political integration with a view to better managing international exchange rate regimes. While the political fragmentation of the region stems firstly from Japanese imperialist expansionist policies of colonization during the 20th century, as well as the political disregard between China and Taiwan, the recent partially offsetting developments were by way of institutional arrangements. In particular, regarding the North and Southeast Asian governing authorities' willingness to provide credible commitments to cooperative targets, there are an increasing number of Asian institutions and with the passing of time, these institutions are incessantly extending their remits. ASEAN consists of Brunei, Cambodia, Indonesia, Laos, Malaysia, Myanmar, the Philippines, Singapore, Thailand and Vietnam. Since its inception in 1967, it has aimed to attain regional peace and stability and to accelerate economic growth. It has been suggested that this forum — in conjunction with China, Japan and South Korea — establish an Asian Financial Institution to promote financial standards and financial development. Furthermore, a complementary initiative with respect to the Asian Bond Markets looks to channel Asian savings to Asian borrowers and hence reduce

[8] This is confirmed by the increasing conformity to parity conditions in the region. For example, while earlier studies such as Glick and Hutchison (1990) found little support for US dollar-based real interest rate parity (RIP) in East Asia, relatively recent studies have documented closer conformity with RIP and PPP in East Asia (e.g., Aggarwal and Mougoue, 1998; Phylaktis, 1999; Shirono, 2008).

the extent to which Asian borrowers rely on the United States and other important extra-regional global economies to extend credit.

The Chiang Mai Initiative constitutes perhaps the most advanced outcome of institution-building in the Asian region, especially with regard to exchange rate coordination, as is shown in the discussion below. APEC (Asia-Pacific Economic Cooperation) consists of the region's finance ministers. Since its inception in 1989, its members have met to share information and promote financial sector development and liberalization. EMEAP (the Executives' Meeting of East Asia–Pacific Central Banks) meets to further regional surveillance and financial market development. This group comprises Australia, China, Hong Kong SAR, Indonesia, Japan, Korea, Malaysia, New Zealand, the Philippines, Singapore, and Thailand. It was established in 1991. Although there is limited current support for close exchange rate arrangements in the region, it has been suggested that EMEAP should consider the establishment of an Asian institution for central banks similar to Europe's Bank for International Settlements (BIS) in Basle. This is seen as a possible move towards a more integrative monetary system for the region. Finally, the Six Markets Group, a forum for the exchange of views amongst the vice ministers of finance, comprise a loose network of cooperation and a consultative forum.

The Chiang Mai Initiative 1996 was a set of "repurchase agreements" for US dollars whereby US securities were used as collateral. As a result, this mechanism was sufficient to withstand a currency attack only to the extent to which this class of collateral was available. The participating governing authorities included those of Hong Kong, Malaysia, Indonesia, Thailand, Japan, Singapore, and the Philippines. Importantly, there was no corresponding limitation placed on these countries' monetary and fiscal policies. The Chiang Mai Initiative of May 2000, which was motivated as a result of the 1997 financial crisis and established within the ASEAN+3 Group, consists of a network of bilateral currency swap arrangements between the finance ministers of the ASEAN + 3. It extends the 1996 initiative. Among other things, this initiative aims to facilitate the increased cooperation amongst Asian governing authorities such that they may more closely cooperate on monitoring capital flows and to develop a regional supervisory mechanism. These swaps supplement existing IMF arrangements and are subject to the latter's conditionality. This facilitates the expeditious availability of liquidity to member governing authorities to act in a pre-emptive measure to dissuade currency attacks and is supported by a pool of reserves amounting to US$40 billion.

In addition, leaders of the ASEAN countries along with those of Japan, Korea, and China presented a proposal for an Asian Currency Unit (ACU) and agreed to create an $80 billion fund in October 2008 as part of their response to the global financial and economic crisis. This agreement called for Korea, Japan, and China to provide 80% of the fund, or $64 billion, with ASEAN members providing the remaining $16 billion. The Chiang Mai Initiative is expected to impart exchange rate stability and, in doing so, may have unwittingly also contributed to closer regional and financial integration. Nonetheless, due to the adversity to political integration in the region, officials have shied away from the possibility that this agreement might act as a platform for regional exchange rate stabilization.

Finally, East Asian financial markets are continuing to develop (e.g., Aggarwal, Jeon and Zhao, 2006) and facilitate possible economic and monetary coordination. Rana (2006), Huang and Guo (2006) and Kawai (2008) report evidence that strengthening trade relations and financial integration has further synchronized business cycles in the region, and thus heightened the symmetry of economic and financial shocks, paving the way for more coordinated exchange rate management in the Asian region. It is generally agreed that the symmetry of shocks is the most important criterion with respect to assessing the potential benefits of forming a currency union.

European Experience and FX Coordination in Asia

The European Monetary System (EMS) served to insulate European currencies from innovations in the US dollar exchange rate. As a result, it may follow that Europe's EMS has implications for the desirability and design of some kind of prospective Asian exchange rate system. In this vein, Bayoumi and Mauro (2001) show that although the economic conditions for an optimum currency area are not very different in North and Southeast Asia to those that existed in Europe prior to the establishment of the EMS, the political conditions do not favor integration. Indeed, as prior research on the EMS concludes, political integration is far more significant than economic coordination (Forssbaeck and Oxelheim, 2003, 2006; Aggarwal *et al.*, 2010).

In contrast, however, since the late 1990s the previously loose links that have traditionally existed between the central banks in the Asian region are becoming stronger. Nevertheless, this chapter does not conclude that an ERM-type system is a promising avenue for further progress, with respect to exchange rate management, in North and Southeast Asia. Rather, similar to the contentions in Moshirian (2009), it is posited here that a collective basket peg exchange rate arrangement, with its greater flexibility and its promise of stable effective exchange rates, is better placed to benefit from the level of North and Southeast Asian macroeconomic and growing institutional convergence.

6.4 Data, Research Design, and the Econometric Models

Data

The data consists of daily bilateral United States dollar and basket currency exchange rates for the Indonesian rupiah, the Korean won, the Philippine peso, the Taiwan dollar and the Thailand baht over the eight-year period from 1 January 1999 through to 29 December 2006. It also comprises, by way of a benchmark, a set of European currencies: the Belgian franc, the Dutch guilder, the French franc and the German mark, expressed in terms of the ECU over the period 1 January 1991 through to 30 December 1998.[9] Globally important currencies including the Euro and the Japanese yen are also examined. All data is sourced from Global Treasury Information Services and World Market Reuters.

[9] The periods for these two sets of exchange rates are selected to be similar with the Asian data starting after the effects of the late 1990s Asian crises, and the European data reflecting important milestones in the move to a monetary and economic union.

The set of select Asian currencies is chosen on the basis of two criteria. *First*, the economies concerned have been long-standing members of ASEAN and are signatories of the Chiang Mai Initiative.[10] Hence, they are committed to regional financial and economic integration. Moreover, Huang and Guo (2006) conclude that the Indonesian rupiah, the Korean won and the Thailand baht are of especial relevance to any future Asian currency zone. *Second*, these currencies exhibit pronounced unilateral European euro and Japanese yen effects as well as United States dollar effects (see Bowman, 2005). Additionally, our goal is to develop a practical recommendation for Asian currencies, and so we have excluded a few otherwise dominant Asian currencies that are tied closely to the dominant non-Asian currency, the US dollar.[11]

The set of select European currencies acts as a reasonable benchmark to assess our Asian results as they were the currencies actively complicit in the process to European currency market integration since the 1970s, and the set is sufficiently small to lend itself to examination with the statistical models used in this chapter. The behaviour of these currencies, during the period examined, is of especial relevance as they have, since 1 January 1999, irrevocably linked their currencies to the Euro.

Consistent with the discussion in Mundell (2003), the basket peg eventuality considered is comprised of an equally-weighted linear combination of the European euro, the Japanese yen and the United States dollar (see Ogawa and Ito, 2002; Williamson, 2005).[12] The United States dollar represents an important trading partner for most

[10] Except Taiwan, which is not internationally recognized as a separate political entity from mainland China even though it is a distinct currency area and it actively seeks to demonstrate its political sovereignty.

[11] The Chinese yuan, the Hong Kong dollar, the Malaysian ringgit, and to a lesser extent the Singapore dollar values are almost entirely determined by changes in the United States dollar, during the sample period studied. Hence, including these rates in a study of the time series properties of a set of exchange rates relative to the US dollar would give misleading results and would not make sense.

[12] In this article we do not estimate optimal weights in a currency basket, leaving that for future research.

Asian countries and should clearly be included in any basket for an exchange rate peg (see Williamson, 2005). The argument in support of the Japanese yen, as an incremental currency of choice, is compelling. *First*, Japan is the largest and most important regional economy with respect to trade (Huang and Guo, 2006) and is of central importance with respect to foreign direct investment (see Urata, 2001). *Second*, growing Japanese yen effects on many of the region's currencies are well-established (see Aggarwal and Mougoue, 1998; Hernandez and Montiel, 2003; Bowman, 2005; Huang and Guo, 2007). *Finally*, researchers at the Bank of Japan and the Japanese Ministry of Finance have also expressed an interest in pursuing this possibility (see Kamada and Takagawa, 2005).[13]

The hypothesis that the notional basket peg should also include the European euro is also cogent for a different set of reasons.[14] *First*, the Euro zone, alongside the United States and Japan, is among the top three trading partners of all the Asian economies concerned (see Williamson, 2005). *Second*, while Euro zone currency effects in Asia are generally of secondary importance after those of the Japanese yen and the United States dollar, such effects are clearly documented (Kearney and Muckley, 2007). A common peg is considered superior to unilateral pegging as it insulates regional trade dynamics from outside disturbances,[15] it yields an environment conducive to enhanced regional monetary integration, and it facilitates the availability of a forward market against, *e.g.*, the United States dollar, for the participating currencies.

---

[13] See, for example, a webpage entirely dedicated to the internationalization of the yen on the Japanese Ministry of Finance website (http://www.mof.go.jp/yen-itiran.htm).

[14] The Euro is a free floating currency and is not managed relative to Asian currencies.

[15] Williamson (2005) indicates that a common basket peg regime, in the East Asia region, outperforms unilateral country baskets in stabilizing effective exchange rates, during 2000–2004. This is tantamount to stabilizing the relative price of traded goods or output with respect to the fluctuation in important global currencies. Unilateral exchange rate pegs imply different yen and dollar weights in the currency baskets which may still cause competitive imbalances.

Research Design

Five simple and intuitive statistical criteria for the successful inception of a basket peg exchange rate regime relative to the alternatives are considered. Specifically, these criteria relate *first* to stability, *second* to pair-wise and multivariate correlations, *third* to the correlations' persistence, *fourth* to volatility transmission, and *fifth* to long-run equilibrium time-series relations in the select aforementioned sets of exchange rates and exchange rate returns expressed in terms of appropriate numeraire (target) currencies.

The greater the stability of the Asian currency sets in terms of the basket currency and the United States dollar and the European currency set in terms of the ECU, the more important is the corresponding numeraire currency in relation to innovations in the Asian or European currency sets. Notwithstanding instability in the currency sets, the larger the pair-wise and multivariate Asian and European rate return correlations and the more pronounced the correlations' persistence relative to the select numeraire currency, the greater the likelihood that this set of currencies might be managed in a more coordinated fashion. With the same motivation in mind, periods of relative tranquility and periods of relative volatility should ideally not coincide across the Asian and European rate returns. After all, independent time-varying volatilities within a candidate bloc are tantamount to an intrinsic dissatisfaction with the requirement of large correlations between the exchange rate returns. A long-run relationship between the Asian rates and the Japanese yen relative to the United States dollar, between the Asian rates (excluding Japanese yen) relative to the basket currency, or between the European currencies and the ECU, is indicative of the presence of a long-run equilibrium. The greater the extent to which these natural criteria are exhibited in the data, the greater the feasibility of the corresponding target exchange rate regime.

The internal long-run dynamics of systems of Asian exchange rates are well-documented (see Aggarwal and Mougoue, 1998; Tse and Ng, 1997). Taken together, these articles reveal long-run relations among sets of Asian currencies with the Japanese yen playing a significant and increasingly influential role. These findings are interpreted as indicative of the potential emergence of a Japanese yen-dominated regional exchange rate system. However, these cited articles rely on asymptotic theory, and thus neglect to consider the impact of GARCH effects on the estimated long-run relations. Given the relatively small sample sizes examined, this is an unreasonable assumption and hence, inference may be misleading (see Hoglund and Ostermark, 2003). In this chapter, we address this shortcoming by simultaneously accounting for GARCH effects when estimating the cointegration vectors, while we also provide updated estimates of these long-run relations since the Asian financial crisis.

Groupings of 3-, 4- and 5-currencies are selected by means of eigenvalue decomposition on each of the standardized variance/covariance matrices of all sets of 3- and 4-Swiss franc exchange rate returns. A Swiss franc numeraire is selected as it is a significant free floating currency. The larger the first eigenvalue of each matrix relative to the summation of the matrix's eigenvalues, the more collinear the variables summarized in that matrix. The groupings are selected with a view to maximizing the collinearity criterion. The same methodology is adopted on a moving window of 250-observations to inspect the evolution of the correlations in the various exchange rate systems examined.[16]

The persistence of the correlations, in each of the exchange rate systems, is estimated using an orthogonal factor generalized ARCH model (see Alexander, 2002). The magnitude of the volatility transmission in the various exchange rate systems is estimated using a multivariate BEKK-specified GARCH model (see Engle and Kroner, 1995).[17] The number of long-run relations tying the system of exchange rates together is estimated using the Johansen (1988) model and also with a

[16] The practical details of the process of establishing a currency union in Asia are beyond the scope of this paper, but can be found elsewhere (see, for example, Volz, 2010).

[17] Yoshi Baba, Robert Engle, Dennis Kraft and Ken Kroner originally specified this model (a synthesis of UCSD Ph.D. theses). As a result, the acronym BEKK is adopted by Engle and Kroner (1995).

variation on the Johansen (1988) econometric methodology, outlined by Gannon (1996). This variation is motivated by the literature in the area of cointegration testing in the context of ARCH effects.

The literature in the area of cointegration testing, in the context of ARCH effects, is in its infancy. The theoretical literature (see Lee and Tse, 1996; Silvapulle and Podivinsky, 2000; Hoglund and Ostermark, 2003) indicates that ARCH effects aggrandize the size of the Johansen (1988) cointegration test. For example, Lee and Tse (1996) indicate that while the Johansen (1988) cointegration test tends to over-reject the null hypothesis of no cointegration in favor of finding cointegration, the problem is generally not very serious. Silvapulle and Podivinsky (2000) report similar results. In contrast, Hoglund and Ostermark (2003) conclude that the eigenvalues of the long-run information matrix for the Johansen (1988) cointegration test are highly sensitive to conditional heteroskedasticity and that, therefore, this multivariate statistic is only reliable in the context of homoskedastic processes.

This latter finding, regarding the size of the cointegration test, becomes increasingly pronounced the more integrated the ARCH process considered. That said, these contributions pertain to low dimensional systems and, as a result, are of limited empirical relevance. For example, empirical contributions (see Alexakis and Apergis, 1996; Gannon, 1996; Pan *et al.*, 1999), across a wider range of system dimensions, tend to indicate that these ARCH effects and their variants exert a significant and deleterious impact on the statistical test's power properties. Specifically, the aforementioned empirical literature identifies significant gains in statistical power once ARCH effects are controlled, when testing for cointegration, using the Johansen (1988) technique.

Econometric Procedures

In the light of the preceding discussion, a modified Johansen (1988) testing procedure is estimated so as to mitigate the deleterious implications of ARCH effects on the estimation of the rank of the long-run information matrix in the specified vector error correction model (henceforth, VECM). Specifically, following Gannon (1996), we adopt a modified test for common roots in which we account for GARCH effects in the correlating combinations of residuals. Consider the p-dimensional VECM:

$$\Delta x_t = \pi x_{t-1} + \Sigma_{i=1}^{k-1} \pi_i \Delta x_{t-1} + \varepsilon_t, \tag{6.1}$$

$$\pi = \Sigma_{i=1}^{k} \pi_i - I, \tag{6.2}$$

$$\pi_i = -\Sigma_{i+1}^{k} \pi_j, (i = 1, \ldots, k-1). \tag{6.3}$$

The residuals, ε_t, are assumed independent normally distributed p-dimensional with mean zero and variance, Ω. The parameters $(\pi, \pi_1, \ldots, \pi_{k-1}, \Omega)$ are unrestricted and are estimated by maximum likelihood estimation. The x_t are vectors of series containing the exchange rates. Now, consider two auxiliary equations:

$$\Delta x_t = \Sigma_{i=1}^{k-1} b_{1i} \Delta x_{t-1} + r_{0t}, \tag{6.4}$$

$$x_{t-1} = \Sigma_{i=1}^{k-1} b_{2i} \Delta x_{t-1} + r_{1t}, \tag{6.5}$$

where b_1 and b_2 are estimated by ordinary least squares (see Johansen and Juselius, 1990). The vectors of series r_{0t} and r_{1t} contain the residuals from the auxiliary regressions. Note that the VECM, Equation (6.1), can now be reformulated as a two-stage estimation process:

$$r_{0t} = \alpha\beta' r_{1t} + error. \tag{6.6}$$

The null hypothesis, H_0, that the components of x_t are cointegrated may be stated as:

$$H_0 : \pi = \alpha\beta'. \tag{6.7}$$

This implies that $q = \text{rank}\ (\pi) < p$. The rows of the (p^*q) matrix β' are the distinct cointegrating vectors of x_t, i.e., $\beta'(x_t)$ are $I(0)$. The elements of α represent the loadings of each of the r cointegrating relations.

The canonical correlations can be estimated from the stacked residuals via Equation (6.6) where the weights, $\omega_{1i},\ldots,\omega_{pi}$ and $\kappa_{1i},\ldots,\kappa_{pi}$, are canonical weights:

$$\hat{j}_i = \hat{\omega}_{1i} r_{01i} + \ldots + \hat{\omega}_{pi} r_{0pi}, \tag{6.8}$$

and

$$\hat{z}_i = \hat{\kappa}_{1i}\, r_{11i} + \ldots + \hat{\kappa}_{pi}\, r_{1pi}, \tag{6.9}$$

where r refers to the residuals from Equations (6.4) and (6.5) and the subscript i refers to the ith pair of canonical variates. Therefore, these variates $\hat{j}_i$ and $\hat{z}_i$ have a zero mean.

Finally, estimate GARCH (1,1) equations for $\hat{j}_i$ and $\hat{z}_i$ for $i = 1,\ldots,q$:

$$\hat{j}_{it} = \rho_i \hat{z}_{it} + u_{it}, \tag{6.10}$$

$$h_{it} = \mathrm{Var}(\hat{j}_{it}/\hat{z}_{it}) = \alpha_{i0} + \alpha_{i1} u_{t-1}^2 + \beta_{i1} h_{t-1}, \tag{6.11}$$

and compare the t-statistic for ρ with the tabulated values of the statistic given in MacKinnon (1991). Hence, an estimate of each eigenvalue, λ_i, is available $\rho_i \approx \sqrt{\lambda_i}$. Neglecting GARCH effects gives inefficient estimates of the λ_is, whereas allowing for GARCH effects partially accounts for simultaneous volatility effects in the system. If there is common volatility across the series entering the system, then linear combinations of the deviations from long-run paths will capture these common factors.

Thus, in order to account for common volatility shocks, the test statistics are estimated from the procedure described in Equations (6.8)–(6.11). We perform the two-stage procedure with and without accounting for GARCH effects. The variates are constructed using canonical coefficients as weights. This procedure provides an estimate, robust to GARCH effects, of the number of cointegrating vectors.

6.5 Empirical Results

This chapter examines groupings of 3- and 4-currencies which exhibit the highest level of multilateral correlation alongside the full 5-currency set. This range of currency sets is examined as a small grouping of eligible currencies is more likely to be politically feasible.[18] The select 3-currency set contains the Korean won, the Philippine peso and the Taiwan dollar; the 4-currency set extends the latter to include the Thailand baht; and the 5-currency set extends to include the Indonesian rupiah. These sets of currencies are extended to include the Japanese yen when the United States dollar exchange rate regime is considered with respect to the criterion of a long-run equilibrium.[19]

Table 6.1 reports summary test statistics. The augmented Dickey–Fuller estimates indicate that these currency returns appear to be stationary, while the currency exchange rates are probably integrated of order one, $I(1)$. This finding statistically motivates the adoption of short- and long-run modeling techniques to examine the outlined criteria. The variances of the exchange rate return series, in terms of the United States dollar and the basket currency, are comparable, while the ECU exchange rate returns exhibit a markedly low level of variance. This reflects the coordinated exchange rate system in Europe in the run-up to the Euro, relative to the regime in Asia, since the 1997–1998 financial crisis. According to a Lagrange Multiplier test, significant ARCH effects are prevalent. This finding motivates a modified test for cointegration to assess the behaviour of long-run

[18] Also, over-specification of the adopted VECM may otherwise imply spurious empirical results with respect to the statistical tests performed in the examination of the fifth criterion regarding long-run relations, as critical values may be too large due to the inclusion of an irrelevant variable (see Richards, 1995; Gannon, 1996).

[19] The Chinese renminbi and the Hong Kong dollar are not included in this statistical analysis as they have mostly been fixed with respect to the US dollar during the period of this study. It is acknowledged that China's 12th five-year plan, disclosed in 2011, further clarifies the Chinese position that the renminbi is expected to experience a gradual appreciation against the US dollar in the future, and hence, if using the methodology adopted in this study in the future, the Chinese renmimbi may constitute a currency of interest.

Table 6.1: Summary statistics.

Currency	Variance	Skewness	Exc. Kurtosis	ARCH	Unit Root
			United States dollar		
IR	1.11	–0.24[a]	12.87[a]	41.82[a]	–40.13[a] [–2.17]
KW	0.16	–0.04	3.66[a]	119.99[a]	–38.13[a] [–0.64]
PP	0.22	–5.57[a]	136.48[a]	65.78[a]	–43.78[a] [–1.79]
TD	0.09	0.33[a]	35.27[a]	335.59[a]	–36.12[a] [–1.28]
TB	0.16	0.14	15.70[a]	130.18[a]	–47.55[a] [–2.06]
JY	0.39	0.00	2.57[a]	3.64[c]	–44.61[a] [–1.99]
			Asian Basket rates		
IR	0.98	0.16[a]	11.84[a]	66.72[a]	–28.44[a] [–2.17]
KW	0.17	0.17[a]	1.09[a]	29.62[a]	–40.62[a] [–1.43]
PP	0.19	1.53[a]	25.22[a]	102.69[a]	–26.01[a] [–1.34]
TD	0.13	–0.02	2.26[a]	82.38[a]	–50.89[a] [–0.65]
TB	0.18	–0.19[a]	4.79[a]	12.11[a]	–46.75[a] [–1.77]
			European Currency Units		
BF	0.03	–1.16[a]	21.51[a]	364.55[a]	–26.75[a] [–1.64]
DG	0.03	–1.61[a]	48.56[a]	363.87[a]	–35.84[a] [–1.62]
FF	0.05	–1.47[a]	23.96[a]	136.87[a]	–42.07[a] [–1.77]
GM	0.03	–1.86[a]	26.46[a]	137.43[a]	–34.67[a] [–1.56]

Notes: The table contains summary statistics concerning the Asian currencies denominated in terms of the United States dollar and the basket currency and four European currencies expressed in terms of ECUs. Currencies are represented as follows: Basket currency = an equally-weighted linear combination of the European euro, the Japanese yen and the United States dollar, BF = Belgian Franc, DG = Dutch Guilder, ECU = European Currency Unit, FF = French Franc, GM = German Mark, IR = Indonesian Rupiah, JY = Japanese Yen, KW = Korean Won, PP = Philippines Peso, TD = Taiwan Dollar, TB = Thailand Baht, and the USD = United States dollar. The currencies expressed in terms of the United States dollar and the Asian Basket rates are examined from 1 January 1999 through to 29 December 2006. The returns expressed in ECUs are examined from 1 January 1991 through to 30 December 1998. For example, IR, under the sub-heading "United States dollar", represents the Indonesian rupiah–United States dollar continuously compounded exchange rate return. A Lagrange multiplier test is performed with respect to first-order ARCH. The unit root summary statistic is the Augmented Dickey–Fuller test statistic; outside the square brackets find the test statistic for the difference of the corresponding currency. The lag length is determined by minimizing the Bayesian Information Criterion. The superscripts a, b and c indicate significance at the 1%, 5% and 10% levels, respectively.

relations in the data, with respect to the fifth criterion. Naturally, it also motivates this chapter's examination of the fourth criterion of volatility transmission within the currency groupings. Finally, while there is evidence of skewness, there is markedly more evidence of excess kurtosis in the unconditional return distributions. We therefore follow Bollerslev (1987) in utilizing a student t-distribution for the exchange rate innovations in our various GARCH models.

Table 6.2 presents the correlation matrices for the Asian currencies, the Japanese yen, and the Euro in terms of the United States dollar; the Asian currencies, excluding Japan, in terms of the basket currency; and the European currencies in terms of the ECU. It appears, from a consideration of the arithmetic mean correlations, that the correlation matrices of the Asian currencies denominated in terms of the basket currency and the European currencies in terms of the ECU are of a similar magnitude, while the United States dollar denominated exchange rate set exhibits relatively lower arithmetic mean correlations. While these preliminary findings reflect the relative importance of the United States dollar in exchange rate determination in Asia, they also reveal the scope for an alternative Asian exchange rate regime as a result of the comparison with the behavior of a set of European currencies in the run-up to the European Economic and Monetary Union (EMU).

Figure 6.1 portrays the levels and returns of the select sets of Asian currencies and the Japanese yen in terms of the United States dollar, and the select set of Asian currencies in terms of the basket currency. It also portrays the set of European currencies in terms of the ECU. Figure 6.2 portrays the bivariate and multivariate correlations in the same sets of exchange rate returns. The Asian exchange rates are rebased to 100 on 1 January 1999 and the European rates are rebased to 100 on 1 January 1991. The Indonesian rupiah, the Korean won and the Philippine peso are relatively unstable when expressed in terms of either numeraire. Taken together, the Asian currencies exhibit significantly less stability than the European currencies. The European currencies range to approximately 10% from the initial base rate, while the Asian currencies expressed in terms of either numeraire are displaced in excess of 30% from the initial base rate.

Table 6.2: Currency correlations.

	IR	KW	PP	TD	TB	JY	EURO
				United States Dollar			
	IR	KW	PP	TD	TB	JY	EURO
IR	1.00	−0.03	0.03	0.11	0.28	0.10	0.02
KW	−0.03	1.00	0.19	0.06	−0.06	0.03	−0.01
PP	0.03	0.19	1.00	0.05	0.01	0.01	0.02
TD	0.11	0.06	0.05	1.00	0.17	0.14	0.10
TB	0.28	−0.06	0.01	0.17	1.00	0.28	0.14
JY	0.10	0.03	0.01	0.14	0.28	1.00	0.30
EURO	0.02	−0.01	0.02	0.10	0.14	0.30	1.00
mean	0.08	0.03	0.05	0.10	0.14	0.14	0.09

	IR	KW	PP	TD	TB
		Basket Currency			
IR	1.00	0.28	0.31	0.30	0.42
KW	0.28	1.00	0.59	0.70	0.52
PP	0.31	0.59	1.00	0.58	0.51
TD	0.30	0.70	0.58	1.00	0.52
TB	0.42	0.52	0.51	0.52	1.00
mean	0.33	0.52	0.50	0.53	0.49

	FF	DG	BF	GM
	European Currency Unit			
FF	1.00	0.17	0.22	0.18
DG	0.17	1.00	0.59	0.77
BF	0.22	0.59	1.00	0.58
GM	0.18	0.77	0.58	1.00
mean	0.19	0.51	0.46	0.51

Notes: The table contains matrices of correlation statistics with regard to the Asian and Euro currency returns denominated in terms of the United States dollar, the Asian regional currency returns in terms of the basket currency, and four European currency returns expressed in terms of ECUs. For example, IR, under the sub-heading "United States dollar", represents the Indonesian rupiah-United States dollar continuously compounded exchange rate return. The returns expressed in the United States dollar and the Asian Basket rates are examined from 1 January 1999 through to 29 December 2006. The returns expressed in ECUs are examined from 1 January 1991 through to 30 December 1998. Currency exchange rates are represented as follows: Basket currency = an equally-weighted linear combination of the European euro, the Japanese yen and the United States dollar, BF = Belgian Franc, DG = Dutch Guilder, ECU = European Currency Unit, Euro = European Euro, FF = French Franc, GM = German Mark, IR = Indonesian Rupiah, JY = Japanese Yen, KW = Korean Won, PP = Philippines Peso, TD = Taiwan Dollar, and TB = Thailand Baht.

This is also demonstrated in clear terms by inspection of the volatility in the returns series. Hence, from the viewpoint of the first criterion, stability, the basket peg and United States dollar regimes provide comparable results, while both regimes appear less promising than did the Euro in the run-up to the EMU.

We turn now to the correlations, which are computed on a moving 250-day window. The heavy lines in Panels A and B of Figure 6.2 represent the 3-, 4- and 5-currency groupings' multivariate correlations. In both instances, the line representing the highest correlation corresponds with the 3-currency set and the multivariate correlation declines with increases in the size of the currency grouping. In Panel C, the heavy line represents the multivariate correlation in the full ECU 4-currency grouping. The mean multivariate United States dollar correlations vary between 0.3 and 0.5, while the mean multivariate basket currency correlations reflect much greater coordination varying between 0.5 and 0.9. In contrast, the mean multivariate ECU returns' correlations vary between a very similar 0.4 and 0.8, but they follow a generally upward trend particularly in the latter period.

Table 6.3 indicates that statistically significant t-distributed GARCH coefficients are estimated on the first and second principal components across the sets of exchange rate returns considered. These t-distributed GARCH (1,1) models indicate that the correlations vary in a persistent manner rather than erratically (see Alexander, 2002).

Taken together, the results presented so far suggest that the US dollar multivariate correlations are generally lower than those of the basket currency, which are similar in magnitude to those of the ECU returns' multivariate correlations. Also, all sets of exchange rate returns exhibit significant persistence in their correlations and thus, comparable results in this regard. These results indicate the superiority of the basket peg exchange rate regime relative to the United States dollar peg exchange rate regime with respect to the second criterion, and the similarity of the performance of the alternative exchange rate regimes with respect to the third criterion.

Table 6.3 also presents results concerning volatility transmission from a t-distributed BEKK specification for the multivariate GARCH (1,1)

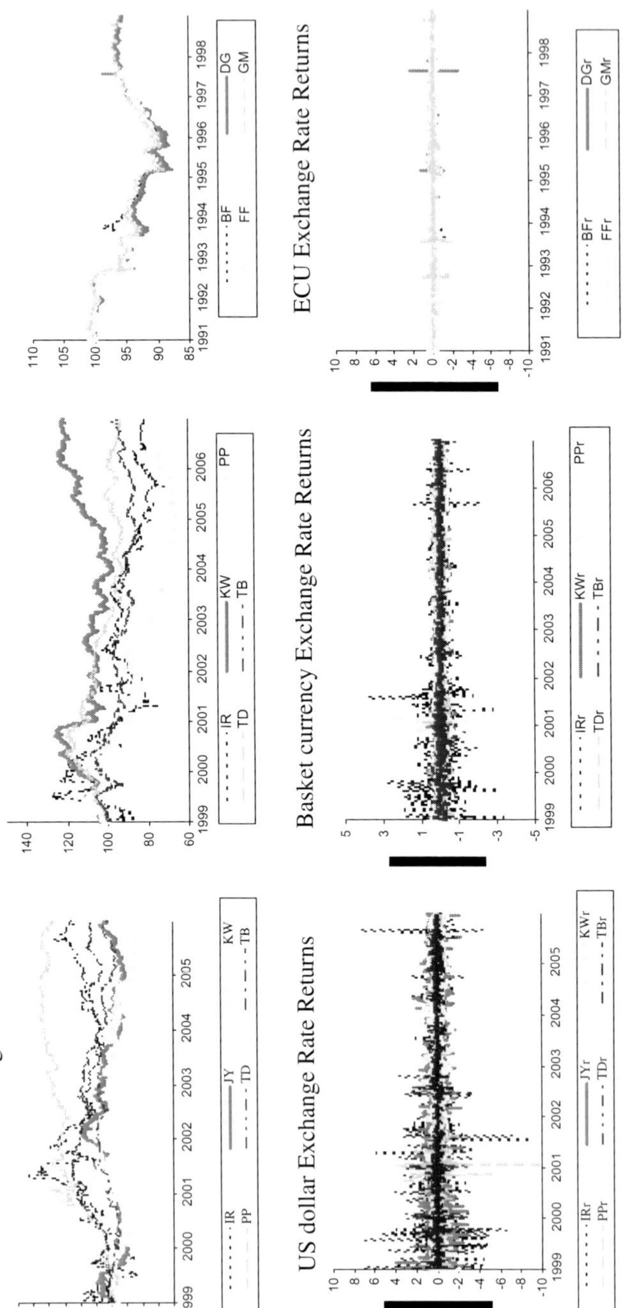
ECU Exchange Rates
BF
FF
DG
GM
Basket currency Exchange Rates
IR
TD
KW
TB
PP
US dollar Exchange Rates
IR
PP
JY
TD
KW
TB
ECU Exchange Rate Returns
BFr
FFr
DGr
GMr
Basket currency Exchange Rate Returns
IRr
TDr
KWr
TBr
PPr
US dollar Exchange Rate Returns
IRr
PPr
JYr
TDr
KWr
TBr

Figure 6.1: US dollar, basket currency and European Currency Unit exchange rates and returns.

Notes: The figure contains graphics corresponding to Asian-US dollar exchange rates and exchange rate returns, and Asian basket currency exchange rates and exchange rate returns, over the period 1 January 1999 through to 29 December 2006, as well as ECU rates and exchange rate returns over the period 1 January 1991 through to 30 December 1998. The Basket currency is an equally-weighted linear combination of the European euro, the United States dollar and the Japanese yen. The terms "IR", "JY", "KW", "PP", "TD" and "TB" correspond to the Indonesian rupiah, the Japanese yen, the Korean won, the Philippine peso, the Taiwan dollar and the Thailand baht exchange rates, respectively. The terms "BF", "DG", "FF" and "GM" correspond to the Belgian Franc, Dutch Guilder, French Franc and German Mark ECU exchange rates, respectively. These terms followed by an "r" indicate continuously compounded percentage exchange rate returns.

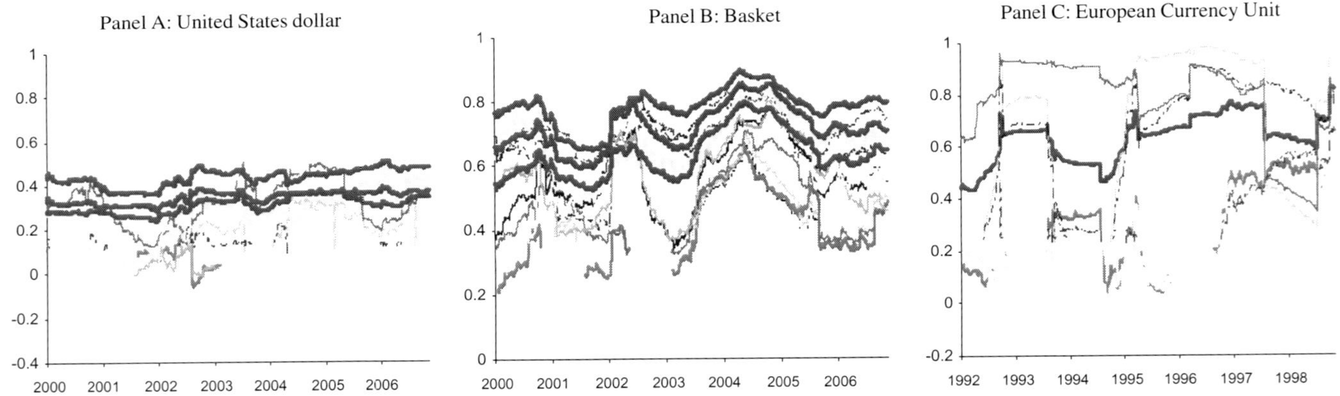

Figure 6.2: Bivariate and multivariate currency return correlations.

Notes: The figure comprises three Panels: A, B and C. The Panels contain bivariate and multivariate correlations estimated in a moving 250-observation window, i.e., an approximate 1-year window, from 1 January 1999 through to 30 December 2006 for the US dollar returns and the basket currency returns and from 1 January 1991 through to 30 December 1998 for the ECU returns. The basket currency is an equally-weighted linear combination of the European euro, the Japanese yen and the United States dollar. The window moves by including the incremental observation and dropping the initial observation for each estimation period. In Panel A, the heavy lines represent the 3-, 4- and 5-currency sets of US dollar returns: namely, a 3-currency set containing the Korean won, the Philippine peso and the Taiwan dollar; a 4-currency set that extends the latter set to include the Thailand baht; and a 5-currency set that extends the 4-currency set to include the Indonesian rupiah. The remaining lines represent the time-varying pair-wise correlations between the US dollar currency returns from the 5-currency set. In Panel B, the same currency groupings are expressed in terms of the basket currency, and the heavy lines represent the aforesaid 3-, 4- and 5-currency sets. The heavy line in Panel C represents the multivariate correlation in the 4-currency set containing the Belgian franc, the Dutch guilder, the French franc and the German mark in terms of the ECU. The remaining lines in Panel C represent the time-varying pair-wise correlations between the ECU currency returns from the 4-currency set.

Table 6.3: Currency correlations.

Panel A: Persistent Correlations	*Asian Currencies [United States dollar numeraire]*						*European Currencies*	
	3-currency		4-currency		5-currency		4-currency	
	PC1	PC2	PC1	PC2	PC1	PC2	PC1	PC2
Eigenvalue	1.22	0.97	1.22	1.16	1.39	1.21	2.38	0.92
Cumulative R^2	0.41	0.73	0.31	0.60	0.28	0.52	0.60	0.83
a	0.04[b]	0.01[a]	0.14[a]	0.05[b]	0.02[a]	0.03[b]	0.02[a]	0.00
b	0.11[a]	0.13[a]	0.29[a]	0.16[a]	0.05[a]	0.08[a]	0.12[a]	0.12[a]
d	0.76[a]	0.75[a]	0.62[a]	0.82[a]	0.88[a]	0.82[a]	0.88[a]	0.89[a]
	Asian Currencies [Basket Currency numeraire]							
	3-currency		4-currency		5-currency			
	PC1	PC2	PC1	PC2	PC1	PC2		
Eigenvalue	1.97	0.52	2.71	0.53	2.93	0.84		
Cumulative R^2	0.66	0.83	0.68	0.81	0.59	0.75		
a	0.02	0.03[a]	0.02	0.02[a]	0.02[b]	0.00[a]		
b	0.02[a]	0.15[a]	0.02[a]	0.13[a]	0.02[a]	0.05[a]		
d	0.96[a]	0.57[a]	0.97[a]	0.83[a]	0.97[a]	0.88[a]		

(*Continued*)

Table 6.3: (*Continued*)

Panel B: Volatility Transmission	*Asian Currencies [United States dollar numeraire]*						*European Currencies*	
	3-currency		4-currency		5-currency		4-currency	
	coeff.	*t-stat.*	*coeff.*	*t-stat.*	*coeff.*	*t-stat.*	*coeff.*	*t-stat.*
	4.26	421.43	3.34	5.82	10.30	159.24	62.24	311.20
	Asian Currencies [Basket Currency numeraire]							
	3-currency		4-currency		5-currency			
	coeff.	*t-stat.*	*coeff.*	*t-stat.*	*coeff.*	*t-stat.*		
	3.43	1374.80	9.71	6347.71	17.06	836.03		

Notes: The table contains two Panels, A and B. Panel A contains T-distributed GARCH (1,1) conditional volatility coefficients "α", "β" and "δ" for the first two principal components of seven sets of exchange rate returns: a 3-currency set containing the Korean won, the Philippine peso and the Taiwan dollar; a 4-currency set that extends the latter set to include the Thailand baht; and a 5-currency set that extends the 4-currency set to include the Indonesian rupiah. Results for these three sets of currencies are presented twice: once with the currencies expressed in terms of United States dollars and once with the currencies expressed in terms of the basket currency, i.e., an equally-weighted linear combination of the European euro, the Japanese yen and the United States dollar. There is also a 4-currency set of European exchange rates comprising the Belgian Franc, the Dutch Guilder, the French Franc and the German Mark. This latter set is expressed in terms of ECUs. The principal components are represented as follows: PC1 = 1st Principal Component, and PC2 = 2nd Principal Component. All exchange rate returns are expressed as continuously compounded returns. The model specification is a vector error correction model (see Johansen, 1988). The superscripts a, b and c indicate significance at the 1%, 5% and 10% levels, respectively. Panel B contains parameter estimates and T-statistics with respect to volatility transmission in respect to the aforesaid seven sets of exchange rate returns. The volatility transmission term is obtained from a BEKK-specified T-distributed multivariate GARCH model (see Engle and Kroner, 1995). The presented coefficient is the summation of the absolute values of the volatility transmission parameters, and the associated T-statistic is computed with a standard error obtained using the delta method.

model. This specification parsimoniously imposes no cross-equation restrictions whilst ensuring a positive definite conditional variance matrix. While it permits the examination of both the direction and the magnitude of volatility transmission, we focus exclusively on a summary measure of the magnitude of volatility transmission. This measurement shows that for the US dollar and basket currency exchange rate sets, generally the larger the set of exchange rates examined, the larger is the magnitude of the volatility transmission. Moreover, it is clear that the volatility transmission in the European currency exchange rate set is significantly more pronounced than in the Asian currency exchange rate sets. That said, the

Table 6.4: Johansen multivariate test for cointegration.

		Critical values		
	Trace	10%	5%	1%
Panel A: US dollar rates				
(i) 4-currency set				
G = 0	41.88	49.65	53.12	60.16
G <= 1	17.71	32.00	34.91	41.07
G <= 2	6.65	17.85	19.96	24.60
G <= 3	1.31	7.52	9.24	12.95
(ii) 5-currency set				
G = 0	87.33[a]	71.86	76.07	84.45
G <= 1	49.73	49.65	53.12	60.16
G <= 2	20.78	32.00	34.91	41.07
G <= 3	7.6	17.85	19.96	24.60
(iii) 6-currency set				
G = 0	120.38[a]	97.87	103.68	110.15
G <= 1	75.47	71.81	76.81	83.74
G <= 2	45.58	49.95	53.95	56.73
G <= 3	24.4	31.93	34.07	37.78
Panel B: Basket rates				
(i) 3-currency set				
G = 0	19.68	32.00	34.91	41.07
G <= 1	9.76	17.85	19.96	24.60
G <= 2	2.29	7.52	9.24	12.95

(*Continued*)

Table 6.4: (*Continued*)

	Trace	Critical values 10%	5%	1%
(ii) 4-currency set				
G = 0	23.70	49.65	53.12	60.16
G <= 1	12.16	32.00	34.91	41.07
G <= 2	2.49	17.85	19.96	24.60
G <= 3	0.04	7.52	9.24	12.95
(iii) 5-currency set				
G = 0	40.25	71.86	76.07	84.45
G <= 1	20.90	49.65	53.12	60.16
G <= 2	9.62	32.00	34.91	41.07
G <= 3	3.26	17.85	19.96	24.60
Panel C: ECU rates				
(iv) 4-currency set				
G = 0	298.21[a]	49.65	53.12	60.16
G <= 1	43.44[a]	32.00	34.91	41.07
G <= 2	15.16	17.85	19.96	24.60

Notes: The table comprises three Panels. Panels A and B contain three sets (i), (ii) and (iii) of US dollar and basket currency rates, respectively, and Panel C contains a set (iv) of ECU rates. In Panel A the terms (i), (ii) and (iii) refer to a 4-currency set containing the Japanese yen, the Korean won, the Philippine peso and the Taiwan dollar; a 5-currency set that extends the latter to include the Thailand baht; and a 6-currency set that extends the 5-currency set to include the Indonesian rupiah. In Panel B the terms (i), (ii) and (iii) refer to a 3-currency set containing the Korean won, the Philippine peso and the Taiwan dollar; a 4-currency set that extends the latter set to include the Thailand baht; and a 5-currency set that extends the 4-currency set to include the Indonesian rupiah. Exchange rate sets (i) through (iii) are observed from 1 January 1999 through to 30 December 2006. In Panel C the 4-currency set (iv) contains the Belgian Franc, the Dutch Guilder, the French Franc and the German Mark in terms of the ECU from 1 January 1991 through to 30 December 1998. The estimated model specification is a vector error correction model. A first order lag is included across models, as indicated by utilizing the Bayesian Information Criterion over lag lengths 1 through 5. This criterion indicates that one lag of returns is included in the estimated vector autoregressive model. Gamma "γ" is the number of cointegrating vectors under the null hypothesis. The critical values are simulated or sourced in Osterwald-Lenum (1992). The superscripts a, b and c indicate statistical significance at the 1%, 5% and 10% levels, respectively.

basket currency exchange rate sets exhibit considerably more volatility transmission than the US dollar exchange rate sets. As a result, the superiority of the basket peg exchange rate regime relative to the US dollar exchange rate regime appears evident with respect to the fourth criterion.

As indicated by the results presented in Table 6.1, there is the possibility of cointegration among our exchange rates. Table 6.4 presents the results from the Johansen (1988) maximum likelihood procedure, a classic set of likelihood ratio "trace" tests, to estimate the rank of the long-run information matrix, *i.e.*, the existence of long-run equilibrium relations driving the long-run movements. Panels A and B present results concerning the select currency sets and the Japanese yen in terms of the United States dollar and the select currency sets in terms of the basket currency, respectively. Panel C presents results concerning the European exchange rates. Following Richards (1995), the order of the associated VECMs is selected using the Bayesian Information Criterion.

Previous research, adopting this statistical test for long-run equilibria, included the Hong Kong dollar and reported the presence of a long-run relationship (see Aggarwal and Mougoue, 1998; Tse and Ng, 1997). However, this prior research may have provided spurious results as the Hong Kong dollar was largely determined by the United States dollar during the corresponding time periods (see Kearney and Muckley, 2007). Nonetheless, our chapter tentatively corroborates those findings by revealing evidence indicative of the existence of a single cointegration vector, at the 10% significance level, in the United States dollar denominated currency systems examined. Our findings also indicate an absence of cointegration relations when the exchange rate systems are expressed in terms of the basket currency. In contrast, compelling evidence of a single cointegration relation is estimated in the European currency dataset, confirming our earlier comparisons of possible Asian FX regimes to the EMS. However, Table 6.1 presents evidence of pervasive and significant ARCH effects. It is possible that these effects have reduced the power of the Johansen (1988) test procedure, hence providing spurious results.

In Table 6.5 the results of a modified test for common roots, in which generalized ARCH effects in the correlating combinations of residuals are accounted for, are presented for the aforementioned exchange rate systems. The results indicate that the European currencies exhibit two cointegrating vectors. The modified test reveals strengthened evidence of cointegration throughout the United States dollar numeraire Asian exchange rate sets, and it also finds significant evidence of cointegration throughout the basket peg numeraire Asian exchange rate sets. Therefore, the modified test reveals starkly different evidence relative to the classic Johansen (1988) "trace" test. It indicates that all of the exchange rate sets exhibit cointegration.[20]

Table 6.5: Modified multivariate test for cointegration with GARCH effects.

				Critical values		
	OLS Coeff.	GARCH Coeff.	T-statistic	10%	5%	1%
Panel A: US dollar rates						
(i) 4-currency set						
rho = 1	0.09	0.12	–2.69	–3.81	–4.1	–4.65
rho = 2	0.06	0.07	–3.62[c]	–3.45	–3.75	–4.29
(ii) 5-currency set						
rho = 1	0.12	0.07	–4.45[b]	–4.13	–4.42	–4.96
rho = 2	0.10	0.09	–5.96[a]	–3.81	–4.1	–4.65
rho = 3	0.09	0.05	–3.36	–3.45	–3.75	–4.29
(iii) 6-currency set						
rho = 1	0.14	0.10	–5.49[a]	–4.42	–4.7	–5.24
rho = 2	0.11	0.09	–5.73[a]	–4.13	–4.42	–4.96
rho = 3	0.10	0.07	–4.66[a]	–3.81	–4.1	–4.65
rho = 4	0.09	0.05	–3.64	–3.45	–3.75	–4.29

(Continued)

[20] We also estimate t-distributed GARCH models with the conditional mean equations containing the currencies, in levels, within each currency set, with a view to statistically testing the standardized residuals for stationarity. The standardized residuals are stationary (at conventional significance levels using MacKinnon (1991) critical values), hence the case for cointegration is preserved. Moreover, this investigation indicates that all variables tend to play an important role in the long-run equilibrium relations. Detailed results are not presented here for brevity but are available from the authors on request.

Table 6.5: (*Continued*)

	OLS Coeff.	GARCH Coeff.	T-statistic	Critical values 10%	5%	1%
Panel B: Basket rates						
(i) 3-currency set						
rho = 1	0.07	0.07	−3.67[c]	−3.45	−3.75	−4.30
rho = 2	0.05	0.03	−1.65	−3.05	−3.34	−3.90
(ii) 4-currency set						
rho = 1	0.10	0.04	−2.96	−3.81	−4.1	−4.65
rho = 2	0.07	0.07	−3.80[b]	−3.45	−3.75	−4.29
rho = 3	0.05	0.02	−1.43	−3.04	−3.34	−3.90
(iii) 5-currency set						
rho = 1	0.10	0.04	−2.64	−4.13	−4.42	−4.96
rho = 2	0.09	0.08	−4.82[a]	−3.81	−4.10	−4.65
rho = 3	0.08	0.07	−3.49[c]	−3.45	−3.75	−4.29
rho = 4	0.04	0.03	−1.50	−3.04	−3.34	−3.90
Panel C: ECU rates						
(iv) 4-currency set						
rho = 1	0.22	0.09	−7.11[a]	−3.81	−4.1	−4.65
rho = 2	0.07	0.04	−3.37	−3.45	−3.75	−4.29
rho = 3	0.03	0.09	−4.22[a]	−3.04	−3.34	−3.90

Notes: The table comprises three Panels. Panels A and B contain three sets (i), (ii) and (iii) of US dollar and Basket currency rates, respectively, and Panel C contains a set (iv) of ECU rates. In Panel A the terms (i), (ii) and (iii) refer to a 4-currency set containing the Japanese yen, the Korean won, the Philippine peso and the Taiwan dollar; a 5-currency set that extends the latter to include the Thailand baht; and a 6-currency set that extends the latter to include the Indonesian rupiah. In Panel B the terms (i), (ii) and (iii) refer to a 3-currency set containing the Korean won, the Philippine peso and the Taiwan dollar; a 4-currency set that extends the latter set to include the Thailand baht; and a 5-currency set that extends the 4-currency set to include the Indonesian rupiah. Exchange rate sets (i) through (iii) are observed from 1 January 1999 through to 30 December 2006. The 4-currency set (iv), presented in Panel C, contains the Belgian Franc, the Dutch Guilder, the French Franc and the German Mark, expressed in terms of the ECU from 1 January 1991 through to 30 December 1998. Coefficients for $\rho = 1 \dots 4$ are the estimated square roots of the eigenvalues, while accounting for t-distributed GARCH effects, of the Johansen (1988) long-run information matrix. The T-statistic critical values are sourced in MacKinnon (1991). The superscripts a, b and c indicate statistical significance at the 1%, 5% and 10% levels, respectively.

Thus, the fifth criterion appears to be satisfied with respect to both the United States dollar exchange rate regime and the basket peg exchange rate regime.

6.6 Move Towards a Multi-polar World

Regional exchange rate regimes are a significant aspect of the global monetary system and have important implications for the nature and management of international financial flows and any imbalances reflected in unsustainable reserve accumulations. In spite of recent strains, the European Economic and Monetary Union has now been in place for about two decades. Does it hold possible lessons for a possible exchange rate regime in Asia? What implications would a currency peg in Asia have for the re-polarization of the global economy?

We have examined several time series properties of select sets of Asian currencies which have demonstrated marked unilateral European euro and Japanese yen effects, alongside important United States dollar effects. Our aim has been to assess the compatibility of these sets of currencies to be in more coordinated exchange rate regimes in light of recent macroeconomic trends. Specifically, a 3-currency set was examined which contained the Korean won, the Philippine peso and the Taiwan dollar, while a 4-currency set extended the latter set to include the Thailand baht. Our 5-currency set extended the 4-currency set to include the Indonesian rupiah. Two more coordinated exchange rate regimes were considered, namely, a United States dollar peg and a basket currency peg, comprised of the European euro, the Japanese yen and the United States dollar.

The behavior of these exchange rate sets was examined using five time series criteria (i.e., stability, correlations, persistence of correlations, volatility transmission, and long-run relations) to assess the extent to which the Asian rates are interdependent relative to the numeraire target currencies proposed by the alternative, more co-ordinated exchange rate regimes. The set of European currencies that have been successful member currencies of the European Economic and Monetary Union since 1 January 1999 acted as a useful benchmark.

Our results document that short- and long-run currency dynamics are more conducive to the feasibility of introducing a common peg for Asian currencies based on an equally-weighted basket of the European euro, the United States dollar and the Japanese yen, compared to the alternative of re-introducing a United States dollar peg exchange rate regime. The benchmark set of European currencies, as expected, performs well on the five criteria, while the Asian basket peg regime also performs well across the outlined criteria, with perhaps the exception of the criterion of stability. In contrast, the US dollar exchange rate regime performs well only on the criteria of the persistence of correlations and long-run relations. Notably, in an advance over prior literature, the evidence for a common Asian basket peg regime is strengthened when the long-run parameters are estimated while accounting for time-varying volatility effects.

The European Monetary System (EMS) served to insulate European currencies from innovations in the US dollar exchange rate. As a result, it may follow that Europe's EMS has implications for the desirability and design of some kind of prospective Asian exchange rate system. Given the current apparent lack of willingness for similar political integration in Asia, an ERM-type system may not be the most promising avenue for further progress with respect to exchange rate management in North and Southeast Asia at this time. Rather, it is posited that a collective basket peg exchange rate arrangement, with its greater flexibility and its promise of stable effective exchange rates, is better placed to benefit from the level of North and Southeast Asian macroeconomic and growing institutional convergence.

In summary, we document that currency dynamics in Asia are conducive to the possibility of introducing a common peg for Asian currencies based on an equally-weighted basket of the European euro, the United States dollar and the Japanese yen — an arrangement that is shown to be better than the United States dollar peg exchange rate regime. Such an arrangement would require exchange rate reserves that are relatively small compared to current levels of currency reserves available in Asia.

These findings clearly have important policy implications for scholars and policymakers interested in Asian financial stability and exchange rate systems. For example, the formation of an Asian currency bloc is a possible precursor to greater economic and political integration in Asia, and indicates a potential move away from global integration of national economies, leading to the likely re-polarization of the global economy. A well-coordinated exchange rate regime in Asia is likely to strengthen economic, financial, and ultimately political ties between the Asian countries. Such strengthening may, but not necessarily, come at the expense of Asian relations with the rest of the world. Such a development would indeed lead to a greater polarization of the world economy with Asia continuing to strengthen as a significant pole in addition to other major poles such as North America, Europe, and perhaps a southern economic bloc consisting of India, Africa, and Latin America. However, this assessment of increasing polarity is accompanied by the major caveat that the exact nature of the future global economy is difficult to forecast.

Acknowledgement

Raj Aggarwal would like to thank his late professor Harry G. Johnson for first instigating his interest in this topic.

References

Aggarwal, R., Jeon, P. and Zhao, X. (2006). Bank exposure to interest rate risks during financial liberalization: evidence from South Korea. *Asia Pacific Financial Markets*, 12(1), 61–90.

Aggarwal, R., Lucey, B. and Muckley, C. (2010). The dynamics of equity market integration in Europe: the impact of political economy events. *Journal of Common Market Studies*, 48(3), 641–660.

Aggarwal, R. and Mougoue, M. (1998). Common stochastic trends among Asian currencies: cointegration between Japan, ASEAN, and Asian Tigers. *Review of Quantitative Finance and Accounting*, 10(2), 193–206.

Aggarwal, R. and Simmons, W. (2006). Economic integration in the Caribbean: evidence from purchasing power parity, 1980–2000. *Journal of Policy Modeling*, 28(3), 277–280.

Alexakis, P. and Apergis, N. (1996). ARCH effects and cointegration: is the foreign exchange market efficient? *Journal of Banking and Finance*, 20(4), 687–697.

Alexander, C. (2002). Principal component models for generating large GARCH covariance matrices. *Economic Notes: Review of Banking, Finance and Monetary Economics*, 31(2), 337–359.

Baele, L., Ferrando, A., Hordahl, P., Krylova, E. and Monnet, C. (2004). Measuring financial integration in the Euro area. European Central Bank, Occasional Paper Series, No. 14.

Bayoumi, T. and Mauro, P. (2001). The suitability of ASEAN for a regional currency arrangement. *The World Economy*, 24(7), 933–954.

Bergsten, C. F. (2009). The dollar and the deficits. *Foreign Affairs*, 88(6), 20–38.

Bollerslev, T. (1987). A conditionally heteroskedastic time series model for speculative prices and rates of return. *Review of Economics and Statistics*, 69(3), 542–547.

Bowman, C. (2005). Yen block or Koala block? Currency relationships after the East Asian crisis. *Japan and the World Economy*, 17(1), 83–96.

Chow, H. K. and Kim, Y. (2003). A common currency peg in East Asia? Perspectives from Western Europe. *Journal of Macroeconomics*, 25(3), 331–350.

Chow, H. K., Kim, Y. and Sun, W. (2007). Characterizing exchange rate policy in East Asia: a reconsideration. *Journal of Asian Economics*, 18(3), 448–465.

Dooley, M., Folkerts-Landau, D. and Garber, P. (2004). The revived Bretton Woods system: the effects of periphery intervention and reserve. NBER Working Paper No. 10332, National Bureau of Economic Research.

Dutta, M. (2000). The euro revolution and the European Union: monetary and economic cooperation in the Asia-Pacific region. *Journal of Asian Economics*, 11(1), 65–88.

Eichengreen, B. (2004). Global imbalances and the lessons from Bretton Woods. NBER Working Paper No. 10497, National Bureau of Economic Research, May.

Eichengreen, B. and Bayoumi, T. (1996). Is Asia an optimum currency area? Can it become one? Regional, global and historical perspectives on Asian monetary relations. Center for International and Development Economics Research (CIDER) Working Paper No. C96-081.

Eichengreen, B. and Bayoumi, T. (1999). Is Asia an optimum currency area? Can it become one? Regional, global and historical perspectives on Asian monetary relations. In: S. Collignon, J. Pisani-Ferry and Y. C. Park (Eds.), *Exchange Rate Policies in Emerging Asian Countries*. London: Routledge.

Eichengreen, B., Rhee, Y. and Tong, H. (2004). The impact of China on the exports of other Asian countries. Working Paper No. 10768, National Bureau of Economic Research.

Engel, C. (2009). Exchange rate policies. Staff Paper No. 8, Federal Reserve Bank of Dallas, November.

Engelmann, D., Hanousek, J. and Kocenda, E. (2008). Currencies, competition and clans. *Journal of Policy Modeling*, 30(6), 1115–1132.

Engle, R. F. and Kroner, K. (1995). Multivariate simultaneous generalized ARCH. *Econometric Theory*, 11, 122–150.

Esaka, T. (2009). Exchange rate regimes, capital controls, and currency crises: does the bipolar view hold? *Journal of International Financial Markets, Institutions & Money*, 20(1), 91–108.

Fischer, S. (2001). Exchange rate regimes: is the bipolar view correct? Paper prepared for the 2001 American Economic Association meetings, Washington, D.C.: International Monetary Fund.

Forssbæck, J. and Oxelheim, L. (2003). *Money Markets and Politics: A Study of European Financial Integration and Monetary Policy Options.* Cheltenham: Edward Elgar.

Forssbæck, J. and Oxelheim, L. (2006). On the link between exchange-rate regimes, capital controls, and monetary policy autonomy in small European countries, 1979–2000. *World Economy*, 29(3), 341–368.

Forssbæck, J. and Oxelheim, L. (2007). The transition to market-based monetary policy: what can China learn from the European experience? *Journal of Asian Economics*, 18(2), 257–283.

Frankel, J. A. (1999). No single currency regime is right for all countries or at all times. *Princeton Essays in International Finance* 215. Princeton, NJ: Princeton University Press.

Frankel, J. A. and Rose, A. K. (1996). Currency crashes in emerging markets: an empirical treatment. *Journal of International Economics*, 41(3–4), 351–366.

Frankel, J. A. and Wei, S. (1994). Yen block or dollar block? Exchange rate policies of the East Asian economies. In: T. Ito and A. O. Krueger (Eds.), *Macroeconomic Linkages: Savings, Exchange Rates and Capital Flows.* Chicago: University of Chicago Press.

Froot, A. K. and Ramadorai, T. (2005). Currency returns, intrinsic value and institutional investor flows. *Journal of Finance*, 60(3), 1535–1566.

Gannon, G. (1996). First and second order inefficiency in Australasian currency markets. *Pacific-Basin Finance Journal*, 4(2–3), 315–327.

Glick, R. and Hutchison, M. M. (1990). Financial liberalization in the Pacific Basin: implications for real interest rate linkage. *Journal of the Japanese and International Economies*, 4(1), 36–48.

Guillermo, A. C. and Mishkin, F. (2003). The mirage of exchange rate regimes for emerging market countries. *Journal of Economic Perspectives*, 17(4), 99–118.

Hernandez, L. and Montiel, P. (2003). Post-crisis exchange rate policy in five Asian countries: filling in the hollow middle? *Journal of the Japanese and International Economies*, 17(3), 336–369.

Hoglund, R. and Ostermark, R. (2003). Size and power of some cointegration tests under structural breaks and heteroskedastic noise. *Statistical Papers*, 44(1), 1–22.

Huang, Y. and Guo, F. (2006). Is currency union a feasible option in East Asia? A multivariate structural VAR approach. *Research in International Business and Finance*, 20(1), 77–94.

Huang, Y. and Guo, F. (2007). Effects of East Asian financial integration: is there a Japanese dominance? *Review of Pacific Basin Financial Markets and Policies*, 20(2), 193–214.

Ito, T., Ogawa, E. and Sasaki, Y. (1998). How did the dollar peg fail in Asia? *Journal of the Japanese and International Economies*, 12(4), 256–304.

Jeon, B. N. and Zhang, H. (2007). A currency union or an exchange rate union: evidence from North East Asia. *Journal of Economic Integration*, 22(2), 256–287.

Johansen, S. (1988). Statistical analysis of cointegrating vectors. *Journal of Economic Dynamics and Control*, 12(2–3), 231–254.

Johansen, S. and Juselius, K. (1990). Maximum likelihood estimation and inference on cointegration — with applications to the demand for money. *Oxford Bulletin of Economics and Statistics*, 52(2), 169–210.

Johnson, H. G. and Swoboda, A. G. (Eds.) (1973). *Economics of Common Currencies*. Cambridge, MA: Harvard University Press.

Kamada, K. and Takagawa, I. (2005). Policy coordination in East Asia and across the Pacific. *International Economics and Economic Policy*, 2(4), 275–306.

Kawai, M. (2002). Exchange rate arrangements in East Asia: lessons from the 1997–1998 currency crisis. *Bank of Japan Monetary and Economic Studies*, 20(1), 167–214.

Kawai, M. (2008). Toward a regional exchange rate regime in East Asia. *Pacific Economic Review*, 13(1), 83–103.

Kearney, C. and Muckley, C. (2007). Is there a yen block emerging in North and Southeast Asia? *International Journal of Finance and Economics*, 12(3), 337–351.

Kwan, C. H. (2001). *Yen Block: Toward Economic Integration in Asia*. Washington, D.C.: Brookings Institution Press.

Lee, T. H. and Tse, Y. (1996). Cointegration tests with conditional heteroskedasticity. *Journal of Econometrics*, 73(2), 401–410.

Ling, H. Y. P. (2001). Optimum currency area in East Asia: a structural VAR approach. *ASEAN Economic Bulletin*, 18(2).

MacKinnon, J. G. (1991). Critical values for cointegration tests. In: R. F. Engle and C. W. J. Granger (Eds.), *Modeling Long-Run Economic Relationships*. Oxford: Oxford University Press.

McCauley, R., Fung, S. and Gadanecz, B. (2002). Integrating the finances of East Asia. *BIS Quarterly Review*, December, 83–96.

McKinnon, R. I. (1963). Optimum currency areas. *American Economic Review*, 53, 717–725.

McKinnon, R. I. (2000). The East Asian dollar standard, life after death. World Bank Workshop on Rethinking the Easy Asian Miracle. *Economic Notes* 29, No. 1.

McKinnon, R. I. (2007). Why China should keep its dollar peg. *International Finance*, 10(1), 43–70.

McKinnon, R. I. and Schnabl, G. (2003). Synchronised business cycles in East Asia and fluctuations in the yen-dollar exchange rate. *The World Economy*, 26(8), 1067–1089.

McKinnon, R. I. and Schnabl, G. (2004). The return to soft dollar pegging in East Asia: mitigating conflicted virtue. *International Finance*, 7(2), 169–201.

Moshirian, F. (2009). Can an Asian-Pacific community, similar to the European community, emerge? *Journal of Banking and Finance*, 33(1), 2–8.

Mundell, R. (1961). A theory of optimum currency areas. *American Economic Review*, 51, 657–665.

Mundell, R. (2003). Prospects for an Asian currency area. *Journal of Asian Economics*, 14(1), 1–10.

Obstfeld, M. and Rogoff, K. (2005). Global current account imbalances and exchange rate adjustments. *Brookings Papers on Economic Activity*, 36(1), 67–146.

Ogawa, E. and Ito, T. (2002). On the desirability of a regional basket currency arrangement. *Journal of the Japanese and International Economies*, 16(3), 317–334.

Osterwald-Lenum, M. (1992). A note with quantiles of the asymptotic distribution of the maximum likelihood cointegration rank test statistics. *Oxford Bulletin of Economics and Statistics*, 54(3), 461–471.

Pan, M. S., Liu, Y. A. and Roth, H. J. (1999). Common stochastic trends and volatility in Asian-Pacific equity markets. *Global Finance Journal*, 10(2), 161–172.

Park, Y. C. and Bae, K. H. (2002). Financial liberalization and economic integration in East Asia. Paper presented to PECC Finance Forum Conference on "Issues and Prospects for Regional Cooperation for Financial Stability and Development," Honolulu, 11–13 August.

Phylaktis, K. (1999). Capital market integration in the Pacific Basin Region: an impulse response analysis. *Journal of International Money and Finance*, 18(2), 267–287.

Rana, P. B. (2006). Economic integration in East Asia: trends, prospects, and a possible roadmap. Working Paper Series on Regional Economic Integration No. 2. Manila: Asian Development Bank.

Richards, A. J. (1995). Co-movements in national stock market returns: evidence of predictability, but not cointegration. *Journal of Monetary Economics*, 36(3), 631–654.

Shirono, K. (2008). Real effects of common currencies in East Asia. *Journal of Asian Economics*, 19(3), 199–212.

Silvapulle, P. and Podivinsky, J. M. (2000). The effect of non-normal disturbances and conditional heteroskedasticity on multiple cointegration and restriction tests. *Journal of Statistical Computation and Simulation*, 65(2), 173–189.

Tse, Y. K. and Ng, L. K. (1997). The cointegration of Asian currencies revisited. *Japan and the World Economy*, 9(1), 109–114.

Urata, S. (2001). Emergence of an FDI-trade nexus and economic growth in East Asia. In: J. Stiglitz and S. Yusuf (Eds.), *Rethinking the East Asian Miracle*. Washington, D.C.: World Bank and Oxford University Press.

Volz, U. (2010). *Prospects for Monetary Cooperation and Integration in East Asia.* Cambridge, MA: MIT Press.

Williamson, J. (2005). A currency basket for East Asia, not just China: policy briefs in international economics. No. PB05–1, Institute for International Economics.

Wilson, P. and Choy, K. M. (2007). Prospects for enhanced exchange rate cooperation in East Asia: some preliminary findings from generalized PPP theory. *Applied Economics*, 39(8), 981–995.

Wyplosz, C. (2001). A monetary union in Asia? Some European lessons. In: D. Gruen and J. Simon (Eds.), *Future Directions for Monetary Policies in East Asia.* Sydney: Reserve Bank of Australia.

Chapter 7

The Rise of China in a Tri-polar World: Can Corruption Co-exist with Economic Growth?

Andrew Delios and Roberto Galang

7.1 Introduction

Since returning to the world economy in the late 1970s, China's economy has gone through multiple transformations. The latest transformation is perhaps the most challenging and most important: to define China's future role in the world economy, particularly *vis-à-vis* other major world regions such as the United States and the European Union.

The importance stems not only from the magnitude of the transition-related challenges facing China's political economy, but it also is a consequence of the shifts in the worldwide balance of economic activity, trade and investment from the US, Europe and Japan, to include China, perhaps at the expense of Japan. This shift currently being faced by the world's major economies has catalyzed the changes that needed to be experienced in China's economic base.

China's importance stems from its well-heralded economic growth over the past 30 years — China has a growing global economic relevance that has become more apparent. Though the country suffered from a brief slowdown brought about by the global recession of 2008, the large stimulus package instituted by the Chinese government allowed the country to rebound economically by the end of 2009. By 2010, the Chinese economy had expanded by 10.3%, accelerating from the 9.2% expansion experienced in the prior year, despite the fact that many parts of the developed world still remained stuck in the economic doldrums. That same year, the country overtook Japan to become the world's second-largest economy.

Accordingly, many analysts and policymakers still see China as a strong market for domestic and foreign investment. The potential for continued GDP growth, the base population of 1.3 billion people and the consequent large market size continue to make China the most promising market among all the world's emerging economies.

There is truth in the above statements, but also limitations as evident in trends witnessed in 2009 and 2010 in Guangdong province. The southern province of Guangdong, which has long enjoyed its favorable geographic position of being adjacent to Hong Kong, saw foreign companies contribute nearly 60% of its output in 2008. Clearly foreign investment is important to this province, but what have foreign investors been doing in the last two years of the 2000s? The answer is divesting, not investing.

China, as a whole, has been experiencing declining foreign direct investment (FDI) inflows since late 2008. Year-on-year, FDI was down 37% in January 2009, 16% in February 2009, and nearly 10% in March 2009. Although FDI had rebounded back to 17.4% to a record-breaking US$105.7 billion in 2010, it remains uncertain whether this trend will continue into the future. More importantly, provinces like Guangdong have been experiencing divestment. In 2008, 4,000 Chinese toy companies closed shop. Toy exporting businesses owned by foreign firms, including those owned by Hong Kong businesspeople, have been closing or going bankrupt because of financial problems or severe order reductions. As a consequence, the number of toy exporting businesses in Guangdong stood at 1,404 companies, with over 3,500 companies having withdrawn from the export market.

These numbers do not lie. China is undergoing a transformation. The Chinese economy is in the process of moving from being the world's manufacturing base, to becoming a more integrated economy with a wider variety of value-added functions. These changes are occurring because China's cost-based advantages are being eroded through economic growth — just as had happened in other economies in the region such as South Korea, Singapore, Taiwan and Hong Kong.

This shift from being a manufacturing and export-oriented economy to a more integrated one is well-recognized by policymakers in China. As reported by Xinhua (2009), Guangdong's vice governor, Wan Qingliang, stated: "More efforts will be paid to enhance capital inflow from developed countries and regions, especially those from top-500 multinational companies in the world, to build regional headquarters, research and development centers, purchasing centers and training bases in Guangdong." Meanwhile, at the national level, according to President Hu Jintao, China has been aiming to build a harmonious society of a new scientific development mode, which means the government has been giving more attention to environmental issues for the purpose of sustainable development.

These are laudable and necessary goals for China's FDI. But are they achievable? Or, put another way, what does China need to do to meet these new goals? Meeting these goals will also mean that China has effectively climbed into the ranks of developed economies, and that it can more effectively be a full economic player in a tri-polar world comprising the US, the European Union and China. Yet, assuming this position means that further developments need to be made to make China an equal and equitable ground for foreign and local companies alike. Moreover, the development that is required is in China's infrastructure — physical, fiscal and regulatory — so that the current set of low value-added manufacturing activities that populate China's economic landscape can be extended to activities of greater sophistication and higher value-added.

Although China's physical and fiscal infrastructure has seen a tremendous upgrading in step with its economic transformation, its regulatory infrastructure remains problematic. In many parts of the country, government corruption remains rampant, political decision-making opaque and private property protection uneven. Numerous studies have consistently demonstrated how a weak institutional environment promotes unnecessary costs and uncertainty to the private sector, lowering investment rates and retarding economic development (e.g., Knack and Keefer, 1995; Mauro, 1995); yet, the miraculous economic performance of China over the past 30 years has turned this conventional wisdom on its head. As the production processes of its firms increase in complexity in the coming years, it remains to be seen whether the Chinese governing institutions can continue to exist in their present condition without fatally undermining the nation's economic potential and its attempts to become the third economic pole, alongside the United States and the countries of the European Union.

This chapter investigates the question as to whether China can continue its impressive economic performance given the deficiencies in its regulatory infrastructure and the continued presence of significant levels of government corruption. The rest of the chapter will be outlined as follows. Section 7.2 describes the changes in manufacturing and related economic activities in China since the turn of the millennium. In Section 7.3, we discuss the current situation pertaining to China's physical, fiscal and regulatory infrastructure. Section 7.4 presents a summary of previous research detailing the relationship between government corruption and investment, particularly how it pertains to the Chinese experience. In Section 7.5, we continue with a comparative empirical analysis on the level of corruption in China and its regions. Finally, Section 7.6 provides concluding remarks on the implications of the government corruption trends in China on its potential rise as the third global economic pole.

7.2 Manufacturing in China in the Late 2000s

What activities were foreign companies conducting in China in the late 2000s? Foreign companies, similar to domestic companies, have been concentrated on manufacturing. This statement does not mean that services, distribution, research and development, and finance and banking activities are absent from the Chinese economy. It means that China has a higher proportion of assembly, basic manufacturing and exporting activities in its economy than most other economies worldwide.

With the heavy levels of domestic and foreign investment in manufacturing, vast integrated production networks have been developed in China in the past 15 to 20 years. The result is an efficient and low-cost base for manufacturing, as has been well-recognized by the media, by businesspeople, and by policymakers and academics alike.

Yet this set of activities represents just a subset of the productive activities required to produce any product, be it an automobile, an air conditioner, a computer or a television. As shown in Figure 7.1, a variety of activities go into the development, manufacture and sale of any product. Products need to be researched, designed and engineered. The manufacturing is often distributed in a series of discrete stages. The sale of a product is undertaken through a local market initiative in branding and distribution. The core functions of research, design and engineering, alongside local market sales and distribution, are the high value-added activities. Distributed manufacturing tends to be low-margin and low value-added. The distributed manufacturing of multinational firms has been transferred to China in large volumes of FDI. The high value-added activities,

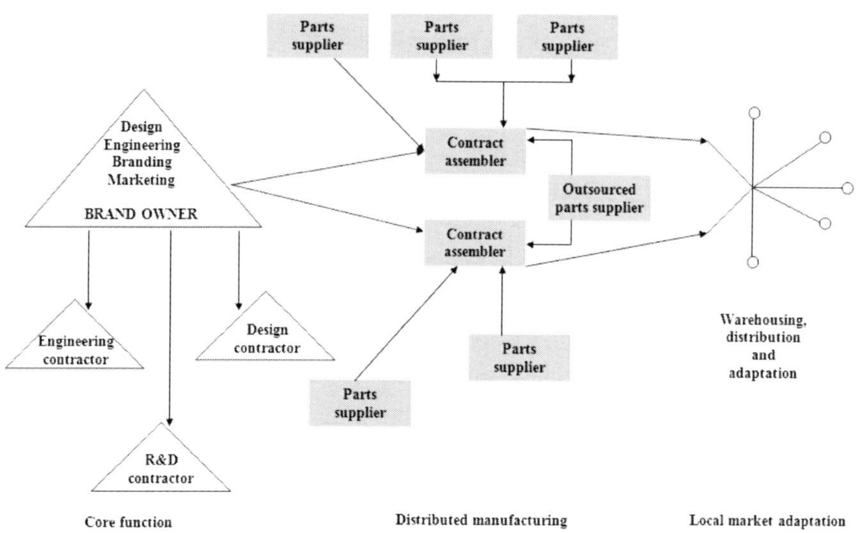

Figure 7.1: A multinational firm's operations.

Source: Peter Buckley (2007). Keynote speech — Lessons from Japanese MNEs? Cross-Cultural Management Practices in East Asia Conference. Leeds, United Kingdom.

particularly at the core function stage, have yet to move to China (see Figure 7.1).

The shift of distributed manufacturing activities to China is a success story on one front, but it also represents a challenge to China on another front. This challenge extends from external environment changes that have created new incentives for foreign subsidiary establishment in China in the later part of this decade.

The changes in the external environment primarily relate to substantial escalations in costs for skilled labor, for land, for property and for other factors of production. Coupled with a rise in the value of the RMB, especially relative to other major Asian currencies not pegged to the US dollar, these escalations in costs have eroded the magnitude of China's cost advantages and altered the feasibility of the types of subsidiaries that can operate profitably in China. As if these changes were not enough, in early 2008, China's new labor contract law took effect. The institution of this law substantially increased the cost of manufacturing in China. This process of factor price escalation has also been exacerbated by the emergence of strong domestic competitors that have increased competitive pressures, and decreased margins, for multinationals focusing on domestic market sales in China.

These characteristics of the external environment influence the comparative advantage of the value-added activities of a foreign subsidiary. A subsidiary performs an activity, or activities, that augments the value of the products and services produced by a multinational firm, and heightens a multinational firm's competitiveness.

A subsidiary can fulfill this role in a multinational firm by conducting a single activity, such as manufacturing, or a full range of value-added activities — research and product design, input sourcing, manufacturing, distribution and marketing. The types of value-added activities a subsidiary performs can be called its role in the multinational firm, or more formally, we can call a subsidiary's set of activities its charter (see Birkinshaw and Hood, 1998). A subsidiary's charter captures the products it produces, the technology it houses, the markets it serves and the functional areas included in its operations.

The consequence of environmental change in China has been a change in subsidiary charters. Subsidiaries with a manufacturing, cost-center charter have been moved inland, but these subsidiaries have also been moved outside of China, to other economies such as Vietnam or Bangladesh. If a subsidiary's core activity has been relocated to another subsidiary inside or outside of China, the subsidiary must either secure a new charter, which can be done if the external environment in China is suited to conducting high value-added activities, or else the subsidiary will be closed.

7.3 Physical, Fiscal and Regulatory Infrastructure

Foreign investors locate subsidiaries in economies that can either support sales or support production activities. If increasing sales is a goal, a foreign investor looks to market size, market growth and to other similar measures of market attractiveness.

If, on the other hand, becoming more efficient and competitive in production is a goal, investors seek a competitive operating environment, where costs are low, where the domestic physical infrastructure is well-developed and where the fiscal infrastructure is favorable for investment, as typified by a regime of low costs, transparent taxes and tariffs.

Yet, as far as higher value-added activities are concerned, foreign investors seek a strong regulatory infrastructure. This regulatory infrastructure facilitates the negotiation and security of contracts by establishing transparency, fairness and independence in the courts of law in a country. The regulatory infrastructure helps to mitigate risks of the unwanted dissemination of outright theft of intellectual property. Its infrastructure also helps to reduce concerns about uncertainty in the policies in the regulatory environment, such laws defining the extent and types of taxes and tariffs faced by domestic and foreign companies. Essentially, the strength of the regulatory infrastructure can be determined by identifying the policy-making process in national and provincial governments, the extent of transparency in government and competitive regulations, the degree of intellectual property protection, the rule of law, and the degree of equity in competitive environments between foreign and domestic companies.

Physical and Fiscal Infrastructure

With regard to the physical and fiscal infrastructures, China has made tremendous strides since opening up its economy 30 years ago. Since the early 1980s, China has placed a high priority on seeking investment from foreign companies. Investment from foreign companies has brought much needed employment to China, alongside a transfer of managerial skills and technology to state-owned enterprises and private firms in China. Furthermore, the 2008 Beijing Olympics and 2010 Shanghai EXPO triggered a new round of infrastructure improvement campaigns. As a result, these two cities and the areas adjacent to these cities have state-of-the-art, world-class facilities and physical infrastructure.

The strong flow of FDI to China was not an accident or a simple consequence of the large market size and the strong growth of the economy. Policymakers took deliberate action to heighten the attractiveness of China through clear and rapid improvements in physical and fiscal infrastructure.

The steps taken to date to facilitate foreign investment in China mostly relate to reducing the difficulty of manufacturing in China. These steps led to substantial improvements in the transportation, financing and communications infrastructure, as well as the development of economic zones that provided tax- and tariff-based cost concessions to foreign investors. Since China's ascension to the WTO in 2001, there has been an additional round of country-wide improvements in the fiscal infrastructure via the reduction of tariffs, equal tax treatments, and the continued opening of new sectors to foreign competition. For example, in the late 2000s, policymakers in China introduced a new corporate income tax. Before 1 January 2008, domestic firms faced a corporate tax rate of 33% and foreign-invested firms were taxed at 15%–24%. After 1 January 2008, domestic and foreign firms faced a unified tax rate of 25%.

These changes are in line with how policymakers developed the fiscal and physical infrastructure in China in their creation of four distinct regimes of FDI in China. The early regime, 1979–1983, began with the establishment of the Joint Venture Law in 1979 and the creation of four Special Economic Zones in 1980. The next regime, 1984–1991, saw 14 coastal cities and the island of Hainan opened to FDI, with foreign investment further encouraged by the passing of the Law on Wholly Foreign-Owned Enterprises in 1986.

The third regime, 1992–1994, was the one in which FDI into China escalated most dramatically. During this regime, the local municipal governments increased incentives for FDI, and new industries such as finance, real estate, tourism, shipping and wholesale and retailing were opened to FDI. From 1995 to the present, we have seen increased competition for FDI arise from other countries in Asia, South America, and the transition economies of Eastern Europe. The State Council in China has continued to refine its definitions of which sectors can receive investment, while re-imposing duties on imported machinery, equipment parts and other materials used in foreign-invested joint ventures, but it has avoided making substantial changes in the regulatory infrastructure.

Regulatory Infrastructure

Without substantial changes in the institutions for investment, the results for the post-1995 regime of FDI have been lackluster. The policy steps taken in the prior three regimes have provided part, but not all, of what needs to be done to attract and retain FDI. Improvements in the fiscal infrastructure, for example, reduce costs so that the baseline for achieving profitable operations is lower. But fiscal incentives stemming from government policies only camouflage systemic problems and can easily be revoked given the lack of constraints on policymakers in China. Physical infrastructure improvements do not provide an advantage that is translatable to the bottom line on a comparative basis across nations. Instead, physical infrastructure improvements have ameliorated the disadvantages of operating a subsidiary in China, such that China's physical infrastructure in the eastern provinces is on par with other locations worldwide.

Foreign investors looking to establish high value-added activities in China necessarily look beyond these improvements in the fiscal and physical infrastructure, for signs that substantive steps, not increased rhetoric, are being taken to enhance China's regulatory infrastructure. Fundamental institutional change would be one of these signs.

In the case where there has been change, it has not always benefited foreign firms. For example, on 30 August 2008, China's National People's Congress passed an anti-monopoly law, which is largely modeled on US and European Union antitrust legislation, though the Chinese version uses a less sophisticated method to determine market dominance. Under the law, competition between and among local or overseas companies has faced an increased level of scrutiny by the Chinese government. The Coca-Cola–Huiyuan case was the first case in which this law affected competitive action, as this new law was used to block Coca-Cola's bid to acquire a domestic company in China, namely Huiyuan.

Even with changes such as these, the institutions in China for governing competition are yet to be well-established. Efforts by the Communist Party of China to demonstrate a stronger resolution to fight against corruption are one positive sign. Yet, observers remain highly concerned about the extent of intellectual property protection, stating that despite the Chinese government's efforts to implement legal reforms in accordance with the WTO Agreement on Trade-Related Aspects of Intellectual Property Rights (TRIPS Agreement), enforcement remains a serious problem.

This problem is not just manifest in the eyes of foreign firms. Domestic consumers in China are well aware of the problems with intellectual property protection in China. China's most savvy new consumers have documented this copycat phenomenon in the new lexicon. Chinese netizens describe the current copycat situation in China as ShanZhai. This word, ShanZhai, literally means "mountain stronghold". However, the word is currently widely used as a noun, adjective or verb to mean or indicate a cloned product. There is a line of "ShanZhai" products ranging from cell phones, TVs to laptop computers. ShanZhai products are not, strictly speaking, knock-offs of branded goods, as they do not use branded names. But they are still essentially copies.

In this sense, the comparatively, even if impressive, easy part of external environmental transition has been instituted. Numerous sectors have been opened to competition, the government officials in China have worked tirelessly to correct infrastructure deficiencies and they have offered fiscal incentives to attract FDI. But these changes merely bring the country up to speed. With increased cost pressures and fewer cost advantages faced in the East, mid-South and North provinces, manufacturing-oriented FDI is exiting to move either inland or overseas. To continue to retain FDI and secure the positioning of high value-added activities in China, more difficult changes need to be made. Institutions need to be developed, the policy environment needs to be made more transparent, and formal and informal rules of competition need to promote a greater level of equity between domestic and foreign firms.

These ideas on the needed changes in China's economy not only reflect normative assumptions about economic development and growth, they are also embedded in a deep academic literature on growth, investment and stability and transparency in the policy environment. Furthermore, these ideas are grounded in data that clearly demonstrate China's laggard position along these dimensions. We turn to each of these two points in the next two sections of this chapter.

7.4 Investment and Corruption

The traditionally held assumption in the social sciences is that governments enact public policies to protect the public, to correct inequitable market practices, and to maximize social welfare. However, the presence of numerous government regulations that were shown to enrich protected and privileged sectors, rather than uphold the common good, led authors to question the validity of this basic assumption (Jordan, 1972; Stigler, 1971). In the worst cases, to enrich themselves and other well-connected individuals, politicians intentionally use the powers of the state to coerce and to tax.

Despite decades of theorization on regulatory capture, studies focusing on corruption, or specifically the sale of government property by government officials for personal gain, were not widely studied in the literature until the mid- to late-1990s (Shleifer and Vishny, 1993). Although some have argued that minimal corruption may help economies grow by facilitating transactions hampered by bureaucratic delay or encouraging corrupt officials to work harder, the great majority of scholars argue that government corruption hampers overall economic development (Klitgaard, 1991; Rose-Ackerman, 1978). Corruption, by diverting subsidies and reducing tax revenues, undermines the ability of governments to enforce their own policies, leading to less equitable income distributions and greater political instability. Thus, the presence of high government corruption is generally both a manifestation and a cause of a weak institutional environment, where the inability of the state to enforce its own laws increases transaction costs among parties, lowers investment rates and diminishes market formation.

In and of itself, corruption — through the amount of money demanded by the multitude forms of government bribery, extortion and other forms of corruption — provides additional costs to investors and consumers, mimicking the imposition of significant government taxes. On top of this, the illegality and secrecy of corruption promotes much unpredictability and greater distortion than an equivalent tax rate increase (Fisman and Svensson, 2007; Shleifer and Vishny, 1993). Thus, numerous studies have shown that the level of theft of public assets in a country lowers economic growth rates by increasing risks and uncertainty and deterring foreign investment (Knack and Keefer, 1995; Mauro, 1995). The significant impact of poor government regulation as a deterrent to economic development has been postulated as the key reason as to why many developing countries are unable to take advantage of the relatively higher returns to capital investments in their areas and converge in income with their developed country counterparts.

These negative economy-level relationships are similarly reflected in the results when verifying the impact of corruption broadly at the firm-level. The government's inability to provide the rule of law or property protection encourages oligarchic control (Fogel, 2006), slows down technology absorption (Henisz and Macher, 2004), leads to lower stock market valuations (Miller *et al.*, 2008) and diminishes firm shareholder value (Weitzel and Berns, 2006). Although corruption diminishes firm value at the macro level, certain firms — particularly firms possessing political resources that provide them with leverage against government officials, such as revenues (Schuler, Rehbein and Cramer, 2002), investment projects (Delios and Henisz, 2003; Vaaler, 2008) and linkages with politicians (Siegel, 2007) — benefit greatly from government corruption.

Despite the common thread in the theoretical and empirical results supporting the negative relationship between economic development and corruption, the unprecedented economic development of China over the past three decades and its position at the top of global foreign direct investment rankings somewhat leads many to question the veracity of these supposed statistical relationships. For example, the impressive economic performance not just of China, but of other Asian countries such as South Korea and Taiwan, over the past 25 years has occurred despite the presence of significant levels of corruption in these countries. Moreover, if corruption is so detrimental to commerce and national development in many countries, why does the population at large tolerate its presence?

One optimistic explanation is that the high levels of government corruption could merely be a transitory phase in China's road to economic development. Economic growth and foreign investments could actually lead to increased corruption in the medium term, as increases in the level of economic transactions present greater opportunities for making money off corruption. The entry of foreigners could also promote greater awareness of the negative impact of corruption, hence leading to higher corruption perception ratings (Robertson and Watson, 2004). Over time, as the economy develops, a growing Chinese middle-class will seek greater political participation and accountability from their government, leading to the decrease in government corruption. This has been the developmental story of wealthier Asian countries like Taiwan and South Korea, as well as of those in the West, where corruption levels decreased as their citizens became better off. However, this sanguine prediction — which generally includes the democratization of the People's Republic — has yet to indicate any green shoots.

As such, experts have sought alternative explanations for the Chinese corruption and economic development conundrum. Another possible answer that comes to mind is that China possesses unique characteristics that implore foreign investors to avoid the country at their own peril. First and foremost is the fact that it contains the largest population in the world, a mind-boggling domestic market of 1.3 billion potential consumers. It also possesses a separate, well-governed financial center in Hong Kong that allows firms to alleviate some of the inherent political risks (Wei and Shleifer, 2000).

At the same time, Chinese corruption may merely be an offshoot — albeit a negative one — of a successful state-led industrial policy where constant government intervention in the economy has helped nurture domestic firm capabilities in consumer electronics and other advanced areas that would most likely not have developed in their absence. Such interventionist industrial policies, which utilize regulations, financial resources and subsidies that are targeted to particular firms or industries, are generally associated with higher levels of corruption, as some subsidies tend to leak out to well-connected but undeserving private entities (Ades and Di Tella, 1997; Gerring and Thacker, 2005). However, in China's case, it could be argued that the fiscal leakage was more than made up for by the performance benefits of the policy, which has allowed China to end up with an export base that is significantly more sophisticated than what would normally be expected for a country at its level of development.

Chinese corruption may have even provided its firms with additional competitive advantages, at least in their present level of development. As stated earlier, the state's limited enforcement of intellectual property laws has permitted Chinese manufacturers to reverse engineer many goods from abroad and leapfrog over the tedious steps required for learning complex technological processes. Some well-connected firms have capitalized on opaque state decision-making to extract additional concessions from their foreign joint-venture counterparts.

Moreover, there is the possibility that Chinese corruption could be different from its developing country counterparts. Previous studies indicate that not all forms of corruption are equally insidious in their impact on economic development. Corruption has been characterized as having two dimensions: pervasiveness or the prevalence of bribery across all government transactions; and arbitrariness or the ambiguity of obtaining the agreed-upon special treatment upon payment of the bribe (Lee and Oh, 2007; Rodriguez, Uhlenbruck and Eden, 2005). These above-mentioned studies show that although the pervasiveness of corruption has a negative relationship to economic development, it is its arbitrariness that has the more detrimental effect on the economy. The strong authoritarian regimes prevalent in many of the Asian miracle countries promoted pervasive corruption that had less arbitrariness than their other developing country counterparts.

Finally, Chinese historical or cultural antecedents may explain the prevalence of corrupt practices that do not necessarily undermine the functioning of the market economy. One supposed argument is that Chinese *guanxi*, or its cultural predilection to facilitate economic transactions through informal social networks, generates interpersonal trust-based relationships among corrupt officials and private citizens that allow illicit payments to be made through more clandestine avenues, but at the same time ensures the delivery of services promised to the bribe-payer (Li and Wu, 2007). In this case, corruption becomes endemic as a culturally accepted practice without much of its negative repercussions, making corruption more difficult to catch and eliminate. Nonetheless, research still argues that corruption can be overcome, recommending certain political approaches such as the commitment of the top leadership and the use of a single, centralized and independent government body, as effective mechanisms to minimizing corruption (Svensson, 2003).

But with a government as massive, powerful and successful as China's, it is difficult to imagine the government being able to find a mechanism or even the willingness to eliminate corruption effectively. Lowering government corruption has proven to be a difficult political task in many countries, as the passage of numerous laws and the creation of corruption-fighting bodies have done little to dent the extent of corruption. As such, the status quo of a corrupt yet economically dynamic China will probably remain in effect for the coming years.

What potential effect could a large, new hegemonic international force that remains a corrupt, developing nation have on the rest of the globe? With deepening economic globalization, national governments are likely to act in concert, leading to regulatory outcomes that become less the sole function of domestic political conditions but instead assimilate much of the regulatory actions conducted in other nations (Schneiberg and Bartley, 2008; Simmons and Elkins, 2004). In many instances, multinational firms, which traditionally have come from developed nations, act as conduits for the propagation of Western global standards and lead to lower incidences of government corruption.

However, the rise of multinational firms from countries where state governance is not as clean may muddle the adoption of anti-corruption measures across the world. The fact is that corruption provides mechanisms through which companies are able to utilize their experiences in dealing with government corruption to their advantage as they expand abroad. Studies indicate how multinational firms from corrupt countries are able to exploit their experiences in accommodating illicit practices at home and successfully enter markets with similarly corrupt institutions, unencumbered by anti-bribery conventions signed by their home governments (Cuervo-Cazurra and Genc, 2008). Thus, we could see a reversal of anti-corruption measures with the increase of successful developing country multinationals.

Already, much has been said about the alleged corrosive effects on global anti-corruption activities by the sudden entry of Chinese investments and multinationals into Middle Eastern, Central Asian and sub-Saharan African countries, particularly those countries run by corrupt governments facing international economic sanctions. With the Chinese government outwardly declaring having no desire to exert pressure on improving governance in these countries, Chinese firms are provided the additional benefit of being free to conduct their business without any home country limitations on their foreign activities. However, it must be noted that much of the Chinese outward investments are in mining, petroleum and other resource production industries that are more prone to violent and corrupt behavior (Kaplinsky, McCormick and Morris, 2006), making it difficult to disentangle whether the source of corruption is due to the institutional or industrial context of the investments.

7.5 Data on Different Dimensions of Corruption

These very points on the commitment of leadership and the use of a central body to address endemic corruption appear to be reflective of trends on corruption levels in China. There are two sets of data that are consistent with these points.

First, numerous agencies that develop measures of corruption of various sorts in national economies, point to a persistent and enduring high level of corruption in China, especially as compared to major economies in the European Union and to the United States. These trends can be found in Tables 7.1 and 7.2.

Table 7.1 depicts longitudinal trends in the corruption perception index as compiled by Transparency International. As can be seen in the table, as compared to most European and North American countries, and indeed many Asian countries, China lags in terms of control of corruption. Importantly, China's relative ranking and absolute score on the index has not changed in the 2000s. China's CPI rank in 2008 was 72nd worldwide, with a score of 3.2, again showing the lack of development as gauged by the corruption perception index.

These data are reinforced by the numbers depicted in Table 7.2, which are drawn from the Worldwide Governance Indicators database of various facets of the strength of a country's institutional environment. Once again, China shows a low ranking on the control of corruption measure, which is consistent (i.e., not improving over time), and leaves China at the same relative country rank for the second half of the 1990s and throughout the 2000s.

Second, the role of leadership commitment in China is evident in terms of the identification and prosecution of individual cases of corruption within China. These data are from the annual reports of Supreme People's Procuratorate of the People's Republic of China,

Table 7.1: Corruption perception index by selected country (2000–2005).

Rank	Country	2005	2004	2003	2002	2001	2000
1	Finland	9.6	9.7	9.7	9.7	9.9	10.0
2	Denmark	9.5	9.5	9.5	9.5	9.5	9.8
3	Singapore	9.4	9.3	9.4	9.3	9.2	9.1
4	Sweden	9.2	9.2	9.3	9.3	9.0	9.4
5	Austria	8.7	8.4	8.0	7.8	7.8	7.7
6	Netherlands	8.6	8.7	8.9	9.0	8.8	8.9
7	United Kingdom	8.6	8.6	8.7	8.7	8.3	8.7
8	Luxembourg	8.5	8.4	8.7	9.0	8.7	8.6
9	Hong Kong	8.3	8.0	8.0	8.2	7.9	7.7
10	Germany	8.2	8.2	7.7	7.3	7.4	7.6
11	USA	7.6	7.5	7.5	7.7	7.6	7.8
12	France	7.5	7.1	6.9	6.3	6.7	6.7
13	Belgium	7.4	7.5	7.6	7.1	6.6	6.1
14	Ireland	7.4	7.5	7.5	6.9	7.5	7.2
15	Japan	7.3	6.9	7.0	7.1	7.1	6.4
16	Spain	7.0	7.1	6.9	7.1	7.0	7.0
17	Malta	6.6	6.8				
18	Portugal	6.5	6.3	6.6	6.3	6.3	6.4
19	Estonia	6.4	6.0	5.5	5.6	5.6	5.7
20	Slovenia	6.1	6.0	5.9	6.0	5.2	5.5
21	Taiwan	5.9	5.6	5.7	5.6	5.9	5.5
22	Cyprus	5.7	5.4	6.1			
23	Malaysia	5.1	5.0	5.2	4.9	5.0	4.8
24	Hungary	5.0	4.8	4.8	4.9	5.3	5.2
25	Italy	5.0	4.8	5.3	5.2	5.5	4.6
26	South Korea	5.0	4.5	4.3	4.5	4.2	4.0
27	Lithuania	4.8	4.6	4.7	4.8	4.8	4.1
28	Czech Republic	4.3	4.2	3.9	3.7	3.9	4.3
29	Greece	4.3	4.3	4.3	4.2	4.2	4.9
30	Slovakia	4.3	4.0	3.7	3.7	3.7	3.5
31	Latvia	4.2	4.0	3.8	3.7	3.4	3.4
32	Bulgaria	4.0	4.1	3.9	4.0	3.9	3.5
33	Thailand	3.8	3.6	3.3	3.2	3.2	3.2
34	Poland	3.4	3.5	3.6	4.0	4.1	4.1
35	Laos	3.3					
36	China	3.2	3.4	3.4	3.5	3.5	3.1

(*Continued*)

Table 7.1: (*Continued*)

Rank	Country	2005	2004	2003	2002	2001	2000
37	Romania	3.0	2.9	2.8	2.6	2.8	2.9
38	Vietnam	2.6	2.6	2.4	2.4	2.6	2.5
39	Philippines	2.5	2.6	2.5	2.6	2.9	2.8
40	Cambodia	2.3					
41	Indonesia	2.2	2.0	1.9	1.9	1.9	1.7
42	Myanmar	1.8	1.7	1.6			

Source: Transparency International.

and the Yearbook of China Prosecution. The Procuratorate began to make public the detailed data about the situation of civil servant corruption from 1988 onwards. In China, the Procuratorate investigated the corruption cases that involved civil servants, so the data in the following figures could specifically reflect the trend of civil servant corruption.

As can be seen in Figures 7.2–7.8, where we show data from the prosecution of corruption or captured incidences of corruption from 1988 to 2009, the trend has been towards year-on-year increases in captured incidences of corruption for most measures of corruption, with the most rapid spikes in incidence in the 1994–1997 period.

Figure 7.2 plots the trend of incidence of corruption, bribery, and embezzlement of public funds. Such crimes include cases where civil servants take advantage of their power to acquire state properties through illegal means, misappropriate public funds for personal use or illegal activities, or misappropriate large amounts of public funds without returning the money within three months. The figure captures the number of civil servants involved in these cases. Overall, there is a downward trend. Although it peaked at 81,110 and 77,231 in 1991 and 1997, respectively, the number of civil servants involved dropped to approximately 30,000 in 1998 and remained stable to 2008.

Figure 7.3 plots the trend of incidence of malfeasance from 1988 until 2009. Malfeasance occurs when civil servants abuse their power or neglect their duties, causing great losses to public property and the

Table 7.2: **Control of corruption by country, World Governance Indicators data (1996–2008).**

Rank	Country	2008	2007	2006	2005	2004	2003	2002	2000	1998	1996
1	Finland	100	100	100	100	100	100	100	100	100	100
2	Singapore	100	96	98	98	98	99	100	98	98	98
3	Denmark	99	99	99	99	99	98	98	97	98	100
4	Sweden	98	98	98	97	98	98	98	99	100	98
5	Netherlands	97	97	96	97	96	97	97	99	99	97
6	Luxembourg	95	97	96	93	95	93	97	95	95	94
7	Austria	94	94	95	96	97	95	94	93	93	95
8	Hong Kong	94	92	93	93	92	91	90	85	86	90
9	United Kingdom	93	94	94	95	94	96	95	97	97	96
10	Germany	93	93	93	94	94	94	94	94	96	95
11	Ireland	92	93	92	92	90	92	91	91	92	94
12	USA	92	92	89	92	93	93	93	93	93	92
13	France	91	89	92	91	91	91	86	91	92	87
14	Belgium	90	91	90	91	92	92	92	92	88	87
15	Japan	86	85	90	85	85	85	83	87	86	85
16	Spain	85	84	83	89	90	90	90	90	88	84
17	Portugal	83	83	83	84	87	87	87	86	87	91
18	Cyprus	83	78	78	74	78	83	82	81	81	92
20	Slovenia	80	81	83	81	83	81	81	80	84	84
21	Estonia	79	81	81	81	83	80	76	74	67	56
22	Taiwan	73	72	73	78	80	76	77	82	80	79
23	Hungary	72	72	72	72	75	74	74	77	76	77

(Continued)

Table 7.2: (*Continued*)

Rank	Country	2008	2007	2006	2005	2004	2003	2002	2000	1998	1996
24	Brunei	71	64	64	63	68	63	66	65	67	69
25	South Korea	70	71	68	70	66	69	70	63	64	71
26	Slovakia	69	66	69	68	70	67	61	64	56	70
27	Poland	68	62	62	61	61	69	67	70	75	72
28	Czech Republic	67	65	67	68	67	70	68	64	69	76
29	Latvia	65	68	68	67	63	64	60	59	62	28
30	Malaysia	63	63	67	64	69	65	68	66	73	74
31	Lithuania	63	61	62	65	67	66	64	67	65	52
32	Italy	62	66	64	63	71	73	74	81	71	71
33	Greece	61	63	65	65	71	71	70	75	75	65
34	Romania	57	56	54	51	49	47	45	46	42	47
35	Bulgaria	52	55	58	60	60	56	56	53	47	24
36	Thailand	43	45	51	54	50	50	46	50	58	43
37	China	41	34	37	33	34	44	43	48	45	54
38	Indonesia	31	29	23	20	19	15	8	14	9	33
39	Philippines	26	22	21	34	32	37	36	36	41	45
40	Vietnam	25	29	23	24	23	33	32	27	29	32
41	Cambodia	9	7	7	9	13	17	17	18	12	8
42	Laos	6	11	11	11	12	13	20	19	28	7
43	Myanmar	1	1	0	0	0	3	3	4	4	6

Source: Transparency International.

Figure 7.2: Incidence of corruption, bribery, and embezzlement of public funds.

Source: Annual reports of Supreme People's Procuratorate of the People's Republic of China.

Figure 7.3: Incidence of malfeasance.

Source: Annual reports of Supreme People's Procuratorate of the People's Republic of China.

Figure 7.4: Incidence of corruption to the amount of 500,000 RMB or greater.

Source: Annual reports of Supreme People's Procuratorate of the People's Republic of China.

Figure 7.5: Incidence of corruption at the cadre level or above (for counties).

Source: Annual reports of Supreme People's Procuratorate of the People's Republic of China.

Figure 7.6: Incidence of corruption at the cadre level or above (for bureaus).
Source: Annual reports of Supreme People's Procuratorate of the People's Republic of China.

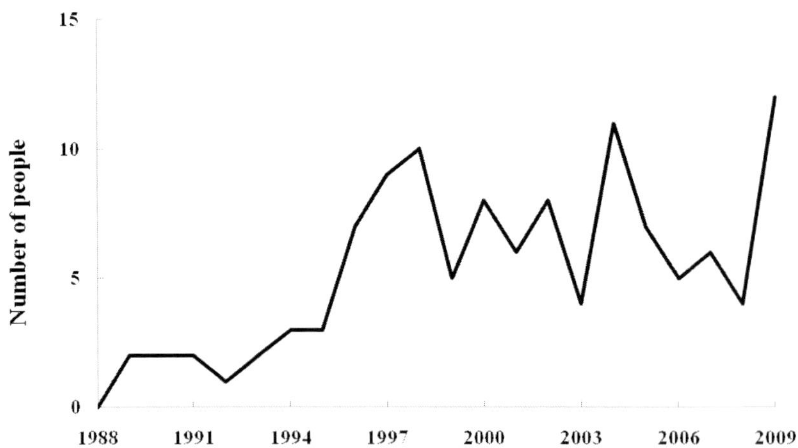

Figure 7.7: Incidence of corruption at the cadre level or above (for provinces).
Source: Annual reports of Supreme People's Procuratorate of the People's Republic of China.

state's and people's interests. Malfeasance is not included in corruption. However, because it involves civil servants, it was included in the Yearbook of China Prosecution, as it can be connected to corruption. The general trend is downward. There are two peaks

Figure 7.8: Recovery of proceeds of corruption crimes (in RMB).

Source: Annual reports of Supreme People's Procuratorate of the People's Republic of China.

in these figures in 1989 and 1997. In 1998, the incidence decreased to 10,000 and remained at that level in subsequent years.

Figure 7.4 shows the incidence of corruption to the amount of 500,000 RMB or greater. The vertical axis describes the number of corruption cases where the amount of money involved exceeded 500,000 RMB. The figure captures a clear increasing trend in the number of cases. It peaked at 19,600 and 19,647 in 1994 and 1997, respectively.

Figure 7.5 describes the general upward trend of incidence of corruption at the cadre level or above for counties. The figure captures the number of people who served as a county-level cadre or above, involved in corruption. The number rose sharply to 3,897 in 1997, from a rather low level at the beginning, and then experienced a considerable decrease. After that, there is an upward trend in the number of people prosecuted for this category of corruption.

Figure 7.6 plots the trend of the incidence of corruption at the cadre level or above for bureaus. The figure captures the number of people who served as a bureau-level cadre or above, involved in corruption. Although there are some small fluctuations after 1997, the overall trend is upward.

Figure 7.7 illustrates the trend of the incidence of corruption at the cadre level or above for provinces. The figure captures the number of people who served as a province-level cadre or above, who were involved in corruption. In the early period, the number was quite low. After 1992, there is an upward trend, but with considerable fluctuation from 1998 to 2009. However, the general trend is upward and it peaked in 2009.

Figure 7.8 describes the situation of the recovery of proceeds of corruption crimes during these periods. At the beginning of the data collection period, the amount was quite low. Then, in 1996, the amount sharply increased. Although it decreased somewhat during the subsequent years, compared with the 1980s, the sums increased considerably.

Across all of the figures, we can see increasing cases of corruption, as particularly captured in Figures 7.4–7.8, but decreasing cases in Figures 7.2 and 7.3. These trends reflect some issues. First, the figures reflect the general anti-corruption stance of leaders in China. Second, the number of people at the cadre level (counties, bureaus, and provinces) and amount of money involved in these cases increased over the years, and showed spikes in 1994–1997 with modest increases to consistent levels through the 2000s. This shows that with the advance of anti-corruption, prosecution became more likely, although we do not know if the absolute level of corruption (prosecuted and non-prosecuted) increased or decreased during this period. What we do know is that prosecutions in terms of numbers of people or dollar amounts remained consistent or grew through the late 1990s and early 2000s.

Interestingly, when we deconstruct these numbers by province (see Table 7.3), we find a similar set of annual trends across each province, suggesting that the prosecution of corruption is driven as much by policy as by rate of incidence. Provinces, or their equivalents such as Shanghai and Beijing, which are also leading economic regions showed fairly low levels of corruption, at least as compared to other provinces. Yet, this trend seems to be isolated to the two major metropolitan areas of Shanghai and Beijing. When we compare the corruption levels for five rich and five poor provinces, as in Figure 7.9,

Table 7.3: Cases of corruption, embezzlement and bribery in China (by province and by year).

	1989	1991	1992	1993	1994	1996	1997	1998	1999	2000	2001	2002	2003	2004	2005	2006
Anhui	2776	3447	2536	1556	2334	2666	3383	1124	1077	1961	1415	1082	1327	1023	1138	1052
Beijing	1090	1285	1083	676	614	836	1185	756	327	519	408	507	599	642	625	321
Chongqing	—	—	—	—	—	—	880	609	742	704	717	693	647	587	511	453
Fujian	1741	3196	1787	1050	1997	1989	2686	954	1064	1336	1264	1040	1092	1146	1099	1081
Gansu	70	96	108	127	476	310	655	596	255	158	151	146	142	173	178	183
Guangdong	1867	1982	1882	950	1505	2123	3030	1306	1286	1625	1595	1637	1298	1426	1697	1480
Guangxi	1172	2152	1610	951	888	1322	2095	1063	1061	1146	1244	1192	1161	1407	1262	1085
Guizhou	1699	3055	2593	1090	1499	2048	3122	945	901	1011	1013	1032	1040	1160	1079	1056
Hainan	317	380	413	177	240	277	239	201	209	250	229	216	189	206	184	177
Hebei	3012	4477	3455	2297	4096	5057	5784	1829	1460	1995	1447	2008	1685	3035	2048	1429
Heilongjiang	2651	5568	3776	2834	3612	3807	4490	1262	1144	2364	1230	1059	2027	1879	1212	1093
Henan	3172	3595	5053	1966	3831	4624	4481	1674	2601	3306	2084	2095	2925	1903	3070	2288
Hubei	3949	4630	4419	1077	2913	3207	2582	1101	1400	2034	1886	1978	1587	1343	1352	1257
Hunan	4725	5722	3973	1197	2455	3272	2513	1137	1017	1528	1101	1278	1082	1053	1048	1100
Neimengu	1041	1433	1271	593	1142	1039	1490	492	500	745	593	489	504	760	624	551
Jiangsu	3080	3253	3011	1778	2459	3323	4219	1474	1252	2522	1521	1341	2047	1812	1767	1456

(*Continued*)

Table 7.3: (*Continued*)

	1989	1991	1992	1993	1994	1996	1997	1998	1999	2000	2001	2002	2003	2004	2005	2006
Jiangxi	1625	2917	1583	933	1088	1407	2933	984	1084	1182	1113	981	1949	1383	1028	1001
Jilin	2360	3630	2467	1373	1851	1596	2294	1099	1250	1474	1077	1074	1049	1267	1038	2091
Liaoning	2335	2829	1928	1037	2068	2447	2641	1055	1045	1889	1516	1773	1746	1772	1364	1294
Ningxia	176	192	179	247	301	258	880	140	105	123	120	125	147	172	176	138
Qinghai	289	318	339	211	261	263	265	167	108	175	143	175	181	176	154	129
Shaanxi	1583	1735	1429	979	1185	2132	2571	1463	1091	1399	1024	1189	1040	1174	976	834
Shandong	4443	5880	3125	1225	1465	5004	5674	2652	2112	3754	2068	2010	2495	2295	2539	2423
Shanghai	123	153	266	360	489	392	545	421	340	378	538	553	305	555	345	478
Shanxi	1686	3924	2345	1019	1217	2396	2895	1194	1097	1316	1071	1020	1071	1258	1091	1189
Sichuan	2300	4030	2439	1099	1818	2453	3573	1307	1366	1628	1386	1660	1708	1755	2024	1336
Tianjin	1090	799	1224	754	796	698	1435	256	309	368	321	349	400	378	311	442
Tibet	125	82	178	70	73	62	61	46	57	57	56	46	44	41	42	46
Xinjiang	940	1088	1165	507	759	1110	1601	689	593	572	654	679	537	629	619	562
Yunnan	2245	2037	2236	991	1530	1763	2258	514	1084	1244	1067	1140	1004	920	804	790
Zhejiang	3022	5016	3005	1090	1736	1960	2482	1132	1319	1456	1058	1154	1394	1368	1316	1014

Source: Yearbook of China Prosecution.
Note: Chongqing was part of Sichuan until 1997.

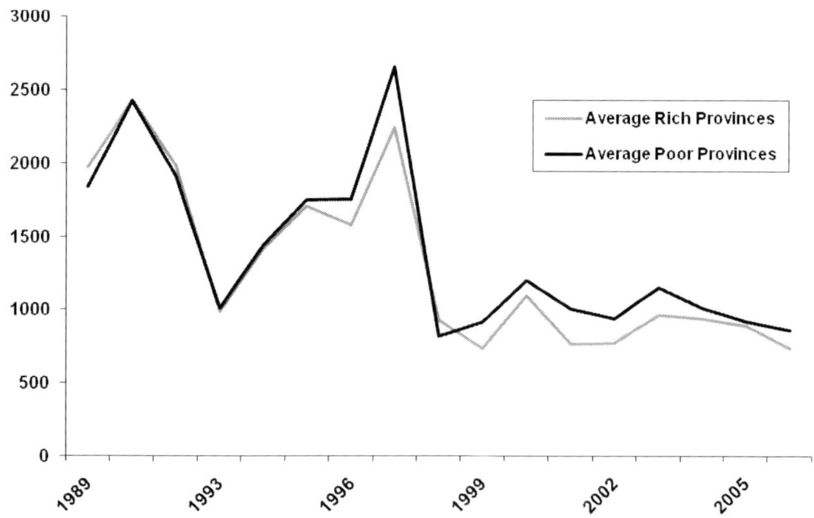

Figure 7.9: Cases of corruption, embezzlement and bribery in China (by wealth of province by year).

Source: Yearbook of China Prosecution.

Note: The five rich provinces (or equivalents) are Shanghai, Beijing, Tianjin, Zhejiang and Jiangsu. The five poor provinces are Gansu, Guizhou, Yunnan, Jiangxi and Anhui.

the data show remarkable similarity across these two provincial groupings, both in terms of levels and temporal trends. The implication is that corruption is not linked to variances in the volume and growth of economic activity across provinces in China, although stronger conclusions cannot be drawn on this point, absent a more sophisticated analysis of provincial levels of corruption and GDP or GDP growth.

Coupling this data with the general trend that China's environment remains stable in modest to high levels of corruption, as reflected in the cross-national data, suggests that leaders are increasing the levels of prosecution of corruption, even though absolute levels of corruption might remain constant, or perhaps in slight decline. Furthermore, the provincial data does show temporal and cross-province variation, but with the exception of the two wealthiest cities (Shanghai and Beijing), corruption seems to be disconnected from the wealth levels of the various provinces, although this conclusion is a tenuous one. The indication is that party officials in China are increasingly targeting corruption, with perhaps the outcome being a de-institutionalization of corruption within China.

7.6 The Third Pole in a Tri-polar World?

Declines in corruption, and more stability and predictability in the formal and informal area of the political and regulatory environment in China, are important for China's development and its positioning in a tri-polar world. If China is to be an equal player to the EU and the US, it needs its major manufacturing areas to become as equally sophisticated and high value-added, eventually, as those of most nations, emerging or otherwise, in the EU and the US.

One question at hand is how long China can continue to grow given persistent and enduring levels of corruption, in particular as high value-added activities move to the wealthier areas of China, and low value-added activities move to the developing provinces. If China does continue to grow as projected, its position as the third economic pole in a tri-polar world is secure. But if its regulatory infrastructure proves to become a deterrent to growth, as has been the case in other countries with similar levels of corruption — that is, if China stops being an anomaly — then its position as the third pole is much less certain.

A secondary form of growth for China is emerging from the economic activities of its domestic firms abroad. There is a clear possibility, as is becoming increasingly accepted in the academic and management literature, that firms have differential capabilities to manage effectively in weak institutional environments. Given the pervasive nature of corruption in China through to the end of the first decade of the 2000s, China's firms might well be enabled to operate effectively in other countries with high levels of corruption and weak institutional environments. This form of differential advantage, founded on the capability to manage a firm well in potentially corrosive environments, could also lead to a polarization of economic activity, in the sense that firms from China could operate well on an FDI and trade basis in places where firms from the United States and European Union have traditionally not performed well or have avoided investment altogether. This latter point is more speculative, as we do not have data to speak conclusively about it, but it is an interesting one, and it speaks further on how the world would look like as a tri-polar one through the growth in China's domestic and foreign economic activity.

References

Ades, A. and Di Tella, R. (1997). National champions and corruption: some unpleasant interventionist arithmetic. *The Economic Journal*, 107(443), 1023–1042.

Birkinshaw, J. M. and Hood, N. (1998). Multinational subsidiary evolution: capability and charter change in foreign-owned subsidiary companies. *Academy of Management Review*, 23(4), 773–795.

Cuervo-Cazurra, A. and Genc, M. (2008). Transforming disadvantages into advantages: developing-country MNEs in the least developed countries. *Journal of International Business Studies*, 39(6), 957–979.

Delios, A. and Henisz, W. J. (2003). Policy uncertainty and the sequence of entry by Japanese firms, 1980–1998. *Journal of International Business Studies*, 34(3), 227–241.

Fisman, R. and Svensson, J. (2007). Are corruption and taxation really harmful to growth? Firm-level evidence. *Journal of Development Economics*, 83(1), 63–75.

Fogel, K. (2006). Oligarchic family control, social economic outcomes, and the quality of government. *Journal of International Business Studies*, 37(5), 603–622.

Gerring, J. and Thacker, S. C. (2005). Do neoliberal policies deter political corruption? *International Organization*, 59(1), 233–254.

Henisz, W. J. and Macher, J. T. (2004). Firm- and country-level trade-offs and contingencies in the evaluation of foreign investment: The semiconductor industry, 1994–2002. *Organization Science*, 15(5), 537–554.

Jordan, W. A. (1972). Producer protection, prior market structure and the effects of government regulation. *Journal of Law and Economics*, 15(1), 151–176.

Kaplinsky, R., McCormick, D. and Morris, M. (2006). The impact of China on Sub-Saharan Africa. Working Paper 291. Brighton: Institute of Development Studies.

Klitgaard, R. (1991). *Controlling Corruption*. Berkeley: University of California Press.

Knack, S. and Keefer, P. (1995). Institutions and economic performance: cross-country tests using alternative institutional measures. *Economics and Politics*, 7, 207–227.

Lee, S. H. and Oh, K. K. (2007). Corruption in Asia: pervasiveness and arbitrariness. *Asia Pacific Journal of Management*, 24(1), 97–114.

Li, S. and Wu, J. J. (2007). Why China thrives despite corruption. *Far Eastern Economic Review*, 170(3), 24–28.

Mauro, P. (1995). Corruption and growth. *The Quarterly Journal of Economics*, August, 681–712.

Miller, S. R., Li, D., Eden, L. and Hitt, M. A. (2008). Insider trading and the valuation of international strategic alliances in emerging stock markets. *Journal of International Business Studies*, 39(1), 102–117.

Robertson, C. J. and Watson, A. (2004). Corruption and change: the impact of foreign direct investment. *Strategic Management Journal*, 25(4), 385–396.

Rodriguez, P., Uhlenbruck, K. and Eden, L. (2005). Government corruption and the entry strategies of multinationals. *Academy of Management Review*, 30(2), 383–396.

Rose-Ackerman, S. (1978). *Corruption: A Study in Political Economy*. New York: Springer.

Schneiberg, M. and Bartley, T. (2008). Organizations, regulation and economic behavior: regulatory dynamics and forms from the 19th to 21st century. *Annual Review of Law and Social Science*, 4(1), 31–61.

Schuler, D. A., Rehbein, K. and Cramer, R. D. (2002). Pursuing strategic advantage through political means: a multivariate approach. *Academy of Management Journal*, 45(4), 659–672.

Shleifer, A. and Vishny, R. W. (1993). Corruption. *The Quarterly Journal of Economics*, 108(3), 599–617.

Siegel, J. (2007). Contingent political capital and international alliances: evidence from South Korea. *Administrative Science Quarterly*, 52(4), 621–666.

Simmons, B. A. and Elkins, Z. (2004). The globalization of liberalization: policy diffusion in the international political economy. *American Political Science Review*, 98(1), 171–189.

Stigler, G. J. (1971). The theory of economic regulation. *Bell Journal of Economics and Management Science*, 2(1), 3–21.

Svensson, J. (2003). Who must pay bribes and how much? Evidence from a cross-section of firms. *The Quarterly Journal of Economics*, 118(1), 207–330.

Vaaler, P. M. (2008). How do MNCs vote in developing country elections? *Academy of Management Journal*, 51(1), 21–43.

Wei, S. J. and Shleifer, A. (2000). Local corruption and global capital flows. *Brookings Papers on Economic Activity*, 2000(2), 303–354.

Weitzel, U. and Berns, S. (2006). Cross-border takeovers, corruption, and related aspects of governance. *Journal of International Business Studies*, 37(6), 786–806.

Xinhua (2009). China's FDI contraction narrows in March following governmental efforts. http://news.xinhuanet.com/english/2009-04/15/content_11191566.htm, accessed 15 April 2009.

Chapter 8

Japan's Role on the New Economic Map: What is Japan's New Identity in the 21st Century?

Yumiko Okamoto

8.1 Introduction

The economic crisis has produced a marked shift in power from the West to the largest emerging markets in the East, currently led by China. The earlier rise of Japan alone was insufficient to achieve such a shift. According to the International Monetary Fund (IMF) (2011), China grew at an annual rate of 10.3% in 2010, despite the global collapse of economic activities. The Chinese economy is now expected to overtake the US economy in around 2027.[1] Given this marked shift in power, Henry Kissinger has called for the US-Chinese relationship to be taken to a new level, and Zbigniew Brzezinski has advocated the development of a G2, a group of two comprising China and the US, to tackle many important global economic and political issues (Economy and Segal, 2009).

The economic crisis has also led to the emergence of the Group of 20 (G20) leaders and the marginalization of the Group of Seven (G7) in the financial arena. The achievements of the G20 — for instance, the establishment of a framework for the regulation of banks — have been quite substantial. However, it remains far from clear how effective the G20 will be in the long run. World leaders should now seriously consider the creation of a better and safer global order. This chapter specifically addresses the role Japan could play in such a new world order.

---

[1] See *Financial Times* (2010).

Though characterized by economic depression, 2009 was a politically exciting year for Japan. For the first time in almost 46 years (excepting the 11 short months between 1993 and 1994 when Morihiro Hosokawa was Prime Minister), the government was headed by a party other than the Liberal Democratic Party (LDP). The economic crisis that has plagued Japan for more than a decade assisted the Democratic Party of Japan (DPJ) in becoming a viable alternative to the LDP. This also caused a departure from the "iron triangle" politics of the LDP, which favored the business and bureaucratic interests in which ruling powers were vested (Kojima, 2010). The emergence of real political competition for the LDP means that Japan now stands a better chance of becoming a two-party system (Funabashi, 2009).

After his inauguration, Prime Minister Michio Hatoyama confirmed his desire to reinforce Japan's economic and cultural identity as an Asian nation and to emulate a European style of governance while maintaining stable political and military ties with the US. Bremmer and Roubini (2009) warned that the Hatoyama government's policies were unrealistic and thus dangerous, advising Japan's government to be less ideological, more realistic, and more willing to compromise. Although the plans and policies announced by the DPJ still appear ill-defined and overly ambitious, what seems clear is that Japan has started to express its desire for a new identity in the 21st century.

In this chapter it is argued that Japan could play at least three important roles in the global economy in the coming decade. One is to continue to act as an economic hub in East Asia. Although China is said to have surpassed Japan when it comes to absolute gross national product (GNP) in 2010, Japan still plays a crucial role as a supplier of parts, machinery and technology to the rest of East Asia. For instance, although China runs a huge trade surplus *vis-à-vis* the rest of the world, China also has huge trade deficits *vis-à-vis* Japan because it still relies on Japan as a source of intermediate goods, machinery and technology.

The second role is to promote Asian economic integration and cooperation. Although Asia has become an engine of economic growth in the post-crisis world, Japan is the only country in Asia that is politically stable and has reached a living standard equivalent to that of Western countries. Many other Asian countries, including China and India, may still face both economic and political uncertainties in the near future. The recent rallies in several Chinese cities in which protesters have vented their anger at Japan is a case in point. Japan needs to take the lead in making Asia a dynamic region open to the rest of the world, and thus a vital contributor to the global economy.

Japan could also play a crucial role as a bridge between East and West (the third role). The rise of China and India, though particularly China, as industrial powers has led to a great deal of political and economic concern in both the East and the West. Since Japan is the only country in Asia that has substantially contributed to building a world economic order by establishing strong ties with Western countries over the previous few decades, it is considered well-positioned to negotiate the gap between the East and the West.

Section 8.2 begins by showing how economic power has started to shift from West to East, using various figures related to gross domestic product (GDP). The chapter argues for the building of a new global governance to reflect this power shift. Then, in Section 8.3, the three roles Japan could play in the post-crisis world are discussed in detail. Section 8.4 summarizes the discussion and concludes the chapter.

8.2 A Shift in Economic Power from West to East

Asia as Leader of the Global Recovery

One year after the most severe recession in recent history, Asia is leading the global recovery (IMF, 2010a). Table 8.1 shows annual percentage changes in the real GDP of major economies and regions in the world. The table shows a distinct trend. The pace of the recovery in advanced economies such as the US, Europe, and Japan has been slow. By contrast, activity in emerging economies rebounded swiftly in 2009 and 2010, particularly in Asia. China's annual GDP growth returned to a double-digit rate in 2010. In addition, India grew approximately 10%, which is one of its highest rates in its recent history, and Asian newly industrialized economies, including Hong Kong,

Table 8.1: Annual percentage changes in real GDP (%).

	1992–2001	2002–2007	2008	2009	2010
United States	3.5	2.6	0.4	–2.6	2.8
Euro Area	2.1	1.9	0.6	–4.1	1.8
Japan	0.9	1.8	–1.2	–6.3	4.3
Asian Newly Industrialized Economies[a]	5.5	5.2	1.8	–0.9	8.2
Developing Asia	7.3	8.8	7.9	7.0	9.3
China	10.3	10.7	9.6	9.2	10.3
India	5.7	8.0	7.3	5.7	9.7
Middle East and North Africa	3.4	5.5	5.1	1.8	3.9
Sub-Saharan Africa	2.8	6.5	5.5	2.8	5.0
Central and Eastern Europe	2.6	5.7	3.0	–3.6	4.2
CIS[b]	NA	7.5	5.5	–6.5	4.2

Source: Author's construction based on data obtained from IMF (2010b) and IMF (2011).
Notes: [a]Asian Newly Industrialized Economies include Hong Kong, Korea, Singapore and Taiwan. [b] CIS stands for Commonwealth of Independent States.

Korea, Singapore and Taiwan, returned to pre-crisis growth rates in 2010.

IMF (2010a) also points out an important difference between patterns of recovery in advanced economies and Asia (excluding Japan). In the former, recovery remains heavily dependent on macroeconomic policy support. In 2010, governments' general fiscal balances, calculated as percentages of GDP, were around –11%, –7% and –10% in the US, the euro area and Japan, respectively.[2] In the latter, the recovery has been reinforced by domestic demand, particularly private demand.

Asia's rapid recovery from the crisis appears to represent a notable break from the past. While in past recessions, such as the one that followed the 1997–1998 financial crisis, Asia's recovery was triggered by exports, this recovery has been driven by robust public and private domestic demand (IMF, 2010a). As many governments in advanced

[2] The source is IMF (2010b, p. 169).

economies plan to begin gradually withdrawing both fiscal and monetary stimulus in the near future, Asia is expected to remain a forerunner in the global recovery effort.

The Renaissance of Asia

Asia's recent contribution to global recovery may not be as surprising as it seems if, as Gill and Kharas (2007) posit, an economic renaissance is beginning in the East. The economic center of gravity — the core of production, trade, and finance — has shifted back towards Asia since the 1960s and 1970s. The pace of change has become so rapid, not only in trade and finance but also in production of ideas, technology and urban development, that, by around 2025, the region may be as large a presence in the world's economy as it was in the early 19th century (Gill and Kharas, 2007).

The idea of a renaissance in Asia originated in various studies conducted by Maddison (2008). Maddison analyzes forces that have determined the per capita income levels of nations throughout the past millennium and projects economic prospects through 2030. According to his research, in the year 1000, Asian countries were at the economic helm; however, the level of per capita income in Western Europe and the US not only became twice as large as the Asian average by 1820, but also became even larger by around 1950. By the 1970s, Japan and Asian Newly Industrialized Economies (Hong Kong, Korea, Singapore and Taiwan) had once again begun growing faster than the West, and some of the ASEAN countries, such as Indonesia, Malaysia and Thailand, joined the force in the 1980s (World Bank, 1993). Moreover, since the 1990s, there has been a major surge in growth in both China and India.

Table 8.2 shows Maddison's estimates for shares of world GDP between 1820 and 2030. It indicates that Asia's share of world income has risen steadily since 1950 and, by 2030, will be close to what it was in 1820 (approximately 53% of the world income). Additionally, as long as its current high rates of economic growth continue, China will be the single largest economy in the world, surpassing the US even before 2030.

Table 8.2: Shares of world gross domestic product, 1820–2030.

	1820	1950	1973	2003	2030
Western Europe	23.0	26.2	25.6	19.2	13.0
USA	1.8	27.3	22.1	20.7	17.3
Australia, Canada and New Zealand	0.1	3.4	3.3	3.1	2.5
Japan	3.0	3.0	7.8	6.6	3.6
Rich	**27.9**	**59.9**	**58.7**	**49.6**	**36.4**
China	32.9	4.6	4.6	15.1	23.8
India	16.0	4.2	3.1	5.5	10.4
Other Asia	7.4	6.8	8.7	13.2	15.4
Eastern Europe	3.6	3.5	3.4	1.9	1.3
Former USSR	5.4	9.6	9.4	3.8	3.4
Latin America	2.1	7.8	8.7	7.7	6.3
Africa	4.5	3.8	3.4	3.2	3.0
Rest	**72.1**	**40.1**	**41.3**	**50.4**	**63.6**
Asia as percentage of world	**59.3**	**14.9**	**24.2**	**40.5**	**53.3**

Source: Maddison (2008, p. 74), cited by Tanaka (2009).
Note: The GDP figures are expressed in 1990 international PPP dollars.

Implications for Global Governance

Regardless of whether China becomes the most prominent global economic presence, the US is expected to remain a major economic power (see Table 8.2); the share the US has in world income is still considered high and is expected to account for 17% of all income in 2030. As such, Henry Kissinger has called for the US-Chinese relationship to be taken to a new level, and Zbigniew Brzezinski has advocated the development of the G2, a group of two comprised of China and the US, to tackle many important global economic and political issues (Economy and Segal, 2009).

Though the US and China may share many interests, they still have significant differences. For instance, they differ in their opinions on the valuation of the renminbi, enforcement of intellectual property rights, and human rights records, among other concerns. As Economy and Segal (2009) emphasize, elevating the bilateral relationship between the US and China without addressing the very real differences between the two countries will lead nowhere.

Despite the relative decline of Western Europe's economic presence, its share in the global economy is still expected to measure approximately 13% by 2030. In addition, the shares of India and other Asian countries will surpass 10% of the world income by 2030. Such countries as Brazil, Russia, and South Africa may rapidly catch up with Asia as well. Thus, the post-crisis world could be described as a multi-polar world.

The economic crisis also corresponded with the emergence of the G20 leaders and the resulting marginalization of the G7/G8 in the financial arena. The achievements of the G20, which include the establishment of a framework for regulating banks, have been quite substantial. They demonstrate that, without the participation of new major players, global financial and economic issues may not be properly addressed. In response to this fact, the G20 leaders in Pittsburgh decided to make the G20 the premier forum for international economic cooperation.[3]

The G20, the members of which account for more than 85% of the global GDP, is more representative and inclusive, and therefore more politically legitimate and operationally effective, than the pre-existing G7/G8.[4] However, it remains to be seen how effective the G20 will be in the long-term. Thus, we should seriously consider how we can create a better and safer global order.

8.3 Three Roles Japan Could Play in the Multi-polar World

Nye (2009) argues that there are three basic ways to affect the behavior of others: coercion, payment, and attraction. The use of coercion and payment requires hard power, while obtaining preferred outcomes through attraction requires soft power. Maddison (2008) predicts that the share of Japan in the world GDP will decline from 6.6% in 2003 to only 3.6% by 2030 unless its underlying economic fundamentals change (see Table 8.2). Given that Japan renounced the use of

[3] See SaKong (2009).

[4] See footnote 3.

coercion to solve conflicts among countries after World War II and that Japan's economy will likely be less dominant than in the past few decades, soft power is the nation's only available option.

I would here like to argue that there are at least three roles Japan could play in the post-crisis world. The first one is to act as a source of new knowledge and technology. The second is to promote economic cooperation and integration in East Asia so that the region continues to be a driving force in the 21st century global economy. The third is to act as a bridge between East and West and as a stabilizing force in East Asia.

The Role of Japan as a Source of Knowledge and Technology

A Shift in Economic Power from Japan to China in East Asia

As power has shifted from the West to the East, the relative rise of China and decline of Japan has become noticeable within East Asia. Figure 8.1 compares the purchasing power parity (ppp)-denominated gross national income of China and Japan over the past two decades. It clearly indicates that while Japan's share of the economic pie hardly expanded after the collapse of the bubble economy in the late 1980s, China's certainly did. A sharp contrast can be found, especially after 2003, during which the rate of China's economic growth accelerated to a great extent. China surpassed Japan to become the second largest economy in the world as early as 2002 in current PPP dollars terms.

The expansion of the Chinese economy is also reflected in its changing business relationships with other countries around the world, in the Asia-Pacific region in particular. Table 8.3 presents a trade matrix that includes the world's major countries. It suggests two fundamental changes in trade relationships among East Asian countries that occurred between the 1990s and 2000s. The first is that, while shares of the US, EU, and Japan in the export market of East Asian countries other than China declined, China's share increased sharply. In other words, over the last decade, China has become an important export destination for all East Asian countries. This is especially true in

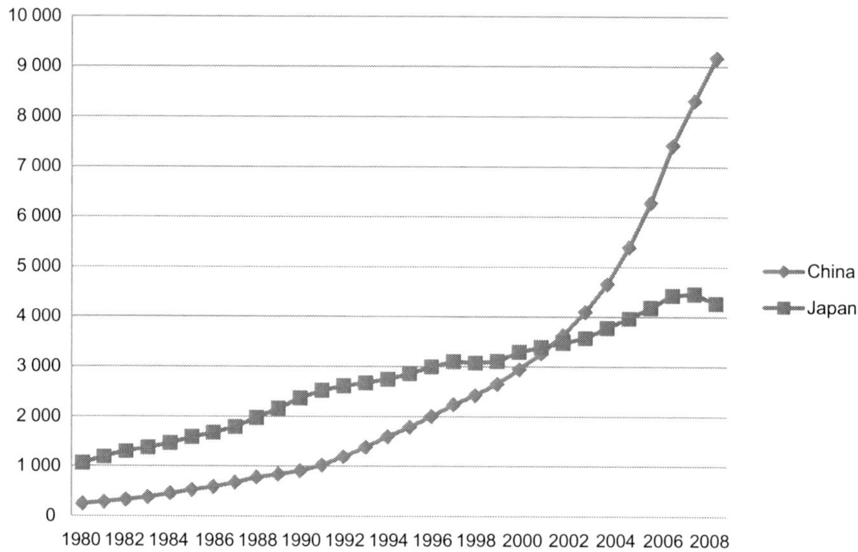

Figure 8.1: A comparison of gross national income for Japan and China (billion current PPP dollars).

Source: The author's construction based on the data of World Bank Indicators Online.

regard to Japan. China's share in exports from Japan increased from only 4.9% in 1995 to 19.6% in 2010.[5]

The second is that, in contrast to other East Asian countries, China's dependence on traditional external markets, such as the US and EU, increased tremendously between 1995 and 2007. This indicates that, although East Asian countries have been closely integrated on the production side with China as a final assembling destination,[6] the demand for final goods and services has come from Western countries. In recent years, this pattern of regional trade and production has become a source of contention, particularly between China and Western countries.

---

[5] China's share in exports from Japan reached 19.6% in 2010, based on data downloaded from UN Comtrade Online.

[6] See Urata (2001) for the FDI-Trade nexus and economic growth in East Asia.

Table 8.3: A trade matrix among East Asian countries, US and EU (%).

Exports from/ Imports to	Year	East Asia	Japan	China	Korea	ASEAN	US	EU(15)	World
East Asia	1995	48.9	8.7	8.4	4.0	15.6	22.4	14.8	100.0
	2007	48.8	6.6	13.3	4.2	12.8	16.2	14.2	100.0
Japan	1995	42.3		4.9	7.1	17.5	27.5	15.9	100.0
	2007	46.8		15.3	7.6	12.2	20.1	13.5	100.0
China	1995	56.5	19.1		4.5	6.6	16.6	12.9	100.0
	2007	37.6	8.4		4.6	7.5	19.1	18.2	100.0
Korea	1995	46.9	13.7	7.4		14.3	19.3	12.2	100.0
	2007	48.0	7.1	22.1		10.3	12.3	11.7	100.0
ASEAN	1995	52.4	14.2	2.7	2.9	23.2	18.6	14.5	100.0
	2007	56.9	10.4	9.3	3.7	24.3	12.2	11.8	100.0
US	1995	29.9	11.0	2.0	4.3	6.8		27.3	100.0
	2007	23.2	5.4	5.6	3.0	5.2		25.3	100.0
EU(15)	1995	7.4	2.1	0.9	0.8	2.2	5.8	58.9	100.0
	2007	6.2	1.2	2.0	0.7	1.5	7.2	59.2	100.0
World	1995	24.5	6.6	2.5	2.7	7.0	15.2	39.6	100.0
	2007	22.7	4.1	6.2	2.4	5.5	13.7	35.7	100.0

Source: Author's construction based on data obtained from Appendix 1 in Yamazawa (2010).
Note: ASEAN here includes Brunei, Indonesia, Malaysia, Philippines, Singapore, Thailand and Vietnam.

The Continuing Role of Japan as a Source of Technology in East Asia

Despite the relative decline of Japan in the global economy *vis-à-vis* China in terms of GNP and world trade, Japan will continue to play an important role in the global economy as a source of new knowledge and technology. Figure 8.2 shows the trend in the value of Japan's technology exports and imports. Around the mid-1990s, China began to emerge as an industrial power and Japan started to run a surplus in technology trade around the world, in addition to trade in goods. During the same period, technology receipts accelerated sharply while payments increased only at a moderate rate (Figure 8.2). As a result, Japan's trade surplus in technology transactions became huge in the late 1990s.

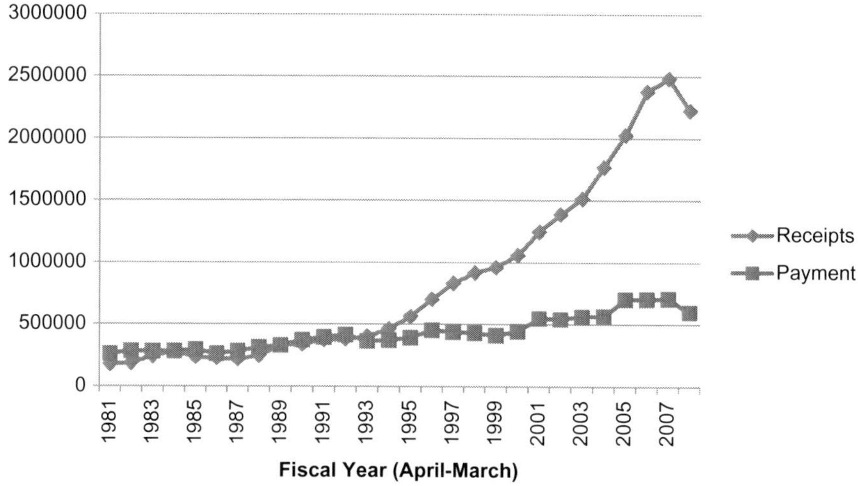

Figure 8.2: Technology receipts and payments (Unit: million yen).

Source: Author's construction based on data obtained from Ministry of Education, Culture, Sports, Science and Technology (2010).

Note: The author uses statistics of the Ministry of Internal Affairs and Communications because it also provides data by country and geographic area.

Moreover, the geographical breakdown of technology export revenue in Figure 8.3 reveals that receipts from Japan sharply increased in all three major regions of the world: North America, Europe, and East Asia. Among the three, Japan's technology trade surplus rose the most in East Asia, as indicated in Figure 8.4, in which East Asia represents over 86% of Japan's technology export revenue.[7] This implies that the role of Japan is, in fact, increasingly significant in the trade of technology, especially in East Asia. In other words, the rise of East Asia as an industrial power is largely due to technology transfers from Japan.

---

[7] This is based on calculations from data available for the Ministry of Education, Culture, Sports, Science and Technology (2010). The trade balance for technology in East Asia cannot be calculated directly because technology payments of Japan *vis-à-vis* East Asia are not available.

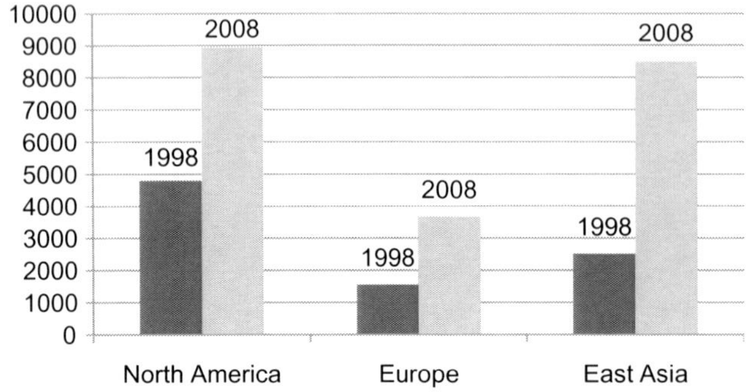

Figure 8.3: Japan's technology receipts by geographic area in 1998 and 2008 (Unit: 100 million yen).

Source: Author's construction based on data obtained from Ministry of Education, Culture, Sports, Science and Technology (2010).

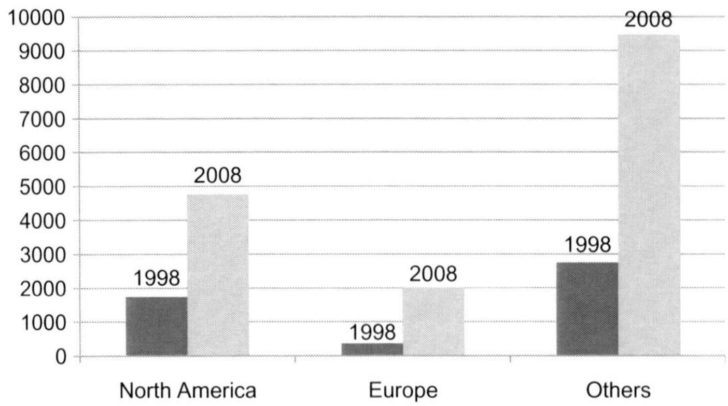

Figure 8.4: Japan's technology trade balance by geographic area in 1998 and 2008 (Unit: 100 million yen).

Source: Author's construction based on data obtained from Ministry of Education, Culture, Sports, Science and Technology (2010).

Note: "Others" include not only East Asia, but other regions. However, East Asia represents more than 88% of Japan's technology receipts of "Others" in 2008.

The Utilization of Japan's Scientific and Technological Capability to Solve Global Issues Related to Energy and the Environment

The dominance of Japan in the global technology trade is expected to continue at least into the immediate future, because one of the key strengths of Japan lies in the production of scientific knowledge and technology. Although the US dominates the field of science and technology, Japan continues to hold second or third place in the output of patents granted and academic articles, as shown in Table 8.4. This implies that Japan will remain a driving global force in the creation of

Table 8.4: Ranks in science and engineering (S&E) article output, and patents granted by USPTO, by selected countries.

	S&E article output			Patents granted	
Country	1995	2007	Country	1995	2008
US	1	1	US	1	1
China	14	2	Japan	2	2
Japan	2	3	Germany	3	3
UK	3	4	South Korea	8	4
Germany	4	5	Taiwan	7	5
France	5	6	Canada	6	6
Canada	6	7	France	4	7
Italy	8	8	UK	5	8
Spain	11	9	China	19	9
South Korea	22	10	Italy	9	10
India	12	11	Netherlands	12	11
Australia	9	12	Australia	13	12
Netherlands	10	13	Israel	15	13
Russia	7	14	Switzerland	10	14
Taiwan	18	15	Sweden	11	15
Brazil	23	16	Finland	16	16
Sweden	13	17	India	30	17
Switzerland	15	18	Belgium	14	18
Turkey	34	19	Austria	17	19
Poland	19	20	Singapore	44	20

Source: National Science Foundation (2010).
Note: USPTO stands for US Patent and Trademark Office.

scientific knowledge and development of technology, at least through the coming decade.

Over the past two decades, Japanese business enterprises have continued to invest in research and development (R&D) despite Japan's gloomy overall macroeconomic situation. Figure 8.5 shows trends in business enterprise R&D as a percentage of value added in industry between 1993 and 2007. The R&D ratio of Japanese business enterprise increased from 2.5% to as high as 3.7% during this period, clearly indicating that the Japanese private sector as a whole had actually intensified its innovation capacity.

At no other time in history have science and technology been considered as instrumental in solving global issues like climate change, poverty, and food and energy securities as they are now. Thus, we could argue that Japan still has the capacity to address both regional and global concerns through the substantial scientific and technological proficiencies it has built up over the last few decades.

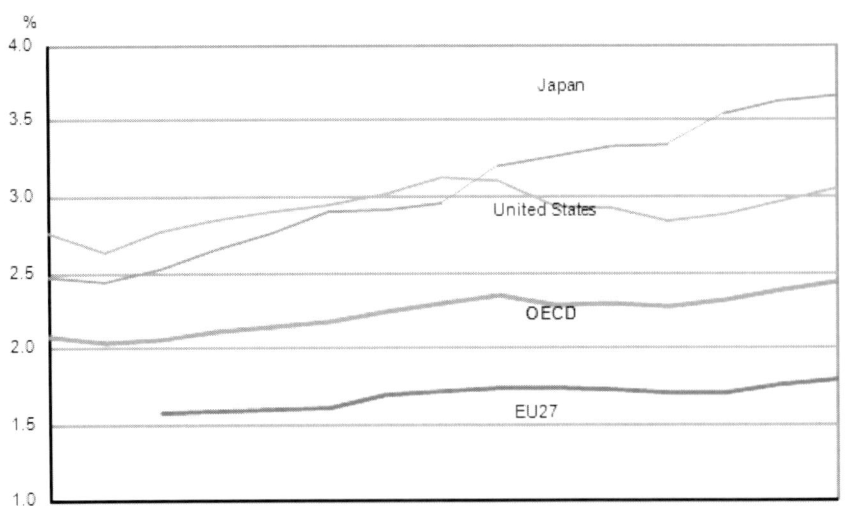

Figure 8.5: Business R&D intensity trends by area, 1993–2007.

Source: OECD (2009).

Note: Business enterprise R&D as a percentage of value added in industry.

Japan's Role in Promoting Asian Economic Integration and Cooperation

As economic power shifts from West to East, it is increasingly important for Asia to make an effort to become a dynamic, politically stable region open to the rest of the world. These characteristics are not only important for the region, but for the rest of the world as well. To achieve stability and openness, it is imperative for Asia to do at least two things: it must remove any bottlenecks prohibiting the region's further growth and establish a region-wide Free Trade Agreement (FTA).

Regional Infrastructure Development in Asia

The Asian Development Bank (ADB) (2009) found that the rapid growth in recent years has put severe pressure on the existing infrastructure, particularly in transport and energy and also in communications. This pressure has exposed the inadequacies of Asia's infrastructure networks and resulted in a bottleneck blocking further growth, a threat to competitiveness, and an obstacle to poverty reduction. Moreover, the ADB (2009) argues that to create a single Asian market where goods, services, capital, information and people move freely, further infrastructure investment is essential.

Under a strong initiative by the government of Japan, particularly the Ministry of Economy, Trade and Industry (METI), the Economic Research Institute for ASEAN and East Asia (ERIA) was launched in Indonesia in 2007. ERIA's main task is to provide policy analyses and recommendations to leaders or ministers in strong partnership with the ASEAN Secretariat and existing research institutes. In August 2010, ERIA announced its recommendation for a comprehensive Asian development plan,[8] the total budget of which will be 25 trillion yen, or 0.3 trillion US dollars. A major part of the plan involves large-scale infrastructure investment in ASEAN

[8] Based on *Nihon Keizai Newspaper* (2010, p. 3).

countries. The recommendation was acknowledged at the East Asian Summit held on October 30, 2010, in Hanoi.[9]

Japan has not only contributed to Asian infrastructure development through the establishment of ERIA, but also through the provision of technical and financial assistance under the Japan International Cooperation Agency (JICA). JICA has a long history of contributing to the infrastructure improvement of developing countries through official development assistance (ODA) programs.

A Region-wide FTA

In contrast to Western Europe and North America, regional economic integration in East Asia has increased as a result of market forces without the help of any institutional framework until recently (Urata, 2009). It has been market mechanisms, rather than regional institutions in the form of regional trade agreements, that have played the most crucial role in creating a dynamic and interdependent region in Asia. Around the turn of the 21st century, Asia started to establish FTAs to promote further economic integration and development.[10]

Table 8.5 summarizes the FTAs in effect, under negotiation, or in early stages of negotiation within the Asia-Pacific region. It clearly demonstrates how bilateral or trilateral FTAs have proliferated in the region.

According to customs union theory, the preferential reduction in tariffs under a regional agreement might induce trade diversion as well as trade creation. In other words, the welfare-related implications of forming an FTA are indeterminate even for agreement participants. Accumulation of bilateral agreements might also increase the probability of a trade diversion effect, making its welfare implications for East Asia uncertain as well; such accumulation could lead to what trade economists call a "spaghetti bowl," or "noodle bowl," effect.

---

[9] Based on "Chairman's Statement of the East Asia Summit (EAS), Ha Noi, Viet Nam, 30 October 2010".

[10] See Chapters 3 and 4 of this volume for the details of EU-Asian trade relations and liberalization initiatives.

Table 8.5: FTAs of the major countries and areas in the Asia-Pacific region.

	Japan	China	Korea	ASEAN	India	US
Asia-Pacific Partners						
China				2003		
Japan			Negotiation	2008	Negotiation com.	
Korea	Negotiation			2007	2009	2010
Hong Kong, Macao		2003, 2004				
Taiwan		2010				
Brunei	2008					
Indonesia	2008					
Malaysia	2006					Negotiation
Philippines	2008					
Singapore	2002	2008	2006		2005	2004
Thailand	2007				Negotiation	Negotiation

(*Continued*)

Table 8.5: (*Continued*)

	Japan	China	Korea	ASEAN	India	US
Vietnam	2009					
ASEAN-wide	2008	2003	2007		2010	
India	Negotiation com.		2009	2010		
Chile	2007	2006	2004		2007	2004
Peru	Negotiation com.	2009	Negotiation			2009
Canada			Negotiation			
Mexico	2005		Negotiation			
Canada · Mexico						1994
US			2010			
Australia	Negotiation	Negotiation	Negotiation			2005
New Zealand (NZ)		2008	Negotiation			
Australia · NZ				2009		
TPP countries						Negotiation

Sources: Author's construction based on information obtained from Bureau of Economic Affairs, the Ministry of Foreign Affairs, Japan (2009) and the Ministry of Economy, Trade and Industry (2010). Information is as of December 10, 2010.
Notes: "Negotiation com." means that the FTA negotiation was completed. TPP stands for Trans-Pacific Partnership.

Recognizing the benefits of region-wide FTAs,[11] several countries have proposed ideas for their creation. At the 1998 summit meeting of ASEAN+3 (China, Japan, and South Korea), the leaders decided to set up the East Asia Vision Group to study visions for economic cooperation and integration. The group recommended the establishment of East Asia FTA (EAFTA). China is said to be a stronger advocate of EAFTA than any other country.

At the ASEAN+6 Economic Ministers' meeting in 2006, Japan proposed the formation of the Comprehensive Economic Partnership in East Asia (CEPEA), which is an economic partnership that features an FTA and includes all of ASEAN+6 (China, Japan, Korea, Australia, India, and New Zealand). CEPEA differs from EAFTA in that membership is wider, and also in that economic cooperation as well as trade and investment liberalization and facilitation are considered central to the agreement.

In addition, at the Asia-Pacific Economic Cooperation (APEC) Leaders' Meeting in 2006, the US proposed the formation of a Free Trade Area in the Asia-Pacific (FTAAP) comprised of 21 APEC member countries. It is thought that the US proposal was motivated by a concern that the US would be excluded from East Asia, causing its economic activities there to decline (Urata, 2009).

Again, unlike Western Europe and North America, East Asia has chosen to advance several different parallel schemes for the time being instead of choosing just one scheme as a pathway to a single Asian market. Given the diversity of the Asia Pacific region, it is quite difficult for countries to agree to adopt a single scheme. Japan continues to play a role in advancing a number of competing integration schemes.

Japan's Role as a Bridge between East and West and as a Stabilizer in East Asia

Amid the new dynamics and challenges that have emerged in the wake of the financial crisis, Japan may also need to play a role as a stabilizer

[11] See Urata (2009) and Bureau of Economic Affairs, the Ministry of Foreign Affairs, Japan (2009) for the details pertaining to region-wide FTA proposals.

in East Asia, as well as a partner in supporting some existing trans-regional frameworks.

The Importance of a US-Japan Alliance

During the 10 short months in which Prime Minister Yukio Hatoyama was in administration, many Asian nations expressed concern over the deterioration of US-Japanese security ties. This indicated that Asian countries increasingly regard a US-Japan alliance as essential to their "common good" (Funabashi, 2010).

Funabashi (2010) presents two reasons that make the US-Japan alliance indispensable to the stability of East Asia. The first pertains to the increasing instability of the Korean peninsula. The Korean situation is expected to become unsustainable as economic crises and further hardships increase for North Korean citizens, and the North Korean regime will likely collapse. In this regard, a close cooperation between the US, Japan, and Korea as well as that between China, Japan, and Korea is regarded as pivotal to maintaining stability in East Asia.

Second, maritime issues are increasingly becoming a source of tension in East Asia. A case in point is the sharp deterioration of China-Japan relations in September 2010, spurred by a dispute over a chain of islands in the East China Sea. Protests over maritime sovereignty erupted in Japan and China in the weeks following the initial dispute. China also temporarily suspended high-level contact with Japan and imposed a de facto halt on exports to Japan of rare earth elements, which are crucial to production of many electronic products. Additionally, at a recent ASEAN regional forum in Hanoi, member nations expressed unease about China's activities in the South China Sea, because "China increasingly perceives the area as its own and denies rival claims to several chains of islands" (Funabashi, 2010). To play a stabilizing role in East Asia, Japan needs to deepen its security ties with the US. In order to achieve this, it must solve its dispute with the US over the military base in Okinawa.

The Establishment of New Directions and Visions for APEC

Amid the new dynamics and challenges unfolding in the region, it is becoming increasingly clear that Asian nations would like to see the US participate in the non-military field of regional strategizing. One example is the planned participation of the US along with Russia at the 5th East Asian Summit, which was held in Hanoi on October 30, 2010. Japan could also play an important role in promoting a trans-regional economic cooperation scheme with the US as a key partner. APEC is one of the most important vehicles for achieving this.

APEC is the premier forum for facilitating economic growth, cooperation, trade, and investment in the Asia-Pacific region. It is the only inter-governmental grouping in the world operating on the basis of non-binding commitments and open dialogue. As of March 20, 2011, APEC has 21 member economies, among them major players in the Asia-Pacific region, namely China, Japan, and the US.

The idea of APEC was first proposed by the Australian Prime Minister in 1989, but Japan has played an instrumental role in the institutional formation of APEC from the start. At the present moment, it is vital that leaders come together once a year, ministers meet more than once a year, and administrative officials meet several times a year to promote cooperation. This kind of frequent and close discussion will positively impact not only economics but also political relations.

Although the profile of APEC significantly diminished after the 1997–1998 Asian financial crisis, APEC has recently regained some of its lost momentum, especially following the APEC Leaders' Meeting in 2006 at which the US proposed the formation of an FTAAP. In 2009, APEC leaders instructed officials to explore a range of pathways to an FTAAP in order to accelerate free and open trade and investment. In 2010, Japan hosted an APEC Leaders' Meeting in Yokohama. As part of it, Japan not only made a critical effort to concretely further regional economic integration, but also worked toward a regional growth strategy. The latter is especially worth mentioning because this is the first time that APEC has adopted a regional strategy of this nature. Japan has pursued both integration- and growth-related objectives simultaneously in an effort to carefully explore how to best ameliorate the potentially negative impacts of FTAs before proceeding with the ambitious creation of an FTAAP (Shiraishi, 2010).

Japan will play a significant role in determining the future directions and new visions for APEC (Shiraishi, 2010) whilst safeguarding the interests of the US in the Asia-Pacific region.

8.4 Japan's Role in the 21st Century: A Shift Towards Soft Power

The economic crisis has produced a marked shift in power from the West to the largest emerging markets in the East, with China in the lead. Given this shift, some analysts have called for the development of a G2, a group of two comprising China and the US, to tackle many important global economic and political issues. However, the world has observed a great deal of friction between these two countries, as evidenced by the Copenhagen climate talks, Google's threat to withdraw from China, and Western concerns about the value of the Chinese currency. A heightened bilateral relationship may not yet be possible for China and the US.

The economic crisis also led to the emergence of the G20 leaders, resulting in the G7's marginalization in the financial arena. The achievements of the G20 — for instance, the establishment of a framework for bank regulation — have been quite substantial. However, how effective the G20 will be in the long-term remains unclear. With no global governance to keep pace with international economic arrangements already in place, Japan should now seriously consider how it can contribute to the development of a better and safer global order.

I have argued here that there are at least three significant roles for Japan to play in the post-crisis era. First, Japan could contribute to the solving of global issues, such as those related to energy and the environment, by utilizing its well-developed scientific and technological capabilities. A careful examination of Japan's technology trade reveals that Japan has succeeded in building up a strong comparative advantage over the years. This is especially true for transactions it has made *vis-à-vis* East Asia. This implies that Asia's development is largely due to a rapid rate of technology transfer from Japan. Furthermore, despite its dismal overall record of economic performance during the last two decades, Japanese companies have continued to spend a certain portion of their own income on R&D. As a result, Japan possesses the technological potential to contribute to the solving of crucial global issues such as climate change.

Second, Japan could promote regional cooperation and integration in East Asia so that the region continues to be not only a driving force in the global economy but also an open trade and investment area for both the rest of the world and its own countries. ADB (2009) warns that without large-scale investment to build up region-wide infrastructure, the high economic growth of East Asia will come to a halt in the near future. Foreseeing this possibility, Japan has begun to play an important role in promoting extensive infrastructure investment in the region, partly through the establishment of ERIA, which completed a comprehensive development plan for Asia in 2010.

Japan has also competed with other countries, such as China, to promote the formation of a region-wide FTA in order to create an area consistent with the World Trade Organization (WTO) and open to the rest of the world. However, unlike the EU and North America, Asia will allow several competing regional integration schemes to exist simultaneously, reflecting the diversity of the region.

The third role for Japan is as a stabilizer in East Asia working in close collaboration with Western countries like the US. An increasing instability in North Korea and uneasiness in East Asian countries about the rise of China's military power has reestablished the need for US-Japan ties, which once deteriorated significantly after Prime Minister Hatoyama took over administrative duties in 2009. Japan is also working to revitalize APEC in order to promote economic cooperation and integration whilst including the US in a non-military capacity.

Putting aside decades of animosity, the political leaders of China, Japan, and Korea met in Fukuoka, Japan in late 2008 to discuss how to handle the financial crisis. The trilateral summit was the first in history and the first opportunity for the leaders of the three nations to meet independently and not on the occasion of other international meetings, such as the ASEAN Summits.[12] Moreover, the three leaders decided to each host the others in the coming years, holding one summit in each member country. They agreed on a joint statement declaring their trilateral partnership and commitment to enhanced cooperation. The second and third China-Japan-Korea Summits were held in China in 2009 and in Korea in 2010, respectively, and both were attended by Prime Minister Hatoyama. Japan hosted the fourth trilateral Summit in May 2011. Prime Minister Kan chaired the Summit. However, the recent deterioration of the Sino-Japan diplomatic relationship reveals that trilateral cooperation is not yet strong enough to build a solid foundation for the prosperity and stability of the global economy.

The world seems to be increasingly characterized as a multi-polar world, as discussed earlier. Amid the new dynamics and challenges, it has become clear that Japan must play several important roles in East Asia, acting not so much as an economic powerhouse but as a stabilizer as well as promoter of economic cooperation, at least until 21st-century superpowers like China and India are ready to take over its role. In other words, Japan must provide for the so-called public or common good of East Asia. Given the existence of a huge income disparity and several sources of political instability in East Asia, Japan still needs to contribute to the prosperity and stability of the region, serving the global society in close collaboration with Western countries.

References

Asian Development Bank (2009). *Infrastructure for Seamless Asia*. Manila: Asian Development Bank.

[12] See "Press Conference by the Deputy Press Secretary, 8 October 2009," downloaded from http://www.mofa.go.jp/, accessed on May 1, 2010.

Bremmer, I. and Roubini, N. (2009). Why Japan needs a Hatobama. *The Wall Street Journal*, December 31, 2009. http://global.factiva.com/ha/default.aspx, accessed January 25, 2010.

Bureau of Economic Affairs, the Ministry of Foreign Affairs, Japan (2009). Japan's current status and future prospect of economic partnership agreement (in Japanese). http://www.mofa.go.jp/, accessed January 23, 2010.

Chairman's Statement of the East Asia Summit (EAS), Ha Noi, Viet Nam, 30 October 2010. http://www.mofa.go.jp/region/asia-paci/eas/pdfs/state101030.pdf, accessed November 1, 2010.

Economy, E. C. and Segal, A. (2009). The G-2 mirage. *Foreign Affairs*, 88(3), 14–23.

Financial Times (2010). January 26, 2010, FT Guide to Davos; Roundtable, p. 10.

Funabashi, Y. (2009). Tokyo's trials. *Foreign Affairs*, 88(6), 106–117.

Funabashi, Y. (2010). Asia's clouded horizon. http://www.eastasiaforum.org, accessed October 25, 2010.

Gill, I. and Kharas, H. (2007). *An East Asian Renaissance: Ideas for Economic Growth*. Washington, D.C.: The World Bank.

International Monetary Fund (2010a). *Regional Economic Outlook: Asia and Pacific*. Washington, D.C.: International Monetary Fund (April).

International Monetary Fund (2010b). *World Economic Outlook: Rebalancing Growth*. Washington, D.C.: International Monetary Fund.

International Monetary Fund (2011). *World Economic Outlook: Update*. Washington, D.C.: International Monetary Fund (January 25, 2011).

Kojima, A. (2010). Japan's political watershed and its economic challenges. http://www.eastasiaforum.org, accessed January 25, 2010.

Maddison, A. (2008). Shares of the rich and the rest in the world economy: Income divergence between nations, 1820–2030. *Asian Economic Policy Review*, 3(1), 67–82.

Ministry of Education, Culture, Sports, Science and Technology (2010). *Indicators of Science and Technology*. Tokyo: Ministry of Education, Culture, Sports, Science and Technology.

Ministry of Economy, Trade and Industry (2010). The maps of FTAs of major countries and regions (in Japanese). http://www.meti.go.jp/policy/trade_policy/epa/othercountry_fta.pdf, accessed March 20, 2011.

National Science Foundation (2010). *Science and Engineering Indicators 2008*. Washington, D.C.: National Science Foundation.

Nihon Keizai Newspaper (2010). September 19, 2010, p. 3.

Nye, J. S. (2009). Get smart. *Foreign Affairs*, 88(4), 160–164.

OECD (2009). *OECD Science, Technology and Industry Scoreboard 2009*. Paris: OECD.

SaKong, I. (2009). Korea and the 20 summit next November. http://www.eastasianforum.org/, accessed January 25, 2010.

Shiraishi, T. (2010). APEC beyond the Bogor goals: proposal for a new vision. IDE-JETRO Policy Brief, submitted to APEC 2010 Third Senior Officials' Meeting (SOM3).
Tanaka, A. (2009). *The Post-Crisis World* (in Japanese). Tokyo: Nihon Keizai Shinbunsha.
Urata, S. (2001). Emergence of an FDI-trade nexus and economic growth in East Asia. In: J. E. Stiglitz and S. Yusuf (Eds.), *Rethinking the East Asian Miracle.* Washington, D.C.: World Bank.
Urata, S. (2009). Institutionalization of regional economic integration in East Asia. Paper presented to the International Conference on Institution Building in Asia for Peace and Development, RIETI and JICA, August 28–29, 2009.
World Bank (1993). *The East Asian Miracle: Economic Growth and Public Policy.* New York: The Oxford University Press.
Yamazawa, I. (2010). *Asia-Pacific Economic Cooperation: New Challenges in the 21st Century* (in Japanese). Tokyo: JETRO.

Chapter 9

India in a Re-polarized World

Shubhashis Gangopadhyay and S. K. Shanthi

9.1 Introduction

This chapter discusses the reforms that have taken place in India in the last two decades from a re-polarization perspective. It discusses the significant changes in policy regarding trade, investment and governance. At one end, India's Constitution envisaged a rule-of-law democracy that allows states to maintain their diversity. At the other end, for a long time, thanks to various central government economic policies on trade, investment, technology and foreign exchange, India has been a highly centrally controlled society.

In the early years, on the political front, India was firmly committed to the Non-alignment Movement during the Cold War years. Economically, however, there was a pro-Soviet stance. Starting with the adoption of the Soviet model for economic development, India maintained excellent trade ties with the Soviet Union. The Soviets also bailed India out during the famine years in the early 1960s by exporting wheat and accepting rupee payments. Geopolitically, the Soviets played "Big Brother" to India. By contrast, India's political and economic relations with the United States were not so cordial, especially after the assassination of President Kennedy. Both countries looked at each other with suspicion, and the distinctly pro-Pakistan stance of the United States did not win any favors in India. The Indo-US ties plunged to new depths when India militarily helped East Pakistan, which was hitherto a part of Pakistan, to become an independent country, Bangladesh, at the latter's request. During this entire period, spanning 1950–1991, all the major European countries more or less toed the US line when it came to India. While sporadic trade and investments from Europe into India did take place, it was very minor. It, therefore, did not make any significant contribution to India's economy which, during this entire period, remained trapped at a low growth rate of 3.2% per annum, with its per capita income growing at around 1.3% per annum.

The reforms unleashed in 1991 have taken India closer to what was originally expected when the country became independent. It is now a much more federal country with states having more power to plan their own destiny.

India's colonial legacy that left it de-industrialized and poor, naturally led to a suspicion of the motives of the West and, hence, to a closed economy that was sceptical of the effects of an open economy that allowed the free inflow of foreign goods and investment. However, the first attempts at liberalizing the economy in the 1980s created an irreversible momentum towards greater openness. As the economy registered greater growth than what it had seen before, it gave confidence to policymakers to push the reform process even further.

At the early 2010s, India boasts of a large young population whose continual entry into the labor force drives the growth of a large domestic market for goods and services. This is obviously an important factor in a world where the West and Japan are burdened by ageing populations in a largely global world. This creates huge opportunities for the world to shift its production of goods and services to India; in the process, developed countries that have the finances and the technology can maintain their living standards from the returns on their investments in India.

In this chapter, we first chronicle the reform process in India over the last two decades and then discuss the current relationship between the EU and India. Section 9.2 discusses the pre-reforms period of India's economic history. Section 9.3 looks at the most important aspects of post-reforms political economy and contains a discussion on the fiscal federalism in India. Section 9.4 contains a fairly detailed discussion of the reforms initiated after 1991 and broadly looks at the banking sector reforms, the capital markets reforms and the external sector reforms. In Section 9.5, a discussion on the impact of reforms on the Indian economy is presented. Section 9.6 focuses on the India-EU trade and investment links over the last few decades. Section 9.7 contains a discussion on India-EU relations in the larger socio-political context, and finally, Section 9.8 concludes.

9.2 India: Pre-Reforms and Political Economy

Domestic Sector

The popular wisdom about India's reform process is that it was initiated in 1991, in the aftermath of a severe balance of payments crisis. The crisis manifested itself in a drop in foreign reserves to a level where India did not have enough foreign reserves to finance more than two weeks' worth of essential imports. The reforms are believed to have encouraged the entry of new private Indian industry and, most importantly, opened up the economy to international trade. However, while there is no dispute that the 1990s experienced major structural changes in the Indian economy, some argue that the process of reforms had started prior to the 1990s.

On the public sector front, the founding fathers of India, most notably the first Prime Minister Mr. Jawaharlal Nehru (a strong believer in the Soviet model of the 1950s), envisaged a mixed economy for India where the public sector would attain the "commanding heights" and set in motion a process of industrialization with the public sector as the leader. During the subsequent decades (ending in the mid-1980s), the public sector was also used as a vehicle for employment generation. But the usual problems associated with public ownership of industrial enterprises affected the performance of these units, many of which never made profits in their entire existence and were provided with budgetary support for their continued survival. Most of the public expenditure needed for investments and for implementing various welfare schemes were debt-funded, and this resulted in the central government getting deep into debt. On the positive side, science and technology received a boost and most of the scientific and research institutions were set up during this period.

Also, the governments, both at the center and at the state levels, set up elaborate public health care and education networks to cater to the needs of the poor, with their effective delivery being different across different states.

Starting from the 1950s, the Indian government had taken an approach of directing the process of industrialization to suit the path of development envisaged in the various five-year plans. The implementation of the industrial strategies involved the use of two policy instruments. First, a number of industrial sectors were reserved for the state sector or public sector units, and private companies were not allowed to invest in them. Second, even where they were allowed to invest, private firms had to have the central government's permission before starting any new production center or increasing current capacity. Such permissions, or licenses, were intended to balance out regional disparities in industrialization.

Over the years, the government added to these basic instruments of industrial policy other initiatives like import substitution, non-tariff barriers against consumer goods imports, and reservation of some industries for the small-scale sector. Investments were also directed through a complex web of subsidies and price supports which resulted in deep inefficiencies, with many private industrial units depending on governmental support to remain in the black. With the economy remaining more or less closed, this resulted in complete lack of competition and competitiveness in the markets.

Many of the policy initiatives that restricted the independent decision-making ability of the Indian private sector, such as bank nationalization, price controls for sugar and other commodities, controlling interest rates, etc., were taken in the 1970s. In 1980, the architect of the 1970s' socialist policies, Indira Gandhi, came back as Prime Minister after being out of power for three years (that followed her 1975 declaration of "emergency" that lasted for two years and during which time most of the democratic rights of citizens were suspended). According to Kohli (2004), Indira Gandhi's 1977 electoral defeat had taught her that it was important to have businesspeople on her side.

External Sector

In the external sector, exchange rates were fixed and the rupee was highly overvalued to benefit the importers, since India had embarked on an import substitution model for development. The government backed up the rupee with tight quantity restrictions on the purchase of foreign exchange by Indians. Whereas the imports of capital goods and other investment goods were favored, the imports of semi-finished or finished goods were subjected to prohibitively high customs duties (exceeding 200% in many cases). While exports did happen, they were largely due to the entrepreneurship of individual exporters rather than due to any favorable government policy. Foreign investments were not encouraged, and even the few corporations which were present in India like Coca-Cola and IBM were asked to wind up their operations by the early 1980s. The rupee did undergo some phased devaluation towards the end of the 1980s, but the exchange rates still did not reflect the demand and supply conditions prevailing in the markets.

Rajiv Gandhi became Prime Minister in 1984 after his mother Indira Gandhi's assassination. He held a strong belief in the role of the private sector in fostering industrialization and economic growth. Indeed, it can be argued that he was the first to unravel the socialist policies put into effect by his mother. The first significant set of liberal economic reforms in the external sector was initiated under his stewardship. Liberalization of this sector began around 1985 when the government forayed into some trade liberalization by allowing Indians to import (at lower customs duties) semi-finished and finished white goods including computers.

9.3 Post-Reforms Political Economy and Fiscal Federalism

In the 1990s, Rajiv Gandhi re-initiated the process of democratic decentralization to revitalize the local bodies which had more or less become defunct since the mid-1960s. During the period between mid-1960s to early 1990s, while the local bodies, both rural and urban, existed, they acted more like agencies of the state governments and implemented their schemes and projects instead of functioning like local self-governments. Their elections were either not conducted or continuously postponed in a majority of the Indian states. The process Rajiv Gandhi initiated resulted in the 72nd and 73rd amendments to the constitution of India in 1992, which paved the way towards strengthening even further the democratic values of this country. Conducting elections in all the local governments by the state election commissions every five years is now mandatory, and women have been given a 33% representation in the local body councils.

The local bodies have also been entrusted with their own sets of functions and administrative powers, which differ widely across states. States like Kerala, West Bengal, Madhya Pradesh and to some extent Karnataka have been more pro-active in transferring and sharing powers and functions out to the local bodies, while many other states have lagged behind in the transfer of powers. For example, in Kerala and Madhya Pradesh, the local governments were entrusted with the task of providing primary education services and also primary health care services. Many argue that the strides the state of Kerala has made in the Human Development Index (HDI) are a result of the empowerment of the local governments.

The Indian governance thus became fully federalist in nature, with fiscal federalism also firmly in place. The central finance commission, which decides on the devolution and revenue-sharing structure between the central and state government (and also to a limited extent directly to the local governments), and the state finance commissions deciding on the same between the state and local governments, are the two arms of the fiscal federalism and they are both constitutional agencies which can function with independence and autonomy from the executive. Like the central finance commission, state finance commissions are also formed every five years in all the states of the country that look into the devolution of funds from the state government's exchequer to the local bodies.

In 1989, Rajiv Gandhi lost power to a coalition government which was, in principle, opposed to most of his economic policies and wanted to concentrate directly on social justice and equity, rather than use economic growth as a means to that end. However, the coalition was inherently unstable, and by 1991 the Congress Party returned to power. But in the interim, Rajiv Gandhi had also been assassinated.

9.4 Economic Reforms

The 1991–1995 government led by Prime Minister Narasimha Rao used the backdrop of the balance of payments crisis to unleash a series of reforms (Parikh, 1997). As a result of these reforms, state monopolies in industries have been dismantled, tariff and non-tariff barriers to imports have been reduced or eliminated, financial markets have been liberalized, and foreign direct investment has been allowed in nearly all sectors.

Financial Markets

The financial market reforms post-1991 were driven by the realization that a strong, dynamic and stable financial sector was necessary to enable the economy to grow and withstand shocks. This meant the gradual unraveling of the financially repressive regime that had prevailed until then. In its place, the reformers wanted a set-up institution, in particular, the banking institutions, that had operational and functional autonomy. To achieve this, government-owned institutions were corporatized, private institutions were allowed to operate in the banking space which until now had been comprised mainly of nationalized public sector banks, foreign institutions were allowed in, and the administered interest rate regime was dismantled. However, in the interest of maintaining financial stability, these changes were introduced through a well thought-out sequence of steps that was both administratively prudent and politically acceptable. The public sector banks, after decades of being in the stranglehold of government regulations and being shored up through budgetary supports, had to start operating in the marketplace without any direct government support and with the regulations being disbanded or phased out and new reform measures instituted in their place.

Foreign Participation in the Banking Sector

The Reserve Bank released a roadmap for foreign banks in March 2005 that was consistent with India's WTO commitments. This aspect of the liberalization was planned to occur in two phases. In the first phase, from March 2005 to March 2009, foreign banks entering India for the first time could set up wholly-owned subsidiaries or operate through branches. For both new and existing foreign banks, India wanted to go beyond the WTO commitment of 12 branches in a year. The first phase was to be both a learning and an experimental phase, to be followed closely to study three interconnected issues. One was the issue of removing constraints on the functioning of such banks and treating them at par with Indian banks as much as possible. Two was the decision regarding the permission to dilute their stake as long as 26% of the paid-up capital of the subsidiary was held by resident Indians. Three, foreign banks could be permitted to enter into merger and acquisition transactions with any private sector bank in India, subject to the overall (foreign) investment limit of 74%. The second phase was scheduled to commence from April 2009. However, that was the time when global financial markets were in turmoil. The start of the second phase was therefore put on hold, and was still so at the beginning of the 2010s.

Reforms were also initiated to widen and deepen the government securities market as well as the money markets. Foreign Institutional Investors (FIIs) can now invest in government securities subject to a maximum ceiling limit of US$10 billion. Simultaneously, large investments were made in technology for quicker settlements and moving on to the Real-Time Gross Settlement Systems in the government securities market. This and many other innovations have resulted in India having a world-class infrastructure for the debt markets and for the equity and other derivative markets.

The banking system in India now consists of three types of institutions, all regulated by the Reserve Bank of India (RBI). These are: (a) publicly owned or privately owned banks along with those owned by RBI itself; (b) development financial institutions and refinancing institutions that were set up either by a separate statute or under the

Companies Act, with four different types of owners — Government, RBI, private or other development financial institutions; and (c) non-bank financial companies (NBFCs), all of which are privately owned. The growth of non-bank financial corporations (NBFCs) was made possible through legislation introduced in 1997 that brought them under the direct supervision of the RBI and eased the laws governing their entry (Mohan, 2005).

The microfinance institutions (MFIs) were for a long time outside any specific regulation. Today, NBFCs form a large part of the MFIs; the rest are non-profit Trusts or NGOs (non-governmental, not-for-profit organizations), co-operative societies and bank-led self-help groups (SHGs). Currently, there is an attempt to create a new regulatory structure under the RBI for MFIs. There is also a discussion on having a separate regulatory body for them.

India has moved towards universal banking as banks and financial institutions have undergone a major shift in their domain of operations. This has led to competition across all financial institutions in both the raising of funds and their disbursement. For instance, while banks have started offering term-loans, financial institutions offer short-term loans. The further reform agenda is to divest the RBI of all its ownership functions.

Impact of Banking Sector Reforms

During the 2008 financial crisis, the Indian banks exhibited their strength in weathering the storm. While both the government and the RBI provided direct support to the financial sector, the support by the government has generally been considerably lower than what was originally anticipated and in comparison to their European counterparts. This has been mostly due to the fact that there was no inherent problem with the Indian financial sector though there was an initial phase of panic among bankers.

Bhaumik and Piesse (2005) concentrate on how ownership changes have affected the banking sector in India. Referring to the literature, they maintain that for an emerging economy, it is not only the efficient allocation of funds that is important; it is also necessary to check for the total amounts of credit disbursed. In other words, the loan portfolio of banks may not be exactly the one that is suitable for a growing economy. They argue that there is evidence of convergence among the different types of Indian banks in terms of financial performance, suggesting growing competition among them. However, more importantly, they argue that, following the new income recognition norms and monitoring of bad loans by the RBI, the banks took the easy route of investing a large part of their portfolio in government securities, more than what was required of them. This was somewhat reversed once debt recovery tribunals were set up around the turn of the century.

Gormley (2007) studies the impact of foreign bank entry into India. He argues that foreign banks were successful in isolating and then working with the better projects. The presence of foreign banks increased the perceived risk for firms left out by them, and this led to a reduction in the supply of credit to firms that could not get foreign bank loans.

Indian financial markets continue to be bank-dominated. Currently, the total assets of the banking sector stand at a whopping US$1 trillion. Indeed, the relative importance of bank assets as a percentage of GDP has continued to grow; this is partly because of banking penetration that has resulted from financial sector reforms and partly because of ongoing deficit financing. On the other hand, the ratio of bank assets to GDP is still low by comparison with other emerging East Asian economies. India has a world-class equity market with the ratio of equity market capitalization to GDP more than trebling to 108% since 1996. (This figure is down from 130% in September 2007, after which India was hit by the global financial crisis.) Over the same period, the Indian banking sector expanded to 74% of GDP from 46.5%. However, the development of both the government and corporate bond markets has lagged behind. The bond market went from 21.3% of GDP in 1996 to a current level of 40% in March 2008. Of this, the government bond market represented 36.1% of GDP, while the corporate bond market was a mere 3.9% of GDP. This, coupled with the lack of credit for firms as explained above, has at the beginning of the 2010s actually held back the economy in a big way.

The government bond market continues to be largely illiquid. The corporate bond market restricts participants and is largely arbitrage-driven (as opposed to driven by strategic needs of issuers) and also highly illiquid. According to Wells and Schou-Zibell (2008), this is surprising because India has world-class infrastructure for equities, equity derivatives and the bond market.

The major challenge faced by the banking sector is financial inclusion. Well over 40% of India's population are currently unbanked and do not have access to the formal banking sector in their monetary management. There is a huge network of unorganized money markets comprised of local money lenders who are currently catering to this population, often charging usurious interest rates ranging from 25% to 120% per annum. Financial inclusion is definitely on the RBI's agenda and it has taken many steps to improve the situation. The results will be known only in due course of time.

Capital Market Reforms

The Controller of Capital Issues (CCI) was abolished and, following the enactment of The Securities and Exchange Board Act (1992), the Securities Exchange Board of India (SEBI) was set up in 1992 as an apex regulator of the Indian capital markets. SEBI is required by law to protect the interests of three groups which constitute the capital market, namely the issuers of securities, the investors (small and big), and the market intermediaries comprised of brokers and others.

SEBI is empowered to draft regulations, conduct investigations and pass rulings on errant market participants. This makes SEBI a very powerful institution; however, to ensure fairness and accountability, there is an appellate process in place in the form of a three-member Securities Appellate Tribunal headed by a former chief justice of a high court, and a further appeal which may be heard at the Supreme Court of India. SEBI has been very active in establishing some very sweeping regulations for the Indian capital markets as required under law.

External Sector Reforms

Since 1991, this sector has undergone a major transformation. During these years, India has gone from being a nearly closed economy to an almost completely open economy. India now has a floating rupee and almost all the restrictions have been removed on the current account which is now fully convertible. Import duties have been reduced steadily to a peak custom duty rate of 12.5%. Indians are now free to import goods and services, except for those that come under a short negative list. The fiscal reforms have, in the meantime, led to a steady growth in direct tax collections for the government, and this has also contributed to the government reducing its reliance on indirect taxes such as customs and excise duties for revenues. However, there are a few remaining restrictions on the capital account and these are to be removed in a phased manner. India's current Prime Minister has announced that capital account convertibility is a goal, and it will be achieved soon.

9.5 Impact of Reforms on the Economy

From a macroeconomic perspective, the impact of the economic reforms on gross capital formation in India has been negligible and found to be statistically insignificant. Ray (2007) and Roland (2005) find that, since the overall start of the reforms in 1991, while the financial repression (McKinnon, 1973) has steadily declined, there is no significant relation between financial development and savings and capital formation, which is contrary to the prediction of the financial liberalization process. A look at the actual data also indicates that the contribution of foreign capital to domestic Indian capital formation is very insignificant. In the year 2009, Gross Capital Formation to GDP ratio stood at 36.5%, and Gross National Savings to GDP ratio stood at 34.9%, up from 22.6% and 22%, respectively, in 1998. This suggests that almost all of the capital formation could be funded by domestic savings alone.

While there is conclusive evidence that poverty has declined in terms of absolute number of people below the poverty line, the income inequality has also increased. The growth-oriented policies and economic liberalization policies discussed above have contributed to the growth in national income, with the decadal average rates of growth jumping to about 8% since 2000 compared to the 3.2% average during the entire period between 1950–1985. Bhalla (2007) goes further and expects a growth rate of 10% to be almost inevitable (these poverty estimates are calculated every five years).

By contrast, India's 128th ranking in the Human Development Index indicates that the country still has far to go in terms of actually improving the standard of living of the masses, especially the rural masses, most of whom have seen little or no change in their economic condition. About 260 million people still live below the poverty line (Kapila, 2007). Social sector policies need to be paid serious attention to. In most states of India there are serious lacunae in the provision of basic amenities like clean drinking water, sanitation and housing for the poor. Investment in rural infrastructure in a majority of the Indian states is less than 5% of the state's GDP, while the overall capital formation in the country stands at around 34%.

From the very beginning (i.e., since becoming independent in 1947), India had tried to use (planned) growth to tackle its poverty problem. However, over the years and especially in the 1970s, India began to rely more and more on re-distribution and targeted programs than on pure growth. Growth was brought back in the 1990s as an important means to end poverty but, unlike in the initial years, India started relying on the market and the private sector to provide the growth impetus. Then, once the growth process was on track, India started attacking poverty issues in a way that it has never done before.

India is now following a poverty alleviation strategy that is very different from the targeted programs of yesteryears. The right-to-development approach discusses five basic demands that a citizen can make on society: (1) the right to freedom from hunger, (2) the right to education, (3) the right to health, (4) the right to civil liberties, and, a slightly controversial one, (5) the right to employment. For the first, India is implementing a Food Security Act, and for the second, a Right to Education Act. One may expect that civil liberties would be better implemented in a democracy. However, in a largely uneducated and hierarchical society, democratic leaders can restrict the rights of the citizens in a number of different ways. A most important way of doing this is to hide information of what the government is doing and how it is conducting its business. The Right to Information Act empowers citizens to demand information from the government; this information has to be provided in a time-bound fashion, and non-compliance by the government administration is a punishable offense. The Indian government has not passed any law regarding the right to health, but it has initiated a national health insurance plan. Under this plan, all poor households receive an insurance policy, the premium for which is paid for by the government. Finally, the government has an employment scheme wherein any adult can ask and get 100 days' employment at minimum wage. However, to get this wage, workers have to provide manual labor that goes into building local public assets; the manual labor requirement acts as a self-selection mechanism.

Every democratic Constitution delineates the rights of its citizens. The way these rights are enforced depends on how the judicial system interprets these directives in the Constitution. However, when specific Acts are enacted, interpretations are no longer required, for these Acts now specify the exact way they are to be enforced. This is important in the Indian context; almost all of the rights discussed here fall in the realm of what the states are required to enforce and are outside the direct control of the central, or the federal, government. What these Acts are doing is that they are giving powers to the central government to develop the infrastructure and institutions necessary to enforce them and for the judiciary to hold the states responsible if these rights are not granted to those living in these states. This is a major change in the way India is addressing its problems of governance and, in the process, that of poverty.

A first paper looking into the pattern of Indian liberalization was by Ansari and Gang (1999). They used aggregate data from the 1970s until the mid-1990s to focus on the nature of the transmission of aggregate shocks, both internal and external, through the economy.

Their results were negative; they found no obvious change in the transmission patterns in their data and concluded that there was no major structural break in the liberalization process since the mid-1970s. However, the major reason for this finding is that they used aggregate data in a country that is very diverse and has a federal structure. This tends to dampen major changes occurring in particular states that are often bigger than many countries.

There are two other hypotheses that have been floated (see Rodrik and Subramanian, 2004; Virmani, 2004; Bhaumik *et al.*, 2008): (i) the structural change in India started in the 1980s; and (ii) the decade of the 1980s was characterized by a pro-incumbent business policy, while the 1990s was characterized by a more pro-entrant policy. Bhaumik *et al.* (2008) make an additional point. They demonstrate that the process of reforms unleashed post-1991 has increased the federal nature of the Indian state. This has led to competition among the Indian states, which in turn has resulted in the poorer states growing faster than before and trying to catch up with the more developed states.

Madsen *et al.* (2010) find that the growth spurt in the Indian economy has been affected by the economic reforms that started in the 1980s and gained momentum after the 1990s. Their results show that financial liberalization, the increase in FDI-GDP ratio and the knowledge flow from abroad following the patent protection rights have influenced growth. Madsen *et al.* further find that the total factor productivity is somewhat lower compared to other OECD countries, but India may catch up if it continues to strengthen its research and development activity, albeit at a distant future.

The most important policy lesson of the 1990s has been that institutional factors have a huge impact on the strategic decision-making process of businesses and that these factors go well beyond the usual institutions of democracy and legal origin. Remember that the nature of parliamentary democracy and legal origin is common across Indian states. However, the initial growth experiences in the Indian states were very different immediately after the 1990s' reform. This could be largely explained by factors like the quality of enforcement of law, policy continuity at the state level in the face of changes in state-level governments at regular intervals, and the quality of governance in general.

The global inflation episode in 2008, followed by the global financial crisis, has resulted in the growth of a strong opposition to fast-track reforms. There has always been a feeling that much of the fruits of liberalization and globalization have completely bypassed certain large sections of the population. The current government, aware of this feeling, undertook far-reaching initiatives for social security and for improving the quality of health and education (and training) of its vulnerable population (referred to previously). Indeed, the experiences of 2008 have vindicated some of India's stubbornness in doing things its own way.

The 2008 inflation resulted in across-the-board food price inflation to levels that were quite rare, though not entirely unprecedented. (India's inflation rates are unique among developing countries in that anything above 10% is usually not seen. In 2008, inflation of food items went up to 15%.) Historically, India has tackled food inflation by imports from abroad and distributed the imports through its subsidized public distribution system (PDS). However, in 2008, the food price rise was mostly due to international sources and, hence, cheap imports were not possible. The government eased the impact of this inflation by holding the PDS prices steady and by increasing the subsidy. Historically, a major objective of the PDS was "food security" which focuses more on access and availability. This approach was a natural outcome of the "forced famine" of 1942–1943 in Bengal when food was diverted away from India to support the war effort. The usefulness of the PDS becomes clear when one compares to what happened in Bangladesh in 2008. Thanks to pressure from all the donor agencies, Bangladesh had dismantled its PDS a few years back. This created havoc in Bangladesh as it tried to tackle the impact of the food inflation without an institutional mechanism to transfer the subsidies required.

The PDS has been lambasted by most foreign observers as inefficient. However, a large part of this inefficiency stemmed from the PDS being viewed as a means to keep food prices cheaper and, hence, being targeted towards the poor. Like any targeted program, it created price distortions, and people who were not poor tried to be identified as poor to get the subsidy.

The financial crisis that followed the inflation re-confirmed India's growth story as being domestic demand-driven. The Indian banks were initially unaffected by the global financial crisis since they were not exposed to the "rogue" instruments that precipitated the crisis. However, the global recession that came with the crisis affected Indian exports. These were mostly in four sectors — textiles, leather, gems and jewellery, and, of course, IT and IT-related services. The first three sectors are very labor-intensive and are geographically concentrated. This meant that employment was adversely affected, as were the regional economies of the places where these sectors were concentrated. This impact was mitigated to an extent by what happened to the Indian rupee during the crisis.

Prior to the crisis, Indian corporations had generated foreign financial obligations to meet their investments abroad. When the financial crisis hit the world, these corporations were suddenly faced with a squeeze on their foreign sources of funds. This therefore created a demand for foreign currency in India, and the Indian rupee depreciated in 2008 by almost 20% within a few months. This obviously was good for the export sector, which was the worst affected by the crisis.

Given India's low reliance on foreign trade (unlike that of, say, China), India was able to weather the storm through its growing domestic demand. Also, the government undertook massive injections of funds into the economy through major infrastructure investments and reductions in taxes at the same time. This increased the fiscal deficit in 2008 which is, at the beginning of the 2010s, being brought back to its original trend. What actually caused a serious problem in India was the panic among the Indian banks. They were unwilling to lend, and the worst affected were the non-bank financial corporations (NBFCs). Indian banks do not lend directly to the small and medium-sized enterprises (SMEs); they lend to the NBFCs which then lend money to the SMEs. Once the banks stopped lending to the NBFCs, the SMEs were starved of money and this affected their levels of activity, hence the slowdown in growth. However, the Reserve Bank of India (as the central bank is called) undertook various steps to encourage banks to continue lending to the SMEs, and this has resulted in India's growth moving back to its earlier trend line.

Thus, India emerged relatively unscathed from the crisis. Some of the other reasons for this could be that India had floating exchange rates and also had a sizable cushion in the form of foreign exchange reserves (which helped to tide over the negative balance on the BOP), though this may not have contributed much to the subsequent growth revisions. More generally, there is evidence to support the intuition that "the transmission of shocks to countries with lower financial linkages to the world (such as low-income countries) tend to occur predominantly through trade, while the financial channel is more relevant for countries with close financial ties to the advanced economies, where the crisis originated" (Berkman *et al.*, 2010).

India has both trade as well as financial linkages with the world, but it is not as well-integrated with the rest of the world compared to other fast-growing economies like China and Brazil. Exports did fall during this period (fell by 21% in February 2009), but the rupee also depreciated by nearly 25% and this managed to stabilize the current account. Also, after many years, the capital account slipped into negative territory, leading to some reduction in the foreign exchange reserves. India lost 2.3% in growth in 2008–2009, i.e., from 9% to 6.7%. The growth rate improved to about 7.5% in 2009–2010 and then to 9% during 2010–2011.

There are some studies that find that in India, the FDI inflows have not made much impact on GDP, but the causality runs from GDP to FDI. However, FDI flows may have led to some growth in exports (Basu and Chakraborty, 2002; Trevino and Upadhyaya, 2003; Basu *et al.*, 2003; Dhakal *et al.*, 2007). The growth in India is almost entirely funded by domestic savings. This meant that in the event of the shock, when foreign capital inflows fell sharply, the domestic economy did not slip into a recession. This combination of factors resulted in the Indian economy being relatively insulated from the shock of the global recession.

9.6 EU-India Trade and Investment Links

The EU has historically been an important trading partner for India. Some countries stand out as more important than others and that is largely because of India's historic links with the UK, France and Germany which also encompassed strong cultural exchanges. However, if one were to look at the first concluded decade of the new century, the EU has been steadily losing out as one of India's major trading partners (see Tables 9.1 and 9.2). This is independent of the problems that followed the global financial crisis. In keeping with India's "look east policy", trade with Asian and ASEAN countries has been steadily increasing over this last decade.

In 2006, the European Commission published a document called *Global Europe: Competing in the World*. Its three main components were harmonization of standards within the EU, importing raw materials from developing countries ("global south"), and signing bilateral free trade agreements (FTAs) outside of the WTO negotiations. This document also singled out India as one of its major targets for closer relationships.

As an obvious follow-up, India and the EU have been holding discussions to sign an FTA between them. Many proponents of this FTA are disappointed with the amount of time it is taking, but this is largely due to two reasons. First, the discussions are being held behind closed doors in both countries with little or no open discussions in the public domain. However, major corporate groups like manufacturers and banks are being consulted. This is obviously raising the concerns of civil societies in both regions, especially after the financial crisis of 2008 when European financial institutions were found to be as greedy as any of the failed institutions in the US.

In both countries, corporate interests are privy to the FTA negotiations. In Europe, major interests like the European Services Forum, the European Banking Federation, the European Federation of Pharmaceutical Industries and Associations, and Business Europe are playing a significant role in driving the negotiations and the agenda. In India, the corporate interests involve manufacturing and services that face non-tariff barriers in trade and investment.

Table 9.1: Regional share in India's exports.

Region	2000	2001	2002	2003	2004	2005	2006	2007	2008	2009
1) Europe	25.94	24.78	24.16	24.54	23.55	24.16	22.86	22.86	22.71	21.40
1.1 EU Countries (27)	24.03	23.17	22.55	22.74	21.85	22.53	21.23	21.17	21.24	20.00
1.2 Other WE Countries	1.87	1.57	1.58	1.73	1.65	1.58	1.58	1.62	1.40	1.33
1.3 East Europe	0.03	0.04	0.04	0.07	0.05	0.05	0.06	0.07	0.07	0.06
2) Africa	4.09	4.93	4.66	4.82	5.05	5.28	6.65	7.07	6.15	6.20
2.1 Southern Africa	0.91	1.06	1.21	1.24	1.51	1.88	2.23	2.21	1.69	2.02
2.2 West Africa	1.74	2.39	2.02	1.99	1.98	1.84	1.94	2.12	1.81	1.80
2.3 Central Africa	0.17	0.21	0.22	0.24	0.19	0.16	0.16	0.16	0.21	0.21
2.4 East Africa	1.26	1.27	1.20	1.35	1.37	1.39	2.33	2.58	2.43	2.17
3) America	24.65	22.95	24.45	20.98	20.10	20.73	19.17	16.96	15.48	14.88
3.1 North America	22.43	20.76	21.99	19.19	17.52	17.82	15.80	13.48	12.15	11.86
3.2 Latin America	2.22	2.19	2.46	1.78	2.59	2.90	3.37	3.48	3.33	3.02
4) Asia & ASEAN	38.69	40.19	44.39	47.60	49.50	48.38	49.86	51.70	52.14	53.76
4.1 East Asia	1.10	1.16	1.15	1.10	1.03	0.97	1.17	0.87	0.95	1.03
4.2 ASEAN	6.52	7.89	8.76	9.12	10.09	10.10	9.97	10.06	10.33	10.53
4.3 WANA	12.62	13.18	14.28	15.95	17.04	16.19	18.23	18.62	22.50	23.46
4.4 NE Asia	14.17	13.29	14.92	14.70	15.83	15.74	15.36	16.25	13.73	14.13
4.5 South Asia	4.27	4.68	5.28	6.73	5.51	5.38	5.12	5.91	4.62	4.61
5) CIS & Baltics	2.35	2.22	1.75	1.62	1.31	1.21	1.17	1.07	1.04	0.89
5.1 CARs Countries	0.18	0.16	0.16	0.24	0.21	0.16	0.15	0.14	0.14	0.16
5.2 Other CIS Countries	2.17	2.06	1.59	1.39	1.10	1.05	1.02	0.92	0.90	0.73
6) Unspecified Region	4.29	4.93	0.59	0.44	0.49	0.24	0.28	0.34	2.49	2.87
Total	100.00	100.00	100.00	100.00	100.00	100.00	100.00	100.00	100.00	100.00

Table 9.2: Regional share in India's imports.

Region	2000	2001	2002	2003	2004	2005	2006	2007	2008	2009
1) Europe	27.55	26.54	24.98	24.04	22.98	22.18	21.63	20.50	18.86	19.05
1.1 EU Countries (27)	21.07	20.71	20.90	19.29	17.31	17.43	16.07	15.28	14.07	13.50
1.2 Other WE Countries	6.47	5.82	4.07	4.73	5.66	4.72	5.52	5.20	4.77	5.53
1.3 East Europe	0.01	0.01	0.01	0.02	0.01	0.02	0.03	0.01	0.01	0.02
2) Africa	3.21	4.11	4.70	3.50	3.01	2.71	6.12	5.93	6.22	7.05
2.1 Southern Africa	2.12	2.88	3.52	2.51	2.06	1.77	1.57	1.92	2.38	3.49
2.2 West Africa	0.89	0.93	0.88	0.74	0.74	0.78	4.40	3.86	3.68	3.42
2.3 Central Africa	0.01	0.01	0.01	0.01	0.02	0.01	0.02	0.02	0.05	0.02
2.4 East Africa	0.19	0.29	0.30	0.24	0.20	0.15	0.13	0.13	0.12	0.12
3) America	7.89	9.11	9.86	8.90	8.82	8.74	10.58	11.76	10.20	9.54
3.1 North America	6.48	7.16	8.16	7.37	6.97	6.96	7.28	9.16	6.92	6.71
3.2 Latin America	1.42	1.96	1.70	1.53	1.84	1.79	3.30	2.61	3.28	2.83
4) Asia & ASEAN	28.61	31.43	30.11	35.36	36.19	34.57	59.14	59.59	62.06	61.54
4.1 East Asia	2.3[illegible]	2.71	2.32	3.52	3.63	3.54	4.08	3.32	3.88	4.48
4.2 ASEAN	8.12	8.53	8.39	9.51	8.17	7.30	9.75	9.01	8.63	9.56
4.3 WANA	6.10	6.17	5.84	6.30	8.54	7.28	27.53	28.62	29.70	27.24
4.4 NE Asia	11.16	12.87	12.71	15.12	14.95	15.51	16.98	17.80	19.25	19.67
4.5 South Asia	0.92	1.15	0.86	0.91	0.89	0.95	0.81	0.84	0.60	0.59
5) CIS & Baltics	1.36	1.43	1.37	1.61	1.76	1.98	2.08	1.51	2.18	2.30
5.1 CARs Countries	0.06	0.06	0.06	0.06	0.06	0.05	0.08	0.04	0.09	0.08
5.2 Other CIS Countries	1.30	1.38	1.31	1.55	1.70	1.93	2.00	1.46	2.10	2.22
6) Unspecified Region	31.38	27.38	28.97	26.59	27.25	29.82	0.45	0.72	0.48	0.52
Total	100.00	100.00	100.00	100.00	100.00	100.00	100.00	100.00	100.00	100.00

Civil societies are largely exempt, as are researchers and the general public. This creates a certain degree of misgiving about the negotiations among the people who are going to be directly affected. For example, a large part of India's population depends on agriculture for their livelihood. There are 35 crops that involve more than 5 million people each (Sharma, 2009). Any agreement that keeps them outside the purview of the negotiations will jeopardize the trade-offs that India can make in its non-agricultural sectors. As is evident in a recent agricultural land acquisition (for industrialization) case in India, it is difficult to move forward in a democracy if people are not involved in the decision-making process.

The second reason for the delay is the approach that the EU is insisting on in the discussions. Though India is only about 7% of the EU economy and has more than 3 times the population, the EU wants to treat India as an "equal partner" in the agreement. This means that all special and differential treatments that WTO agreements entail are to be suspended in this agreement. At the same time, the European agricultural subsidies have to be maintained, as well as the standards governing the import into the EU of food and agricultural products. India, and other developing countries, has long maintained that these standards act as non-tariff barriers, especially because there is no harmonization of these standards across European countries.

Europe's focus on raw material imports from the "global south" is viewed with suspicion in India. India's colonial history has been marked by the forced de-industrialization of India's indigenous industry by the British and the latter's extraction of raw materials to feed its industry back home. To state upfront in its 2006 publication that its objective is to import raw materials from countries like India and gain market access for its finished products and services, has certainly not won many enthusiastic supporters among the general public in India.

In addition to agriculture, another major area of concern is the EU's insistence on WTO plus conditions in services and investment. The Indian government is interested in liberalizing most services trade as long as Mode 1 (that support outsourcing through BPOs) and Mode 4 (that allow movements of professionals) services trade are liberalized by the EU. However, such movements of people will ultimately be decided outside the FTA by the respective country governments, as political decisions. The recent experiences in the UK regarding Indian doctors have created grave doubts about the commitment of European countries to such movements.

These misgivings, on both sides, are unfortunate because they act as serious impediments to a process of reforms in India that is beneficial to both the populations.

By contrast, the Indo-US trade relations have been improving at a phenomenal rate. The total Indo-US trade shot up by threefold from US$13.7 billion in 2001 to US$41.4 billion in 2007, thus registering an average growth of about 30% per annum. Following the global crisis, this growth sharply declined to 7.4% and has begun to show signs of revival since 2009.

On the FDI front, Hunya and Stollinger (2009) find that while the EU is well-positioned as a direct investor both globally and in the BRIC economies, its position in India and China is low and not particularly dynamic. They find that geographical distances matter and while large corporations may be willing to invest in far away countries like India and China, for the SMEs in the EU, policy initiatives may be needed to increase their presence there. This is all the more desirable since India and China have huge potential and are capable of realizing much better returns on the FDI. However, there are bottlenecks in the form of ownership controls and sectoral caps on FDI in these countries, especially in industries like finance and telecom which may be of interest to the EU investors. The EU trade policy should work towards improving the situation.

The flow of FDI from EU to India has been fairly erratic and unpredictable. The share of FDI to India out of the total FDI of EU was an abysmal 0.02% in 2003, and limited to a few large EU members like Netherlands, UK, Germany, France, Italy and Sweden. The total FDI flow to India from EU was Euro 2.881 billion, and the FDI from India to EU in the same year stood at Euro 940 million (after peaking at Euro 10.118 billion in 2007). Given that the EU is very outward-looking in its approach, and given India's strong historical linkages with the biggest members of the EU, it is surprising that

India has received such little investments from there. The global economic crisis saw a further reduction in the FDI flows to India from EU to Euro 2.4 billion. The EU accounted for about 27% of total FDI to India in 2009. In a recent announcement in March 2009, the EU requested a further opening up of the Indian economy for investments. Their ambassador Mr. Smadja is quoted to have said that the proposed comprehensive FTA with India will bring more predictability in the investment relations.

9.7 India-EU Relations

India and EU have a lot in common. The EU that India sees is one region with 27 countries speaking in 23 languages. Its constituents also vary widely in size, ranging from a population of only 0.4 million in Malta to 81 million in Germany. Correspondingly, India has 28 states (+7 Union Territories that are governed directly from Delhi) and speaks in 22 officially recognized languages. Its smallest state, Sikkim, has 0.5 million people and its largest, Uttar Pradesh, has 166 million. While the EU is a set of countries coming together, India has a very federal structure wherein the states have their own and different histories, traditions, cultures and languages like the EU constituents.

Both are multi-cultural, multi-ethnic, multi-religious and strongly dedicated to democratic principles and the rule of law. India's national integration in 1947 was an experimental nature, with its constituents' desire to escape the clutches of their colonial masters; of course, now some point out that cricket and Bollywood are the two major cementing factors along with federalism and commitment to maintaining unity of principles across the many diversities among its states. Similarly, the seeds of European integration were sowed immediately after the ravaging conflict during World War II, and the current integration is being fed by the desire to achieve shared goals. Indeed, many of the issues that the EU faces today — harmonization of standards and a common "legal language" — were problems faced by the Indian state in the early years. Unfortunately, while all these common characteristics and shared goals create huge potential for cooperation and engagement, the actual reality is that India and the EU have historically not been very relevant to each other.

The huge internal diversity within the EU is important in order to understand what it is that the EU actors — businesses, governments and civil societies — are missing about India. First, aggregate data on India is highly misleading and the data from different states need to be looked at separately. Second, looking at Delhi to solve some of the business irritants regarding India is tantamount to coming to Brussels to set up a factory in Sweden. On the other hand, the EU must appreciate that given that its constituents have differing standards for imports from India, Indian actors are unwilling to treat the EU as one region. Finally, given India's historical ties with some of the member states (like Germany, France, UK), it will take some time for India to start thinking about the EU as an entity.

Fioramonti (2007) analyzes the Indian media to infer what Indians think about the EU. EU as an entity is still unknown to India and this is largely because of the lack of congruence amongst Indian actors about how they view the EU. While businesses are willing to consider the EU as a possibly integrated market in some areas, the political circles find it more convenient to view the EU as an entity only when it comes to international politics and diplomacy. And both are much belabored views. For businesses, as mentioned in the previous section, the lack of harmonization in non-tariff barriers destroys the notion of the EU as an integrated region. For the government and intellectuals, engaging with the US is more efficient since when it comes to India, the EU appears to have no independent views other than toeing the US line anyway. More importantly, while it pays to have the US on its side, India has not seen any obvious fruits of EU support.

Raja Mohan (2006) emphasizes that "India's relations with Europe have been limited by the fact that New Delhi is fairly unimpressed with Europe's role in global politics." This feeling was re-affirmed by the opposition to the Indo-US nuclear deal from many EU members. The mitigating factor was the support it got from the UK and France. Indeed, France was the first, and well before the US, to see a market for high-tech goods in India. Consequently, when

India conducted its nuclear tests in 1998, France shielded India from G-8 anger. The growing threat of international terrorism and India's economic rise has resulted in the UK being more accommodating of India's foreign policy and global aspirations.

India has been trying to tell the whole world about the threats of cross-border terrorism, having faced its consequences for more than two decades since the 1990s. However, the US, because of its support to China, and by extension to Pakistan, was unwilling to take India's complaints seriously. Things changed after 9/11, though the US had by then already deviated from its past position of blindly supporting Pakistan by siding with India when Pakistani forces infiltrated into Kargil in 1999. Pakistan claimed that these were Kashmiri insurgents fighting against India. However, India was able to give conclusive proof that the Pakistani armed forces were directly involved in both the planning of the attack and participating in it. Since the EU was essentially toeing the US line pre-Kargil, and it was the US that came out in support of India in 1999, the EU was once again sidelined in India as a region that is more interested in following the US. Hence, India focused its attention on the US.

What happened post-Kargil was a natural outcome of India's changing approach to foreign policy following the reforms. Two important things happened in 1991; first, India gave up its socialist leanings on economic matters and embraced the market system, and second, the Cold War had come to an end. India therefore took stock of the new global environment and moved determinedly towards a greater involvement with its East and the United States. This was an important deviation from its past, when both of these attitudes were not popular with the political elite (Jaffrelot, 2006). The focus on these two approaches left no space for engaging with the EU. Fortunately, though late, such an engagement was initiated with the India-EU summit that took place in Lisbon in 2000, and in 2004 the two parties signed a Strategic Partnership Agreement. This has led to major cooperation in cultural and intellectual exchanges (in science and engineering) and the setting up of a scholarship fund to pay for Indian students studying in the EU. However, the number of Indian students in the US is many, many times more than those in the EU.

Jaffrelot (2006) refers to four initiatives that need to be taken to improve relations between the EU and India. First, EU must engage with India as one entity and member states should not deal directly, and independently, with India. This is a necessity given India's size, its growing economy, and its role in the region and among other developing countries (like Brazil or South Africa). Second, the EU has to give up its obvious pro-China economic and political bias since this is contradictory to its apparent concerns regarding democracy and civil liberties. While the US has historically been pro-China since 1971, it has of late been suspicious of the growing dominance of China in the region. Third, the EU should directly help India to solve some of its social and economic problems and not simply criticize, or ignore, India because of its shortcomings in these areas. Two obvious sectors are infrastructure and the environment; in both of these, the EU has immense expertise whereas India is struggling very hard to cope with them. Finally, two initiatives that will go a long way because they are both "symbolic and substantive" are higher education and work experience. Indian students in the US move seamlessly into the US job market and then, by the time they move back to India, they usually have an established network of friends and colleagues in the US who share a common understanding and vision about the objectives of the two countries. Unfortunately, such possibilities within the EU are in their infancy.

One opportunity that should not be missed has been opened up by the current Indian government's welfare reforms. India is moving away from a regime of targeted programs for certain sections of the population to a rights-based approach to development. In the latter, all citizens are conferred certain rights, independent of whether or not they are poor. The enactment of laws that India is now going through makes it imperative for the administrative machinery to enforce these rights as, otherwise, empowered citizens can take the administrators to court. In a rule-of-law society, this is an important method of implementation and it leaves the politics out of the process of ensuring the basic rights of citizens. If one were to look at the EU, in most of its member states, the welfare system does not target any particular group of citizens. Thus, education and health are free regardless of whether one is rich or poor. Intellectual exchanges regarding a targeted approach versus a universal approach and the benefits of the European welfare system could be an important avenue for bringing the two societies together. The EU then will participate in some of the most far-reaching initiatives that India is undertaking in its push towards development. Such intellectual cooperation will have much greater impact than conferences on trade and investment where the positions taken by each of the parties are usually more adversarial than consultative!

9.8 Conclusions: Scope for Closer Indo-European Ties in the Re-polarization Process

Looking ahead, India's outlook is very bright. The macro-fundamentals are very strong and the investment climate is very positive, driven by reforms of almost all the sectors of the Indian economy, as discussed in the preceding sections. New opportunities for investments are being created all the time, such as the civilian nuclear deal opening up opportunities for major investments in nuclear energy, and the opening up of the higher education system to foreign universities, to name only two. Unlike other Asian economies, India's growth took off due to the private sector, with the IT and ITES sector acting as the vehicle of this higher growth. India's growth path also is somewhat different from the traditional path of countries transitioning from agrarian to manufacturing with services becoming important at a later stage. India has gone from being an agrarian economy to a services-led economy, with its share of manufacturing stagnating at around 20%. However, in the wake of the financial crisis, the first sector to start posting strong growth rates has been the manufacturing sector, which is not as well-integrated with the rest of the world as the IT and ITES industry is.

On the political front, since 1991, successive governments, while belonging to different political parties, have shown their commitment to the liberalization process and there is no danger of any policy reversals. India's strength has always been its strong English-educated and skilled manpower base. In the next decade, the percentage of people below 40 years is expected to be about 65.

The EU has not played a significant role in India's growth story thus far. The strengthening of economic ties with the EU is contingent on several developments, most notably the FTA between EU and India. While India has strong ties with a few individual members of the EU like France, Netherlands and UK, the EU is not a cohesive entity and the trade and investment ties appear to be more bilateral in nature.

India has come a long way from being the economically dependent country that it once was to a robust one with its strong growth driven primarily by domestic consumption. It is now a very attractive market for global players from the EU and the rest of the world. FDI continues to flow in, drawn by the attractive return on investments. In this context, it can be argued that the EU has largely ignored India. But it cannot continue to do so in the years to come. The proposed FTA with India shows that the EU is taking active steps to counteract history.

In a re-polarized world, India would like to see itself growing in global importance not only economically but politically as well. Its aspiration for a permanent seat on the UN Security Council is well-known. India has strengthened its trade ties with other South East Asian countries and the trade and investment flows with them have been rising at a steady pace. India also has a healthy trade relationship with China, and both countries have expressed a desire to take the trade levels to new highs. At the same time, India has forged ties with Brazil (in South America) and South Africa (on the African continent).

By contrast, India's economic ties with the major countries of the EU have stagnated if not deteriorated in the last two decades. Part of the reason for this is the formation of the Union itself, which might have led to trade diversion away from countries like India. Going forward, India's relationship with the rest of the world, and with the EU in particular, will be based on mutual benefit. It will also depend on how cohesive the EU becomes as an entity to engage and negotiate with, as opposed to being a collection of nations, at least in the eyes of countries like India. The EU for its part needs to think about where it wants to stand *vis-a-vis* India.

Given India's history of political non-alignment, India would love to think that it can be a torch-bearer for countries that want to be independent of superpowers and be free to pursue their own goals. In the past, India has wanted to play this role but was sidelined by the lack of any economic strength to force the world to listen to it. The current high and consistent growth rates have given India the chance to fulfil its goals. As ageing populations look more and more at investments outside their home countries, India feels that it can get the clout it needs for a changed world order since developed countries will have to invest abroad in fast-growing economies. Historically, the Indian government has not been close to the US government, especially since 1971 and the Bangladesh war when most developed countries, led by USA, maintained a distance from the genocide happening there since China opposed the Bangladesh freedom struggle. That has had a profound influence on the Indian government's thought process; it has realized that national business and commerce interests usually overshadow the oft-repeated loftier goals of democracy and rule of law. India's experiences during its own colonial past are thereby reinforced and, therefore, it is unlikely that India will be a part of any pole unless it is one where the less developed countries belong to. However, in spite of its many internal problems, India likes to think it is more like the European countries in terms of their focus on individual rights and, hence, there is scope for closer Indo-European ties.

References

Ansari, M. I. and Gang, I. N. (1999). Liberalization policy: fits and starts or gradual change in India. *Comparative Economic Studies*, 41(4), 23–46.

Basu, P. and Chakraborty, C. (2002). Foreign direct investment and growth in India: a co-integration approach. *Applied Economics*, 34(9), 1061–1073.

Basu, P., Chakraborty, C. and Reagle, D. (2003). Liberalization, FDI, and growth in developing countries: a panel cointegration approach. *Economic Inquiry*, 41(3), 510–516.

Berkman, P., Gelos, G., Rennhack, R. and James, P. W. (2010). The global financial crisis: explaining cross-country differences in the output impact. IMF Working Paper WP/09/280.

Bhalla, S. (2007). *Second among Equals: The Middle-Class Kingdoms of India and China*. Washington, D.C.: Institute of International Economics.

Bhaumik, S. K. and Piesse, J. (2005). Are foreign banks active in emerging credit markets? Evidence from the Indian banking industry. William Davidson Institute, Working Paper No. 774.

Bhaumik, S. K., Gangopadhyay, S. and Krishnan, S. (2008). Policy, economic federalism, and product market entry: the Indian experience. *The European Journal of Development Research*, 20(1), 1–30.

Dhakal, D., Rahman, S. and Upadhyaya, K. P. (2007). Foreign direct investment and economic growth in Asia. *Indian Journal of Economics and Business*, 6(1), 15–26.

Fioramonti, L. (2007). Different facets of a strategic partnership: how the EU is viewed by political and business elites, civil societies and the press in India. *European Foreign Affairs Review*, 12(3), 349–362.

Gormley, T. A. (2007). The impact of foreign bank entry in emerging markets: evidence from India. Mimeo, Washington University.

Hunya, G. and Stollinger, R. (2009). Foreign direct investment flows between the EU and the BRICs. The Vienna Institute for International Economic Studies, Research Report 358, December 2009.

Jaffrelot, C. (2006). India and the European Union: the charade of a strategic partnership. CNRS Working Paper.

Kapila, U. (2007). *Indian Economy: Performance and Policies*. New Delhi: Academic Press.

Kohli, A. (2004). Politics of economic growth in India: 1980–2000. Paper presented at a conference on State Politics in India in the 1990s, India International Center, New Delhi, December 16–17.

Madsen, J. B., Saxena, S. and Ang, J. B. (2010). The Indian growth miracle and endogenous growth. *Journal of Development Economics*, 93(1), 37–48.

McKinnon, R. I. (1973). *Money and Capital in Economic Development*. Washington, D.C.: Brookings Institution.

Mohan, R. (2005). Financial sector reforms in India. *The Chartered Accountant*, February, 962–972.

Parikh, K. (Ed.) (1997). *India Development Report*. New Delhi: Oxford University Press.

Raja Mohan, C. (2006). Will the West engage. *Foreign Affairs*, July/August 2006.

Ray, A. (2007). A time series analysis of long-term capital formation in India. *Vidyasagar University Journal of Commerce*, 12 (March).

Rodrik, D. and Subramanian, A. (2004). From “Hindu growth” to productivity surge: the mystery of the Indian growth transition. Discussion Paper No. 4371, Centre for Economic Policy Research.

Roland, C. (2005). Banking sector liberalization in India. Paper presented at the 9th Capital Markets Conference, Indian Institute of Capital Markets, 2005.

Sharma, H. R. (2009). Rural non-farm employment in Himachal Pradesh, 1971–2001: a district-level analysis. *Indian Journal of Agricultural Economics*, 64(2), 208–228.

Trevino, L. J. and Upadhyaya, K. P. (2003). Foreign aid, FDI and economic growth: evidence from Asian countries. *Transnational Corporations*, 12(2), 119–135.

Virmani, A. (2004). Economic reforms: policy and institutions, some lessons from the Indian experience. Working Paper No. 121, Indian Council for Research on International Economic Relations, New Delhi.

Wells, S. and Schou-Zibell, L. (2008). India's bond market — development and challenges ahead. Working Paper Series on Regional Economic Integration, No. 22, Asian Development Bank.

Chapter 10

Chindia FDI in Africa: Implications for Europe and Re-polarization

Raj Aggarwal and Rym Ayadi

10.1 Introduction

Africa has both some of the poorest and some of the fastest growing economies. The future of Africa is considered very bright as it is a large and populous continent with much potential (Mahajan, 2009). In addition, China and India have been some of the fastest growing large economies for the last few decades, but a few decades ago they were not unlike what Africa is today in terms of its potential. Between 1985 and 2008, Africa's share in attracting overseas investment grew from \$2.4 billion to \$87.6 billion (UNCTAD, 2010b). Consequently, the rising roles of China and India in Africa are of much interest. Unfortunately, there is inadequate past literature on this topic (Onyeiwu and Shrestha, 2004). This chapter is an attempt to fill this gap in the literature.

Although, historically speaking, European ex-colonial powers have been the key economic players in Africa, the past decade has witnessed a significant increase in the economic involvement of China and India (hereafter alternatively referred to as Chindian or the Asian drivers) in the continent. This increased economic involvement has manifested itself in the fields of trade and foreign direct investment (FDI). As much as aid might be considered as an important part of the countries' involvement in Africa, this paper focuses particularly on trade and FDI, with a view to highlighting how the increasing resource needs of these two developing economies shape their economic involvement in Africa.

This chapter documents the rise of FDI from China and India (Chindia) in Africa since 2000. It contends that this growing presence of Chindian FDI is likely to change and reduce the relative role and influence of Europe in the continent, further leading to an increased multi-polarization of the global economy.

While the resource needs of China and India are similar, their patterns of engagement differ significantly, reflecting their different political structures. In the Chinese case, it is the government who is the dominant actor driving FDI to Africa. On the other hand, it is the private Indian companies, with the support of the Indian Diaspora in Africa, that are responsible for the rapid increase of the country's position in the continent. Regardless of their diverging patterns of involvement, it is important to draw attention to the fact that both countries implement their know-how in infrastructure-building to create a favorable environment for the satisfaction of their resource needs. Thus, this chapter analyzes the dynamics of Africa's international economic landscape as a result of the above-mentioned changes in FDI and trade patterns. Not only does this study contribute to a better understanding of China's and India's economic involvement in Africa, it also provides insights for Europe's future African policies.[1]

Section 10.2 provides an overview of the African economic landscape, focusing on FDI inflows and stocks in the continent. Section 10.3 highlights the growing Chinese and Indian trade and investment ties with Africa and their characteristics of ownership, entry and integration of local labor. Section 10.4 delves into the drivers of Chindian investments in Africa, with particular attention devoted to the role of natural resources, governments and Diasporas. Section 10.5 analyzes the mixed effects of Sino-Indian trade and investment with the continent, while Section 10.6 concludes by deriving implications for FDI

---

[1] While the current data falls short of creating a solid basis for a clear assessment of the impacts of Chinese and Indian economic relations with Africa, it nevertheless points at implications for EU's policies in the continent.

theory and assessing the policy implications of the changing economic scene in Africa for the EU.

10.2 African Economy and FDI Inflows

Africa consists of 54 countries[2] with a combined population of over one billion, accounting for one-sixth of the worldwide population and 4.04% of world GDP in 2010 (IMF, 2010). The continent can be better analyzed according to two sub-regional categories (North and Sub-Saharan Africa) and one country (South Africa).[3] This distinction presents different pictures as regards GDP, integration in the world economy, and political stability. Compared to Sub-Saharan Africa, the five North African countries are wealthier and relatively more integrated in the world economy. With the exception of Algeria, North African countries enjoyed relative political stability over the 1990s,[4] contrasting with violent conflict situations in a number of Sub-Saharan African countries (e.g., Democratic Republic of Congo, Eritrea, Liberia, Sierra Leone and Sudan). South Africa presents yet another picture: it is today the richest economy in the continent; it has managed to maintain political stability in the aftermath of decolonization; and it is by far the more integrated economy, ranking 34th in world trade in 2009 (WTO Trade Profiles, 2009). Table 10.1 summarizes some economic statistics for the various African regions.

Given Africa's size, its overall performance in attracting FDI during the 1990s was bleak and picked up only in 2000. Throughout the 1990s, the continent accounted for 5% of cumulative FDI inflows in developing economies, compared to a share of 22% and 17% for South America and South East Asia, respectively. Moreover, reflecting the continent's differences, FDI has been unequally distributed: cumulative inflows amounted to $9 billion in South Africa compared

---

[2] Since July 2011, South Sudan became an independent State.

[3] See Appendix 10.A for general data on African economies.

[4] Such stability was questioned after the 2011 uprisings in the region which have resulted in a wave of downgrading of the political risk in these countries. In the long run, if successful, the democratization process is likely to lead to better political risk.

Table 10.1: Africa basic indicators, 2010.

Indicators	North Africa[5]	Sub-Saharan Africa[6]	South Africa[7]	Africa
Total population (thousands)	166.578,89	791.665,42	50.109,82	1.008.354,13
Total land area (thousands of km^2)	6.017,19	23.084	1.221,04	30.322,57
Population density (pop/km^2)	27.68	34.29	41.04	33
Total GDP based on PPP valuation (US$ Million, 2010)	1.099.131	2.462.046	524.341	4,085,518.00
Average GDP per capita (PPP valuation, US$, 2010)	8.522,25	3.509,92	10.505,33	4.126,40
Annual real GDP growth (average over 2001–2011, estimation)	4.6	4.72	3.4	4.3
Total FDI inflows, 1990–2000 (US$ Million, current prices)	22.201,67	73.726,97	9.390,50	105.319,14
Total FDI inflows, 2001–2009 (US$ Million, current prices)	108.541,90	351.829,18	36.402,23	496.773,31

Sources: African Economic Outlook (2009 and 2011), IMF (2010), UNCTAD FDI statistics online.

[5] Algeria, Egypt, Libya, Morocco, Tunisia.

[6] Angola, Benin, Botswana, Burkina Faso, Burundi, Cameroon, Cape Verde, Central Afr. Rep., Chad, Comoros, Congo, Congo Dem. Rep., Côte d'Ivoire, Djibouti, Equatorial Guinea, Eritrea, Ethiopia, Gabon, Gambia, Ghana, Guinea, Guinea Bissau, Kenya, Lesotho, Liberia, Madagascar, Malawi, Mali, Mauritania, Mauritius, Mozambique, Namibia, Niger, Nigeria, Rwanda, São Tomé & Príncipe, Senegal, Seychelles, Sierra Leone, Somalia, South Sudan (since July 2011), Sudan, Swaziland, Tanzania, Togo, Uganda, Zambia, Zimbabwe.

[7] South Africa.

to an average of $4.4 billion and $1.5 billion for North Africa and Sub-Sahara.[8] The low attractiveness of the continent during the 1990s has been explained by a number of deterrent factors: political instability, macroeconomic mismanagement, lack of transparency, unfriendly regulatory frameworks, poor GDP growth, lack of infrastructure, high degree of protectionism, excessive reliance on commodities, and weak governance standards.[9] Since the early 2000s, following structural reforms, improvement of economic management, incentives to develop the private sector, important changes in governance legislation in doing business and long-awaited peace building efforts as well as resource endowments in a context of high commodity prices, FDI inflows have taken off (Fitch Ratings, 2010). Furthermore, during this period, many African economies adopted a proactive approach to FDI in extractive industries, mostly by opening up their mining privatization programs (United Nations Economic Commission for Africa, 2009).

These changes and developments have reinforced resource-seeking FDI and, in recent years, overseas FDI to Africa has been substantially directed to oil-producing countries. It is important to note that Africa benefits from important oil and gas endowments as it accounts for, respectively, 10% and 8% of the world's proven reserves, making the continent the most endowed in hydrocarbons after the Middle East and Eurasia (figures for 2009; British Petroleum, 2010). Between 2001 and 2009, Algeria, Angola, Congo, Equatorial Guinea, Gabon, Libya, Nigeria and Sudan[10] accounted for 30% of total inflows geared to the continent. When taking into account oil, gas and minerals, resource-rich countries accumulated up to 65% of the total FDI stock in 2009.[11] For example, South Africa has the largest proven gold and

---

[8] See also Appendix 10.B for data and figures on inward FDI to Africa and developing economies for the period 1990–2009.

[9] See, for example, Dupasquier and Osakwe (2005), Ibi Ajayi (2006), Onyeiwu and Shrestha (2004), Bende Nabende (2002), Krugell (2005), and Basu and Srinavasan (2002).

[10] Data collected before the independence of South Sudan.

[11] South Africa (24.32% of total FDI stock in Africa in 2009), Nigeria (13.42%), Egypt (12.96%), Sudan (3.75%), Algeria (3.37%), Angola (3.21%), Libya (3.01%), Congo (2.56%), Zambia (1.85%). See Appendix 10.D for inward FDI stock by country.

platinum reserves (respectively 12% and 88% of world total), and it ranks 4th after Botswana, Congo and Australia in terms of diamond reserves (United States Geological Survey, 2010).[12]

Overall, one-third of FDI in Africa has been for natural resource extraction. The remaining two-thirds of foreign capital have been invested in manufacturing, services and telecommunications (UNCTAD, 2010a), with a recent slow but steady rise of offshoring activities (A.T. Kearney, 2010). The better economic performance witnessed since the early 2000s has also translated into the slow emergence of an African middle-class that could number as many as 300 million out of a total population of 1 billion, which in turn is likely to trigger more market- and efficiency-seeking FDI in the future.

Foreign capital invested in Africa has historically originated mainly from the OECD countries, despite the fact that the continent is a marginal destination for developed countries' investors. The US, UK, France, Germany, Netherlands, and to a lesser extent Spain and Italy, were the main providers of foreign capital to the continent. Their cumulative FDI stocks amounted to $152 billion in 2009,[13] with investments driven by resource acquisition. For instance, with the aim of reducing oil dependency towards the Middle East by 75%, American companies have actively engaged in exploration ventures in Africa. EU-based FDI follows the same trend: after years of sanctions towards Libya, EU-based companies have now turned to the country for its hydrocarbon reserves.[14] From the African economies' perspective,

[12] See Appendix 10.C for Africa's resource endowments.

[13] See Appendix 10.E for OECD outward FDI stock in Africa.

[14] After sanctions were lifted, the EU became Libya's main oil buyer, with 85% of the country's production entering the European market. The uprising that began on 17th February 2011 translated into radical cuts in oil production: from a daily figure of 1.6 million barrels/day, Libyan production dropped to 0.5 million barrels/day. Major shifts in both production and exports' direction are unlikely, since EU companies are the main operators of Libyan oil fields, particularly after the ouster of Muammar Gaddafi and the successful transition of the National Council for Transition to power. EU's — and especially France's — shares in Libyan oil production are likely to increase as a result of its early support to the opposition movement.

Table 10.2: Shares of FDI stock of OECD countries in Africa, 2009.

	UK	France	USA	Netherlands	Italy	Spain	Rest of the world
Share of FDI stock (%)	13.3	9.53	6.54	3.22	1.74	1.52	64.5

Source: Authors' calculations based on UNCTAD and OECD database "Direct Investment by Country".

since the 1990s, France has been the leading investor in Morocco; United Kingdom's companies have important stakes in South Africa, Madagascar and Zambia; Italy takes the lead in Tunisia; while Egypt sources a significant share of its foreign capital in the United States. Table 10.2 presents the shares of the major OECD countries in inward African FDI.

10.3 Growing Chinese and Indian Ties in Africa

Since 2000, investors originating from Asia have become key players in African economies, with China, Singapore, Malaysia, and India accounting for a combined FDI stock of $30 billion in 2008 (UNCTAD, 2010b).[15] At the same time, the OECD countries' share of FDI stock in Africa accounted for $156 billion, a share of 36% of total FDI stock in the continent in 2007. Yet, this figure masks important reshufflings: for example, the OECD countries' share of FDI inflows to Algeria declined from 93% in 1999 to 63% in 2001, and in Egypt, their share has fallen from 83% in 2001 to 67% in 2006 (UNCTAD, 2008). However, due to data limitations and differences in FDI definitions, it is difficult to assess the real importance of Asian-based investors in the continent (UNCTAD, 2010b).

India has historically been more involved in Africa compared to China, as the continent accounted for 17% of its outward FDI between 1975 and 1990; Chinese emergence in the African economic landscape took off dramatically in 2000. The total Chinese FDI

[15] See Appendix 10.F for outward FDI stock of developing countries in Africa.

inflows to Africa which were below $100 million in 2003, quadrupled to reach $400 million in 2005 (UNCTAD, 2007). In 2008, Chinese FDI stocks in the continent amounted to $7.8 billion (UNCTAD, 2010b). The sectoral distribution of the Chinese and Indian investors follows the same patterns described above, with large interests in the oil and extractive activities (Goldstein *et al.*, 2006).

Commercial (Trade) Ties

Over the last decade, Asian drivers have been emerging as important commercial partners in Africa. Indeed, the total trade between China and Africa doubled in less than a decade (from $1.2 billion in 2001 to $2.7 billion in 2008). Yet, the total Sino-African trade remains behind EU's and India's, accounting respectively for $307 billion and $30 billion.[16] On the export side, 85% of Africa's exports to China originate from Sub-Saharan economies. Among them, oil-rich economies, who also account for a significant share of the total FDI stock, seem increasingly dependent on their crude oil exports to Beijing. As shown in Table 10.3, in the exports of Angola, Sudan, Nigeria and Congo directed to China, oil accounts for a share between 85% and 99% (Goldstein *et al.*, 2006; Jenkins and Edwards, 2006).

In contrast, import patterns of African countries are more diversified. While imports of all African countries from China amounted to approximately $7 million in 2001, they grew more than tenfold between 2001 and 2008 to reach $1.6 billion. As regards the import basket of goods originating from China, African countries import

Table 10.3: Share of fuels exports to China and imports from China as a percent of total exports and imports for selected African countries, 2009.

Item	Angola	Sudan	Nigeria	Congo
Share of fuels in total exports to China (%)	99.60	99.34	85.24	99.34
Share of China in total imports (%)	15.60	21.18	15.76	9.07

Source: UNCTAD Stat online database.

[16] See Appendix 10.G for trade between Africa and China, India and the EU.

manufactured goods (45% of total imports), machinery and transport equipment (24%) and other products (24%) (Wang, 2007) — a slightly different pattern from the EU, whose exports to Africa are composed of machinery and transport equipment (43% in 2009), manufactured goods (12%), chemicals (11%) and mineral fuels (10%).[17]

As for India's trade patterns with Africa, these are more balanced than China's. As of 2008, India was the 7th largest trader with Africa, while China was at the number one spot, followed by France, Germany, USA, Italy, and UK. Furthermore, India is increasing its share in total African trade: its exports to Africa have grown at a compound annual growth rate (CAGR) of 20% since 1990, more rapidly than African trade with China (16%), Brazil (13%), the United States (7%), the European Union (6.5%), United Kingdom (4.5%) or Japan (4.6%). The rate of this increase in Africa-India trade has been especially significant since 2000, with this trade increasing threefold from $8 billion in 2000 to $30 billion in 2008. In aggregate terms, in contrast to China's trade deficit with Africa valued at $5.6 billion in 2008, India had a large trade surplus of $2 billion in 2008. India's Ministry of Commerce and Industry expects bilateral trade with Africa to double to $70 billion by 2013, while the Associated Chambers of Commerce and Industry of India expect two-way trade to surpass $150 billion (Nanji, 2010).

As far as exports to India are concerned, a number of African countries have become increasingly reliant on Indian demand for their products, in particular the relatively small economies like Guinea Bissau, Eritrea, Sierra Leone, Benin, Togo and Senegal. However, India's influence is not just confined to smaller African economies. For example, Egypt (10%), South Africa (6%), Nigeria (4.3%), and Angola (3%) each send a large share of their total exports to India. Indicative of India's importance, nearly two-fifths of African nations rank India as a top five export destination (WTO, 2009). Similarly, Indian exports

[17] Figures are taken from European Commission Directorate-General for Trade (DG Trade), "African Caribbean Pacific (ACP) bilateral trade with the EU", 2010. Although the figures encompass Caribbean and Pacific economies, their similarities with African economies, which are reflected in the EU's approach to Economic Partnership Agreements (EPAs), allow for some generalization.

to Africa are also somewhat concentrated. South Africa is the recipient of one-fifth of India's exports to Africa. Kenya, Mauritius and Tanzania account for a cumulated one-third of Indian exports to Africa, while Egypt and Nigeria are the destinations for 16% and 12% of India's exports to Africa, respectively (Freemantle and Stevens, 2009).

Chinese and Indian trade with Africa has been rising very rapidly in recent decades. However, this growing Chindian-African trade is only one aspect of the strong economic relations between the large African continent and the Sino-Indian geographical ensemble. Indeed, the growing Chindian-African trade stems from the rising levels of Chinese and Indian direct investments in Africa.

Investment Ties

China and India invested in Africa unequally in the past, but the continent's share of their outward investment has risen significantly since the turn of the century. Chinese investments in Africa started from a very low base and increased rapidly only at the end of the 1990s: for the 1990–1995 period, the OECD reported an estimate of only $14 million of total outflows to the continent, while for the second half of the 1990s they were estimated at $107 million per annum. Since 2000, Chinese outward FDI (OFDI) to Africa has increased substantially, reaching an average level of $326 million per annum between 2003 and 2006 (OECD, 2008). Indian OFDI in Africa has been more important than China's. Through the 1980s and 1990s it amounted to $703 million, accounting for 39% of the country's FDI outflows (Pederson, 2008). Furthermore, it increased at a compound annual growth rate (CAGR) of 43% per annum since 1997, from a somewhat pedestrian $205 million in 1997 to over $11 billion in 2007 (Freemantle and Stevens, 2009).

The Asian drivers' economic expansion with annual growth rates since 2000 of 7% for India (Nanji, 2010) and 10% for China and the concomitant increase in demand for raw materials explain why both countries invest in Africa's resource-rich countries. But despite the figures reported, it is difficult to accurately report the "real" amount of Chinese and Indian FDI in Africa due to definition issues and data limitation.[18] Data on a project basis reported by UNCTAD (2007) provide us with insights on the investment patterns of both countries.[19] Between 2002 and 2005, a total of 34 projects implying the setting up of new production facilities were conducted by Chinese investors in Africa. Ten of them targeted the energy sectors of Algeria, Egypt, Nigeria, and Sudan. But these countries, which, together with Angola are among the main recipients of Chinese capital and providers of oil, also benefited from the setting up of new production facilities in textiles, automotive industries, machinery, logistics, telecom and

[18] Aggregate data on FDI match the IMF definition: "*Direct Investment is the category of international investment that reflects the objective of a resident entity in one economy in obtaining a lasting interest in a company located in another country*" (IMF, 1993, p. 86); however, UNCTAD (2010b, p. 80) reports that FDI across developing countries may be "*wrongly estimated because of the way in which Trans National Corporations (TNCs) structure their investments, e.g., for tax reasons. Significant amounts of OFDI from developing countries are directed towards offshore financial centers who act as a gateway towards worldwide investments.*" Another issue arises from the nationality criteria used for FDI. Three different criteria can be used to define the nationality of a company: its place of incorporation, the location of its headquarters, or the location of its owners. Statistics of FDI inflows capture this notion regardless of nationality, but it is not unusual that many Southern TNCs locate their headquarters or are incorporated in developed countries while their main activities take place in developing countries, including Africa. Given that India has signed a double taxation avoidance treaty with Mauritius, it might be possible that a share of its investments in Africa is channeled through the island. On the other hand, given Africa's marginal share in total Chinese OFDI, it might be possible that Chinese investments to the continent are channeled through developed economies where Chinese companies are incorporated.

[19] The data are taken from UNCTAD (2007) and have been provided by the LOCO Monitor developed by OCO Consulting. Data on FDI projects are gathered from a comprehensive set of more than 9,000 sources, and cover only investment projects implying the setting up of new production facilities. They do not take into account the expansion of existing facilities, acquisitions by Chinese and Indian businesses of existing facilities, or the investments in neighboring countries of Chinese and Indian businesses already established in Africa. Although few operations report the total capital invested, the projects can be interpreted as investments implying "fresh" outflow of capital from China and India to Africa. Chinese and Indian greenfield FDI projects concluded between 2002 and 2005 are reported in Appendix 10.H. Aggregate figures on Chinese and Indian OFDI are also reported.

infrastructures. While the bulk of Chinese investments have been resource seeking (Goldstein *et al.*, 2006), Chinese FDI is distributed along a wide array of activities ranging from light manufacturing to trade, services, telecommunications and agriculture (Wang, 2007). India follows an even more diversified pattern of engagement in the continent. While investing at par with its Chinese counterparts in extractive industries with 11 projects, the country's businesses conducted 16 projects in services and 22 in manufacturing against, respectively, 2 and 15 by China for the considered period (Pal, 2009).

Ownership, Entry and Integration of Local Labor

Reflecting China's political system, a large number of Beijing companies operating in Africa are state-owned. State-Owned Enterprises (SOEs) are almost exclusively responsible for all the Chinese deals in extractive industries, either by setting up facilities or by acquiring assets, while small and medium-sized companies (SMEs) are active in the other sectors (Kaplinsky and Morris, 2009). Among the 800 Chinese companies reported to have activities in Africa, 100 large SOEs operate in extractive industries (UNCTAD, 2007). In addition, managers of Chinese companies, especially larger ones, are often connected to provincial governments and follow guidelines from the Party and central government. Consequently, it is not easy to verify to what extent the corporate governance structure of Chinese businesses is independent from the state.[20]

In contrast, Indian companies tend first to be privately owned, and second, to follow more market-seeking motives. For example, according to Aguiar *et al.* (2009) of the Boston Consulting Group (BCG), while only one privately-owned Chinese company makes the list of the top 100 FDI source companies from rapidly developing economies, India's share has more or less equal numbers of private

[20] The European Commission's approach to anti-dumping cases against China illustrates the linkages between state actors and private businesses in China. The country has not yet been granted market economy status in trade investigations, as it has failed to demonstrate that its businesses operate away from state influence (European Commission Directorate-General for Trade, 2007).

and public companies, along with strategic investors. Only one Indian company out of the 192 in the BCG's list was state-controlled (Aguiar *et al.*, 2009). The Tata group is illustrative of this market-seeking rationale and longer engagement in Africa. More than a century ago Mohandas Gandhi found his calling there, and today many Indian companies find South Africa the perfect gateway to the rest of the continent. As a case example of this strategy, the Tata Group is present in 11 African countries. Its investments in Africa are closing in on the half-billion-dollar mark. Tata plans on taking that to close to a billion dollars over the next few years, with a base in South Africa which is believed to be the gateway for Tata's operations in the entire continent (Mahajan-Bansal *et al.*, 2009).

There are also significant variations as regards the entry mode of Chinese and Indian investors. Differences in ownership structures translate into commercial risks being perceived differently and into different business strategies. Chinese firms tend to enter new markets in Africa by building new facilities, creating business entities that are vertically integrated, buying supplies from China rather than from local markets, and selling in Africa mostly to government entities. They rarely facilitate the integration of their workers into the African socioeconomic fabric. In Algeria, for example, following important investments in infrastructure, the Chinese workforce is estimated to range somewhere between 45,000 and 100,000 immigrant workers (*Washington Times*, 2010). The non-recourse to local labor creates increased social tensions in a country where the unemployment rate reaches almost 14%.[21]

On the other hand, Indian firms are more integrated locally. Most Indian companies in Africa acquire established businesses, are less vertically integrated, prefer to procure supplies locally or from international markets (rather than from Indian suppliers), engage in far more sales to private African entities, and encourage the local integration of their workers. As cited in Broadman (2007), in a 2006 survey of 450 business owners in Africa, almost half of the respondents who were ethnically Indian had taken on African nationalities (with most of the other half retaining their Indian nationality), compared with only 4%

[21] See Souiah (2010).

of firm owners who were ethnically Chinese (the other 96% had retained their Chinese nationality). This finding suggests that, reflecting their long history in Africa, Indian businesspeople are substantially more integrated into the African business community than are the relatively new Chinese business managers and owners (Broadman, 2008).

India is arguably a more collaborative and sustainable partner, while China is considered more opportunistic and more willing to work even with failed states (Halper, 2010). Indian companies investing in Africa are more integrated with the local economy, whereas Chinese companies operate almost as free-standing enclaves (Nanji, 2010). The main reason for the former's collaborative approach is that India has been trading with the African continent for hundreds of years. During the British colonial period, thousands of Indians were taken to Africa to work. Today, about two million people of Indian descent live in Africa, many of them running their own businesses. More than one million Chinese workers are currently based in Africa, but they are relatively recent arrivals. On the whole, India has a far better reputation in Africa than China, which has been criticized for using predominantly imported Chinese labor in its African projects and for a cavalier attitude toward the human rights records of the regimes with which it deals. However, despite admirable measures such as a pledge to develop a project to link remote African schools and medical centers to Indian institutions via the Internet, India could easily lose its superior reputation by succumbing to temptations (Walker, 2008). Perhaps temptations could be high, given the highly resource-seeking motives driving both countries into Africa.

10.4 Key Drivers of Chinese and Indian Investment in Africa

Natural Resources: A Driver of Chinese and Indian Investments in Africa and Their Entanglement with Infrastructure Projects

The Asian drivers' growth has translated into high demand for raw materials which are increasingly sourced from Africa (Goldstein *et al.*, 2006). In 2009, China was the second highest oil consumer in the world behind the United States (EIA website, China page) and while in the 1990s it was an oil producer, its dependency on foreign crude is expected to reach 50% in 2030. In the same year, India was ranked fourth (EIA website, India page), and its dependency on foreign crude is expected to reach 92%. Besides oil, both countries' growth increases their other raw materials needs such as copper, zinc, gold, platinum and diamonds. Chinese and Indian energy SOEs (including China National Petroleum Company, CNPC; China Petroleum and Chemicals, SINOPEC; and India's Oil and National Gas Corporation, ONGC) as well as public and private mining companies are therefore increasingly entering into exploration ventures in Africa. They concluded a series of deals guaranteeing them long-term commodity supplies in exchange for non-equity investments such as loans and guarantees in the awarding of public contracts to build the continent's lacking infrastructures. By doing so, Chinese and Indian companies are ensured long-term access to raw materials.

Examples of concessions against non-equity investments, loans, and infrastructure constructions are manifold and help to explain the trade patterns between the Asian drivers and Africa. For instance, China issued a loan to Angola backed by oil supplies amounting to 10,000 barrels per day for 17 years. Administered by the Angolan Ministry of Finance, the loan is intended to rebuild the country's infrastructure which was devastated after a 26-year civil war which ended in 2002. Tied to this loan is the condition to award 70% of the contracts to Chinese companies investing $400 million in the country's telephone infrastructure, housing programs, roads and public buildings' rehabilitation. As a consequence of this oil-backed engagement and investments, Angola has surpassed Saudi Arabia as China's primary oil supplier with more than 2.12 tons of crude being shipped to Beijing (Corkin, 2008). Algeria is also illustrative of such practices. In 2003, CNPC and the Algerian state-owned Sonatrach signed a contract under which the Chinese company would invest $31 million between 2004 and 2007 to prospect for oil and gas in the country. In exchange for prospection services, Sonatrach would guarantee a stable flow of hydrocarbon supplies to China.[22] In addition, the China State Construction Engineering Corp. is building the east-west roadway, and other Beijing-based consortia are building housing programs in Algiers' suburbs, as well as a new airport, hotel resorts, railways and water supply networks.[23]

The Indian ONGC has acquired shares in oil exploration ventures in Nigeria and Libya and has formed partnerships with China and Malaysia through investing in Sudan's hydrocarbon sector. Overall, ONGC holds shares in blocks in Congo, Egypt, Libya, Nigeria, Sao Tomé and Principe and Sudan. ONGC also financed an oil pipeline from Khartoum to Port Sudan in 2004. Furthermore, in the same year, the company invested $12.5 million in offshore drilling in Cote d'Ivoire and obtained permission to conduct geological studies in Mauritius. In Nigeria, ONGC, in partnership with Mittal Energy Ltd., struck a $6 billion infrastructure deal with the government. As part of the deal, ONGC Mittal receives access to production blocks in exchange for a refinery, a power plant, and railway lines. Other agreements include India's National Thermal Power Corporation (NTPC) establishing coal- and gas-based power plants to satisfy growing demand for power in Nigeria, Africa's most populous country. As part of the agreement, NTPC will have access to Nigerian gas for its plants in India. Complementing these ONGC and NTPC ventures, private energy companies such as Reliance Industries are pursuing refinery opportunities in both Angola and Nigeria. As a consequence, imports from Angola have increased 185% since 1998; meanwhile, Nigeria has become India's second-largest supplier of oil, providing 15% of India's total import demand, and no less than 80% of India's imports from Africa originate from Nigeria, South Africa, Egypt, Algeria, Angola and Libya (Freemantle and Stevens, 2009).

---

[22] *Washington Times* (2010).

[23] Souiah (2010). Furthermore, to improve future access to imported food, China has also invested in and leased large tracts of agricultural land in Africa.

As far as non-oil mining is concerned, Zambia provides examples of Chindian investors entering the country's extractive industries in exchange for infrastructure deals. In 2005, when Zambia conducted its mine privatization program, the China Nonferrous Metal International Mining Company (CNMC) invested $100 million to acquire the Chambeshi deposit located around the Southern African copper belt. Today, expansion plans go further, with investment announcements valued at around $500 million to develop copper mines. At the same time, the Chinese company ZTE is investing in Zambia's telecommunication infrastructure, and China announced an $800 million investment to build a special economic zone including manufactures of cell phones, TV sets and other electronic items (Carmody, 2009). India is also wooing the country's copper potential, with Vedanta having invested more than $750 million in the country's mines as of 2008.

Given the experience of both Chinese and Indian companies of working in developing country environments, some expect them to be well-suited to overcoming Africa's challenging conditions. The Chinese and Indian revival of African infrastructures may prove to be a supportive factor for further development, and increased attention is being deployed towards the continent beyond extractive industries.[24] With the creation of road, telecom, and urban networks, the cost of operating in these countries will decrease and make any new involvement in other activities more profitable. However, as was previously documented, such investments may not have been possible without the series of supportive factors. While for China, government policies play a key role, Indian multinational companies' managerial know-how, technology, and financial resources are complemented by the country's deeply rooted African Diaspora.

[24] UNCTAD (2010b) reports that Chinese companies have started to invest recently in African agriculture. Being important grain importers, their investments are aimed at securing food supplies. While this trend is recent, estimates of its magnitude are difficult to report, since it is difficult to verify whether the announced investments have actually been realized.

State as a Supportive Factor in Chinese Investments

In the case of China, Beijing's policies can be viewed as two series of pull factors for increased investment in Africa. These are to be found in the Forum on China-Africa Cooperation (FOCAC) and in the evolution of regulations affecting OFDI. In addition, Chinese internal market regulations can be analyzed as a push factor for overseas investment.

While China's engagement with Africa has attracted wide public attention, it is far from being a new trend. In fact, Beijing's former political ties with Africa are the building ground for the increased Sino-African ties. In the aftermath of the Bandung Conference of Non-Aligned Countries, China started to engage with African countries by providing aid in exchange for political support in the nascent United Nations (Lum *et al.*, 2009). Sino-African relations have resulted in a number of government buildings, "white elephant" presidential palaces, Olympic stadiums, and the emblematic Tanzania-Zambia railway being built by Chinese contractors. Ties deepened progressively with changes in China's leadership, by integrating more and more African partners within joint venture agreements. In 1991, relations went a step further by advocating the principles of mutual benefit, economic development and non-interference in any matter related to state sovereignty (Congressional Research Service, 2008).

Since 2000, Sino-African relations have culminated within the framework of the FOCAC, which is a platform of dialogue between China and Africa on various issues such as international affairs, politics, economics and social development. Housed within the Ministry of Foreign Affairs, it is the vehicle through which Sino-African relations are conceptualized. Aid and external assistance are central to Sino-African relations under Beijing's motto of mutual benefit, economic development and non-interference in home affairs. Although this chapter does not cover aid and external assistance issues, a brief look at how they are managed by China is necessary so as to understand the key supportive factors behind the increased involvement of the country's state-owned and private businesses in Africa.

First of all, Chinese practices of development assistance differ significantly from the OECD's definition of aid[25] (Brautigam, 2010). Indeed, China's assistance to Africa consists of packages comprising a mix of grants, interest-free loans, bilateral state loans and partially commercial low-interest loans, strongly supported by the country's $262 billion trade surplus in 2007.[26] These resources are used to finance infrastructures in the partner countries. The financial component of Chinese aid to Africa is often conditional and obliges African countries to acquire Chinese goods, services or credit. Such conditionality impacts recipient countries' trade balance negatively, as some projects promoted in Africa require up to 50% of materials to be sourced in China (Lum *et al.*, 2009).

The management of the Chinese aid system also does not comply with international donor standards. In China, it is the Department of Foreign Aid within the Ministry of Commerce (MOFCOM) who organizes the aid programs in cooperation with the Ministry of Foreign Affairs. Under the MOFCOM, China's export-import bank (CHEXIM) administers the country's foreign aid loan program. As a policy bank, it offers subsidies for export credits and foreign investment; although these practices do not qualify as aid by OECD standards, they do by Chinese standards. In addition to CHEXIM, the China Development Bank (CDB) is another policy bank actively involved in China's foreign aid practices. It runs the $5 billion China-Africa Development Fund (CAD) established in 2007, with a view to encourage Chinese FDI in the fields

[25] For the OECD, official development assistance (ODA) is defined as: *Grants or Loans to countries and territories on Part I of the DAC List of Aid Recipients (developing countries) which are: (a) undertaken by the official sector; (b) with promotion of economic development and welfare as the main objective; (c) at concessional financial terms [if a loan, having a Grant Element (q.v.) of at least 25 per cent]. In addition to financial flows, Technical Co-operation (q.v.) is included in aid. Grants, Loans and credits for military purposes are excluded. For the treatment of the forgiveness of Loans originally extended for military purposes, see Notes on Definitions and Measurement below. Transfer payments to private individuals (e.g., pensions, reparations or insurance payouts) are in general not counted* (OECD Online Glossary).

[26] Xin Hua News (2008).

of agriculture, manufacturing, infrastructure, natural resources and industrial parks.

The divergent practices in China's external assistance make it difficult to account for "real" development assistance and by how much it influences the FDI dynamics in Africa. For example, when looking at FDI on a project basis, given the conditions put forward by Chinese aid, it is very likely that a significant number of the projects announced were a direct result of the FOCAC framework. Indeed, the FOCAC summits held every three years often come with commitments to finance infrastructures, and their cumulative value for the period 2001–2007 reached almost $16 billion (UNCTAD, 2010b). Depending on the investment vehicles used in project financing, it is difficult to state whether these joint ventures qualify as FDI. Consequently, the Chinese government policy towards Africa can be seen as a strong pull factor of the increased investments in the continent. This is especially true for projects involving a high level of sunk costs, as subsidized and soft loans provided by CHEXIM and CAD decrease the cost of capital for the companies entering Africa. At the same time, the principle of non-interference as a pillar of Chinese diplomacy and external assistance and the friendly Sino-African relations within the FOCAC provide an informal framework guaranteeing stability for Chinese businesses.[27]

In addition to the Chinese policy towards Africa, Beijing's regulations on overseas investments can be analyzed also as a pull factor of FDI. Before the FOCAC was formally established, the growing foreign exchange reserves drained by China's trade surplus *vis-à-vis* the rest of the world helped the country to launch the "go out policy" in 2000, under which Chinese firms are allowed and encouraged to expand internationally. After the "go out policy" was launched, OFDI flows from China increased from less than $2 billion in 2000 to reach $52 billion in 2008 (Davies, 2009). Furthermore, during the 1990s, China's industrial structure evolved rapidly and became increasingly

---

[27] The FOCAC summits, gathering high-level Chinese officials and African heads of state, are reported to be a channel through which important business decisions are concluded.

modern, urging the government to actively push overseas expansion of domestic companies. As the trade surplus and reserves grew, the Chinese central government adopted a series of measures to encourage overseas investment whilst providing the Chinese investors with a wide range of incentives, such as tax advantages, preferential or even soft loans, and abolition of foreign exchange quotas. Beijing also facilitated an import-export regime on materials necessary for overseas production processes. A key element of the "go out" policy is the encouragement of investments in certain strategic areas, among which resource exploration and extraction fit with China's main African partners (UNCTAD, 2007). In addition, while China's policy towards Africa and overseas capital are direct factors helping to explain Beijing's involvement in Africa, China's internal regulations can be viewed as indirect factors helpful in explaining the country's wave of FDI to Africa.

The distorted economic system prevailing in China affects SOEs and private business differently, notwithstanding the 2004 Constitution which guarantees equal treatment between the two categories. Through local policies regulating the supply of goods in the internal market, provincial governments issue trade permits more easily for SOEs than for private businesses. Consequently, the two categories of business do not operate in the same market *de facto*: contrary to SOEs, private companies face administrative obstacles in their own market equivalent to non-tariff barriers (Alon, 2010).

Similar distortions apply in the capital markets. On financial grounds, the prevalence of state-owned banks in collecting deposits also translates into a discriminatory framework in which SOEs are favored against private companies. In order to survive and grow, the latter have been compelled to develop a wide range of informal skills and managerial expertise allowing them to operate in complex, developing and low-income consumer markets. While private companies face institutional barriers, large SOEs benefit from official Beijing support and are well-positioned to implement the country's strategic objectives. Consequently, Chinese internal policies have created different firm-specific advantages according to the companies' ownership structure. It is in this respect that Chinese internal market policies can be viewed as a push factor for outbound investment. Although more research is needed to verify this, an unpublished survey from the Chinese Ministry of Foreign Trade and Cooperation (MOFTEC) quoted by UNCTAD (2007) provides some support for this hypothesis.[28] Despite lower returns on investment in Africa than in other locations, more than half of Chinese companies operating in the continent were at least covering costs, and only a small proportion recorded losses or was involved in disputes. This underlines the Chinese firm-specific advantages in entering low-income consumer markets, in dealing with high bureaucratic involvement and operating in informal environments.

These pull and push factors are supportive of Beijing's involvement in Africa. They create a strong state or quasi-state led pattern of engagement through numerous initiatives, incentives, and robust firm-specific advantages, allowing Chinese companies to enter the continent relatively easier than its traditional partners. On the other hand, India is relatively less present in Africa than China, and benefits from radically different supportive factors for its operations.

Supportive Factors of Indian Investments: Private Companies and the Diaspora

While Sino-African ties are mostly contemporary, politically driven and gained momentum at the turn of the century, Indo-African ties are deep-rooted. India has a long economic history with Africa going back millennia when traders travelled back and forth between East African

[28] On empirical grounds, Alon (2010) regresses Chinese outbound FDI on a series of factors, among which include the ownership structure of the investing companies. According to his model, both public and private firms are likely to enter large markets in both developed and developing countries. For private firms, large markets are twice as important compared to for SOEs. For SOEs, natural resources and new technologies matter relatively more than for private companies, thus confirming the theoretical predictions of the author as well as the characteristics described above relating to Chinese FDI in Africa. In addition, the author notes that a share of FDI directed to Africa might be used to export goods to China in order for private companies to circumvent internal market regulations.

coastal towns and counterpart towns on the west coast of India across the Indian Ocean. These traders carried a wide range of goods, fulfilling commercial needs on both continents. With the arrival of the British and other European colonial powers in both India and Africa starting in the 18th century, these Africa-India trading ties deepened considerably. As is usually the case, trading ties also reflect cultural interchanges between the trading regions. These cultural interchanges expanded greatly in the 19th century after the colonial Europeans imported large numbers of Indians to work as indentured servants on African farms run by Europeans. Many of these Indians chose to stay in Africa after they had fulfilled their initial contracts with the Europeans, thus forming an Indian Diaspora with deep multi-generational roots in Africa. In fact, the Indian Diaspora in South Africa provided the initial employment for a young, recently graduated British lawyer of Indian origin named Mohandas Karamchand Gandhi — later known to the world as the father of the non-violence movement, Mahatma (great soul) Gandhi.

The Indian Diaspora in Africa has played an important role as a facilitator of FDI. India's Ministry of External Affairs describes non-resident Indians (NRI) as Indian citizens who have migrated to other countries, persons of Indian origin (PIO, not Indian citizens) who are born outside India, or persons of Indian origin who reside outside India. A Person of Indian Origin (PIO) is usually not a citizen of India. As of 2005, the NRI and PIO population across the world was estimated to be over 30 million, with 2.8 million in Africa (Freemantle and Stevens, 2009). While the Indian Diaspora in Africa has had its difficulties in the past, a cursory analysis of the locations of these NRIs and PIOs in Africa correlates strongly with the countries on the continent which offer the strongest ties with India.

According to the Indian Ministry of External Affairs, the distribution of the Indian Diaspora in Africa includes major concentrations (in thousands, estimated as of 2008) in South Africa (1,300), Mauritius (855), Reunion (220), Kenya (100), Uganda (90), Tanzania (90), and other (130). Included in the "other" category are the following countries: Nigeria, Madagascar, Mozambique, Libya, Zimbabwe, Botswana, Zambia and Seychelles (Freemantle and Stevens, 2009). Clearly, India's

Diaspora networks are strongest in South Africa and East Africa (Kenya, Uganda and Tanzania), offering Indian MNCs preferential access into these markets.

Compared to the Chinese government, the Indian government lags behind in providing political support for commercial bilateral engagements. Its role seems to be limited to acting as a catalyst to facilitate the trade and investment activities of Indian companies. It has issued grants and loans to African countries for the improvement of crucial infrastructure such as railways, IT, telecom, and power systems (Beri, 2003). As of 2009, India had extended more than $3 billion of concessional lines of credit to African countries. During the 2009 India-Africa Business Partnership Summit held in New Delhi, it was reported that India had committed to make a further $5.4 billion in credit available over the next five years. Over the same period, India would also allocate $500 million for projects in higher and vocational education, science, IT, agriculture, and renewable energy in Africa. In addition, India has donated $1 billion to connect 53 African countries with satellite and fiber-optic networks to promote virtual medical and educational programs (Nanji, 2010). India has agreed to enhance its budget for technical assistance and training programs and to expand opportunities for African students to pursue studies in India. Since 2009 India has also supported the short-term training of over 1,100 Africans in India in a variety of technical fields, and the program plans to train 1,600 trainees per year. India has also pledged to support Africa in its quest to gain a permanent seat on the United Nation's Security Council (Dubey, 2008).

10.5 Implications of the Chinese and Indian Trade and FDI in Africa

The rise of Chindian FDI into Africa and the relative displacement of traditional European colonial powers as the only major investors in Africa have had many implications. In addition to important implications for the continuing role of Europe in Africa, this new source of FDI also poses some challenges for traditional FDI theory. Furthermore, the rise of Chinese and Indian economic activity in

Africa implies that the world is moving towards a multi-polar structure. Next, we examine these implications.

The Mixed Effects of Chindian FDI on African Economies

The important engagement of the Asian drivers, supported by their respective political initiatives and characteristics, has had important effects on African economies, which are to be analyzed through trade channels, as a significant share of both countries' FDI is tied to resource extraction and long-term commodity supplies.

For the most targeted countries by Chinese and Indian investors, the bilateral trade patterns raise concerns over a possible Dutch Disease Syndrome (Corden and Neary, 1982). For the Dutch Disease Syndrome to manifest, two preconditions must be met. First, the real exchange rate need to appreciate to the extent that it will damage the competitiveness of undifferentiated manufactured goods. Second, the terms of trade appreciation resulting from the increase of commodity prices need to be stable rather than transitory. As manufactured goods are not exported by these African economies, the first condition is not met. Regarding terms of trade, abstracting from 2009 and the global downturn, they have been on the rise since 2003. Should this trend be sustained over the coming years, commodity-exporting African economies would not have any incentive to engage in economic diversification as a high exchange rate would deter their competitiveness. It remains to be seen whether this pattern will be sustained (Goldstein *et al.*, 2006).

Rather than the Dutch Disease Syndrome, four issues may arise from the increased Chinese and Indian demand for commodities. First, extractive industries are capital-intensive and prevent the emergence of a manufacturing sector. Second, skills in resource extraction are specific, which limits spillovers to other sectors. Third, imperfect capital markets create a situation in which the proceeds of the traded resources are not channeled towards the development of human capital but are rather kept in the hands of the resource-controlling elite. Fourth, volatility of commodity prices might impede the emergence of other productive and tradable activities. If these issues need to be carefully monitored in the medium and long run, there was no supportive evidence of these two sets of drawbacks until 2007 (Goldstein *et al.*, 2006).

Increased exports of commodities against imports of manufactured goods can also exert competitive pressures on domestic industries. Here again, there does not seem to be univocal evidence of significant threats being posed to Africa by China and India (Jenkins and Edwards, 2006; Goldstein *et al.*, 2006). Typologies of "winners" and "losers" have been developed to analyze Chinese and Indian trade with African economies (Stevens and Kennan, 2006; Goldstein *et al.*, 2006). "Winners" are the countries for which the number of sectors benefiting from cheaper imports outweighs the number of sectors undergoing losses due to decreased market shares in export markets or higher prices due to increased Chinese demand for the product considered. The results show that the majority are in fact "winners", while 6 countries experience neutral effects, and only one country is reported to be a "loser".[29] However, these are only rough estimations; until today, there is no quantitative assessment on the welfare effects of increased Chinese- and Indian-linked effects of trade and investment on African economies. Nevertheless, some qualitative studies find negative effects associated with increased Chinese and Indian presence in Africa. In the retailing and trade sectors, the trend reported in Senegal on Chinese workers locating in the informal sector and competing with local retailers is not an exception (Hazard *et al.*, 2009); Cameroon and Zambia are also subject to the same effects (Khan and Baye, 2008; Mwanawina, 2008).

Indian investments in Africa are believed to be more transparent and socially beneficial than the Chinese investments. Allegations of corruption, un-transparent practices in bidding, lack of respect for social

[29] Goldstein *et al.* (2006) report that Angola, Benin, Burkina Faso, Cameroon, Congo, Democratic Republic of Congo, Ghana, Guinea, Mali, Mauritania, Mauritius, Niger, Nigeria, Senegal, South Africa, Sudan, Tanzania, Togo, Uganda and Zimbabwe are "winners". Chad, Ethiopia, Kenya, Madagascar, Mozambique and Zambia experience neutral effects, and only Malawi is reported to be a "loser".

standards, non-recourse to local labor, and non-integration of Chinese workers are often cited as one of the main drawbacks associated with Chinese FDI in Africa. Examples include South Africa, where some infrastructure deals were claimed to be corrupted (Burke *et al.*, 2008). In Angola, while China issued a $2 billion loan to the government for infrastructure investments in 2004, two years later $1.8 billion was reported to have been spent without disclosure (Corkin, 2008). In Zambia, despite employing more local workers than elsewhere, Chinese companies have been heavily criticized after a series of industrial accidents stemming from non-respect of security standards in the country's copper mines (Carmody, 2009).

Policy Implications for the EU in the Context of Re-polarization

The rise of the Asian drivers, and especially the growing role China has in Africa's economic landscape, challenges EU's relations with the continent. The EU's involvement in Africa is structured along different frameworks. For North Africa, relations are shaped by several schemes. In 1995, the Barcelona Process associated North Africa, along with the Mashrek countries, Israel and Turkey, under a cooperation framework based on free trade and political dialogue. Association Agreements between the EU and individual countries are a key instrument for achieving these goals. Following the EU's enlargement in 2004, North African countries were integrated in the European Neighborhood Policy, which sought to deepen relations between the two regions. Country-specific action plans, comprising a set of mutually agreed reforms and financial support for their implementation, are the instrument of this cooperation. Four years later, in 2008, the Union for the Mediterranean (UfM) was launched with a view to responding to criticisms over the convalescence of the Barcelona Process and its lack of tangible outcomes.

Reflecting the radically different socio-economic conditions of the two parts of the African continent, relations with Sub-Saharan Africa are structured along different frameworks. Under the Lomé Conventions, African Caribbean and Pacific (ACP) countries were given aid managed by the European Investment Bank,[30] and duty-free access from some of their agricultural and mining products. Whereas the Lomé Conventions were restricted to aid and trade, the Cotonou Agreement signed in 2000 was much deeper in scope: it established the basis for a political dialogue and instituted the principle of good governance. Under these agreements, trade preferences were no longer unilaterally granted by the EU. Contrary to the Lomé Conventions, ACP countries agreed to open up their markets and sign WTO-compatible trade agreements, hence the Economic Partnership Agreements (EPAs). Under the latter, aid is tied to market liberalization and achievements in good governance. At the political level, the EU deepened relations with Sub-Saharan Africa in 2007 with the enactment of the Africa-EU Strategic Partnership.[31] The Partnership foresees cooperation in eight areas: peace and security; democratic governance and human rights; regional integration and infrastructure; millennium development goals; energy; climate change; migration mobility and employment; and science information society and space. Sub-Saharan Africa benefits from periodical action plans for the implementation of the objectives set in the partnership.

While the two parts of Africa are targeted differently by the EU in both political and economic terms, Chinese policies integrate them all in their respective frameworks. Nearly all African countries[32] are part of the FOCAC and are thus potential beneficiaries of Chinese initiatives. However, the highly visible presence of Beijing in Africa increasingly raises concerns. Chinese investments are often loaded with state influence, especially in strategic sectors, and it is difficult to clearly differentiate between business relations, foreign policy objectives and

[30] The Lomé Conventions committed the EU on aid and investment amounts to be channeled to ACP countries. Under the four conventions, commitments amounted to: Lomé I: 3ECU billion, Lomé II: 5.5ECU billion, Lomé III: 8.5ECU billion, and Lomé IV: 12ECU billion. In addition to these amounts, two further schemes were created, aimed at providing compensatory finance to ACP states against negative fluctuations in agricultural (Stabex) and mineral prices (Sysmin).

[31] European Commission (2007).

[32] Exceptions are: Burkina Faso, Gambia, Republic of the Congo, Sao Tomé Principe and Swaziland.

development assistance. Non-interference in state sovereignty, lack of transparency in development aid and business-led initiatives, lack of interest in governance, as well as human rights and social issues, all raise fears that Beijing's involvement in Africa could lead to a neo-colonialist pattern of relations.

The emergence of China as a provider of aid and as one of the leading investors in Africa exerts significant pressure on the EU's African policies. Beijing's exclusive focus on economic interests often hinders the efforts of the EU and other international donors, provides some countries with leverage against European and Western partners, and contributes to the maintenance of sluggish governance practices. Angola's loan obtained from China in 2004 is a case in point. In a different fashion, Algeria is another example where increased Chinese involvement challenges European policy. While the Association Agreement (AA) concluded with the EU in 2005 aims at bilateral tariff dismantling, the gains stemming from increased relations with China between 2005 and 2010 are being put forward by Algeria to exert pressure on Brussels and obtain more favorable conditions from the EU in 2010.[33]

Nevertheless, despite Beijing's higher involvement, the EU still maintains its influence in the continent. Europe's specificity and force in Africa lies in its focus on social standards in international relations. In this regard, to maintain its influence in the continent, actions must target several levels. At the political level, the EU should continue to exert pressure on African governments for institutional reform, good governance, transparency and respect of social standards. Given the sensitiveness toward state sovereignty after China's arrival in the continent and the exacerbation of autonomy sentiments, it will certainly not be easy for the EU to compete directly with China by advocating

[33] At the 10th EU/Algeria Inter-Parliamentary meeting held on 6–7 October 2010, Algerian deputies explicitly said that the increased trade and investment relations with China in particular, and Asian actors in general, are resulting in the EU losing ground in the country. Their remark was made amidst a context where the AA is being renegotiated on Algeria's request. The country is currently pushing for a review of the tariff dismantlement schedule and calling for more EU-based FDI.

the benefits arising from stable environments. Nevertheless, efforts on good governance should be maintained in coordination with other partners engaged in the continent. Support for civil society movements, non-government organizations and non-state actors should be maintained for their efforts in raising awareness on social issues. The progressive establishment of democratically based political systems will be a supportive factor of this strategy. The Zambian example shows that, despite massive Chinese investment in copper mines and industrial zones, civil society discontent and active pressure for the respect of social conditions have been efficient in curbing China's attitude. EU's trade with Africa can serve as a strong leverage of such a strategy.

While actual Chinese involvement raises concerns, African economies may turn out to be "winners" from their ties with Beijing. The infrastructure deficit is currently being addressed and additional improvements are very likely to trigger more FDI, by decreasing the cost of doing business, thus helping to address the excessive reliance on commodities and economic diversification needs. The steady increase in inflows directed toward the continent in the last decade augurs that investments are profitable, and a straightforward way of supporting capital flows to Africa is to engage more with African governments in the promotion of local investment opportunities. A strengthening of the EU-Africa Business Forum[34] with annual periodicity would be helpful. In this regard, the forum should also be open to other emerging economic partners such as Singapore, Malaysia, and Arab investors. While China's FOCAC has been operational since 2000, the EU lags behind as its business-led forum only dates back to 2007. Also, a higher visibility of the European Investment Bank (EIB) activities in the ACP and overseas countries and territories (OCTs) would be valuable; as of 2011, only three EIB offices are operating in Sub-Sahara.[35]

[34] The Africa Business Forum was launched by the European Commission in 2007 and is held every two years. Its main aim is the promotion of investment opportunities in Africa to boost investor confidence.

[35] Regional offices are operational in Dakar (Senegal), Nairobi (Kenya) and Tshwane-Pretoria (South Africa).

China's ties with Africa are also challenging Beijing's own practices in aid whilst highlighting the benefits of the EU's approaches. The EU and its member states have a longer experience on the African continent, and hence, have more field knowledge than their Chinese counterparts. Chinese officials dealing with aid are now turning increasingly to European experts for guidance in aid management. Moreover, it is arguable that with the deepening of Sino-African ties, the actual perpetuation of poor social practices and sluggish governance will hinder Chinese interests as they develop in the future. In this regard, there may be scope for cooperation between China and other actors involved in the continent on governance and social rights. To do so, the EU should continue to exert pressure on China to make the country align with the international standards outlined in the 2005 Paris Declaration of Donors on Aid Effectiveness. The EU's relations with China on trade grounds can indeed serve as a strong leverage in negotiations (Wissenbach, 2009).

On trade grounds, the EU also has an interest in developing increased ties with Beijing as it remains by far Africa's main trading partner. EPAs are the cornerstone of Africa-EU relations, and as of 2011 some African countries are still reluctant to sign them. As China develops production facilities in the continent and increases commercial flows, it will have an active interest in being eligible to supply goods to the EU via its African partners. Hence, the EU's engagement with China in Africa can be an opportunity to resume the conclusion of EPAs via Beijing. However, despite EU's critical importance in Africa on trade grounds, a positive signal must be given to Sub-Saharan economies in order to restore influence. This is especially the case as China had announced in 2009 that it would phase-in zero tariff treatment to 95% of the goods originating from Africa's less developed economies having diplomatic relations with Beijing, starting with 60% of the products in 2010. While tariff liberalization is already scheduled in the EPAs, the EU should rather make an effort to curb qualitative requirements for African exports (Holslag *et al.*, 2007).

Last but not least, the 2011 turmoil in North Africa questions the Asian (especially the Chinese) drivers' global ambitions and their non-interference doctrine. Libya's uprising, triggered by poor economic conditions and lack of political rights, has urged the international community to react. While France, the United Kingdom and the Arab League pushed for the United Nations Security Council Resolution 1973 legitimizing a military intervention in the country, both China and India abstained from voting on it, hence missing an opportunity to gain importance on the international stage. While their respective level of engagement in Libya and other North African countries is small compared to other African countries, their position creates a discrepancy between economic importance and their political significance. Indeed, their focus on strictly economic interests and their hesitation to support the resolution paints them as important economic actors lacking the political caliber to be globally important. In contrast, traditional Western actors are still important partners of African economies, and their combination of economic and political leadership and support for democratization is likely to reinforce their presence on the continent.

10.6 Conclusions

This chapter has reviewed the major features of the rising Chinese and Indian trade and direct investment with Africa. The rise in Africa of these relatively new, mostly resource-focused Asian trade and investment sources is displacing traditional European trade and investment with Africa. The analysis presented here also shows that African trade and investment from China differs greatly from African trade and investment from India, with the former driven much more by Chinese government policies and the latter much more by private economic forces. Furthermore, as the following examples show, the rise of these Asian-African trade and investment flows has important policy, business, and scholarly implications.

Implications for FDI Theory

Traditional FDI theory was developed amidst a context where a vast majority of overseas direct investment was undertaken by large companies from the developed and industrialized economies. A number of factors have changed this situation, and FDI theory is therefore being modified to accommodate the new forms, sources, and destinations for FDI. As noted in Aggarwal (2008), globalization today is very different and is now technologically driven.

First, is the rise of new communication and work-flow technologies based on the microprocessor, and the mutually reinforcing interaction of such technologies with the forces driving globalization. These communication and work-flow technologies have clearly made it much easier for business to globalize.

Second, technological growth is accelerating because of globalization, as new technologies are much more profitable being deployed over larger global markets. Many of these new technologies also further decrease the costs of globalization through enabling communication and work-flow technologies (cheaper and more powerful microprocessors can be used in new products as well as in communication equipment).

Third, is the decline of socialism and central planning in most countries as they move to market-driven economic systems. This adds a large number of new economic agents, many of which find globalization attractive. Fourth, globalization is also encouraged by the savings resulting from specialization and trade, which are often augmented by economies of scale and learning effects.

These are four powerful and mutually reinforcing forces that are accelerating globalization. As Friedman (2005) notes, globalization 1.0 was when countries globalized after the voyages of discovery at the end of the 15th century. At that time, it took the resources of a whole country to support and finance globalization. This led to globalization 2.0 when large companies could globalize in the late 19th and 20th centuries. During this time, vast commercial empires went global with the rise of companies like the Singer Sewing Machine Company and Standard Oil, later followed by numerous others like IBM, Coca Cola, KFC, and McDonald's. The new millennium is an age of globalization 3.0, when Internet-connected individuals and small "born global" companies can and have become global. Companies from small and under-developed countries can now also be global companies.

Thus, the traditional context of FDI where large companies from large, well-developed economies globalized, is being supplemented by numerous upstart companies ranging from small "born global" industrialized country companies to entrepreneurial global companies from the developing countries. In this context, traditional assumptions of the flow of technology, market segmentation, ethnocentric staffing, and organizational structures may no longer be universally true. FDI theory must therefore make allowances for these new types of global economic agents that have different ways of overcoming the liability of foreignness.

South-South FDI (e.g., Chinese and Indian FDI in Africa) is an example of this new context and presents a number of challenges to traditional FDI theory (Aggarwal, 2009). First, this FDI is often not driven by the need to exploit home country technology or brands in an overseas market, as is the case for traditional MNCs. Second, the Chinese and Indian resource-seeking FDI in Africa is better understood by invoking less-than-perfect markets for resources where long-term supply can best be insured with ownership rights instead of trade in free and efficient markets for commodities. Third, these south-south investments are also associated with non-traditional roles for the home governments. In the case of China, it includes the provision of subsidized government-directed financing to government-owned companies for acquisitions overseas and, less explicit but nevertheless important, home government support for overseas acquisitions in Africa by Indian companies.

Finally, since 2000, traditional economic drivers of FDI are being supplemented by institutional factors. In the current context, there may be mutually reinforcing feedback between Chinese and Indian trade and investment in Africa, with both rising because the other is. To some extent, India and China are rivals for the same raw materials and there may be some competitive imitation. Such herding behavior among private companies has been well-documented (e.g., Bikhchandani *et al.*, 1998; Graham, 1978; and Haveman, 1993).

Implications for Global Economic Polarization

Africa is a vast and under-studied continent, with both some of the poorest and some of the fastest growing economies. Historically, the

European colonial powers have been the major investors in Africa, but European economic relations with Africa have had a mixed record. However, historical trends in African economics seem to be changing, especially with the rise of the Asian economies, particularly China and India. With the growth of their economies, these two countries have seen their trade, investment and other economic activity in Africa rise rapidly.

For most of the second half of the 20th century the world has been a bi-polar world — one consisting of countries with the free enterprise-based economic system headed by the US, and the second consisting of socialist countries headed by the former Soviet Union (there were very few countries with mixed systems). After about 1989, with the breakup of the Soviet Union and the move by most socialist countries towards free enterprise, there was briefly only one superpower, the US, and perhaps the only and dominant pole. In terms of trade and FDI, historically there have been clear geographic (north-south) patterns, with North America dominating in South America, Europe dominating in Africa, and Japan dominating in Asia.

At the beginning of the 21st century, we have again seen a move towards a multi-polar world economy. In addition to North America, there is now at least the still united EU. It is expected that in the near future these two poles will be supplemented by a third, Asian pole of China, India, and Japan. Others believe that we are headed for a multi-polar world economy. But if the relative decline of north-south trade and investment ties and the rise of south-south economic ties, exemplified by increasing Chinese and Indian trade and FDI with Africa, is moving the world closer to a multi-polar structure, the lack of engagement of the Asian drivers on more political grounds reinforces the already high importance of traditional poles. In this chapter we have documented the recent rise of FDI from Asia, especially from China and India, in Africa and contend that this growing presence of Chindian trade and FDI is likely to change and reduce the relative role and influence of Europe in the continent. These changes are also likely to strengthen South-South economic ties and further lead to an increased multi-polarization of the global economy.

Acknowledgement

Valuable research assistance by Salim Gadi is acknowledged.

References

African Economic Outlook (2009). Basic indicators. http://www.africaneconomicoutlook.org/en/data-statistics/.

Aggarwal, R. (2009). Economic development, business strategy, and corporate restructuring in India. *Journal of Indian Business Research*, 1(1), 14–25.

Aggarwal, R. (2008). Technology, globalization, and business education. *American Journal of Business*, 23(2), 5–12.

Aguiar, M., Bailey, C., Bhattacharya, A., Bradtke, T., de Juan, J., Hemerling, J., Koh, K. W., Michael, D. C., Sirkin, H. L., Stern, C., Tratz, A., Waddell, K. and Waltermann, B. (2009). *The 2009 BCG 100 New Global Challengers: How Competition from Rapidly Developing Economies are Contending Global Leadership.* Boston Consulting Group.

Alon, T. M. (2010). Institutional analysis and the determinants of Chinese OFDI. Federal Reserve Bank of San Francisco.

A.T. Kearney (2010). The shifting geography of offshoring.

Basu, A. and Srinavasan, K. (2002). Foreign direct investment in Africa — some case studies. IMF Working Paper, No. 02/61.

Bende Nabende, A. (2002). Foreign direct investment determinants in Sub-Saharan Africa: a co-integration analysis. *Economics Bulletin*, 6(4), 1–19.

Beri, R. (2003). India's Africa policy in the post-cold war era: an assessment. *Strategic Analysis*, 27(2), 216–232.

Bikhchandani, S., Hirschleifer, D. and Welch, I. (1998). Learning from the behavior of others: conformity, fads, and information cascades. *Journal of Economic Perspectives*, 12(3), 151–170.

Brautigam, D. (2010). China, Africa and the international aid architecture. African Development Bank Working Paper, No. 107, April.

British Petroleum (2010). BP statistical review of world energy 2010.

Broadman, H. G. (2008). China and India go to Africa. *Foreign Affairs*, 87(2), 95–109.

Broadman, H. G. (2007). *Africa's Silk Road: China and India's New Economic Frontier*. Washington, D.C.: The World Bank.

Burke, C., Naidu, S. and Nepgen, A. (2008). Scoping study on China's relations with South Africa. Center for Chinese Studies, University of Stellenbosch.

Carmody, P. (2009). An Asian-driven economic recovery for Africa? The Zambian case. *World Development*, 37(7), 1197–1207.

Congressional Research Service, Library of Congress (2008). China's foreign policy and soft power in South America, Asia and Africa. Study prepared for the Committee on Foreign Relations, United States of America Senate, Washington, D.C., April 2008.

Corden, M. W. and Neary, P. J. (1982). Booming sector and de-industrialization in a small open economy. *Economic Journal*, 92, 825–848.

Corkin, L. (2008). AERC scoping exercise on China-Africa relations: the case of Angola. Center for Chinese Studies, University of Stellenbosch.

Davies, K. (2009). While global FDI falls, China's outward FDI doubles. *Columbia FDI Perspectives*, No. 5, 26 May 2009. Vale Columbia Center on Sustainable International Investment.

Dubey, A. J. (2008). Foreign policy of India with special reference to India's Africa policy. Working Paper, Institute of International Politics and Economics, Jawaharlal Nehru University.

Dupasquier, C. and Osakwe, P. N. (2005). Foreign direct investment in Africa: performance, challenges and responsibilities. African Trade Policy Center Working Paper No. 21, United Nations Economic Commission for Africa.

Energy Information Administration of the United States (EIA) website, China page. http://www.eia.doe.gov/countries/country-data.cfm?fips=CH#data. Accessed 18 March 2011.

Energy Information Administration of the United States (EIA) website, India page. http://www.eia.gov/countries/country-data.cfm?fips=IN#data. Accessed 18 March 2011.

European Commission (2007). The Africa-EU strategic partnership: a joint Africa-EU strategy. Draft endorsed by the Africa-EU Ministerial Troika meeting, 31 October 2007.

European Commission Directorate-General for Trade (2010). ACP-EU bilateral trade statistics, September.

European Commission Directorate-General for Trade (2007). Market economy status of the People's Republic of China in trade defense investigations. Commission Staff Working Paper.

Fitch Ratings (2010). Sub-Saharan Africa: a brighter outlook? Fitch Ratings Special Report, 6 July 2010.

Freemantle, S. and Stevens, J. (2009). Unpacking the nuances of India-Africa engagements. Economics Africa: BRIC in Africa, Standard Bank, 31 August 2009.

Friedman, T. L. (2005). *The World is Flat: A Brief History of the 21st Century*. New York: Farrar, Straus, and Giroux.

Goldstein, A., Pinaud, N., Reisen, H. and Chen, X. (2006). The rise of China and India: what's in it for Africa? OECD Development Center Studies.

Graham, E. M. (1978). Transatlantic investments by multinational firms: a rivalistic phenomenon. *Journal of Post-Keynesian Economics*, 1(1), 82–99.

Halper, S. (2010). Beijing's coalition of the willing: failed states as an opportunity for China. *Foreign Policy*, July-August, 100–102.

Haveman, H. A. (1993). Follow the leader: mimetic isomorphism and entry into new markets. *Administrative Sciences Quarterly*, 38, 593–627.

Hazard, E., DeVries, L., Barry, M. A., Anouan, A. A. and Pinaud, N. (2009). The developmental impact of the Asian drivers on Senegal. *World Economy*, 32(11), 1563–1585.

Holslag, J., Geeraerts, G., Gorus, J. and Smis, S. (2007). Chinese resources and energy policy in Sub-Saharan Africa. Report for the Development Committee of the European Parliament, Vrije Universiteit Brussel.

Ibi Ajayi, S. (2006). Foreign direct investment in Sub-Saharan Africa: origins, targets, impact and potential. African Economic Research Consortium.

International Monetary Fund (IMF) (1993). Balance of Payments Manual.

International Monetary Fund (IMF). Direction of Trade Statistics Database.

International Monetary Fund (IMF) (2010). World Economic Outlook Database, October 2010.

Jenkins, R. and Edwards, C. (2006). The economic impacts of China and India on sub-Saharan Africa: trends and prospects. *Journal of Asian Economics*, 17(2), 207–225.

Kaplinsky, R. and Morris, M. (2009). Chinese FDI in Sub-Saharan Africa: engaging with large dragons. *European Journal of Development Research*, 21(4), 551–569.

Khan, S. A. and Baye, F. M. (2008). China-Africa economic relations: the case of Cameroon. AERC Scoping Studies on Africa-China Relations.

Krugell, W. (2005). The determinants of foreign direct investment in Africa. In: B. M. Gilroy, T. Gries and W. A. Naudé (Eds.), *Multinational Enterprises, Foreign Direct Investment and Growth in Africa*. Heidelberg: Physica-Verlag.

Lum, T., Fischer, H., Gomez-Granger, J. and Leland, A. (2009). China's foreign aid activities in Africa, Latin America and Southeast Asia. Report for the United States' Congress, February, Washington, D.C.

Mahajan, V. (2009). *Africa Rising: How 900 Million African Consumers Offer More Than You Think*. New York: Pearson Publishers.

Mahajan-Bansal, N. and Suri, S. (2009). The siege of Africa. *Forbes Asia*, 5(15), 132–137.

Mwanawina, I. (2008). China-Africa economic relations: the case of Zambia. AERC Scoping Studies on Africa-China Relations.

Nanji, M. (2010). India and Africa collaborating on trade and investment for mutual benefit. *FinanceAsia*, April, 17–19.

OECD. Direct Investment by Country Database. Organization for Economic Cooperation and Development, Paris.

OECD (2008). Investment policy reviews: China 2008. Organization for Economic Cooperation and Development, Paris.

OECD Online Glossary: Official development assistance. http://www.oecd.org/glossary/0,2586,en_2649_33721_1965693_1_1_1_1,00.html#1965586. Organization for Economic Cooperation and Development, Paris

Onyeiwu, S. and Shrestha, H. (2004). Determinants of foreign direct investment in Africa. *Journal of Developing Societies*, 20(1–2), 89–106.

Pal, P. (2009). Surge in Indian outbound FDI to Africa: an emerging pattern in globalization? Indian Institute of Management, Calcutta. http://www.iimcal.ac.in/research/download/OFDI_Partha-pal.pdf.

Pederson, J. D. (2008). The second wave of Indian investments abroad. *Journal of Contemporary Asia*, 38(4), 613–637.

Souiah, F. (2010). La société Algérienne au miroir des migrations Chinoises. *Moyen Orient Magazine*, No. 7, August-September.

Stevens, C. and Kennan, J. (2006). How to identify the trade impact of China on small countries. *International Development Studies Bulletin*, 37(1), 33–42.

UNCTAD (2007). Asian foreign direct investment in Africa: towards a new era of cooperation among developing countries. United Nations Conference on Trade and Development, New York and Geneva.

UNCTAD (2008). World Investment Directory 2008. United Nations Conference on Trade and Development, New York and Geneva.

UNCTAD. FDI statistics online database. United Nations Conference on Trade and Development, New York and Geneva.

UNCTAD. Stat online database. United Nations Conference on Trade and Development, New York and Geneva.

UNCTAD (2010a). World investment report 2010. United Nations Conference on Trade and Development, New York and Geneva.

UNCTAD (2010b). Economic development in Africa report 2010. South-South Cooperation: Africa and the New Forms of Development Partnership. United Nations Conference on Trade and Development, New York and Geneva.

United Nations Economic Commission for Africa (2009). Africa's mining regimes: framework report. Report by the International Study Group established under the auspices of the African Union and the United Nations Economic Commission for Africa.

United Nations Security Council Resolution 1973. (2011). United Nations, New York.

United States Geological Survey (2010). Mineral commodity summaries, January 2010.

Walker, M. (2008). Indian ocean nexus. *Wilson Quarterly*, 32(2), 21–28.

Wang, J. Y. (2007). What drives China's growing role in Africa? IMF Working Paper No. 07/211.

Washington Times (2010). China leads Algeria construction boom. 27 January 2010.

Wissenbach, U. (2009). The EU's response to China's Africa safari: can triangular cooperation match needs. *European Journal of Development Research*, 21, 662–674.

WTO Trade Profiles (2009). World Trade Organization, Geneva.

Xin Hua News (2008). China's 2007 trade surplus hits record. 11 January 2008.

Appendix 10.A: Africa basic indicators, 2009.

Country	Population (thousands)	Land area (thousands of km^2)	Population density (pop/km^2)	GDP based on PPP valuation (US$ Million)	GDP per capita (PPP valuation, $)	Annual real GDP growth (average over 2001–2009)
Algeria	34,895	2,382	15	256,542	7,352	3.7
Angola	18,498	1,247	15	100,459	5,431	11.6
Benin	8,935	115	78	13,454	1,506	4.1
Botswana	1,950	582	3	25,764	13,214	3.9
Burkina Faso	15,757	274	58	19,395	1,231	5.4
Burundi	8,303	28	298	2,853	344	3.0
Cameroon	19,522	476	41	46,347	2,374	3.3
Cape Verde	506	4	125	2,002	3,959	6.1
Central Afr. Rep.	4,422	623	7	3,471	785	1.9
Chad	11,206	1,284	9	17,067	1,523	8.4
Comoros	676	2	302	821	1,215	1.9
Congo	3,683	342	11	15,614	4,239	4.5
Congo Dem. Rep.	66,020	2,345	28	21,304	323	4.7
Côte d'Ivoire	21,075	322	65	33,766	1,602	0.9
Djibouti	864	23	37	1,955	2,262	3.8
Egypt*	82,999	1,001	83	471,509	5,681	4.9
Equatorial Guinea	676	28	24	21,188	31,331	20.5
Eritrea	5,073	118	43	3,813	752	0.8
Ethiopia*	82,825	1,104	75	72,196	872	8.0
Gabon	1,475	268	6	21,951	14,886	1.9
Gambia	1,705	11	151	2,003	1,175	5.0

(Continued)

Appendix 10.A: (*Continued*)

Country	Population (thousands)	Land area (thousands of km^2)	Population density (pop/km^2)	GDP based on PPP valuation (US$ Million)	GDP per capita (PPP valuation, $)	Annual real GDP growth (average over 2001–2009)
Ghana	23,837	239	100	36,558	1,534	5.5
Guinea	10,069	246	41	10,473	1,040	2.8
Guinea Bissau	1,611	36	45	817	508	1.1
Kenya	39,802	593	67	62,423	1,568	4.1
Lesotho	2,067	30	68	2,482	1,201	3.1
Liberia	3,955	111	36	1,093	276	1.3
Libya	6,420	1,760	4	99,491	15,497	4.4
Madagascar	19,625	587	33	18,230	929	3.0
Malawi	15,263	118	129	8,395	550	4.9
Mali	13,010	1,240	10	15,898	1,222	5.7
Mauritania	3,291	1,026	3	8,157	2,479	3.9
Mauritius	1,288	2	631	17,489	13,576	3.7
Morocco	31,993	711	45	151,855	4,747	5.1
Mozambique	22,894	802	29	21,746	950	8.0
Namibia	2,171	824	3	13,737	6,327	4.3
Niger	15,290	1,267	12	10,392	680	5.0
Nigeria	154,729	924	167	327,822	2,119	8.2
Rwanda	9,998	26	380	9,526	953	6.5
São Tomé & Príncipe	163	1	169	339	2,083	6.1
Senegal	12,534	197	64	20,841	1,663	3.8
Seychelles	84	0.455	185	1,480	17,563	0.9

(*Continued*)

Appendix 10.A: (*Continued*)

Country	Population (thousands)	Land area (thousands of km^2)	Population density (pop/km^2)	GDP based on PPP valuation (US$ Million)	GDP per capita (PPP valuation, $)	Annual real GDP growth (average over 2001–2009)
Sierra Leone	5,696	72	79	4,509	792	10.1
Somalia	9,133	638	14	…	…	…
South Africa	50,110	1,221	41	487,107	9,721	3.6
Sudan	42,272	2,506	17	95,466	2,258	7.1
Swaziland	1,185	17	68	5,806	4,900	2.2
Tanzania	43,739	945	46	53,167	1,216	6.9
Togo	6,619	57	117	6,071	917	1.8
Tunisia	10,272	164	63	89,010	8,666	4.6
Uganda	32,710	241	136	46,632	1,426	7.7
Zambia	12,935	753	17	19,606	1,516	5.4
Zimbabwe	12,523	391	32	2,193	175	–5.4
Africa	1,008,354	30,323	33	2,825,691	2,802	5.3

Sources: United Nations, Department of Economic and Social Affairs, Population Division, World Population Prospects, The 2008 Revision. ADB Statistics Department, Various domestic authorities and IMF World Economic Outlook (March 2010).

Note: * Fiscal year July (n-1)/June (n). ** Fiscal year April (n)/March (n+1).

Appendix 10.B: FDI in Africa and developing economies, 1990–2009 ($ million).

Year	Africa	Developing economies	Share of Africa in FDI to developing economies (%)
1990	2,793.01	35,095.65	7.96
1991	3,448.86	39,770.02	8.67
1992	3,770.39	53,167.23	7.09
1993	5,443.14	76,834.55	7.08
1994	6,104.83	103,501.67	5.90
1995	5,655.40	115,943.16	4.88
1996	5,687.04	147,077.80	3.87
1997	10,772.58	190,723.95	5.65
1998	8,986.32	190,729.50	4.71
1999	11,670.58	228,079.39	5.12
2000	9,394.83	256,465.22	3.66
2001	18,799.04	214,696.48	8.76
2002	15,008.87	176,063.06	8.52
2003	19,783.81	183,911.74	10.76
2004	20,854.10	291,919.08	7.14
2005	37,115.72	330,129.87	11.24
2006	53,586.95	434,365.87	12.34
2007	61,429.82	564,929.90	10.87
2008	69,532.78	630,012.53	11.04
2009	55,718.11	478,349.04	11.65

Source: UNCTAD, FDI Statistics Online Database.

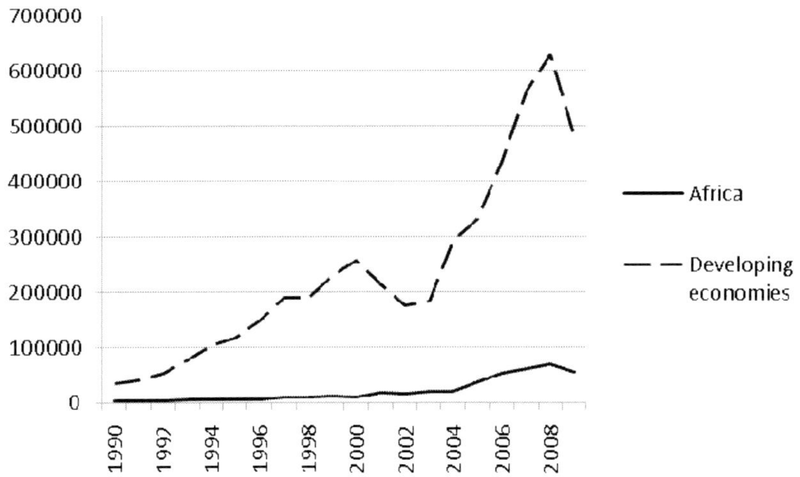

Source: UNCTAD, FDI Statistics Online Database.

Appendix 10.C: Africa's, comparator countries'/regions' and world's proven reserves in selected minerals, oil and gas.

Diamond reserves in 2009	Kilograms (percent)
Congo Kinshasa	150 (25.8)
Botswana	130 (22.4)
South Africa	70 (12)
Australia	70 (12)
World	580
Share of Africa (%)	*60*
Platinum metals reserves in 2009	Kilograms (percent)
South Africa	63,000,000 (88)
Russia	6,000,000 (8.4)
World	71,000,000
Share of Africa (%)	*88*
Gold reserves in 2009	Kilograms (percent)
South Africa	6000 (12.7)
Russia	5000 (10.6)
Ghana	1600 (3.4)
World	47,000
Share of Africa (%)	*16*

Source: USGS, Commodity Summaries, January 2010.

Country	Oil (thousand million barrels)	Share in Africa's total reserves
Libya	44.3	34.7%
Nigeria	37.2	29.1%
Angola	13.5	10.6%
Algeria	12.2	9.6%
Sudan	6.7	5.2%
Egypt	4.4	3.4%
Gabon	3.7	2.9%
Republic of Congo (Brazzaville)	1.9	1.5%
Equatorial Guinea	1.7	1.3%
Chad	0.9	0.7%
Tunisia	0.6	0.5%
Other Africa	0.6	0.5%
Total Africa	127.7	100.0%

Appendix 10.C: (*Continued*)

Region	Oil (thousand million barrels)	Share of world total
Total Middle East	754.2	56.6%
Total S. & Cent. America	198.9	14.9%
Total Europe & Eurasia	136.9	10.3%
Total Africa	127.7	9.6%
Total North America	73.3	5.5%
Total Asia-Pacific	42.2	3.2%
Total World	1333.1	100.0%

Country	Gas reserves (trillion cubic meters)	Share in Africa's total gas reserves
Nigeria	5.25	35.6%
Algeria	4.50	30.5%
Egypt	2.19	14.8%
Libya	1.54	10.4%
Other Africa	1.27	8.6%
Total Africa	14.76	100.0%

Region	Gas reserves (trillion cubic meters)	Share of world total
Total Middle East	76.18	40.6%
Total Europe & Eurasia	63.09	33.7%
Total Asia-Pacific	16.24	8.7%
Total Africa	14.76	7.9%
Total North America	9.16	4.9%
Total S. & Cent. America	8.06	4.3%
Total World	187.49	100.0%

Source: BP Statistical Review of World Energy 2010.

Appendix 10.D: Inward FDI stock in Africa by country in 2009 ($ million).

Country	FDI stock	Share (%)
Ethiopia (former)	—	—
Mayotte	—	—
Saint Helena	—	—
Western Sahara	—	—
South Africa	125,085.36	24.29
Nigeria	69,089.09	13.42
Egypt	66,709.30	12.95
Morocco	40,719.36	7.91
Tunisia	31,857.13	6.18
Sudan	19,296.42	3.74
Algeria	17,344.37	3.36
Angola	16,515.20	3.20
Libyan Arab Jamahiriya	15,508.36	3.01
Congo	13,166.60	2.55
Zambia	9,503.93	1.84
U.R of Tanzania	7,266.30	1.41
Equatorial Guinea	6,678.55	1.29
Ghana	6,570.79	1.27
Côte d'Ivoire	6,222.91	1.20
Uganda	4,987.81	0.96
Mozambique	4,689.20	0.91
Liberia	4,605.50	0.89
Cameroon	4,402.63	0.85
Namibia	3,988.30	0.77
Ethiopia	3,790.11	0.73
Madagascar	3,495.86	0.67
Chad	3,386.68	0.65
Dem. Rep. of the Congo	3,057.96	0.59
Mauritania	2,141.64	0.41
Kenya	2,129.07	0.41
Mauritius	1,889.13	0.36
Guinea	1,614.32	0.31
Zimbabwe	1,603.55	0.31
Senegal	1,378.10	0.26
Niger	1,362.70	0.26
Gabon	1,267.37	0.24
Seychelles	1,113.89	0.21
Cape Verde	1,093.30	0.21

(*Continued*)

Appendix 10.D: (*Continued*)

Country	FDI stock	Share (%)
Mali	1,086.73	0.21
Lesotho	1,075.48	0.20
Botswana	981.46	0.19
Togo	914.33	0.17
Burkina Faso	867.97	0.16
Djibouti	851.70	0.16
Malawi	820.74	0.15
Swaziland	808.97	0.15
Benin	694.93	0.13
Gambia	637.58	0.12
Sierra Leone	459.52	0.08
Somalia	454.19	0.08
Rwanda	411.93	0.08
Eritrea	382.75	0.07
Central African Republic	296.66	0.05
Sao Tome and Principe	181.73	0.03
Guinea-Bissau	181.25	0.03
Burundi	71.45	0.01
Comoros	48.96	0.00
Total	514,759.10	100

Source: UNCTAD, FDI Statistics Online Database.

Note: Figures may not add due to rounding.

Appendix 10.E: FDI stocks of OECD countries in Africa in 2009 ($ million).

Country	FDI stock	Share (%)
United Kingdom	56,536.10	36.08
France	40,453.20	25.8
United States	27,764.00	17.71
Netherlands	13,680.20	8.73
Italy	7,372.20	4.7
Spain	6,434.50	4.1
Sweden	2,567.60	1.6
Denmark	1,285.80	0.8
Greece	377.70	0.24
Poland	131.00	0.08
Finland	79.40	0.05
Slovak Republic	2.10	0.00
Iceland	1.50	0.00
Czech Republic	0.20	0.00
Total	156,682.1	100

Source: OECD, Direct Investment by Country Database.
Note: Figures may not add due to rounding.

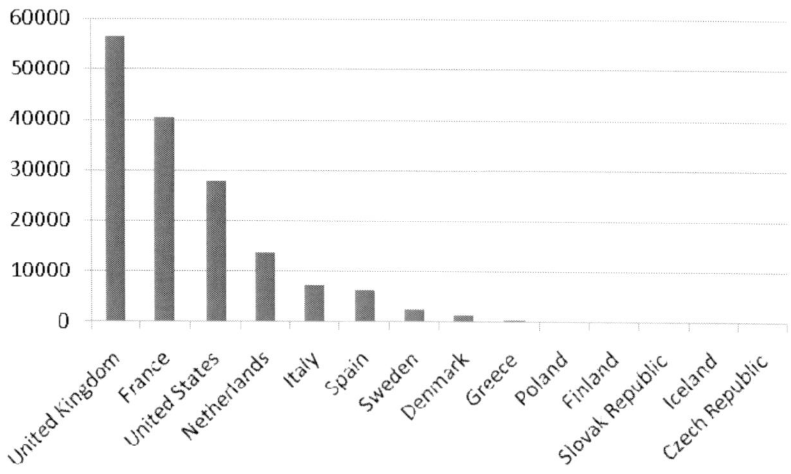

Source: OECD, Direct Investment by Country Database.

Appendix 10.F: Outward FDI stocks of developing countries in Africa in 2008 ($ million).

Country	FDI stock	Share (%)
Singapore	9,829	31
China	7,804	25.3
Hong Kong China	5,268	17
Malaysia	3,718	12
India	2,652	8.6
Republic of Korea	516	1.6
Taiwan Province of China	436	1.41
Thailand	227	0.73
Chile	195	0.63
Pakistan	93	0.3
Brazil	82	0.26
Total	30,820	100

Source: UNCTAD (2010b).
Note: Figures may not add due to rounding.

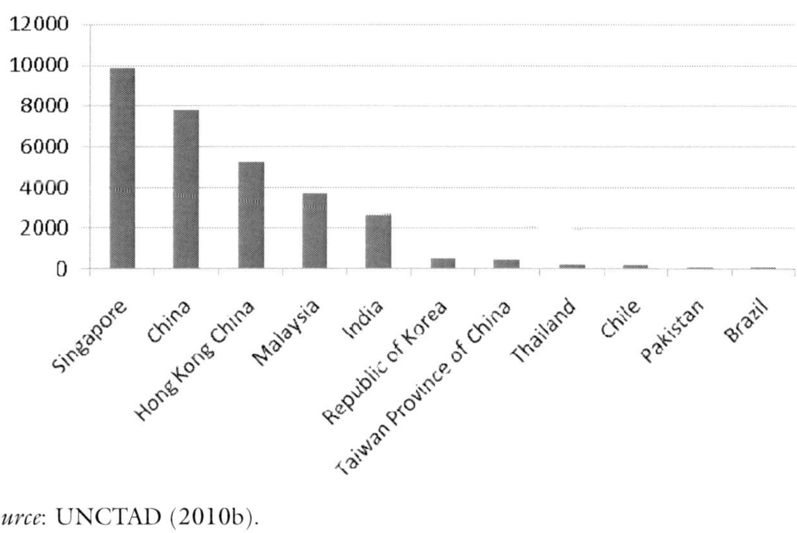

Source: UNCTAD (2010b).

Appendix 10.G: Africa's trade with the EU, China and India, 2000–2009 ($ million).

Exports	China	European Union	India
2000	4,266.09	54,439.40	5,309.29
2001	3,583.22	52,007.30	3,376.11
2002	4,139.57	54,309.80	3,634.54
2003	7,703.91	61,683.70	3,808.35
2004	11,735.74	77,071.30	1,927.46
2005	17,646.30	90,545.40	2,953.19
2006	25,684.60	102,878.00	8,294.10
2007	33,428.92	112,777.00	13,312.00
2008	44,518.62	151,054.00	16,393.70
2009	32,004.07	97,034.50	12,837.70
Imports	**China**	**European Union**	**India**
2000	4,272.27	48,956.30	1,621.47
2001	4,751.85	50,725.90	1,861.42
2002	5,727.27	52,997.40	2,330.55
2003	8,724.17	67,481.00	3,098.76
2004	12,862.49	79,435.00	4,142.39
2005	18,334.76	87,790.10	6,089.31
2006	26,560.47	101,202.00	9,045.96
2007	37,256.53	133,394.00	12,118.40
2008	50,147.83	156,317.00	14,373.00
2009	49,107.11	132,240.00	12,589.50

Source: IMF, Direction of Trade Statistics Database, 2010.

Appendix 10.H: Chinese and Indian total FDI outflows for the period 1990–2009 ($ million) and Greenfield investments concluded in Africa between 2002 and 2005.

Year	China	India
1990	830	6
1991	913	–11
1992	4000	24
1993	4400	0.350641
1994	2000	82
1995	2000	119
1996	2114	240
1997	2562.49	113
1998	2633.807	47
1999	1774.313	80
2000	915.777	514.4454136
2001	6885.398	1397.43655
2002	2518.407	1678.039428
2003	2854.65	1875.779518
2004	5497.99	2175.366588
2005	12261.17	2985.487528
2006	21160	14284.98907
2007	22468.86	17233.03143
2008	52150	18498.7082
2009	48000	14896.71586

Source: UNCTAD, FDI Statistics Online Database.

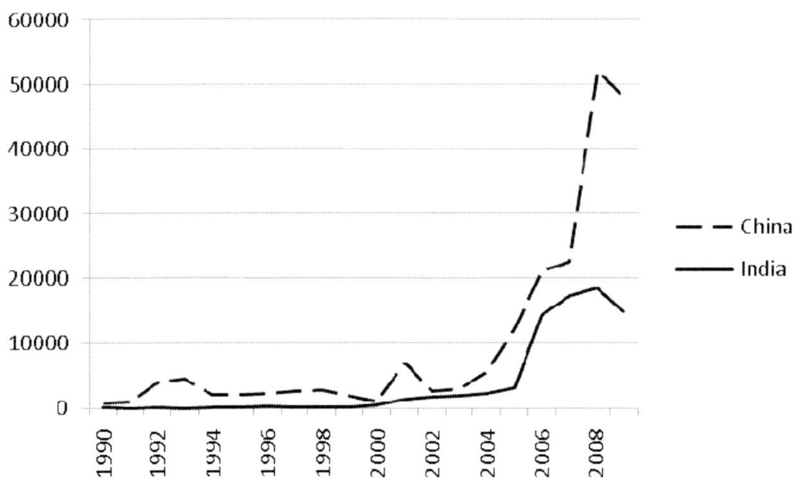

Source: UNCTAD, FDI Statistics Online Database.

Chindian Investments in Africa, 2002–2005.

Year	Name of source company	Home country	Destination (host country)	Industry	Number of projects	Investment value ($ million)	Employment
2002	Veronica Laboratories	India	Kenya	Pharmaceuticals	1	..	..
2002	Indian Oil (IOC)	India	Mauritius	Energy	1	..	..
2002	Mahindra & Mahindra (M&M)	India	South Africa	Automotive OEM	1	..	..
2002	Tata Group India	India	South Africa	Metals/Mining	1	40	..
2002	Hidesign	India	South Africa	Textiles	1	..	..
2002	Infosys Technologies	India	Mauritius	IT and software	1	25	1500
2002	CMEC	China	Nigeria	Energy	1	390	..
2003	Beijing General Research Institute of Mining and Metallurgy (BGRIMM)	China	Zambia	Chemicals	1	8	..
2003	China National Petroleum (CNPC)	China	Algeria	Energy	1	350	..
2003	China Petroleum and Chemical (Sinopec)	China	Nigeria	Energy	1	..	..
2003	Aditya Birla	India	Egypt	Plastics and rubber	1	..	1000
2003	Hindusthan Seals	India	Egypt	Plastics and rubber	1	..	..
2003	KK Birla Group	India	Egypt	Chemicals	1	..	..

(*Continued*)

(Continued)

Year	Name of source company	Home country	Destination (host country)	Industry	Number of projects	Investment value ($ million)	Employment
2003	LML	India	Egypt	Other Transport OEM	1	..	..
2003	ONGC	India	Libyan Arab Jamahiriya	Energy	1	30	..
2003	Hindusthan Seals	India	Morocco	Plastics and rubber	1	..	..
2003	Bank of India	India	Kenya	Financial services	1	..	..
2003	Infosys Technologies	India	Mauritius	IT and software	1	10	..
2003	Tata Group	India	South Africa	Metals/Mining	1	53	..
2003	State Bank of India (SBI)	India	South Africa	Financial services	1	..	..
2003	Bharat Biotech	India	South Africa	Biotechnology	1	..	..
2003	Ramco Systems	India	South Africa	IT and software	1	10	..
2003	Bank of Baroda	India	United Rep. Of Tanzania	Financial services	1	..	..
2003	Hindusthan Seals	India	United Rep. Of Tanzania	Plastics and rubber	1	..	..
2003	China National Petroleum (CNPC)	China	Sudan	Energy	1	1000	..
2003	China National Petroleum (CNPC)	China	Niger	Energy	1	..	..

(Continued)

(*Continued*)

Year	Name of source company	Home country	Destination (host country)	Industry	Number of projects	Investment value ($ million)	Employment
2003	Tianjin Litong Elevator	China	Egypt	Machinery and industrial goods	1	3	..
2003	Shenzhen Topway Solar	China	Uganda	Machinery and industrial goods	1	..	..
2003	Shanghai Baosteel Group	China	Zimbabwe	Metals/Mining	1	300	2000
2003	Yue Yang Paper	China	Uganda	Paper and packaging	1	10	114
2003	ZTE	China	Egypt	Telecom equipment	1	..	..
2004	Liming Chemical Industriam	China	United Rep. Of Tanzania	Chemicals	1	..	..
2004	China National Petroleum (CNPC)	China	Sudan	Energy	1	..	..
2004	Indian Oil (IOC)	India	Mauritius	Energy	1	..	..
2004	HDFC	India	Mauritius	Business services	1	..	..
2004	Tata Group	India	Mauritius	Hotels, tourism and leisure	1	..	..
2004	Hinduja Group	India	Mauritius	IT and software	1	..	..
2004	Mahindra & Mahindra (M&M)	India	South Africa	Automotive OEM	1	..	..

(*Continued*)

(Continued)

Year	Name of source company	Home country	Destination (host country)	Industry	Number of projects	Investment value ($ million)	Employment
2004	Usha Martin	India	South Africa	IT and software	1	..	..
2004	ICICI Bank	India	South Africa	Financial services	1	..	..
2004	Indusind Bank	India	South Africa	Financial services	1	..	..
2004	Syndicate Bank	India	South Africa	Financial services	1	..	..
2004	Teledata Informatics	India	South Africa	IT and software	1	..	9
2004	Hatsun Agro Product (HAPL)	India	Seychelles	Food and drink	1	..	..
2004	Dabur	India	Nigeria	Consumer products	1	..	..
2004	ONGC	India	Sudan	Energy	1	200	..
2004	Indian Oil (OIC)	India	Nigeria	Energy	1	..	..
2004	Jinchuan	China	South Africa	Metals/Mining	1	..	..
2004	ZTE	China	Algeria	Telecom equipment	1	..	..
2004	ZTE	China	Nigeria	Telecom equipment	1	..	..
2005	SAIC Chery Automobile	China	Algeria	Automotive OEM	1	..	..
2005	Brilliance Auto Hong Kong	China	Egypt	Automotive OEM	1	..	..
2005	Changchun Construction Group	China	Madagascar	Building materials, ceramics and glass	1	..	..
2005	Lenovo	China	Kenya	Business machines and equipment	1	..	..

(Continued)

(Continued)

Year	Name of source company	Home country	Destination (host country)	Industry	Number of projects	Investment value ($ million)	Employment
2005	Lenovo	China	Kenya	Business machines and equipment	1	..	..
2005	AUCMA Group	China	Kenya	Consumer electronics	1	2	52
2005	China Petroleum and Chemical (Sinopec)	China	Egypt	Energy	1	..	..
2005	Hutchison Whampoa Hong Kong	China	Egypt	Logistics and distribution	2	..	..
2005	Indian Oil (IOC)	India	Mauritius	Energy	1	1	..
2005	China Nonferrous Metal Int'l Mining	China	Zambia	Metals/Mining	1	100	..
2005	ZTE	China	Rwanda	Telecom equipment	1	..	..
2005	ZTE	China	Angola	Telecom equipment	1	300	..
2005	ZTE	China	Angola	Telecom equipment	1	..	..
2005	ZTE	China	Angola	Telecom equipment	1	..	..
2005	ZTE	China	Angola	Telecom equipment	1	..	..
2005	ZTE	China	Zambia	Telecom equipment	1	..	..
2005	Huawei Technologies	China	Egypt	Telecom equipment	1	..	..
2005	ZTE	China	Kenya	Telecom services	1	..	..
2005	China Textile Machinery Group (CTMC)	China	Egypt	Textiles	1	13	900

(Continued)

(*Continued*)

Year	Name of source company	Home country	Destination (host country)	Industry	Number of projects	Investment value ($ million)	Employment
2005	Bank of India	India	United Rep. Of Tanzania	Financial services	1	..	..
2005	Mahanagar telephone Nigam (MTNL)	India	Mauritius	Telecom Equipment	1	23	..
2005	Metropolis Health Services Group	India	Kenya	Pharmaceuticals	1	..	..
2005	ONGC	India	Egypt	Energy	1	..	..
2005	Tata Group	India	Morocco	Chemicals	1	..	..
2005	Tata Group	India	Morocco	Automotive OEM	1	25	2070
2005	National Thermal Power (NTPC)	India	Nigeria	Energy	1	..	..
2005	Bharti group	India	Seychelles	Telecom services	1	8	..
2005	Tata Group	India	South Africa	Automotive OEM	1	..	..
2005	Tata Group	India	South Africa	Automotive OEM	1	..	..
2005	Murugappa Group	India	Tunisia	Chemicals	1	180	..
2005	Numeric power Systems	India	Mauritius	Electronic components	1	..	..

Source: UNCTAD (2007), based on LOCO Monitor.

Chapter 11

Low-Carbon Revolution of Chinese Economy: External Challenges vs. Internal Barriers

Libo Wu, Weiqi Tang and Wenshi Yu

11.1 Introduction

To achieve the target of 20% reduction on energy consumption for per unit of economic output over the 11th five-year plan period (2006–2010), China has undertaken great changes in its policy schemes, legal systems and institutional settings. The main underlying driving forces inducing these changes arise from the international climate negotiations, the instability of the world energy market, the serious local environmental degradation and the unsustainability of the Chinese energy system. All of these challenges are regarded as long-term threats to China's sustainable development. Hence, the Chinese government has set the target of developing an energy-saving and environment-friendly society as a central part of its policy scheme. In the national 12th five-year plan, the Chinese government has maintained its energy-saving target, and has also established the carbon emission intensity reduction target for all the provinces. This is a big step for a developing country in the stage of rapid industrialization, urbanization and motorization. It seems that the Chinese government is trying its best to disentangle economic growth from resource consumption and environmental degradation.

However, there are still some intrinsic barriers deterring the low-carbonization process in China. Firstly, the coal-based energy supply system is the most significant impediment for low-carbon transformation. Potential alternatives such as fossil fuel substitute, renewable energy deployment and carbon capture and storage technology are all hindered by high costs. Secondly, the rapid industrialization and urbanization process is a significant barrier from the demand side for the low-carbonization process. As an open but dual-structure economy, China's comparative advantages are its relatively cheaper labor force and resources, which determine the domestic industrial structure and China's position in the international specialization hierarchy. Therefore, to enhance the overall welfare level of all Chinese people, the government must achieve a balance between economic development and environmental protection. Thirdly, a significant barrier deterring low carbonization arises from the property of public goods. Since carbon emission controlling measures can lead to great economic and social benefits but not all of these benefits can be completely maintained by the party who take these measures, the market-based pricing mechanism will become ineffective without government intervention. Such intrinsic public-goods attribute leads to the dilemma of international climate cooperation and also the lack of incentives and actions on a regional level. Climate change has been one of the most serious challenges calling for more involvement in mitigation and adaption activities. Multilateral agreement on climate change for the post-Kyoto era is definitely needed. Since such international common solutions are so critical for all of the world's economies regarding their energy use, land use and water management ways, climate change must be one of the most prominent driving forces for the global re-polarization process. As a theoretical speculation on the low-carbon revolution in China, this chapter will first provide a thorough overview of the energy supply situation in China, and then move to a theoretical discussion of the external challenges, internal status and barriers for low-carbon revolution in China. Finally, the impacts of the Chinese low-carbonization process on the re-polarization process of the whole world will be explored.

The outline of the remaining sections is as follows. Section 11.2 focuses on the energy reserve in China. Section 11.3 addresses the issue of China's energy supply and demand in the world context. Section 11.4 refers to the realistic response to climate change and low-carbon economy all over the world. Then, Section 11.5 introduces two theoretical restrictions of the low-carbon economy. Section 11.6 turns to China's industrial structure optimization and low-carbon economic growth. Finally, Section 11.7 discusses the relationship between international trade, international investment and China's low-carbon economic growth.

11.2 Energy Reserve in China

Table 11.1 summarizes the energy reserve situation in China. It is obvious that China is a coal-based country and that the oil and natural gas supply is partly dependent on foreign energy markets.

Table 11.1: Energy reserve in China.

	Total primary energy (bill. TOE)	Raw coal (bill. ton)	Crude oil (bill. ton)	Natural gas (bill. m^3)	Hydro (bill. kilowatt)
Total reserve	2832.6	5059.22	100.0	38140.00	5922.18
Structure %	100.0	89.3	3.5	1.3	5.9
World total	73416.6	119574.84	5117.28	7933082.71	41309.5
Share of China %	3.9	4.2	2.0	0.5	14.3
Verified reserved (technically)	576.17	1007.7	16.00	2060.60	1923.3
Structure %	100.0	87.4	2.8	0.3	9.5
World total	23078.8	35274.96	2567.46	2663007.52	11754.9
Share of China %	2.5	2.9	0.6	0.1	16.4
Ratio of verification	20.3	19.9	16.0	5.4	
Resource guaranteed period	349.2	398.3	86.0	29.8	
Remaining verified reserved (economically)	97.43	114.50	3.27	1366.89	1260
Structure %	100.0	58.8	3.4	1.3	36.5
World total	9683.3	984.21	140.28	149381.10	7305.3
Share of China %	10.1	11.6	2.3	0.9	17.2
Resource guaranteed period	59.05	45.2	17.6	19.8	
Production in 2007	1.65	2.53	0.186	69.2	496.5
Structure %	100.0	76.63	11.31	3.91	7.24

Source: BP statistical review full report 2008; China Energy Statistical Yearbook 2008.

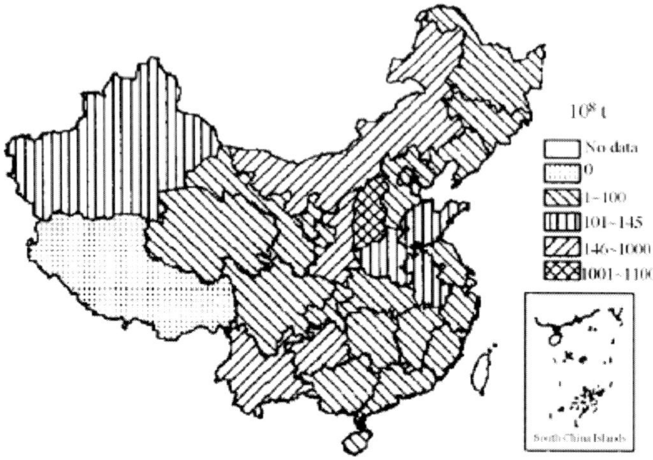

Figure 11.1: China's coal reserve distribution in 2004.

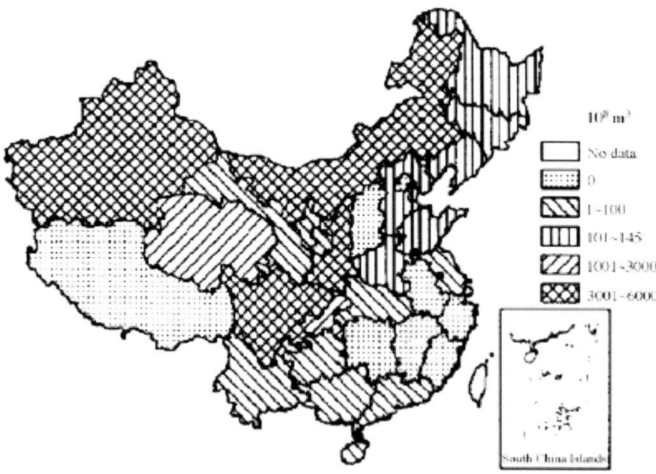

Figure 11.2: China's natural gas reserve distribution in 2004.

Figures 11.1–11.3 show the regional distribution of various energy reserves in China. The coal reserves are mainly concentrated in the northern part of China, eastern China is full of water resources, while most of the oil reserves are located in western China. The diverse spatial distribution of energy sources makes the transportation issue essential to the Chinese energy supply system.

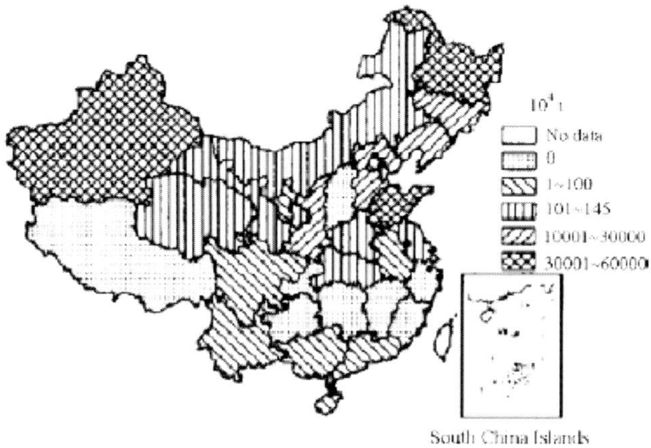

Figure 11.3: China's petroleum reserve distribution in 2004.

11.3 China's Energy Supply and Demand in the World Context

Energy Supply

Primary energy production in China has increased rapidly in recent years. The total primary energy production in 2000 was 1848.96Mtoe, and it increased by 81.91% to 3363.50Mtoe in 2007 (NBS, 2008). Production of primary electricity (hydro and nuclear power) also increased by 97.95%, from 139.33Mtoe in 2000 to 275.80Mtoe in 2007.

Figure 11.4 shows the growth of primary energy production in China. As we can see, the growth rate accelerated sharply since the beginning of this century. The average annual growth rate of primary energy production in the 1980s was 5.34%; in the 1990s it dropped to 2.17%; whereas the average annual growth rate from 2000 to 2007 was 8.92%. Primary electricity also increased rapidly. The average annual growth rate was 8.21% in the 1980s; it dropped to 5.97% in the 1990s; and then increased to 10.25% in this century. Indeed, the share of primary electricity in total primary energy production increased from 7.2% in 2000 to 8.2% in 2007 (see Figure 11.5).

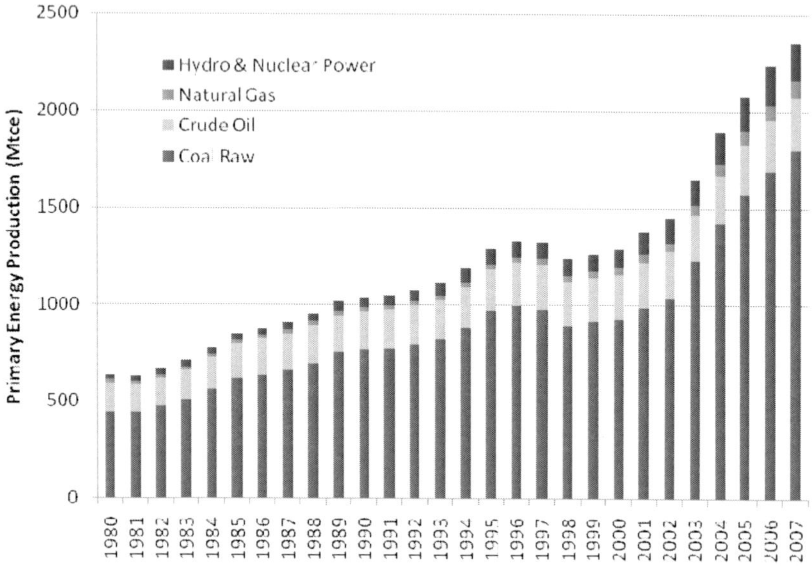

Figure 11.4: Primary energy production of China (2008).

Source: China Energy Statistical Yearbook 2008.

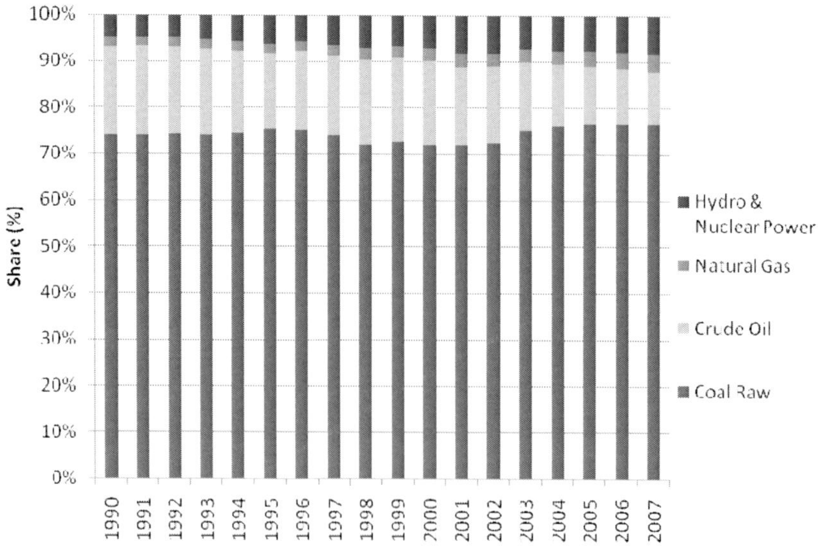

Figure 11.5: Share of primary energy production (2008).

Source: China Energy Statistical Yearbook 2008.

China's natural gas production in 2000 was 52.54Mtoe, accounting for 2.8% of total energy production, and in 2007 natural gas production increased to 135.46Mtoe. The annual growth rate of natural gas production from 2000 to 2007, 14.26%, was the highest among all kinds of primary energy. But the absolute value remained relatively low, so its portion in total energy production was still low at 3.9%. The change was insignificant, as we can see in Figure 11.4.

The growth rate of electricity, 11.04%, was also very high. Electricity production in 2000 was 139.33Mtoe, and that in 2007 was 275.8Mtoe. Since 2000, over 70% of energy industry investment in China has been imputed to the power sector, and the absolute value of investment is increasing rapidly (see Section 11.6 for more details on energy industry investment in China). This will surely further stimulate the electricity production capacity in China.

China's crude oil production in 2007 was 380.07Mtoe (186.32Mt), slightly increasing by 14.22% from 332.76Mtoe (163.00Mt) in 2000. The share of crude oil in total primary energy production dropped from 18.1% in 2000 to 11.3% in 2007. Meanwhile, final consumption of petroleum products increased by 62.97%, from 224.39Mt in 2000 to 365.70Mt in 2007. Booming consumption of petroleum boosted demand for crude oil, and hence, crude oil consumption in China increased by 56.23%, from 217.83Mt in 2000 to 340.31Mt in 2007. The foreign dependence of crude oil in China exceeded 50% in 2007.

From Figures 11.4 and 11.5, we can easily see that China's energy structure is highly dependent on coal. Coal is the most widely used primary energy in China. Though its share in total primary energy production has decreased dramatically since the 1970s, it has stayed at around 70% since the 1990s. More than half (50.47%) of the coal consumption in China is utilized for power generation.

Table 11.2 shows a comparison of energy indicators across four important regions: the US, OECD Europe, China and India. China's energy production in 2007 accounted for 14.83% of the world total — the biggest share among the four regions — and her 5.6Gt CO2 emission was the second largest, slightly smaller than that of the USA's (5.7Gt). China's energy consumption per capita was very low compared to the world average, but her energy intensity of economic output was extremely high.

According to Table 11.2, China's energy consumption per capita in 2007 was 1.43toe/cap, slightly lower than the world average (1.8), and

Table 11.2: China's energy system in a global context in 2007.

	United States	OECD Europe	China	India	World
General Indicator					
Population (millions)	300	540	1312	1110	6536
Land area (million km^2)	9.83	5.23	9.6	3.29	147.9
GDP (billion 2000 US$ using exch. rates)	11265	10090	2092	703	37759
GDP (billion 2000 US$ using PPPs)	11265	12564	8685	3671	57564
GDP/Population (2000 US$ per capita)	37550	18685	1595	633	5777
Energy as a Whole					
Total primary energy supply (Mtoe)	2321	1885	1879	566	11740
Energy production (Mtoe)	1654	1095	1749	436	11796
Net imports (Mtoe)	730	857	136	135	3
Total self-sufficiency	0.71	0.58	0.93	0.77	1
TPES/GDP (toe per thousand 2000 US$)	0.21	0.19	0.9	0.8	0.31
TPES/GDP (toe per thousand 2000 US$ PPP)	0.21	0.15	0.22	0.15	0.2
TPES/population (toe per capita)	7.74	3.49	1.43	0.51	1.8
Coal					
Total coal supply (Mtoe)	606		1303	220.5	
Coal production (Mtoe)	614		1249	198	
Net imports (Mtoe)	–8		54	21.24	
Coal and peat self-sufficiency	1.01		0.96	0.90	

(*Continued*)

Table 11.2: (*Continued*)

	United States	OECD Europe	China	India	World
Total coal supply/GDP (toe per thousand 2000 US$ PPP)	0.05		0.15	0.06	
Total coal supply/ population (toe per capita)	2.02		0.99	0.20	
Oil					
Total oil supply (Mtoe)	937	696	344	136	4029
Oil production (Mtoe)	318.58	250.56	185.76	39.44	4029
Net oil imports (Mtoe)	0.06	0.05	0.08	0.14	0
Oil self-sufficiency	0.34	0.36	0.54	0.29	1
Oil supply/GDP (toe per thousand 2000 US$)	0.08	0.07	0.16	0.19	0.11
Oil supply/population (toe per capita)	3.13	1.29	0.26	0.12	0.62
Gas					
Total gas supply (Mtoe)					
Gas production (Mtoe)					
Net imports (Mtoe)					
Gas self-sufficiency	0.86	0.55	1.03	0.75	1.01
Total gas supply/GDP (toe per thousand 2000 US$)					
Total gas supply/GDP (toe per thousand 2000 US$ PPP)					
Total gas supply/ population (toe per capita)					

(*Continued*)

Table 11.2: (*Continued*)

	United States	OECD Europe	China	India	World
Power					
Hydro power supply (Mtoe)					
Nuclear power supply (Mtoe)					
Thermal power supply (Mtoe)					
Wind power supply (Mtoe)					
Solar PV and CSP supply (Mtoe)					
Electricity consumption/ GDP (kWh per 2000 US$)	0.36	0.33	1.28	0.79	0.46
Electricity consumption/ population (kWh per capita)	13515	6206	2040	503	2659
Electricity consumption (TWh)	4052	3350	2676	558	17377
CO2 Emissions					
Total emission (Gt)	5.7	4.1	5.6	1.25	28
CO2 emissions/ population	19.00	7.59	4.27	1.13	4.28
CO2 emissions/GDP (toe per thousand 2000 US$)	0.51	0.41	2.68	1.78	0.74
CO2 emissions/GDP (toe per thousand 2000 US$ PPP)	0.51	0.33	0.64	0.34	0.49
Energy Efficiency					
Energy consumption per unit of steel			726		
Energy consumption per unit of cement			181		
Energy consumption per unit of glasses					

Source: IEA, Beyond 2020.

much lower than that of the US and OECD Europe. More specifically, since China's energy structure is highly dependent on coal, her oil and electricity consumption per capita was much lower than the world average, but that of coal could be higher (unfortunately we do not have the data).

Although energy consumption per capita was low, China's economic output was highly energy-intensive. The energy consumption per unit GDP of China was 0.9toe/thousand US$ (in 2000 constant price), almost three times higher than the world average (0.31).

The shift from coal to electricity in China's energy structure is an issue of consequence in the global context of CO2 emissions reduction. Total investment in both the energy industry and the power sector has been increasing rapidly in recent years, and this will surely further stimulate the growth of the electricity sector in China.

Energy Consumption

Energy consumption in China has also been increasing rapidly since 2000, as Figure 11.6 shows. The final energy consumption in 2000

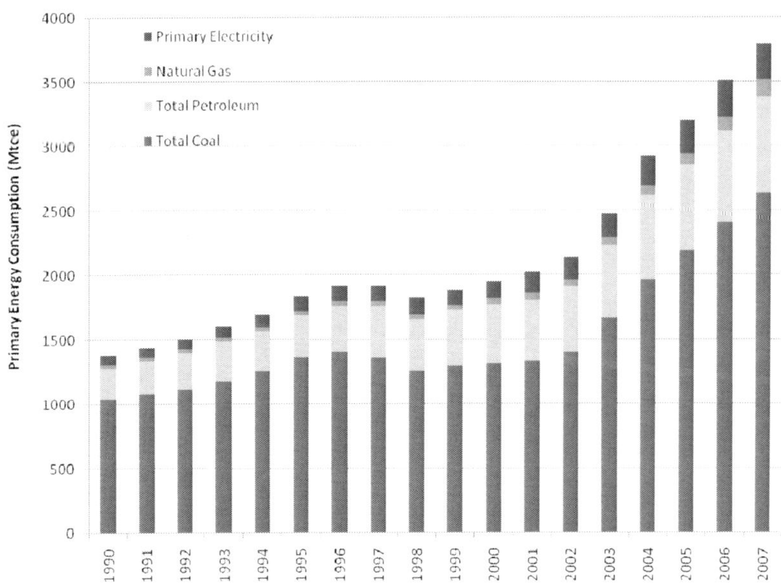

Figure 11.6: Final energy consumption of China (end-use).

Source: China Energy Statistical Yearbook 2008.

was 1951.2Mtoe, while in 2006 it was 3507.63Mtoe; the yearly increase rate was 10%. Natural gas had the highest yearly growth rate of 15%, and that of electricity was 13%.

China has witnessed tremendous economic growth in recent years, but this growth was highly energy-intensive compared to other developed economies in the world. China's energy consumption increased from 1347.14TWh in 2000 to 3271.18TWh in 2007, almost tripling within 7 years, and the average annual growth rate was 13.51%. However, China is gradually taking steps to decrease energy intensity in economic growth.

As we can see in Table 11.3, the energy consumption elasticity in China grew above 1 in 2003 (1.53), 2004 (1.59) and 2005 (1.02),

Table 11.3: Electricity consumption elasticity of China in 2007.

Year	Growth rate of energy consumption	Growth rate of electricity consumption	Growth rate of GDP	Energy consumption elasticity	Electricity consumption elasticity
1985	8.1	9.0	13.5	0.60	0.67
1990	1.8	6.2	3.8	0.47	1.63
1991	5.1	9.2	9.2	0.55	1.00
1992	5.2	11.5	14.2	0.37	0.81
1993	6.3	11.0	14.0	0.45	0.79
1994	5.8	9.9	13.1	0.44	0.76
1995	6.9	8.2	10.9	0.63	0.75
1996	5.9	7.4	10.0	0.59	0.74
1997	−0.8	4.8	9.3		0.52
1998	−4.1	2.8	7.8		0.36
1999	1.2	6.1	7.6	0.16	0.80
2000	3.5	9.5	8.4	0.42	1.13
2001	3.4	9.3	8.3	0.41	1.12
2002	6.0	11.8	9.1	0.66	1.30
2003	15.3	15.6	10.0	1.53	1.56
2004	16.1	15.4	10.1	1.59	1.52
2005	10.6	13.5	10.4	1.02	1.30
2006	9.6	14.6	11.6	0.83	1.26
2007	7.8	14.4	11.9	0.66	1.21

Source: China Energy Statistical Yearbook 2008.

but it decreased sharply in 2006 (0.83) and 2007 (0.66). Electricity consumption elasticity, on the other hand, stayed above 1 from 2000 onwards, which means electricity consumption grew faster than GDP did. Since the Chinese final energy consumption structure is shifting away from coal to electricity, we can expect this trend to last for a longer period of time.

The energy consumption elasticity of industry was 0.845 in 2007, and electricity consumption elasticity was 0.902. The highest energy consumption elasticity was in the manufacturing sector, especially in Manufacture of Communication Equipment, Computers and Other Electronic Equipment (1.029).

China is currently in the middle of its industrialization progress; the end-use energy consumption by the industry sector was about 70% in 2006 and is increasing, as Figures 11.6 and 11.7 show. The share of transportation is also increasing in China. Since the industry sector in China will continue to develop over a long period of time, the only practical way for China to implement energy conservation and CO_2 emission reduction is to speed up the technology development for energy and manufacturing industries.

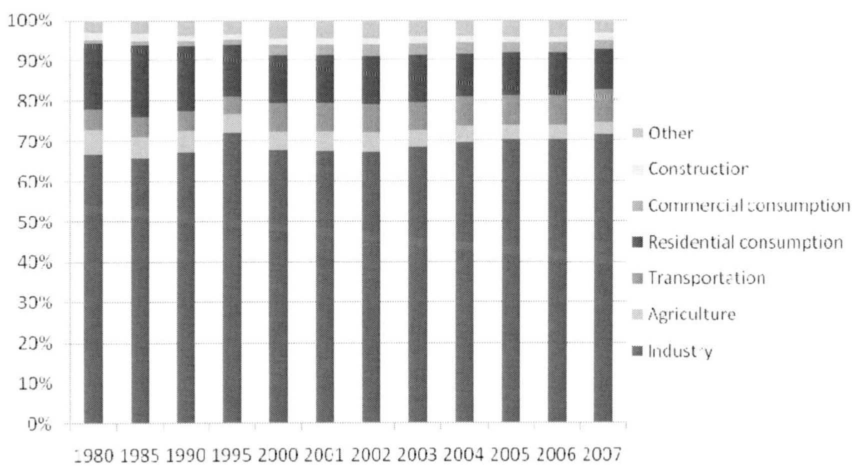

Figure 11.7: Share of total final energy consumption by sector.

Source: China Energy Statistical Yearbook 2008.

Energy Import and Export

China has been an energy net importer since 1997, and the energy import deficit has kept increasing rapidly since then, as shown in Table 11.4. The fast economic growth in China and other emerging economies requires large amounts of energy consumption. According to IMF statistics, China became the second largest crude oil consumer in 2003 and the second largest crude oil importer in 2005. In 2007, the foreign dependence of oil supply in China increased to nearly 50% (see Figure 11.8 and Table 11.4). Saudi Arabia is the biggest source of China's imported crude oil. 45% of the total imported crude in 2007 came from the Middle East, 32.5% came from Africa, and 3.5% came from the Asia-Pacific area. China is seeking to import more crude from other regions including Russia, the mid-Asia area and Latin America, and the pipelines between China and Russia are currently under construction. Vladimir Putin, the prime minister of Russia, said in April 2009 that the first oil pipeline between China and Russia was expected to reach the border within several weeks. This pipeline was planned to be put into use in 2010, and can transport up to 15Mt crude oil to China. China and Russia also signed an energy credit contract in February 2009. Under this contract, Russia will export 300 million tons of oil to China between 2010 to 2030.

Energy Efficiency

China's oil consumption has doubled over the past decade, and its economic growth is highly energy-intensive (see Figure 11.9). The current energy consumption per US$1,000 GDP of China is 0.57 tons of oil equivalent (toe), higher than those of Germany (0.09), Japan (0.12) and the US (0.17). The energy efficiency of industries in China is also very low; energy consumption per unit of output for cement is 53% higher than the world's average, that of glass is 47% higher, petro-chemicals 45%, and alkali 34%. Table 11.5 shows the detailed inter-regional comparison of energy efficiency for some key industrial products and services. As we can see in Table 11.5, China's

Table 11.4: Net energy import and foreign dependence ratio in China.

	Total Energy		Crude Oil		LPG		Coal		Electricity	
Year	Net import (Mtce)	Foreign dependence (%)	Net import (Mt)	Foreign dependence (%)	Net import (Mt)	Foreign dependence (%)	Net import (Mt)	Foreign dependence (%)	Net import (TWh)	Foreign dependence (%)
1985	−54.34	−0.0699			−0.02	−0.0122	−30.71	−0.0371	−7.15	−0.0765
1990	−45.65	−0.0474	2.92	0.0249	−0.01	−0.0043	−15.29	−0.0150	1.84	0.0143
1995	−13.20	−0.0102	17.09	0.1148	2.25	0.3004	−26.98	−0.0202	−5.39	−0.0272
2000	47.00	0.0343	70.27	0.3309	4.80	0.3513	−52.89	−0.0412	−8.33	−0.0357
2001	23.26	0.0164			4.87		−87.47	−0.0670	−8.39	−0.0290
2002	47.52	0.0316	69.41	0.3079	6.21	0.3818	−72.64	−0.0530	−7.40	−0.0240
2003	73.47	0.0423	91.02	0.3652	6.34	0.3531	−82.93	−0.0508	−7.36	−0.0228
2004	149.46	0.0728	122.72	0.4269	6.38	0.3164	−68.05	−0.0354	−6.08	−0.0151
2005	155.05	0.0688	126.82	0.4215	6.14	0.3047	−45.55	−0.0212	−6.18	−0.0138
2006	202.46	0.0821	145.18	0.4502	5.36	0.2426	−25.17	−0.0107	−6.88	−0.0140
2007	246.06	0.0942	163.16	0.4794	6.95	0.2986	−2.17	−0.0008	−10.32	−0.0192

Source: China Energy Statistical Yearbook 2008.

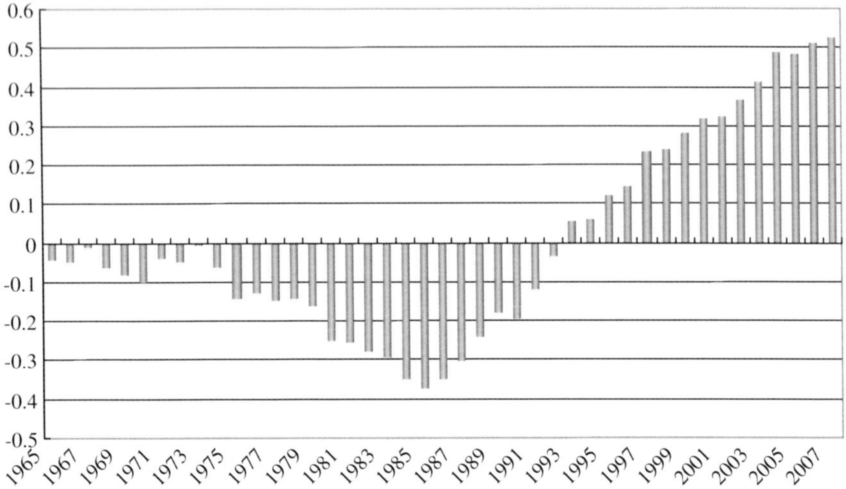

Figure 11.8: Foreign dependence of oil supply in China.

Source: China Energy Statistical Yearbook 2008.

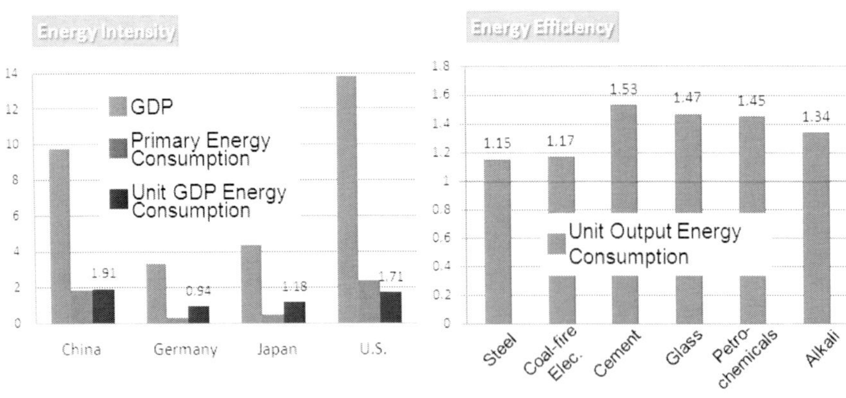

Figure 11.9: Cross-country comparison of energy intensity and energy efficiency.

consumption of energy for per unit of electricity supply, chemical industry products, steel and cement is higher than in developed economies like the US and Japan. China's energy efficiency of transportation is also much lower than that of the US.

However, great improvements have been made in several industries and for the economy as a whole. The energy intensity of China's economic growth has declined dramatically since the National Development and Reform Commission included an energy conservation goal in its 11th five-year plan, requiring a 20% cut in unit GDP energy consumption. The energy efficiency of producing key industrial products has also improved, as seen in Table 11.5 where energy

Table 11.5: Energy efficiency comparison of key industrial products and services.

Country	1980	1985	1990	1995	1999	2000	2003
Coal Consumption for Power Supply (Thermalpower Plant) (gce/kW·h)							
China (over 6MW)	448	431	427	412	399	392	380
United States	378	376	373	376			
Japan	339	338	332	331	322		312
Specific Energy Consumption for Ethylene (kgce/tn)							
China	2013		1580	1277		1212	889.8
Japan	1100		857	870		714	629
Specific Energy Consumption for Steel Production (kgce/tn)							
China (key enterprises)	1201	1062	997	976		781	726
Japan	705	640	629	656		646	646
United States	880	761	757				
United Kingdom	794	721	677	721			
France	826	764	707	735			
Specific Energy Consumption for Synthetic Ammonia (kgce/tn)							
China	1431		1343	1284		1200	
United States	1320		1000	970		970	
Specific Energy Consumption for Cement (kgce/tn)							
China (large, medium)	218.8	208	201	199.2		181	181
Japan	135.7	123.4	122.6	124.4		125.7	128.4
Oil Consumption for Trucks (l/102tn-km)							
China							
Gasoline Trucks	8.7	7.7	7.1	7.06			
Diesel Oil Trucks	6.2	5.8	4.8	4.82			
United States	3.43	3.36	3.5	3.54			

consumption for per unit of electricity supply, chemical products, steel and cement production in China has decreased. Thus, the gap between China's energy efficiency and that of the US is narrowing.

China's energy conversion efficiency was 69.04% in 2000 and increased to 71.25% in 2007, and that of the electricity sector also increased from 37.36% in 2000 to 40.24% in 2007. More importantly, the energy intensity of China's economic growth is decreasing. The energy consumption per unit GDP in 2005 was 1.22Mtce/10,000 RMB, but in 2007 it decreased by 13% to 1.064%. The energy consumption per unit industrial-added-value also decreased by 3% in 2006, from 2.59Mtce/10,000 RMB in 2005 to 2.53Mtce/10,000 RMB in 2006. Unfortunately, data for industrial-added-value of 2007 is unavailable so far.

However, the electricity consumption per unit GDP has shown no evidence of decreasing consistently. That of 2005 was 1,358.5kWh/10,000 RMB, in 2006 it was 1,388.8, and in 2007 it was 1,310.9. The shift in China's energy consumption structure toward electricity may be the reason for this.

Energy Pricing System in China and Subsidies

Energy prices in China have increased sharply in recent years. According to *GTZ International Fuel Prices, 6th Edition — Data Preview*, the retail price of gasoline in 2005 was 48 US-cents per liter; that increased to 69 cents in 2007 and 99 cents in 2009. In 2005, the retail price of gasoline in China was above the world average but lower than that of the US, among those economies offering normal gasoline subsidies. But in 2007 and 2009, the gasoline retail price in China was higher than that of the US, and was among those economies imposing gasoline taxation. This upward trend can also be found in diesel retail prices. Figures 11.10 and 11.11 show the ranking of gasoline and diesel retail prices in different countries. The retail price of diesel in China in 2009 was 101 cents per liter, much higher than that of the US and most developed countries. Although retail prices of diesel and gasoline are under strict price control, still the high prices may reflect the growing energy demand from the traffic

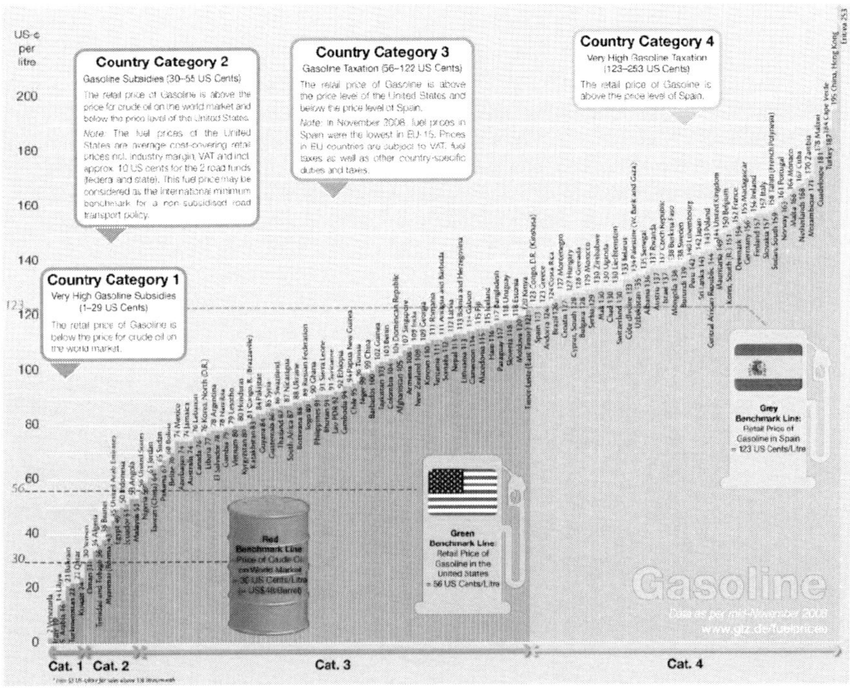

Figure 11.10: The ranking of gasoline retail prices in different countries.

sector. Figure 11.12 illustrates projections for the growth rate of traffic demand for energy in different regions, and that of China is the highest at over 5%.

As for electricity prices, China is implementing various policies aiming at energy conservation and environmental protection. Such policies include a differential price policy, adopting higher electricity prices in highly energy-intensive industries, lowering the on-grid price of small and old units, and increasing the on-grid price of units with desulphurization equipment. Table 11.6 lists electricity prices in different regions in China. Average retail prices increased by 1.03% from 2006 to 2007, which was a direct result of the policies aiming at energy conservation and environmental protection.

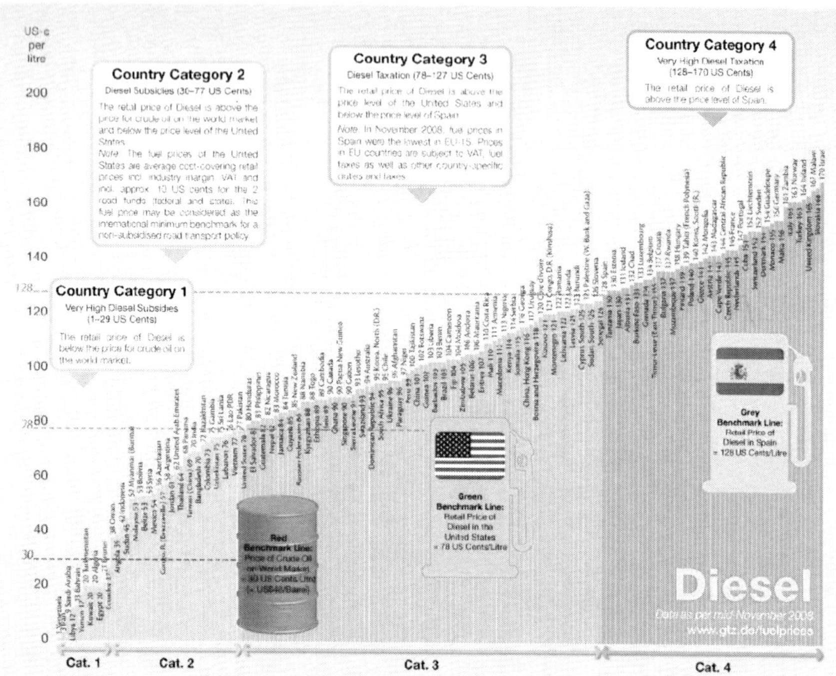

Figure 11.11: The ranking of diesel retail prices in different countries.

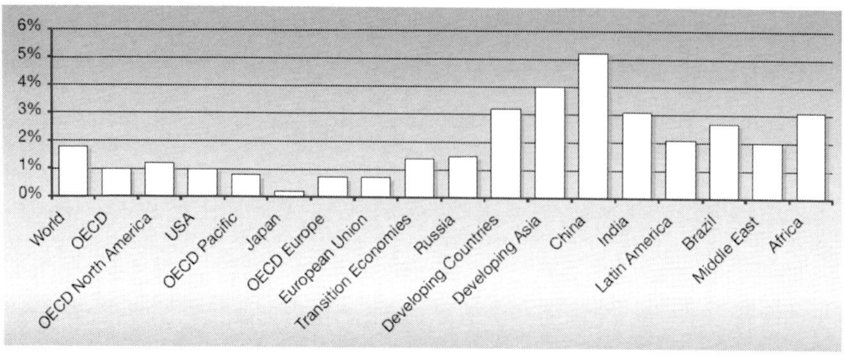

Figure 11.12: Annual growth rate of energy demand in the transportation sector, 2004–2030.

Table 11.6: Electricity prices in different regions of China in 2007 (RMB/MWh).

	Benchmark on-grid prices				
Grids	Not desulphurized	Desulphurized	Wholesale price	Transmission price	Retail price
Huabei Grid					
Jingjingtang	335.4	350.4	525.32	156.18	527.76
Hebei	335	350	440.92	95.28	458.50
West-Mongolia	250.9	265.9	352.61	97.68	316.65
Shanxi	260.4	275.4	408.63	123.47	394.55
Shandong	339.9	354.9	478.48	90.59	504.51
Dongbei Grid					
Liaoning	347.1	362.1	508.55	151.05	520.15
Jilin	341	356	485.62	136.24	495.27
Heilongjiang	341.7	356.7	482.22	160.78	472.10
East-Mongolia	324.6	339.6			316.65
Xibei Grid					
Shangxi	285	300	420.74	123.80	417.15
Gansu	235.8	250.8	356.65	129.22	362.12
Ningxia	236.4	251.4	358.72	130.83	374.37
Qinghai	240	255	291.43	108.75	293.08
Xinjiang	235	250	417.13	193.58	395.65
Huadong Grid					
Shanghai	400.4	415.4	649.60	196.76	656.71
Zhejiang	404.5	419.5	569.28	111.52	578.56
Jiangsu	375	390	590.13	160.75	571.70
Anhui	356	371	503.37	126.54	487.12
Fujian	364	379	490.13	113.65	482.58
Huazhong Grid					
Hubei	367	382	516.75	154.25	511.64
Hunan	387.5	402.5	496.41	149.60	495.88
Jiangxi	370	385	506.82	126.29	504.38
Henan	334.2	349.2	429.24	82.70	419.38
Sichuan	332.8	347.8	465.76	147.08	458.63
Chongqing	322.3	337.3	507.04	173.80	480.56

(*Continued*)

Table 11.6: (*Continued*)

Grids	Benchmark on-grid prices: Not desulphurized	Benchmark on-grid prices: Desulphurized	Wholesale price	Transmission price	Retail price
Nanfang Grid					
Guangdong	438.2	453.2	681.90	180.93	701.32
Guangxi	361.8	376.8	449.70	111.57	438.03
Yunnan	255.3	270.3	392.33	140.36	365.80
Guizhou	272.6	287.6	377.29	95.01	355.98
Hainan	372.4	387.4	615.23	215.44	615.37

11.4 Realistic Response to Climate Change and Low-Carbon Economy

After decades of development, the international community has gradually formed an international environmental management system as a form of governance for global environmental issues. Its framework is relatively clear, but its effectiveness, efficiency and relevance remain controversial. Within the international environmental management system, active agents are usually divided into three levels. The first type of agents include the UN General Assembly, UN Economic and Social Council, UN Environment Program, UN Commission on Sustainable Development and the UN Development Department Program, as well as specialized agencies such as the Food and Agriculture Organization of the United Nations (FAO), World Health Organization (WHO), United Nations Educational, Scientific and Cultural Organization (UNESCO) and the World Meteorological Organization (WMO). In addition, the World Bank, World Trade Organization, inter-governmental international organizations of regional or sub-regional level such as the OSCE, the European Union, and other regional financial institutions such as regional development banks are also included. The second type of agents are the nations, who play an important role as the main participants in international environmental cooperation, while in many cases they themselves are the object of global environmental governance. Nowadays, most nations have established their own environmental ministry/office/department and other specialized agencies, thus demonstrating their own governance function as well. The third type of agents consist of the major groups of civil society, e.g., non-governmental organizations, the private sector, the media, the scientific community, etc., who are also important participants in global environmental governance.

The international environmental management system is based mainly on multilateral environmental agreements (MEAs). A total of 14 MEAs was established as of 2007 covering ozone layer protection, climate change, biodiversity, wildlife, marine resources and other aspects of the environment. MEAs can be considered as a kind of international convention; once signed, the Contracting States must comply with and implement the Convention. However, it is often the case in the actual operation that states unilaterally withdraw from the agreement or violate the principles of the convention — the Bush administration unilaterally withdrawing from the Kyoto Protocol in 2001 is perhaps the most well-known example. But in recent years, with the gradual deepening of scientific research, the evidence for global climate change continues to increase and more active agents are significantly enhancing their international negotiation and cooperation activities. Nevertheless, the most critical reason why the 2009 climate change conference in Copenhagen ended in failure lies in the fact that there is huge disagreement over the responsibility sharing of the governance of the global environmental crisis.

"Responsibility sharing" is currently one of the most sensitive issues in the international environmental management system. The 2005 report by the United Nations Environment Program shows that the goal of environmental governance as set by the United Nations has not been realized under the framework of the international environmental management system. The progress made in environmental protection presently is mainly in the advances in the air and water quality protection in Europe and the United States, whereas the overall global environment is worsening, especially in developing countries. Specifically, the MEAs fail to effectively deal with the following issues: climate change effects on migratory waterbirds; commercial fishing from an environmental perspective; High Seas fishing effects on marine species such as marine mammals and birds; management of coastal zones; population, poverty and urbanization effects on the coastal resources; deforestation; tropical timber trade; the absence of confirmation of locales with marine value under the World Heritage List; river ecosystems and the relationship between poverty, corruption and environmental management practices; etc.

Numerous studies have demonstrated that the environmental governance systems of major cities which are adopted as models by many developing countries turn out to be unsustainable from the global perspective. Take London, New York or Tokyo as an example; although the quality of the environment in these cities is better than historical levels and compared to the rest of the world, this improvement comes at the expense of foreign residents in developing countries and future generations. Dhakal (2004) found that, when we compare the direct CO2 emissions of urban production and consumption, emissions per capita in Beijing was 30% higher than in Tokyo; but when it comes to the comparison of the city's total CO2 emissions of the goods and services consumed in its production processes, Tokyo is 46% higher than Beijing. In fact, Tokyo's direct greenhouse gas emission is only one-third of the total emissions of its final consumption.

Economic globalization has enabled international industrial transfer, making it possible for the cities in developed countries to shift industry and services with low value-added, high energy consumption and high pollution to developing countries or to other less developed domestic regions. While the developed cities employ electricity and other "clean energy" within their own region, they effectively transfer the thermal power plants' emissions, nuclear power plants' environmental risks, and hydropower plants' ecological risks to other areas. Accompanied by continued growth in demand for material goods, this environmental governance model will lead to more serious global environmental problems in the future.

Developing countries and less developed areas will therefore pay a higher cost in terms of environmental resources due to backward technology, low-cost resources, and lack of environmental standards. Furthermore, as a result of the distorted pricing mechanism caused by this global division of labor, the magnified social costs can hardly be calculated in the product's final price. Developing countries will have little choice but to participate in this international division of labor, as it means making full use of their own comparative advantages of labor, resources and environment, although it will inevitably hasten global and regional environmental degradation. China's reform and opening-up since 1978 is following this development path whilst creating the greatest economic miracle.

Therefore, the existing international environmental management system is not sustainable. When contrasting the climate change risks faced by the various countries, regions and cities against their respective historical contribution to pollution and climate change, there exists a serious asymmetric phenomenon. This phenomenon is perhaps the biggest obstacle to reaching an agreement on climate change in the international community. In the documentary "An Inconvenient Truth", Dhaka, Mumbai, Bangkok, Shanghai and other cities in Asia are considered to face extremely high risks of climate change; however, will these cities therefore carry out an exact roadmap of emission reduction? Compared with those cities in developed, Western countries facing smaller climate change risks but with huge historical contributions to pollution, more Asian leaders would like to see those Western countries who have historically contributed to pollution bear more responsibility for climate change. As the world's largest developing economy and the world's largest emitter of carbon dioxide, China has been at the teeth of the storm in international climate negotiations in recent years. Should China shoulder such moral commitments and undertake more effective emission reduction obligation in the post-Kyoto era? We can give a profound interpretation of this series of questions only after considering all the facts.

In 2007 China's total primary energy consumption ranked second in the world, reaching 16.8%. The world's largest energy consumer as of 2007 was still the United States, who accounted for 21.3% of the world's total consumption. Russia ranked third in the world's total primary energy consumption with a share of 6.2%. As for the energy structure, coal dominated China's energy consumption in 2007, accounting for 70.4% of total consumption; crude oil was in second place with a percentage of 19.8%. In the USA, on the other hand, the main energy source was crude oil, accounting for 39.9% of total consumption; natural gas and coal came second and third with a proportion of 25.2% and 24.3%, respectively. In short, China is the world's largest consumer of coal and hydroelectricity and the world's second largest consumer of crude oil, while the United States is the world's largest consumer of crude oil, natural gas and nuclear power and the second largest coal consumer. With regard to crude oil imports, China was the world's third largest importer in 2007, accounting for 8.2% of the total world imports. The US was the world's largest importer with 25.3%, followed by Japan with 10.3%. The crude oil import dependence of the United States, Japan and China was, respectively, 53.2%, 89.6% and 44.3%.

According to the 2007 forecasts of the International Energy Agency (IEA, 2007), China will in future overtake the United States to become the world's largest energy consumer. China's energy demand is expected to increase at an average annual rate of 5.1% before 2015, and in 2030 the total energy consumption is estimated to reach 2.2 times that in 2005 with the transport sector's oil demand quadrupled and the total number of motor vehicles septupled, reaching 270 million. It is expected that new car sales in China will surpass that of the United States by 2015.

Carbon dioxide, mainly discharged from the burning of fossil fuels, is one of the most important greenhouse gases. Since China's energy structure is highly dependent on coal, its carbon dioxide emission per unit of energy consumption is significantly higher than that of other nations that mainly rely on crude oil and natural gas. IEA statistics show that China surpassed the US as the world's largest emitter of carbon dioxide in 2007. Furthermore, China's contribution to the incremental carbon dioxide emissions from 2000 to 2006 was 58%, while India's was only 6%. Therefore, China is indeed a country with fast-growing energy consumption and greenhouse gas emissions; however, in terms of China's historical trend, the total emissions and emission per capita are still at a rather low level.

According to the 2008 statistics of BP, in terms of the total world energy consumption from 1965 to 2007, America's share amounted to 25.6%, while Europe's share was 36.7% and Japan's was 5.3%. China only accounted for 9.07%. In terms of carbon dioxide emissions, IEA statistics indicate that the emissions of the United States and European Union from 1900 to 2005 made up more than half of global total emissions, while China's proportion was only 8%. Even on the basis of forecasts, China's accumulated emissions will only reach 16% of the world total by 2030, whereas that of the US and EU will reach 25% and 18%, respectively. As for emissions per capita, China's emissions per capita is only one-fifth of that of the United States, and is estimated to be one-third by 2015 and one-half by 2030.

All these above-mentioned figures suggest that, for China and other emerging economies, the logical starting point on which to formulate their own diplomatic strategy for energy and the environment is either the historical perspective or the realistic perspective, or both. From the historical perspective, China's total energy consumption levels and carbon dioxide emissions are fairly low, with even lower emissions per capita. Therefore, from a broad sense of equality and intergenerational equity, if the world's major industrialized countries do not take substantive action to reduce emissions, China also has no reason to.

However, this static method ignores the potential crises and challenges that China currently faces in reality and will face in the future, hence the realistic perspective. In recent years, the international commodity market has evidently demonstrated the trend that "what China buys, its price goes up; what China sells, its price goes down". Copper, iron ore and crude oil are the most obvious examples. The international copper price has risen by five times from 2002 to 2006 since China has become the world's largest copper consumer; similarly, the price of crude oil has risen by 2.8 times (excluding depreciation of the dollar) from 2002 to April 2008, and China is the world's second largest oil consumer. This continuing rise in commodity prices has greatly increased the cost of China's economic operations, with developed countries on one hand blaming China for its price control of basic resources leading to excessively growing demand, and on the other hand enjoying resource dividends brought by the cheap "Made in China" brand. At the same time, it must be noted that China's energy efficiency is relatively low. In the 30 years since its reform and opening up, China has accounted for 10.1% of the world's total energy consumption while creating only 2.9% of world economic output, resulting in much higher energy consumption per unit of output than the world average, even higher than that of developed countries. Faced with the pressure of the rising price of energy and other basic resources and for the sake of China's own interests, saving energy and reducing consumption is an inevitable choice. Reducing reliance on traditional energy resources through the appropriate transformation of economic growth can effectively enhance the efficiency of economic growth as well as decrease the opportunities for international speculators to take advantage of Chinese factors of production to artificially inflate commodity prices.

As one of the countries that is confronted with the highest climate change risks, China must not underestimate any hazard caused by greenhouse gas emissions. Since 2008, the frequency of extreme weather events in various regions of China has significantly increased, many of them derived from climate disasters caused by rising global surface temperatures, inducing huge economic losses. Consequently, saving energy and reducing consumption in China has a double benefit. Reducing emissions of carbon dioxide will bring real environmental and health benefits to China, and in turn translate into higher economic profits. Hence, effectively employing the international mechanisms and reducing carbon dioxide emissions to achieve energy saving would constitute a win-win strategy.

Why are developed countries so concerned about climate change? Firstly, continuously rising crude oil prices affect the all-important issue of energy supply, forcing the world's major economies to fundamentally consider energy saving as a way of dealing with the climate change crisis. Secondly, each industrialized nation hopes to fully develop its own new energy sector within the international emission reduction framework, and developing countries like China and India will become major markets for these new energy products. Therefore, involving the developing countries in any post-Kyoto agreement means opening doors for new energy product imports, which undoubtedly provides the greatest reassurance for new energy technologies with long R&D cycles and high costs.

Given the above, the issue of whether to develop a low-carbon economy deserves careful and deep consideration. China's current economic growth and industrial structure is codetermined by endogenous endowment conditions, external objective constraints and the stage of economic development. The double impact of the financial crisis and the climate change crisis is forcing a comprehensive reconstruction of the world economic system; at the same time, China's internal imbalance accumulated over its three decades of rapid economic growth also need adjustment. In this new round of adjustment, "low-carbon" is turning into an economic concept, not just an environmental concept, affecting the establishment of a new world economic order. "Low-carbon" is quickly becoming the standard within the international financial and trading system through which countries can gain increasing support from other economies. Consequently, as the world's largest developing country and carbon dioxide emitter, China should pay more attention to corresponding strategies and mechanisms and advocate a policy system, market mechanism and legal system that is not only beneficial to its own economic development, but also effectively compatible with international mechanisms for energy saving and promoting a low-carbon economy.

11.5 Two Theoretical Restrictions of Low-Carbon Economy

The logical starting point of the low-carbon economy development is the unsustainable carrying capacity of the environmental resources brought by the "high-carbon economy". However, in order to reverse this unsustainablity, it is necessary to fundamentally transform the pattern of fossil fuel use for human existence and evolvement that has been in use since the Industrial Revolution. This will inevitably involve fairly high socioeconomic costs. The "Stern Review: Economics of Climate Change" (hereafter referred to as the Stern report), released in October 2006, is based on climate science and adopts a cost-benefit analysis framework to assess the socioeconomic costs of climate change itself as well as the adaptation and mitigation strategies in response to climate change. The Stern report indicates that the benefit of taking forceful action on climate change as soon as possible is greater than the cost. If no action is taken, the cost and risk resulting from climate change will damage global GDP by 5%; the loss will even reach 20% or more if we take a wider range of risks and impacts into consideration. In addition, the average governance cost before 2050 will be about 1% of GDP each year if we want to maintain the surface concentration of carbon dioxide at 550 ppm. However, the Stern report has been much criticized in the academic field, especially with regard to the utility function and discount rate involved in its cost-benefit analysis, although it still receives much attention from the policy-making level.

Nordhaus (2007), a well-known climate change economist from Yale University, has criticized the Stern report as being a political product with fuzzy logic rather than a strictly academic research. In particular, in the cost-benefit analysis, the Stern report set the social discount rate at a level close to zero, which greatly overestimated the economic benefits of responding to climate change and underestimated its costs. In fact, the choice of discount rate is the first theoretical constraint of low-carbon economics, reflecting different selection criteria in the intergenerational wealth distribution. Taking action against climate change today may create higher initial costs as well as lower variable costs, but higher yields; whereas taking action in the future creates the contrary. Hence, the principle of maximizing net income only guarantees the largest "cake" for multi-generations to share, but fails to appropriately allocate between generations. Choosing a relatively high discount rate de-emphasizes the future environmental benefits, while a lower discount rate will enhance environmental benefits but at the risk of impairing the ability of modern economic development, affecting wealth accumulation of future generations and reducing future generations' capacity to deal with environmental risk simultaneously.

It is also noted that if the future climate risk can be identified, then the above-mentioned issues will be of less concern; but in the case of uncertain climate risk, the second theoretical constraint of climate change economics — risk aversion — will be involved. Any socioeconomic cost-benefit analysis is based on a risk-neutral assumption, but in fact, attitudes to risk vary considerably among different income groups, ages and educational backgrounds. This in turn will directly impact the establishment of international climate change cooperation mechanisms. The risk of climate change itself shows some uncertainty, although the 2007 IPCC report has significantly enhanced the credibility of the scientific evidence for climate change. Nevertheless, there still exists some doubt, and an "environmental conspiracy theory" has been widely reported or speculated upon from time to time. Under these circumstances, the groups or countries with higher income will be risk-averse, while those with lower income will have a high appetite for risk, leading to differences in social costs and benefits. It is fairly possible that the cost of carbon dioxide emissions reduction in developing countries will be more than 1% of GDP each year.

Thus, as can be seen, the development of a low-carbon economy is, at present, largely viewed from a purely theoretical mechanism. In order to make worldwide behavioral agents involved in carbon dioxide emissions pay their reasonable social cost at the practical level, it is necessary to make the process of economic growth generate the following market signals: (1) For consumers, the market signals should guide them to consume as little high-carbon products and services as possible; (2) For producers, market signals should lead them to produce, research and develop low-carbon goods instead of high-carbon ones; (3) Market signals should guide future investors and innovators to invest in low-carbon technologies and industries, and conduct innovation of the relevant mechanisms. It seems that all of these low-carbon market signals can be facilitated through "carbon pricing". However, the general equilibrium theory reveals that this process involves various segments of the economy such as department production, final consumption, government spending, international trade, tax allocation, etc., and all the factors in these relevant segments must cooperate to make the low-carbon economy "economic".

11.6 China's Industrial Structure Optimization and Low-Carbon Economic Growth

China achieved remarkable economic progress from 1980 to 2000 with an average annual GDP growth rate of more than 9%, while the average annual growth rate of energy consumption was only 3.9%. Development practice in industrialized countries shows that energy consumption tends to grow faster than GDP at the initial stage of industrialization. During the period 1981–2002, the average elasticity of energy consumption in industrialized countries was less than 1, or even less than 0.5; China was the only developing country to achieve an energy elasticity of 0.44, whereas the coefficient in India and Brazil was 0.84 and 1.45, respectively. With the arrival of the 21st century, however, China's transitioning economy has demonstrated investment-driven features accompanied by strong growth in energy demand. Since 2002, China's energy consumption has grown at a rate faster than that of GDP. In the subsequent four years, China's GDP growth rate (in constant 2000 prices) was 9.1%, 10.0%, 10.1% and 9.9%, while the annual growth rate of energy consumption reached 9.9%, 15.3%, 15.2% and 12.7% (Zhuang, 2006). Moreover, elasticity of energy consumption was more than 1 for these four successive years, reversing China's historical trend of elasticity of less than 1. From 2001 to 2005, China's energy intensity also increased from 4,121 to 4,177 tons of standard coal per ten thousand RMB.

This rapid growth of energy consumption increases the risk and cost of a country's economic operations and will devastate economic development in the event of energy supply shocks if it is not effectively curbed. The two major energy crises that erupted in the 1970s and 1990s and the subsequent lag in economic development in the oil-consuming countries are obvious examples. It is fully proven that energy and economic development are closely related, and energy may be both an engine for and a constraint of economic growth. In addition, considerable pollution associated with energy consumption forms a serious threat to the natural environment and may even develop into large-scale environmental pollution incidents in some regions. On this account, the PRC's 11th five-year plan proposed binding indicators to reduce energy consumption per unit of GDP by 20% and to reduce the total discharge of major pollutants by 10%. However, in the starting year of the 11th five-year plan period, China failed to achieve these targets determined earlier. Even more serious, industry, especially the sectors with high energy consumption and high pollution, grew too quickly from 2007 onwards. Six major industries, namely electricity, steel, nonferrous metals, building materials, oil processing and chemicals, accounting for nearly 70% of the country's total industrial energy consumption and sulfur dioxide emissions, increased by 20.6% in the first quarter with an acceleration of 6.6 percentage points.

In response to this tough situation, the State Council issued a "comprehensive work program of energy reduction" which proposed a total of 45 highly targeted initiatives from ten aspects for saving energy and reducing consumption, among which the "industrial structure optimization and adjustment" was given priority. Five key breakthroughs in structural energy saving and emissions reduction were introduced during the second year of the 11th five-year plan period, and they were as follows: control the rapid growth of industries with high energy consumption and high pollution; accelerate the elimination of backward production capacity; improve policies promoting the industrial structure adjustment; actively advance the adjustment of the energy structure; and accelerate the development of the services sector and high-tech industry.

According to the research by He Jiankun and Zhang Xiliang (He and Zhang, 2005; He *et al.*, 2006), China's rising energy elasticity in the 21st century is mainly caused by the transformation of the industrial structure. The accelerated development of industry, especially heavy industry; the enlarged scale of infrastructure construction in the urbanization process; urban residents' consumption upgrade in housing and automobile consumption; as well as dramatic changes to the industrial structure in the short run; all are among the main reasons behind China's increased GDP energy intensity. In terms of technical efficiency of energy conversion and utilization, China has demonstrated an overall improvement in recent years, with the unit energy consumption of major energy-consuming products continuing to drop. Therefore, the rise in GDP energy intensity in China in recent years is induced mainly by the structural transformation rather than the reduced efficiency of energy technology. In other words, it is a result of dramatic changes in the industrial structure, staged particularly in the heavy and chemical industries.

Thus, the five major industrial restructuring initiatives introduced under the "comprehensive work program of energy reduction" are evidently to the point. However, after in-depth analysis, it is not difficult to find reasons for anxiety, although the vision of the industrial structure adjustment is quite encouraging. The industrial structure adjustment method of "Off, stop, merge, transfer" will certainly interfere with China's increasingly improved market economy system at this stage, and there is still some doubt on its own social costs and benefits. On the other hand, relying on the "invisible hand" alone to promote the optimization and upgrading of the existing industrial structure will inevitably lack the support of an efficient resource pricing system, market access system as well as the fiscal and taxation system. It should also be noted that China's industrial structure is confronted with a series of quasi-rigid constraints at this stage. Into the 21st century, China's industrial structure appears "heavy" — the proportion of secondary industry has increased with heavy industry occupying a significantly rising percentage, thus resulting in the "high energy consumption" state of China's industrial structure, which has the characteristic of being quasi-rigid and is fairly difficult to reverse in the short term.

There are a few factors contributing to the "heaviness" of China's industrial structure. First, the accelerating urbanization process provides rigid demand. China's urbanization process since the mid-1990s has increasingly speeded up, thereby stimulating the development of pillar industries with high energy consumption. China faced an urbanization rate of 36.22% in 2000 and 42.99% in 2005 (National Bureau of Statistics of China, 2006). There exist tight links between urbanization and industrialization. The industrialization process requires emerging labor resources, demand markets as well as a logistics, sales and distribution system, of which the carrier must be the city. At the same time, the urbanization process requires large-scale infrastructure and housing construction, which also leads to increased demand for energy-intensive materials such as steel, cement and chemical materials. This continued growth of energy-intensive industries has deepened the "heaviness" of China's industrial structure.

Second, international industrial transfer promoted by FDI still prominently favors heavy industry. The industrial distribution of FDI flows into China in 2005 showed that manufacturing was still the absolute leader, accounting for 67.36% of FDI inflow, while the real estate industry rose to second place with a proportion of 10.26%; the FDI inflow of other tertiary industries occupied only 10.18% (National Bureau of Statistics of China, 2006). The above indicates that the "heavy" feature of FDI is still prominent, playing a significant role in pushing China's industrial structure towards heavy chemical industries. The current trend of international industrial transfer in China mainly relates to the transfer of heavy industry and modern services industry, although, of course, the former is ahead of the latter in both speed and scale. When it comes to China's current ability to undertake international industrial transfer, manufacturing is still the dominant sector, especially in the economic and technological development zones of the middle and western regions of China, which are in urgent need of FDI inflows for investment in infrastructure construction.

Third, the relatively lagged service industry development in China exacerbates the "heaviness" of the overall economic structure. China's relatively lagged service industry is clearly evident in the low proportion of the tertiary industry within the industrial structure, and is indirectly expressed in the low added-value of the tertiary industry itself. From the perspective of the Chinese service industry structure, business dining, transportation and other traditional services still account for more than 40%, but financial services, tourism, real estate, information, radio and television, press, publishing and other modern services make up a relatively low proportion, despite many Chinese cities enjoying a high pace of development. Financial services and the information industry are key elements in the process of undertaking international industrial transfer; however, China's industrial upgrading in this field is still lagging behind as a result of relatively slow institutional transition.

Fourth, the employment structure in China goes against the structure of economic development, thereby continuously imposing constraints on the industrial structure upgrading. In China's current industrial structure, the primary, secondary and tertiary industries account for 12.6%, 47.5% and 39.9% respectively, whereas in the employment structure, the corresponding proportion of the primary, secondary and tertiary industries is 44.8%, 23.8% and 31.4% (China Statistical Yearbook, 2006). In other words, while China's output structure is beginning to integrate with that of the developed economies, its employment structure is still in the initial stage of industrialization. The backward labor productivity in the primary industry effectively slows down the speed of surplus labor that could otherwise be transferred to the secondary industry and the services sector. In addition, an inadequate supply of qualified labor further decelerates the development of the modern services industry and information industry. In order to meet the requirement of future industrial upgrading and transformation, the demand for highly skilled labor will continue to expand. The current labor supply, both in overall quality and structure, imposes constraints on the growth of the modern services industry.

The above therefore proves that the "heavy" characteristic of China's current industrial structure has an intrinsic rationality. Thus, the phenomenon of "high energy consumption, high emission" can hardly be avoided. How, then, should we optimize the industrial structure adjustment? The answer to this question depends not only on the basic orientation of international and domestic factor/commodity markets, but also on the basic direction of international and domestic capital flows. In order to achieve targeted results, macro-industrial policy must be implemented on the basis of the endogenous/exogenous motivation of industrial restructuring. In essence, industrial restructuring is a process of industry differentiation and recombination deduced by various industry carriers allocating capital, labor, technology and system elements based on the "cost-benefit" principle. Therefore, when establishing the macro-industrial policy aimed at saving energy and reducing consumption, we should consider the policy's relevance, rationality and effectiveness from four dimensions, namely the capital, labor, technology and system elements. It is also recommended to start from the time series combination and spatial sequence combination of industrial development to screen and judge the scope, timing, and intensity of various policy combinations.

The complexity of energy consumption and waste emissions is most evident in the industrial sectors. Diversified production processes, complex manufacturing techniques, innovative product structure, changing production technologies — any transformation is likely to impact the behavior of energy consumption and waste discharge. To construct the macro-industrial policy system for energy saving and emissions reduction, it is necessary for resource and environmental economics, industrial ecological economics and industrial economics to provide support. Resource and environmental economics needs to answer the following questions: How can we dissect and forecast the change law of an economy's total energy consumption, energy consumption per unit of output, total waste emissions, emissions per unit of output, etc.? What role do industrial structure factors play in the process of leading the change law? Industrial ecological economics needs to provide a response as to how different industries can rationally combine in space and time to improve resource utilization efficiency as well as reduce waste emissions. Meanwhile, industrial economics needs to clarify how to allocate the capital, labor, technology and system elements in order to make the industrial structure develop in a direction towards eco-efficiency optimization. Only by focusing on the interactive relationship between energy consumption, waste emissions and economic growth as well as industrial structure optimization and upgrading, can we establish a specific, reasonable and feasible macro-industrial policy system for energy saving and emissions reduction.

Using the factor decomposition model (Index Decomposition Analysis) and input-output decomposition model (Input-Output Decomposition Analysis), energy economists have carried out in-depth studies on the historical trends of total energy consumption and consumption per unit of output in major industrialized countries as well as China, India and other developing countries. Although the factors that different models explain can vary, all factors can be divided into three categories: scale factor, structure factor and efficiency factor. Among these three factors, the scale factor is relatively more distinct and is always positively correlated with the total energy consumption, whereas the structure factor and efficiency factor display violent fluctuations. The deeper the industry is decomposed, the more likely it is to resolve the contribution of the structure factor.

Since the late 1990s, China has become the focus of most studies (see, e.g., Fisher-Vanden *et al.*, 2004). The reason for this lies mainly in the fact that, since 1996, China's energy supply and total energy consumption has decreased instead of increased, which is in sharp contrast with its average annual growth of 10% (Sinton and Fridley, 2000; Wu *et al.*, 2005). However, widely different conclusions are reached in the various studies on the historical movement trend of China's total primary energy supply, final energy consumption, energy consumption per unit of output and other factors. Some studies suggest that China's industrial restructuring has negatively promoted energy consumption since the 1980s, which is a major factor leading to China's high growth and low energy consumption (Zhang, 2003; Ang, 2004), while other studies have found that sub-industry efficiency is the main factor driving this trend and that adjustment of industrial structure actually plays a positive role in promoting energy consumption.

In the mid-to-late 1990s, a number of Chinese state-owned enterprises with energy use inefficiency were replaced by foreign-funded enterprises with relatively high efficiency; furthermore, the implementation of the "off, stop, merge, transfer" policy rapidly eliminated backward production capacity. These events weakened the positive effect of the industry structure factor in promoting energy consumption whilst relatively enhancing the negative effect of the efficiency factor, resulting in a decline in total energy consumption. Since entering the 21st century, the negative effect of the efficiency factor has been continuous, but the positive effect of the structure factor has been strengthened by the "heavy" industry, causing energy consumption to enter a new period of rapid growth. According to Wu *et al.* (2005, 2006), the contribution rate of the industry structure factor to energy consumption has reached 30%–50%. Thus, it can be seen from the large-scale existing research that the role that industrial restructuring plays in energy saving and emission reduction is significant, regardless of whether it positively or negatively affects energy consumption.

The concern over the relationship between industrial structure, energy consumption and economic growth as well as its evolution law dates back to the Petty–Clark law in classical industrial economics. The Petty–Clark law first explained the internal association of national income per capita and industrial structure. The American economist Kuznets then expanded on this by revealing the theoretical basis and empirical test results for the law that the industrial structure and labor sector structure changes with economic growth in his "National Income and Its Components", "Modern Economic Growth", "Quantitative Aspects of the Economic Growth of Nations" and other literatures. He pointed out that in order to provide a reasonable explanation for economic growth, it is necessary to understand and measure the changes in production structure. Influential factors include domestic demand structure, foreign trade structure and production technology. Lewis (1994) believes that in countries where the economy is composed of a weak modern capitalist sector and a powerful traditional agricultural sector, it is necessary to expand the modern capitalist sector and shrink the traditional agricultural sector in order to promote economic development. In his masterpiece, "Theory of Economic Growth", he comprehensively analyzes economic factors and non-economic factors that affect economic development and proposes the theoretical model of a dual economic structure to explain the economic issues facing developing countries.

Chenery (1961), a US economist, also describes the interdependence between industrial sectors in the process of economic growth and reveals the important role that industrial structure plays in economic development. He believes that changes in industrial structure impose the most direct and important influence on economic growth. An economy's industrial structure is manifested through the proportion of the primary, secondary and tertiary industries along with any upgrades within these industries. Hence, from this perspective, economic development itself can be regarded as a series of interrelated changes in economic structure.

Based on Kuznets, Lewis and Chenery's theory, many scholars have conducted empirical research centered on economic growth, industrial structure and the evolution of industrial structure since the 1990s (see, e.g., Grossman and Helpman, 1991). With the third wave of international industrial transfer, the evolution of industrial structure, especially in developing countries like China, is driven more and more by economic globalization. Thus, the research focus has gradually shifted to the dynamic mechanisms for international industrial transfer and the interaction between international industrial transfer and domestic industrial structure. In recent years, more focus has been devoted to the following issues: the spatial geographic patterns of industrial agglomeration; the effect of industrial agglomeration on industrial restructuring; the relationship between industrial structure evolution and industrial competitiveness issues, etc. Unfortunately, energy consumption and waste emissions are rarely covered in studies on industrial restructuring and industrial transfer. Thorough and systematic research on this aspect is also very rare in China. In other words, energy consumption and waste emissions have not entered into the "Industrial Economics Perspective".

It is in the emerging field of industrial ecological economics that in-depth studies centered on energy consumption, waste emission and industrial production behaviors have been conducted (see Behrens *et al.*, 2007; Ohl *et al.*, 2007; Groenenberg *et al.*, 2005; Ramos-Martin *et al.*, 2007; Greening *et al.*, 2007; Jollands and Harmsworth, 2007; Murphy *et al.*, 2007). With the help of the product lifecycle assessment (LFA), material flow analysis (MFA), energy flow analysis (EFA), ecological footprint (EF) and other methods, industrial ecological economics has carried out research on resource use and waste emission in the production process. Presently, Japan, the United States, Brazil, and a few European countries have established national material flow accounts to monitor the lifecycle of the material flows of the whole country as well as of the leading industries. Japan has also begun recycling efforts since 2000. In order to promote the development of a recycling economy, Japan strived to carry out material flow analysis, invested large funds in database building, and consequently achieved a breakthrough. In the case of China, however, the current studies merely focus on individual production processes or industries; material flow analysis at the national level has not been carried out.

With the resource and environmental issues becoming increasingly prominent, considerable theoretical and empirical research based on Kuznets' inverted U-theory has appeared in environmental economics. These studies set various pollutant emissions as the target variable, while per capita GDP, industrial structure, population, environment control capacity, policy and other factors make up the explanatory variables. These studies then employ linear and nonlinear econometric models to analyze the correlation between pollutant emissions, economic development and industrial structure characteristics (Shafik and Bandyopadhyay, 1992; Pasche, 2002; Lindmark, 2002; Taskin and Zaim, 2001; Muradian and Martinez-Alier, 2001). This type of research was once at the forefront of environmental economics; however, it is now entering its bottleneck stage. Whether the inverted U-shaped relationship exists or not, depends on the complexity of the econometric model rather than the target countries or the timing. As for China, in the matter of whether the pollutant emissions comply with Kuznets' theory, the answer varies among different pollutants. But from the overall perspective, keeping in mind the constraints of China's current economic development stage and industrial structure, we can say with some certainty that the majority of emissions have not reached the Kuznets turning point. Even though individual pollutants may show a slow growth or even decline in the short-term, there is still a high possibility of a rebound.

Econometric models are also largely employed in studies on the correlation between energy consumption, economic growth and industrial structure. This type of research places more emphasis on the causal relation and correlation between economic growth, industrial restructuring, employment restructuring, product price adjustments and total energy consumption and energy consumption structure. This research specializes in analyzing historical relationships between variables, but fails to provide future trend forecasts. Moreover, the results are usually very sensitive to the model's estimation method. Some Chinese scholars use this model to check for the existence of cointegration relationship and Granger causality between economic growth, structural adjustment and energy consumption (Tehrani Nejad, 2007; Bockermann *et al.*, 2005; Lee and Chang, 2007).

Regarding the macroeconomic evaluation of industrial policies and energy environmental policies, the international analysis tools that are currently widely used can be divided into three categories, namely the "Top-down" model, the "Bottom-up" model and the industry-specific simulation/optimization model (Tehrani Nejad, 2007; Bockermann *et al.*, 2005; Böhringer *et al.*, 2006; Ohl *et al.*, 2007; Gielen and Taylor, 2007; Hanson and Laitner, 2004; Groenenberg *et al.*, 2005; Wing, 2006; Adeyemi and Hunt, 2007; Edenhofer *et al.*, 2005; Ayres and van den Bergh, 2005; Murphy *et al.*, 2007). The computable general equilibrium (CGE) model, as the most typical "Top-down" model, can provide analysis on a particular industrial policy's impact on macroeconomic growth. China has begun to study energy and environmental issues using the existing CGE model, but is facing problems in the design of policy parameters. The most typical "Bottom-up" model is the MARKAL model, which can simulate industrial distribution mechanisms and technology roadmaps guided by a specific energy-saving and emissions reduction target. The MARKAL model can also provide answers as to how the promotion of new industry technologies can affect energy consumption and waste emissions. China has established its own MARKAL model through cooperation with foreign research institutions (Wing, 2006; Groenenberg *et al.*, 2005), and is undertaking part of the theoretical advisory missions for policy-making. At the Asian Energy and Environment Modeling Forum (AEEMF) held in 2007, it was agreed that the policy persuasion of China's current energy and environmental macroeconomic model is fairly limited; the simulation technologies need to be improved, and the selection of policy parameters and the updating of technical data also need to be urgently deepened.

In short, it can be said that macro-industrial policy studies for energy saving and emissions reduction involve four key points: economic growth, industrial structure, technological progress, and energy saving and emissions reduction. The logical thinking in establishing the policy system is as follows: optimize industrial structure on the basis of ensured economic growth; advance technological progress on the basis of optimized industrial structure; and make sure that energy saving and emissions reduction is an inevitable result of the sustained economic growth, rationalized industrial structure and upgraded technological progress.

To this end, we provide the following three-pronged interpretation of the establishment of a macro-industrial policy system for energy saving and emissions reduction.

First, dissect the evolutionary characteristics of economic growth, energy consumption and waste emission at the different stages, making clear that industrial structure transformation is essential in order to lead the evolution of energy consumption and waste emission patterns.

Starting from the evolutionary characteristics of economic growth, especially in relation to the total amount, structure and efficiency, we can describe the path of industrial structure transformation and the benchmark for leading industries at the different stages of economic development. Table 11.7 provides an analysis of the periodical characteristics of energy consumption and waste emissions according to the stage of economic development.

In contrast to the traditional Kuznets theory and follow-up empirical research, here we abandon the existing simulation studies of energy consumption that set various pollutant emissions as the target variable. Instead, we focus on the characteristics of energy and environmental issues and the corresponding evolution laws at the different stages of economic development. The seven-stage economic growth model presented in Table 11.7, jointly led by total economic output and industrial structure, describes the corresponding characteristics of energy consumption and pollutant emissions as well as the spatial and temporal evolution law at the various stages. It not only clearly defines the corresponding energy and environmental problems at the different stages, but also distinctly depicts the impact of phase jumps caused by industrial restructuring on the

Table 11.7: Periodical characteristics of energy consumption and waste emissions.

Stage of economic development	Characteristics of energy consumption and environmental pollution	Evolution law
Stage 1: Stage led by agriculture	Low total energy consumption, single structure, low efficiency; Environmental pollution is mainly agricultural pollution: animal manure, straw burning, fertilizer and pesticide residues	Energy consumption and environmental pollution show an inverted U-type relationship; Traditional Agriculture → Oil Agriculture → Recycling Agriculture
Stage 2: Stage led by light and textile industries	Relatively low total energy consumption, single structure, improved efficiency; Environmental pollution is mainly of industrial "three wastes"	Industrial expansion stage: energy consumption and environmental pollution show an inverted U-type relationship, with increasing energy consumption and enhanced environmental pollution. Industrial optimization stage: slowly growing energy consumption and reduced environmental pollution. Industrial transfer and recession stage: decreased energy consumption and less environmental pollution
Stage 3: Stage led by the heavy and chemical industry, with focus on raw materials, fuels and energy and other basic industries	Relatively high total energy consumption, single structure, gradually improving efficiency; Environmental pollution is still of industrial "three wastes"	Industrial expansion stage: increasing energy consumption and enhanced environmental pollution. Industrial optimization stage: slowly growing energy consumption and reduced environmental pollution. Industrial transfer stage: constant energy consumption and further

(*Continued*)

Table 11.7: (*Continued*)

Stage of economic development	Characteristics of energy consumption and environmental pollution	Evolution law
		reduced environmental pollution. According to China's existing natural resources, industrial optimization stage intertwines with the industrial transfer stage; energy consumption and environmental pollution will fluctuate for a long period
Stage 4: Stage led by the heavy and chemical industry, with low degree of processing and assembling	Low-tech machinery, steel, shipbuilding and other heavy and chemical industries with low-level processing and assembling. Higher total energy consumption, diversified structure, gradually increasing efficiency; Environmental pollution is mainly of industrial "three wastes", with living pollution beginning to appear	Industrial expansion stage: increasing energy consumption and enhanced environmental pollution. Industrial optimization stage: slowly growing energy consumption and reduced environmental pollution. Industrial transfer stage: constant energy consumption and further reduced environmental pollution. According to China's existing natural resources, industrial optimization stage intertwines with the industrial transfer stage; energy consumption and environmental pollution will slowly increase
Stage 5: Stage led by the heavy and chemical industry, with high degree of processing and assembling	High-tech precision machinery, fine chemicals, petrochemicals, computers, aircraft manufacturing, automobiles, machine tools and other industries with high added-value.	Industrial expansion stage: increasing energy consumption and enhanced environmental pollution. Industrial optimization stage: slowly growing energy consumption and reduced environmental pollution. According to China's existing

(*Continued*)

Table 11.7: (*Continued*)

Stage of economic development	Characteristics of energy consumption and environmental pollution	Evolution law
	High total energy consumption, diversified structure, relatively high efficiency; Environmental pollution is of industrial "three wastes", the transport sector pollution, and living pollution	natural resources, industrial optimization stage intertwines with the industrial transfer stage; energy consumption and environmental pollution will continuously increase
Stage 6: Stage led by the tertiary industry	Services, transportation, tourism, business, real estate, finance and insurance, information and other industries. Lower total energy consumption, diversified structure, relatively high efficiency; Environmental pollution is mainly from transportation, construction, commercial and residential sectors	Industrial expansion stage: increasing energy consumption and enhanced environmental pollution. Industrial optimization stage: slowly growing energy consumption and further reduced environmental pollution. According to China's existing natural resources, industrial optimization stage intertwines with the industrial transfer stage; energy consumption continuously increases, but the impact on the environment is relatively weak
Stage 7: Stage led by the information industry	The economy enters into a post-industrialization era	Industrial expansion and industrial optimization have a weak impact on energy consumption and environmental pollution; but energy consumption continues to increase due to the expansion in transportation energy

energy and environmental issues. This "Energy and Environment Evolution Model" from the perspective of the "growth model" is not only currently lacking in the theoretical field, but also deserves more attention at the policy-making level.

Second, dissect the endogenous and exogenous driving forces of China's industrial structure evolution, highlighting the framework, pillars and focus of the macro-industrial policy for energy saving and emissions reduction.

The evolution of industrial structure is driven mainly by domestic demand, international trade, international industrial transfer, factor prices and technological progress factors. These driving forces can promote the evolution of industrial structure by releasing certain market signals, or by receiving aid from the relevant government departments to accelerate and enhance the effect. In terms of China's current situation, its industrial restructuring will undoubtedly be influenced by market arrangements as well as government arrangements. The government can further be divided into two categories: central government-led and local government-led. The basic characteristic of China's economic reform is that of a "progressive reform model", i.e., incomplete reform. On one hand, the basic role of market mechanisms continues to be strengthened and dominates in some Chinese industries; thus, structural adjustment against the principles of market economy will hardly achieve the desired performance or obtain the support of those industry sectors. On the other hand, due to the incompleteness of China's "progressive reform", industrial structure adjustment will inevitably require government intervention. In particular, when faced with property rights, investment and financing issues, corporate cross-border asset reorganization and employment disputes, it is almost impossible to solve these problems without the active involvement and influence of the government. Therefore, China's industrial restructuring is doubly affected by both market arrangements and government arrangements.

The industries involved in energy saving and emissions reduction usually exhibit high energy consumption, high pollution and a large proportion of backward production capacity, while the degree of marketization tends to vary among these industries. Hence, under the general guidelines of saving energy and diminishing backward production capacity, the design of the macro-industrial policy must take into account the varying degrees of marketization of the different industries. The macro-industrial policy system must differentiate between short-term policies and long-term policies. For example, in order to achieve the 11th five-year plan target of reducing energy consumption per unit of GDP by 20%, we can adopt short-term policies like the "off, stop, merge, transfer" method led by the government and other non-market means; but in order to guide the industry structure towards low consumption, low emission and high output in the long run, market mechanisms must be engaged as well. In addition, for industries with relatively high external dependence, it is reasonable to raise the FDI entry barriers with respect to energy and environmental indicators so as to guide the industries to develop in a more rationalized and sophisticated direction. As for industries with relatively low external dependence, it is possible to accelerate the pace of international industrial transfer and, in doing so, realize the elimination of backward production capacity.

Third, dissect the labor allocation, capital formation, technological progress and system transition mechanisms of industrial structure adjustment, highlighting the correct path to energy saving and emissions reduction in both time and space.

As previously mentioned, industrial restructuring is essentially a process of industry differentiation and recombination deduced by various industry carriers allocating capital, labor, technology and system elements based on the "cost-benefit" principle. When establishing the macro-industrial policy, it is necessary to start from these four dimensions — capital, labor, technology and system elements — in considering the policy's relevance, rationality and effectiveness. In regards to the allocation of labor, industrial structure adjustment refers to the labor transition amongst the different industry sectors as well as the cultivation and input of incremental labor. The potential demand for labor in leading industries with eco-efficiency, environmental efficiency and economic efficiency should be met first, as this would encourage the development of a "greener" industrial structure.

In terms of capital formation, industrial structure adjustment refers to the reallocation of capital within different industries, spaces and time periods, i.e., capital reconstruction. In the case of China, since the capital market is still weak, the government should limit the investment to industries with high energy consumption and high pollution, while offering preferential policies for capital demand in the information industry, service industry and advanced manufacturing, so as to build a "light and green" capital market.

In terms of technological progress, industrial restructuring means giving priority to the cultivation of technologies that are closely related to industrial development. Although China has strong research capabilities in high-tech and basic technologies, its technological structure is extremely imbalanced due to weak intermediate technology, especially industrial technology, thereby adding to the difficulty of industrial upgrading and structural transformation. The imbalanced technological structure also results in a relatively low degree of specialized division of labor, and creates difficulties for forward and backward integration processes. The key here is in expanding independent research while simultaneously encouraging absorption of innovations; taking advantage of FDI's technology spillover effect to promote the rapid development of intermediate technology; and further advancing international cooperation mechanisms such as CDM and TR to deepen the technology spillover effect.

As for system transition, industrial structure adjustment refers to industrial reconstruction of organizational structure and management structure. In China's current industrial development, the performance of resources and the environment is rarely assessed or monitored. The issue of how to reflect resource and environmental performance in organizational and management structure is fundamental to achieving energy-saving and emissions reduction. The Clean Development Mechanism, the ISO international environment quality certification system, annual environmental reports, public participation and other tools can help promote the low-carbon development path, which is the future transition direction of China's industrial system.

In short, starting from the time series combination and spatial sequence combination of industrial development to screen and judge the scope, timing and intensity of various policy combinations, forms the basic precondition for judging the path and prospects of China's industrial structure optimization. We can promote this process through the following three mechanisms. First, the rationalization mechanism of China's industrial structure: correct the imbalance in the proportion of the different industries, the imbalance between upstream and downstream within the industry chain, and structural lags in the industry growth rate based on the allocation efficiency of industrial resources. Second, the upgrading mechanism of China's industrial structure: advance the upgrading of industrial structure at the national level, regional level and industry level through industrial agglomeration and the establishment of eco-industrial parks. Third, the internationalization mechanism of China's industrial structure: starting from the dynamic comparative advantages and competitive advantages of the relevant industries, explore the new growth point of industrial international competitiveness as well as potential possibilities for international industrial transfer, so as to provide a theoretical basis for the enhanced exogenous driving force of industrial structure optimization.

11.7 International Trade, International Investment and China's Low-Carbon Economic Growth

From the perspective of environmental externalities, environmental pollution will inevitably lead to the destruction of environmental resources and human living conditions. Moreover, due to the "public property" feature of environmental resources, environmental pollution will bring damage to all various owners of the resources. As a result of the global political and economic inequality, cross-border transfer of pollution frequently occurs from developed to developing countries, mainly through economic means including industrial investment transfer and international trade transfer amidst the backdrop of economic globalization.

Industrial investment transfer is when developed countries base emerging high value-added industries in their own countries, while transferring sunset industries with high energy consumption and high pollution to developing countries through cross-border cooperation. Take asbestos, a strong carcinogen, as an example. The use of asbestos is currently controlled in Europe and America; however, its overall worldwide consumption is not decreasing. In fact, MONBIL

Company from the United States and Europe's largest asbestos manufacturing companies have established joint ventures in India and are exporting to Southeast Asia. International trade transfer can be divided into two cases: the first is when developed countries purchase primary products, whose production is prohibited within their own domestic environmental law, through international trade, thereby transferring resource destruction and environmental pollution to other countries; the second is when developed countries transport waste that is difficult to dispose and degrade to developing countries by paying high disposal fees.

Why does this international transfer of environmental pollution occur? One reason lies in the international economic and political inequality: developing countries have little alternative but to bear the brunt of it. However, the value transfer hidden by international trade liberalization and economic globalization is the more convincing cause.

The international community's concern over trade and environmental issues has reached two climaxes. The first climax occurred in the 1970s, triggered by the OECD countries' implementation of strict environmental control policies focusing on the impact of environmental regulation on international competitiveness. The second climax began in the 1990s, driven by the enhanced trend of global economic integration, development of the concept of sustainable development, growing public awareness and interest in global environmental issues, the maturing of environmental organizations and other factors. The areas of concern now extended from international competitiveness only to international competitiveness and environmental regulation (e.g., transfer of polluting industries, control and comparative advantage), trade and cross-border pollution, product standards as non-tariff barriers, trade in dangerous goods, the impact of trade openness on environmental degradation and natural resource utilization, etc. These trade and environmental issues led to a variety of conflicts, mainly between free traders and environmentalists (Qin, 2005).

Free traders argue that trade liberalization will benefit the environment, since it can help improve resource use efficiency, promote economic prosperity and transfer environmental technology freely, thus helping to solve global environmental problems. In their view, the trading system itself is not intrinsically harmful to the environment; rather, it is the poorly designed environmental policies that cause tensions between trade and the environment. According to the "Environmental Kuznets Curve Hypothesis", growth in per capita income will eventually lead to the improvement of environmental quality, which implies that free trade, as an important way to stimulate economic growth, should be upheld.

Environmentalists, however, believe that trade is a significant factor in damaging the environment, inducing environmental deterioration in developing countries by cross-border transfer of pollution through trade. The "Hypothesis of Pollution Haven" states that in conditions of complete free trade, polluting enterprises will choose to operate in countries with lower environmental standards, thus resulting in environmental crises in these countries. The "race to the bottom" hypothesis states that in order to attract or retain investment, countries will compete to lower their environmental standards, thereby bringing about the "Prisoner's Dilemma" situation. Meanwhile, the "Factor Endowment Hypothesis" (Brian *et al.*, 2003) states that countries specialize in production on the basis of their relative abundant elements and then export the relevant products. According to this theory, the abundant capital makes developed countries become exporters of contaminated products; but, on the other hand, strict environmental regulations mean that developed countries have to import contaminated products. Therefore, the environmental consequences of trade patterns depend on which of these two effects dominates.

The hypotheses above only focus on the changes in economic structure brought about by trade liberalization, when in actual fact, in order to evaluate the overall impact of trade on the environment, we must consider other mechanisms affecting the environment as well. Grossman and Krueger (1992) propose decomposing the economic effects of trade into the three effects of scale, portfolio and technology. Scale effects will lead to environmental degradation; the portfolio effect on the environment depends on the country's comparative advantages; while technology effects have a positive impact on the environment. Thus, in the matter of whether international trade liberalization is beneficial to the environment, the answer is uncertain.

As an export-oriented economy, China has to rely on some energy-intensive sectors in order to obtain profits within the international specialization chain. This in turn is strengthened by China's intrinsic impediments with regard to factor endowments. While the Chinese government is taking active measures to promote the low-carbon revolution, the most urgent task is to cultivate market incentives from the final consumption sector for a "green" transformation. Pollution reduction targets based on a top-down system lead to great costs for enterprises. Following the 12th five-year plan, the Chinese government should release more market-oriented mechanisms and institutional settings.

References

Adeyemi, O. I. and Hunt, L. C. (2007). Modelling OECD industrial energy demand: Asymmetric price responses and energy-saving technical change. *Energy Economics*, 29(4), 693–709.

Ang, B. W. (2004). Decomposition analysis for policymaking in energy: Which is the preferred method? *Energy Policy*, 32(9), 1131–1139.

Ayres, R. U. and van den Bergh, J. C. (2005). A theory of economic growth with material/energy resources and dematerialization. *Ecological Economics*, 55(1), 96–118.

Behrens, A., Giljum, S., Kovanda, J. and Niza, S. (2007). The material basis of the global economy: Worldwide patterns of natural resource extraction and their implications for sustainable resource use policies. *Ecological Economics*, 64(2), 444–453.

Bockermann, A., Meyer, B., Omann, I. and Spangenberg, J. H. (2005). Modelling sustainability: Comparing an econometric (PANTA RHEI) and a systems dynamics model (SuE). *Journal of Policy Modeling*, 27(2), 189–210.

BP Statistical Review Full Report 2008.

Brian, R., Copeland, M. and Taylor, S. (2003). Trade, growth and the environment. *Journal of Economic Literature*, 42(1), 7–71.

Böhringer, C., Hoffmann, T. and Manrique-de-Lara-Peñate, C. (2006). The efficiency costs of separating carbon markets under the EU emissions trading scheme: A quantitative assessment for Germany. *Energy Economics*, 28(1), 44–61.

Chenery, H. B. (1961). Comparative advantage and development policy. *The American Economic Review*, 51(1), 18–51.

Dhakal, S. (2004). Urban energy use and greenhouse gas emissions in Asian megacities: Policies for a sustainable future. Institute for Global Environmental Strategies (IGES).

Edenhofer, O., Bauer, N. and Kriegler, E. (2005). The impact of technological change on climate protection and welfare: Insights from the model MIND. *Ecological Economics*, 54(2–3), 277–292.

Fisher-Vanden, K., Jefferson, G. H., Liu, H. and Tao, Q. (2004). What is driving China's decline in energy intensity? *Resource and Energy Economics*, 26(1), 77–97.

Gielen, D. and Taylor, M. (2007). Modelling industrial energy use: The IEA's energy technology perspectives. *Energy Economics*, 29(4), 889–912.

Greening, L. A., Boyd, G. and Roop, J. M. (2007). Modeling of industrial energy consumption: An introduction and context. *Energy Economics*, 29(4), 599–608.

Groenenberg, H., Blok, K. and van der Sluijs, J. (2005). Projection of energy-intensive material production for bottom-up scenario building. *Ecological Economics*, 53(1), 75–99.

Grossman, G. E. and Helpman, E. (1991). Quality ladders in the theory of growth. *Review of Economic Studies*, 58(1), 43–61.

Grossman, G. M. and Krueger, A. B. (1992). Environmental impacts of a North American free trade agreement. Woodrow Wilson School, Princeton, NT.

GTZ (2009). *International Fuel Prices, 6th Edition — Data Preview*.

Hanson, D. and Laitner, J. A. (2004). An integrated analysis of policies that increase investments in advanced energy-efficient/low-carbon technologies. *Energy Economics*, 26(4), 739–755.

He, J. K. and Zhang, X. L. (2005). Analysis on the impact of the structural changes in the manufacturing industry. *Environmental Protection*, (12), 37–41.

He, J. K., Liu, B., Chen, Y., Xu, H. Q., Guo, Y. *et al.* (2006). National assessment report on climate change (III): Integrated evaluation of strategies on response to climate change in China. Advances in Climate Change Research, 2006-04.

International Energy Agency (2007). *World Energy Outlook*.

International Energy Agency. Beyond 2020 database.

Jollands, N. and Harmsworth, G. (2007). Participation of indigenous groups in sustainable development monitoring: Rationale and examples from New Zealand. *Ecological Economics*, 62(3–4), 716–726.

Lee, C.-C. and Chang, C.-P. (2007). Energy consumption and GDP revisited: A panel analysis of developed and developing countries. *Energy Economics*, 29(6), 1206–1223.

Lewis, P. M. (1994). Economic statism, private capital, and the dilemmas of accumulation in Nigeria. *World Development*, 22(3), 437–451.

Lindmark, M. (2002). An EKC-pattern in historical perspective: Carbon dioxide emissions, technology, fuel prices and growth in Sweden, 1870–1997. *Ecological Economics*, 42(1–2), 333–347.

Muradian, R. and Martinez-Alier, J. (2001). Trade and the environment: From a 'Southern' perspective. *Ecological Economics*, 36(2), 281–297.

Murphy, R., Rivers, N. and Jaccard, M. (2007). Hybrid modeling of industrial energy consumption and greenhouse gas emissions with an application to Canada. *Energy Economics*, 29(4), 826–846.

National Bureau of Statistics of China (2006). China Statistical Yearbook.

National Bureau of Statistics of China (2008). China Statistical Yearbook.

Nordhaus, W. D. (2007). Review: A Review of the "Stern review on the economics of climate change". *Journal of Economic Literature*, 45(3), 686–702.

Ohl, C., Krauze, K. and Grünbühel, C. (2007). Towards an understanding of long-term ecosystem dynamics by merging socio-economic and environmental research: Criteria for long-term socio-ecological research sites selection. *Ecological Economics*, 63(2–3), 383–391.

Pasche, M. (2002). Technical progress, structural change, and the environmental Kuznets curve. *Ecological Economics*, 42(3), 381–389.

Qin, Z. (2005). *International Trade and Environment: The Problems of International Trade.*

Ramos-Martin, J., Giampietro, M. and Mayumi, K. (2007). On China's exosomatic energy metabolism: An application of multi-scale integrated analysis of societal metabolism (MSIASM). *Ecological Economics*, 63(1), 174–191.

Shafik, N. and Bandyopadhyay, S. (1992). Economic growth and environmental quality: Time series and cross-country evidence. The World Bank Policy Research Working Paper Series No. 904.

Sinton, J. E. and Fridley, D. G. (2000). What goes up: recent trends in China's energy consumption. *Energy Policy*, 28(10), 671–687.

Taskin, F. and Zaim, O. (2001). The role of international trade on environmental efficiency: A DEA approach. *Economic Modelling*, 18(1), 1–17.

Tehrani Nejad M., A. (2007). Allocation of CO2 emissions in petroleum refineries to petroleum joint products: A linear programming model for practical application. *Energy Economics*, 29(4), 974–997.

Wing, I. S. (2006). The synthesis of bottom-up and top-down approaches to climate policy modelling: Electric power technologies and the cost of limiting US CO2 emissions. *Energy Policy*, 34(18), 3847–3869.

Wu, L. B., Kaneko, S. and Matsuoka, S. (2005). Driving forces behind the stagnancy of China's energy-related CO_2 emissions from 1996 to 1999. *Energy Policy*, 33(3), 319–335.

Wu, L. B., Kaneko, S. and Matsuoka, S. (2006). Dynamics of energy-related CO_2 emissions in China during 1980 to 2002. *Energy Policy*, 34(18), 3549–3572.

Zhang, Z. X. (2003). Why did the energy intensity fall in China's industrial sector in the 1990s? *Energy Economics*, 25(6), 625–638.

Zhuang, G. Y. (2006). Role of China in global carbon market. *China & World Economy*, 14(5), 93–104.

Chapter 12

The New Financial Architecture: The Role of Market Discipline for Governance

Apanard Penny Prabhavivadhana and Clas Wihlborg

12.1 Introduction

There are many aspects to market discipline within the financial sector. In the recent global financial crisis, the failure of market discipline to rein in risk-taking of financial institutions has received the most attention. Another aspect is the role of markets in providing incentives for corporate managers and owners to work on behalf of various stakeholders in the corporation, including society at large. In this chapter we discuss the interaction among markets, corporate and financial sector law, and the political system in order to identify distinguishing characteristics and determinants of corporate governance systems in Asia. Our analysis focuses particularly on impacts of the global re-polarization process of economic power towards Asia (see Figure 12.1) on the corporate governance systems. We pose the question whether the greater economic weight of Asia in the global economy leads to a corresponding greater weight of Asian models for corporate governance. Asian models — presuming such models can be identified — may gain influence not only because Asia's weight in the world economy is growing, but also because other countries may try to emulate characteristics of successful economic systems. On the other hand, weaknesses in Asian governance systems may be exposed over time in global competition. If so, will Asian systems converge towards an Anglo-Saxon system or a Continental European system?

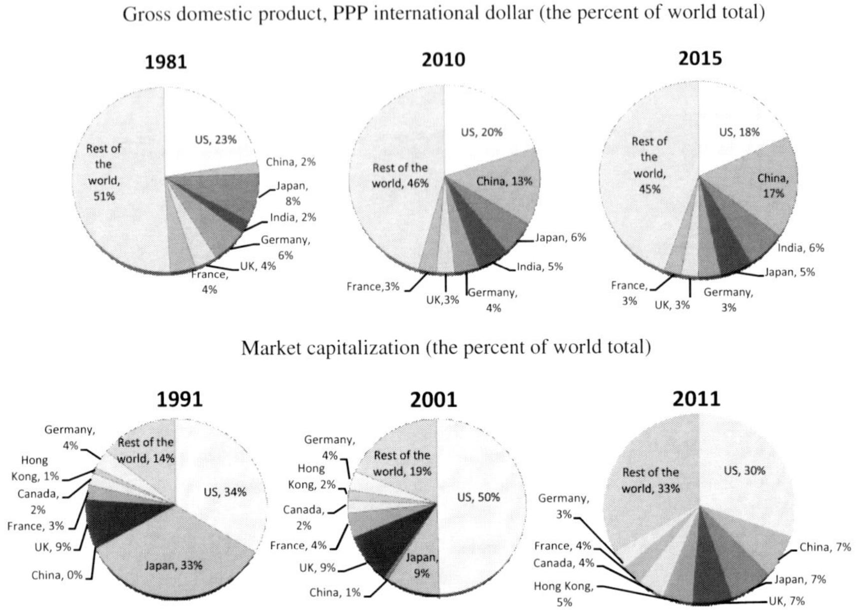

Figure 12.1: The shift of the distribution of global economic and financial activities, selected years.

Sources: World Economic Outlook Database, International Monetary Fund, and Bloomberg.

Note: The 2010 and 2015 GDP data are forecasts. The market capitalization data in 2011 are as of the end of March.

The recent financial crisis has broken a trend towards the Anglo-Saxonization of the financial architecture in Europe and Asia. In Europe, this trend has been evident in the financial reforms within the EU post-1992. In Asia, the woes of the Japanese banking system after the expansive 1980s and the Asian financial crisis in 1997–1998 enhanced the role of the Anglo-Saxon (A-S) model as the one to emulate following a period when the Japanese system, in particular, seemed successful. Many American observers in the late 1980s blamed the A-S financial system for US loss of competitiveness relative to both Japan and Europe. For example, Porter (1992) has argued that the attention to stock market values made American managers myopic in their investment decisions.

Financial systems and associated corporate governance structures do not change overnight. These structures are defined by formal as well as informal rules and are intrinsically linked to legal systems, cultural factors and political governance. La Porta *et al.* (1997, 1998, 1999, 2000) are the main proponents of a focus on legal regimes to explain corporate governance characteristics and aspects of economic performance. One contradictory view is presented by Rajan and Zingales (2003). They note that stock markets developed just as well in civil law- as in common law countries in the late 19th century and through the first half of the 20th century. Thus, corporate governance systems may not be as rigid as implied by the legal regime view.

Trade openness and interest group politics are emphasized by Rajan and Zingales as alternative explanations of financial market developments and corporate governance systems. Roe (2003) argues that corporate governance structures can be explained by the influences of various interest groups through the political process. He argues that powerful interest groups within the corporate sphere are not going to abdicate their powers without fundamental — even revolutionary — shifts in the political process. The influence of these groups may be exercised in different ways and, therefore, is not linked to a specific legal arrangement.

In spite of the rigidities of power structures, fundamental change can occur in the time perspective of several decades. A series of small, seemingly innocuous reforms can possibly accumulate to systemic changes over time if they all go in the same direction. Thus, is the current shift of mood away from the A-S system going to be long-lasting, or will the Anglo-Saxonization in Europe and Asia continue after a temporary setback? Much depends on what happens in the United States as the main A-S model economy. The current financial reforms in the United States may also weaken the traditional A-S model. In fact, it can be argued that this model has been weakening for some time. We return to these issues below.

In Section 12.2 we discuss agency costs and why the reduction of agency costs from shareholders' point of view tends to enhance the competitiveness of a corporate governance system. Thereafter, in

Section 12.3 we consider three aspects of market discipline in corporate governance systems which can influence economic performance of corporations as well as important characteristics of corporate governance systems over long periods. In Section 12.4 Asian corporate governance systems are compared to A-S and Continental Western European systems in terms of commonly used criteria for market-based (outsider-oriented) systems and bank-based (insider-oriented) systems.

The political dimension is brought into the picture in Section 12.5. The question here is whether Asian countries can be characterized in terms of relatively stable, generally accepted social objectives in the way Roe (2003) characterized Western European countries as "social democrat", wherein employees' interests have stronger weight than in the United States. We argue that the objectives of the large corporations in many Asian countries are strongly interlinked with perceived national objectives. Thus, we talk about "the nationalist corporation" in relatively developed Asian countries, while "the corrupt corporation" may be a more fitting description in less developed Asian countries with weak legal and political structures. Each type of corporation is associated with specific restrictions on market discipline, and these restrictions are presumably imposed by the political process.

In Section 12.6 we turn to a comparison of performance of different corporate governance systems in terms of dynamic characteristics. We follow Morck, Wolfenzon and Yeung (2005), arguing that long-term growth is best served by dynamic economic systems that enable new firms and ownership structures to develop and be weeded out or survive in a trial-and-error process.

The consequences of re-polarization of economic power towards Asia for corporate governance are discussed in the concluding Section 12.7. Two hypotheses stand against each other. One is that the increased economic power of Asia will strengthen the role of national interests in governance in Asia as well as in other countries. Another is that governance systems in Asia will become increasingly outsider-oriented (market-based) over time when political processes respond to global economic competition, wherein the most dynamic governance structures provide an edge.

12.2 Agency Costs in Corporate Governance Systems

In this section we discuss how the concept of agency costs from shareholders' point of view can be used to evaluate corporate governance systems, even if these systems are not focused on shareholder wealth maximization. We take the perspective of agency theory and consider, to begin with, the corporate manager as an agent of shareholders as well as of other stakeholders in a corporation. In the standard A-S oriented model of financial markets, the manager is viewed as the agent of shareholders and the main issue to be resolved by the corporate governance structures is to align the interests of shareholders and managers who have an interest in pursuing "private benefits". A broader view is to consider management as an agent for diverse stakeholder groups and the interests of these groups must be balanced one way or the other. Theoretically, it is more convenient to view management as an agent for shareholders and broaden the concept of "private benefits" to include influences by other stakeholders inducing management to pursue their interests at the expense of shareholders. These interests could be related to social concerns or objectives of employees or other interest groups. The pursuit of non-shareholders' interest beyond what is specified in contractual arrangements, law and social norms can be thought of as agency costs from shareholders' point of view, even if the managers' objectives are not linked to private benefits in the narrow, self-oriented sense. The "optimal" corporate governance structure would maximize the sum of benefits to non-shareholders minus the loss to shareholders of managers' pursuit of private benefits.

Shareholder wealth maximization would be consistent with social wealth maximization if other stakeholders' interests are reflected in contractual arrangements, law, regulation and social norms constraining management behavior. This situation requires well-functioning markets for ownership and control, imposing discipline on managers, as well as well-functioning markets for labor, inputs and output. Not least, the political processes that determine law and regulation must reflect people's preferences. Obviously, the ideal political and economic governance mechanisms that would induce managers to pursue social welfare maximization by maximizing shareholder wealth do not and will never exist.

Two kinds of deficiencies in corporate governance systems from a social welfare's point of view can be identified based on the reasoning above. First, there are agency costs in the management–shareholder relationship as noted above. Second, corporate activities create externalities for a variety of stakeholders, and these externalities are not always reflected in law and regulation. Valuation of these externalities requires that there is a degree of social consensus about their identification and magnitude. If there is no consensus about the social value of the externalities created by shareholder wealth-maximizing managers, the only criterion we can use to evaluate corporate governance systems is shareholder wealth maximization. In democracies we would generally presume that if externalities are not addressed in law, regulation or social behavioral norms, social agreement on their nature is lacking. Shareholder wealth maximization is, then, the appropriate criterion for evaluating corporate governance systems.

The non-existence of the perfect political process that designs laws and regulations as remedies for externalities creates incentives for groups associated with specific stakeholders in corporations to argue for special consideration of their interests in corporate governance. Thus, stakeholder groups may argue for and obtain legislation that force or induce managers to serve their interests at the expense of shareholders. Examples include managers pushing for takeover defenses to protect their interests at the expense of shareholders, and employees pushing for a voice on corporate boards. In either case, agency costs are created from shareholders' point of view.

The argument in the following is based on the assumption that social welfare is best served if agency costs are minimized from shareholders' point of view. Thus, it is assumed that rules for governance are not systematically aimed at reducing negative externalities (or increasing positive externalities) of corporate activities. Instead, governance rules are likely to reflect the ability of particular interest groups to influence rules of governance through the political process. We return to this issue in Section 12.4.

All corporate governance systems have weaknesses in the sense that they allow for agency costs by inducing managers to serve either their own interests or the interests of other stakeholders at the expense of shareholders. In the next section we discuss the role of market discipline in limiting managers' ability to impose agency costs.

12.3 Channels of Market Discipline in Corporate Governance

We consider in this section three channels of market discipline that may influence the degree to which management works to maximize shareholder wealth and the mechanism by which managers are allocated to firms and functions in an efficient way.

Channel 1: Markets for corporate control including markets for equity, corporate debt and managers. Contractual arrangements among shareholders, owners, and debtholders are determined in these markets, influencing incentives of management and the agency costs. The greater the weight of these markets in influencing management behavior and, thereby, agency costs, the more "outsider-oriented" or "market-based" is the corporate governance system. With dispersed ownership and separation of ownership and control, the threat of hostile takeovers through markets for equity disciplines management to maximize shareholder wealth. Markets for corporate debt are important because, for example, leveraged buy-outs and other forms of takeovers are often financed through these markets. Furthermore, contractual arrangements with debtholders are important in bankruptcy and influence shareholders' incentives. Markets for managers determine the level and structure of executive compensation and, thereby, incentives.

Corporate and credit market law and regulation influence the effectiveness of equity and credit markets from the point of view of reducing agency costs of different kinds. Corporate law may enable managers to resist hostile takeover bids. Markets for public debt may be non-existent in bank-dominated systems where banks monitor and influence management more directly than through contractual arrangements. Similarly, the market for managers may be more or less non-existent where managers are restricted to move within a corporation or among corporations within a group under common control. In this case, we talk about "insider-based" or "relationship-based" systems. Concentrated (block) ownership, dual-class shares, pyramid structures, interlocking directors and cross-ownership are common in these systems. Even if the direct discipline of markets on managers' incentives is lacking, equity and credit markets provide channels for indirect market discipline.

Channel 2: Competition for funding in stock markets and banking. Stock market valuation affects the cost of capital for a corporation. Thus, if agency costs increase and shareholders notice that managers extract private benefits, the firm's cost of capital increases as well. Similarly, the value of a conglomerate is reduced by lack of transparency over the ability of managers within the conglomerate to deviate from shareholder wealth maximization.

The corporations with concentrated ownership are often closely associated with a bank and, therefore, rely less on equity financing. In this case, competition among banks over depositors' funds could substitute for competition for funds in equity markets.

Depositors are protected by explicit and implicit deposit insurance in many countries. Furthermore, restrictions on investing in other countries limit the range of choice for households. If so, neither competition in equity markets nor in banking would provide effective discipline on managers' behavior, and the scope of private benefit extraction would increase. An additional channel of market discipline exists, however.

Channel 3: Competition in goods and labor markets. Managers' extraction of "private benefits", whether they serve themselves or other stakeholders, would normally be associated with reduced productivity of a firm and, as a result, a higher cost level and reduced competitiveness. If competition restricts the firm's ability to raise price, management's ability to divert resources away from "productive uses" is also restricted. Goods market competition is, in the end, the disciplining device that provides competition among corporate governance systems. Thus, greater protectionism in international trade and hindrances to competition domestically contribute to the conservation of corporate governance systems associated with substantial agency costs.

What can be said about the relative merits of insider- and outsider-oriented corporate governance systems from the point of view of wealth maximization? Table 12.1 describes the main characteristics associated with idealized descriptions of the two systems. A first critical factor is the ability of management to extract private benefits (assuming goods market discipline is not perfect). In an outsider-based system with dispersed ownership, the efficiency of the market for hostile takeovers disciplines management. Thus, the ability of management to limit the threat of hostile takeovers by means of, for example, poison pills, increases its ability to entrench itself. According to Gilson and Kraakman (2005), the Delaware Supreme Court has become increasingly friendly to takeover defenses after a period of frequent hostile takeovers with far-reaching consequences for industrial structure during the 1980s. The more far-reaching the structural effects of the takeover are expected to be, the greater the likelihood that the courts will accept defenses and allow management to prevent a shareholder vote on a bid. Thus, management has become increasingly entrenched in the United States over the last two decades.

In an insider-oriented system, concentration of ownership tends to be relatively high and, therefore, the controlling owner is likely to have incentives more closely aligned with most shareholders. However, if a block shareholder can keep control with a relatively small share of the equity, the incentive to extract private benefits increases. Dual-class shares and pyramid structures of ownership are means by which block shareholders can obtain control with a relatively small ownership share. Under these circumstances, entrenchment of a controlling minority shareholder and associated management is a strong possibility.

Table 12.1: Summary of characteristics of stylized corporate governance models.

Characteristics	Anglo-Saxon/ Market-based/ Outsider-oriented	Relationship-based/Insider-oriented (Continental European-Japanese model)
Objective	Wealth maximization	Utility maximization
Principal	Shareholders	Stakeholders (shareholders, creditors, employees, customers)
Ownership structure	Widely dispersed ownership; Separation between ownership and control	Concentrated ownership; banks and/or other corporations are major shareholders
Decision-making structures	Managers have a large amount of freedom in making decisions	Decision making relies on consensus and the use of committees
Mechanisms for disciplining managers/ Market for corporate control	Managers are disciplined by the market if their performance is poor; Threat of hostile takeovers	Managers are linked to controlling owner; protection from direct market discipline but subject to indirect market discipline
Role of banks	Banks play a minimal role in corporate ownership; Arm's-length banking	Bank ownership or board membership; Close links in both corporate finance and control
Family-controlled firms/ Private ownership and control	General separation of equity holding and management in public firms, but "going private" is an opportunity	Family ownership important only for small- and medium-sized enterprises. Dual-class shares and pyramids common
Disclosure and accounting rules	Relatively strong investor protection rules	Group affiliation (family-owned firms or family controlled by financial institutions) often comes with worse transparency

(*Continued*)

Table 12.1: (*Continued*)

Characteristics	Anglo-Saxon/ Market-based/ Outsider-oriented	Relationship-based/Insider-oriented (Continental European-Japanese model)
Management boards	One-tier board	Two-tier boards; executive and supervisory responsibility separate
Role of stock market	Market for takeover as well as valuation; Strong role in corporate finance	Valuation providing indirect market discipline
Main source of agency costs	Managerial entrenchment; Private benefit extraction by manager if market for control is weak	Private benefit extraction by controlling block shareholder
Sample countries	United States, United Kingdom	Continental Western Europe, Japan, S. Korea

Sources: Authors' adaptation of Carnat (2004) and Allen (2005).

A second critical factor when evaluating the insider- and outsider-based systems of corporate governments is their ability to apply relevant information when allocating financial resources to projects. As Boot and Thakor (2000) have pointed out, the outsider-based system is able to utilize dispersed information that becomes revealed in market trading. Profit opportunities in the stock market provide incentives for various individuals to become informed about firms and the factors affecting the value of their projects. The outsider-oriented system is essentially pluralistic.

The advantage of the insider-based system is that the responsibility for the allocation of financial resources in a larger entity comprising several firms and possibly a bank lies with a few well-informed individuals with inside information about the available projects. Thus, each system has an advantage with respect to different kinds of information.

Similar reasoning can be applied on the efficiency of the market for managerial skill. Within the insider-based system there is an internal market for managers who can move among the different entities within the industry group, while the market for managers in the outsider-based system becomes broader and more dependent on dispersed information.

The conclusion of this discussion is that it is not possible on *a priori* grounds to say that one corporate governance system is superior to another. The stronger the degree of competition in goods markets, the greater is the likelihood that the system we observe is the result of competition among governance structures. If there is little competition in goods markets, entrenchment within both systems could be the result of low sensitivity of the cost of capital to equity market valuation, and of little competition among banks.

Morck, Wolfenzon and Yeung (2005) have pointed out that entrenched groups within a particular corporate governance system are likely to be able to exercise political power as well and, thereby, hinder market discipline on different levels through the political process. We return to this issue in Section 12.5. We argue there that one way to evaluate the efficacy of corporate governance systems is to analyze their contribution to industrial dynamics based on trial and error in a competitive environment.

12.4 Corporate Governance Systems and Market Discipline in Asia in Comparison with Anglo-Saxon and Continental European Countries

The trend towards adopting aspects of the A-S corporate governance system was apparent in Asia prior to the recent global financial crisis. A poor system of corporate governance in Asia had in part contributed to the 1997–1998 Asian financial crisis. Lack of adequate transparency, unreliable financial reports, and weak internal control sheltered banks, financial companies and corporations from market discipline (Zhuang, 1999). IMF recommended that developing countries abandon the Asian relationship-oriented business model and, instead, adopt more

Table 12.2: List of countries.

Asia	Western Europe	Central and Eastern Europe	Anglo-Saxon
High-income	Austria	Bulgaria	Australia
Hong Kong	Belgium	Czech Republic	Canada
Japan	Denmark	Estonia	Ireland
South Korea	Finland	Hungary	New Zealand
Singapore	France	Latvia	United Kingdom
Taiwan	Germany	Lithuania	United States
	Greece	Poland	
Lower-income	Italy	Romania	
China	Luxembourg	Slovenia	
India	Netherlands	Slovakia	
Indonesia	Norway		
Malaysia	Portugal		
Philippines	Spain		
Thailand	Sweden		
	Switzerland		

of the US model oriented towards shareholder wealth maximization (Singh and Zammit, 2006).

Table 12.2 lists the countries included in the analysis below. We distinguish among High- and Lower-income Asian countries, Continental Western European countries, Central and Eastern European countries, and Anglo-Saxon countries. Asian countries are divided into two groups, although Asia is a very diverse region in terms of levels of economic development, corporate governance and political governance. In 2010, the annual income per capita varied from lower than $2,000 in India and the Philippines to more than $40,000 in Japan and Singapore. Tables 12.3 and 12.4 show the data on characteristics of corporate governance. The data in Table 12.3 show that the average percentage of family control of nationally listed corporate assets is highest for the group of lower-income Asian economies (56% and 61% for the control thresholds of 10% and 20%, respectively). The percentage of family controlled firms for high-income Asia is lower, but still higher than in Continental Europe and Anglo-Saxon groups of countries.

Table 12.3: Ownership concentration (percent of firms in sample widely held and under family control using different criteria for control).

Country	Control inferred at 10%		Control inferred at 20%		Source	No. of firms in the study's sample	Survey year
	Widely held	Family control	Widely held	Family control			
High-income Asia							
Hong Kong	0.6	64.7	7	66.7	CDL	330	1998
Japan	42	13.1	79.8	9.7	CDL	1,240	1998
S. Korea	14.3	67.9	43.2	48.4	CDL	345	1998
Singapore	1.4	52	5.4	55.4	CDL	221	1998
Taiwan	2.9	65.6	26.2	48.2	CDL	141	1998
High-income Asia							
Hong Kong	10	70	10	70	LLS	20 largest firms	1995
Japan	50	10	90	5	LLS	20 largest firms	1995
S. Korea	40	35	55	20	LLS	20 largest firms	1995
Singapore	5	45	15	30	LLS	20 largest firms	1995
Lower-income Asia							
Indonesia	0.6	68.6	5.1	71.5	CDL	178	1998
Malaysia	1	57.5	10.3	67.2	CDL	238	1998
Philippines	1.7	42.1	19.2	44.6	CDL	120	1998
Thailand	2.2	56.5	6.6	61.6	CDL	167	1998

(*Continued*)

Table 12.3: (*Continued*)

Country	Control inferred at 10%		Control inferred at 20%		Source	No. of firms in the study's sample	Survey year
	Widely held	Family control	Widely held	Family control			
Continental Western Europe							
Austria	5	15	5	15	LLS	20 largest firms	1995
Belgium	0	50	5	50	LLS	20 largest firms	1995
Denmark	10	35	40	35	LLS	20 largest firms	1995
Finland	15	10	35	10	LLS	20 largest firms	1995
France	30	20	60	20	LLS	20 largest firms	1995
Germany	35	10	50	10	LLS	20 largest firms	1995
Greece	5	65	10	50	LLS	20 largest firms	1995
Italy	15	20	20	15	LLS	20 largest firms	1995
Netherlands	30	20	30	20	LLS	20 largest firms	1995
Norway	5	25	25	25	LLS	20 largest firms	1995
Portugal	0	50	10	45	LLS	20 largest firms	1995
Spain	15	25	35	15	LLS	20 largest firms	1995
Sweden	0	55	25	45	LLS	20 largest firms	1995
Switzerland	50	40	60	30	LLS	20 largest firms	1995
Anglo-Saxon							
Australia	55	10	65	5	LLS	20 largest firms	1995
Canada	50	30	60	25	LLS	20 largest firms	1995

(*Continued*)

Table 12.3: (*Continued*)

	Control inferred at 10%		Control inferred at 20%				
Country	Widely held	Family control	Widely held	Family control	Source	No. of firms in the study's sample	Survey year
Ireland	45	15	65	10	LLS	20 largest firms	1995
New Zealand	5	45	30	25	LLS	20 largest firms	1995
United Kingdom	90	5	100	0	LLS	20 largest firms	1995
United States	80	20	80	20	LLS	20 largest firms	1995
	Average				Study	Total firms	Survey year
*High-income Asia**	14.6	49.4	33.9	45.1	CDL	2,136	1998
High-income Asia	26.3	40.0	42.5	31.3	LLS	20 largest firms	1995
Lower-income Asia	1.4	56.2	10.3	61.2	CDL	703	1998
Continental Western Europe	15.4	31.4	29.3	27.5	LLS	20 largest firms	1995
Anglo-Saxon	54.2	20.8	66.7	14.2	LLS	20 largest firms	1995

Sources: LLS = La Porta, Lopez-de-Silanes and Shleifer (1999); CDL = Claessens, Djankov and Lang (2000).
Note: * Excludes Taiwan for comparability between the studies of CDL and LLS.

Table 12.4: **Shareholder and creditor rights (higher value = stronger rights).**

	Legal origin	Shareholder rights (0–5)	Strength of investor protection (0–5)	Creditor rights (0–5)	Private monitoring index
Source	DMS	LLSV/DLLS	WB	DMS	BCL
High-income Asia					
Hong Kong	English	5	4.5	5	8
Japan	German	4.5	3.5	2.5	9
South Korea	German	4.5	2.7	3.8	11
Singapore	English	5	4.7	3.8	9
Taiwan	German	3	2.7	2.5	9
Lower-income Asia					
China	German	1	2.5	2.5	n/a
India	English	5	3	2.5	n/a
Indonesia	French	4	3	2.5	9
Malaysia	English	5	4.4	3.8	9
Philippines	French	4	2	1.3	n/a
Thailand	English	4	3.9	2.5	10
Continental Western Europe					
Austria	German	2.5	2	3.8	n/a
Belgium	French	3	3.5	2.5	7
Denmark	Scandinavian	4	3.2	3.8	n/a
Finland	Scandinavian	3.5	2.9	1.3	8

(Continued)

Table 12.4: (*Continued*)

	Legal origin	Shareholder rights (0–5)	Strength of investor protection (0–5)	Creditor rights (0–5)	Private monitoring index
Source	DMS	LLSV/DLLS	WB	DMS	BCL
France	French	3.5	2.7	0	n/a
Germany	German	3.5	2.5	3.8	9
Greece	French	2	1.7	1.3	n/a
Italy	French	2	2.9	2.5	9
Luxembourg		2	2.2	n/a	7
Netherlands	French	2.5	2.4	3.8	11
Norway	Scandinavian	3.5	3.4	2.5	8
Portugal	French	2.5	3	1.3	7
Spain	French	5	2.5	2.5	9
Sweden	Scandinavian	3.5	2.9	1.3	7
Switzerland	German	3	1.5	1.3	7
Central and Eastern Europe					
Bulgaria	German	3	3	2.5	7
Czech Rep.	German	4	2.5	3.8	n/a
Hungary	German	2	2.2	1.3	9
Latvia	German	4	2.9	3.8	9
Lithuania	French	4	2.5	2.5	10
Poland	German	2	3	1.3	n/a
Romania	French	5	3	2.5	n/a

(*Continued*)

Table 12.4: (*Continued*)

	Legal origin	Shareholder rights (0–5)	Strength of investor protection (0–5)	Creditor rights (0–5)	Private monitoring index
Source	DMS	LLSV/DLLS	WB	DMS	BCL
Slovak Rep.	German	3	2.4	2.5	n/a
Slovenia	German	n/a	3.4	3.8	8
Anglo-Saxon					
Australia	English	4	2.9	3.8	9
Canada	English	4	2.9	3.8	n/a
Ireland	English	5	4.2	1.3	10
New Zealand	English	4	4.2	1.3	10
United Kingdom	English	5	4.9	5	10
United States	English	3	4	5	10
Average					
High-income Asia		4.4	3.6	3.5	9.2
Lower-income Asia		3.8	3.1	2.5	9.3
Continental Western Europe		3.1	2.6	2.2	8.1
Central and Eastern Europe		3.4	2.7	2.6	8.6
Anglo-Saxon		4.2	3.8	3.3	9.8

Sources: DMS = Djankov, McLiesh and Shleifer (2007); DLLS = Djankov, La Porta, Lopez-de-Silanes and Shleifer (2008) (the shareholder rights data in this study is updated from La Porta, Lopez-de-Silanes, Shleifer and Vishny, LLSV, 1998); WB = World Bank's *Doing Business* (http://www.doingbusiness.org/); BCL = Barth, Caprio and Levine (2006).
Note: The strength of investor protection and creditor rights are rescaled to 0–5 for comparability.

Family control and political connections of firms in Asia are often viewed as evidence of poor corporate governance. These characteristics also allow cronyism and corruption. Figure 12.2 shows the plot between the level of corruption and the extent of family controlled firms. The scatter plot suggests the expected positive relationship between ownership concentration and corruption. Asian economies with a higher share of family controlled firms also have relatively high levels of corruption (most Asian economies are on the top left in Panel A of this Figure). This relationship is weaker in Panel A of Figure 12.2 which includes the sample of Continental Western European countries (R-square = –0.51) than when the sample of Asian countries alone is included (not shown). Among the (relatively few) Anglo-Saxon countries, a greater share of family controlled firms is actually associated with lack of corruption (Figure 12.2, Panel B).

Table 12.4 shows legal origin, shareholder rights, strength of investor protection, creditor rights and a private monitoring index reflecting market transparency for each country and country group. High-income Asia and the Anglo-Saxon countries have similar relatively high scores for these characteristics, although transparency seems superior in the Anglo-Saxon countries as shown by the private monitoring index. Continental Western Europe scores lower than High-income Asia in all dimensions. Even Lower-income Asia scores higher than Western Europe in all dimensions. Thus, it seems that Asian countries have adopted some Anglo-Saxon characteristics in their legal frameworks for corporate governance. The effect on agency costs of these characteristics is likely to depend on the degree of market discipline exerted through financial markets, competition and international trade.

Market Discipline and Competition as Constraint

The Economic Freedom Index is a very general measure of the degree to which markets are allowed to function without hindrance by governments. A high degree of freedom is associated with low entry and exit restrictions and high contractual effectiveness. Although the index is an imperfect measure of market discipline, it can be of interest in comparing economic freedom indices for the country groups in different dimensions.

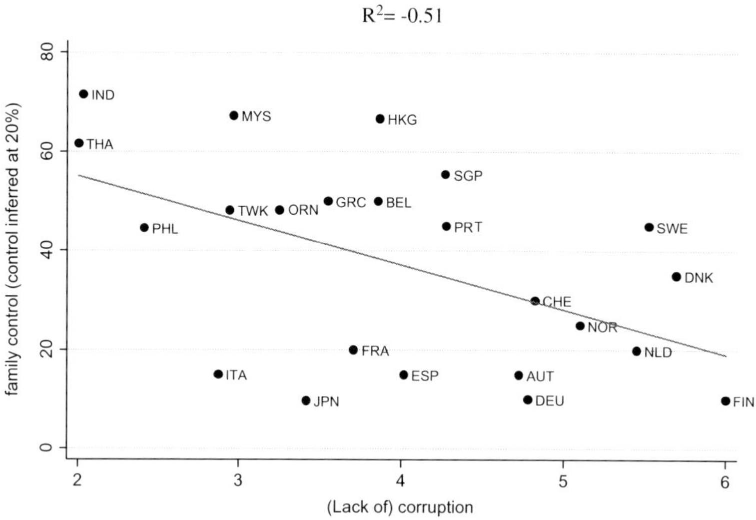

(a) *Relationship-Based*

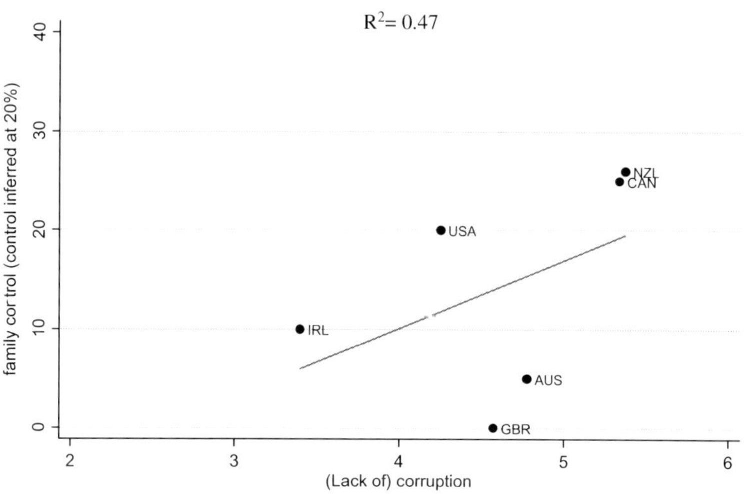

(b) *Anglo-Saxon*

Figure 12.2: Ownership concentration measured by family control (20%) and (lack of) corruption.

Sources: The data for family control are from La Porta, Lopez-de-Silanes and Shleifer (1999) and Claessens, Djankov and Lang (2000). The data for (lack of) corruption are from International Country Risk Guide (the shown index is rescaled from the original data so that a higher value indicates a lesser degree of corruption).

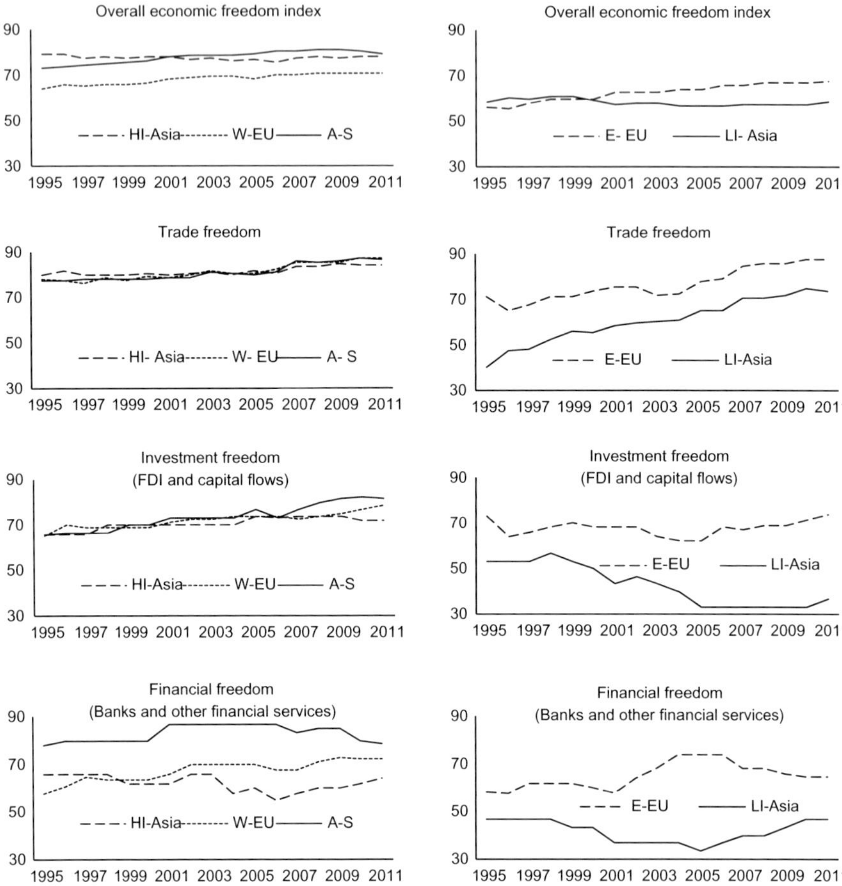

Figure 12.3: Economic, trade, investment and financial freedom index, 1995–2011, by country group.

Source: The 2011 Index of Economic Freedom, Heritage Foundation.
Note: HI-Asia = High-income Asian countries, W-EU = Continental Western European countries, A-S = Anglo-Saxon countries, LI-Asia = Low-income Asian countries, and E-EU = Central and Eastern European countries. See Table 12.2 for the list of countries in each group.

Figure 12.3 shows that the overall economic freedom index is relatively low in Continental Western Europe in comparison with A-S countries and High-income Asian countries, while Asian lower-income countries have a lower index than European emerging economies (the top two graphs). Looking at financial freedom referring to banks and other financial services, the A-S countries stand out with the highest index. The Western European index has been increasing as a result of EU reforms and it has surpassed the index for High-income Asia since 2000 (the bottom two graphs). These data are consistent with the view that market discipline on corporate governance of the first as well as the second kind is associated with the A-S countries in particular.

High-income Asia and, more recently, Continental Western Europe have liberalized financial markets and, thereby, strengthened market financial discipline of the second kind. The ownership structures in these countries indicate that market discipline of the first kind is lacking in both these country groups, however. The lower-income Asian economies stand out as having the lowest level of financial freedom.

The Trade Freedom Index, shown in the upper middle graphs in Figure 12.3 for different country groups and in Figure 12.4 for six lower-income Asian countries in our sample, can be viewed as a measure of market discipline of the third kind. A high index Figure implies high openness to global competition in goods markets. Such openness would presumably expose weak governance systems to competition. All high-income countries in our sample have a high degree of trade freedom (the left, upper middle graph, Figure 12.3). The lower-income Asian countries have long been more protected from global

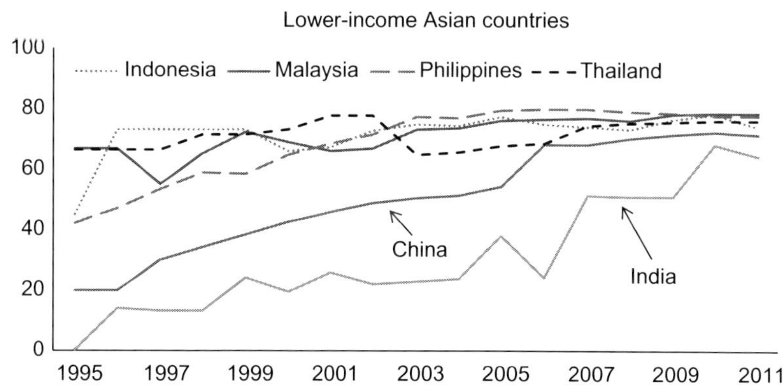

Figure 12.4: Asian Trade Freedom Index, 1995–2011, by country.
Source: The 2011 Index of Economic Freedom, Heritage Foundation.

competition. Figure 12.4 shows that this situation has been changing across the board. The trend toward increased trade freedom is present for all the lower-income Asian countries and is most pronounced for India and China. This trend may have implications for the long-run development of corporate governance systems since global competition constrains the ability of various stakeholders to extract benefits that create agency costs.

12.5 Interaction between Corporate and Political Governance: The "Manager-Entrenched", the "Social Democrat", the "Nationalist" and the "Corrupt" Corporation

In this section we begin by reviewing Roe's (2003) theory for political determinants of corporate governance. Also following Roe, we discuss the differences between the US and Western Europe. Thereafter, we apply the theory to Asian economies under assumptions about political forces in these economies. An important question is how homogeneous the countries in Asia are with respect to political preferences. It is quite possible that the differences among Asian countries are larger than the difference between any one Asian country and, say, the United States. A first distinction amongst Asian countries would be to differentiate between high-income and lower-income countries. We return to these issues.

The theory Roe (2003) develops does not explain each particular aspect of a corporate governance system but focuses on corporate objectives and corporate governance characteristics that support these objectives. Roe focuses particularly on ownership structure and the legal characteristics supporting this structure. The theory applies most directly to industrialized countries where property rights and contractual enforcement are sufficiently strong for the legal framework to have legitimacy and effectiveness.

The starting point of the theory is that political systems work to achieve social peace and respond to interest groups to reduce and resolve social conflicts. In order to achieve social peace, the political system must develop legal institutions wherein the rules are considered reasonably fair and where economic activity leads to generally acceptable outcomes. Countries may differ in terms of general attitudes and preferences with respect to, for example, income inequality, acceptance of state authority, concentration of power and wealth, self-reliance and competition.

The US and Europe; the "Manager-Entrenched" and the "Social Democrat" Corporations

The main distinction Roe makes amongst political systems is between the European "social democratic" attitudes favoring the rights and interests of those currently employed, and the American attitudes favoring ownership and the opportunity of the individual, acceptance of income inequality and distrust of collectives, big corporations, big banks and big government. For example, in the United States, big corporations have been broken up, legislation has hindered the creation of financial conglomerates, banks' close involvement with firms has been discouraged, individual ownership of stocks has been encouraged, and so on. The US political attitudes have not discouraged political and legislative involvement in the economic sphere, but the involvement often favors the "fair" treatment of the "average American" lacking first-hand information about products (liability rules) or companies (investor protection, disclosure).

Roe's thesis with respect to corporate governance is that the American political process has prevented banks from deep involvement in firms through, for example, lender's liability rules, as well as enabled and encouraged the wide dispersion of ownership through, for example, pension systems, constraints on cross-ownership and interlocking directors, and reliance on own savings to overcome potential unemployment and to finance life after retirement.

The European countries, meanwhile, have developed towards "social democracies", whether the governments have been literally social democrat or conservative, because social peace has required acceptance and even encouragement of strong unions, reliance on collective solutions to social insurance, legislation favoring "job security" and, in some countries, direct employee representation on corporate boards. At the same time, the concentration of economic power in corporations has not been discouraged. The antidote to concentrated economic power in the private sector has been nationalization, concentration of economic power in unions and direct employee influence on investment decisions. Concentrated economic power in the private sector has actually been viewed as an advantage because the government can more easily directly influence corporate decision-making when there are relatively few large units dominating economic life, and unions have a more well-defined party to negotiate with. The concentration of economic power has been allowed to exceed the concentration of wealth by means of, for example, dual-class shares and pyramid structures. Economic inequalities have been addressed through the tax system. Ownership of shares has been viewed with some suspicion since such ownership would create a conflict of interest for the employee trying to extract maximum benefits through union negotiations or government influence.

As a result of the different political attitudes in the United States and Europe, the corporate governance systems and supporting legal frameworks have developed towards the systems we have described: dispersed ownership in the United States versus relatively concentrated ownership in the social democratic Europe; weak banks with arm's-length relations to customers in the United States versus strong universal banks in Europe with direct links to corporations through ownership or board membership; financial innovations to develop competing forms of financing in the United States versus resistance by banks to the development of competing securities markets in Europe; high market capitalization and many publicly traded firms in the United States versus relatively low market capitalization and fewer publicly traded firms in Europe.

The dispersed ownership in the United States creates separation of ownership and control. To avoid agency problems from management entrenchment, the threat of hostile takeovers must be an accepted reality and/or executive compensation schemes must support shareholder wealth maximization. However, the tendency towards greater acceptance of takeover defenses has been strong during the last few decades, according to Gilson and Kraakman (2005).

Thus, the scope for the manager-entrenched corporation in the US has been increasing.

The concentration of ownership in Continental Europe may potentially prevent the agency problem associated with separation of ownership and control. The concentration of ownership may substitute for the threat of hostile takeovers in aligning shareholders' and managers' interests, but it also allows block owners to extract private benefits. There are also political pressures on the corporations to support employees' interests to a greater extent than in the United States. Thus, shareholder wealth maximization cannot be the sole objective of management; rather, this objective must be balanced with employment and job security considerations. Therefore, there is an agency problem relative to the shareholder model. This agency problem is not that management extracts literally private benefits (although this agency problem exists too as noted above), but the agency costs take the form of a tradeoff between shareholder wealth and benefits to employees in place. It is possible that the owners have accepted the agency costs associated with benefits to employees by having kept the ability to extract some private benefits for themselves.

We may call the European corporation with its mixed objectives the "social democrat corporation." Since it is inherently burdened with agency costs, markets for goods and labor must not be perfectly competitive as noted in Section 12.2. If they were highly competitive, the corporations would have to sacrifice the support of employees in place. The political process in social democracies will therefore tend to be supportive of a degree of protectionism against foreign competition as well as restrictions on competition domestically in goods and labor markets. Even if the state does not actually restrict competition, it may not resist corporate attempts to restrict competition.

The European Social Democracies are obviously not all the same. The Anglo-Saxon United Kingdom implemented a number of reforms under Margaret Thatcher undermining the power of the unions, thereby weakening the influence of employees in place. The direct influence of the state also varies considerably. France is well-known for its close relations between corporate power and state power. This close relation may create greater political acceptance of agency costs in the form of both private benefits to controlling owners and benefits to employees. The socialist influence has also been stronger in France and Italy than in, for example, Scandinavia and the United Kingdom. Relatively strong communist unions have favored direct state ownership and control in Southern Europe to a greater extent than in the Northern part. Thus, there are substantial differences in the corporate governance structures as well as in attitudes towards free trade across Europe.

The European Union has been in the process of reforming the legal foundations of corporate governance with the objective of creating systems closer to the A-S system. However, the process has been slow and has met with resistance to varying degrees among EU members. The financial crisis may put a stop to this process, and political leaders like President Sarkozy in France have expressed great satisfaction that this process comes to a halt. These developments seem consistent with the work of Morck, Wolfenzon and Yeung (2005), who describe how the groups with economic power influence the political process to sustain their own power and conserve the corporate structures. In the absence of strong public opposition to this power, the corporate governance structures are likely to change only slowly.

Asia and the "Nationalist" and "Corrupt" Corporations

What would the theory of political determinants of corporate governance predict about Asia? Can political attitudes and forces be identified which can explain and predict corporate governance in Asian countries?

There are clearly great differences among Asian countries in terms of political attitudes based on social norms and history. India is certainly different from East Asia, and the relatively high-income East Asian countries are different from the lower-income countries in the region. We would classify India as a version of the social democracies in Europe but lacking the strong legal structures of Western Europe.

The East Asian countries from Japan in the north to Indonesia and the Philippines in the south share some cultural characteristics that may explain aspects of corporate governance. For example, the acceptance of authority is relatively high whether it comes from the state or from elders, and the acceptance or appreciation of pluralism as a positive force is weak. Like most European countries, East Asian countries have had a privileged aristocracy and the acceptance of the power of the few is widespread. In communist countries like China, the party or the state has taken the role of the old aristocracy. In other countries, relatively few families have amassed wealth and economic power. As in France, these families tend to be closely associated with the state.

These observations with respect to East Asia would indicate that corporate governance systems in many ways would be similar to those in Western Europe and France in particular, but social peace may be predicated on different preferences than in Europe. Democratic traditions are weaker in most Asian countries, if not non-existent. Therefore, the objectives of the corporations need not reflect the majorities' attitudes (favoring employees in place) to the same extent as in Europe. Several Asian countries have a paternalistic tradition, however, with the implication that those with economic power and wealth have a responsibility to provide for the well-being of their employees or dependents in other ways. Social peace may also depend on these concerns. In these countries, we expect strong similarities with Europe's social democracies, although the political processes differ.

In other countries, lack of democracy and less paternalistic traditions would lead to different corporate objectives. The strong relations to the state may lead to corporations' interests becoming closely associated with nationalistic objectives of the political elite. Such objectives of "the nationalist corporation" can also gain widespread political support in countries where the reliance on authority is strong.

Nationalist objectives can vary. One could be a strong, visible presence in the global economy. Another could be mercantilist objectives in international trade. China, for example, seems to work toward both objectives, while South Korea seems to focus more on the former objective.

Whether the nationalist corporation has the objective of global recognition and market share, maximization of exports relative to imports, or employees' well-being, there are strong agency costs associated with the fulfillment of each objective. The corporations must therefore be protected to some degree from market discipline in financial markets as well as in goods markets. Hence, a degree of financial repression can be expected as well as formal or informal constraints on free trade. Financial repression as well as protectionism need not be overt. Financial innovation can be hindered by means of "moral suasion" in direct contacts between business leaders and government officials. Protectionism can take the form of preferences for domestic suppliers, costs associated with border controls of product standards, etc.

Fan (2010) describes the dominating Asian corporate governance model as characterized by family ownership and family control of management. The head of the family leading the corporation develops strong ties to the government that helps protect the interests of the corporation. Fan points out that this governance model implies strong challenges associated with succession of control from one generation to another because relationships develop over time and are partly lost in succession. Fan shows that the stock market value of Hong Kong and Singapore enterprises falls dramatically from about 60 months prior to succession to the time of succession. The average monthly accumulated stock return over this period is negative 1.2 percent in Hong Kong and negative 0.4 percent in Singapore. In Taiwan, the succession period does not affect the stock return much, however. Thus, there are great differences among Asian countries. These differences could be the result of differences in the importance of relationships of the departing family member in control, as well as of the strength and nature of the relationship between corporations and governments.

In the relatively lower-income Asian countries with weak democracies and weak legal infrastructure, the nationalist objectives and the objectives of the few powerful families are likely to be highly intertwined. These conditions create the foundations for the "corrupt corporation". The overlap between the controlling families and the politically powerful implies that the state can be used directly to serve the interests of the corporations owned by the families. The corrupt corporation may, for example, be granted monopoly in a market or rights to valuable land at low cost. The nationalist corporation may also be served by the government, but in more subtle ways through a democratic process that favors particular corporate interests.

Both the nationalist corporation and the corrupt corporation are associated with agency costs. We would expect the corrupt corporation to have particularly high agency costs and, therefore, require substantial state intervention to enable owners to extract benefits. Since the owners are often closely associated with the political powers, the main disciplinary device on the ability of owners of corrupt corporations to extract benefits would be free trade and competition. As noted above, the tendency towards greater trade openness has been strong in the lower-income Asian countries during the last decade.

We cannot predict the relative magnitude of agency costs in manager-entrenched, social democrat and nationalist corporations. The different types of corporations can coexist in a country or any particular corporation may have all three characteristics to some degree. The so-called "Corporate State" first associated with Mussolini's Italy can be thought of as a system wherein the leaders of the government, the corporations and the unions find commonality of interests and define these interests as the national interests. Italy before WWII was an extreme case, but elements of the Corporate State may exist in both European and Asian countries to different degrees. The governance rules in the Corporate State would be set in unison among the three leadership groups and have elements of both social democrat and nationalist governance.

12.6 Corporate Governance and Industrial Dynamics

If economic growth were determined by corporate governance systems alone, the systems of several Asian countries would seem to be superior or, at least, improving at a very fast rate. The evidence of fast growing Asian economies and financial systems is presented in Table 12.5 as well as in Figure 12.1. Table 12.5 reports the economic growth rates in our sample countries by decade. Both high- and lower-income Asian economies have experienced relatively high economic growth. Only the Eastern European countries in the 2000s

Table 12.5: Average real GDP growth (%), by decade.

	1980s	1990s	2000s	2010–2014 (Est.)
High-income Asia				
Hong Kong	6.5	3.6	4.0	4.7
Japan	3.8	1.5	0.7	1.9
Korea, Rep.	7.7	6.3	3.9	4.5
Singapore	7.5	7.6	3.9	6.0
Taiwan	8.2	6.5	2.5	5.5
Lower-income Asia				
China	9.7	10.0	9.7	9.7
India	5.6	5.6	6.9	8.4
Indonesia	5.7	4.3	4.9	6.6
Malaysia	5.9	7.2	4.6	5.4
Philippines	2.0	2.8	5.1	4.9
Thailand	7.2	5.3	4.0	5.0
Continental Western Europe				
Austria	1.9	2.5	1.7	1.7
Belgium	2.2	2.3	1.5	1.8
Denmark	1.9	2.4	1.0	2.1
Finland	3.5	1.6	2.2	2.0
France	2.3	1.8	1.4	1.9
Germany	1.9	2.3	0.7	2.0
Greece	0.8	1.9	3.7	0.2
Italy	2.1	1.4	0.6	1.2
Luxembourg	4.9	4.8	3.4	2.9
Netherlands	1.8	3.1	1.5	1.8
Norway	2.8	3.6	2.0	1.8
Portugal	3.7	3.4	0.8	0.9
Spain	2.7	2.8	2.7	1.4
Sweden	2.6	1.8	2.0	3.4
Switzerland	2.5	1.1	1.5	2.1
Central and Eastern Europe				
Bulgaria	3.7	–5.3	4.8	3.3
Czech Republic	2.3	–0.2	3.5	3.0
Hungary	1.5	0.2	2.9	2.4
Latvia	n/a	1.3	5.4	3.1
Lithuania	n/a	–0.7	5.3	8.6

(*Continued*)

Table 12.5: (*Continued*)

	1980s	1990s	2000s	2010–2014 (Est.)
Poland	0.1	2.7	3.7	4.0
Romania	1.6	–2.3	4.8	2.8
Slovak Republic	n/a	4.5	4.9	4.3
Slovenia	n/a	4.2	3.6	2.4
Anglo-Saxon				
Australia	3.3	3.3	2.7	3.3
Canada	3.0	2.4	2.2	2.5
Ireland	2.4	7.0	3.9	2.3
New Zealand	1.8	2.5	2.6	2.9
United Kingdom	2.4	2.2	1.9	2.3
United States	3.1	3.1	1.8	2.7
Average				
High-income Asia	6.7	5.1	3.0	4.5
Lower-income Asia	6.0	5.9	5.8	6.7
Continental Western Europe	2.5	2.4	1.8	2.0
Central and Eastern Europe	1.8	–0.7	4.4	4.1
Anglo-Saxon	2.7	3.4	2.5	2.7

Source: World Economic Outlook Database, International Monetary Fund.

have comparable growth rates. The economic growth forecast (2010–2014) also indicates that the Asian economies will keep growing at a relatively high pace.

The correlation coefficient of 0.54 between the share of family-controlled firms and average economic growth rates in the 2000s in Table 12.6 supports the argument of a positive relationship between the Asian corporate governance model and economic growth. In the same table, the correlation between the share of widely-held corporations and economic growth in the 2000s is negative (the correlation coefficients are –0.28 and –0.34 for the control thresholds of 10% and 20%, respectively).

Simple correlations can be misleading, however. Over long periods, economic growth may be associated with improvements of corporate governance systems as well as with types of system. Furthermore, economic

Table 12.6: Correlations.

	Shareholder rights	Strength of investor protection	Creditor rights	Widely held (10%)	Family control (10%)	Widely held (20%)	Family control (20%)	Private moni-toring	Corporate stability index	Corporate continuity index	Corporate survival index	U.S. Outward position/ GDP (2009)	Inward position/ GDP (2009)	Growth 2000s
Strength of investor protection	0.56	1												
Creditor rights	0.32	0.40	1											
Widely held (10%)	0.17	0.14	0.39	1										
Family control (10%)	0.02	0.08	−0.14	−0.64	1									
Widely held (20%)	0.28	0.13	0.19	0.93	−0.69	1								
Family control (20%)	0.02	0.10	−0.07	−0.64	0.94	−0.71	1							
Private monitoring	0.35	0.23	0.36	0.40	−0.33	0.34	−0.32	1						
Corporate stability index	−0.34	−0.41	0.07	0.38	−0.53	0.42	−0.54	0.01	1					
Corporate continuity index	−0.33	−0.35	−0.22	−0.17	−0.10	−0.11	−0.14	0.10	0.45	1				
Corporate survival index	−0.32	−0.36	0.10	0.20	−0.24	0.16	−0.16	−0.16	0.80	0.38	1			
U.S. Outward position/GDP (2009)	0.19	0.27	0.15	0.32	−0.14	0.20	−0.17	0.27	0.05	0.05	0.07	1		
Inward position/ GDP (2009)	−0.13	0.06	−0.15	−0.17	0.14	−0.23	0.18	−0.36	−0.05	−0.07	0.10	0.53	1	
Growth 2000s	0.06	−0.03	−0.003	−0.28	0.54	−0.34	0.54	0.15	−0.62	−0.19	−0.49	0.04	−0.20	1
Growth 2008–2010	−0.19	−0.17	−0.09	−0.25	0.46	−0.34	0.54	−0.12	−0.38	−0.25	−0.29	−0.42	−0.32	0.57

Note: Widely held of high-income Asia is from LLS. The highlighted cells indicate correlations with proxies of dynamic corporate governance variables.

growth is explained by a variety of factors that have little relationship with corporate governance systems.

In the following we consider dynamic aspects of countries' economies as evidence of efficacy of corporate governance systems. First, we follow He, Morck and Yeung (2003) and argue that effective corporate governance does not conserve inefficient industrial structures but enables change in corporate control, exit and entry of firms. We also expect that financial crises are associated with lower output costs in countries where corporate governance allows greater dynamics. He, Morck and Yeung (2003) develop three indices for lack of long-term industrial dynamics: Corporate Stability Index, Corporate Control Continuity Index and Corporation Survival Index. They provide empirical evidence that these indices are negatively related to economic growth. Table 12.7 presents the index figures for our sample of countries.

The "corporate stability index" indicates the top 10 firms' share of employment of workers in 1996 relative to the top 10 firms' share in 1975. A higher index figure indicates greater stability of employment patterns. A higher value for the "corporate control continuity index" indicates that a higher percentage of top 10 firms were controlled by the same individual or family in both years of 1976 and 1996. The "leading corporation survival index" indicates the percentage of the top 10 firms in 1975 that remained in the top 10 list in 1996.

The corporate governance characteristics presented above do not show historical developments since the 1970s, but it can be assumed that the relative position of the countries in different dimensions has remained rather stable if we do not include Central and Eastern Europe. Based on the discussion of corporate governance systems, we expect that countries with relatively strong Anglo-Saxon characteristics are more dynamic to the extent that managers are not strongly entrenched and, therefore, the stability-index numbers should be relatively low for these countries. The simple correlations in Table 12.6 show that all three stability indices are negatively correlated with shareholder rights and strength of investor protection. The picture is more ambiguous for other characteristics.

Table 12.7: Corporate sector stability indexes.

Country	Corporate stability indexes	Corporate control continuity indexes	Leading corporation survival indexes
High-income Asia			
Hong Kong	0.39	0.10	0.71
Japan	0.77	0.34	0.73
South Korea	0.50	0.42	0.38
Singapore	0.17	0.11	0.22
Taiwan	0.19	0.19	0.39
Lower-income Asia			
India	0.17	0.17	0.18
Indonesia	0.09	0.09	0.24
Malaysia	0.09	0.00	0.28
Philippines	0.24	0.14	0.26
Thailand	0.35	0.35	0.61
Continental Western Europe			
Austria	0.59	0.28	0.59
Belgium	0.26	0.09	0.41
Denmark	0.60	0.20	0.49
Finland	0.60	0.26	0.53
France	0.39	0.20	0.56
Germany	0.72	0.30	0.76
Greece	0.41	0.36	0.40
Italy	0.60	0.60	0.48
Netherlands	0.65	0.50	0.79
Norway	0.33	0.15	0.31
Portugal	0.20	0.09	0.34
Spain	0.39	0.15	0.46
Sweden	0.50	0.73	0.61
Switzerland	0.80	0.05	0.83
Anglo-Saxon			
Australia	0.49	0.12	0.67
Canada	0.37	0.11	0.25
Ireland	0.34	0.34	0.29
New Zealand	0.26	0.00	0.09
United Kingdom	0.31	0.00	0.23
United States	0.50	0.00	0.53

(*Continued*)

Table 12.7: (*Continued*)

Country	Corporate stability indexes	Corporate control continuity indexes	Leading corporation survival indexes
Average			
High-income Asia	0.41	0.23	0.49
Lower-income Asia	0.19	0.15	0.31
Continental Western Europe	0.50	0.28	0.54
Anglo-Saxon	0.38	0.10	0.34

Source: He, Morck and Yeung (2003). A higher value of the Corporate Stability Index indicates a higher percentage of the workers employed by the top 10 firms of 1996 who also worked in the top 10 firms of 1975. A higher value of the Corporate Control Continuity Index indicates a higher percentage of top 10 firms who were controlled by the same individual or family in both years of 1976 and 1996. The Leading Corporation Survival Index indicates the percentage of the top 10 firms of 1975 that remained in the top 10 list in 1996.

Table 12.8 shows the results of regressions with the three corporate stability indices as dependent variables. The independent variables in each regression are corporate governance characteristics (shareholder rights, creditor rights, share of widely-held firms or share of family-controlled firms) and freedom index data (trade, investment and financial freedom indices). The latter are expected to reduce agency costs through market discipline. The level of real GDP in 1995 is included as a control variable in each regression. Regressions are estimated using the Ordinary Least Squares (OLS) method with the robust standard errors, based on the country sample listed in Table 12.7.

The results in Table 12.8 confirm the pattern observed in simple correlations. Shareholder rights are negatively associated with all types of stability. In this sense, the A-S model seems to contribute to industrial dynamics. The creditor rights variable is insignificant in all regressions. Other results indicate that characteristics associated with the A-S model impact negatively on industrial dynamics. The share of widely-held firms is positively associated with corporate stability and insignificant in other regressions. When we substitute family control for widely-held firms, we

Table 12.8: Regression results: Indicators of industrial dynamics, corporate governance and freedom indices.

Dependent variable	Corporate stability	Control continuity	Corporate survival	Corporate stability	Control continuity	Corporate survival
Constant	0.241	0.320	0.139	0.404	0.469	0.101
	(0.369)	(0.202)	(0.752)	(0.221)	(0.111)	(0.823)
Real GDP 1995	–0.001	0.003*	0.001			
	(0.636)	(0.096)	(0.858)			
Shareholder rights	–0.111**	–0.079*	–0.074	–0.070**	–0.070*	–0.062
	(0.003)	(0.086)	(0.176)	(0.030)	(0.081)	(0.140)
Creditor rights	0.015	0.012	0.011	0.008	0.019	0.002
	(0.661)	(0.755)	(0.851)	(0.835)	(0.609)	(0.968)
Widely held 20	0.004*	0.001	0.001			
	(0.068)	(0.542)	(0.661)			
Family control 20				–0.004**	–0.002	–0.000
				(0.018)	(0.153)	(0.947)
Trade freedom	0.006	0.009**	0.006	0.005	0.008*	0.007
	(0.279)	(0.036)	(0.253)	(0.279)	(0.057)	(0.195)
Investment freedom	0.000	–0.005	0.001	–0.000	–0.004	0.000
	(0.908)	(0.153)	(0.880)	(0.978)	(0.151)	(0.970)
Financial freedom	–0.001	–0.003	0.000	–0.000	–0.004*	0.001
	(0.800)	(0.233)	(0.995)	(0.910)	(0.099)	(0.858)
Observations	28	28	28	28	28	28
F-Statistics	3.534	1.547	1.657	5.942	2.721	1.765
Prob > F	0.012	0.208	0.177	0.001	0.037	0.151
R-squared	0.470	0.276	0.231	0.460	0.318	0.218

Note: The numbers in parentheses are the p-value. *,** indicate the significance levels of 10% and 5%, respectively.

find that family control is negatively associated with corporate stability and control continuity, although the latter coefficient is not strongly significant. These results may be explained by differences in the correlations between ownership concentration and industrial dynamics in different corporate governance systems. Most of the countries in our sample have non–A-S governance systems. It is possible that ownership concentration is positively associated with industrial dynamics within the group of countries where stock markets do not play much of a role in corporate control.

Turning to the relationships between freedom indices and stability indices, we observe that trade freedom is positively associated with control continuity, in contradiction to our hypothesis with respect to the impact of third-level market discipline. Investment freedom and financial freedom are negatively associated with control continuity as expected. The other stability indices do not seem to be related to any freedom index.

Looking at average levels of stability in the different country groups, the data conform more strongly to expectations based on the discussion above. Setting lower-income Asia aside, the Anglo-Saxon countries on average show the least stability (strongest dynamics) in all three dimensions. Comparing High-income Asia and Continental Western Europe, the Asian countries appear more dynamic in terms of corporate change (corporate stability and survival) but less dynamic in terms of control continuity. These observations conform with the observation made above that the high-income Asian countries have adopted Anglo-Saxon characteristics as well as economic freedom to a greater extent than Europe.

The lower-income Asian countries actually have the least stability of top 10 corporations and survival. These countries were in an earlier stage of industrialization during the index period. We expect a relatively low level of industrial stability in less mature industrialized countries independent of corporate governance systems.

Another indicator of industrial dynamics is the degree to which firms in a country are open to foreign takeovers and ownership. As an imperfect proxy, we compare inward positions of Foreign Direct Investment (FDI) relative to GDP in Table 12.9. Although there is

Table 12.9: Inward FDI as indicator of dynamic corporate governance.

Country	Inward position/GDP (2009)
High-income Asia	
Hong Kong	n/a
Japan	3.9
South Korea	14.1
Singapore	n/a
Taiwan	n/a
Lower-income Asia	
India	13.5
Indonesia	20.1
Malaysia	n/a
Philippines	n/a
Thailand	n/a
Continental Western Europe	
Austria	74.9
Belgium	n/a
Denmark	48.5
Finland	35.4
France	39.5
Germany	29.9
Greece	12.7
Italy	18.6
Netherlands	81.8
Norway	39.9
Portugal	47.7
Spain	43.0
Sweden	74.9
Switzerland	101.2
Anglo-Saxon	
Australia	42.7
Canada	39.3
Ireland	109.7
New Zealand	55.0
United Kingdom	48.5
United States	18.9

(*Continued*)

Table 12.9: (*Continued*)

Country	Inward position/GDP (2009)
Average	
High-income Asia	9.0
Lower-income Asia	16.8
Continental Western Europe	59.3
Anglo-Saxon	52.4

Source: OECD.

substantial variation within country groups, the table shows that High-income Asian countries have substantially lower levels of FDI/GDP than Anglo-Saxon countries and Continental Europe. These data may be seen as a confirmation of the characterization of the corporate governance system as nationalistically oriented.

Finally we turn to the performance of different corporate governance systems during financial crises. Figure 12.5 plots the relationship between the output costs associated with the Asian financial crisis (measured by the accumulated GDP growth loss during 1997–1998) and the share of family-controlled firms. It shows that Asian countries with a high share of family-controlled firms experienced greater severity of the crisis. This bivariate relationship, as well as the relationship in Figure 12.2 between ownership concentration and (lack of) corruption, is consistent with arguments and findings in existing literature that the corporate governance systems in Asia are associated with a higher level of corruption and that the systems partly contributed to the crisis severity.

The Asian corporate governance model that seemed to be a weakness during the Asian financial crisis seems to have performed relatively well during the most recent crisis. Figure 12.6 shows the relationship between the extent of ownership concentration and the output costs of the recent financial crisis (measured by accumulated real GDP growth during 2008–2009). The plots for countries with relationship-oriented corporate governance (Panel A) indicate that countries with a higher share of family-controlled firms (lower share of widely-held ownership) suffered less during the recent global

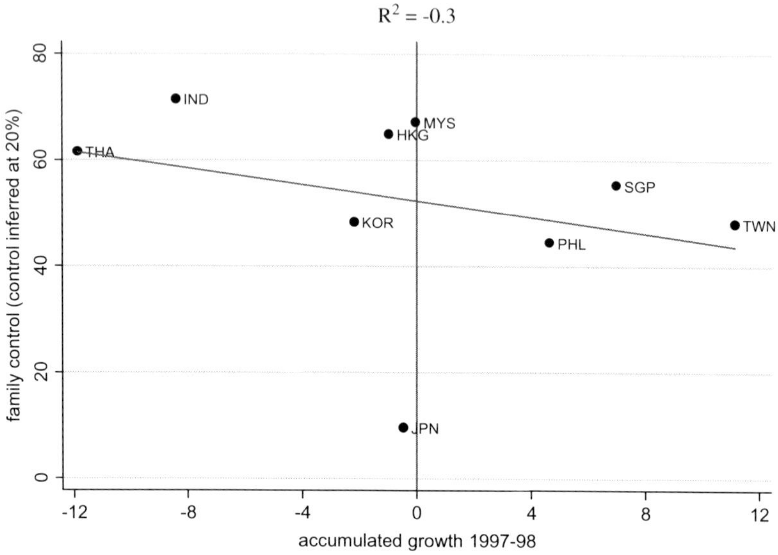

Figure 12.5: Ownership concentration and 1997–1998 crisis growth in Asian countries.

Sources: The data for family control are from La Porta, Lopez-de-Silanes and Shleifer (1999) and Claessens, Djankov and Lang (2000). The GDP growth rate data are from the World Economic Outlook Database, International Monetary Fund.

financial crisis. Among Anglo-Saxon countries in Panel B, there is no clear relationship between ownership structure and growth during the crisis years.

The bilateral relationships for the crisis episodes are possibly suggestive but must be interpreted with caution. One reason is that the relationships are simply bilateral. Another reason is that the two crisis episodes were different and originated in different countries.

12.7 Conclusions; Re-polarization and Dynamics of Corporate Governance Systems

Neither corporate governance systems nor effectiveness of corporate governance are easily characterized and measured. We have used traditional characteristics of corporate governance systems as well as

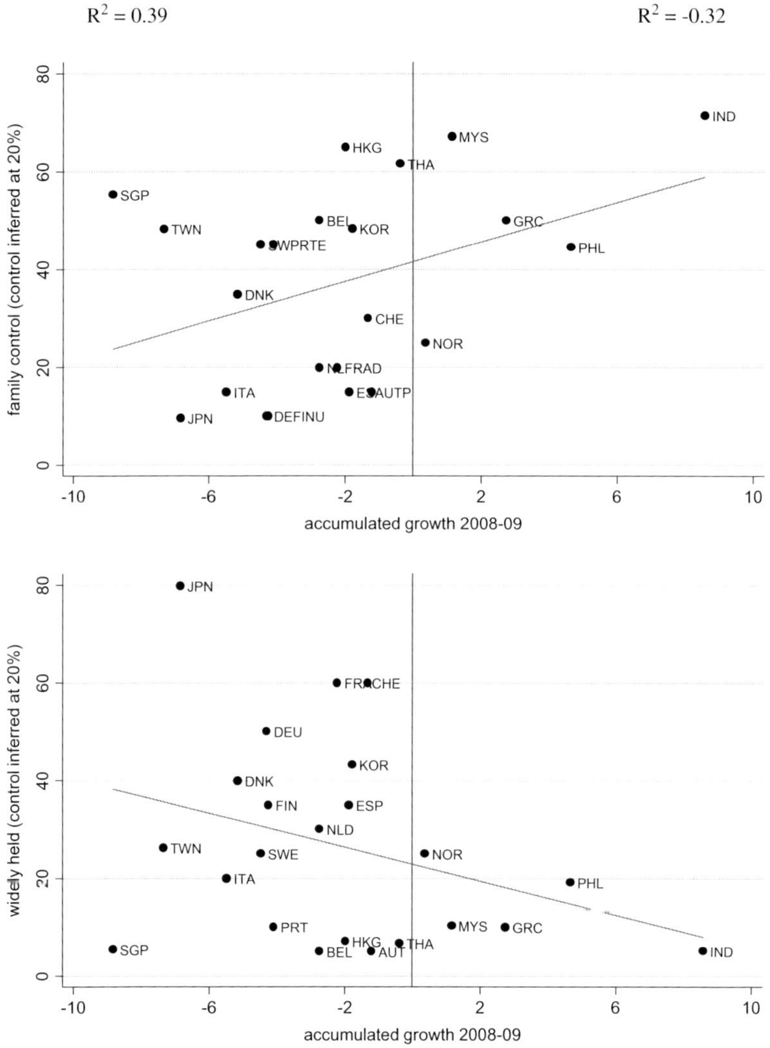

(a) *Relationship-Based*

Figure 12.6: The current financial crisis and 2008–2009 growth by country in relationship-based and A-S models.

Sources: The data for family control are from La Porta, Lopez-de-Silanes and Shleifer (1999) and Claessens, Djankov and Lang (2000). The GDP growth rate data are from the World Economic Outlook Database, International Monetary Fund.

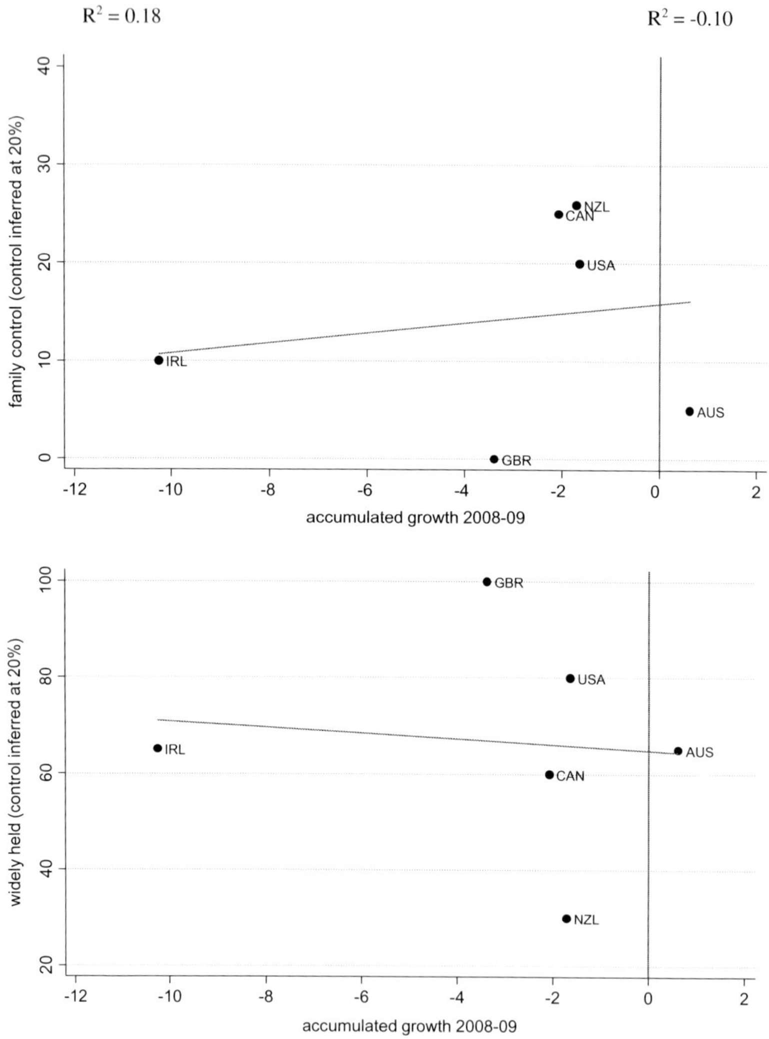

(b) *Anglo-Saxon*

Figure 12.6: (*Continued*)

characteristics based on a political economy view of corporate governance to broadly identify sources of agency costs in different systems. We have also noted that agency costs under any system are constrained by market discipline. Political influences of dominating interest groups may at the same time constrain the impact of market discipline on corporate governance systems. In the end, market and political forces in a country combine to create a set of formal and informal rules for corporate governance, with a tendency to serve the interests of groups dominating the political system. Stronger political powers of these groups and weaker market forces tend to be associated with agency costs in corporate governance.

The pure Anglo-Saxon model of corporate governance is, in theory, expected to be the least vulnerable to agency costs and, in this sense, this model serves as the benchmark for efficacy of corporate governance. However, the countries characterized as Anglo-Saxon do not conform exactly to the pure model because they are vulnerable to managerial entrenchment. Thus, agency costs arise in any system. Following Roe (2003), we characterized Continental Western European countries as "social democrat" with corporate governance systems favoring those currently employed. In the same vein, we characterized corporate governance in high-income Asian countries as "nationalist" based on the interests and values of political elites in these countries. The weak legal and political institutions of lower-income Asian countries make "corrupt corporations" possible.

Using these characterizations of corporate governance systems, we argued that countries with strong Anglo-Saxon characteristics would have relatively efficient corporate governance with relatively low agency costs. The High-income Asian countries and the Continental Western European countries would be expected to have less effective corporate governance than Anglo-Saxon countries, but more effective than countries allowing more corruption.

Re-polarization, defined as increasing economic weight of Asia relative to Europe, in particular, would in this view require continuous improvement of corporate governance systems. Increased freedom of trade and competition would contribute to this process, while politically entrenched nationalist interests would slow down the process. The data presented indicate that the Asian countries have adopted some Anglo-Saxon characteristics at a faster pace than Continental Europe.

A contrasting view is that the fast long-run economic growth of the Asian economies can be partly explained by the Asian corporate governance model which allows a long-term relationship between firms and banks and, therefore, a relatively long-term view of investment decisions. This argument also states that government support and intervention (e.g., entry restrictions) help firms and industries to achieve an extraordinarily high level of growth. In addition, a long-term, co-operative relationship between owner/management and labor helps increase the willingness of workers to work hard, accept innovative change and participate at enterprise level in proposing corporate improvement. If this view is believed by the political elites in Europe and the US, re-polarization would likely lead to imitation of Asian corporate governance in Europe and the US. The political atmosphere after the financial crisis provides fertile ground for the view that governments should adopt a more active role in shaping the industrial dynamics. It is too early to tell, however, whether the post-crisis political attitudes to economic governance will be lasting.

In evaluating the efficacy of corporate governance systems, we did not use GDP growth since growth depends on a large number of other factors. Instead, we argued that effective corporate governance models with low agency costs are associated with greater dynamics (less stability) of industrial and control structures. Thus, we expected characteristics associated with Anglo-Saxon corporate governance and stronger market influences through economic openness to contribute to stronger industrial dynamics.

The empirical evidence presented was only partially supportive of the hypotheses. It seems, however, that the stronger adoption of some Anglo-Saxon characteristics in higher-income Asian countries may have contributed to a more dynamic industrial environment than in Continental Western Europe. At the same time, the view of corporate governance as nationalistic was supported by the relatively low level of foreign direct investment relative to GDP in these countries.

If the tendency towards increased economic freedom in both Asia and Europe is allowed to continue after the financial crisis, agency costs will be constrained by market discipline. In this view, re-polarization will be associated with adoption of Anglo-Saxon governance at a faster pace in Asia than in Continental Europe. But if the backlash created by the crisis against the Anglo-Saxon model continues to last, the nationalist governance model of Asia may inspire more government involvement in industrial policy and governance based on the economic success of many Asian countries.

References

Allen, F. (2005). Corporate governance in emerging economies. *Oxford Review of Economic Policy*, 21(2), 164–177.

Barth, J. R., Caprio Jr., G. and Levine, R. (2006). *Rethinking Bank Regulation; Till Angels Govern*. Cambridge: Cambridge University Press.

Boot, W. A. and Thakor, A. V. (2000). Can relationship banking survive competition? *Journal of Finance*, 55(2), 679–713.

Carnat, L. (2004). The emerging Europe corporate governance model: Anglo-Saxon, Continental, or still the century of diversity? *Journal of European Public Policy*, 11(1), 147–166.

Claessens, S., Djankov, S. and Lang, L. H. P. (2000). The separation of ownership and control in East Asian corporations. *Journal of Financial Economics*, 58(1–2), 81–112.

Djankov, S., La Porta, R., Lopez-de-Silanes, F. and Shleifer, A. (2008). The law and economics of self-dealing. *Journal of Financial Economics*, 88(3), 430–465.

Djankov, S., McLiesh, C. and Shleifer, A. (2007). Private credit in 129 countries. *Journal of Financial Economics*, 84(2), 299–329.

Fan, J. P. H. (2010). The great succession challenge of Asian business. Keynote Speech at the Business Forum of The Australasian Finance & Banking Conference, December 15.

Gilson, R. J. and Kraakman, R. (2005). Takeovers in the boardroom: Burke versus Schumpeter. Harvard Law School, John M. Olin Center for Law, Economics, and Business, Discussion Paper No. 517

He, K., Morck, R. and Yeung, B. (2003). Corporate stability and economic growth. Frank J. Petrilli Center Research in International Finance, Working Paper, Fordham University.

La Porta, R., Lopez-de-Silanes, F., Shleifer, A. and Vishny, R. (1997). Legal determinants of external finance. *Journal of Finance*, 52(3), 1131–1150.

La Porta, R., Lopez-de-Silanes, F., Shleifer, A. and Vishny, R. (1998). Law and finance. *Journal of Political Economy*, 106(6), 1113–1155.

La Porta, R., Lopez-de-Silanes, F. and Shleifer, R. (1999). Corporate ownership around the world. *Journal of Finance*, 54(2), 471–517.

La Porta, R., Lopez-de-Silanes, F., Shleifer, A. and Vishny, R. (2000). Investor protection and corporate governance. *Journal of Financial Economics*, 58(1–2), 3–27.

Morck, R., Wolfenzon, D. and Yeung, B. (2005). Corporate governance, economic entrenchment, and growth. *Journal of Economic Literature*, 43(3), 655–720.

Porter, M. E. (1992). Capital disadvantage: America's failing capital investment system. *Harvard Business Review*, 70(5), 65–74.
Rajan, R. and Zingales, L. (2003). The great reversals: the politics of financial development in the twentieth century. *Journal of Financial Economics*, 69(1), 5–50.
Roe, M. J. (2003). *Political Determinants of Corporate Governance: Political Context, Corporate Impact.* Oxford: Oxford University Press.
Singh, A. and Zammit, A. (2006). Corporate governance, crony capitalism and economic crises: should the US business model replace the Asian way of doing business? *Corporate Governance: An International Review*, 14(4), 220–233.
Zhuang, J. (1999). Corporate governance in East Asia and some policy implications. EDRC Briefing Notes, No. 14, Economics and Development Resource Center, Asian Development Bank.

Chapter 13

EU and Vietnam: From a Parental to a Competitive Relationship?

Ari Kokko

13.1 Introduction

The relationship between the European Union and Vietnam is interesting for several reasons. Most importantly, Vietnam is a rapidly developing emerging economy that is becoming an interesting market and production location for European business, as well as a notable exporter with the European market as one of its main targets. Few developing economies have been able to match the economic performance of Vietnam; China is the only country that has clearly been able to exceed the Vietnamese growth record since the early 1990s. This change in Vietnam's development status — from one of the least developed countries 25 years ago to an emerging economy in the early 2010s — has had an inevitable effect on the relationship between the EU and Vietnam.

A quick glance at the evolution of the links between the EU and Vietnam might suggest that it illustrates the re-polarization discussed in this volume. From the early 1990s until the mid-2000s, the relationship seemed amicable — the European approach to Vietnam may even be described as "parental". The bilateral relation was mainly centered on official development assistance (ODA), with more than a dozen EU countries and the EU Commission supporting Vietnam with grants, credits, and technical assistance. Much of the support was aimed at facilitating Vietnam's internationalization — infrastructure, private sector development, and trade reform (e.g., support for Vietnam's WTO accession) were important areas of collaboration. Since the mid-2000s, however, attention has turned to more contentious issues. A few of the main bilateral donors have terminated or are planning to terminate their bilateral ODA programs in Vietnam. For example, in the case of Sweden, this has partly been as a form of protest against Vietnam's lack of progress in human rights and democracy. Increasing friction has been noted also in the economic area. A number of highly publicized EU anti-dumping cases have restricted the ability of Vietnamese firms to penetrate the EU market. Leather shoes, bicycles, and fluorescent lamps are examples of Vietnamese export products that have allegedly been "dumped" on the European market, according to the EU Commission. It appears that the parental relationship has been replaced by a more competitive one, in line with the re-polarization theme of this volume.

The purpose of this chapter is to examine how this changing relationship between the EU and Vietnam should be understood. Is it a shift from a "parental" to a "competitive" relationship? Or will it be possible to maintain a development-oriented relationship even in a more polarized world economy? Section 13.2 below provides a background by briefly describing Vietnam's macroeconomic development during the past two decades. Section 13.3 looks at the aid relationship. One of the arguments presented in this section is that the bilateral relationship was never a "parental" one, largely because of Vietnam's historical experiences from the aid relationship with the Soviet Union. Instead, there was substantial tension between the donor community and Vietnam during most of the period after Western aid re-commenced in the early 1990s. Section 13.4 turns to the trade relationship. It begins by outlining Vietnam's trade policy environment before 2007, and continues with a discussion of how it has changed as a result of WTO membership. The EU's increasing use of anti-dumping tariffs against Vietnamese exporters in recent years could be an indication of a less friendly and more competitive attitude towards Vietnam. However, we argue in this section that the anti-dumping measures used by the EU are not primarily directed at Vietnam, but rather at China. This means that Vietnam is affected by the re-polarization of the world economy through its links with China, but that the relation with the EU is perhaps not as confrontational as the increasingly frequent trade conflicts may suggest.

Section 13.5 concludes, stressing the fact that the re-polarization of the world economy forces small countries like Vietnam to navigate in a much more complex international environment than in the past. In the Vietnamese case, re-polarization has meant that the country has inadvertently been caught in the shadow of China.

13.2 The Macroeconomic Context

Vietnam's macroeconomic development during the past decades has been remarkably successful, with rapid economic growth and reasonably stable prices. Real annual GDP growth has averaged nearly 7.5 percent since 1990, with the official growth rate reaching 5.3 percent in 2009 and 6.8 percent in 2010, in spite of the global financial crisis. As a result, real per capita incomes have quadrupled over the past 20 years — nominal per capita income has grown from about $100 in 1990 to over $1,100 in 2010. After some years of high inflation following the liberalization of state-controlled prices in the mid-1980s, the inflation rate dropped to single-digit levels, and has remained at below 10 percent for most of the period since 1990. The main exception was a temporary inflation peak in 2008, when prices rose by 23 percent.

In the early 1990s, growth was fuelled by the opportunities opening up as decision-making power was decentralized and the contacts with market economies — and their multinational corporations — started growing. The domestic private sector emerged as an important actor in the late 1990s, and the number of registered private enterprises started growing rapidly after the introduction of a new enterprise law in 2000. This law was not only a sign that private enterprise had become politically acceptable, but it also simplified the complex licensing procedures that had been required to set up new private firms. As a result, the modern private sector is the most dynamic part of the Vietnamese business community today, particularly with regard to employment creation. Since the mid-2000s, growth has been fuelled mainly by high investment rates — more than one-third of GDP is devoted to investment — and rapid export expansion. Vietnam's export volume nearly quintupled between

Table 13.1: Macroeconomic development in Vietnam (1990–2010).

	1990	1995	2000	2005	2010
GDP (billion $)	6	21	31	53	105
Real GDP growth (%)	5.1	9.5	6.8	8.4	6.8
GDP per capita ($)	98	288	402	635	1220
Inflation rate (GDP deflator)	72.8	17.0	3.4	8.0	11.8
Merchandise exports (billion $)	2.4	5.4	14.5	32.7	72.2
Merchandise imports (billion $)	2.7	8.2	15.6	37.8	79.3
Current account (% of GDP)	–4.0	–8.3	3.6	–1.5	–3.8
External debt (% of GDP)	359.6	122.6	41.1	36.2	42.5
GDP composition by economic sector (% of GDP)					
Agriculture	38.7	27.2	24.5	20.9	21.3*
Industry and construction	22.7	28.8	36.7	39.5	40.0*
Services	38.6	44.0	38.8	38.0	38.7*
GDP composition by ownership (% of GDP)					
State	31.7	40.2	38.5	38.4	35.1*
Non-state	63.0	53.5	48.2	45.6	46.5*
FDI	5.3	6.3	13.3	16.0	18.4*
Structure of investment by ownership (% of total investment)					
State investment	34.2	38.3	58.2	51.5	40.6*
Non-state investment	33.7	29.4	19.4	32.2	33.9*
FDI	32.1	32.3	22.4	16.3	25.5*

Note: * Data for 2009; Data for 2010 are estimates.
Sources: EAEP (2006); CIEM (2006); World Bank Databank, http://data.worldbank.org/country/vietnam.

2000 and 2010, and exports amounted to about 70 percent of GDP by 2010. Table 13.1 summarizes the data on these achievements, together with some additional information about the structure of the Vietnamese economy.

Foreign investors have been important for both investment and export growth since the mid-1990s. The inflows of FDI grew rapidly from around 1993, and the annual FDI inflows amounted to $1.5–$2.5 billion by 2007, with an increase to over $6 billion per year during the period 2008–2010. Foreign-invested enterprises accounted for nearly one-fifth of GDP, nearly one-third of total investment, and more than half of total exports including crude oil (excluding crude oil, the FDI share of exports is about one-third) by 2010. Yet, the state sector still holds a dominant position in the Vietnamese economy. In fact, the state's share of GDP was larger at that time than at the beginning of the market-oriented reform process. The main reason for this paradoxical observation is that agriculture has been considered a part of the non-state sector since the abolishment of collective agriculture in the late 1980s — the productivity growth rate of the agricultural sector has been much lower than that of the manufacturing sector, where state-owned enterprises are concentrated.

It is not only in the economic sphere that Vietnam has recorded substantial improvements during the past two decades. The country's health indicators have improved substantially since the late 1980s. For instance, life expectancy at birth increased from about 65 years in 1990 to about 74 years in 2010. The total fertility rate has declined sharply over the same period, from 3.8 to below 2. Child mortality and maternal mortality rates have diminished even faster. Many vaccine-preventable diseases have also been brought under control through broad immunization programs, and the share of deaths caused by infectious disease declined from over one-half in the mid-1980s to about one-third in 1999 (MoH, 2002). Some diseases like polio and infant tetanus have been eliminated altogether (MoH, 2002; SRV, 2005).

In spite of the overall success, there are also areas where the remaining challenges are serious. Macroeconomic stability is one example. The high GDP growth rate reflects high aggregate demand, and there is a chronic risk that bottlenecks in the domestic economy will generate inflationary pressures. The situation since 2008, when the inflation rate rose above 20 percent, has revealed some of the weaknesses in this area. It would have been hard for Vietnamese authorities to reduce inflation without a significant reduction in the growth rate even under "normal" circumstances, but the onset of the global financial crisis made it even more difficult to find an appropriate balance between price stability and growth. The contractionary policies that were introduced to reduce inflation coincided with the fall in export demand brought about by the financial crisis, and the policy stance was therefore quickly reversed: both monetary and fiscal policy became expansionary in late 2008. However, Vietnamese authorities did not respond equally quickly to the recovery in global demand that started in 2009, and chose instead to maintain a relatively loose monetary policy through 2010. The result was a relapse into high inflation, which necessitated a sizable devaluation of the currency in early 2011.

The continuing dominance of the state sector is another challenge. Although the state sector controls much of the country's investment resources, there are worries that the investments are not efficient. The direct employment generated through state investment is small — the total employment in the state sector amounts to about 10 percent of the labor force and has barely increased over the past decade — and complaints about problems at all stages in the public investment process, ranging from planning to implementation, have been common (CIEM, 2006). One of the long-term responses to these weaknesses is the *equitization* of state-owned enterprises (SOE), which is intended to establish harder budget constraints and more efficient and business-oriented management practices in the state sector. However, the annual equitization targets have systematically been missed, and there are numerous problems slowing down the process. The most important ones appear to be resistance from SOE managers, problems regarding the valuation of state assets, and legal uncertainties connected to the restructuring and equitization of the largest government conglomerates, the so-called General Corporations. To maintain high growth rates, it will be necessary to accelerate the pace of SOE reform in the coming years.

Yet another potential problem is related to the country's external balance. In spite of the high export growth rates, Vietnam's merchandise trade balance recorded deficits of 13–15 percent of GDP in 2007–2009. Adding other current account transactions (services and transfers, e.g., overseas remittances and ODA), the deficit was reduced to about 8–9 percent of GDP (with lower deficits in 2010 because of the financial crisis, as shown in Table 13.1). While Vietnam does not appear to have any problems in covering this deficit in the short run — the inflows of FDI and foreign credits are normally more than sufficient to cover the current account balance, and external debt is not alarmingly high — it is essential that the import surplus is used to raise the country's long-term competitiveness. The concerns in this area are related to the efficiency of investment, including state investment. Much of the trade deficit is probably connected to investments in SOEs and public infrastructure, which could be expected to raise future production capacity. However, this expectation assumes that the investment resources are used for projects that yield a sufficiently high social return. For investments in state-owned industry, a key question is whether enterprises will be able to survive in the more competitive climate that can be expected as Vietnam's trade barriers are gradually reduced in the future. The fact that the capital inflows to Vietnam have been high throughout the period 2008–2010 — easily comparable to those in China on a per capita basis — does not reduce these concerns. On the contrary, the availability of large amounts of capital makes it important to invest available funds efficiently, since there are often important lock-in effects of investments. Once large amounts of funds are committed to specific projects, they create interest groups that benefit from these investments and that are likely to try to maintain *status quo* even when it would be socially beneficial to change the direction of policies. Some of the difficulties in the negotiations over Vietnam's WTO membership prior to 2007 were probably caused by investment decisions made in the state sector in the mid-1990s: much investment was targeted at sectors where Vietnamese producers were competitive only thanks to protection from imports (see Kokko, 1997).

The emerging income and welfare gaps in Vietnam make up a further policy challenge. Although the overall growth performance of the economy has been laudable — and although Vietnam has managed to cut the incidence of poverty by more than half since the late 1980s — there are worries about the distribution of income and wealth. High economic growth is a strong priority for the Vietnamese leadership, for several reasons. A high economic growth rate provides some degree of legitimacy to Vietnam's one-party Communist rule; it may be argued that alternative political systems might be less efficient, consuming more resources in the political struggle between parties and interest groups and leaving less for productive investments. Even more importantly, a high growth rate is considered as a precondition for social stability. Given that initial wealth, human skills, and opportunities are not perfectly equally distributed in any society, and that economic development is a process where relative prices are in constant change, it can be argued that a certain minimum growth rate is necessary to ensure that all (or almost all) social groups benefit from economic development. Growth rates lower than this minimum might leave some groups worse off, which would cause discontent and might result in political protests and opposition against a system that is not perceived as "fair", hence the need to generate sufficiently high growth. However, it is clear that income inequality has been rising in Vietnam as a result of the economic reform process (see, e.g., Glewwe *et al.*, 2004). This is true in both a geographical and a social dimension — some regions are growing substantially faster than others, at the same time as some social groups fare much better than others. Geographically, growth is concentrated in Vietnam's two urban centers: Hanoi and Ho Chi Minh City. The so-called *socialization* of health and education (which actually entails moving a larger part of the financing burden from the state budget to the users of the services, i.e., the relevant social groups) is an example of a policy that may have contributed to increasing social gaps (Kokko and Tingvall, 2008). There is no doubt that some of these gaps will need to be addressed by policymakers to ensure continued smooth macroeconomic development.

13.3 Relations with the EU: Development Assistance

In spite of Vietnam's rapid development during the past two decades, it remains a relatively small and poor economy. The country's nominal GDP in 2010 was only $105 billion, which is comparable to the purchasing power of a medium-sized European city like Stockholm or Copenhagen. Adding the long distance between Vietnam and Europe, it is not surprising that the economic relations between the two regions have been of limited importance for both parties. Vietnam has not been an important market for European firms, and Europe's foreign direct investment in Vietnam has been small compared to that of regional investors like Japan, Malaysia, Singapore, and Taiwan. Nevertheless, the political relations between the EU and Vietnam have been remarkably strong. The historical colonial links between France and Vietnam, coupled with the contacts established during the 1970s and 1980s between Vietnam and several Eastern and Central European countries (within the framework of the COMECON) as well as the (Northern) European political support to Vietnam during the American War, have all contributed to various kinds of interactions and contacts. A large part of these relations have been centered on ODA.

It is not only the EU that provides aid to Vietnam; in fact, Vietnam has become one of the favorite aid recipients of many multilateral and bilateral donors over the past decade. During the period 2005–2008, it was among the world's four largest recipients of ODA together with Iraq, Afghanistan, and Ethiopia. Many countries that receive substantial amounts of aid have developed more or less "parental" relationships with their donors. The implicit assumption is often that the donor has superior knowledge of policy making and macroeconomic management, and that the recipient should follow the policy advice provided by the donors. Often, aid disbursements have even been conditional on specific reforms — the aid programs have essentially been "owned" by the donor community. However, this has not been the case in Vietnam.

Aside from its good economic performance — donors are pleased to see progress in economic development and poverty reduction — Vietnam is popular because it is perceived as a "good" aid recipient. In fact, Vietnam is sometimes identified as the "best practice" example of ODA management and recipient ownership of the development agenda (Forsberg, 2007; GRIPS, 2002; UNDP, 1996). Over the past few years, most donors have accepted the priorities and objectives defined by the Vietnamese government and have aligned their activities with the official development strategy (Jacquemin and Bainbridge, 2005).

Vietnam's strong ownership and the present framework for ODA management are largely based on experiences from the 1970s and 1980s, when the country became heavily dependent on the Soviet Union. Since that time, Vietnam has been careful to avoid similar dependency in the relations with other foreign countries — a prime rule for engagement with foreign countries has been to preserve the autonomy of the nation.

The economic sanctions that were introduced by the West and many Asian countries after the Vietnamese decision to send troops to Cambodia in 1978 led to the withdrawal of most of the ODA that had started to flow into the country after the end of the Vietnam War in 1975. Sweden, Finland, and the UNDP were the only Western donors that continued to support Vietnam, albeit at a small scale. Thus, Vietnam was forced to move closer to the Soviet Union and the European communist bloc for external assistance and trade relations. Throughout the 1980s, when the weaknesses in the centrally planned economy resulted in stagnation and macroeconomic instability, the Vietnamese economy survived primarily thanks to Soviet aid. According to Pike (1987), at its peak in the mid-1980s, Soviet aid made up about 10 percent of GDP and covered more than 40 percent of the government budget and 75 percent of total public investment. At the same time, the share of trade with the Soviet Union reached about 70 percent of Vietnam's total foreign trade. The support from Sweden, Finland, and the UNDP is estimated to have reached only about one-tenth of what was provided by the Soviet bloc.

The reliance on aid from the Soviet bloc forced Vietnam to implement a political agenda — both domestically and internationally — that was largely outlined by the Soviet Union. However, the substantial aid flows did not contribute much to Vietnam's ability to create a sustainable foundation for economic development. The disintegration of the Soviet Union at the end of the 1980s, which ended the aid inflows from the Communist bloc, therefore had a severe impact on the country. The economy stagnated at the same time as inflation accelerated. One particularly troublesome consequence was a fall in food production — although few people suffered from starvation, it is clear that a majority of the population was below the food poverty line. These circumstances eventually led to the introduction of the market-oriented reform package that became known as *Doi Moi*. Together with the withdrawal of Vietnamese troops from Cambodia in 1989, the reforms contributed to the return of aid from Western countries a few years later. The government quickly facilitated the normalization of relationships with major donors and introduced aid as an important external resource for the ongoing reform process.

Yet, the relations with donors were managed very cautiously. The Vietnamese strategy aimed to avoid too much dependency on one power, and the government also hesitated to deal with donors as a unified bloc. This caution remained for a long time after the *Doi Moi* reforms, in order to avoid the risk that foreign assistance could be used to influence Vietnam's domestic affairs. The principles laid down by the Politburo stated that the relations with external actors should contribute to "self-determined integration, bringing into play the nation's internal forces and taking most advantage of integration in order to strengthen effectiveness of international cooperation, ensuring independence and ownership as well as national interests" (Communist Party of Vietnam, 2001). Consequently, the government has generally resisted development projects where a donor's policies and aid disbursements are tied to strong political or economic conditions. Strong autonomy and ownership of ODA policies have been maintained to avoid aid dependency.

Another explanation for the strong sense of recipient ownership is that many donors represented in Vietnam in the early 2010s arrived after the market-oriented reforms were initiated by the Vietnamese leadership. This is important for Vietnam's relations to donors, since it is clear that foreign aid was not the initial driver of the economic advances that have taken place over the past two decades. Moreover, the reforms resulted in rapid economic development that enabled Vietnam to avoid taking on substantial amounts of foreign debt. Taken together, these factors have strengthened Vietnam's bargaining position, making Vietnam different from many other aid recipients and their relations to donors: the Vietnamese government controls its agenda to a higher degree. Donor support remains strong, with annual aid flows increasing from a few hundred million dollars in 1990 to over

$2.5 billion per year since 2007. Japan, ADB, and the World Bank have accounted for 70–75 percent of total aid inflows during the past decade, with the EU contributing most of the remainder.

Although the purely financial aspects of foreign aid have been important for Vietnam, it is important to note that the donor community plays a more important role than just financing Vietnamese development. Over time, donors have become important policy dialogue partners and have influenced Vietnamese policy-making in various ways (UNDP, 2005). This is also the area where the EU has made the biggest impact on Vietnam. As we will argue below, the EU has probably been more important as a catalyst for institutional change than what is reflected by its financial contributions to Vietnamese development.

Institutional Design: ODA in a Centrally Planned Economy

Given Vietnam's political and historical heritage, it is not surprising that the Vietnamese government has aimed to maintain strong central control of its development agenda, even after the introduction of market-oriented reforms in the business sphere. In the area of development cooperation, central planning has until recently been the fundamental tool of the government to manage and regulate socio-economic policy and development. The Ministry of Planning and Investment (MPI) was at the center of the country's institutional framework for development planning. MPI drafted and formulated the overall national development strategies and short-term plans, and was responsible for the management of public investment and resource allocation. Its main task was to manage the government's development priorities and to balance stakeholder interests between sectoral and regional concerns, as well as between national and international actors. The integration of ODA into the government's development programs was an important part of this task. The concentration of power within the MPI suited the central planning system, but was also a wish from donors, especially multilateral donors such as UNDP and the WB.

In practice, the integration of ODA and government preferences was handled using Vietnam's national development plans as instruments. Based on the socio-economic development plan and the 5-Year Public Investment Programs (PIP) (both of which were drafted by MPI), MPI prepared a priority list of national projects calling for ODA investment during the current five-year planning period. This priority list was, in principle, a "menu" that donors could use for selecting development projects. It was clear that all donor projects were expected to conform to the framework outlined by Vietnam's development plans. The resulting structure for ODA management had three main characteristics:

(i) The state regulated not only domestic development planning, but also the allocation of aid and the relations with donors. The central position of MPI was instrumental in creating strong ownership. If donor and aid management had been outside the body responsible for national economic planning, it would have been more difficult to align aid flows with Vietnamese development priorities. In addition, donors were given a window for policy dialogues, making it possible for donors to have some impact on national development planning.

(ii) MPI was mainly responsible for the coordination and management of loan aid, which has constituted 60–70 percent of total ODA in financial terms from 1996 (UNDP, 2005). This arguably gave more influence to donors like the WB and Japan, who accounted for most of the loan aid to Vietnam. Smaller bilateral donors, who provided more technical assistance and grant aid projects, were in a weaker position to influence Vietnamese development policy. They participated in the top-level dialogue, e.g., as contributors to multilateral credit packages, but most of their direct contacts were with sectoral and provincial authorities. Heads of line ministries and provincial people committees were only entitled to approve smaller technical projects.

(iii) The incentives and capacity of line ministries and provincial agencies were formally constrained by the centralization of power to the MPI. Overall, the government exercised a system in which it planned, steered and controlled local governments through the provision of public services and infrastructure, including those investments that were financed by ODA. Aid was a strongly politicized process, where provinces had to turn to Hanoi in order to convince MPI that their development projects were of higher priority than others, and that they should be included in the priority lists presented to donors (Dapice, 2002).

Did ODA Undermine Central Planning?

Although the institutional set-up concentrated power in the hands of MPI, it turned out to be difficult to maintain central control of ODA in an environment undergoing rapid structural change. Instead, the general framework for development planning and the role of MPI have slowly begun to change in recent years. The centralization of power to the center not only constrained the dynamism of provincial development and the economic autonomy and accountability of local authorities, but it also created other problems. For example, the dominance of MPI created a strong bias towards physical investment and economic growth, with much less attention paid to social issues and "pro-poor" expenditures than what most donors desired. Among the donors, it was mainly the World Bank, the Asian Development Bank, and Japan that collaborated directly with MPI. These donors were the largest creditors to Vietnam, and they also had a strong focus on infrastructure and other investments that were relatively easy to adapt to the Vietnamese central plan. The European Union's aid portfolio was divided between the EU Commission and a dozen bilateral donor agencies, each of them with their own specific development agenda. Although the EU provided some loans for infrastructure development, the emphasis was on "softer" issues, and there was a preference for technical assistance and institutional support rather than investment credits. These projects were more difficult to administer as part of the central planning system. Some decentralization was therefore allowed, so that donors and various domestic actors (mainly provincial authorities and line ministries) could agree about smaller aid projects without the need for MPI approval.

The emphasis on growth and infrastructure was very obvious in the investment programs undertaken during the 1990s. "Modernization and industrialization" were the main objectives of the 5- and 10-year plans, and a large share of available resources was invested to create the infrastructure needed for economic growth. During the first half of the 1990s, the focus was on water and sanitation; during the second half of the decade it shifted to energy; and after 2000, priority was given to transportation. Social issues had lower priority, and were handled through various national programs that targeted the poor mountainous areas in the northern and central parts of the country. Yet, the bulk of resources, including the ODA funds, were deployed in regions that were already relatively wealthy, since it was expected that the growth effects would be larger there.

Over the past decade, two processes have contributed to change the form and content of Vietnamese central planning. One is related to the increasing bargaining power of provincial authorities regarding the use of ODA. In the same way that European regions discovered that contact with Brussels could strengthen their bargaining positions in negotiations with national authorities, Vietnamese provinces recognized that cooperation with EU (and other) donors could strengthen their bargaining power with respect to the MPI and Hanoi. Instead of waiting for MPI to add their favorite project to the list of prioritized ODA projects, provinces could first elicit funding (or at least commitments) from donors, and then turn to MPI to get the projects formally approved in the central plan. These practices turned out to complicate central planning, since many ODA projects require counterpart funding from the national budget. ODA could no longer be seen as a resource that was generated by the center and then distributed across the country, according to the priorities in the central plan. Instead, it was necessary to get advance information about what donors and provincial authorities were discussing and to assess the possible consequences of these negotiations for public expenditure before the central plan could be finalized.

It can be argued that the EU played a particularly important role in this process. Unlike Japan, ADB, and the World Bank, which operate large centralized programs where concessional credits are the main form of aid, the EU carries out many small projects in different sectors and provinces, relying much more on technical assistance and support for institution-building. In recent years, the aggregate EU portfolio has included 15 bilateral donors as well as the EU Commission, each with a variety of projects with different objectives and targets. The effects of each individual aid project have probably been small, although it is impossible to assess what their aggregate impact on Vietnamese development has been. However, at the macro level, it is clear that the aid relationship with the EU has had a very important impact on Vietnam. The fragmentation of EU aid has actually contributed to transforming Vietnamese central planning towards a more consultative process whereby provincial authorities and other interest groups have been strengthened at the expense of MPI. If the EU had acted in a more coordinated manner, pooling its resources into fewer but larger projects, it is likely that MPI would have taken a more direct role in the implementation of these projects. In that case, European ODA would instead have strengthened MPI's (and the central government's) ability to uphold central planning.

The other process is related to the increasing emphasis on poverty alleviation among donors. Since the late 1990s, the donor community has shifted its focus from demands for structural adjustment to calls for poverty reduction, with particular emphasis on health care, education, and social sectors. The aggregate Vietnamese response to the tendency towards decentralization described above and the stress on poverty reduction has been the introduction of a special planning document that summarizes the new strategies in this field — the Comprehensive Poverty Reduction and Growth Strategy (CPRGS). This document can be said to have three roles. Firstly, it presents a summary of Vietnam's overall development strategy. A large part of ODA is made up of credits and budget support, which basically contribute to all expenditure categories in the Vietnamese government budget. Budget support is fungible by nature, and it is therefore impossible to identify exactly which expenditure items it finances. Therefore, donors need a comprehensive summary of all areas that are influenced by ODA. Secondly, CPRGS functions as a more concrete and detailed plan for domestic development than the relatively abstract 5- and 10-year plans. This provides incentives for local development initiatives, since it improves the ability of provincial and local authorities to develop plans that are consistent with the policies of the central government. Thirdly, it makes it easier for donors to align their ODA programs with the national development plan in areas other than infrastructure and physical investment.

The process for formulating the CPRGS is also different from the standards used to develop the old central plans. Instead of only expressing the objectives of the central government, the CPRGS is a consensus document that is discussed at a large number of seminars in different parts of the country. Various interest groups, including the donor community, are allowed to present their views and argue for their specific causes. Since the CPRGS has become an integral part of the general 5-year plan, it can be argued that the whole planning process has been changed in the direction of increasing participation from civil society. Even though there is still an ambition to plan the future, there has been a shift in focus from inputs and investments to targets, objectives, and priorities.

What, then, were the priorities during the first decade of the 21st century? In its introductory remarks, the CPRGS states eight broad objectives for the country's socio-economic development for the period up to 2010 (SRV, 2003). These are to:

(i) Promote rapid and sustainable economic growth coupled with attainment of social progress and equity;
(ii) Create an equal business environment for all types of enterprises from all economic sectors;
(iii) Continue with structural reforms to bring about a transformation of the nation's economic structure. This objective includes further integration with the international economy and strengthening the competitiveness of Vietnamese industries;
(iv) Provide poor households with opportunities to raise their income by accelerating broad-based growth of agriculture, industry, and services;
(v) Encourage human development and reduce inequality;

(vi) Solve the particular problems of urban poverty with regard to employment, income, and housing;
(vii) Develop and expand social protection and safety nets for the poor; and
(viii) Undertake public administration reform.

In comparison with earlier strategy documents, there is clearly a stronger emphasis on equity and social issues, although economic growth remains the prime objective. Just a few years after the introduction of the CPRGS, it is possible to discern some changes in the pattern of ODA utilization. In particular, there has been a reduction in the share of large-scale infrastructure and an increase in the share of funds directed directly to provinces. Provincial authorities have been given permission to negotiate directly with foreign donors, instead of using MPI as a middleman. Policy and institutional support have emerged as the most important forms of aid. Pro-poor spending, including projects focusing on education, health, and area development, has also increased.

Effects of European ODA

The most important conclusion regarding the impact of European development cooperation with Vietnam is arguably related to the changes in Vietnamese central planning. It is difficult to identify the precise effects of the EU's various aid projects on growth and poverty reduction in Vietnam, but it is obvious that the fragmented nature of EU aid has influenced power relations in Vietnamese society. Instead of channeling all ODA through MPI and the central government, individual EU members have sought out local partners and established collaboration with various interest groups throughout the country. This has strengthened the capacity of provinces and line ministries and increased their bargaining power with respect to MPI, which has necessitated changes in the planning process. Instead of a centrally controlled process where resources are distributed to various actors according to the intentions of the central planner, economic planning has began to transform into a consultative process that includes large parts of society, including the donor community. In the long run, assuming that demands for democratization and human rights will grow stronger over time, this may well be the most important effect of EU aid in Vietnam.

This unintended consequence of aid fragmentation may be a reason to think carefully about what is the optimal degree of aid coordination in countries with authoritarian political regimes. The donor community has for several years stressed the need for stronger aid coordination, and it has also been included as a major objective, e.g., in the 2005 Paris Declaration on Aid Effectiveness. However, we now know that stronger coordination of EU development assistance in Vietnam would likely have strengthened MPI and the central government, and delayed the necessary reforms of the planning system. It would have allowed Vietnamese authorities to exercise stronger ownership of EU-financed aid projects (which is also a major objective of the Paris Declaration) and might even have resulted in higher aid efficiency, at least as defined by the Vietnamese government's objectives. It is not obvious that this type of development would have been better than what has been achieved with the more fragmented ODA approach of the European Union.

13.4 Relations with the EU: Trade and Trade Policy

Trade and trade policy are two areas where Vietnam has seen dramatic changes since the introduction of market-oriented reforms in the late 1980s. The volumes of imports and exports have increased more than twenty-fold since 1990, with the ratio of trade to GDP exceeding 130 percent since 2005. This development is explained mainly by policy changes undertaken unilaterally by Vietnam. The market-oriented reforms introduced in the late 1980s gradually resulted in a shift from import substitution towards an increasingly export-oriented development strategy. The import regime has been cautiously liberalized, with a reduction in the general level of protection and increasing reliance on tariffs rather than quotas, temporary import restrictions, and other discretionary policy interventions.

The donor community has supported both of these policy changes, and several of the largest donors — including the European Union and many of the individual EU countries — have included trade reform as an explicit target in their country strategies for Vietnam. Much of the support for policy reform before 2007 focused on Vietnam's application for WTO membership, although a substantial share of the ODA in infrastructure, industry, and agriculture can also be interpreted as support for internationalization.

Vietnam's trade performance has, of course, also been affected by the policies of its trade partners — foreign market access is essential to achieve export success. The most significant event in this area was arguably the lifting of the US trade embargo in 1994. This facilitated a rapid increase in international trade with many countries that had earlier been hesitant to break the embargo, and made it possible for the World Bank and IMF to establish their aid and policy support programs in Vietnam. However, market access remained a problem even after the lifting of the embargo. Not being a member of the WTO until 2007, Vietnam was not guaranteed Most Favored Nation (MFN) treatment, and was therefore forced to negotiate bilateral or regional trade agreements with its trade partners to ensure predictable market conditions. As shown in Table 13.2, by the end of 2004, Vietnam had signed a total of 57 bilateral agreements covering most of its trade relations, including the ASEAN Free Trade Agreement and bilateral agreements with the US, Japan, and the EU. The need for bilateral trade agreements has diminished since Vietnam's accession to the WTO, as it guarantees MFN treatment in all other member countries.

Table 13.2: Number of bilateral and multilateral trade agreements.

	Asia	Africa	Europe	America	Total
Before 1990	1	5	0	0	6
1990–1995	11	2	6	1	20
1995–2000	7	2	3	3	15
2000–2004	4	8	3	1	16
Total	23	17	12	5	57

Source: Ministry of Trade, Vietnam.

Vietnam and the EU established diplomatic relations in 1990, after the Vietnamese withdrawal of troops from Cambodia, and a series of trade agreements have followed since then. An agreement on trade in textiles (connected to the MFA) was signed in 1992, a more comprehensive framework agreement on trade and economic cooperation was established in 1995, and this trade agreement was revised in 2004 when Vietnam and the EU completed the bilateral negotiations related to Vietnam's WTO membership application. The agreement granted EU members MFN treatment in the Vietnamese market, while Vietnam was given access to EU's GSP tariffs, which are often substantially lower than MFN tariffs.[1] The European GSP tariffs are classified into four categories, depending on how sensitive the products are considered to be. For the most sensitive items in the GSP list, including mainly agricultural products, the preferential tariffs are about 15 percent lower than the MFN tariffs, leaving substantial trade barriers protecting European producers. In particular, the escalation of tariffs leaves high levels of protection for processed food products, making it difficult for developing countries to move into higher value-added activities. For less sensitive products, mainly manufacturing products, GSP tariffs are lower, in many cases fixed at zero. These preferences have been maintained also after Vietnam's accession to the WTO.

Yet, although GSP tariffs are lower than MFN tariffs, it is hard to determine how much of a competitive advantage they provide for Vietnam. Firstly, the EU's average MFN tariffs are already low, at 3–4 percent for manufacturing products, which leaves little room for preferences. Secondly, almost all countries have more favorable access to the EU market than what is provided by the MFN rules. A few years ago, the US, Canada, Japan, Australia and New Zealand were the only countries that had MFN treatment in the EU market; in the last couple of years, however, this list has been extended to include Hong Kong and China, Singapore, Taiwan, and South Korea, who have graduated from the GSP system. Thirdly, African, Caribbean,

[1] The Generalized System of Preferences (GSP) lowers tariffs for exporters from developing countries. GSP tariffs are set at 50 percent of MFN tariffs.

and Pacific (ACP) countries and Least Developed Countries (LDCs) have access to even more beneficial trade rules through the Cotonou Agreement and the *Everything But Arms* (EBA) Agreement. There are also rules of origin and other restrictions (such as technical standards and phytosanitary regulations) that make it difficult to fully use the preferences, particularly in the food industries. This notwithstanding, Vietnam has been very successful in penetrating the EU market, and exports to the EU grew from about $600 million in 1995 to nearly $11 billion in 2008, making the EU the top export destination next to the US.

World Trade Organization

In spite of the large number of bilateral agreements that Vietnam signed from the early 1990s to 2004, there is no doubt that the long-lasting negotiations with the WTO were at the center of the trade policy agenda for most of this period. Vietnam applied for WTO membership in January 1995, and the accession negotiations in the WTO Working Party progressed concurrently with various bilateral negotiations from 1998. Several of the bilateral agreements signed after this time, including those with the US and the EU, were actually part of the preparations for WTO membership. In the bilateral agreement signed with the US in 2001, most rules were modeled on the WTO, and a substantial share of the adjustment to the WTO was achieved simply by extending these bilateral rules to other member countries. The 2004 trade agreement with the EU was even more directly connected to the WTO, since it resulted from the bilateral negotiations in the WTO accession process.

In May 2006, Vietnam reached a bilateral "agreement-in-principle" with the US, completing the negotiations with 28 WTO Working Party members and clearing the way for a final accession bid. Vietnam formally joined WTO in early 2007. Vietnam's history as a planned economy is one reason why the accession process was slow and complex. The WTO is based on market principles and it has been difficult to integrate its rules and regulations into Vietnam's existing legal framework, which is largely obsolete. Another problem was the privileged position of SOEs, which is not consistent with rules on national treatment and non-discrimination. Yet another reason was the size of the Working Party for Vietnam's WTO negotiations. In all, 68 countries decided to take part in the negotiations, which suggests that many countries expect Vietnam to become a significant actor in the future. Many of these countries have been concerned about future competition from Vietnamese companies, arguing that safeguards against rapid Vietnamese export expansion are needed, at the same time as they have pressed for improved access to Vietnam's domestic market, particularly in the service sector. Obviously, these views were not always easy to reconcile with Vietnam's wish to reform slowly and maintain a leading role for the state. Considering Vietnam's apparent success in securing reasonably good access to the most important foreign markets through bilateral agreements, it is therefore relevant to ask why it spent so much time and effort to be accepted as a WTO member. There are at least three arguments that have appeared in the Vietnamese debate.

Firstly, even though bilateral agreements have provided good market access, they were considered as less predictable than WTO membership. In particular, bilateral agreements did not automatically adjust to the progress made in multilateral agreements. For instance, not being a WTO member, Vietnam could not automatically benefit from the abolishment of garment quotas that resulted from the termination of the WTO's Agreement on Textiles and Clothing on January 1, 2005. Most of Vietnam's important trade partners did lift the quotas on Vietnamese clothing exports as well, but this was generally done on the basis of unilateral decisions that might be reversed later on. As a WTO member, Vietnam would have been able to request the same treatment in all trade-related areas as other WTO members.

Secondly, some of Vietnam's bilateral trade agreements were subject to regular review and could be cancelled or changed because of arguments not related to trade. For instance, Vietnam did not have unconditional "normal trade relations" with the US. The Jackson–Vanik amendment of the US Trade Act of 1974 restricts trade with countries that do not fulfill US definitions of "freedom of emigration", and the US President had to grant an annual waiver for Vietnam in order to allow Vietnamese products to enter on MFN terms. With WTO membership, Vietnam gained permanent normal trade relations.

Thirdly, although many of Vietnam's bilateral agreements outlined rules for the use of trade remedies (safeguards, countervailing duties, and anti-dumping tariffs), there were seldom any rules or procedures for dispute settlement. For instance, Vietnam could not challenge US or EU decisions about anti-dumping tariffs outside the US or EU court systems. As a WTO member, Vietnam has access to WTO's dispute settlement system, where qualified expert panels make impartial assessments of complaints, with strict time schedules for the various stages of the dispute settlement process.

The general perception in Vietnam is that the need for a functioning dispute settlement system has increased over time. As long as Vietnam was a weak exporter, it did not pose any threat to local industries in foreign markets, and foreign governments could afford to provide generous rules for market access. As Vietnam has gradually grown to become a stronger competitor, however, with notable market shares in some sectors, the implementation of rules has become less generous and the need for a functioning dispute settlement system has become more obvious.

WTO accession has provided a stronger and more predictable position for Vietnam in foreign markets, but it has also required other reforms of Vietnamese trade rules. In particular, Vietnam has been forced to improve market access — the average tariffs have fallen substantially — and deepen commitments in several areas. The bilateral trade agreement with the US required that approximately 4 percent of Vietnam's tariffs would be bound, but the WTO has required binding all tariffs. Vietnam has also added new commitments regarding the use of technical barriers to trade and rules of origin; the WTO's agreement on trade in services (GATS) is more comprehensive than the BTA; there are additional provisions on trade-related intellectual property rights (TRIPS); and the agreement on agriculture calls for stronger discipline in the use of state aid and export subsidies. Moreover, Vietnam has conformed to the WTO rules for the use of trade remedies. Most of these provisions benefit Vietnamese business and consumers as well as foreign exporters. In particular, lower levels of protection, increasing transparency, and higher predictability have clearly promoted investment, growth, and development in areas where Vietnam has comparative advantages.

The accession agreement also included some safeguards that can be considered troublesome. For instance, Vietnam was forced to accept the designation as a "non-market economy" for a substantial period after accession — until 2018. This is a potential problem when any of Vietnam's trade partners decide to apply anti-dumping tariffs on Vietnamese exports. The domestic price structure in a country categorized as a "non-market economy" is assumed to be so distorted that it is impossible to use domestic prices to determine whether the country is dumping goods. Instead, the cost calculations needed to determine whether there is dumping (and how high anti-dumping tariffs should be) can be based on cost calculations from third countries. Given the relatively strong competitiveness of Vietnamese exporters in labor- and resource-based industries, it is always possible to find third countries where costs are higher than in Vietnam. In other words, Vietnam is highly vulnerable to anti-dumping accusations, and is not able to rely on WTO's dispute resolution mechanism to challenge partner countries that decide to impose anti-dumping duties on Vietnamese goods.[2]

Summarizing the development of Vietnamese trade policies and the trade policy environment in which Vietnamese exporters operate, it is safe to conclude that the changes in recent years have been conducive to development. Vietnam's own trade policies have been simplified and liberalized, which has reduced the distortions caused by the import-substituting policy that characterized the economy until the late 1990s. Foreign countries have been willing to provide market access on favorable terms, creating a potential for export-led growth. The total volume of exports has increased rapidly, and the export

[2] Several countries, including the ASEAN members, Australia, New Zealand, India and Argentina, have granted Vietnam market economy status, but the US, EU and Japan still consider the country a non-market economy.

structure has become more diversified, with a shift from primary products to manufacturing. Import capacity has also grown accordingly, allowing Vietnam to use foreign technologies and intermediate products to upgrade its production structure and accelerate the rate of industrial development. Moreover, the developments in the trade arena have been essential for creating a favorable environment for FDI since the early 2000s. Vietnam has been able to attract very substantial amounts of foreign investment, as noted in Table 13.1.

Interactions between ODA and Trade

The discussion in the previous two sections suggests that there is substantial coherence between the aid and trade policies of many of the donor countries that are active in Vietnam. The policy advice given by donors has stressed the need for trade reform, both in order to promote exports and to reduce the distortions caused by protectionism. Accordingly, ODA resources have been used directly to promote trade reform — including support for Vietnam's application for WTO membership — and indirectly to ease the costs caused by trade reform and to improve the competitiveness of Vietnamese exporters and import-competing firms.

At the same time, most donor countries have been reasonably generous in providing market access for Vietnamese exporters. Unlike most other developing countries, Vietnam did not have any automatic market access or MFN guarantees in foreign markets before its WTO accession in 2007. Instead, through their bilateral market access negotiations, Vietnam's trade partners have been able to decide what level of trade preferences they want to extend to Vietnam. In most cases, the choice has been to allow Vietnamese goods to enter on GSP terms. This relatively favorable treatment has facilitated a rapid increase in Vietnamese exports, which in turn has had a strong positive effect on Vietnamese development. The main exception is in processed agricultural products, where many export destinations remain highly protected. The access to foreign markets has made Vietnam an attractive location for efficiency-seeking FDI, facilitated various contacts that have contributed to technology transfer and learning effects, and generated hard currency earnings that have been translated into substantial import capacity.

Development over Time: From Aid Recipient to Competitor

Many of the bilateral trade relations between Vietnam and the OECD countries were established at a time when Vietnam's export capacity was low, and Vietnamese producers could not pose any threat to local firms in foreign markets. Hence, providing generous rules for market access was not very costly, but could be politically convenient, both with regard to domestic interest groups and in an international context. Over time, however, the situation has changed due to Vietnam's increasing export capacity and the diversification of Vietnam's exports. As Vietnamese firms are beginning to take advantage of the market access preferences in their partner countries, they are also beginning to cut into the market shares of local firms.

Consequently, Vietnam's increasing export competitiveness has begun to cause friction in some foreign trade relations. Most of Vietnam's bilateral trade agreements include rules for the use of trade remedies, such as safeguards and anti-dumping tariffs, and they have also been used with increasing frequency. As seen in Table 13.3, Vietnam was subject to five trade conflicts with foreign countries between 1994 and 2001, three of which resulted in the imposition of anti-dumping tariffs. Between 2002 and 2008, the frequency of trade disputes increased dramatically, with 23 new cases initiated by Vietnam's trade partners, several of them by the European Union and the US. After the onset of the global financial crisis, there has been another distinct increase in the number of anti-dumping complaints, with 14 new cases filed against Vietnam between August 2008 and March 2010.

In most of the dispute cases, Vietnam has denied dumping and argued that the low prices of its products were due to low labor costs and other sources of comparative advantage. These arguments have rarely been successful, however, and over 70 percent of the disputes have resulted in the imposition of anti-dumping tariffs on Vietnamese exporters. One reason is that Vietnam has had a weak bargaining

Table 13.3: Trade disputes (1994–2008).

No.	Year	Product	Country	Conclusion
1.	1994	Rice	Colombia	No anti-dumping tariffs applied — no harm to local rice producers shown
2.	1998	Glutamate	EU	Anti-dumping tariff of 16.8%
3.	1998	Shoes, sandals	EU	No anti-dumping tariff applied — small market share
4.	2000	Gas lighters	Poland	Anti-dumping tariff of EUR0.09/lighter
5.	2001	Garlic	Canada	Anti-dumping tariff of $1.48/kg
6.	2002	Shoes and soles	Canada	No anti-dumping tariff applied — no harm to local producers shown
7.	2002	Lighters	South Korea	Complaint withdrawn
8.	2002	Lighters	EU	Complaint withdrawn
9.	2002	Catfish	USA	Anti-dumping tariffs of 36.84%–63.88%
10.	2003	Zinc oxide	EU	Anti-dumping tariffs of 93%
11.	2003	Chains	EU	Anti-dumping tariff equal to difference between EUR325/1000 chains and price stated in the invoice
12.	2003	Shrimp	USA	Anti-dumping tariff of 4.3%–25.7%
13.	2004	Motorcycle and bicycle tubes/tyres	Turkey	Anti-dumping tariffs of 29%–49%
14.	2004	Bicycles	EU	Anti-dumping tariffs of 15.8%–34.5%
15.	2004	Steel pipes and steel goods	EU	No anti-dumping tariffs imposed
16.	2004	Stainless steel fasteners	EU	Anti-dumping tariff of 7%
17.	2004	Fluorescent lamps	EU	Anti-dumping tariff of 66.1%
18.	2004	Surfboards	Peru	Anti-dumping tariff of USD5.2/unit

(*Continued*)

Table 13.3: (*Continued*)

No.	Year	Product	Country	Conclusion
19.	2005	Leather shoes	EU	Anti-dumping tariff of 16.8% from July 2006
20.	2005	Fluorescent lamps	Arab Union	Anti-dumping tariff of USD0.32/unit
21.	2005	Bicycle spokes	Argentina	Anti-dumping tariff of 81%
22.	2006	Driving belt	Turkey	Anti-dumping tariff of USD4.55/kg
23.	2006	Fabric footwear	Peru	
24.	2007	Gas lighter	Turkey	
25.	2007	Fluorescent lamps	India	
26.	2007	CD-R	India	Anti-dumping tariff of INR3.04–3.23/unit
27.	2008	Uncovered innerspring	US	
28.	2008	Flat yarn of polyester	India	

Source: Ministry of Trade, Hanoi, personal communication; Le and Tong (2009).

position in the dispute resolution processes. Anti-dumping complaints are treated as domestic cases in the courts of Vietnam's trade partners. Prior to 2007, Vietnam's bilateral trade agreements did not include provisions for impartial dispute settlement of the kind found in the WTO. Instead, Vietnam was restricted to challenging the anti-dumping decisions of its trade partners in the courts of the partner countries, according to the specific laws of those countries.

The accession to the WTO has not resulted in any great improvement of the Vietnamese bargaining position. As noted earlier, the accession agreement defined Vietnam as a "non-market economy", which means that importing countries can claim that there is dumping as soon as Vietnamese firms charge prices that are lower than those in "comparable" market economies. For instance, the EU's decision to levy anti-dumping decisions on imports of Vietnamese leather shoes was based on cost and price comparisons with Brazilian shoe producers.[3] Similarly, the catfish and shrimp conflicts with the US were based on arguments that Vietnam's non-market economy status provided unfair advantages to Vietnamese producers.

While some industries still benefit from public support that is not compatible with fair trade arguments (e.g., shipbuilding, where the state-owned Vinashin has received substantial amounts of state-guaranteed credit on unclear terms), most private enterprises do not, and it is clear that these regulations may constitute a formidable obstacle for Vietnamese export companies in the future. The problem, from the Vietnamese perspective, is that individual private companies can be subject to anti-dumping remedies even if there is no challenge against their individual pricing decisions or business practices; instead, the grounds for anti-dumping tariffs may be that Vietnamese land prices or electricity prices are not market-determined, or that labor costs do not reflect the underlying market conditions. This is likely to have harmful development effects. Although there are no detailed analyses of the consequences for Vietnam of foreign anti-dumping actions, it is possible to identify two likely outcomes. Firstly, the imposition of tariffs raises the price of Vietnamese products, which reduces sales, production, and incomes in Vietnam. Given that most of the industries and product groups involved in trade disputes are labor-intensive, the cost in terms of unemployment can be substantial. For instance, Vietnamese industry sources estimate that the EU tariffs on leather shoes resulted in tens of thousands of lost jobs even before they were introduced, as EU customers cancelled orders in anticipation of the anti-dumping tariff. The effects on poverty are likely to be severe too — most of the workers in the labor-intensive industries have low levels of education, but earn salaries that are larger than the earnings in agriculture or the informal sector.

Secondly, the threat of anti-dumping tariffs will affect competition and pricing decisions. This is a particularly severe problem for

[3] The anti-dumping case involving leather shoes was initiated before Vietnam joined the WTO, but the EU already applied a non-market economy rule for Vietnam at that time.

those cases where the anti-dumping claims are based on "non-market economy" arguments. Instead of following normal business principles, where products are priced on the basis of demand conditions and production costs, Vietnamese producers may be forced to engage in strategic behavior, where one objective may be to limit growth rates and market shares in order to avoid the imposition of trade remedies. A possible consequence is the emergence of export cartels to coordinate the behavior of the individual firms. An alternative outcome is stronger state intervention and export controls on the Vietnamese side. Both these outcomes are undesirable from a development perspective. The development of an export cartel is likely to affect competition in the domestic market as well, limiting growth and raising prices for local consumers. A solution whereby the degree of state interference increases because of trade policy concerns is also highly undesirable, and is in stark contrast with the general trend in Vietnamese economic development, where private enterprise and market-determined decisions are promoted.

Can the EU Live with Successful Developing Countries?

The WTO accession clause designating Vietnam as a non-market economy until 2018 is one of the clearest examples of a situation where the trade policies of Western countries, including the EU, are in obvious disagreement with ODA and development policies.[4] While ODA and the development dialogue in general promote an increasing market orientation, trade policies freeze Vietnam's status as a non-market economy for an extended period, without any regard for what happens in Vietnam. A likely consequence is that the momentum for

[4] In extreme cases, Vietnam's trade partners might refer to the non-market economy clause if Vietnamese exporters rely heavily on ODA-financed infrastructure, or benefit from technical advice, financing, or other business services provided through aid-financed programs. It is also interesting that the general view in the development economics literature is that non-market conditions constitute a general disadvantage rather than a competitive advantage. By contrast, trade legislation accommodates the view that non-market conditions could create advantages in all sectors.

domestic reform is weakened; the argument will be "Why reform if our reforms are not recognized by our trade partners?" The EU has decided not to follow Australia, New Zealand, and several other countries that have recognized Vietnam as a market economy. Should this be interpreted as a new stage in the relations between the EU and Vietnam — a stage that is better characterized by competition and conflict rather than cooperation?

Although Vietnam is a rapidly developing country that may be expected to play an increasingly important global role in the future, there is still a long way to go before this potential is realized. Vietnam is a small economy — in spite of its nearly 90 million inhabitants, it accounts for less than 0.7 percent of EU imports. There is little scope for claiming that Vietnam could pose a serious competitive challenge to the EU, except in very narrowly defined industrial sectors. Hence, it is unlikely that conflicts and competition related to trade and economic relations could motivate a shift in the EU's relationship with Vietnam at this time.

This positive statement appears to contradict the picture suggested by the EU's use of anti-dumping tariffs against Vietnam and the EU's unwillingness to recognize Vietnam as a market economy. This apparent contradiction is probably explained by the relation between the EU and China. Whereas Vietnam does not pose any significant challenge to European firms, there is no doubt that China does. Chinese exporters have captured dominant positions in a wide range of manufacturing industries and account for 27 percent of the EU's imports of manufacturing goods. Moreover, trade with China exhibits large imbalances, with the EU deficit reaching nearly EUR170 billion in 2010 — only about EUR35 billion less than the US trade deficit with China the same year. Understandably, the EU is concerned about competitiveness, employment, and macroeconomic balance in its relations with China.

This concern spills over to the relationship with Vietnam. One reason is the similarity in history and economic structure between China and Vietnam. Both countries have a past as planned economies, and both operate state-dominated market economies where state-owned enterprises play important roles. It will be difficult for the EU to motivate different treatments of Vietnam and China in a WTO context. Given that China is more important, it is clear that the common policy approach will mainly focus on China. Hence, it is unlikely that the EU will unilaterally revise Vietnam's non-market economy status.

Moreover, Vietnam and China are linked when it comes to current trade and investment patterns. Several of the anti-dumping tariffs faced by Vietnam are brought about by these links. Bicycles, leather shoes, and fluorescent lamps are examples of cases where the EU had first initiated anti-dumping proceedings against China, and where the Chinese producers (or foreign investors operating in China) have subsequently moved to Vietnam.[5] In cases where this migration of production has not occurred, Vietnam has generally not been subject to the same trade remedies as China. For example, comparing the frequency of anti-dumping actions, it is notable that China was targeted by the EU 122 times during 2000–2010 whereas Vietnam was named only 9 times.[6] Another notable observation is that the EU has refrained from levying any new anti-dumping tariffs on Vietnam since 2006 (but the tariffs on Vietnamese leather shoes have been extended during this period), although the global financial crisis has contributed to a distinct increase in the use of trade remedies during the last two years.

A cautious conclusion from these observations is that the relationship between the EU and Vietnam is more amicable than what the increasing frequency of trade disputes might suggest. This relationship is to some degree obscured by the European need to manage the more competitive relations with China — overall, it will be difficult to provide special preferences to Vietnam. The exception from this generalization is the ongoing negotiation between the EU and Vietnam regarding a preferential trade agreement. Although restrictive rules of origin will probably limit the ability of Vietnam to utilize the trade preferences under this type of agreement, it would

---

[5] See http://www.vnnnews.net/anti-dumping-mud-sticks-on-firms.

[6] For data on EU anti-dumping cases, see http://trade.ec.europa.eu/doclib/docs/2010/january/tradoc_145673.pdf.

still provide distinct structural benefits to Vietnam. Most importantly, it would make it possible for the EU to recognize Vietnam as a market economy without having to extend the same treatment to China. In addition, it would include an investment agreement that would make Vietnam a more attractive location for European investors. The outcome of these negotiations are of great interest not only for the EU and Vietnam, but also for other developing countries and emerging markets worried about the possibilities to pursue export-oriented development strategies, with the EU as a major export destination. A successful result will demonstrate that the EU's trade preferences towards developing economies are not only temporary promises that will be deflated if the partner economy is actually able to achieve sustained growth and create the capacity to utilize the preferences.

13.5 Vietnam: Caught between The West and The East

The relationship between the EU and Vietnam is in a process of change in the early 2010s. The rapid development of the Vietnamese economy is altering the basic setting for the interactions between the two regions. As long as Vietnam was a weak developing economy with limited capability for internationalization, the EU's contacts with Vietnam were mainly related to development aid. Both the EU Commission and more than a dozen member countries had bilateral aid programs in Vietnam, with various specific targets depending on the overall policy preferences of the individual donors. The general objective was to promote sustainable growth and progress in social development. Like all other aid relationships, it could be argued that this relationship was to some extent "paternal", in the sense that it involved a more developed partner that contributed both physical resources and knowledge about "development" to a less developed partner. However, because of historical reasons, Vietnam was concerned that the external powers might interfere with domestic affairs, and it therefore established a structure for aid management that would guarantee Vietnamese ownership of the country's development agenda. Aid was made into an integral part of the economic planning process, and aid management was centralized to the Ministry of Planning and Investment. The possibility to use aid and explicit conditions in order to influence Vietnamese policy was limited.

Nevertheless, the EU's ODA investments turned out to have a fundamental impact on the Vietnamese economy, although not in a manner that was explicitly intended by the EU. The fragmentation of the EU's aid portfolio into more than 15 different bilateral programs, each made up of several components, meant that the Vietnamese government had to decentralize responsibility for a large share of the ODA projects to regional and sectoral authorities. Over time, this contributed to increasing the relative strength and bargaining power of actors outside the central government, and led eventually to thorough reforms of the central planning system. It became impossible to impose a central plan when various regional and sectoral authorities could act independently to secure promises of external resources from the donor community.

Since the early 2000s, Vietnam has started to develop a notable export capacity and has increased its attractiveness as a low-cost production location for foreign multinational enterprises. The emergence of Vietnamese products in the European marketplace has coincided with a designation of Vietnam as a "non-market economy" and the introduction of European anti-dumping tariffs against selected Vietnamese exports — goods like bicycles, leather shoes, and fluorescent lamps. This implies that the European attitudes towards Vietnam may have changed, so that the focus on supporting Vietnamese development through ODA has been replaced by a more complex relationship, where Europe feels a need to protect its own markets from competition from Vietnam.

Yet, there is reason to believe that the bilateral relationship will not necessarily deteriorate towards a more competitive and antagonistic association. The reason is that the protectionist reactions from the European side are probably not focused primarily on Vietnam, but rather on China. Most of the anti-dumping cases brought against Vietnam are extensions of cases initiated against China, and the designation of Vietnam as a non-market economy follows a similar policy with respect to China. Hence, it can be argued that Vietnam has been caught in the global re-polarization process, stuck between the West and the East, in the shadow of China. It is neither in the interest of Europe nor Vietnam to cement this state of affairs. There is no reason for Europe to push Vietnam to become a part of the Chinese sphere of interest — on the contrary, it is in Europe's interest to maintain good relations with Vietnam, and to signal to other developing countries that good relations with the EU are possible even when emerging economies are successful enough to win market shares in the European market. That would be a highly encouraging signal in a world where many other developments suggest a stronger polarization between different growth centers and spheres of interest.

It is also in Vietnam's interest to maintain close relations with Europe. For historical reasons, Vietnam has no wish to become more dependent on China. Strong economic and political links with Europe would serve to mitigate Chinese influence and bargaining power. The negotiations over a preferential trade agreement between the EU and Vietnam that commenced in 2010 could, if concluded successfully, form the base for a more positive relationship. In particular, it would allow the EU to differentiate between Vietnam and China — under the current WTO framework, this is not possible.

References

CIEM (2006). *Vietnam's Economy in 2005.* Hanoi: Statistics Publishing House.

Communist Party of Vietnam (2001). *Politburo Resolution*, No. 07-NQ/TW 2001:3, Central Party Committee, Hanoi.

Dapice, D. (2002). Helping Vietnam to make better choices. Discussion Paper, Kennedy School of Government, Harvard University, Cambridge, MA, August.

EAEP (East Asian Economic Perspectives) (2006). Recent trends and prospects for major Asian economies. Special Issue, 17(February).

Forsberg, L. T. (2007). Defining strong ownership: institutional determinants and stakeholder interests in Vietnamese development planning. Lund University, Lund.

Glewwe, P., Agrawal, N. and Dollar, D. (Eds.) (2004). *Economic Growth, Poverty, and Household Welfare in Vietnam.* Washington, DC: World Bank.

GRIPS (2002). Japan's development cooperation in Vietnam — supporting broad-based growth with poverty reduction. National Graduate Institute for Policy Studies, Tokyo.

Jacquemin, A. and Bainbridge, B. (2005). Perceptions of development partners and evidence on aid effectiveness. Mimeo, DFID, London. http://www.dfid.gov.uk/mdg/aid-effectiveness/newsletters/vietnam-report.pdf.

Kokko, A. (1997). *Managing the transition to free trade: Vietnamese trade policy for the 21st century.* Macroeconomic Reports 1997:4, Swedish International Development Cooperation Agency, Stockholm.

Kokko, A. and Tingvall, P. (2008). The welfare state. In: A. Kokko (Ed.), *Vietnam: 20 Years of Doi Moi.* Hanoi: The Gioi Publishers.

Le, T. T. V. and Tong, S. Y. (2009). Vietnam and anti-dumping: regulations, applications and responses. EAI Working Paper No. 146, National University of Singapore.

MoH (2002). *Vietnam Health Report 2002.* Hanoi: Ministry of Health.

Pike, D. (1987). *Vietnam and the Soviet Union: Anatomy of an Alliance.* Boulder, CO: Westview Press.

SRV (2003). *The Comprehensive Poverty Reduction and Growth Strategy.* Hanoi: Socialist Republic of Vietnam.

SRV (2005). *Vietnam: Managing Public Expenditure for Poverty Reduction and Growth.* Public Expenditure Review and Integrated Fiduciary Assessment, Vol. 2: Sectoral issues. Hanoi: Socialist Republic of Vietnam and the World Bank.

UNDP (1996). *Developing Capacities in Aid Coordination and Management: Vietnam — A Successful Government-UNDP Partnership.* New York: Management Development and Governance Division, United Nations Development Program.

UNDP (2005). *Vietnam Development Cooperation Report 2004.* Hanoi: United Nations Development Program.

Chapter 14

The Role of SWFs in Shaping the Neo-polar World: The Asia–Europe Perspective

Michael Keller

14.1 Introduction

The European Union is the world's leading exporter of international investment capital. However, in recent years, developing countries have continuously gained in relative importance as sources of foreign direct investment (FDI) (UNCTAD, 2009). Global investment flows include investments by sovereign wealth funds (SWFs), for which the emergence of developing countries as dominant investors is particularly striking.

Although SWFs have been present in Europe for many decades (Lyons, 2008), their activities in international capital markets, including Europe, have increased greatly only since 2007 (Kern, 2008) and thus play an important role in explaining the neo-polar world. In fact, a closer look at the geographical origin of the funds reveals a bi-polar situation with Asia and the Middle East completely dominating the increasingly important phenomenon of global SWF investments, whereas Europe's role is limited to Norway's Government Pension Fund. Compared to the Middle East, Asia is far more dominant in the debate about the re-polarization of the world economy. It is thus the main aim of this chapter to analyze this phenomenon with a particular focus on Asian SWF investments in Europe. Using *inter alia* our own database on SWFs, we will identify the Asian SWFs operating in Europe, take a closer look at their characteristics, point out the particular role of China, and discuss the concerns they evoke and the policy developments regarding the regulation of SWFs in European countries.

SWFs are government vehicles with the central objective of high risk-adjusted returns. According to our survey for the period 2007–2009, about 200 cases of effective investments by SWFs or deals in negotiation can be identified within the EU.[1] Europe is typically characterized by an open policy regarding the movement of capital. This liberal approach towards FDI seems to reach a limit when it comes to investments by SWFs, however (Chaisse and Gugler, 2010). This scepticism may be linked to the fact that the most important funds are from emerging countries in Asia and the Middle East. In 2007, assets managed by Asian SWFs already approached $600 billion, and it was no longer possible to ignore that they were becoming substantial players on European markets (Subacchi, 2007).

Investment activities by SWFs are considered "one of the most controversial financial issues" today (Park, 2008, p. 1). In developed countries from Europe to the United States, the advent of SWFs from emerging countries has given rise to growing concerns about the lack of transparency of SWFs, their potential geopolitical and strategic objectives and geographical shifts of economic power (Chaisse and Gugler, 2010). At the policy level, responses to these concerns include strict legislation at the national level of some European countries such as Germany and France, the promotion of a multilateral approach by the European Commission, as well as a voluntary code of conduct for SWFs at the international level, which reflects the fact that SWFs are now conceived as an important global issue.

The chapter is organized as follows. Section 14.2 presents some basic facts and main features regarding SWFs. Section 14.3 provides a descriptive analysis of Asian SWF investments in Europe, assessing their importance and characteristics. Moreover, the particular role of Chinese SWFs with respect to the re-polarization debate is pointed

[1] The survey is part of a research project based at the Center for Competitiveness of the University of Fribourg/Switzerland, led by Prof. Dr. Philippe Gugler and including Prof. Dr. Julien Chaisse from the Chinese University of Hong Kong. For more information, please visit the following website: http://www.unifr.ch/competitiveness.

out. Section 14.4 briefly discusses the main concerns raised at the European level and the policy developments in Europe regarding SWFs. Section 14.5 concludes.

14.2 Main Features Regarding SWFs

Definition of SWFs

According to UNCTAD (2008, p. 20), no "universally agreed-upon definition" of SWFs exists. Their objectives tend to vary, although most of them originated from the idea of wealth preservation. SWFs' investment strategies are quite different from those of private equity funds and multinational enterprises (MNEs). Miracky *et al.* (2008, p. 11) consider that a SWF is a government vehicle that meets three criteria: "(1) it is owned by a sovereign government; (2) it is managed separately from funds administered by the sovereign government's central bank, ministry of finance, or treasury; and (3) it invests in a portfolio of financial assets of different classes and risk profiles, including bonds, stocks, property, and alternative instruments." A significant part of assets is invested abroad in higher-risk asset classes.

SWFs may be considered as "part of a continuum of sovereign government investment vehicles that runs along a spectrum of financial risk from Central Banks as the most conservative and risk-averse, to traditional pension funds, to special government funds, to SWFs, and finally to state-owned enterprises, which are the least liquid and highest-risk investments" (Miracky *et al.*, 2008, p. 14) (see Figure 14.1).

Types of SWFs

Based on their dominant investment types, SWFs may be divided into two main categories: FDI and portfolio investments. Most investments by SWFs are not FDI. FDI by SWFs was $26.5 billion in 2009, accounting for around 0.5% of their total assets and only 0.7% of total FDI flows. Private equity funds invested more than

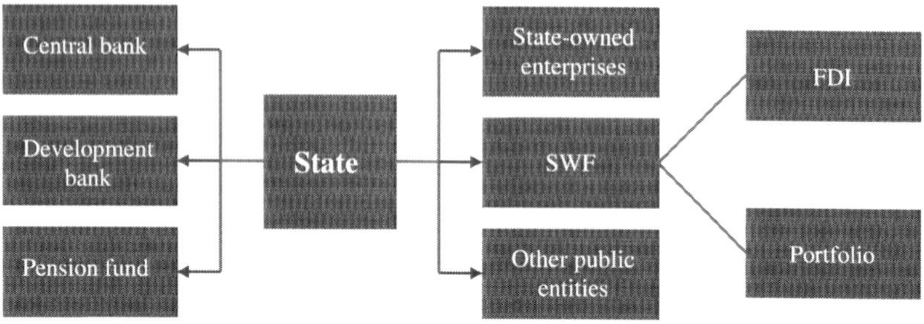

Figure 14.1: SWFs and government activities.

Source: Adaption based on Kern (2008, p. 2).

\$460 billion in FDI in the same year, despite being much smaller in size. FDI by SWFs has registered a constant growth even during the financial market crisis (UNCTAD, 2010). In 2010, however, it dropped to \$10 billion and was expected to increase again in 2011 (UNCTAD, 2011).

The majority of SWF investment is in portfolios with professional management to generate a sustainable income stream. Portfolio investments include equities, bonds and alternative asset classes (UNCTAD, 2008). During the period 2007–2009, important investments took place in the financial sectors of developed countries, due to the financial market crisis and the associated liquidity needs of numerous banks in Europe and in the United States (UNCTAD, 2010). For example, the Government of Singapore Investment Corporation (GIC) acquired a \$9.8 billion stake in the Swiss bank UBS (UNCTAD, 2008, pp. 23–24).

SWFs are different from private equity funds (Blundell-Wignall *et al.*, 2008), although both have become important players in global investment activities. Table 14.1 shows a comparison of SWFs with private equity funds and their main differences. The volume of SWFs was nine times larger than that of private equity funds in 2007. In addition, SWFs are also growing more rapidly due to increasing foreign exchange reserves and trade surpluses. According to UNCTAD (2008, p. 22), "non-economic rationales sometimes combine with economic motivations in investment decisions by SWFs." Furthermore, home country governments directly control SWFs, which is not the case

Table 14.1: Comparison between SWFs and private equity funds, 2007.

Item	SWFs	Private equity funds
Volume	$5,000 billion	$540 billion
FDI	$10 billion	$460 billion[1]
Main source economies of FDI	United Arab Emirates, Norway, Saudi Arabia, Kuwait, Singapore, China, Hong Kong (China) and Russian Federation	United States, United Kingdom
Largest funds involving FDI	Istithmar PJSC (United Arab Emirates), Dubai Investment Group, Temasek Holdings (Singapore), GIC (Singapore)	KKR, Blackstone, Permira, Fortress, Bain Capital, Carlyle (United States)
Investment strategy	Shifting from passive to active investors. Have tended to hold investment-grade, short-term, liquid sovereign assets in the major currencies, particularly United States treasury securities, but are now becoming strategic investors, with a preference for equities. Also investing in bonds, real estate, hedge funds, private equity and commodities. Still limited involvement in FDI. Concentrated in developed countries	Shorter time frame (exit within 5–8 years) than public companies and traditional TNCs, but play a more active role in the management of invested companies than SWFs. At the same time, inclined to look for options that offer quick returns, akin to those of portfolio investors. Buy larger and also public-listed companies, but also invest in venture capital. Undertake FDI through buyouts. FDI is expanding in developing countries

Source: UNCTAD (2008, p. 22).
Note: [1] Cross-border M&As only.

for private equity funds. In most cases, SWFs are able to hold stakes longer than private equity funds.

SWFs: Global Trends

The increased integration among the world's main regions has advanced the rise of emerging countries over the past few years. Countries with large current account surpluses have built up large holdings of official reserve assets and embarked on SWF investments (Subacchi, 2007, p. 2). SWFs are not a new phenomenon, particularly in resource-rich countries, but "they have recently gained prominence in various emerging countries, reflecting those countries' large balance of payment surpluses" (Subacchi, 2007, p. 2). The major wave, starting in 2000 and intensifying since 2007, has led to the formation of around 20 SWFs, most of which are funded by capital inflows based either on large trade surpluses (e.g., China) or on high energy prices (in particular in the Middle East). Indeed, the size and dynamic of their capital flows, including SWF investments, is one of the characteristics that put the emerging countries of Asia and the Middle East on the main stage of the world economy and into the spotlight of global markets.

SWF trends reflect the key changes in global capital flows. The size of SWFs is estimated to total $4 trillion in 2011 compared to $500 billion in 1990 (PREQIN, 2011; UNCTAD, 2009). Although the funds are heavily invested in their home countries and only account for about 1% of total FDI flows, they are set to become important players in global markets due to the impressive increase in their size (UNCTAD, 2009). The financial market crisis and the global economic downturn in 2008 and 2009 led to a short-term decline of SWFs' total assets in 2009. However, starting with the improving world equity markets in the latter half of 2009, their asset portfolios have since recovered (UNCTAD, 2010). Their considerable size is expected to grow further in the years ahead. Some studies estimate that the amount could surpass $10 trillion in 2015 (Miracky *et al.*, 2008, p. 18), even though many analysts have adopted a slightly more moderate view of SWFs' growth prospects during the crisis. Currently, there are some 70 such funds in 44 countries and their assets range from $20 million to more than $600 billion (UNCTAD, 2010). Their holdings are, however, concentrated in a few countries such as Saudi Arabia, the United Arab Emirates, Kuwait, Singapore, China and Norway. As China is expected to play a key role in the re-polarization process of the world economy, the Chinese SWFs are likely to become the biggest funds in the world, surpassing GIC (Singapore), Norway's Government Pension Fund and Abu Dhabi Investment Authority (UAE) (PREQIN, 2011).

Norway's GPF, previously called The Petroleum Fund of Norway and holding the surplus wealth produced by Norwegian petroleum income, is amongst the largest SWFs in the world. However, its role in the re-polarization debate is somewhat marginal. Research by Deutsche Bank (Kern, 2008) showed that specific GPF-investments in foreign European countries are absent from the screened financial news coverage. In fact, virtually all of the funds of publicly reported total SWF investments between 1995 and 2008, as identified by Deutsche Bank (Kern, 2008), have been contributed by Asian (66%) and Middle Eastern SWFs (34%), leaving no space for Norwegian investments. This absence from the statistics reflects a relatively low interest in GPF-investments due to its high transparency and its commitment to a role as a pure financial investor with non-strategic holdings (Norway Ministry of Finance website, 2010). Moreover, it points out the limits of the currently available sources of comparable data. Nevertheless, it also mirrors the current state of affairs in the scientific argument on the emergence of new economic powers: even though Europe is still an important economic player in absolute terms (in the case under consideration: Norway's GPF), its role as an economic pole is receding in relative terms due to the developments in emerging countries (in the case under consideration: growth of SWFs from Asia and the Middle East).

14.3 Asian SWFs in Europe

Investments by SWFs in international capital markets, including Europe, have increased greatly over the last few years (Kern, 2008). The phenomenon has caught the attention of economists, policymakers and the financial community. In spite of scarce authorized information and data on the subject, it has become the object of numerous studies in recent years. A wider public, at latest, realized the potential influence of SWFs during the financial and economic crisis starting in 2007. The need for international investors in the European Union is likely to continue to grow in the near future as a result of the European sovereign debt crisis. It is the aim of this section to identify the role Asian SWFs play in this process and to assess the importance and the characteristics of Asian SWFs operating in Europe. Moreover, the particular role of Chinese SWFs will be pointed out.

Reliable information on SWFs and their operations, in particular their asset sizes, asset allocation and investment strategies, is very scarce (Kern, 2008). This lack of information on SWFs is partly due to a lack of transparency and clear communication on the part of the funds themselves (Chaisse and Gugler, 2010). Assessing the importance and the objectives of SWFs on the basis of such fragile data is thus delicate, and results and figures should be treated with caution. However, some studies have tried to quantify investments by SWFs, and we will partially rely on such studies to provide an outline of the importance (in terms of value) of Asian SWFs in Europe.

In order to identify the characteristics of Asian SWF investments in Europe, we will additionally rely on the results of our own survey of publicly available sources for the period 2007–2009. Based on this survey, the Center for Competitiveness of the University of Fribourg/Switzerland has established a database of cases of effective investments by SWFs as well as deals in negotiation and rejected deals within the EU.

Importance and Characteristics of Asian SWF Investments in Europe

In October 2008, assets managed by Asian SWFs were estimated to account for around $1 trillion, representing 30% of worldwide sovereign assets (Kern, 2008). This made Asia the second most important region in terms of SWF assets, next to the Middle East, which was estimated to control almost half of the overall volume of SWF assets in October 2008. Europe followed far behind, with 16% of total sovereign assets, driven by SWFs from Russia and Norway (Kern, 2008). The volume of assets as such provides a somewhat static picture of the importance of SWF investments. To capture the degree of activity of SWFs in recent years, it is far more interesting to take a look at actual investment undertaken by SWFs.

In terms of value of investment transactions, Asian SWFs seem to be the most active sovereign investors in the world. According to Kern (2008, p. 7), Asian SWFs contributed 66% of the funds of total global SWF investments (value) between 1995 and 2008, whereas Middle Eastern SWFs only contributed 34%. This is in line with the estimation of Miracky *et al.* (2008) for the period 2000–2008, which presumed that Asian SWFs invested $150 billion worldwide over this period, whereas funds based in the Middle East and North Africa (MENA) region invested some $100 billion.

However, there is a striking difference between Asian SWFs and funds from the Middle East with respect to the targets of their sovereign investment. Asian SWFs invested heavily in their home region from 2000 to the first quarter of 2008. $75 billion, representing half of total investment by value, took place in Asia. Most of the remaining Asian investment, $74 billion, went to Europe and the United States. Middle Eastern SWFs, on the other hand, invested only $19 billion inside their home region, whereas almost three-quarters of Middle Eastern SWF investment by value, $72 billion, went to Europe and North America (Miracky *et al.*, 2008, pp. 37–38).

We now narrow our focus to SWF investments in Europe. As a result of different investment patterns with respect to target regions, the dominant investment activity of Asian SWFs at the global level is less impressive if only investments with European companies as targets are taken into account. In fact, Asian and Middle Eastern SWFs accounted for almost equal shares of the total value of SWF investments in Europe between 1995 and 2008, with 48% and 52% of total volume, respectively (Kern, 2008).

As noted by Kern (2008), data on the *value* of actual investments undertaken by SWFs have to be treated with even greater caution than data on the volume of assets as such. Given this difficulty with respect to data on investment *value*, it is appropriate to complement the analysis with a survey of the mere *number of transactions*. We therefore resort to our own database of publicly reported investments by SWFs within the EU for the period January 2007–December 2009. Overall, we identified about 200 reports of investments by SWFs in Europe for this period. These include effective investments, deals in negotiation and rejected deals. 154 cases of effective investments or deals in negotiation remained after having excluded all rejected deals and deals which turned out to be false rumors.

23% of these reported transactions concerned investments by Asian SWFs (China and Singapore), whereas investments by Middle Eastern and North African SWFs (Bahrain, Kuwait, Libya, Qatar and UAE) accounted for 61% of all cases (see Figure 14.2). The remaining transactions came in equal shares from European SWFs (Russia and Ireland) and from funds with an unspecified origin.

This result based on the *number of transactions* contrasts with Kern's (2008) estimation, which put the share of Asian SWF investments in Europe between 1995 and 2008 at 48% in terms of *value*. Even though our database covers operations reported over a more limited but recent time period, we may thus assume that compared to

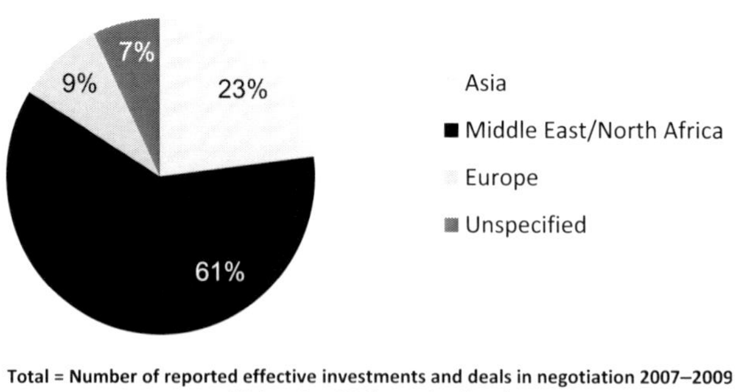

Figure 14.2: Origins of SWF investments in Europe.

Source: Elaboration based on the database of the Center for Competitiveness, University of Fribourg.

Middle Eastern SWFs, Asian SWFs invested infrequently in Europe, but in bigger volumes at once.

In order to identify the characteristics of Asian SWF investments in Europe, and to compare them with the funds from the Middle East, we have to go into more detail regarding the targets of the investments. We first provide a breakdown of the transactions in our database by targeted *countries* (Figure 14.3). In 80% of our covered transactions (2007–2009), the United Kingdom was the target of Asian SWF investments. Germany and Switzerland followed jointly at a wide interval, with 6% each. This concentration on UK targets can also be observed for Middle Eastern SWFs, albeit to a much lesser extent. The UK was the target of Middle Eastern SWF investments in only 45% of the reported transactions, and Middle Eastern investments generally followed more diversified patterns with respect to targeted countries. According to our database, Germany, Italy, France and Switzerland were all targeted in 5%–14% of the reported cases of Middle Eastern SWF investments in Europe.

Further insight is gained by a breakdown of the transactions in our database by targeted *sectors* (Figure 14.4). In line with Kern's (2008)

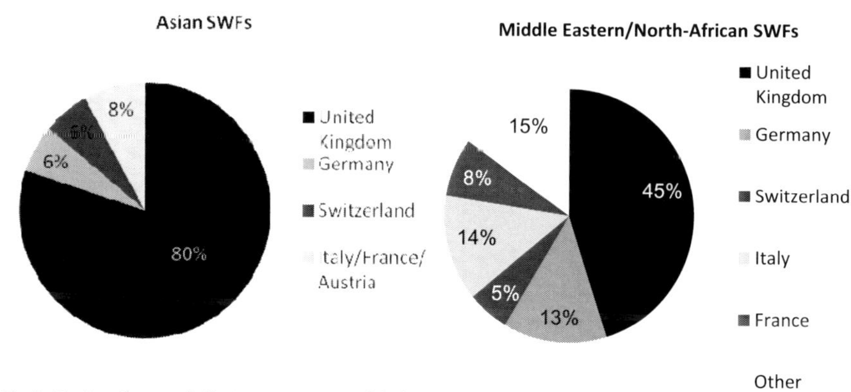

Total = Number of reported effective investments and deals in negotiation 2007-2009.

Total = Number of reported effective investments and deals in negotiation 2007-2009.

Figure 14.3: Target countries of SWF investments in Europe.

Source: Elaboration based on the database of the Center for Competitiveness, University of Fribourg.

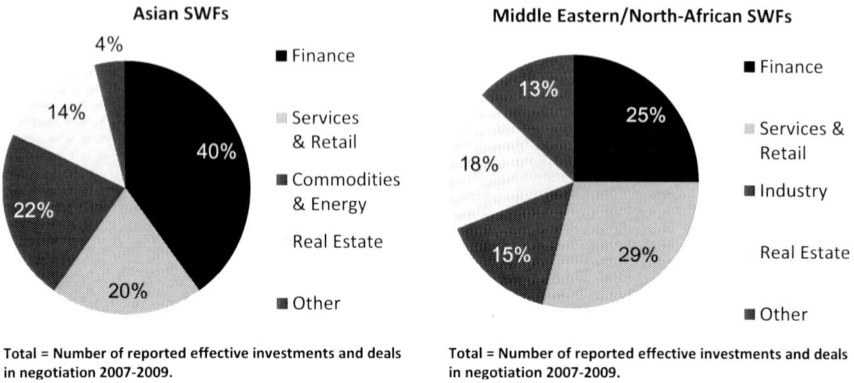

Figure 14.4: Targeted sectors of SWF investments in Europe.

Source: Elaboration based on the database of the Center for Competitiveness, University of Fribourg.

results at the global level, Finance was by far the most frequent target (40%) of Asian SWF investments in Europe for the 2007–2009 period. This contrasts with the situation for Middle Eastern SWF investments, for which Finance was only the second most important target (25%), following Services & Retail with 29%. On the whole, Asian SWF investment patterns in Europe varied markedly from their Middle Eastern counterparts in the composition of targeted sectors. Asian SWFs focused more on Finance, whereas Real Estate and Services & Retail played a minor role. In addition, Industry was completely absent from Asian SWFs' targeted sectors in Europe, whereas it accounted for 15% of Middle Eastern SWF investments (mainly car industry). The reverse was true for Commodities & Energy, absent from Middle Eastern investments, but a rather important target for Asian SWFs (22%). This provides some broad evidence for the claim that concerns about strategically sensitive sectors such as Finance and Commodities & Energy are more of an issue in the Asia-Europe perspective than for the European relationship with the Middle East.

Asian SWF Investments in Europe: A Closer Look

Our database of publicly reported investments by SWFs within the EU for the period 2007–2009 allows for a closer look at the involved funds.

Table 14.2: Asian SWFs investing in Europe, 2007–2009.

SWF	Country	Worldwide Assets ($Billion)	Investments[1] in Europe, 2007–2009
SAFE Investment Company	China	567.9	10
China Investment Corporation (CIC)	China	409.6	4
Government of Singapore Investment Corporation (GIC)	Singapore	247.5	13
Temasek Holdings	Singapore	157.2	3

Source: Elaboration based on the database of the Center for Competitiveness, University of Fribourg, and data from http://www.swfinstitute.org, 2011.
Note: [1]Number of reported transactions including deals in negotiation (University of Fribourg database).

The origin of a small fraction of all Asian investments in our database is not specified. For the rest, however, we are able to identify the investing SWF by name. In fact, Asian SWF investments in Europe between 2007 and 2009 included deals by four different funds from China and Singapore (Table 14.2). These funds were all among the global top 15 SWFs ranked by assets in 2007 (Subacchi, 2007). Furthermore, some minor Asian SWFs, not appearing in our database, exist in Brunei, South Korea, Malaysia and Taiwan. None of them, however, reached a volume of total assets exceeding $30 billion in 2010 (PREQIN, 2011).

The scope of the identified investments in terms of acquired ownership varied considerably, ranging from less than 1% to the 100% acquisition of UK-based Chapterhouse Holdings Limited, whose primary asset is the Merrill Lynch Financial Center in London, by the Government of Singapore Investment Corporation (GIC, 2007).

Table 14.3 lists the top investments in our 2007–2009 database by ownership percentage, for which ownership data is available. As for data with respect to investment values, the figures on ownership should be treated with caution. The list serves as an indicative sample of showcase investments of Asian SWFs in Europe.

Clearly, the Government of Singapore Investment Corporation was the most active SWF in the European market between 2007 and

Table 14.3: Top investments by Asian SWFs in Europe, 2007–2009.

SWF	Target	Country	Ownership
GIC	Chapterhouse Holdings	UK	100%
Future Fund	Bull Ring Shopping Centre, Birmingham	UK	33%
Temasek	Standard Chartered	UK	19%
CIC	Songbird Estates	UK	19%
GIC	Springer Science + Business Media	Germany	18%
GIC	Sintonia Holding	Italy	14%
CIC	Blackstone Group	UK	12.5%
GIC	Brixton	UK	10.4%
GIC	UBS	Switzerland	9%

Source: Elaboration based on the database of the Center for Competitiveness, University of Fribourg.

2009. It has been around for a long time, established in 1981 out of growing reserves due to a high national savings rate (Subacchi, 2007). The fund is wholly-owned by the Government of Singapore and is composed of three major sovereign wealth enterprises: GIC Asset Management Pte. Ltd., GIC Real Estate Pte. Ltd., and GIC Special Investments Pte. Ltd. (GIC Report 2008/2009). Each of these enterprises focuses on a specific investment area to build and preserve a sound expertise. GIC does not own the assets under its management, but manages them on behalf of the Government of Singapore and the Monetary Authority of Singapore. The Ministry of Finance, as a representative of the Government of Singapore, determines the investment objective, risk parameters and investment horizon for the portfolio. It does not interfere in GIC's investment decisions, but holds the GIC Board responsible for the overall performance of the portfolio.

Recent investments by GIC in Europe include the participation in the acquisition of Springer Science and Business Media, the German magazine publisher, in Europe's biggest private equity deal of the year 2009; and an investment in Switzerland-based Glencore, the world's dominant commodity trader, in December 2009 (Financial Times, 2009b; Financial Times, 2009c).

Temasek Holdings, the second Singapore SWF, has been in existence since 1974, established by the Ministry of Finance (the sole shareholder) to manage direct stakes in local industries. Since then, the fund has been expanding in foreign markets, including Europe, with a particular focus on financial groups (Subacchi, 2007; Financial Times, 2008a). Temasek's mission is relatively clear: "to create and maximize long-term shareholder value as an active investor and shareholder of successful enterprises" (Temasek website).

China's SWFs came into operation later. The SAFE Investment Company, a subsidiary of the State Administration of Foreign Exchange, was established in 1997 (Financial Times, 2008a; Subacchi, 2007), and the China Investment Corporation (CIC), a wholly state-owned company headquartered in Beijing, in 2007 as a way to diversify China's foreign exchange reserves, hold less in US currency and increase risk-adjusted returns. CIC comprises two distinct and separate entities: the investment management operation (CIC) investing globally; and Central Huijin Investment Ltd., a wholly-owned subsidiary company "investing exclusively in domestic state-owned financial institutions on behalf of the state in order to improve governance and preserve and enhance the value of state-owned financial assets" (CIC Annual Report, 2008).

CIC's most recent move in our covered data was the investment of €800 million into Apax Partner, a British private equity firm, in December 2009. It joined GIC from Singapore and Future Fund, the Australian SWF established in 2006, which together had bought 7.7% of Apax earlier in 2009 (Financial Times, 2009a).

SAFE, on the other hand, has long conservatively managed China's rapidly swelling foreign reserves, but since 2008 it has emerged as a "powerful and more aggressive investor, chasing the kind of returns offshore that CIC was mandated to go after" (Financial Times, 2008a). It came into prominence with a series of investments in Commodity & Energy firms and utilities, such as Total, a French oil firm, BG Group, a UK-based oil and gas firm, BP, a British energy company, and Drax Group, a British electrical power generation company owning England's largest power station (Financial Times, 2008b). These deals never comprised acquisitions of stakes exceeding 2%, however.

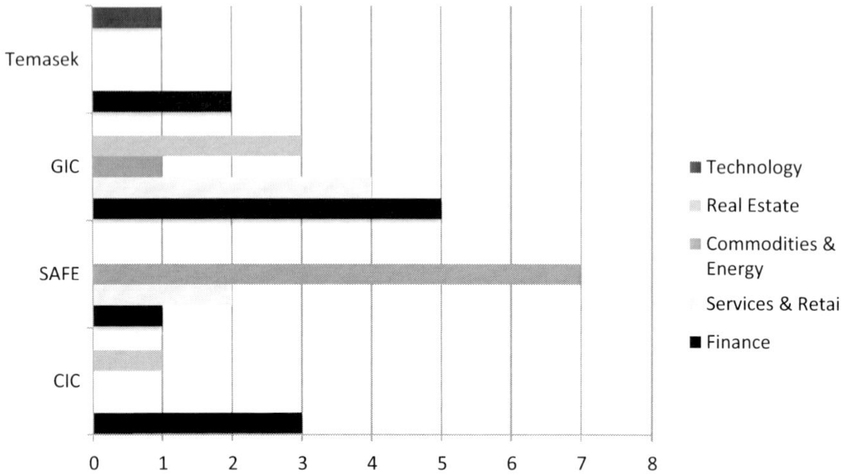

Figure 14.5: Asian SWFs in Europe, number of reported effective investments and deals in negotiation, 2007–2009, by targeted sectors.

Source: Elaboration based on the database of the Center for Competitiveness, University of Fribourg.

A systematic look at the number of reported effective investments and deals in negotiation in 2007–2009 by *targeted sectors* unambiguously reveals differing characteristics of Asian SWFs investing in Europe (Figure 14.5). GIC, the most active fund in Europe, made the most balanced investments, covering Finance, Services & Retail, Real Estate, and Commodities & Energy as targets. Finance was the most important target of all funds except for SAFE, which in turn accounted for virtually all of the investments in Commodities & Energy between 2007 and 2009.

The Particular Role of Chinese SWFs

Whereas Singapore plays a marginal role in the scientific debate on the re-polarization process of the world economy, China is one of the frequently cited candidates to take the place of the main global economic pole. It is thus important to take a special look at the two Chinese SWFs identified in the previous section. The main question regarding Chinese SWFs and the global re-polarization process can be formulated as follows: Do Chinese SWF investments reflect a pure financial consideration (i.e., the maximization of the return on investment) or a strategic and geopolitical objective?

The investment strategies of Chinese SWFs suggested by the analysis of Asian investments in Europe, as presented in the previous section, have been confirmed by a recent study of Chinese SWF investments at the global level (Gugler *et al.*, 2010). The main targets of CIC and SAFE's investments include *financial companies*, firms active in the *commodities and energy sector*, and general investments in *resource-rich regions* and regions of *particular importance in the global economy*. In order to approach the question of whether the government influences Chinese SWF investment decisions, we briefly analyze the government's policy towards Chinese outward FDI and compare this strategy with the identified investments undertaken by CIC and SAFE.

Chinese outward investments in general are based on a specific policy for outward FDI (OFDI), adopted and implemented by the Chinese government, called the "*Go Global*" policy. This strategy aims to encourage and promote the internationalization of capable Chinese firms through different preferential measures (such as the facilitation of access to foreign exchange or the preferential loans) in order to enhance their international competitiveness (Buckley *et al.*, 2008; Poncet, 2007). Furthermore, in 2004, the Ministry of Foreign Affairs (MoFA) and the Ministry of Commerce (MOFCOM) established an overseas investment guidance catalogue orienting OFDI towards specific industries and countries. According to Schüler-Zhou *et al.* (2010, p. 4), the catalogue ensures that all Chinese OFDI benefits the Chinese economy by securing access to *natural resources*. In terms of investment locations, the host countries have to fulfill some requirements: (i) *have a close relationship with China*, (ii) *have complementarities to the Chinese economy*, (iii) be important *trading partners of China*, (iv) have signed *investment and taxation agreements*, and (v) be part of an *important economic region in the global economy* (Schüler-Zhou *et al.*, 2010, p. 4). It is interesting to note in this context that in the 12th Five-Year Plan (March 2011), the Chinese

Government has revealed a shift in focus from the export-led sectors to increasing domestic consumer demand. This shift might indicate a change of priorities in the use of foreign exchange reserves in the future, with less scope for strategic considerations.

Combining the results found in analyzing the actual investments by CIC and SAFE with the objectives defined in the "*Go Global*" policy by the Chinese Ministry of Commerce, it seems obvious that the Chinese government influences its investment decision process in certain ways. Securing access to natural resources that are scarce in China has long been one of the main objectives of the Chinese government in order to ensure its development as a global economic pole (Zhan, 1995), and this is omnipresent in the identified investment patterns of Chinese SWFs, in particular of SAFE. CIC, however, maintains that it is a pure financial investor, maximizing the investment income and having no strategic interest in controlling the invested firm (CIC Annual Report, 2008). Due to the lack of transparency, it is difficult to find a concluding classification of the funds as either pure financial investors or strategic investors. Nevertheless, a certain amount of strategic consideration seems to be confirmed by the data (Gugler *et al.*, 2010). This uncertainty about strategic and geopolitical objectives underlying Chinese investments is representative of the concerns towards SWF investments raised in European recipient countries in general. These concerns are discussed in further detail in the next part of this chapter.

14.4 European Concerns about SWFs and Policy Developments

Although SWF investments have been welcomed in Europe for their stabilizing effects during the financial crisis, concerns prevail in the general attitude of European institutions towards SWFs (Chaisse and Gugler, 2010). The emergence of SWFs reflects a shift in financial power from private to public actors, which raises several concerns. Some critics are warning that investment by SWFs amounts to nationalization through the back door: "Why should we privatize our industries and utilities and see them fall into the hands of foreign governments such as the Chinese government?" (Whyte and Barysch, 2007, p. 1). Generic concerns may be divided into three main categories: threats to national safety and security, lack of transparency, and, most importantly in the context of the re-polarization of the world economy, difficulties to accept a trend, which reflects the geographical shifts of economic power. It is the aim of this last part of the chapter to briefly present these concerns and the corresponding policy responses in European countries.

Concerns about National Safety and Security and Lack of Transparency

A first concern about SWFs is linked to the suspicion that the management of some SWFs may not be motivated by wealth maximization only, but also by "nationalistic considerations" (Aizenman and Glick, 2008, p. 23), and may be used as a financial instrument to achieve a political objective (Aizenman and Glick, 2007; Beck and Fidora, 2008; Weisman, 2008). As shown previously, such concerns about strategic and political interests are common in the case of China. The desire to obtain control over critical infrastructure within a recipient country raises particular issues of market integrity and national security (Greene and Yeager, 2008, p. 247).

Röller and Véron (2008) have argued that SWFs could create a threat to national security through mergers and acquisitions. However, as stated by UNCTAD (2008, p. 25), "most states already reserve the right to refuse mergers and acquisitions for national security reasons." Many European countries (e.g., France, Germany, United Kingdom) already have a legal framework that allows restrictions or withdrawal of a foreign investment for national safety and security reasons. Another argument often used by opponents to SWFs concerns recently privatized firms. It is feared that efficiency-improvements from such privatizations may be "rolled back as a result of SWF investments." Other concerns are based on the fact that some of the SWFs come from countries that "lack a free market or respect of human rights and sound environmental standards" (UNCTAD, 2008, p. 25).

A second concern is the low level of transparency of many SWFs. Their operations are often carried out in opaque ways. In general, SWFs seldom publish data on their investments. They normally do not disclose information about their exact size, composition and strategy.

The Government of Singapore Investment Corporation (GIC) and Temasek, the second Singaporean government-controlled investment institution, have pioneered the use of SWFs. Both funds were notorious for their low degree of transparency in the beginning of their existence (Chaisse and Gugler, 2010). According to a 2008 assessment by Standard Chartered (see Figure 14.6), however, the degree of transparency of Singaporean SWFs has improved in recent years. On the other hand, the China Investment Corporation (CIC) reached a somewhat lower level of transparency in this same assessment. This is in line with the Linaburg–Maduell Transparency Index developed at the Sovereign Wealth Fund Institute, which uses a scale between 1 (lowest transparency) and 10 (highest transparency). With an index of 7, CIC just failed to meet the recommended minimum

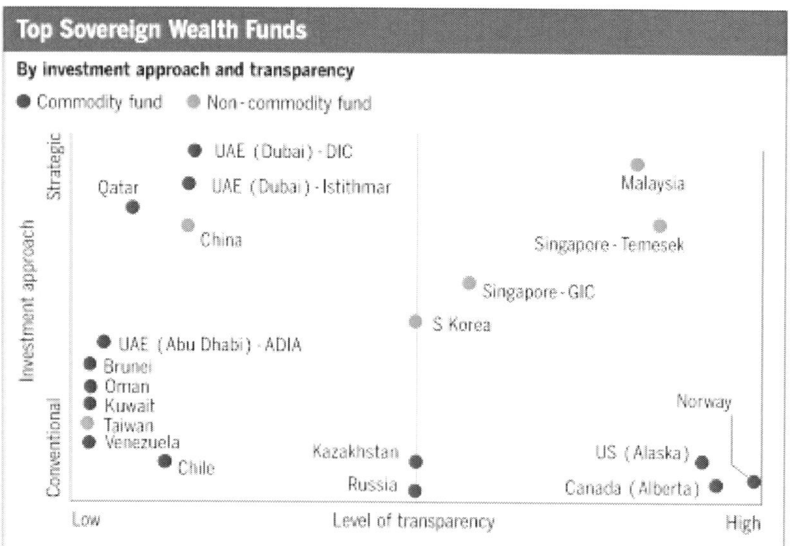

Figure 14.6: Sovereign wealth funds: Strategy and transparency.
Source: Standard Chartered, 2008.

transparency rating of 8 in 2010. The transparency of the second Chinese SWF, SAFE, was clearly rated insufficient in the same year, reaching a score of only 2 (SWF Institute, 2010).

In general terms, it has been observed that "SWFs do not meet the standards set by local financial institutions, which demand rigid governance structures and disclosure. As a result, we can infer that if SWFs align their governance practices with those of the local financial institutions, legitimacy would be granted" (Monk, 2008, p. 13). Recent experience shows that the lack of transparency of some SWFs can lead to defensive reactions, as observed in European countries such as Italy (Financial Times, 2008c), Germany, France and the UK (Die Zeit, 2008).

Reluctance to Accept the New Economic Order

Alongside concerns about national security and transparency, the significant wave of SWF investments from emerging countries such as Asian ones to developed economies such as European ones is, finally and most importantly, a sign of the shift in the balance of power in the world economy. New emerging market giants like China are becoming heavyweights on the new economic map that has previously been dominated by Western industrialized countries. Capital has "historically tended to flow from the core of an economic system to its periphery [...] sovereign wealth funds play a potentially important role in this apparent reversal. The sense that capital is increasingly flowing from the periphery to the core is raising a variety of political sensitivities in the core countries" (Hildebrand, 2008). It has been the norm for Western companies ("North") to invest in developing countries ("South") in recent decades. The present capital surpluses in some of these countries now lead to a situation where the "South" seeks out investment opportunities in the "North" (Ruet, 2009, p. 84). This can happen through private sector investment. However, privately-owned companies of a sufficient size to invest significantly in industrialized countries are often scarce in emerging and developing countries. These investments are thus increasingly being made by SWFs (Chaisse and Gugler, 2010).

As noted by Miracky *et al.* (2008, p. 18), "unsurprisingly, the combination of sovereign ownership, large size and impressive growth prospects, appetite for risk, and lack of transparency constitutes a perfect storm for political controversy. Much of the controversy originates in the fact that most new SWFs come from emerging countries outside the OECD. This raises the possibility of new alignments in global affairs between the established powers that became dominant after World War II versus those now emerging."

It should be noted that concerns as well as the nature of expected impacts regarding SWFs differ upon the origin of the funds. Until recently, SWFs originated largely from countries such as Norway, Singapore, Kuwait and the United Arab Emirates. These countries were generally considered to be friendly to the West and their investments were mainly concerned with boosting commercial returns (Whyte and Barysch, 2007). But newcomers, notably the SWFs from China, are growing rapidly, and their investment approach is feared to be more strategic and political in nature (Gugler *et al.*, 2010; PREQIN, 2011).

Policy Developments

In response to the main concerns generated by SWFs, international organizations as well as national governments have started to study what kind of regulations should be adopted. The present debate around SWFs may erroneously suggest that, as far as Europe is concerned, no rules exist to regulate those funds.

In a 2008 communication, the European Commission declared that EU law provides a "comprehensive regime to regulate the establishment and the actions of foreign investors, which covers SWFs in exactly the same way as any other foreign investor."[2] The communication reminds that free movement of capital is a fundamental freedom

[2] Communication from the Commission to the European Parliament, the Council, the European Economic and Social Committee and the Committee of the Regions. A common European approach to Sovereign Wealth Funds, COM/2008/0115 final, 27 February 2008, p. 5.

in the European common market, which can only be contradicted in clearly limited cases and which does not apply only between Member States but also prohibits restrictions on the movement of capital between third countries and Member States. However, this principle is limited by derogations and safeguard clauses that provide a *marge de manoeuvre* for national governments to restrict FDI, including FDI by SWFs (Chaisse and Gugler, 2010).

As indicated above, several European governments have become alarmed about SWFs. Some EU Member States are planning to adopt specific legislation on SWFs or have already adopted new laws and measures, which differ from one country to the other (Financial Times, 2008c; Greene and Yeager, 2008). The legislation in the UK and in France already allows fending off investments from SWFs. In Germany, a new law that entered into force in April 2009, following rumors that SWFs could buy some German firms including Deutsche Bank, Deutsche Telecom or Deutsche Bahn (Die Zeit, 2008), gives the federal government the right to prohibit any investment from non-EU or EFTA countries exceeding 25% of a company's stakes, in case "public security" or "public order" is at risk.[3]

With its 2008 communication, and in opposition to such national legislations, the EC promotes an EU common approach to SWF issues that emphasizes the free movement of capital principle and the commitment to an "open investment environment, support of a multilateral framework, use of existing instruments, respect of EC Treaty obligations and international commitments and finally, proportionality and transparency."[4] This common approach has been welcomed by the European Parliament and the European Economic and Social Committee, who underlined, however, "that the lack of transparency of certain SWFs may not allow a proper understanding of their

[3] Thirteenth Act amending the Foreign Trade and Payments Act and the Foreign Trade and Payments Regulation, 18 April 2009.

[4] Communication from the Commission to the European Parliament, the Council, the European Economic and Social Committee and the Committee of the Regions. A common European approach to Sovereign Wealth Funds, COM/2008/0115 final, 27 February 2008.

structure and motivation"[5] and that "the Commission should work together with the Member States and the supervisory authorities to improve the transparency of these funds, understand their motives and make sure they are not pursuing political objectives."[6]

In addition, all EU institutions have come to the conclusion that SWFs have an international scope and that the EC is thus not the level at which a final decision on a binding regulation should and could be taken. Hence, the EU actively supports a multilateral approach to address SWF issues. In particular, the EC seeks a code of conduct that would be developed jointly at the global level by the recipient countries and by the SWFs themselves.

The international reflection on the role of SWFs was launched in 2007 by the G7 Finance Ministers and backed in the same year by the G20. Since then, the IMF and the OECD have both worked on the definition of best practices, with the European Commission being actively involved in their work. In a joint effort with the IMF, the International Working Group on Sovereign Wealth Funds (IWG), an international group comprising 23 nations including China, Singapore, Russia, Kuwait and the United Arab Emirates,[7] was established in April 2008 to identify and draft a set of principles — called the Santiago Principles — that work as a voluntary code of conduct for SWFs (Chaisse and Gugler, 2010).

In the Asia-Europe perspective, it is worthwhile to note that GIC, Temasek and CIC are actively participating in the IWG. As reported by the Deputy Chairman and Executive Director of GIC, Dr. Tony Tan Keng Yam, in the GIC Report 2008/2009: "GIC supports efforts to enhance trust and the understanding of SWFs as financially-oriented investors. (…) GIC continues to support the

---

[5] Resolution of European Parliament on sovereign wealth funds, P6_TA-PROV(2008)0355, Strasbourg, 9 July 2008, point 2.

[6] Opinion of the European Economic and Social Committee, Section for Economic and Monetary Union and Economic and Social Cohesion (ECO/204). Opinion on financial integration: the case of European stock markets (own-initiative opinion), CESE 283/2008, 13 February 2008, para. 1.5.

[7] The IWG is now called International Forum of Sovereign Wealth Funds (IFSWF).

objectives of the Santiago Principles through the International Forum of Sovereign Wealth Funds established by the IWG to contribute to the development and maintenance of an open and stable investment environment."

14.5 Conclusion about the Role of SWFs in the Re-polarization of the Global Economy

What is the role played by SWFs in the re-polarization process of the global economy? What can we learn from SWF trends about how the new economic map will look like after the current financial and economic turmoil?

Developing countries have continuously gained in relative importance as sources of FDI in recent years. This emergence of developing countries as dominant investors is particularly striking in the case of sovereign wealth funds (SWFs). SWF investments in international capital markets, including Europe, have increased since 2007, are expected to grow further, and thus play an important role in explaining the neo-polar world. A closer look at the geographical origin of the funds reveals a bi-polar situation with Asia and the Middle East completely dominating the publicly available coverage of the increasingly important phenomenon of global SWF investments. Compared to the Middle East, Asia is far more dominant in the debate about the re-polarization of the world economy and hosts one of the frequently cited candidates to take the place of the main global economic pole in the future: China.

The size of SWFs is estimated to be about $4 trillion today, compared to $500 billion in 1990, and their considerable size is expected to grow further in the years ahead and could surpass $10 trillion in 2015. Virtually all of the funds of publicly reported total SWF investments between 1995 and 2008, as identified by Deutsche Bank (Kern, 2008), have been contributed by Asian (66%) and Middle Eastern SWFs (34%).

A closer look at Asian SWFs has revealed that Asia is of great importance in the context of sovereign investments in Europe, with Asian SWFs accounting for about half of all SWF investments in

Europe, although the Middle East may still be closer to the focal point of attention. It has been shown that Asian SWFs are a particular issue for the UK, being the country most targeted by Asian investments. Moreover, Asian SWFs have been shown to differ from Middle Eastern ones in terms of targeted sectors. Finance as well as Commodities & Energy, sectors of potential strategic importance, have attracted particular attention from Asian SWFs.

Our database of publicly reported investments by SWFs within the EU for the period 2007–2009 has allowed us to identify the most important SWFs in the Asia-Europe perspective. Asian SWF investments in Europe between 2007 and 2009 included deals by four different funds from China and Singapore: Government of Singapore Investment Corporation (GIC), Temasek Holdings, China Investment Corporation (CIC) and SAFE Investment Company.

Whereas Singapore plays a marginal role in the scientific debate on the re-polarization process of the world economy, it is important to take a special look at the Chinese SWFs. Do Chinese SWF investments reflect a pure financial consideration (i.e., the maximization of the return on investment) or a strategic and geopolitical objective? The identified investments undertaken by CIC and SAFE have been compared in this chapter to the Chinese government's official policy towards outward FDI. Although it is difficult to find a concluding classification of the funds as either pure financial investors or strategic investors due to the lack of transparency, it has been shown that one of the main objectives of the Chinese government in order to ensure its development as a global economic pole — the access to natural resources — is omnipresent in the identified investment patterns of Chinese SWFs.

Although SWF investments have been welcomed in Europe for their stabilizing effects, before and during the financial crisis, concerns prevail in the general attitude of European institutions towards SWFs. These concerns reflect the importance of investment issues in the re-polarization process of the world economy. European concerns about SWFs may be divided into three main categories: threats to national safety and security, lack of transparency, and difficulties in accepting geographical changes of economic power. It has been shown that concerns differ upon the origin of the SWFs. Middle Eastern countries were generally considered to be friendly to the West and their investments, were mainly concerned with boosting commercial returns. Chinese investments, on the other hand, have been subject to particular concerns due to the fact that they originate from a potential geopolitical rival. The policy responses to these concerns include *inter alia* strict legislation at the national level of some European countries, the promotion of a multilateral approach by the European Commission as well as a voluntary code of conduct at the international level. They all reflect the fact that SWFs are now conceived as an important global issue.

SWFs heavily invest in their home countries and only account for a still limited share of total global FDI flows. It is therefore difficult to grant them directly with a key role in the re-polarization process of the global economy. However, SWF trends impressively reflect the key changes to the global economic map. The analysis suggests an emergence of developing countries as dominant investors, notably including China from the list of the candidates to become the main global economic pole. The particular role of Chinese SWF investments is reflected in the special concerns they raise with respect to their potential geopolitical objectives.

Acknowledgements

I would like to thank all the persons involved in the research project on SWFs at the Center for Competitiveness of the University of Fribourg/Switzerland, in particular Prof. Dr. Philippe Gugler, Prof. Dr. Julien Chaisse and Laura Vanoli, research assistant, for their contributions to this chapter.

References

Aizenman, J. and Glick, R. (2007). Sovereign wealth funds: stumbling blocks or stepping stones to financial globalization? Federal Reserve Bank of San Francisco, *Economic Research*, Issue 38.

Aizenman, J. and Glick, R. (2008). Sovereign wealth funds: stylized facts about their determinants and governance. NBER Working Paper No. 14562, December.

Beck, R. and Fidora, M. (2008). The impact of sovereign wealth funds on global financial market. European Central Bank, ECB Occasional Paper No. 91.

Benoit, B. (2008). Berlin foreign investors bill clears hurdle. *Financial Times*, August 20, 2008.

Blundell-Wignall, A., Hu, Y. and Yermo, J. (2008). Sovereign wealth and pension fund issues. OECD Working Papers on Insurance and Private Pensions, No. 14. OECD Publishing.

Buckley, P. J., Cross, A. R., Tan, H., Liu, X. and Voss, H. (2008). Historic and emergent trends in Chinese outward direct investment. *Management International Review*, 48(6), 715–748.

Burton, J. (2007). Singapore's wealth fund flattered by imitation. *Financial Times*, September 4, 2007.

Chaisse, J. and Gugler, P. (2010). The regulation of sovereign wealth funds in the European Union: can supranational level limit the rise of national protectionism? In: K. Sauvant (Ed.), *Sovereign Investment: Concerns and Policy Reactions*. London: Oxford University Press, Forthcoming.

Chesterman, S. (2008). The turn to ethics: disinvestment from multinational corporations for human rights violations — the case of Norway's sovereign wealth fund. *American University International Law Review*, 23, 577–615.

China Investment Corporation (CIC) (2008). *Annual Report 2008*. Beijing.

Council of the European Union, revised version of the Presidency Conclusions of the Brussels European Council (13/14 March 2008), 7652/1/08 REV 1, Brussels, 20 May 2008.

Council of the European Union, Economic and Financial Affairs, 2857th Council meeting, 7192/08, 4 March 2008.

Die Zeit (2008). Chinesen wollen die Deutsche Bahn. *Die Zeit*, September 4, 2008.

European Commission (2008). Communication from the Commission to the European Parliament, the Council, the European Economic and Social Committee and the Committee of the Regions. A common European approach to sovereign wealth funds. COM/2008/0115 final, 27 February 2008.

European Economic and Social Committee (2008). Opinion of the European Economic and Social Committee. Section for Economic and Monetary Union and Economic and Social Cohesion (ECO/204). Opinion on financial integration: the case of European stock markets (own-initiative opinion). CESE 283/2008, 13 February 2008, para. 1.5.

European Parliament (2008). Resolution of European Parliament on sovereign wealth funds. P6_TA-PROV(2008)0355, Strasbourg, 9 July 2008, point 2.

Financial Times (2008a). Temasek eyes further investment in Western banks despite losses. *Financial Times*, August 22, 2008.

Financial Times (2008b). Beijing's shadowy pool for buying up best assets. *Financial Times*, September 12, 2008.

Financial Times (2008c). Italy set to curb sovereign wealth funds. *Financial Times*, October 21, 2008.

Financial Times (2009a). CIC in €800m offer to Apax. *Financial Times*, December 2, 2009.

Financial Times (2009b). EQT and Singapore fund seal €2.3bn Springer buy. *Financial Times*, December 11, 2009.

Financial Times (2009c). Glencore takes step closer to flotation. *Financial Times*, December 23, 2009.

GIC (2007). Merrill Lynch completes sale of main London office campus to GIC. GIC News Releases, June.

GIC website. Report on the Management of the Government's Portfolio for the Year 2008/2009. http://www.gic.com.sg, accessed February 22, 2010.

Greene, E. and Yeager, B. (2008). Sovereign wealth funds — a measured assessment. *Capital Markets Law Journal*, 3.

Gugler, P. and Boie, B. (2009). The rise of Chinese multinational enterprises. In: J. Chaisse and P. Gugler (Eds.), *Expansion of Trade and FDI in Asia: Strategic and Policy Challenges*. London: Routledge, Contemporary Asia Series.

Gugler, P., Keller, M. and Vanoli, L. (2010). Chinese SWFs: at the crossroad between the visible and the invisible hand? Conference Paper submitted at the 4th China Goes Global Conference, Harvard University, Cambridge.

Hildebrand, P. M. (2008). The challenge of sovereign wealth funds. http://www.voxeu.com/index.php?q=node/881.

International Monetary Fund (IMF) (2008). Sovereign wealth funds: a work agenda. www.imf.org/external/np/pp/eng/2008/022808.pdf.

Kern, S. (2008). *SWFs and Foreign Investment Policies — An Update*. Deutsche Bank Research.

Kimmitt, R. M. (2008). Public footprints in private markets: sovereign wealth funds and the world economy. *Foreign Affairs*, January/February.

Lyons, G. (2008). State capitalism: the rise of sovereign wealth funds. *Law and Business Review of the Americas*, 14(5).

Miracky, W., Dyer, D., Fisher, D., Goldner, T., Lagarde, L. and Piedrahita, V. (2008). Assessing the risks: the behaviours of sovereign wealth funds in the global economy. Monitor Group.

Monk, A. (2008). Recasting the sovereign wealth fund debate: organizational legitimacy, institutional governance and geopolitics. Oxford University Centre for the Environment, Working Papers in Employment, Work and Finance, No. WPG08-14.

Nicolas, C. (2006). European coordination at the World Bank and International Monetary Fund: a question of harmony? ADS Consultants Report, Brussels: 8–10.

Norway Ministry of Finance website. Norway's position in the debate on sovereign wealth funds. http://www.regjeringen.no/en/dep/fin/Selected-topics/The-Government-Pension-Fund/Norways-position-in-the-debate-on-Sovere.html?id=487466, accessed October 15, 2010.

Park, D. (2008). Developing Asia's new sovereign wealth funds and global financial stability. ADB Briefs, No. 1, October.

Poncet, S. (2007). Inward and outward FDI in China. Panthéon-Sorbonne-Economie, Université Paris 1 CNRS and CEPII, Working Paper.
PREQIN (2011). *2011 Preqin Sovereign Wealth Fund Review*. London.
Rodan, G. (2006). Singapore: globalization, the developmental state and politics. In: G. Rodan, K. Hewison and R. Robison (Eds.), *The Political Economy of South-East Asia: An Introduction*, 3rd edn. Melbourne: Oxford University Press.
Röller, L. H. and Véron, N. (2008). Safe and sound: an EU approach to sovereign investment. Bruegel Policy Brief, November.
Ruet, J. (2009). The reshaping of global capitalism by MNEs from emerging countries. In: J. Chaisse and P. Gugler (Eds.), *Expansion of Trade and FDI in Emerging Asia: Strategic and Policy Challenges*. London: Routledge, Contemporary Asia Series.
Schüler-Zhou, Y., Brod, M. and Schüller, M. (2010). Heading for Europe? Push and pull factors for Chinese FDI in EU. In: I. Alon, M. Fetscherin and P. Gugler (Eds.), *Chinese International Investments*. Palgrave Publisher, Forthcoming.
Subacchi, P. (2007). *Asian SWFs in Europe: Much Ado about Nothing?* Chatham House.
SWF Institute (2011). SWF Institute website. Retrieved from http://www.swfinstitute.org/what-is-a-swf/.
Temasek website. Temasek Review 2009. http://www.temasekholdings.com.sg, accessed February 22, 2010.
UNCTAD (2008). *World Investment Report 2008*. Geneva.
UNCTAD (2009). *World Investment Report 2009*. Geneva.
UNCTAD (2010). *World Investment Report 2010*. Geneva.
UNCTAD (2011). *World Investment Report 2011*. Geneva.
Weisman S. (2008). Sovereign wealth funds promise to avoid geopolitical goals. *International Herald Tribune*, March 21, 2008.
Whyte, P. and Barysch, K. (2007). What should Europe do about sovereign wealth funds? *Centre for European Reform Bulletin*, Issue 56, October/November.
Zhan, J. X. (1995). Transnationalization and outward investment: the case of Chinese firms. *Transnational Corporations*, 4(3), 67–100.

Chapter 15

Stuck in the Middle: A Challenge of Re-polarization for Europe and Indonesia

Janti Gunawan, Elizabeth L. Rose and Rebecca Piekkari

15.1 Introduction

Economic re-polarization raises concerns on many levels, including humanitarian, business, and environmental. Developed economies represented in the European Union (EU) and its executive body, the European Commission (EC), have strong motivation — and arguably moral responsibility — to take steps to manage such a global development. Targeted development-oriented investment in less developed countries, especially pertaining to the enhancement of a low-carbon economy, offers the potential to create friendly linkages across regional borders (United Nations Conference on Trade and Development, 2010).

The EC has allocated extensive financial resources to programs that support the United Nations' Millennium Development Goals (MDG). In this chapter, we describe one such initiative in Indonesia — an international public-private partnership involving the development of a tourism venue. This cooperation includes a French public-private venture created with EC funding, the Indonesian government, an international non-governmental organization, and a potential joint venture between private investors from France and Indonesia. The project addresses both economic and environmental needs in a geographically unique, but economically disadvantaged, region of the country. This case study offers an insider's perspective on one European linkage with

Indonesia, which, as a founding member of ASEAN,[1] is an important economic player in the region. By focusing on Indonesia and ASEAN, we emphasize that "Asia" is more than just the economic powerhouses of Japan, Singapore, South Korea, China, and India. Yet, Indonesia as an economically less powerful nation may offer fruitful opportunities for bridging the gap between the EU and Asia in a tri-polar world, leveling the power balance in the new economic order and locating new allies further afield. Through Indonesia, which has the world's largest Muslim population, we offer an example of a successful bilateral European-Asian relationship that transcends religious differences.

In this chapter, we argue that both Indonesia and Europe face being "stuck in the middle" as the world is being re-polarized, albeit for different reasons. Within Asia, Indonesia is faced with regional competitors, some of whom enjoy lower labor costs and others who have the benefit of more developed infrastructure (e.g., Lee and Tan, 2006). Europe, in turn, risks being marginalized by the longstanding members of the Triad — the US and Japan — and by the new emerging economic powers of China and India. From this perspective, both Europe and Indonesia could benefit from increased mutual economic collaboration, particularly with careful selection of projects. For example, environmental issues in Western Europe are quite advanced, while Indonesia has a real need for development in this area. Hence, collaboration focusing on environmental sustainability in the tourism sector, which is a sector targeted for growth in Indonesia, seems to have especially strong potential for the development of more extensive ties between Europe and Asia.

The remainder of this chapter is organized as follows. In Section 15.2, we introduce the context of Indonesia. Section 15.3 deals with existing and prior linkages between Europe and Indonesia, and we then introduce the focal linkage in Section 15.4. The following sections (15.5 and 15.6) explore the European and Indonesian aspects of the project, and Section 15.7 concludes with a discussion

[1] Current ASEAN members are Brunei Darussalam, Cambodia, Indonesia, Lao PDR, Malaysia, Myanmar, Philippines, Singapore, Thailand, and Vietnam.

of the potential for future connections between Europe and Indonesia in the tourism sector.

15.2 Indonesian Context

Consisting of an archipelago of more than 17,000 islands, Indonesia is the world's fourth most populous nation, with approximately 235 million inhabitants. Its inhabitants include approximately 400 ethnic groups that speak over 700 languages, and give Indonesia the largest Muslim population (86% of Indonesians). The nation's per capita GDP was approximately US$4,300 in 2010, compared to the EU average of over US$32,900. Indonesia's most recent (2009) Gini index is 39.4, and 13.3% of the population lives below the poverty line (CIA, 2011). Unemployment is at approximately 7.1%, with youth unemployment at over 20%, which is especially problematic.

Although Indonesia is a Muslim country, its government and laws follow democratic principles. This is arguably an outcome of more than three centuries of largely European occupation (Dutch, Portuguese, and English). Indonesia, which has been a republic since 1945, has experienced three post-independence institutional environments. The Sukarno era (1945–1965) was characterized by domestically-focused political changes, international isolation, and nationalism. This era saw the rise of state-owned enterprises that remain important players in the current Indonesian business environment. During the Soeharto era (1966–1998), Indonesia was more open to foreign cooperation, as evidenced by the liberalization of foreign exchange and trade policies, and the development of export-oriented policies and the encouragement of inward foreign direct investment (FDI), especially in the manufacturing sector. Prior to the launch of export-oriented policies, the Indonesian economy was heavily dependent on oil and other natural resources. Following the policy changes, agriculture remained extremely important to the domestic economy (as is the case today), but the manufacturing sector became a key driver. Indonesia's inward FDI has been dominated primarily by Japanese and US firms, in the automotive and mining sectors, respectively. The third era, starting with the financial crisis of 1998, has brought a more democratic situation to Indonesia, although the business environment is still quite changeable. Following massive divestment by US and European firms, inward FDI flows have returned to at least pre-crisis levels. Domestically, extensive decentralization in 2001 altered the institutional situation, creating a friendlier business environment, with the government establishing free trade and economic partnership agreements and facilitating the development of industry clusters. However, challenges remain with respect to creating effective coordination mechanisms among the national, provincial, and local governments (Winters, 2010).

With a 6.2% growth in GDP in 2010 (Biro Pusat Statistik, 2010a), Indonesia is weathering the global financial crisis better than most countries. Its key industries are petroleum and natural gas, textiles, apparel, footwear, mining, cement, chemical fertilizers, plywood, rubber, food, and tourism. Indonesia's export-oriented economy generated US$116.51 billion in 2009. Some 19% of Indonesia's exports go to the EU. Although this is a very small portion of overall imports by EU countries, the EU remains an important source of FDI in Indonesia, with European firms having moved to replace US divestment following the financial crisis. Japan is Indonesia's largest export market, accounting for over 20% of exports. This is consistent with the strong Japanese FDI presence in the country. Indonesia is thus likely to experience spillover economic effects of the 2011 tsunami disaster in Japan, and may need to search for greater diversification in its export markets, in order to buffer its own economy.

While viewing Asian markets as key to their success, Indonesian firms have to balance their difficult "stuck in the middle" position within the region. In terms of providing cheap labor, Indonesia can no longer compete with other emerging economies in Asia, such as Vietnam. On the other hand, Indonesia also faces a challenge in relation to its more developed Asian neighbors, which compete effectively based on their more advanced infrastructure. This puts pressure on Indonesian businesses to look for innovative approaches beyond the region, with Europe, for example.

The Muslim world does not seem to contribute significantly to the Indonesian economy. Despite being the largest Muslim country,

Indonesia has rather limited business relationships with other Islamic nations. Most such economic relations are associated with Indonesian workers employed in other predominately Muslim countries, such as Malaysia and Saudi Arabia. However, many employment situations in these countries involve the protection of these unskilled and informal Indonesian workers and their human and employment rights.

This situation seems to present an opportunity for the EU. As major investors, European firms have been key players in the Indonesian economy. However, the rising activity of other Asian nations, including Japan, China, and ASEAN members, means that EU members face the risk of having their relative standing in the Indonesian economy reduced, as noted in the European External Action Service (2006).

15.3 The EU and Indonesia — Past and Existing Connections

The EU's development activities for Indonesia are strongly connected to its region-to-region strategy through ASEAN. Via the Development Co-operation Instrument (DCI), the EU has allocated over €5.187 billion to Asia for the period 2007–2013, with 81% of the allocation planned for development assistance for individual countries. Guided by the Millennium Development Goals (MDGs), the DCI aims to work toward eradicating poverty and promoting democracy, whilst encouraging high standards of governance and respect for human rights and the rule of law in target countries and regions. For the DCI's activities in Asia, five thematic programs supplement the MDGs: Investing in People (diseases, health, gender, education, culture, employment, and youth); Environment (and sustainable use of natural resources); Non-State Actors/Local Authorities in Development; Food Security; and Migration and Asylum.

More specific to Indonesia, recent EU developmental assistance (on the order of €6 million per annum) is aimed at reducing poverty and its impact on the Indonesian population. Key foci have included basic education and sustainable management of the country's natural resources: forests, water, and the natural environment (particularly in rural areas). The EU has funded programs to aid the development of stronger institutions related to governance, addressing a broad range of issues such as the management of trade, access to justice, and public administration reforms to facilitate the delivery of basic services (e.g., health and education). In addition, the assistance includes broader issues such as the environment, human rights, gender equality, and conflict prevention. Examples of EU-funded projects in Indonesia — including developmental assistance, disaster relief, and other types of support — are shown in Table 15.1.

Of course, not all of the linkages between Europe and Indonesia are established at a purely governmental level. European businesses play an important role in the Indonesian economy, and hybrid forms of cooperation, including both public and private entities, are now evolving. One field in which such hybrid approaches are developing is tourism. Cutting across traditional sectors, tourism has the potential to play an important role in the development process, as it incorporates trade, investment, and education, and facilitates the transfer of knowledge. The development of the tourism sector involves economic, social, and political players, leading a recent World Tourism Organization conference to conclude that partnerships between the public and private sectors are especially critical for the development of tourism-related projects. As a large country, in terms of both population and land mass, and home to some remarkable natural environments, Indonesia has real tourism potential. However, the development of its tourism sector is rather slow, relative to other ASEAN countries. Figure 15.1 shows the number of tourist arrivals in ASEAN countries from 2006 to 2009. Indonesia, with a population of 231 million, was visited by approximately six million tourists in 2009. In contrast, Malaysia, with a population of 27.7 million, welcomed 23.6 million tourists during the same year. With approximately 10% of the tourists coming from Europe, this suggests the presence of unexplored tourism potential. Carefully constructed partnerships in the Indonesia tourism sector may well offer benefits for both Indonesian and European interests.

Table 15.1: Selected EC support for Indonesia in the 21st century.

Focus	Description	Amount
Education	Working with central and local authorities to improve the quality of basic education	€20 million
Health	Developing improved access to community health services in Jambi, South Sumatra and Papua	€35 million
Trade	Facilitating EU-Indonesia trade by providing technical expertise and twinning with EU laboratories, to remove barriers to trade	€8.5 million
	Helping to enhance the efficiency and transparency of customs management systems	€3.5 million
Environment	Working toward improved water resource management	€10 million
	Negotiating an EU-Indonesia voluntary partnership agreement to ensure the traceability of legal forestry export products	€15 million
Civil society	Assisting local organizations with regional programs, including delivering aid to uprooted people, education, trade and investment, and the environment	€62 million
	Small grants in support of human rights and democracy	€3.6 million
	Support for local elections and reforms of local governance systems to further the peace process in Aceh, following momentum developed in the aftermath of the 2004 tsunami	€25 million
Disaster relief	Reconstruction efforts in Java (in addition to immediate humanitarian and rehabilitation aid), following the 2006 earthquakes	€30 million
	Reconstruction efforts in Aceh and North Sumatra, following the 2004 tsunami (regenerating communities, restarting livelihoods, repairing large infrastructure)	€200 million

Source: http://eeas.europa.eu/delegations/indonesia.

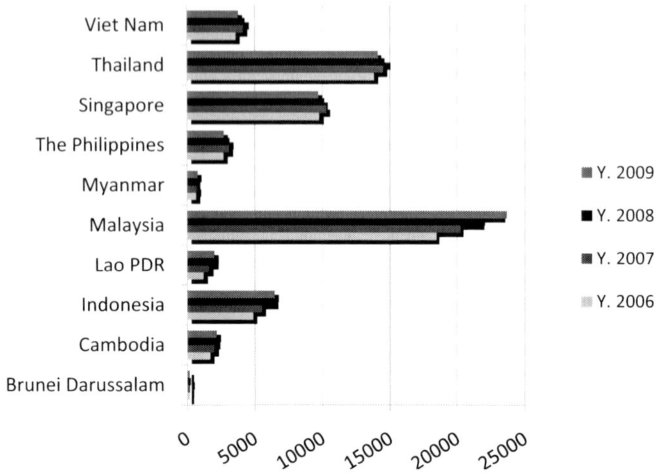

Figure 15.1: Tourist arrivals in ASEAN countries, 2006–2009.
Source: ASEAN Secretariat (www.aseansec.org).

15.4 A New European-Indonesian Connection Through a Public-Private Partnership

Public-private partnership (PPP) collaborations aim to provide mutually beneficial outcomes for governments, private entities, and communities, through the joint development of large-scale projects as diverse as infrastructure and pharmaceutical development (Kim *et al.*, 2005). PPPs take various forms, allowing different parties to bring unique contributions to the partnerships (WTO, 2003). The benefits of PPPs include the sharing of risk and the potential for faster innovation. In the context of an international PPP (IPPP) that involves a partner from a developed economy contributing to a project in a developing economy, knowledge transfer is another important outcome, providing the potential to create long-term benefits for the recipient country. The implementation of PPPs is typically of a limited duration, with a clearly defined end-point, and the key driver is generally the lack of local financial capacity to fund expensive projects such as development (Kim *et al.*, 2005).

The PPP that we consider in this chapter is in the tourism sector. Initiated by the United Nations' International Labor

Organization (ILO), the partnership involves the Indonesian government, and private entities in both Indonesia and France. Indonesia faces challenges with respect to fostering its economic development while dealing with a particularly high rate of youth unemployment. Building on an earlier multi-year youth employment project undertaken with European funding (the US$2.7 million Netherlands-ILO Cooperation Program), the ILO's Indonesian operation initiated the Job Opportunities for Youth (JOY) project. One component of JOY, "Local Economic Development" (LED), aims to provide inputs and examples for initiatives to combat youth unemployment, while improving local economies and facilitating young people's entry into the labor market through various programs that pertain to enterprise development and capacity development training. Two LED pilot projects are currently located at the foot of Mount Bromo, in East Java. Mount Bromo is the region's icon, and tourism, with the volcano as its focus, has been identified as a key sector for achieving the goals of the LED and JOY projects. Feasibility studies and LED fora show that the area has considerable potential for tourism, based on its unique natural, rugged beauty and volcanic activity. However, the limited local facilities and the decentralization of tourism promotion and attendant need for coordination among national, regional and district governments impose serious constraints on the region's ability to attract tourists.

A defining feature of Indonesia's location is associated with the fact that it has the world's largest number of active volcanoes, formed at the junction of the Eurasian and Indo-Australian tectonic plates. While theme parks are booming in the country, none of them has a volcanic theme. This gap has led to an investigation into the feasibility of using a PPP arrangement to create a replication of Vulcania — a volcano-themed park in Saint-Ours-les-Roches, Auvergne, France — in the Bromo region of East Java. Such a project would establish a new EU-Asia connection that differs to most, in that it is focused on the service sector and is driven by locational attributes, rather than the availability of low-cost labor.

15.5 The Auvergne Vulcania PPP in France

The model for the proposed project in Indonesia is the Vulcania park in France. Vulcania was based on the idea of Katia and Maurice Krafft, French volcanologists who died in 1991 while filming an eruption in Japan. Building on the Kraffts' concept of establishing a volcanic museum in the Chaîne des Puys, an ancient seismic region in central France, the regional government decided to establish a hybrid educational/amusement park with a volcanic theme, using a PPP arrangement. Not surprisingly, given the scale and cost of the project, taking Vulcania from plan to fruition was a decade-long endeavor. The involvement of globally renowned architect Hans Hollein increased the project's visibility. However, the involvement of former French President Valéry Giscard d'Estaing was arguably the key to making Vulcania a reality. Giscard d'Estaing offered the project both strong, highly visible support and considerable political clout that spanned different levels of government.

Established to serve both entertainment and educational purposes, Vulcania was itself developed using a PPP framework. The park's construction was paid for by the regional government of Auvergne, the French government, and the EU, while the Auvergne Regional Council owns the park. The Vulcania park is managed under a PPP involving the Auvergne regional council in conjunction with large, local private companies (e.g., bottled water producers, airlines, Michelin) that have clear interests in the region's economic growth. Operational since 2002, Vulcania has adapted its strategy in response to commercial realities. Reacting to feedback that the park was perceived to be overly scientific, more entertainment (e.g., 3-D movies) has been added to the visitor experience. The current mix of education and entertainment has yielded a financially successful operation. Over 80% of the park's visitors come from outside the region, and approximately 40% report having come to the area especially to visit the park. In the 50 years before the park's opening, Auvergne ranked 15th out of 22 regions in France, with respect to income from tourism. In 2002, with no substantial change apart from Vulcania, Auvergne reached 8th place on this measure, and has remained there since. While impossible to assess accurately, the Vulcania park is widely viewed as providing strong economic benefit to the Auvergne region, with some estimates in excess of €50 million per annum.

The Vulcania tourism investment was aimed at promoting local economic development in a rather remote area, by creating local jobs and assisting entrepreneurship, whilst providing educational opportunities related to the topic of volcanoes. Three levels of government collaborated to finance the €118 million project: regional (85%), Europe (10%), and national (5%). Under the agreement, the Auvergne regional government owns the park and manages the financing of the investment. The design and construction of the park was contracted to private partners, and the operation is conducted through a PPP, under which the park is managed privately, with an annual fee paid to the regional government.

The Vulcania model seems to offer potential for the Mount Bromo project. There are, of course, challenges. Following the 2001 transition of Indonesia's governance processes from fully centralized to fully decentralized, both national and local governments are still learning how to develop integrated approaches to planning and implementation. The ILO's involvement in the initial investigation of the project is intended to overcome some of these obstacles.

15.6 The Vulcania Indonesia International PPP

Situated on the "Pacific ring of fire", which is host to approximately 90% of the world's earthquakes, Indonesia has the largest number of active volcanoes in the world. However, as tourism strategies are decentralized to the regional level, there has not been an integrated approach developed for promoting the Bromo area. The governance systems thus present a challenge, as the national, provincial and four district governments are all involved in any development of the Bromo area. While the public sector faces the need to address issues including infrastructure and the development of knowledge, staff, and community, financial constraints and the lack of clear policies present obstacles. The ILO has established LED programs in which partnerships among the public sector, the private sector, and communities underlie all activities on the ground. The ILO's experience with coordinating among various stakeholders suits the PPP environment, and may assist the project with respect to overcoming institutional limitations and improving stakeholders' benefits. Additional challenges include low literacy levels among the local people, particularly in light of the educational component of a Vulcania-type park experience, and limited financial and institutional resources.

Mount Bromo is a key part of the Bromo Tengger Semeru National Park, located in East Java, to the southeast of Surabaya (Indonesia's second-largest city). The park's name is derived from two of its three mountains — Mounts Semeru and Bromo — and the local indigenous people, the Tenggerrese. The area consists of five volcanoes (four of which are active), and a range of ecosystems including savanna, forest, desert, river, and lake. The local culture is also very specific, as the region is inhabited by one of the few substantial Hindu populations in predominately Muslim East Java. The people who live in the surrounding area are generally very poor. While the area covers four districts (Probolinggo, Lumajang, Pasuruan and Malang), tourism is actively promoted primarily in the district of Probolinggo, which, along with Malang, has the most well-established infrastructure.

Given that Mount Bromo itself is located within an area that is both a national park and culturally protected, the plan is to locate the theme park at some distance from the volcano. This generates a strong need for effective coordination among the four district governments, in order to define the location of the proposed Vulcania-type investment, and to maximize the benefit of the project for the four communities. Of course, the intent of utilizing an international PPP vehicle to create the park means the addition of another important voice. The private partner will certainly require input on how to establish an effective and cost-efficient coordination framework with stakeholders across districts and different levels of infrastructure and capacity, while providing excellent service to customers.

The idea is to use the park as a magnet, to draw people and to provide them with both entertainment and education about volcanoes, in the hope that they will then be interested in exploring

Mount Bromo and the surrounding area. Income would then be generated for the local community through a multiplier effect, as tourists would be expected to use local transportation, eat at local food stalls, and purchase local souvenirs.

Large-scale PPP projects tend to have the government and the private sector as key drivers behind the agreement. The situation for Vulcania Indonesia is a bit different, with the community, spearheaded by the ILO, serving as the driver. There are, of course, real challenges associated with establishing linkages that are strong enough to effectively replicate a well-established project from a developed European country in a developing country in Asia, through the vehicle of a somewhat non-traditional IPPP.

Large projects may employ PPPs at various stages, including pre-establishment (e.g., design, research, product development, advocacy), construction, and operation (Kim *et al.*, 2005). In the case of the Vulcania Indonesia project, it seems likely that IPPPs will be involved in all of these stages. Given the fact that the focal Mount Bromo is located in a national park, and that access to the area is controlled by four separate districts, the IPPP for the Vulcania Indonesia project has a complex collection of stakeholders, including several layers of government (district, provincial, national), the international partner (Vulcania France), private enterprise (national and/or international), and communities (both local and an international NGO). In order for Vulcania Indonesia to achieve the economic potential suggested in preliminary feasibility studies, each of the stakeholders has important contributions to make to the project. Table 15.2 displays the result of a situational analysis, considering the various stakeholder groups and their resources and roles.

A successful PPP in the tourism sector requires contributions from various stakeholders (Franco and Estevao, 2010). Developing a Vulcania park in Indonesia will require a complex, multi-stage IPPP; importantly, each stage has the potential to provide spillover development benefits. Firstly, the planning of the project will need to include a variety of actors. While the project is likely to be privately-owned, the government is interested in a vehicle that will promote volcanic education and assist with much-needed local economic development. Thus,

Table 15.2: Contributions of various partners for Vulcania Indonesia.

	Local/provincial/ national government	Vulcania France and international agencies	Private partners	Local communities and ILO
Resources to be contributed	Land, law	Technical expertise (hardware, software)	Financial resources, managerial skills, business networks	Labor, unique culture, hospitality
Resources lacking	Finance, knowledge (technical, managerial) necessary to design, build and operate the park		Knowledge regarding Indonesian regulations pertaining to investment, infrastructure, promotion, and transportation	Financial, capacity (knowledge) management
Strategic role	To integrate various programs and expertise regarding volcanic activity in Indonesia	To transfer knowledge and develop a common understanding of environmentally-friendly investment	To promote the companies internationally	To promote local culture and learning whilst developing sustainability

a consortium that includes public, private, and community involvement seems necessary for the facilitation of the proposed park's multiple objectives. The consortium will require competent and visionary leadership that is willing and able to work across the many levels of stakeholders and operate within the often complicated institutional environment of Indonesia. This is effectively the role that was assumed by Valéry Giscard d'Estaing for Vulcania in France; a comparable "champion" has not yet emerged for Vulcania Indonesia.

Considering the fact that governance systems in Indonesia are still in the developing stage — including the strategic and operational alignment for government coordination and public-private cooperation among national, regional and district levels — Vulcania Indonesia has the opportunity to serve as a model not only for the province of East Java, but more broadly for Indonesia and other nations facing similar levels of development. Thus, the planning stage for the project will involve the fostering of democratic processes, which also represents a significant development for a Muslim-populated country such as Indonesia.

Secondly, design and construction will clearly be undertaken through contracts with private partners. An international design competition would provide Indonesian architects and developers with useful exposure to worldwide benchmarking, with respect to both technical and aesthetic aspects of designing tourism venues.

Thirdly, operation and management is expected to involve both public and private players. The partnership with Vulcania in France will allow the European stakeholder to assume a strategic role, sharing specific expertise and introducing international standards of conduct to tourism operators in the region of the Bromo Tengger Semeru National Park. Improved standards with respect to tourism should then expand to much of East Java, given that tourists will be interacting with service providers in the wider area, both before and after the Vulcania Indonesia experience. Working with international partners, both public and private, is also expected to provide local and national government agencies with the opportunity to learn by observing good governance in practice. These particular European-Indonesian ties in the context of a community-based tourism initiative, have the potential for extra impact; in addition to effects related to economic and human resource development, it will also help to smooth the relationships between parties with different religious backgrounds by promoting common values.

To date, the key stakeholders in Indonesia — national, regional, and local governments, in addition to the community — have agreed to structure Vulcania Indonesia as a PPP, using land that belongs to the village government and the community. With financing coming primarily from the Indonesian national budget and expertise from Vulcania France, the park will be owned by stakeholders that include the provincial and four district governments; negotiations regarding ownership shares are ongoing. Agreement between Vulcania France and the Indonesian government is expected, following the East Java governor's recent visit to Auvergne. The ILO will no longer play a substantial part in the project as Vulcania Indonesia progresses, due to the completion of its broader project in Indonesia; efforts are currently under way to ensure that the leadership role it has played will be assumed by a governmental stakeholder.

15.7 Conclusion: A New Europe-Indonesia Linkage for Bridging the Gap in a Tri-polar World?

Tourism is important to Indonesia; it is the country's third most important non-oil/gas source of foreign revenue. In 2010, tourism accounted for nearly 20% of the employment of productive-aged people in Indonesia (Biro Pusat Statistik, 2010b). Despite its importance to the country, however, the sector remains underdeveloped. Indonesia welcomed approximately 6.4 million international visitors in 2009, compared to 10 million for Singapore and over 20 million for Malaysia. Given that nearly a third of the international visitors fly directly to Bali, which is a relatively self-contained destination, tourism in the rest of Indonesia is far from reaching its potential. The fact that the Mount Bromo area is a several-hour drive from the East Java capital of Surabaya means that adding the Vulcania park to an international tourist's itinerary would probably add at least two days to the average of 8.6 days spent in the country. Thus, in addition to the clear benefits that the Vulcania Indonesia IPPP would have for the economically disadvantaged districts in its vicinity, it would also be likely to have a positive impact on tourism in the larger East Java region.

Developing the tourism sector is particularly important for Indonesia. Typical of countries progressing along a development path, hourly wage rates in Indonesia have increased to a level such that Indonesia is no longer attracting manufacturing FDI based primarily on low-cost labor. Its reported 2010 wage rate was US$0.82, as compared to US$0.59, US$0.39, and US$0.31 for near-neighbors Vietnam, Cambodia, and Bangladesh, respectively.[2] As the manufacturing sector transitions from a focus on labor-intensive production for foreign firms to a more balanced portfolio, Indonesia's stuck-in-the-middle position (i.e., neither cheap labor nor fully-developed infrastructure) may be eased by a stronger focus on its abundant natural resources. Tourism is one way in which to utilize those natural resources in a sustainable manner.

Interestingly, Indonesia's position is not dissimilar to that of EU countries, with respect to wage rates. Among EU member nations, the World Bank-reported mean wage rate for 2009 was US$8.09, with a standard deviation of US$2.92. The 95% confidence interval for the EU mean (US$6.99, US$9.20) is fully lower than the mean wage rates for the other Triad countries (Japan at US$9.36 and the US at US$12.77), suggesting that the EU mean is significantly ($p < 0.05$) lower than the other two means. Using the same approach, the EU mean wage is, however, significantly higher than those of emerging powers China (US$1.93) and India (US$0.91). Closer to home, the computed 95% confidence interval for the mean wage rates for the EU does not overlap with that for several potential EU candidates[3] (US$2.27, US$3.58) or a collection of 11 less developed nations in the vicinity of Western Europe[4] (US$1.14, US$2.84),

---

[2] As reported by the World Bank; see http://www.sfgsa.org/Modules/ShowDocument.aspx?documentid=7753 for international wage rates.

[3] Albania, Bosnia and Herzegovina, Montenegro and Serbia.

[4] Azerbaijan, Belarus, Georgia, Kazakhstan, Kyrgyz Republic, Moldova, Russia, Tajikistan, Turkmenistan, Ukraine, Uzbekistan.

suggesting that the EU mean wage is significantly higher than those of these two neighboring groups. Thus, a strong argument can be made that the EU also faces a stuck-in-the-middle situation.

Indonesia's record with respect to managing its environment is not particularly strong; developing and institutionalizing more sustainable practices across a broad range of industries thus has the potential to create substantial impact. Given the unique nature of the Mount Bromo area and the natural focus of the Vulcania park, there is a clear imperative to adopt an environmentally sensitive approach to the project. This suits both the EC's focus on environmentally sustainable development and the ILO's focus on the creation of "green" jobs in the effort to combat high unemployment (especially for youth) in Indonesia. The educational component of the project has the potential to increase the environmental awareness of local stakeholders and the community at large, through both example and the development of educational programs and media on the subject of seismic and volcanic activity and environmental sustainability.

IPPPs involve collaboration across institutional and national environments. The Vulcania IPPP has players from both developed and developing countries, which provides spillover benefits for the Indonesian partners and possibilities for learning about a range of international-standard practices such as the development of guidelines, project management, environmentally-friendly design and operation, enterprise management, service provision for tourism, and human resource management (involving issues associated with both gender and human rights). Governance-related spillovers have the potential to be especially important for this particular IPPP, given the Indonesian government's focus on reducing corruption. Such sharing of expertise represents small, but potentially important, steps to mitigate both economic and political re-polarization. Compared to relatively simple aid packages, IPPPs involve both ongoing operational linkages and the possibility for broader and more institutionalized change. Moreover, in this age of religion-driven terrorism, undertaking such a project in the Bromo area, where people of multiple ethnicities and religions live in peace, is of particular importance. It demonstrates and promotes good practice of managing a diverse workforce in a global economy.

Indonesia is strongly embedded in Asia. While it possesses enduring linkages to Japan and is influenced by businesses in the West, these linkages are giving way to a more regional focus. In order to improve its position in the global economy and overcome the situation of being "stuck in the middle" in Asia, Indonesia faces a strong need to select, in a strategic manner, suitable partners. We argue that the EU finds itself in a parallel troubled position in the new tri-polar world, in which economic power is more diffused across a broader range of countries than was previously the case. Therefore, the EU is also on the lookout for support and new partners which would level its position and bridge the gap in relation to Asia. It is important to note that Asia consists of more than Japan, South Korea, Taiwan, China, and India. Some ASEAN members may offer interesting possibilities for the development of peaceful, mutually beneficial economic linkages. The Vulcania Indonesia case is based on an economic initiative between Europe and a Muslim country that is in a developing stage. While past ties between Europe and Indonesia have not always led to positive outcomes, this IPPP represents a large, new Europe-Indonesia connection that offers both economic and social benefit.

Acknowledgements

We are grateful to Matthieu Cognac, the ILO's youth employment specialist, for his valuable comments on an earlier version of this chapter.

References

ASEAN Secretariat. http://www.aseansec.org.

Biro Pusat Statistik (2010a). *Trends of the Selected Socio-Economic Indicators of Indonesia.* Jakarta: Biro Pusat Statistik.

Biro Pusat Statistik (2010b). *Labour Force Survey.* Jakarta: Biro Pusat Statistik.

Cetinski, V., Peric, M. and Sugar, V. (2009). The European dimension of public-private partnership and experiences in tourism of the Republic of Croatia. *Tourism and Hospitality Management*, 15(1), 85–100.

CIA (2011). The world factbook. https://www.cia.gov/library/publications/the-world-factbook/fields/2172.html.

European External Action Service. For EU support to Indonesia, http://eeas.europa.eu/delegations/indonesia. Accessed March 2011.

European External Action Service. For EU-Indonesia relations, http://ec.europa.eu/external_relations/indonesia/index_en.htm. Accessed March 2011.

European External Action Service (2006). Indonesia-European Community Strategy Paper, 2007–2013.

Franco, M. and Estevao, C. (2010). The role of tourism public-private partnerships in regional development: a conceptual model proposal. *CADERNOS EBAPE. BR*, 8(4), 600–612.

General Services Agency. For international wage rates, http://www.sfgsa.org/Modules/ShowDocument.aspx?documentid=1644. Accessed March 2011.

Kim, D. K., Kim, C. and Lee, T. H. (2005). Public and private partnership for facilitating tourism investment in the APEC region. APEC Tourism Working Group and Ministry of Culture and Tourism, Republic of Korea, College of Hotel and Tourism Management, Kyung Hee University.

Lee, H. H. and Tan, H. B. (2006). Technology transfer, FDI and growth in the ASEAN regions. *Journal of the Asia Pacific Economy*, 11(4), 394–410.

United Nations Conference on Trade and Development (2010). *World Investment Report: Investing in a Low-Carbon Economy*. Geneva: United Nations Publications.

Vulcania homepage. For the Vulcania park in Auvergne, France, http://www.vulcania.com/. Accessed March 2011.

Widodo, T. (2007). European presence in Indonesia. *Asia Europe Journal*, 5(3), 381–399.

Winters, M. (2010). Development Partners' Working Group on Decentralization and Local Governance (DPWG-DLG) report — country profile: Indonesia. USAID.

WTO (2003). *Cooperation and Partnerships in Tourism: A Global Perspective*. Madrid: World Tourism Organization.

Chapter 16

The Reform and Reconstruction of China's Social Security System

Chun Ding

16.1 Introduction

This chapter addresses the reforms implemented in China to help enable the country to become one of the key economic powers in the decades to come. It starts by discussing below China's social and economic development versus the reform and perfection of its social security system since the beginning of its reform and opening up. In Section 16.2 the current conditions, problems, and challenges of China's social security system are scrutinized. The relation between the perfection of the social security system and the sustainable social and economic development is then discussed in Section 16.3. In Section 16.4 it is concluded that China's social security system needs to be further improved to ensure that China maintains a sustainable economic development and a position as an important part of the tri-polar world after the current re-polarization.

The General Conditions of China's Economic and Social Development Since the Beginning of Its Reform and Opening Up

Since the beginning of China's process of reform and opening up in 1978, rapid economic growth at an annual average rate of 9.8% has been maintained in China for over 30 years. As seen in Figure 16.1, China's GDP in 2010 amounted to RMB39.7983 trillion, an equivalent of US$5.8791 trillion, 25 times the size of its GDP in the year 1978 (The Central People's Government of the People's Republic of

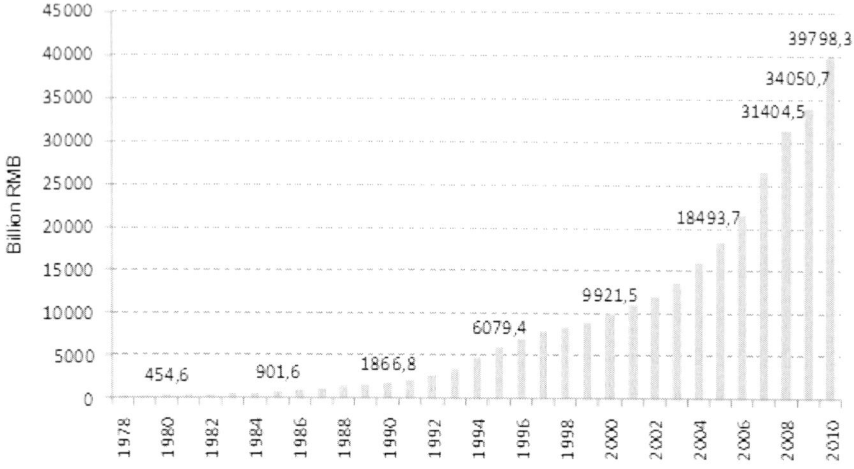

Figure 16.1: The growth of China's GDP in current prices, 1978–2010.
Source: National Bureau of Statistics of China, *China Statistical Yearbook* (various years).

China, 2011a). China has now become the 2nd largest economy in the world, second only to the US and surpassing Japan in terms of total volume of the economy. Its share of GDP to the world total has increased to 5.0% in 2005 and even to 9.5% in 2010, from a mere 1.8% in 1978 (The Central People's Government of the People's Republic of China, 2011b).

Following this rapid economic growth, a series of profound changes are emerging, which fundamentally alter China's social and economic structure. The major changes are as follows:

(1) The transition from a centrally planned economy to a market economy has been achieved. China's non-public-owned enterprises, which are usually regarded as the major players and representatives of a free market economy, already accounted for 71% of total GDP in 2008, a dramatic increase from a mere 1% in 1985 (National Bureau of Statistics of China). At the same time, the public-owned sector of China's economy, including state-owned and collective-owned enterprises, has shrunk by a large margin.
(2) Due to the unprecedented speed of industrialization, the structure of China's national economy has been tremendously

modified, with the manufacturing sector now propping up the whole economy as the major pillar, and the service sector expanding quickly after the transitional process of industrialization was largely finished. Measured in terms of the share of output against the total, China's overall structure of the primary, secondary, and tertiary industries has been optimized from a 28.2%–47.9%–23.9% ratio in 1978 to 11.3%–48.6%–40.1% in 2008 (National Bureau of Statistics of China). Compared to the data of 1978, the share of the primary industry has been reduced by 16.9%, while the share of the tertiary industry has increased by 16.2%.

(3) After its entry into the WTO and other related events, China has successfully integrated its own economy into the system of the world economy and achieved its economic internationalization. The share of its overall volume of import and export to the world total increased from a mere 0.79% in 1978 to 7.88% in 2008. As seen in Figure 16.2, China's total value of import and export in 2008 reached the level of US$2.5616 trillion, 123.1 times the size of its total volume of foreign trade in 1979 (National Bureau of Statistics of China). In terms of China's foreign exchange reserve, after surpassing the level of US$10 billion in 1990 (see Figure 16.3), it is now approaching the level of US$3 trillion,

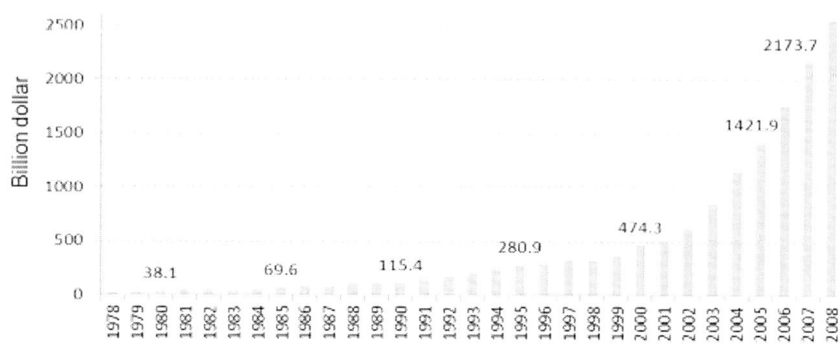

Figure 16.2: The change in the volume of China's import and export.

Source: National Bureau of Statistics of China, *China Trade and External Economic Statistical Yearbook 2009*.

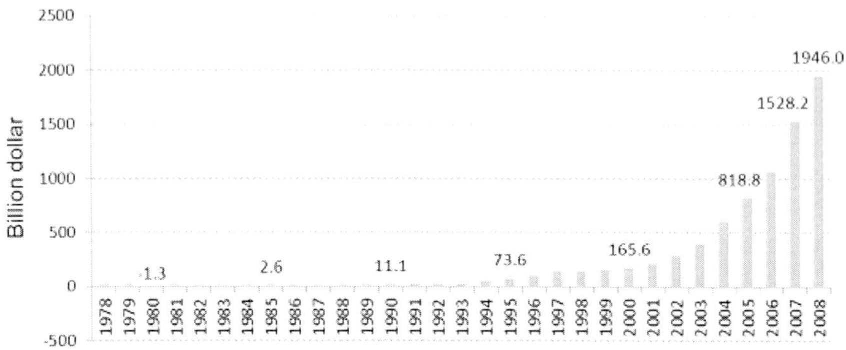

Figure 16.3: The change in China's foreign exchange reserve.

Source: http://www.locpg.hk/rszg/jjjs/200812/t20081202_3593.asp.

ranking China's foreign exchange reserve as the largest among all the countries in the world.

(4) Amid the industrialization, China's urbanization process is also being accelerated, drastically changing China's former rural-urban binary structure. China's urbanization rate increased from 19.4% in 1978 to 43.1% in 2008 (National Bureau of Statistics of China). Since the beginning of this new century, the urbanization rate has been increasing at an average speed of 1% per year.

At the same time, the living standards of the common Chinese people have also been raised significantly. In 1978, China's GDP per capita was only US$241 if calculated by annual average exchange rate, whereas in 2008 it had already reached US$3,194. In 2008 the urban average disposable income and the rural average disposable income were RMB15,781 and RMB4,761, respectively, an increase by 8.15 times and 7.93 times from 1978 levels if calculated by comparable prices. Meanwhile, the actual consumption level of common residents in China increased from RMB184 per capita per year in 1978 to RMB7,103 per capita per year in 2007 (see Figure 16.4).

The reform and reconstruction of China's social security system has been organized and implemented against the backdrop of China's fast pace of economic reform and growth. Therefore, on the one hand, China's continuous economic growth provides a solid material

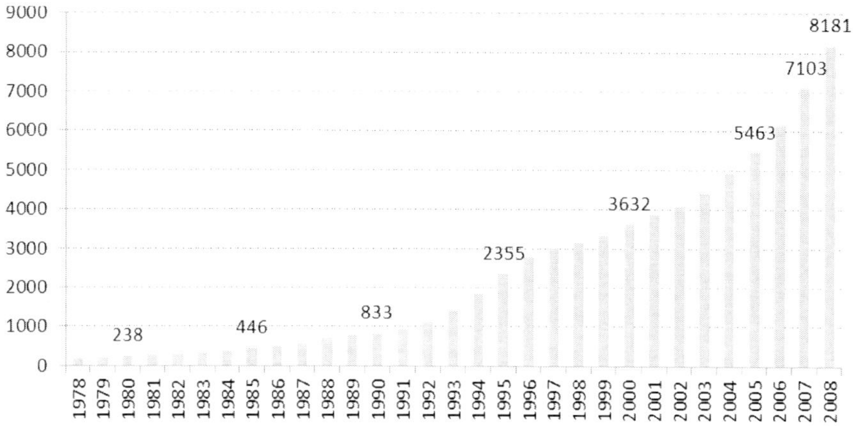

Figure 16.4: The change in the consumption level of Chinese residents.
Source: National Bureau of Statistics of China, *China Statistical Yearbook 2009*.

basis for the adjustment and modification of its social security system; on the other hand, the resulting affluence and prosperity brought by such quick economic growth has in turn nurtured a huge demand and strong initiative for the reform and reconstruction of China's social security system.

The History of Evolution, Reform, and Improvement of China's Social Security System

The Period of the Centrally Planned Economic System (1950–1978)

The People's Republic of China was founded in 1949. Several years later, in 1951, the State Council of the newly established People's Republic issued Labor Insurance Regulations, which brought into effect a set of labor insurance regulations targeted at employees of enterprises in urban areas, and a public-funded social security system targeted at employees of non-profit institutions and public servants. The Labor Insurance Regulations covered almost all the employees working for state-owned and collective-owned enterprises and non-profit institutions, as well as their family members, and included a wide variety of items such as pension, disease relief, work-related injury compensation, and welfare for maternity. However, the coverage of this set of regulations was rather limited, as it excluded those urban residents not employed by public-owned institutions, and common peasants, who accounted for over 80% of the total population of China. Under these circumstances, there existed a tremendous gap between those social groups inside and outside the official social security system. When this system was originally established, public-owned enterprises were responsible for paying social security fees, which could be used nationwide. Later, the operational model was changed and the public-owned enterprises directly provided security for their own employees. During the 1960s, a rural cooperative medical treatment system was established, based on a rural collective economy with a low level of security. Attaching great importance to primary medical treatment and public health and hygiene, this rural system was characterized by low-level investment, high-level return, and extensive coverage, and was highly praised by WHO.

Undoubtedly, China's social security system during this period was properly adapted to and articulated into its actual economic and political conditions, because China at that time operated a centrally planned economic system. This social security system indeed offered substantial security to urban workers and employees, but it was often criticized for its over-dependency on public-owned enterprises and government, its narrow coverage, and its low level of benefits.

The Period of Reform (1978–)

The stage of urgent response and original probing for reform (1978–1993)

China's economic reform, launched in 1978 with the final objective of building a market economy, dealt a huge impact on the social security system established under the former centrally planned economic system. Therefore, a series of urgent measures were adopted in response to the dramatic changes brought about by the economic reform. The changes and urgent measures were as follows:

(1) In China's rural economic reform, a contract system with responsibility linked to output was initiated and soon promoted

nationwide, which gradually replaced the former rural collective economic system. Amid such changes, the former rural cooperative medical insurance system, whose coverage was diminished to less than 5% of the total rural population in the mid-1980s from a previous share of 90%, automatically collapsed. Furthermore, during the market-oriented economic reform, a large number of public-owned institutions (mostly state-owned or collective-owned enterprises) almost inevitably went bankrupt due to their deteriorating financial situation in the increasingly intensified market competition, so they could no longer provide effective social security for their employees. At the same time, a large number of non-public-owned institutions (private enterprises, joint ventures, and other forms of foreign-funded enterprises) emerged during China's transition from a centrally planned economic system towards a market-oriented system. For example, the number of employees of private enterprises that were excluded from the network of the original social security system increased from 150,000 in 1978 to 7.6 million in 1991 (Chen and Wang, 2010). However, the free flow of labor was still obstructed. The human resources could not flow freely between public-owned institutions and non-public-owned enterprises due to a large gap between the benefits offered by the social security system of public-owned institutions and the inadequate conditions of social security of non-public-owned enterprises.

(2) In this sense, China's enterprises of different ownerships could not compete with each other on level ground. Public-owned enterprises were obligated to provide adequate benefits of social security for their employees, which increased their operational cost by a large margin and gave them a huge disadvantage in competing against non-public-owned enterprises, who were not burdened by such obligations. This situation ran contrary to the purpose of market-oriented reform, which aimed at bringing public-owned enterprises into a model of being self-responsible for any loss and profit sustained through their operations in the market.

(3) As China's population aged, the former "Pay-As-You-Go" model of financing for social security was faced with a serious challenge

> posed by financial sustainability. Some significant reform of the original social security system became inevitable. During this stage, the market competition mechanism was put into effect, and non-public-owned enterprises (such as private and foreign-funded enterprises) were invigorated by reform policies. Under these circumstances, many public-owned enterprises were bankrupted or forced to close down. As these public-owned enterprises were the only financial sources of social security benefits for their employees, the financing and payment of social security benefits, pensions and medical treatment fees, in particular, became a big problem for their employees and retirees. Hence, some attempts were made to probe a practical way to make possible social pooling and unified management of the social security fund (mainly the fund for pension and medical treatment), which meant that the fund should be paid by various enterprises but managed in a regionally unified way. Due to these measures, the social security benefits of the employees of some enterprises were no longer affected by the operational condition of those individual enterprises. In this sense, the function of social security was no longer attached to enterprises, but was returned to society instead. Meanwhile, the unemployment insurance was also introduced.

During this stage, all the reform measures were concentrated on some specific purpose for a specific branch of social security (such as pension and medical treatment), so as to offer supportive service to the reform of enterprises. These reform measures could therefore be viewed as an urgent response to economic reform and related social changes. In terms of institutional reform and re-arrangement, different measures and methodologies with strong regional characteristics were taken in different regions due to the diverse and unique problems facing these regions. Generally speaking, there was a lack of overall or systematic contemplation in the measures of social security reform taken at this stage; rather, they were the result of a backlash effect in the economic and social transition created by the reform towards a market economy.

The stage of building the framework of an urban social security system (1993–2002)

Economic reform during this stage was characterized by the establishment of the status of market economy in China. Therefore, the main aim of the reform at this stage was to reconstruct a social security system that could be integrated with the general structure of a market economy. Gradually, the general framework of an urban social security system was developed, which consisted of such social security branches as pension, medical treatment, unemployment benefits, maternity benefits, and work-related injury benefits. The largest institutional innovation during this stage was a new model of financing that combined the partial "Pay-As-You-Go" system, jointly financed by both corporate employers and employees, with a social pooling fund connected to a partial accumulation system and an individual saving account. This institutional innovation was applied to urban pensions and medical insurance systems, replacing the previous Pay-As-You-Go system that was financed solely by enterprises themselves. In accordance with this new design applied to the new old-age insurance system, the operational details were as follows. Both corporate employers and employees had to pay their share of the fund into an old-age insurance account, but the share paid by employers should be different from that paid by employees (usually different percentages of wages obtained by employees). The fund paid by employers and employees should be deposited into a social pooling fund and a private saving account of the individual employees, in accordance with a regulated ratio. After retirement, employees could then take out some money regularly from their individual old-age insurance accounts as their pension, but the actual amount of money they could get differed in accordance with the actual accumulations in their old-age insurance accounts. This new model of financing fully reflected the principle of combining social solidarity with self-responsibility. Meanwhile, the individual old-age insurance system was especially designed to deal with the needs of an aging population (the structure and details can be found in Figure 16.5).

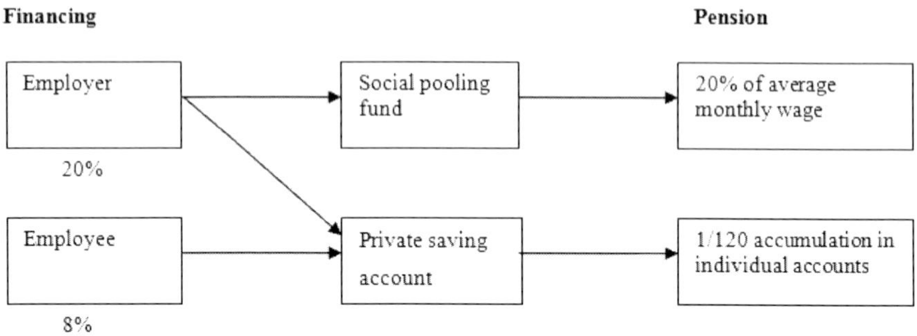

Figure 16.5: Institutional arrangement of old-age insurance system for urban employees.

China's urban employees' medical insurance system, initiated in 1998, was also constructed on a financing model of combining a social pooling fund with a private medical insurance account. Under this system, the medical insurance fare should be jointly paid by both employers and employees, and deposited into a social pooling fund as well as the individual employee's private medical insurance account. The share paid by the employee should be deposited into his own private account, while 30% of the share paid by the employer should be deposited into his employee's private account, with the rest of the employer's share collected to establish a social pooling fund. Clarification was made on those items of medical treatment that should be paid by social pooling fund and those that should be paid by private account. According to the regulations of this system, the social pooling fund of medical insurance should be used to pay for large medical expenses and hospitalization fares, while the private medical insurance account should be used to pay for small medical expenses and clinic treatments. Deductible level and ceiling standard were also established in the social pooling fund for the payment of medical treatment. At the same time, the coverage and payment levels of the insurance systems of unemployment benefits, work-related injury compensation, and maternity welfare were also expanded correspondingly.

During this stage, the reform policies of the social security system showed more characteristics of systematic adjustment than the urgent responsive measures of the previous stage. Social security reform was no longer regarded as a means to support economic reform, but was viewed as an integral part of the overall construction of China's market economy. More and more characteristics of active and initiative reform could be found in the establishment of the insurance systems of urban social security, and in the institutional innovation of combining a social pooling fund with a private insurance account in the insurance systems.

The stage of construction of a nationwide social security system (2003–)

As of this stage, China's market-oriented economic reform has been largely achieved. The fiscal capacity of the government has also increased by a huge margin due to continuous economic growth and enormous accumulation of wealth in the treasury. At the same time, the common Chinese people have gradually become more aware of their rights related to social security, and so their demand for social security has become even stronger. More and more social groups are appealing loudly for a complete social security system. The official objective for reform at this stage is the development of a "Harmonious Society", and the top priority of all the reform measures taken during this period is to remedy the existing inadequacies and insufficiencies of the social security system. It is widely agreed that some form of innovative institutional arrangement will need to be created to fill the vacuum produced by deficiencies in the original social security system, and that the standard of that institutional arrangement should be continuously improved. The key point here is to construct a comprehensive nationwide social security system that is adapted and articulated to China's unique system of market economy. The specific measures are as follows:

(1) In urban areas, the old-age insurance and medical insurance systems have been expanded from covering only urban employees to include unemployed urban citizens. Those urban citizens not employed by any institution are covered by another social security scheme that offers a status of beneficiary which is slightly lower than those systems for employees.

(2) The reconstruction and perfection of the rural social security system is emphasized. The new types of rural cooperative medical insurance system and rural old-age insurance system for retirement have been quickly promoted all over China. Because rural income level is usually lower than that of urban areas, these two new types of insurance systems are deliberately designed differently from those of urban areas. The funds for these two new types are raised by individual payment, collective support, and government finance.

(3) For the migrant workers moving back and forth between rural and urban areas, various provincial and local governments have formulated a variety of special social security schemes in accordance with their respective fiscal capacities, including diverse schemes for work-related injury compensation, medical insurance, and old-age insurance.

(4) For the large numbers of the poverty-stricken population newly formed in the process of economic reform, China's government has made a great effort to establish and improve the rural and urban minimum subsistence allowance system that is targeted at specific social groups with the lowest income, so as to ensure that these poverty-stricken social groups can be relieved and supported by institutional arrangements.

(5) The housing security system has begun to be implemented. On the whole, the reform of China's social security system during this stage has been characterized by its unprecedented systematic complexity and foresightedness, effectively shaking off its former auxiliary role subordinate to and supportive of economic reform. Instead, it has now emerged to play a major role in China's overall reform for the purpose of establishing a nationwide social security system beneficial to every citizen. In 2004, the right of obtaining social security protection was included in the Chinese Constitution as one of the basic rights of China's citizens. In 2006, China's government set up a clear objective to establish a complete social security system covering all of China's citizens by 2020. From 1 July 2011, the Social Security Law of China has been put into effect.

As mentioned previously, the top priority of all the reform policies taken during this period is to remedy the existing inadequacies and deficiencies of the social security system. Based on the continuous improvement of the urban and rural social security systems, more measures will be adopted in future so as to accelerate the solution of the problems faced by urban residents outside the existing social security network, migrant workers, and rural dwellers. Meanwhile, further anti-poverty measures will be actively implemented, and the housing security system will be established. In short, a nationwide social security system adapted and articulated to China's unique system of market economy will, in time, be comprehensively and completely established.

16.2 The Current Conditions, Problems, and Challenges of China's Social Security System

Due to a sustained effort lasting over 20 years now, the framework of a multi-lateral social security system has been largely established in China. This framework regards social insurance as its core and includes a series of institutional arrangements, such as social relief, social welfare, special care and replacement, and housing guarantee. The social insurance of this system consists of two layers of institutions. In urban areas, this social insurance includes a series of schemes for pension, medical treatment, unemployment benefits, and maternity benefits; while in rural areas, it includes rural old-age insurance and new rural cooperative medical insurance (the structure and details can be found in Figure 16.6).

Statistics show that at the end of 2010, in China's urban areas, the numbers of people who had participated in urban basic old-age insurance for retirement, urban basic insurance for medical treatment, unemployment insurance, work-related injury insurance, and maternity insurance were, respectively, 256.73 million, 432.06 million, 133.76 million, 161.73 million, and 123.06 million. In that same year, about 96.3% of China's rural population had participated in the new type of rural cooperative medical insurance, and approximately 102.77 million people in rural areas nationwide had joined the new type of rural old-age insurance for retirement. Furthermore, a total of 23.11 million urban residents and

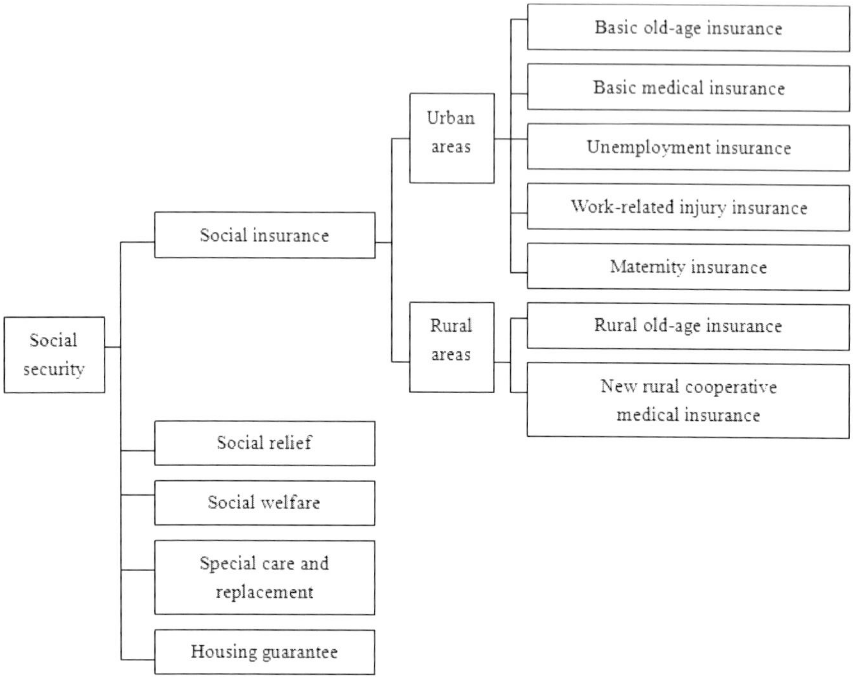

Figure 16.6: Framework of a multi-lateral social security system.

52.284 million rural residents have been integrated into the protection net of the official minimum subsistence allowance system (The Central People's Government of the People's Republic of China, 2011a). Recent World Bank data shows that 70% of the achievements in global poverty reduction have been made by China (Xinhua Daily Telegraph, 2011), and the poverty-stricken population in China's rural areas has been reduced from 30.7% of its total rural population to a mere 3.8% at the end of 2009 (Permanent Mission of The People's Republic of China to The United Nations Office in Geneva and Other International Organizations in Switzerland, 2010).

Current Problems of China's Social Security System

(1) Despite the quick pace of development of China's social security system in recent years, the coverage of present institutional

Table 16.1: The coverage of China's various social insurance schemes, 2008.

Social groups participating in insurance schemes	2008 (10,000 persons)	2008 coverage (%)
Employees of governmental institutions	1155.5	100
Employees of non-profit institutions	2790.5	100
Urban basic old-age insurance	16587.5	63.16
Rural social old-age insurance	5595.1	9.84
Urban basic medical insurance	19995.6	76.13
New rural cooperative medical insurance	81517.6	91.53
Unemployment insurance	12399.8	47.21
Work-related injury insurance	137878.2	52.49
Maternity insurance	9254.1	35.23

Source: 2008 Statistical Bulletin for the Development of Human Resources (Labor) and Social Security Affairs, Almanac of China's Statistics.

arrangements of social security is still limited. The old-age insurance system, which might be regarded as the most important insurance scheme for social security, can be taken as an example. In 2008, the coverage rate of the basic old-age insurance scheme for urban employees was 63.16%, while the coverage rate of the rural old-age insurance scheme was only 9.84% (see Table 16.1). In addition, the present basic insurance standard for social security is relatively low. For example, with regard to the old-age insurance system, in 2005 the monthly pension for the enterprise retirees insured by the urban old-age insurance was only RMB730 per capita, while the monthly wage of on-job urban employees was RMB1,533 per capita (National Bureau of Statistics of China).

(2) China's social security system is in a state of fragmentation, which poses another big problem. This state of fragmentation is reflected in the differences between rural and urban schemes of social security, the gaps between high standards of social security in advanced areas and lower standards in backward areas, and the discrepancy in social security treatment between employees of public sectors and those of private sectors. The differences between rural and urban schemes of social security

are evident in the apparent differences of categories and standards between urban insurance schemes and rural ones. The regional gaps in social security standards mean huge differences between different regions in terms of institutional arrangement, premium standard, and allowance payment standard. There is also a tremendous discrepancy in social security treatment between employees of public sectors and those of private sectors. Take old-age insurance as an example. The retirees of China's public sector enjoy a special mechanism of pension adjustment different from the one implemented for retirees of the private sector. The pension level of retirees of the public sector is directly connected to the wage growth of on-job employees in the public sector, which means that their pension can increase in line with any increases in the wage level of the public sector. However, there is no pension growth mechanism designed for retirees of the private sector. As a result, the gap between the pension level of the public sector's retirees and that of the private sector's retirees becomes increasingly wider. In fact, the ratio between the pension level of the public sector's retirees and that of the private sector's retirees increased from 1.2 times in 1996 to 2.1 times in 2005 (China Business Times, 2011).

(3) Serious financing problems also occur in the transitional process of China's social security system from a Pay-As-You-Go system to a mixture of partly Pay-As-You-Go and Partly-Capital-Funded system. Take old-age insurance as an example. No new institutional arrangement has ever been made over the source of funds for those retirees who had obtained their regular pension from the previous Pay-As-You-Go system, so their pensions are now being paid by their original employers and present old-age insurance participants who are currently working for their original employers. Therefore, their original employers and the present participants of old-age insurance who are now working for these employers have to assume a very heavy burden under the present Partly-Capital-Funded system of old-age insurance. At the same time, empty accounts appear in the accounts of old-age insurance.

Challenges Facing China's Social Insurance System

An aging population is one of the challenges facing China's social security system. In accordance with the definition of an aging society commonly accepted by the international community (which defines an aging society as one where the population over 60 years old and over 65 years old account for, respectively, 10% and 7% of the total population), China entered into this stage in 1999, owing to its rapid economic growth, extension of average lifespan, and continuous implementation of its one-child policy.

Compared to those developed countries in the West, the speed of the aging of China's population is rather ahead of its pace of growth of affluence, which seems to be a unique characteristic of the aging process of China's population. Upon entering the stage of an aging society, most Western countries had already completed their industrialization processes and owned a quite solid economic basis. China, however, entered the ranks of an aging society when it had not yet fully achieved its industrialization and its economic basis remained weak. When China became an aging society, its GDP per capita was US$825, only half that of France, one-ninth that of the US, and one-twelfth that of Japan when these countries first entered the stage of an aging society.

Thus, China has entered the stage of an aging society before gaining full affluence. Its relatively weak economic basis cannot provide adequate resources for its social security system, so the aging of its population exerts an enormous pressure on the financing of its social security, particularly its pension fund. Serious deficits have already appeared in the pension account of Shanghai, where the extent of aging of the population is most evident. [At the end of 2009, elderly people who were over 60 years old accounted for 22.5% of the total population with domicile registration in Shanghai, those over 65 years old accounted for 15.8% of the total, while those over 80 years old accounted for 4% of the total (News at Noon, 2010).] In 2008, the Shanghai Municipal Government spent an extra RMB1.7 billion to fill the deficit gap in the pension account, accounting for 18% of its fiscal expenditure that year (Zhao, 2009).

Moreover, the aging of China's population is not slowing down. It is anticipated that the number of China's elderly people over 60 years old will reach 438 million in 2050, accounting for 31.1% of its total population, and its population of over 65 years old will expand to 320 million in 2050, accounting for 22% of its total population at that time. At this rate, the deficit of the pension account, which has already occurred in Shanghai, will gradually appear in other cities and places around China as well (Ding, 2010). A calculation made by a special research group of the Ministry of Labor and Social Security reveals that the pension deficit of China's present social security system will increase from RMB51.1 billion in 2004 to RMB441.3 billion in 2033, given a steady pace of annual growth (Taikang Life).

Additional research shows that two-thirds of a man's total health expenditure is spent after the age of 60 (Ding and Zhou, 2010). In this sense, the expenses of the whole society on medical treatment will increase drastically once the population of that society ages. This brings almost inevitable pressure to the problem of financing for China's medical insurance and social security system.

Urbanization is another challenge facing China's social security system. The fast pace of urbanization in China has in turn helped improve the rural economy, because those migrant workers who work outside their own home villages effectively increase the income level of rural areas. Approximately 40% of the total net income per capita of peasants is obtained from their work in urban areas as migrant workers, which forms a large share in the overall structure of peasants' income (Hu, 2009). At present, there are over 130 million migrant workers employed in urban areas all over China, and there are also tens of millions of urban residents doing so-called flexible jobs. It is still not clear whether those migrant workers should be covered by the social security system of urban areas or that of rural areas. In recent years, special policies have been enacted for migrant workers to participate in work-related injury insurance and medical insurance for serious diseases. However, the proportion of migrant workers participating in old-age insurance is still relatively low. According to the 2010 Investigation and Policy Suggestion for the New Generation of Migrant Workers in Enterprises, only 67.7% of the new generation of migrant workers participated in the old-age insurance system, lower than the proportion of urban workers by 23.7% (Wang, 2011).

China's current level of urbanization is still considered inadequate compared to global levels. Therefore, its urbanization process will continue to proceed, with large space ahead for further development in the future. Correspondingly, the overall scale of migrant workers who hope to find a job in urban areas will also expand further. The current "fragmented" institutional arrangement of China's social security system has regarded migrant workers as a special social group, keeping them outside the normal network of the social security system. Given these circumstances, cautious contemplation therefore needs to be made on institutional design and reform of the current social security system so that it can cover the large migrant population who travel back and forth between urban and rural areas in search of jobs.

Urbanization also creates a secondary problem, namely with regard to rural pension and retirement. In the past, no complete social security system had been established in China's rural areas, and elderly people in rural areas depended heavily on their land and their family for their own security of living upon reaching old age. The urbanization process, however, has rapidly reduced arable land in China, and a large proportion of the labor force of rural youth and adults has migrated to urban areas in search of jobs and a higher standard of living. In this way, the rural aging population is even larger than the urban aging population. China's National Commission for the Aging Problem estimates that China's rural aging population is larger than that of urban areas by 1.24% (Hu, 2009). At the same time, the rural family structure has been greatly changed, dealing a huge impact on the original family-supported security for rural elderly people. Therefore, institutional rearrangement and reconstruction should be accelerated so as to fill the social security vacuum created by the fast pace of urbanization.

16.3 The Relation between the Perfection of the Social Security System and the Sustainable Social and Economic Development

The Perfection of China's Social Security System is the Preliminary Condition of Its Social Stability

China's fast economic development and drastic social transition have not only brought a huge growth of wealth and affluence, but have also caused tremendous impacts on various aspects of its society. One such impact is the apparently widened gap between the poor and the rich due to the imbalance of distribution of income and benefits. The income gap has continuously widened between poor and rich social groups, urban and rural areas, as well as between different regions of China. Since 1978, China's Gini Coefficient — an important index used to measure the inequality and imbalance in the distribution of wealth and affluence in a society — has increased relentlessly. In 2008, its Gini Coefficient reached 0.469, indicating a severe imbalance in the income distribution of the whole society (National Bureau of Statistics of China). In that same year, the ratio between the 20% of the total population who enjoy the highest income level and the 20% of the total population who have the lowest income level reached 5.71:1 (China Reform Forum). Meanwhile, the gap between rural and urban areas of China has also expanded in recent years. In 1978, the income gap between China's urban areas and its rural areas was 2.57:1 (Li and Feng), while in 2005 that gap increased to 3.22:1 (China Business Times, 2011). In 2009, the ratio of GDP per capita of Zhejiang Province, a fairly affluent coastal province of China, compared to that of Gansu Province, which is located in the barren hinterland, reached 3.45:1 (National Bureau of Statistics of China).

At the same time, social instability has been gradually built up by those marginalized social groups, such as the nearly 10 million unemployed workers who lost their jobs during China's transition from a centrally planned economy to a market system, the peasants who lost their land in China's process of urbanization, and the approximately 135 million migrant workers who are excluded from the official social security system and therefore lack steady income sources and a sense of belonging. As the elements that might lead to instability are accumulated further, doubts have begun to arise over China's prospects for achieving social stability. In recent years, more and more collective upheavals and even riots have emerged in China. Official statistics reveal that there were nearly 90,000 collective upheavals in the year 2009 alone (China.org.cn, 2010). Meanwhile, public order has deteriorated too, as reflected by the rising crime rate of those marginalized social groups. Out of the total number of criminals convicted in Beijing in 1980, the share of non-locals was a mere 3.41%, before increasing to 9.28% in 1985 and then to 23.3% in 1988. In 1999, migrant workers accounted for 53.43% of the total number of criminals convicted in Shanghai; in Canton, this ratio was 52.29%. Although the total numbers of non-locals in China's metropolises have not increased generally, and have even decreased on some occasions, the ratio of non-local criminals to the total number of criminals convicted in these metropolises has been steadily increasing (Ling, 2005).

Undoubtedly, a variety of factors could be attributed to the phenomena of imbalanced income distribution and social instability. However, it cannot be denied that one of the major contributing factors is the lack of a complete and highly efficient social security system.

Traditionally, the value of social stability has always held great importance in Chinese culture. Nevertheless, social frictions and conflicts seem to be unavoidable in the process of economic transition. The common people's demand for social stability appears to grow stronger in the face of social and economic transition. According to a study by the China Investigation Center for Public Opinions of the Globe, it was revealed that over 80% of the Chinese people interviewed in that study agreed with the notion that "stability means blessing, while turbulence means calamity". It is widely recognized that a complete social security system can be used as a valve to release the dissatisfactions and discontents of certain social groups, and can be operated as a special device of shock absorption for the purpose of defusing the tension created by social frictions (Ducan, 2011). Therefore, a complete and perfect social security system needs to be constructed so as to promote the re-distribution of wealth and affluence in China's social and economic development in the future. Such a social security system can achieve social justice and promote social stability to some degree, whilst providing a stable social environment for the sustainable development of China's market economy.

The Improvement and Perfection of China's Social Security System is the Fundamental Guarantee of Its Sustainable Economic Development

The Improvement of China's Social Security System Contributes to Its Economic Transition from Investment- and Export-Oriented Growth to Consumption-Oriented Growth

China's rapid economic growth in the past 30 years has been fueled by investment and export. Since China's entry into the WTO, the leading role played by export and investment in the mechanism driving China's economic growth appears more and more prominent. From 1979 to 2006, the contribution rates of investment and net export to economic growth in China were, respectively, 35.2% (during 1979–2005, the global contribution rate of investment was just 23.5%) and 8% (National Bureau of Statistics of China). However, this growth mechanism driven by investment and export is apparently unsustainable, as explained below.

In China, the government usually plays a dominant role in investment. However, after many years of huge expansion of government-led investment, the efficiency of such investment has obviously decreased. Meanwhile, China's government, especially at the provincial and local level, is being confronted with budget pressures amid growing fiscal imbalances. At the end of June 2010, the total amount of calculable debt of China's provincial and local government was RMB8.42 trillion. According to China's National Audit Office, the debt rate of local government has reached a level as high as 364.77% (Ba, 2011). In addition, the negative effects of government-led investment, such as the crowding-out effect towards private investment, should not be ignored.

The dependency of China's economy on its foreign trade has also been continuously strengthened, especially after its entry into the WTO. China's rate of dependency on foreign trade increased to 59.2% in 2008 from a much lower level of 12.5% in 1980. Meanwhile, China's trade friction with other countries has intensified as a result of the enormous expansion of its total export volume and dramatic growth of trade surplus (Zhong, 2010). In 2010, 66 cases of trade relief survey were filed against China, involving a total value of US$7.7 billion (Qing, 2011). China's continuous trade surplus has also led to sustained international pressure for large-margin appreciation of the RMB — a key demand of China's trade partners. Under these circumstances, therefore, China's model of export-oriented economic growth is now faced with unprecedented obstruction.

At present, China's government and its citizens have reached a consensus that domestic consumption should be valued as a driving force that can boost sustainable economic growth and replace the obstructed exports and increasingly inefficient investment. In fact, China's government has tried various methods to encourage domestic consumption, but this has only resulted in a temporary increase of consumption, without achieving any long-term and stabilized trend of consumption growth. Undoubtedly, Chinese citizens' high saving rate is the most direct cause leading to the sluggish pace of consumption growth. An investigation conducted by McKinsey & Company on 6,000 households in over 30 cities of China indicates that most people who were investigated affirmed their saving ratio as one-fourth of their household income. When asked about the reason for such a high saving rate, 50% of the people who were investigated explained that they saved for "emergency medical treatment expenses for family members", while another 43% showed a strong concern for "life after retirement". This investigation confirms that one of the important reasons leading to China's repressed total consumption and diminished desire of common residents for domestic consumption is the incomplete social security system with narrow coverage and low level of security, which strengthens common people's cautiousness and prudence. An empirical study by a Chinese scholar (Xiuyun, 2006) shows that a relatively strong negative correlation exists between China's social security expenditure and household saving rate, such that the household saving rate will be reduced by 1.779% for every increase of social security expenditure by 1% (Ma, 2010).

The Improvement of the Social Security System Contributes to the Reduction of Economic Volatility

First, as is known to all, social security itself should be regarded as an automatic stabilizer of economic fluctuation that plays a role in reducing economic volatility.

Second, the construction and improvement of the social security system based on government fiscal spending can create strong positive externalities, which may boost economic growth indirectly. Research has shown that for every RMB10 billion of social security spending in China, output can increase by RMB15.5 billion (Jin, 2010). At the same time, more jobs can be created from the increased social security spending.

Third, data reveals that the margin of fluctuation of China's domestic consumption is usually much lower than that of investment. Therefore, China's economy will become more stable and will run more smoothly if a complete social security system is established, which can boost the growth of consumption and correspondingly reduce the weight of influence of investment volatility over the economy.

Finally, the growth of domestic consumption will also reduce the weight of influence of exports over China's economy. In this way, China's trade partners' economic volatility, which is transmitted to China usually through exports, will be reduced, and more certainty will be assured for a smooth operation of China's economy.

The Perfection of the Social Security System Contributes to the Shaping of an Efficient and Unified National Labor Market and the Process of Urbanization

Currently, China's social security system is highly fragmented with extremely complex and messy institutions. The institutional arrangement, financing, and benefits of various types of schemes, social contributions, and other forms of social security are all very different from one another. Such mess and disorder in China's social security system seriously obstruct the free flow of labor across boundaries of various regions and professions, effectively blocking the optimal allocation of human resources and posing a major impediment to the establishment of a unified national labor market, a dream that is still far from reality. At the same time, the rural-urban binary structure, the highly differentiated and disordered social security system, and the lack of a unified national arrangement for the social security of migrant workers, have all posed negative effects in relation to China's urbanization process. Thus, a nationally uniform institutional arrangement is needed and should be implemented as early as possible.

16.4 China Needs More Reforms of Its Social Security System to Become a Part of the Tri-polar World After the Current Re-polarization Process

China's economic reform is the direct driving force that propels the whole process of reform and improvement of its social security system. In keeping with China's economic transition from a centrally planned economy towards a market-oriented system and its rapid economic growth, the reform of China's social security system has evolved from the original stage of urgent response to economic and social changes, through the stage of preliminary probing for reform (1978–1993), and the stage of building the framework of an urban social security system (1993–2002), to the stage of construction of a nationwide social security system (2003–). This reform has progressed from making small modifications in specific branches of social security, such as old-age insurance and medical insurance, to constructing an overall social security system that can cover the whole country. Throughout this evolutionary process, many difficulties and tough issues have to be handled and resolved. At the beginning of the 2010s, significant achievements have been made in China's reform of its social security system. There has emerged a preliminary structure of a multi-level complete social security system aimed at offering social security benefits to every citizen, combining social pooling with individual private accounts, adapted and articulated to China's unique system of market economy, and with its coverage relentlessly expanding. Meanwhile, relatively good achievements have also been made in the field of anti-poverty. Of course, China's social security system is still not perfect, and it still faces various problems and challenges, such as the lack of proper methods to further expand its coverage and improve its security level, and the fragmentation of institutional arrangements. Therefore, more contemplation needs to be made over how to effectively expand its coverage and unify the social security's institutional structure nationwide. Foresightedness is necessary as well to handle the challenges brought by the aging society and urbanization processes.

Currently, a consensus has been reached in China that the model of China's economic growth should be upgraded from an investment- and export-driven model to a domestic consumption-driven one, so as to bring a new propelling force to its sustainable economic growth. In China's 12th five-year plan for social and economic development during 2011–2015, strategic adjustment of China's economic structure has been regarded as a top priority, and a social security system covering its whole population has also been proposed. This arrangement clearly regards domestic consumptive demands as a strategic focus, and thus, one of the most important means to achieve this plan is to perfect China's national social security system. A complete social security system is regarded as an important pre-condition and guarantee for this transition, and is also viewed as an effective tool to reduce China's economic fluctuation. At the same time, a complete social security system can further contribute to the shaping of a nationally unified labor market in China and the process of urbanization.

As for the re-polarization, it will take China until at least 2020 to implement the necessary reforms. This means that until then, China will focus on its social and economic construction and gradually approach its role as the Third Pole.

Acknowledgements

The author expresses his sincere thanks to Mr. Fei Chen for his help in collecting the relevant material for this chapter.

References

Ba, S. (2011). Survey on local government's debt in China. Available at: http://www.iceo.com.cn/column/28/2011/0210/208746.shtml. Accessed April 2, 2011.

Chen, J. and Wang, Y. (2010). *Report on the Development of China's Social Security*. Beijing: Social Sciences Press.

China.org.cn (2010). The crucial reasons of collective upheavals are conflicts between government officials and commoners. Available at: http://www.china.com.cn/book/zhuanti/qkjc/txt/2010-01/13/content_19228539.htm. Accessed April 2, 2011.

China Business Times (2011). Discover the old-age insurance system. Available at: http://news.xinhuanet.com/2011-02/25/c_121120704_4.htm. Accessed April 2, 2011.

China Reform Forum. Worldwide comparative studies on the national income distribution. Available at: http://www.chinareform.org.cn. Accessed April 2, 2011.

Ding, C. (2010). Institutional construction on the system of special care and care insurance for China's elderly. In: S. Langsdorf, R. Traub-Merz and C. Ding (Eds.), *Altenpflege und Pflegeversicherung, Modelle und Beispiele aus China, Deutschland und Japan*. Shanghai: Press of Shanghai Academy of Social Sciences.

Ding, C. and Zhou, T. (2010). Problems and reform of medical treatment insurance systems against the background of globalization. In: H. Zhou (Ed.), *International Comparative Studies on Social Security*. Beijing: Press of China's Labor and Social Security.

Ducan, C. (2011). Chinese people give much credit to 'stability'. *Global Time*, No. 2388, 2011-03-04.

Hu, X. (2009). *Towards Harmony: The Development of China's Social Security System in 60 Years*. Beijing: Press of China's Labor and Social Security.

Jin, S. (2010). Sustained growth of domestic consumption: A consequence only after the further perfection of the social security system. Available at: http://www.studa.net. Accessed April 12, 2011.

Li, S. and Feng, F. Empirical studies on the gap between rural and urban areas and economic development of China. Available at: http://www.chinacity.org.cn. Accessed April 12, 2011.

Ling, H. (2005). The issue of crime committed by migrant workers in China's process of urbanization. Available at: http://www.wenhuacn.com/article.asp?classid=11&articleid=1201. Accessed March 15, 2011.

Ma, Q. (2010). Discussion on the effect of social security system on consumer demand in China. Available at: http://www.ectime.com.cn/emag.aspx?titleid=12225. Accessed April 12, 2011.

National Bureau of Statistics of China. China statistical yearbooks (past years). Available at: http://www.stats.gov.cn/. Accessed April 12, 2011.

News at Noon (2010). March 26, 2010.

Permanent Mission of The People's Republic of China to The United Nations Office in Geneva and Other International Organizations in Switzerland (2010). China makes new 10-year plan of anti-poverty. Available at: http://www.china-un.ch/chn/bjzl/t716885.htm. Accessed April 2, 2011.

Qing, F. (2011). 10 years after its accession to the WTO, China's trade friction with other countries has intensified. Available at: http://news.cnstock.com/cmjx/201103/1181498.htm. Accessed April 2, 2011.

Taikang Life. Available at: http://www.taikang.com.

The Central People's Government of the People's Republic of China (2011a). Economic and society development report No. 1. Available at: http://www.gov.cn/gzdt/2011-03/01/content_1813927.htm. Accessed April 2, 2011.

The Central People's Government of the People's Republic of China (2011b). Economic and society development report No. 17. Available at: http://www.gov.cn/gzdt/2011-03/24/content_1831096.htm. Accessed April 2, 2011.

Wang, L. (2011). Integration of rural and urban social security: a chasm waiting to be filled. *First Financial Daily*, March 7th, 2011.

Xinhua Daily Telegraph (2011). April 1, 2011.

Zhao, F. (2009). Aging population increasing, 1.7 billion RMB shortage in pension account of Shanghai. Available at: http://finance.qq.com/a/20090401/000092.htm. Accessed April 2, 2011.

Zhong, S. (2010). View on China's rate of dependency on foreign trade. Available at: http://finance.people.com.cn/GB/10933378.html. Accessed April 12, 2011.

Index